McGRAW
MICROCOMPUTING

Annual Edition
1992–1993

Timothy J. O'Leary
Arizona State University

Brian K. Williams

Linda I. O'Leary

Mitchell McGRAW-HILL
New York St. Louis San Francisco Auckland Bogotá Caracas Hamburg
Lisbon London Madrid Mexico Milan Montreal New Delhi Paris
San Juan São Paulo Singapore Sydney Tokyo Toronto Watsonville

To
Pat and Tuff—T.J.O.
Stacey—B.K.W.
My sister, Ann—L.I.O.

McGraw-Hill Microcomputing: Annual Edition 1992–1993

Copyright © 1992, 1991, 1990, 1989 by McGraw-Hill, Inc. All rights reserved. Printed in the United States of America. Except as permitted under the United States Copyright Act of 1976, no part of this publication may be reproduced or distributed in any form or by any means, or stored in a database or retrieval system, without the prior written permission of the publisher.

All inquiries should be addressed to Mitchell/McGraw-Hill, 55 Penny Lane, Suite 103, Watsonville, CA 95076, (408) 724-0195 or (800) 435-2665.

1 2 3 4 5 6 7 8 9 0   KGP KGP   9 0 9 8 7 6 5 4 3 2 1

ISBN 0-07-048838-X

See Illustration Credits on pages 269–270.
Copyrights included on these pages by reference.

Sponsoring editor: Roger Howell
Editorial assistant: Laurie Boudreau
Production director: Betty Drury
Project manager: Greg Hubit, Bookworks
Text and cover designer: Merrill Haber
Illustrator: Pat Rogondino
Photo researcher: Monica Suder & Associates, San Francisco
Compositor: York Graphic Services
Printer and binder: Arcata Graphics Kingsport

ISSN 1040-4511

ABOUT THE AUTHORS

Timothy J. O'Leary *(left)* has been a professional educator since 1975. He is currently an Associate Professor in the department of Decision and Information Systems at Arizona State University. He has written several books and articles on computers and information systems.

Linda I. O'Leary is a professional trainer in the area of computers. She has developed computer training manuals for corporations and presented seminars on the use of many computer software packages. She has also coauthored a book on Lotus 1-2-3.

Brian K. Williams is a professional writer and has coauthored six books about computers. The holder of degrees from Stanford University, he was for many years an editor and manager for several book publishers before turning full time to writing. He lives in Incline Village, Nevada.

ABOUT THE BOARD

Bob Autrey *(left),* Chuck Riden, and Jerry Booher are members of the McGraw-Hill Microcomputing Advisory Board. They are university and community college instructors who teach microcomputing courses. Their ongoing input has been invaluable to the development of this project.

CONTENTS IN BRIEF

Preface xiii

1
You and Computer Competency 1

2
Applications Software: Basic Tools 17

3
Systems Software 36

4
The Central Processing Unit 54

5
Input and Output 77

6
Secondary Storage 95

7
Communications 113

8
Files and Databases 133

9
Information Systems 148

10
Systems Analysis and Design 164

11
Programming and Languages 182

12
Emerging Applications: Power Tools 203

13
Workplace Issues, Privacy, and Security 222

14
Your Future: Using Information Technology 238

Glossary 249
Index 262

Microcomputer Disk Operating System — DOS1
with Introduction to the Labs

   Overview: Getting Started with Your Microcomputer
   Lab 1 Using the Disk Operating System (DOS)
   Lab 2 Managing Your Hard Disk
   Summary
   Index

WordPerfect 5.1 — WP1

   Overview: Word Processing
   Lab 1 Editing a Document
   Lab 2 Creating and Formatting a Document
   Lab 3 Merging and Refining Documents
   Lab 4 Creating a Research Paper
   Summary
   Index

Lotus 1-2-3 Release 2.2 — SS1

   Overview: Electronic Spreadsheets
   Lab 1 Creating a Worksheet: Part 1
   Lab 2 Creating a Worksheet: Part 2
   Lab 3 Managing a Large Worksheet
   Lab 4 Creating and Printing Graphs
   Lab 5 Creating Templates and Macros
   Summary
   Index

dBASE III PLUS — DB1

   Overview: Database
   Lab 1 Creating a Database
   Lab 2 Modifying, Editing, and Viewing a Database
   Lab 3 Sorting, Indexing, and Summarizing Data
   Lab 4 Creating a Professional Report
   Summary
   Index

Local Area Network — NET1

   Overview: Local Area Network
   Lab 1 Using a Local Area Network
   Summary
   Index

For detailed Table of Contents, refer to the beginning of each individual application software tutorial.

CONTENTS

Preface xiii

■■ 1 ■■
You and Computer Competency 1
End Users and Computer Competency 2
Four Kinds of Computers 3
The Five Parts of a Microcomputer System 4
Software 5
    Applications Software 6
    Systems Software 6
Hardware 7
    Input Devices 7
    The System Unit 8
    Secondary Storage 8
    Output Devices 10
    Communications Devices 11
Data 11
Connectivity 12
A Look at the Future 12
    Powerful Software 12
    Powerful Hardware 12
    Connectivity 12
    Emerging Microcomputer Applications 13
    Workplace Issues, Privacy, Security, and Your Future 13

Review Questions 16
Discussion Questions 16
Visual Summary 14–15

■■ 2 ■■
Applications Software: Basic Tools 17
Using Software Off the Shelf 17
    The Cursor and Scrolling 18
    Menus 18
    Format 18
    Special-Purpose and Function Keys 18
Word Processing 20
    Word Wrap and the Enter Key 21
    Search and Replace 21
    Block and Move 21
    Other Features 21
Spreadsheets 23
    Format 24
    Formulas 24
    Recalculation 24
    Windows 24
    Other Features 25
Database Managers 25
    Retrieve and Display 26
    Sort 26
    Calculate and Format 26
    Other Features 26
Graphics 27
    Analytical Graphics 27
    Presentation Graphics 28
Communications 29
    Data Banks 30
    Message Exchanges 30
    Financial Services 31

Integrated Packages 31
A Look at the Future 32

Review Questions 32
Discussion Questions 33
Visual Summary 34–35

■ ■ **3** ■ ■
Systems Software 36
Why Learn About Systems Software? 36
Four Kinds of Programs 38
DOS: The IBM Personal Computer Standard 39
    Advantages 40
    Disadvantages 41
DOS with Windows 41
    Advantages 42
    Disadvantages 43
OS/2 43
    Advantages 45
    Disadvantages 45
Macintosh Operating Systems 45
    Advantages 46
    Disadvantages 47
Unix: The "Portable" Operating System 47
    Advantages 48
    Disadvantages 48
A Look at the Future 50

Review Questions 51
Discussion Questions 51
Visual Summary 52–53

■ ■ **4** ■ ■
The Central Processing Unit 54
The Four Types of Computer Systems 54
    Microcomputers 54
    Minicomputers 59
    Mainframes 60
    Supercomputers 60
The CPU 60
    The Control Unit 61
    The Arithmetic-Logic Unit 61
Primary Storage 61
    Registers 61
    The Processing Cycle 62
The Binary System 63
    Units of Measure for Capacity 64
    Binary Coding Schemes 64
    The Parity Bit 64
The System Unit 65
    System Board 65
    Microprocessor Chips 66

    RAM Chips 69
    ROM Chips 70
    System Clock 70
    Expansion Slots and Boards 70
    Bus Lines 71
    Ports 72
A Look at the Future 72

Review Questions 73
Discussion Questions 76
Visual Summary 74–75

■ ■ **5** ■ ■
Input and Output 77
Input: Keyboard Versus Direct Entry 77
Keyboard Entry 78
    Keyboards 78
    Terminals 79
Direct Entry 80
    Pointing Devices 80
    Scanning Devices 81
    Voice-Input Devices 83
Output: Monitors, Printers, Plotters, Voice 84
Types of Monitors 84
    Monochrome Monitors 84
    Graphics Monitors 85
Printers 86
    Dot-Matrix Printer 86
    Daisy-Wheel Printer 87
    Laser Printer 88
    Ink-Jet Printer 88
    Chain Printer 88
    Printer Features 89
Plotters 89
    Flatbed Plotter 90
    Drum Plotter 90
    Electrostatic Plotter 90
Voice-Output Devices 90
A Look at the Future 90

Review Questions 91
Discussion Questions 91
Visual Summary 92–93

■ ■ **6** ■ ■
Secondary Storage 95
Data Organization 96
Four Kinds of Secondary Storage 97
Diskettes 97
    The Disk Drive 97
    How a Disk Drive Works 98
    Drive A and Drive B 99
    The Parts of a Diskette 99
    Taking Care of Diskettes 101

Hard Disks   101
  Internal Hard Disk   101
  Hard-Disk Cartridges   103
  Hard-Disk Packs   103
Optical Disks   105
  CD-ROM   105
  WORM   105
  Erasable Optical Disks   106
Magnetic Tape   106
  Magnetic Tape Streamers   106
  Magnetic Tape Reels   106
A Look at the Future   108

Review Questions   109
Discussion Questions   109
Visual Summary   110–111

■ ■ 7 ■ ■
Communications   113
Communications and Connectivity   114
  Fax Machines   114
  Electronic Bulletin Boards   114
  Electronic Mail   115
  Voice-Messaging Systems   115
  Sharing Resources   116
  Databases   116
  Commercial Services   117
  Groupware   117
User Interface   117
  Modems and Communication Speeds   117
  Types of Modems   118
Communications Channels   119
  Telephone Lines   119
  Coaxial Cable   119
  Fiber-Optic Cable   119
  Microwave   120
  Satellites   120
Data Transmission   120
  Bandwidth   120
  Serial and Parallel Transmission   121
  Direction of Data Transmission   121
  Modes of Transmitting Data   122
  Protocols   123
Network Configurations   124
  Star Network   124
  Bus Network   125
  Ring Network   125
  Hierarchical Network   125
Network Types   126
  Local Area Network   127
  Metropolitan Area Network   127
  Wide Area Network   128
A Look at the Future   129

Review Questions   129
Discussion Questions   132
Visual Summary   130–131

■ ■ 8 ■ ■
Files and Databases   133
Files   133
  Data Organization   133
  The Key Field   134
  Batch Versus Real-Time Processing   134
  Master Versus Transaction Files   135
  File Organization   135
Database   136
  The Need for Databases   136
  Software for a Database Management System   137
  The Data Dictionary   137
  Query Language   137
DBMS Organization   138
  The Hierarchical Database   138
  The Network Database   139
  The Relational Database   139
Types of Databases   140
  The Individual Database   140
  The Company, or Shared, Database   141
  The Distributed Database   141
  The Proprietary Database   141
  Costs   142
Database Uses and Issues   142
  Data for Strategic Uses   142
  Importance of Security   142
A Look at the Future   144

Review Questions   144
Discussion Questions   145
Visual Summary   146–147

■ ■ 9 ■ ■
Information Systems   148
The Information Revolution   148
How Information Flows in an Organization   149
  Functions   150
  Management Levels   152
  Information Flow   153
The Levels of Computer-Based Information Systems   154
Transaction Processing Systems   155
Management Information Systems   157
Decision Support Systems   158
  The User   158
  System Software   158
  The Data   158
  The Decision Models   158
Executive Information Systems   159
A Look at the Future   160

Review Questions   161
Discussion Questions   161
Visual Summary   162–163

■ ■ 10 ■ ■
Systems Analysis and Design   164
Systems Analysis and Design   165
Phase 1: Preliminary Investigation   166
  Defining the Problem   167
  Suggesting Alternative Systems   168
  Preparing a Short Report   168
Phase 2: Analysis   168
  Gathering Data   168
  Analyzing the Data   170
  Documenting the Systems Analysis Stage   171
Phase 3: Design   172
  Designing Alternative Systems   173
  Selecting the Best System   173
  Writing the Systems Design Report   173
Phase 4: Development   173
  Developing Software   174
  Acquiring Hardware   174
  Testing the New System   174
Phase 5: Implementation   174
  Types of Conversion   174
  Training   176
Phase 6: Maintenance   176
Prototyping   177
A Look at the Future   178

Review Questions   178
Discussion Questions   178
Visual Summary   180–181

■ ■ 11 ■ ■
Programming and Languages   182
Programs and Programming   182
  What Is a Program?   183
  What Is Programming?   183
Step 1: Define the Problem   184
  Determining Program Objectives   184
  Determining the Desired Output   184
  Determining the Input Data   185
  Determining the Processing Requirements   185
Step 2: Make-or-Buy Decision   186
Step 3: Design the Program   186
  Top-Down Program Design   187
  Pseudocode   188
  Flowcharts   188
  Logic Structures   190
Step 4: Code the Program   191
  The Good Program   191
  Which Language?   191
Step 5: Debug the Program   193
  Syntax Errors   193
  Logic Errors   193
  The Debugging Process   194

Step 6: Document the Program   194
Five Generations of Programming Languages   195
  Machine Languages: The First Generation   195
  Assembly Languages: The Second Generation   196
  Procedural Languages: The Third Generation   196
  Problem-Oriented Languages: The Fourth Generation   197
  Natural Languages: The Fifth Generation   198
A Look at the Future   198

Review Questions   199
Discussion Questions   202
Visual Summary   200–201

■ ■ 12 ■ ■
Emerging Applications: Power Tools   203
Desktop Managers   203
Project Management Software   204
Desktop Publishing   205
New Media: Hypertext and Multimedia   208
  Hypertext   208
  Multimedia   209
CAD/CAM   211
  Computer-Aided Design   211
  Computer-Aided Manufacturing   212
Artificial Intelligence   213
  Robotics   213
  Knowledge-Based and Expert Systems   214
  Artificial Reality   216
A Look at the Future   217

Review Questions   218
Discussion Questions   219
Visual Summary   220–221

■ ■ 13 ■ ■
Workplace Issues, Privacy, and Security   222
Workplace Issues   223
  Physical Health Matters   223
  Mental Health Matters   224
  Design with People in Mind   225
Computers and Privacy   226
  Use of Large Databases   226
  Use of Electronic Networks   227
  The Major Laws on Privacy   227
Threats to Computers   228
  Computer Criminals   229
  Computer Crime   230
  Other Hazards   232
Security   232
  Restricting Access   233

Anticipating Disasters 233
 Backing Up Data 234
 Security for Microcomputers 234
A Look at the Future 234

Review Questions 235
Discussion Questions 235
Visual Summary 236–237

■ ■ 14 ■ ■
Your Future: Using Information Technology 238
Being a Winner 238
Technology and Organizations 239
 New Products 239
 New Enterprises 240
 New Customer and Supplier Relationships 240
Technology and People 240
 Cynicism 241
 Naïveté 241
 Frustration 242
How You Can Be a Winner 242
 Stay Current 242
 Maintain Your Computer Competence 242
 Develop Professional Contacts 243
 Develop Specialties 243
 Be Alert for Organizational Change 244
 Look for Innovative Opportunities 244
A Look at the Future: The Rest of Your Life 245

Review Questions 245
Discussion Questions 248
Visual Summary 246–247

Glossary 249
Index 262
Illustration Credits 269

PREFACE

The Audience for This Book

This book is designed for students, both majors and nonmajors, enrolled in a one-quarter or one-semester first course on computers and information processing or an introductory computer course with a microcomputer orientation. There are no prerequisites.

Why This Is Different: An Extremely Flexible, Annually Revised Set of Materials for Teaching Computer Competency

This set of materials is, we think, quite distinctive in a number of ways.

1. It Is Designed to Provide Maximum "Customization" for Instructors. The instructional materials come in four versions, giving instructors maximum flexibility. You are now holding one of the following versions:

- **Text plus labs.** *McGraw-Hill Microcomputing: Annual Edition* consists of 14 chapters covering computer concepts; several labs covering DOS; a selection of popular word processing, spreadsheet, and database programs; and a simulation of a communications program on a local area network (LAN). This standard spiral-bound version includes labs on WordPerfect 5.1, Lotus 1-2-3 Release 2.2, dBASE III PLUS, DOS, and LAN.
- **Text only.** *McGraw-Hill Computing Essentials: Annual Edition* describes basic concepts about computers. With 14 chapters, the book is concise yet also comprehensive. We have tried to include all the significant topics usually covered in an introductory course, without being too cursory or too technical.
- **Labs only.** *McGraw-Hill Microcomputing Labs: Annual Edition* consists of several labs covering DOS; a selection of the most popular word processing, spreadsheet, and database programs; and a simulation of a communications program on a local area network (LAN). This standard spiral-bound version includes labs on WordPerfect 5.1, Lotus 1-2-3 Release 2.2, and dBASE III PLUS software.
- **"Customized" lab software options.** All parts of the Annual Edition "System" are available in self-standing "modules." You can put these modules together in any combination to make your own customized textbook. Along with the *Essentials* (or concepts) module, the following Lab Software options are available:

xiii

DOS Versions up to 5.0
DOS Version 5.0
WordPerfect 4.2
WordPerfect 5.0
WordPerfect 5.1
WordStar 4.0
Lotus 1-2-3 Release 2.01
Lotus 1-2-3 Release 2.2
Quattro Version 1.01
VP-Planner
VP-Planner Plus
SuperCalc4
dBASE III PLUS
dBASE IV Release 1.1
Microsoft Works Release 2.0 on the IBM PC and compatibles
Microsoft Windows 3.0
Microsoft Windows 3.1

A McGraw-Hill sales representative can explain this "customization" feature in more detail.

2. It Is Revised Annually. All writers in the field of computers and information processing struggle constantly with fast-changing equipment and software. Our mailboxes are glutted with periodicals and new-product announcements. However, textbooks usually are revised only once every 2 or 3 years. This is fine for many academic subjects, but it can be a handicap in this one. With computers, a year's developments can mean changes in many areas. We were delighted, therefore, when McGraw-Hill suggested that our book be revised *every year*. This allows us—and our readers—to keep pace with cutting-edge developments. And it allows us to support instructors by describing the latest in ideas and technology.

NEW TO THE TEXT FOR THIS EDITION: New developments have led to the following changes in this year's edition:

- **An entirely new chapter, Chapter 13, "Workplace Issues, Privacy, and Security."** Such issues as *ergonomics, repetitive strain injury, "technostress," safeguarding of medical and credit records, security and privacy laws, "hackers" and "crackers," computer viruses, software piracy*, and *disaster recovery plans* have become more important in recent times. We cover them all in this brand-new chapter.

- **New material on operating systems.** Chapter 3, "Systems Software," has been revised to describe the latest developments in operating systems, including *Windows, DOS 5.0*, and the increasing popularity of the *graphical user interface*.

- **More on hardware and software.** Chapter 4, "The Central Processing Unit," goes into more detail on the fast-growing area of portable computers—*transportables, laptops, notebooks,* and *pocket personal computers*. We also describe the latest development in supercomputers, *massively parallel processing*. The importance of the *RISC chip* is also described. Chapter 12, "Emerging Applications: Power Tools," introduces the subject of *project management software*.

- **More on trends and the future.** New charts and graphs have been added to show trends in hardware and software purchases and other areas. The sections at the end of each chapter, "A Look at the Future," have been updated to cover such subjects as *pen-based computers that read handwritten text, hand-held wireless computers, HDTV, data-compression technology*, and *image processing*.

NEW TO THE LABS FOR THIS EDITION: Coverage of the following additional packages: Lotus Release 2.3, Quattro 1.01, dBASE IV version 4.0, Microsoft Windows Version 3.0, and Microsoft Windows 3.1.

3. The Purpose of This Book Is to Create Computer Competency. This book is not about "computer literacy," a notion that has been around for a few years. Rather, it is about *computer competency*. It means, we hope, that when students complete the book and the course, they will have the competency in computer-related skills that will allow them to walk into an office and immediately be of superior value to employers.

Our goal, then, is to produce students who are . . .

- **Microcomputer-trained.** They will be able to operate microcomputers in ways that will make them the most productive employees for most organizations.
- **Familiar with brand-name software.** They will know the most popular brands of applications software—especially word processors, spreadsheets, and database managers.
- **Grounded in fundamental concepts.** They will have a basic working vocabulary and knowledge of computer and information concepts appropriate for most organizations. This means they will have some understanding not only of microcomputers but also of mainframes, end-user applications, management information systems, decision support systems, knowledge-based systems, systems analysis and design, and other topics that have transformed and expanded microcomputing.

4. The Book Reflects the Popular Wishes of the Marketplace. Some hardware and software is no doubt better designed and more efficient than others. However, our concern in this book is with *what is most popular with employers*. Therefore, we have selected our topics for the text and software for the labs according to the following criteria.

- **Industry barometers.** Many indicators show which products are most favored. Examples are number of units of software shipped last year as reported by industry pulse-takers, popularity of particular brands as measured among readers in magazine polls, and specific hardware and software stressed by professional training firms. We have looked at as many of these barometers as possible.
- **Survey of schools.** McGraw-Hill has formally surveyed the colleges and schools that we think are likely candidates for our approach to find out what they want. This research has been extremely valuable to us.
- **Direct feedback.** The labs in particular have benefited from the kind of improvements that can come only from personal feedback. All the labs were thoroughly planned with the help of the McGraw-Hill Microcomputer Advisory Board—instructors who teach the course in the kinds of schools and institutions to which we are directing our efforts. These instructors contributed advice and tested the labs with their students. Thus, when any directions were found to be troublesome, we were able to make crucial adjustments in the final drafts. Similarly, the 14 chapters of the text benefited from our extensive interaction with members of the Advisory Board, along with the comments of later reviewers.

5. The Basic Philosophy Is: "Learn by Doing." We believe readers of this book have four attributes.

- **Readers think jobs come first.** Our readers, we think, are principally interested in learning the skills necessary to obtain administrative or managerial jobs, or to do better in their present jobs. They are not computer enthusiasts, concerned with systems theory, the history of computing, and so on. Thus, the labs, for example, are set in a job environment—a health club—and the activities follow actual business practices suggested by experts in the field who reviewed the labs.

- **They want readable material.** We have worked to make the text easily readable: Sentences are short. Headings are used frequently. Ideas are set off in "bite-size" paragraphs. Sections are summarized at the beginning.
- **They learn visually.** We believe people learn best by being able to *see* how things work. Thus, at the end of every text chapter, we present a *Visual Summary* that shows how topics and concepts fit together.
- **They learn by doing.** We think students using this material also learn best by *doing* rather than by *reading*. "Hands on" is important. That is why we have put so much effort into designing the labs. The labs are intended not only to teach particular software packages but also to demonstrate how and why they are used in a real-world environment.

Professional Development of the Project

This book was conceived and written by a development team consisting of the following professionals:

- An educator
- A writer
- A computer trainer
- The McGraw-Hill Microcomputer Advisory Board

As mentioned, the Advisory Board consisted of community college and university instructors who were intensely involved from the beginning in planning, developing, and testing the project.

Learning Aids

The learning aids are practical, designed to reinforce the acquiring of computer competency.

Some special features of the text are:

- **Competency objectives.** Both text chapters and labs begin with a description of the goals—"Competencies," we call them—that the reader should hope to achieve.
- **Section summaries.** Sections are summarized in large type at the beginning.
- **Visual Summaries.** Key ideas of each of the 14 chapters are summarized with words and pictures, not just words.

Some special features of the labs are:

- **Overview to applications.** Before each of the major divisions of software—operating system, word processing, spreadsheets, and database—we present a few pages of description on the purposes and generic commands of this software.
- **Case study.** We describe a short case study on which the lab directions and exercises will be based.
- **Step-by-step solutions.** We describe in detail the solution to the case in order to demonstrate the capabilities of the software package.
- **List of key terms.** New terms introduced in the lesson are summarized.

- **Problems.** The lesson concludes with practice problems that show the applicability of the software to business problems.

Diskettes Provided

Two types of diskettes are provided:

- **Data diskettes.** Data diskettes are provided to the instructor and are freely copyable. The first lab shows students how to duplicate these diskettes for their own use during the course. This is an integral part of the first lab and teaches students the skills of formatting and copying. Students are expected to provide their own blank diskettes for duplication.
- **Program diskettes.** Educational versions of popular applications software are offered by McGraw-Hill in two ways: (1) At no extra charge, a master diskette can be provided to the instructor. Students can then duplicate this diskette in the first lab. (2) For a modest extra fee, copies of certain applications software—dBASE III PLUS, Quattro, SuperCalc4, and a choice of either WordPerfect 4.2 or WordStar 4.0—can be packaged with the book and sold as a set to the student.

Teaching Materials: The Support Package

Teaching Materials are available separately for *Computing Essentials* and also for each of the lab modules in the McGraw-Hill Microcomputing series.

Each *Teaching Materials* volume consists of the following:

- **Instructor's Manual.** The Instructor's Manual offers lecture notes to accompany the *Essentials* or the individual labs. It also provides specific suggestions on how to teach the *Essentials* text or the labs texts, such as presenting problems students commonly encounter and ways to expand and extend each lab's content.
- **Printed Test Bank.** The printed test bank contains true-false or multiple-choice questions for the *Essentials* text or the lab texts.
- **Overhead Transparency Masters.** Applicable artwork from the text is provided as masters for making overhead transparencies.

  Other support materials available are:

- **Instructor's Data Disk Set.** Includes 5¼- and 3½-inch disks containing the data files for all lab modules.
- **Overhead Transparencies.** A set of four-color transparencies is available.
- **Videotapes.** A sales representative can describe the videotapes available from the McGraw-Hill series, *Computers at Work*.
- **Computerized Test Bank.** Includes the test banks for the *Essentials* text as well as for all lab modules.
- **Computer Resource Library.** A hypercard stack that contains dynamic presentation material for the computer concepts part of the class as well as basics of applications software material.
- **Computerized Glossary of Terms.** An on-line "electronic" look-up of 1400 terms.

Acknowledgments

We were very fortunate to have a great deal of fine input and ongoing advice from the McGraw-Hill Microcomputer Advisory Board: Bob Autrey, Mesa Community College;

Jerry Booher, Scottsdale Community College; and Chuck Riden, Arizona State University, Mesa Community College, and Dobson High School. A special thanks goes to those industry professionals who have given invaluable insights into the use of microcomputers in today's work life. They include Bill Bauer, Ernst & Whinney; Brian Corke and Gene Kunkle, Sun State Seafoods; and Ernie Ziak, Western Reserve Family Sports Center.

We are also grateful for the helpful comments and criticisms of reviewers: Henry Altieri, Norwalk State Technical College; Harvey Blessing, Essex Community College; Cathy Brotherton, Riverside Community College; Tim De Clue, Southwest Baptist University; Kevin Duggan, Midlands Technical College; Jeanine Englehart, Coastline Community College; J. Patrick Fenton, West Valley College; Nancy Gillespie, Glassboro State College; Carla Hall, St. Louis Community College–Florissant Valley; Peter Irwin, Richland College; Barbara Jauken, Southeast Community College; Cynthia Kachik, Santa Fe Community College; Philip E. Lowry, University of Nevada–Las Vegas; Deborah Ludford, Glendale Community College; Brian Monahan, Iona College; Don Myers, Vincennes University; Dean Orris, Butler University; James Payne, Kellogg Community College; Allan Peck, Springfield Technical Community College; James Phillips, Helena Vocational Technical Center; Rick Phillips, Roosevelt University; Leonard Presby, William Paterson College; Lorilee Sadler, Indiana University; Sandra Stalker, North Shore Community College; Hamilton Stirling, University of South Florida at Saint Petersburg; Douglas Topham; Michael Trombetta, Queensborough Community College; and Jeannetta Williams, Piedmont Virginia Community College. We are particularly grateful to David Adams from Northern Kentucky University for his expert assistance and advice on the Macintosh operating system.

A special note of thanks goes out to Shelley Langman of Bellevue Community College for her detailed review of this revision.

In addition, we are extremely appreciative of all the efforts of the McGraw-Hill and Mitchell staff and others who worked on this book: Roger Howell, Laurie Boudreau, and Steve Mitchell for their enthusiastic support of the 1991–1992 edition; Betty Drury and Jane Somers for their production supervision; Mel Haber for his splendid interior and cover designs; and James Hill, Karen Jackson, Eric Munson, and Seib Adams for their past and present editorial and marketing support.

We are also grateful for the contributions of those outside McGraw-Hill and Mitchell: Jim Elam for his dedication and thoughtful suggestions; Colleen Hayes for her thorough software evaluation and recommendations; Greg Hubit for his project management; Karl Konrad for his excellent programming support; Pat Rogondino for her illustrations and design support; Peg Sallade for permission to use parts of her research paper, "Acquatic Fitness"; Monica Suder and Associates for photo research; Lura Dymond for copyediting; Dorothy Wilson for proofreading; and York Graphic Services for composition.

Finally, a book of this nature could not be done without the superb contributions of equipment manufacturers and software developers, who furnished us photographs of their products without charge. In particular, we want to give special thanks to Jessie O. Kempter and the IBM Corporation in White Plains, New York.

Write to Us

We welcome your response to this book, for we are truly trying to make it as useful as possible. Write to us in care of: Information Systems Editor, Mitchell/McGraw-Hill, 55 Penny Lane, Watsonville, CA 95076.

Timothy J. O'Leary
Brian K. Williams
Linda I. O'Leary

CHAPTER 1
You and Computer Competency

Computer competency: This notion may not be familiar to you, but it's easy to understand. The purpose of this book is to help you become *competent* in computer-related skills. Specifically, we want to help you walk into a job and immediately be of value to an employer. First we describe why learning about the computer is important to your future. Then we describe the five parts of a microcomputer system: people, procedures, software, hardware, and data.

Ten years ago, most people had little to do with computers, at least directly. Of course, they filled out computerized forms, took computerized tests, and paid computerized bills. But the real work with computers was handled by specialists—programmers, data-entry clerks, and computer operators.

Then microcomputers came along and changed everything. Today it is easy for nearly everybody to use a computer. People who use microcomputers today are called "end users" (see Figure 1-1 on p. 2). Some examples:

- Microcomputers are common tools in all areas of life. Writers write, artists draw, engineers and scientists calculate—all on microcomputers. Businesspeople do all three.
- New forms of learning have developed. People who are homebound, who work odd hours, or who travel frequently may take courses by telephone-linked home computers. A course need not fit within the usual time of a quarter or a semester.
- Expert knowledge is readily at hand. Whatever your field or prospective field—from animal husbandry to tax law—programs probably exist that can offer you advice. Powerful "expert systems" make the wisdom of professionals available to you.

What about you? How can microcomputers enhance *your* life?

COMPETENCIES

After you have read this chapter, you should be able to:

1. Explain computer competency.

2. Distinguish four kinds of computers: microcomputer, minicomputer, mainframe, and supercomputer.

3. Explain the five parts of a microcomputer system: people, procedures, software, hardware, and data.

4. Distinguish applications software from systems software.

5. Describe hardware devices for input, processing, storage, output, and communications.

6. Describe the categories of data: character (byte), field, record, and file.

7. Explain computer connectivity.

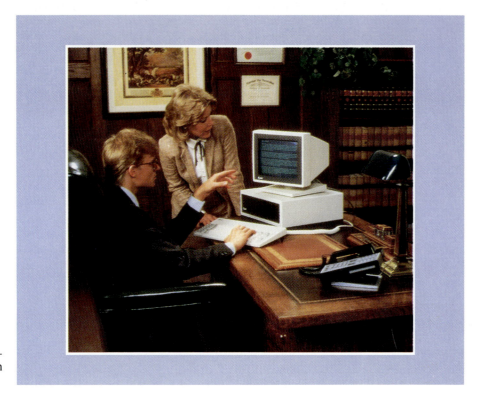

FIGURE 1-1
End users: people are using microcomputers to meet their information needs.

End Users and Computer Competency

By Gaining Computer Competency, End Users Can Use Microcomputers to Improve Their Productivity and Their Value in the Workplace.

End users are people who use microcomputers or have access to larger computers. If you are not an end user already, it is almost certain that you will become one in the near future. That is, you will learn to make use of prewritten computer programs to meet your unique needs for information. Let us point out two things here.

- By "prewritten programs," we mean programs that you can buy rather than those you have to write yourself. A video game on a diskette is an example of a prewritten program. But here we describe work-related programs, such as word processing for typing documents and electronic spreadsheets for analysis.
- By "needs," we mean various organizing, managing, or business needs. That is, they are *information-related* or *decision-making* needs. Becoming **computer competent**—learning how to use the computer to meet your information needs—will improve your productivity. And it will make you a more valuable employee.

How much do you have to know to be computer competent? Clearly, in today's fast-changing technological world, you cannot learn everything—but very few people need to. You don't have to be a computer scientist to make good use of a microcomputer.

Indeed, that is precisely the point of this book. Our goal is not to teach you everything there is to know but only what you *need* to know. Thus, we present only what we think you will find most useful—both now and in the future.

Four Kinds of Computers

Computers Are of Four Types: Microcomputers, Minicomputers, Mainframes, and Supercomputers.

This book focuses principally on microcomputers. However, it is almost certain that you will come in contact at least indirectly with other kinds of computers, too. Thus, we describe many features that are common to these larger machines.

Computers are categorized into four types: *microcomputers, minicomputers, mainframe computers,* and *supercomputers*. We discuss these in detail later in the book, but here let us give a quick description for purposes of comparison.

- **Microcomputers** are small computers that can fit on a desktop. They are often called **personal computers.** Some microcomputers are small enough to be portable (*laptops* and *notebooks*). Until recently, the more powerful microcomputers, those used by engineers and scientists, were called **workstations.** However, the distinction between personal computers and workstations is now blurring. The demand for some types of microcomputers has been growing spectacularly over the years (see Figure 1-2).

- **Minicomputers** are refrigerator-size machines that fall in between microcomputers and mainframes in their processing speeds and data-storing capacities. Medium-size companies or departments of large companies typically

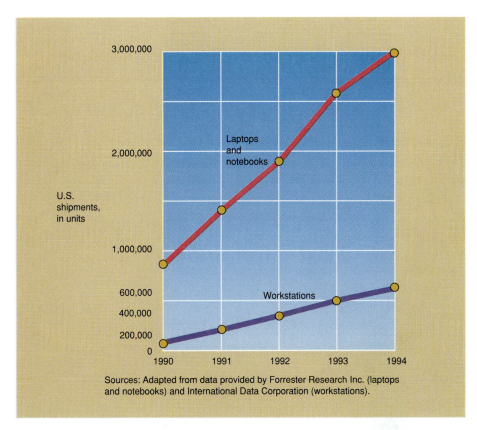

FIGURE 1-2
Increased demand for microcomputers—laptops/notebooks and workstations.

use them for specific purposes. For example, they might use them to do research or to monitor a particular manufacturing process. Smaller-size companies typically use minicomputers for their general data processing needs, such as accounting.

- **Mainframe computers** are large computers occupying specially wired, air-conditioned rooms and capable of great processing speeds and data storage. They are used by large organizations—businesses, banks, universities, government agencies—to handle millions of transactions. For example, insurance companies use mainframes to process information about millions of policies.
- **Supercomputers** are special, high-capacity computers used by very large organizations principally for research purposes. Among their uses are weapons research, oil exploration, and worldwide weather forecasting.

Let us now get started on the road to computer competency. We begin by describing the microcomputer as a system.

The Five Parts of a Microcomputer System

A Microcomputer System Has Five Parts: People, Procedures, Software, Hardware, and Data.

When you think of a microcomputer, perhaps you think of just the equipment itself. That is, you think of the video display screen or the keyboard. There is more to it than that. The way to think about a microcomputer is as a *system*. A **microcomputer system** has five parts, as shown in Figure 1-3 and as described below: *people, procedures, software, hardware,* and *data.*

- *People:* It is easy to overlook people as one of the five parts of a microcomputer system. Yet that is what microcomputers are all about—making people, end users, more productive.
- *Procedures:* **Procedures** are manuals containing rules or guidelines to follow when using software, hardware, and data. Procedures are also used for connecting to other computer systems. These manuals are usually written by computer specialists for particular organizations. Software and hardware manufacturers also provide manuals with their products. An example is the Lotus 1-2-3 Reference Manual.

FIGURE 1-3
The five parts of a microcomputer system.

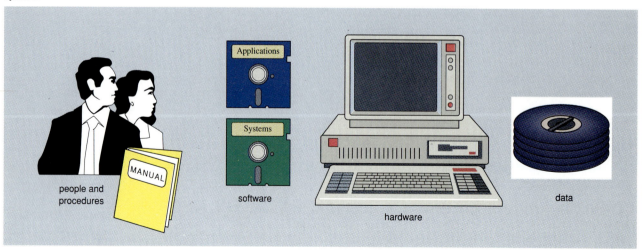

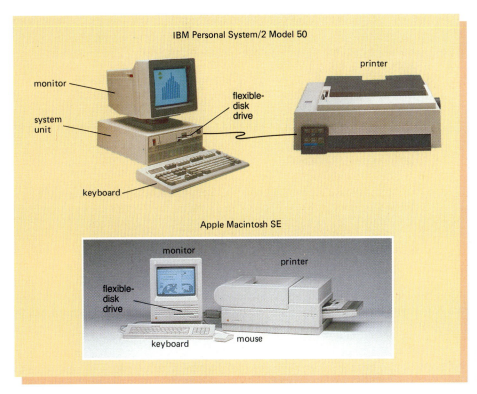

FIGURE 1-4
Two well-known microcomputer hardware systems.

- *Software:* **Software** is another name for a program or programs. A **program** is the step-by-step instructions that tell the computer how to do its work. The purpose of software is to convert *data* (unprocessed facts) into *information* (processed facts).
- *Hardware:* The **hardware** consists of the equipment: keyboard, monitor (video display screen), printer, the computer itself, and other devices. Figure 1-4 shows hardware for two well-known microcomputer systems—the IBM PS/2 Model 50 and the Apple Macintosh SE.
- *Data:* **Data** consists of the raw, unprocessed facts that are input to the system. Examples of raw facts are hours you worked and your pay rate. After data is processed through the computer, it is usually called **information.** An example of such information is the total wages owed you for a week's work.

In large computer systems, there are specialists who deal with writing procedures, developing software, and creating data. In microcomputer systems, however, end users often perform these operations. To be a competent end user, you must understand the essentials of software, hardware, and data.

Software

Software Is of Two Kinds. Applications Software, Which May Be Custom-Written or Come in Packaged Form, Does "End-User" Work. Systems Software Does "Background" Work.

Software, as we mentioned, is another name for programs. Programs are the instructions that tell the computer how to process data into the form you want. In most cases, the words *software* and *programs* are interchangeable.

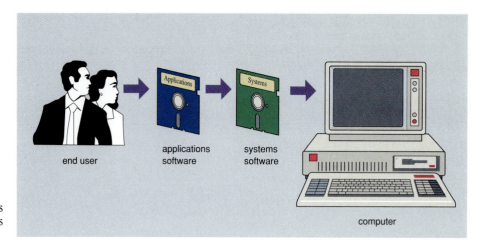

FIGURE 1-5
End users interact with applications software. Systems software interacts with the computer.

There are two major kinds of software—*applications software* and *systems software*. You can think of applications software as the kind you use. Think of systems software as the kind the computer uses (see Figure 1-5).

Applications Software **Applications software** might be described as "end-user" software. Applications software performs useful work on general-purpose tasks such as word processing and cost estimating.

Applications software may be *packaged* or *custom-made*.

- **Packaged software** consists of any program that has been prewritten by a professional programmer and is typically offered for sale on a diskette. There are over 12,000 different types of applications packages available for microcomputers alone.
- **Custom-made software,** or **custom programs,** is what *all* software used to be. Twenty years ago organizations hired computer programmers to create all their software. The programmer custom-wrote programs to instruct the company computer to perform whatever tasks the organization wanted. A program might compute payroll checks, keep track of goods in the warehouse, calculate sales commissions, or perform similar business needs.

There are certain general-purpose programs that we call "*basic tools*" in this book. These programs are widely used in nearly all career areas. They are the kind of programs you *have* to know to be considered computer competent. We discuss these in Chapter 2.

The most popular so-called basic tools are:

- *Word processing* programs, used to prepare written documents
- *Electronic spreadsheets,* used to analyze and summarize data
- *File and database managers,* used to organize and manage data and information
- *Graphics programs,* used to present data visually, as charts and graphs
- *Communications programs,* used to transmit and receive data
- *Integrated programs,* which combine some or all of these programs in one package

Systems Software The user interacts with applications software. **Systems software** enables the applications software to interact with the computer (refer to Figure 1-5).

Systems software is "background" software. It includes programs that help the computer manage its own internal resources.

The most important systems software program is the **operating system,** which interacts between the applications software and the computer. The operating system handles such details as running ("executing") programs, storing data and programs, and processing ("manipulating") data. Systems software frees users to concentrate on solving problems rather than on the complexities of operating the computer.

Microcomputer operating systems are in the process of changing as the machines themselves become more powerful and outgrow the older operating systems. Today's computer competency, then, requires that you have some knowledge of the four most popular microcomputer operating systems:

- *DOS,* the standard operating system for International Business Machines (IBM) and IBM-compatible microcomputers.
- *OS/2,* the operating system developed for IBM's more powerful microcomputers.
- *Macintosh operating system,* which runs only on Apple Corporation's Macintosh computers.
- *Unix,* an operating system originally developed for minicomputers. Unix is now important because it can run on many of the more powerful microcomputers.

Hardware

Microcomputer Hardware Consists of Devices for Data Input, Processing, Storage, Output, and Communications.

Microcomputer hardware—the physical equipment—falls into five categories. They are *input devices, the system unit, secondary storage, output devices,* and *communications devices.* Because we discuss hardware in detail later in the book, we will present just a quick overview here.

Input Devices **Input devices** are equipment that translates data and programs that humans can understand into a form that the computer can process. The most common input devices for the microcomputer are the keyboard and the mouse (see Figure 1-6). The **keyboard** on a computer looks like a typewriter keyboard, but it has additional

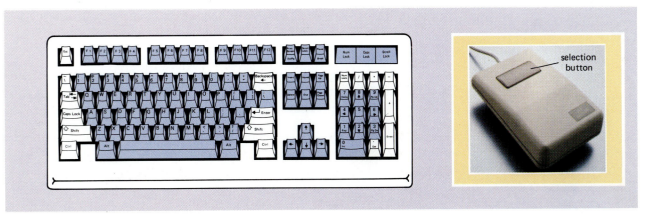

FIGURE 1-6
Microcomputer keyboard and mouse.

8
You and Computer Competency

FIGURE 1-7
An open system cabinet of an IBM PS/2 Model 30.

FIGURE 1-8
Relative size of a microprocessor chip.

FIGURE 1-9
5¼-inch flexible diskette.

FIGURE 1-10
3½-inch flexible diskette.

specialized keys. A **mouse** is a device that can be rolled about on the desktop. It directs the **cursor,** or pointer, on the display screen. A mouse has selection buttons for entering commands. It is also used to draw figures.

The System Unit The **system unit** is housed within the computer cabinet (see Figure 1-7). The system unit consists of electronic circuitry that has two parts.

- The **central processing unit (CPU)** controls and manipulates data to produce information. A microcomputer's CPU is contained on a tiny (⅛-inch-square) *microprocessor,* or "microscopic processor." Microprocessors are called *integrated circuits* or *processor chips* (see Figure 1-8).
- **Primary storage,** also known as **memory,** holds data and program instructions for processing the data. It also holds the processed information before it is output. Primary storage is located in the system unit on tiny *memory chips.*

Secondary Storage Primary storage is part of the system unit and is used to hold data and instructions only *temporarily.* That is, the data and instructions exist only as long as the electrical power to the computer is turned on. **Secondary storage** devices store data and programs *permanently.* These devices are located outside of the central processing unit, although they may still be built into the system unit cabinet.

For microcomputers, the most important kinds of secondary storage "media" are as follows:

- **Flexible diskettes** (also called "floppy disks") hold data or programs in the form of magnetized spots on plastic platters. The two sizes in most common use are 5¼-inch and 3½-inch diskettes (see Figures 1-9 and 1-10). The

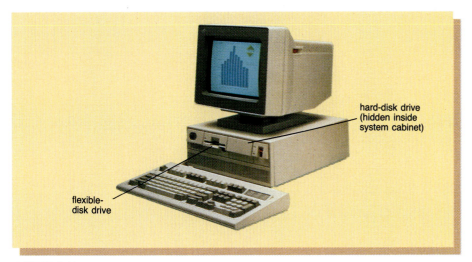

FIGURE 1-11
Two kinds of disk drives: flexible and hard. Hard disks are not removable from the drives.

newer, smaller size, which can fit in a shirt pocket, is more durable and can hold more and therefore is gaining rapidly in popularity.

A flexible diskette is inserted into a **disk drive** (see Figure 1-11). This mechanism **reads** data from the diskette. That is, the magnetized spots on the diskette are converted to electronic signals and transmitted to primary storage inside the computer. A disk drive can also **write** data. That is, it can take the electronic information processed by the computer and record it magnetically onto the diskette.

Flexible-disk drives are usually built into the system cabinet, but they also may be separate units outside it.

■ A **hard disk** contains one or more metallic disks encased within a disk drive. Like flexible disks, hard disks hold data or programs in the form of magnetized spots. They also *read* and *write* data in much the same way as do flexible disks. However, the storage capacity of a hard-disk unit is many times that of a flexible disk.

Flexible diskettes are inserted and removed from their disk drives and are stored separately. The hard disk, by contrast, typically is not removable. Hard-disk drives are usually built into a system cabinet (see Figure 1-11), but there are also external hard-disk drives.

Many microcomputer systems have two flexible-disk drives. One drive is referred to as drive A and the other as drive B (see Figure 1-12). Many other microcomputer systems have one flexible-disk drive and one hard-disk drive. The flexible-disk unit is referred to as drive A and the hard-disk unit as drive C.

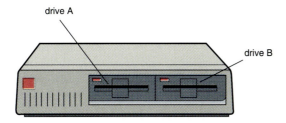

FIGURE 1-12
Drives A and B on an IBM personal computer.

FIGURE 1-13
Newer monitors show crisp images and vivid colors.

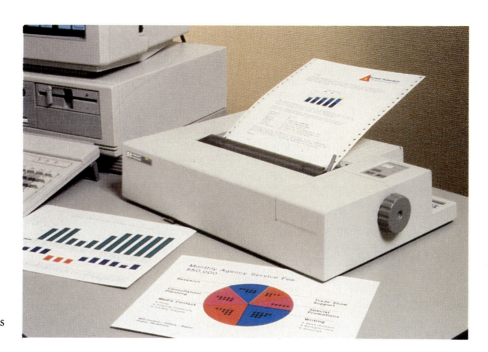

FIGURE 1-14
Some printers can print color images on paper.

Output Devices Output devices are pieces of equipment that translate the processed information from the CPU into a form that humans can understand. One of the most important output devices is the **monitor,** or **video display screen,** which may resemble a television screen. The quality of monitors has improved dramatically. Many monitors now offer crisp images and vivid colors (see Figure 1-13). Another important output device is the **printer,** a device that produces printed paper output. Some printers can also print in color (see Figure 1-14).

FIGURE 1-15
External modem connecting a microcomputer and a telephone.

Communications Devices Communications hardware sends data and programs from one computer or secondary storage device to another. Many microcomputers use a **modem** (pronounced "*moh*-dem"). This device translates the electronic signals from the computer into electronic signals that can travel over a telephone line. A modem at the other end of the line then translates the signals for the receiving computer. A modem may be located inside a microcomputer's system cabinet. It may also be a separate unit (see Figure 1-15).

Data

Data Is Organized into Characters, Fields, Records, and Files.

To be a competent end user, you must understand the essentials of hardware, software, and data. Now that we know the first two, let us describe what data is.

Data consists of the characters that are input to the computer system. Data is organized into four increasingly sophisticated levels, as follows:

- A **character** is a letter, number, or special symbol—for example, M, 3, or $.
- A **field** is an item of data consisting of one or more logically related characters. An example of a field is your last name, social security number, or driver's license number.
- A **record** is a collection of related fields. For example, all information on a driver's license would be one record. All information on a registration card for one college course would be another record.
- A **file** is a collection of related records. For example, all driver's licenses issued or renewed in your state today make one file. All information about a student's courses and grades in the registrar's office makes another file.

These categories of data can be collected together into a sophisticated structure known as a **database.** A database is a collection of integrated data.

Connectivity

Connectivity Is the Microcomputer's Ability to Communicate with Other Computers and Information Sources.

Connectivity is the capability of the microcomputer to use information from the world beyond your desk. Connectivity is a concept, not a thing. Data and information can be sent over telephone or cable lines and through the air. Thus, your microcomputer can be *connected* to other microcomputers, to many computerized data banks, and other sources of information that lie well beyond your desk.

Connectivity is a very significant development, for it expands the uses of the microcomputer severalfold. Central to the concept of connectivity is the **computer network.** A network is a communications system connecting two or more computers and their peripheral devices. All major companies have **local area networks** (**LANs**), in which computers within the same building or organization are connected by communications lines. In addition, a microcomputer may be linked to regional, national, and international networks.

With all these possible connections at your disposal, perhaps you can begin to see how important connectivity is. By using a modem and communications software, you can transmit information to other computers. You can exchange messages with other microcomputer users. (Some arrangements require a fee, but some are free, except for telephone line charges.) You can receive all kinds of information from data banks and databases—electronic libraries and catalogs—connected with large computers. Indeed, connectivity is changing the very nature of how large computers are being used.

A Look at the Future: You and Computer Competency

Computer Competency Is Understanding the Rules and the Power of Microcomputers. Competency Enables You to Take Advantage of Increasingly Productive Software and Hardware and the Connectivity Revolution That Are Expanding the Microcomputer's Capabilities.

The purpose of this book is to help you be computer competent not only in the present but also in the future. Having competency requires your having the knowledge and understanding of the rules and the power of the microcomputer. This will enable you to benefit from three important developments: more powerful software, more powerful hardware, and connectivity to outside information systems.

Powerful Software The software now available can do an extraordinary number of tasks and help you in an endless number of ways. More and more employers are expecting the people they hire to be able to use it. Thus, we spend the next two chapters describing applications software—what we call "basic tools"—and systems software.

Powerful Hardware Microcomputers are now much more powerful than they used to be. Indeed, the newer models have the speed and power of room-size computers of only a few years ago. However, despite the rapid change of specific equipment, their essential features remain unchanged. Thus, the competent end user should focus on these features. Chapters 4 through 6 explain what you need to know about hardware: the central processing unit, input/output devices, and secondary storage.

Connectivity The principle of *connectivity* is a revolutionary development. No longer are microcomputers and competent end users bounded by the surface of the desk.

Now they can reach past the desk and link up with other computers to share data, programs, and information. Accordingly, we devote Chapters 7 through 9 to discussing connectivity: communications, files and databases, and information systems.

To competently develop access to information beyond your desktop, you must understand how information systems are created and modified. This is done with the techniques of systems analysis and design. The most successful end users not only use existing systems to generate information; they also know how to improve on these systems. They know how to evaluate and integrate new technology to improve the quality and accessibility of information. This is called *systems analysis and design*. We cover this subject in Chapter 10.

One part of systems analysis and design may include the creation of new software—specially designed programs. We describe the process of developing new software in Chapter 11.

Emerging Microcomputer Applications In addition to certain applications programs called "basic tools," we need to explore some emerging applications programs—what we call "power tools." These are programs that, until recently, were not available on microcomputers, only on mainframe computers. However, as microcomputers have become more powerful, these programs have become more available and less expensive. Learning to use this kind of software will enable you to distinguish yourself from other computer-competent people. It will enable you to work productively in innovative ways that will place you among the computer-competent of the future.

In Chapter 12, we describe the following examples of so-called power tools. *Desktop managers* are used to increase the efficiency of the end user, replacing the usual desktop "accessories" of calculators, address books, and the like. *Project management software* is used to plan, schedule, and control the people, resources, and costs of a project. *Desktop publishing* is used to create professional-quality résumés, reports, newsletters, and other publications mixing both text and graphics. What has come to be called "new media" includes hypertext and multimedia, which enable users to link related pieces of information in exciting ways. *Hypertext* is software that can connect any text or picture file with any other. *Multimedia* can link text, graphics, video, or sound. *CAD/CAM* is used to design and manufacture products.

The field of computer science known as *artificial intelligence (AI)* attempts to develop computer systems that can mimic or simulate human thought processes and actions. AI includes robotics, knowledge-based and expert systems, and artificial reality. *Robotics* is the field of study concerned with developing and using robots. *Knowledge-based systems* and *expert systems* in effect capture the knowledge of human experts and make it accessible to others through a computer program. They extend one's capacity to perform certain jobs at the level of an expert. *Artificial reality* consists of interactive sensory equipment (headgear and gloves) and software that allows one to experience alternative realities to the physical world.

Workplace Issues, Privacy, Security, and Your Future Very few parts of society now exist in which computers are not an important presence. Consequently, we must now consider their relationship to our personal lives. Chapter 13 describes workplace issues, including how we can avoid certain physical and mental health matters associated with computers. The chapter also considers privacy issues, such as the spread of personal information without your consent. Finally, it discusses security matters, such as computer-related crimes.

The final chapter, Chapter 14, shows you how to keep up and stay ahead—to stay computer competent in the future.

CHAPTER 1
You and Computer Competency

V I S U A L   S U M M A R Y

People and Procedures

People

People are competent end users working to increase their productivity. **End users** use microcomputers and prewritten programs (such as word processing and spreadsheet programs) to solve information-related or decision-making problems.

Procedures

Procedures are manuals and guidelines that guide and instruct end users on how to use the software and hardware.

Software

Software is another name for **programs**—instructions that tell the computer how to process data. Two kinds of software are applications software and systems software.

Applications Software

Applications software is "end-user" software that helps perform useful work. Such software may be **packaged** (prewritten) or **custom-made** (written by a programmer). Examples of general-purpose packaged software ("basic tools") are:
- *Word processing* programs—to prepare written documents.
- *Electronic spreadsheets*—to analyze and summarize data.
- *File and database managers*—to organize and manage data and information.
- *Graphics programs*—to present data visually, as charts and graphs.
- *Communications programs*—to transmit and receive data.
- *Integrated programs*—combine some or all of the preceding programs in one package.

Systems Software

Systems software is "background" software that helps a computer manage its internal resources. An example is the **operating system**, which interacts between applications software and the computer. Four popular microcomputer operating systems are:
- *DOS*—today's standard operating system for IBM and IBM-compatible microcomputers.
- *OS/2*—new operating system developed for IBM's most powerful microcomputers.
- *Macintosh operating system*—runs on Apple's Macintosh computers.
- *Unix*—runs on many powerful microcomputers.

Visual Summary

Computers Are of Four Types:

- **Microcomputers**—desktop or portable size, known as **personal computers** or **workstations**.
- **Minicomputers**—medium-size machines for medium-size organizations and departments within larger organizations.
- **Mainframes**—large machines for large organizations.
- **Supercomputers**—high-capacity machines for research.

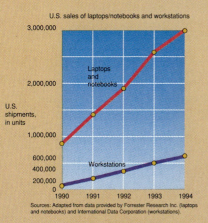

Hardware

Input Devices

Input devices take data and put it into a form the computer can process. Especially important is the **keyboard**, a typewriter-like keyboard with specialized keys.

The System Unit

The **system unit**, housed in a microcomputer's cabinet, consists of electronic circuitry with two parts:
- **The central processing unit (CPU)**—controls and manipulates data to produce information.
- **Primary storage** (**memory**)—temporarily holds data for processing, program instructions for processing the data, and processed data before it is output.

Secondary Storage

Secondary storage permanently stores data and programs. Two storage "media" are:
- **Flexible diskettes**—removable flexible 5¼-inch or 3½-inch plastic disks.
- **Hard disk**—nonremovable, enclosed disk drive.

Output Devices

Output devices output processed information from CPU. Two important output devices:
- **Monitor**—TV screen–like device to display results.
- **Printer**—device that prints out images on paper.

Communications Devices

These send and receive data and programs from one computer to another. A device that connects a microcomputer to a telephone is a **modem**.

Data and Connectivity

Data

Data consists of characters that are input into the computer system. Data organization:
- **Character**—letter, number, special character.
- **Field**—set of related characters (e.g., person's name).
- **Record**—set of related fields (e.g., name and address).
- **File**—set of related records (e.g., all names and addresses of companies applied to for work).
- **Database**—a collection of integrated data.

Connectivity

Connectivity is a concept describing the ability of end users to tap into resources well beyond their desktops. With **computer networks**—communications connections—microcomputers can be linked to other microcomputers, minicomputers, or mainframes to share data and resources. Connectivity greatly expands the power of end users.

Review Questions

1. What is *computer competency?*
2. Who are *end users?*
3. What are *prewritten programs?*
4. Distinguish among the four kinds of computers: microcomputers, minicomputers, mainframes, and supercomputers.
5. Describe the five parts of a microcomputer system.
6. Distinguish between applications software and systems software.
7. How do packaged software and custom-made software differ?
8. Name some principal kinds of packaged software—what we call software "basic tools."
9. Name the five categories of microcomputer hardware.
10. What common input device will you probably use?
11. What are the two parts of the system unit, and what do they do?
12. What is the difference between primary storage and secondary storage?
13. Distinguish between flexible diskettes and hard disks.
14. What is the difference between a program diskette and a data diskette?
15. What is a monitor?
16. What output device produces images on paper?
17. What does a modem do?
18. What are the four increasingly sophisticated levels of data?
19. What is *connectivity?*
20. Give three important reasons why gaining competency in microcomputers is important.
21. What are some software "power tools" that are emerging for microcomputer end users that formerly were found only on mainframes?

Discussion Questions

1. Motivation is everything. No matter how much you think you *ought* to learn something, knowledge comes harder if you don't really *want* to learn it. Here is a chance to pinpoint *why* you want to gain computer competency. Imagine your dream career. How do you think microcomputers, from what you already know, can help you do the work you want to do?

2. Video games have become a big part of some people's leisure time. But microcomputers have also become a big part of other kinds of after-work pursuits. Many hobbyists use microcomputers linked by telephones to so-called electronic bulletin boards to share interests such as travel or science fiction. Others catalog their music collections, books, and baseball cards. Others use electronic spreadsheets to track sports statistics or investment ideas. What kind of after-hours interests do you have? Assuming you could afford one, how could a microcomputer bring new skills or value to those interests?

CHAPTER 2
Applications Software: Basic Tools

Think of the microcomputer as an *enabler*. People may not consider themselves as being very good at typing. Or at doing calculations, drawing charts, or looking up information. A microcomputer, however, enables you to do all these things—and much more. All it takes is the right kind of software—the programs that go into the computer. We describe the most important ones here.

Not long ago, all the things you can now do with a microcomputer were performed mostly by trained specialists. Secretaries typed professional-looking business correspondence. Market analysts used pencils and paper and calculators to project sales. Graphic artists drew colored charts. Data processing experts stored files of records on large computers. Now you can do all these tasks—and much more—with just *one* microcomputer. And many of these tasks can be done with just *one* applications program.

Using Software Off the Shelf

Some Features Are Common to All Kinds of Applications Packages.

Word processing, electronic spreadsheets, database managers, graphics programs, communications programs, and software that combines all five tasks are *general-purpose applications packages*. That is, they may be used by many people for many different kinds of tasks. This is why we have called them "basic tools." Packaged software is also called **off-the-shelf software.** Some well-known software publishers are Lotus Corporation, famous for spreadsheets; Borland (database); and WordPerfect and Microsoft (word processors).

Some features are common to most packaged programs. The following are the most important.

COMPETENCIES

After you have read this chapter, you should be able to:

1. Explain the features common to all kinds of applications software.

2. Describe applications software for word processing, spreadsheets, database managers, graphics, and communications.

3. Describe integrated software that combines all these tasks.

```
Dear New Sports Club Member:

     Congratulations on your new membership in the Sports Club.
All of us on the staff welcome you and encourage you to
participate in the many tournaments, leagues and club
activities offered throughout the year.

     Each month you will receive a newsletter about the upcoming
events at the club. If you have questions about the event
or would like to sign up to participate in an event, just call or
come in to the front desk personnel.

     The club facilities include 18 lighted tennis courts,
5 racquetball courts, an Olympic-size swimming pool, Nautilus
equipped weight room, and basketball court. For your comfort
while using the club, the men's and ladies' locker rooms
each have showers, a sauna, and a steam room. A spa for both men
and women is located between the locker rooms. The lounge and
cafe are open to serve you throughout the day and evening.

     On behalf of the staff of the Sports Club, I hope
your association with the Club is long and enjoyable._             — cu

        1 Full Text; 2 Page; 3 Options; 4 Printer Control; 5 Type-thru; 6 Preview: 0
```

FIGURE 2-1
A word processing screen, with cursor and menu bar (WordPerfect 5.0).

The Cursor and Scrolling   The *cursor* is a blinking symbol on the screen (see Figure 2-1). It shows where you may enter data next. You can move the cursor around using cursor control keys, such as the directional arrow keys on many keyboards. You can also move the cursor using a mouse.

Scrolling is a feature that lets you move quickly through the text forward or backward. Thus, you can look at a screen full (20–22 lines, as shown in Figure 2-1) of your work. By issuing a command, you can then move ("scroll") through the screen and into the following screens.

Menus   Most software packages have **menus,** which list commands available for manipulating data. Menus are of two kinds:

- **Menu bar:** This is a line or two across the top or bottom of the screen listing commands available (see Figure 2-1).
- **Pull-down menu:** This is a list of commands that "drops down" from a menu bar at the top of the screen (see Figure 2-2).

Most applications programs also offer a **Help menu** or **Help screen** (see Figure 2-3). Help menus present a choice of step-by-step explanations on how to perform various tasks. Help menus are particularly useful when you need assistance but don't have an instruction manual handy.

Format   You can change the **format,** or "look," of your work. For instance, the line spacing in a letter can be altered. It can be double spaced or single spaced. Top, bottom, left, and right margins can be made narrower or wider. In a spreadsheet, the width of columns can be changed.

Special-Purpose and Function Keys   Computer keyboards have **special-purpose keys,** such as *Esc* ("Escape") and *Ctrl* ("Control"). Special-purpose keys are used to enter

your words on a diskette or hard disk. Then you turn on the printer and print out the results on paper.

The beauty of this method is that you can make any changes or corrections—before printing out the document. Even after your document is printed out, you can easily go back and make changes. You can then print it out again. Want to change a report from double spaced to single spaced? Alter the width of the margins on the left and right? Delete some paragraphs and add some others from yet another document? A word processor allows you to do all these with ease. Indeed, *deleting, inserting,* and *replacing*—the principal correcting activities—can be done just by pressing keys on the keyboard.

Once it was thought that only secretaries would use word processors. However, they are used extensively in managerial and professional life. Indeed, it has been found that, among the basic software tools, word processors produce the most productive gains.

Popular word processing packages include WordPerfect, Word, and MacWrite. Some interesting features shared by most word processors are described in the following sections.

Word Wrap and the Enter Key One outstanding word processing feature is **word wrap.** On a typewriter, you must decide when to finish typing a line. You indicate the end of a line by pressing a carriage return key. A word processor decides for you and automatically moves the cursor to the next line. As you keep typing, the words "wrap around" to the next line. To begin a new paragraph or leave a blank line, you press the Enter key.

Search and Replace A **search** command allows you to find any word or number that you know exists in your document. When you search, the cursor will move to the first place where the item appears. If you want, the program will also search for the item everywhere it appears in the document. For example, in one word processing program (WordPerfect), if you wanted to find *Chicago* in your text, you would position the cursor at the beginning of the document and then press the *F2* function key. After the word *Search* appears at the bottom of your screen, you type *Chicago*. Then press *F2* again. The cursor will then move to the word's first occurrence.

The **replace** command automatically replaces the word you search for with another word. For example, you could search for the word *Chicago* and replace it with the word *Denver*. You can do this at every place the word *Chicago* appears or only in those instances where you choose to do so. The search and replace commands are useful for finding and fixing errors—for example, if you misspell a client's name. They also may be used to revise a document intended for one person to go to another person.

Block and Move In writing a rough draft, typewriter users find they must use "cutting and pasting." That is, they use scissors and glue or tape when moving text from one place to another. This creates a revised draft on paper. Then this revised draft must be completely retyped. Word processors eliminate this double effort.

On a word processor, the portion of text you wish to move is a **block.** You mark the block by giving commands that produce **highlighting,** a band of light over the area (see Figure 2-5 on p. 22). The task of moving the block is called a **block move.**

The block command may also be used to delete text or to copy chunks of text into another document. All this occurs before the document is printed out. You can imagine the savings in time and effort.

Other Features Almost all applications software provides commands for enter, search, and move. These features are not limited to word processors. Some other features you'll usually find in word processing packages are:

- Right margins may be **justified**—that is, evened up, like the margins in this book. Or they may be **unjustified,** given a "ragged-right" appearance like correspondence typed on a standard typewriter.

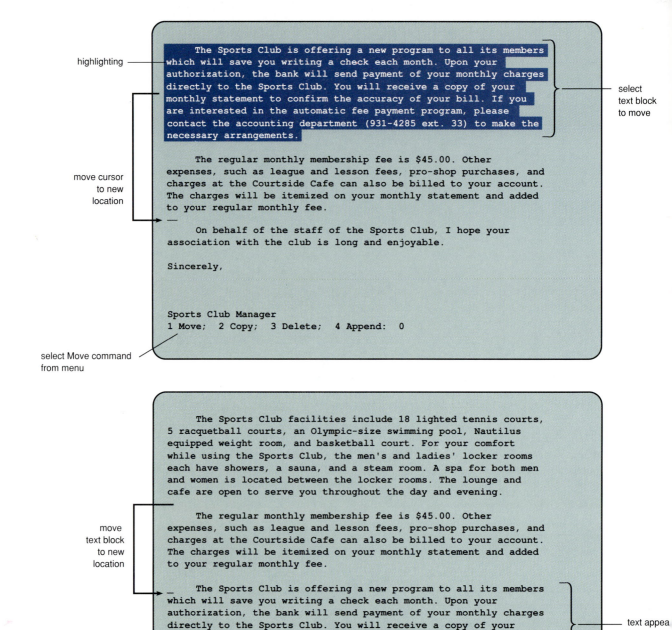

FIGURE 2-5
Example of highlighting text to identify a block, which may then be moved to another location.

- ■ Headings may be centered. A word may be typed <u>underlined</u> or **boldface** (extra dark lettering) for emphasis.
- ■ Spelling can be checked automatically, by running your text through a **spelling-checker** program.

- **Thesaurus** programs enable you to quickly find the right word or an alternative word by presenting you with an on-screen thesaurus.
- A **mail-merge** or **form-letter** feature allows you to merge different names and addresses so that you can mail out the same form letter to different people.
- **Desktop publishing** capabilities are available with some advanced word processing programs, such as WordPerfect 5.1. This feature enables you to mix text and graphics to produce newsletters and other publications of nearly professional quality.
- **Outlining programs** (sometimes called "idea processors") allow you to use Roman numerals, letters, and Arabic numbers to write an outline. You put in the main topic head, then the subtopics, sub-subtopics, and the like. If you decide to change the placement or importance of an idea, you simply move the block of text. The outline numbers and letters are resequenced automatically.
- Some programs have an **importing** feature. Files may be retrieved ("imported") from nontext programs such as spreadsheets and graphics and added to the word processing program. (The process of saving a file in a form that can be retrieved by another program is called **exporting**.)

Spreadsheets

A Spreadsheet Is an Electronic Worksheet Used to Organize and Manipulate Numbers and Display Options for "What-If" Analyses.

The **electronic spreadsheet** is based on the traditional accounting worksheet. Paper worksheets have long been used by accountants and managers to work up balance sheets, sales projections, and expense budgets. The electronic spreadsheet has rows and columns that can be used to present and analyze numeric data. (Numeric data involves numbers rather than words.) A screen of one electronic spreadsheet, the Lotus 1-2-3 package, is shown in Figure 2-6.

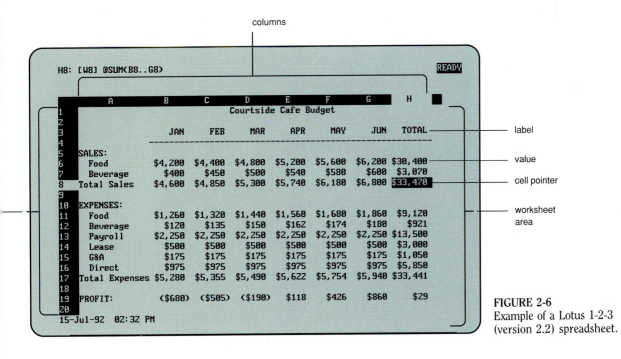

FIGURE 2-6
Example of a Lotus 1-2-3 (version 2.2) spreadsheet.

Electronic spreadsheets allow you to try out various "what-if" kinds of possibilities. That is a powerful feature. You can manipulate numbers by using stored formulas and calculate different outcomes. For example, a restaurant manager can figure out whether the business will make a profit or loss by projecting the cost of food and beverage sales over a six-month period (see Figure 2-6). The manager can then subtract expenses from sales. Expenses might include such things as payroll for employees, lease of restaurant space, and purchases of food and beverage supplies. If the expenses are too high to produce a profit, the manager can experiment on the screen with reducing some expenses. For example, the number of employees and hence payroll costs might be reduced.

Spreadsheet packages are used by financial analysts, accountants, contractors, and others concerned with manipulating numerical data. Popular spreadsheet programs are Lotus 1-2-3, Quattro Pro, Excel, and SuperCalc.

As Figure 2-6 shows, a spreadsheet has several parts. The **worksheet area** of the spreadsheet has **column headings** across the top and **row headings** down the left-hand side. The intersection of a column and row is called a **cell.** The cell holds a single unit of information. The position of a cell is called the **cell address.** For example, "*A1*" is the cell address of the first position on a spreadsheet, the topmost and leftmost position. A **cell pointer**—also known as the **spreadsheet cursor**—indicates where data is to be entered or changed in the spreadsheet. The cell pointer can be moved around in much the same way that you move a cursor in a word processing program. In Figure 2-6, the cell pointer is located in position H8.

Some common features of spreadsheet programs are described below.

Format   Column and row headings are known as **labels.** Usually a label is a word or symbol, such as a pound sign (#). A number in a cell is called a **value.** Labels and values can be displayed or formatted in different ways. A label can be centered in the cell or positioned to the left or right. A value can be displayed to show decimal places, dollars, or percent (%). The number of decimal positions (if any) can be altered, and the width of columns can be changed.

Formulas   One of the benefits of spreadsheets is that you can manipulate data through the use of formulas. **Formulas are instructions for calculations.** They make connections between numbers in particular cells. For example, the spreadsheet in Figure 2-6 on p. 23 is concerned with computing sales of food and beverages for a restaurant. The formula in Figure 2-6 is shown at the top of the screen: *H8: @SUM(B8. .G8).* This means sum, or add, the values in cells B8 through G8 (total sales from January to June). The total is then placed in cell H8.

Recalculation   **Recalculation** is one of the most important features of spreadsheets. If you change one or more numbers in your spreadsheet, all related formulas will recalculate automatically. Thus, you can substitute one value for another in the cells affected by your formula and recalculate the results.

By manipulating the values, you can use spreadsheet formulas to explore your options. For example, consider Figure 2-6. If the January-to-June sales are *estimates,* you can change any or all of the values in cells B8 through G8. The total in cell H8 will change automatically.

For more complex problems, recalculation enables you to store long, complicated formulas and many changing values and quickly produce alternatives. A contractor might need to keep the cost of building a house within a budget. The contractor can run cost calculations on various grades of materials and on the going pay rates for labor.

Windows   The screen-sized area of a spreadsheet that you are able to view is called a **window** or a **page.** Only about 20 rows and 8 columns of a spreadsheet are visible on the video display screen at one time. The total size of the spreadsheet can be much larger. Lotus 1-2-3, for instance, contains 256 rows and 8192 columns.

Other Features Most electronic spreadsheets also include additional capabilities for visually displaying and rearranging data. Among them are the following features:

- *Data displayed in graphic form:* Most spreadsheets allow users to present their data in graphic form. That is, you can display numerical information as pie charts or bar charts (as we describe on p. 27).
- *3-D graphics:* Some spreadsheet programs even permit you to display data in graphs and charts that have a three-dimensional look.
- *Graphics on worksheet:* A new feature gives users the ability to place graphical elements such as lines, arrows, and boxes directly onto the worksheet. You can thereby create charts and graphs directly on the worksheet (rather than display them separately).
- *Consolidation feature:* Data may be consolidated from several small worksheets into one large worksheet. Thus, you can work with small worksheets, which are more manageable, and summarize the data on a large worksheet.
- *Dynamic file links:* Some software offers **dynamic file links,** which allow you to link cells in one worksheet file to cells in other worksheet files. Whenever a change occurs in one file, the linked cells in the other files are automatically updated.

Database Managers

A Database Manager Organizes a Large Collection of Data So That Related Information Can Be Retrieved Easily.

A *database* is a large collection of data that has been entered into a computer system and stored for future use. The computerized information in the database is organized so that the parts that have something in common can be retrieved easily. We describe databases in detail in Chapter 8.

A **database manager** or **database management system** (**DBMS**) is a software package used to set up, or *structure,* a database. It is also used to retrieve information from a database. A screen from one kind of database manager, dBASE, is shown in Figure 2-7, p. 26. This database contains information about a health club's members. The top part is a menu. The entire list of member names and addresses is called a *file.* Each line of information about one member is called a *record.* Each column of information within a record is called a *field*—for example, last name, first name, street, and city.

To see the value of a computerized database, imagine that you are a filing clerk in a large corporation. The boss asks to see a list of all employees who have been with the company fewer than three years. The employee records are stored on paper, in alphabetical order by last name. It might take you days or weeks to assemble this information by hand, going through rows of four-drawer filing cabinets.

When the same information is held in an electronic database, you can get the information "on line" in a few minutes. You instruct the database software to scan just one field in every employee's record: the hire date. The computer can then print out a list of all current employees hired within the past three years.

Database management programs are used by salespeople to keep track of clients. They are also used by purchasing agents to keep track of orders and by inventory managers to monitor products in their warehouses. Database managers are used by many people inside and outside of business, from teachers to police officers. Popular database management programs include dBASE, Paradox, and FoxPro.

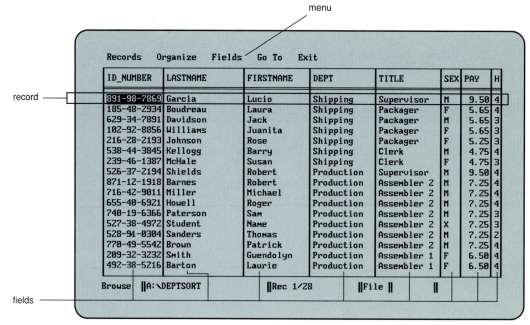

FIGURE 2-7
A database containing records (dBASE IV). Each person's name and address may be entered in any order. These records can then be sorted in logical ways, such as by hometown or alphabetically by last name.

Database managers have different features, depending on their sophistication. A description of the principal features of database manager software for microcomputers follows.

Retrieve and Display A basic feature of all database programs is the capability to locate records in the file quickly. In our example, the program searches each record for a match in a particular field to whatever data you specify. The records can then be displayed on the screen for viewing, updating, or editing. For example, if an employee moves, the address field needs to be changed. The record is quickly retrieved by searching the database to find the employee record that matches the name field you specify. Once the record is displayed, the address field can be changed.

Sort Database managers make it easy to change the order of records in a file. Normally, records are entered into the database in the order they occur, such as the date a person is hired. This may not be the best way, however. There are a number of ways you can quickly rearrange the records in the file. For example, you might want to print out an entire alphabetical list of employees by last name. For tax purposes, you might want to list employees by social security number.

Calculate and Format Many database programs contain built-in math formulas. In the office, for example, you can use this feature to find the highest or lowest commissions earned. You can calculate the average of the commissions earned by the sales force in one part of the country. This information can be organized as a table and printed out in a report format.

Other Features Among other capabilities offered by some database management programs are the following:

- *Customized data-entry forms:* A person new to the database program may find some of the descriptions for fields confusing. For example, a fieldname may appear as "CUSTNUM" for "customer number." However, the form on the screen may be customized so that the expression "Enter the customer number" appears in place of "CUSTNUM." Fields may also be rearranged on the screen, and boxes and lines may be added.
- *Professional-looking reports:* A custom-report option enables you to design the elements you want in a report. Examples are the descriptions appearing above columns and the fields you wish to include. You can even add graphic elements, such as a box or line, so that the printed report has a professional appearance. Although the database itself may have, say, 10 fields, the report can be customized to display only the 5 or so important fields.
- *Program control languages:* Most people using a database management program can accomplish everything they need to do by making choices from the menus. Many database management programs include a programming control language so that advanced users can create sophisticated applications. In addition, some programs, such as dBASE IV, allow direct communication to specialized mainframe databases through languages like SQL (Structured Query Language).

Graphics

A Graphics Program Can Display Numeric Data in a Visual Format for Analytical or Presentation Purposes.

Research on communications shows that people learn better when information is presented visually. A picture is indeed worth a thousand words—or numbers. The projected rise in the popularity of graphics programs is shown in Figure 2-8.

There are two types of graphics programs. *Analytical* graphics programs are used to analyze data. *Presentation* graphics programs are used to create attractive finished graphs for presentations or reports. As a microcomputer user, you will probably be particularly interested in analytical graphics.

Analytical Graphics **Analytical graphics** make numerical data much easier to grasp than when it is in the form of rows and columns of numbers. Graphics may take the form

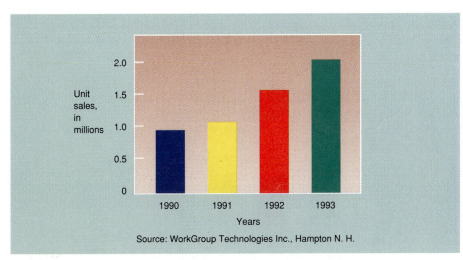

FIGURE 2-8
Graphics on the rise: rise in sales of graphics software packages.

28
Applications Software: Basic Tools

of *bar charts, line graphs,* and *pie charts* (see Figure 2-9). For instance, in Figure 2-9, the numbers to the left of the bar chart show the actual sales figures during a 12-month period. The bar chart itself, however, gives an instant visual profile of those same figures. The line graph in Figure 2-9 shows a visual profile in another way. The pie chart in Figure 2-9 shows the proportion of international accounts as slices of pie. Another kind of chart (not shown here) is the *high-low graph*. This kind of graph shows a range—for instance, of house prices. All these pictorial devices make information much easier to grasp compared to when it is presented in columns of numbers.

Most analytical graphics programs come as part of spreadsheet programs, such as Lotus 1-2-3. Thus, they are used by the same people who use spreadsheets. They are helpful in displaying economic trends, sales figures, and the like for easy analysis. Analytical graphics may be viewed on a monitor or printed out.

Presentation Graphics You can use **presentation graphics** to communicate a message or to persuade other people, such as supervisors or clients. Thus, presentation graphics are used by marketing or sales people, for example.

Presentation graphics look more sophisticated than analytical graphics, using color, titles, a three-dimensional look, and other features a graphic artist might use (see Figure 2-10). Using special equipment, you can convert graphics displays into slides or transparencies. High-end presentation graphics packages even include animation capabilities. These packages allow you to create and edit animated graphics on your microcomputer and then run them on your VCR.

bar chart

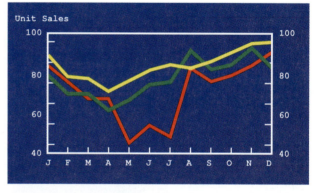

line graph

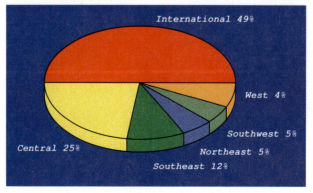

pie chart

FIGURE 2-9
Three types of analytical graphics.

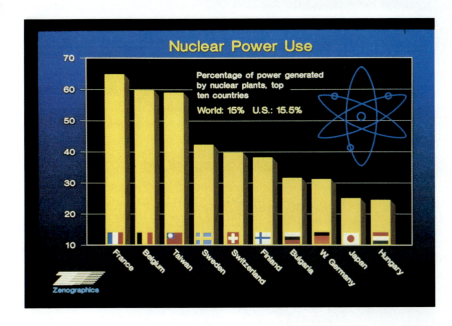

FIGURE 2-10
Example of presentation graphics.

Popular business graphics packages are Harvard Graphics, Freelance Plus, Draw Applause, and Graph Plus.

Communications

Communications Software Lets You Send Data to and Receive Data from Another Computer.

Communications software enables a microcomputer with a modem to send and receive data over a telephone or other communications line. Program menus show you the steps to take. A sample menu from the Crosstalk Mk.4 2.0 communications program is shown in Figure 2-11. A sales representative, for instance, might use this software to retrieve an

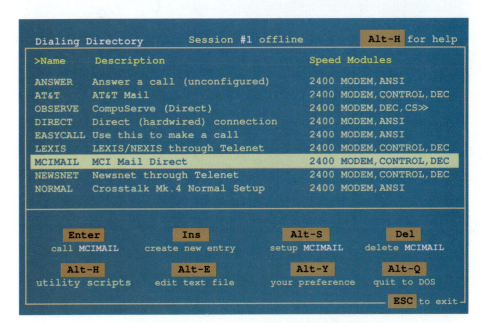

FIGURE 2-11
A menu from the communications program Crosstalk Mk.4 2.0.

electronic file from a distant, telephone-linked information source. The file might be something such as a list of clients. The representative could then copy the file to his or her own diskette or hard disk.

Communications programs are used by all kinds of people inside and outside of business. Examples are students doing research papers, travelers making plane reservations, consumers buying products, investors getting stock quotations, and economists getting government statistical data. Popular communications software includes ProComm, Smartcom, and Crosstalk.

Communications programs give microcomputers a powerful feature, as we have mentioned—namely, that of *connectivity.* Connections with microcomputers open up a world of services previously available only to users of mainframe computers. We devote all of Chapter 7 to explaining computer communications. Here, let us briefly note some features about microcomputer communications programs.

Data Banks With a communications program, you can access enormous computerized databases: data banks of information. Some of these, such as Dialog, resemble huge electronic encyclopedias.

Message Exchanges Communications programs enable you to leave and receive messages on *electronic bulletin boards* or to use *electronic mail services.* Electronic bulletin boards exist for people interested in swapping all kinds of software or information. Such people might be job seekers, lawyers, feminists, rock music fans, or students—the possibilities are almost endless.

Many organizations now have "electronic mailboxes." For instance, you can transmit a report you have created on your word processor to a faraway company executive or to a college instructor. Figure 2-12 shows an example of a message list an employee might receive on an electronic mail system. This is a directory of messages received during part of one day. To read the first message, you might type the command "READ 1."

```
Sports Club Electronic Mail System

New Mail
================================================================
    1:  Memo "MEET" from KAREN          Monday, Dec 4,   6:25 am

    2:  Memo "COMP" from ANN            Monday, Dec 4,   6:42 am

    3:  Memo "MEMB" from FRED           Monday, Dec 4,  10:05 am

    4:  Memo "2" from KAREN             Monday, Dec 4,  11:13 am

    5:  Memo "CAFE" from DONNA          Monday, Dec 4,   1:19 pm




================================================================
          Please enter a command. Press <F1> for help.
```

FIGURE 2-12
Example of an electronic mail screen.

Financial Services With communications programs, you can look up airline reservations and stock quotations. You can order discount merchandise and even do home banking and bill paying.

Integrated Packages

Integrated Software Is an All-in-One Applications Package That Includes Word Processing, Spreadsheet, Database Manager, Graphics, and Communications.

We have described five important kinds of applications software. What happens if you want to take the data in one program and use it in another? Suppose you want to take information stored in the database manager and use it in a spreadsheet. This is not always possible with separate applications packages, but it is with integrated software.

An **integrated package** is a collection of applications programs that work together and share information from one program with another. With an integrated package, you can use the database manager to pull together relevant facts. An example of such facts might be the annual membership fees for a sports club for different years. You can then use the spreadsheet to compare these membership fees (see Figure 2-13). You can use the word processing program to write a memo about these membership fees for different categories of members. You can use this program to merge into the memo totals from the spreadsheet. Finally, you can use the communications program to send the memo to another computer.

Some popular integrated packages are Works, First Choice, Symphony, Enable, Framework, and SmartWare II. End users who are just beginning to learn about applications software find integrated packages quite helpful. These packages can easily exchange data between programs, and they share a common structure. These factors

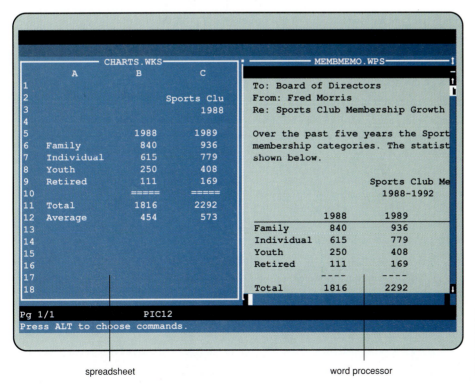

FIGURE 2-13
Example of a memo prepared with the integrated package called Works 2.01. Spreadsheet figures are merged into text.

make them easy to learn and convenient to use. However, each application in an integrated package is generally less powerful than separate applications software, such as a word processing package. Recent developments in microcomputers make it easier for a user to share data between different applications programs. We will describe these developments in Chapters 3 and 4.

A Look at the Future

Tutorials, Special Software, and Hardware Add-ons Help Students Learn Complex Software Tasks.

Applications software is one of those areas in which there are always new developments. How, then, can you keep up with newer versions?

Of course you can always take a class, which is often the easiest way. Many software manufacturers also produce *tutorials*—step-by-step directions and practice sessions. These may be available on diskettes or videotape cassettes. In the future, as software features multiply, the pressure will increase to make the learning process more efficient.

Already some *attempts at simplification* are being marketed. An add-on console (The Simplifier) can be plugged into a microcomputer keyboard. Its special cartridges contain instructions for students to help interpret complex commands in spreadsheet programs. Assistance is also available for learning other complex tasks. For instance, one word processing program (Wordbench) forces students to learn to write by limiting the writing space, prohibiting users from going back to edit, and not allowing writers to see the words as they are written. In addition, the Help command has been made more useful in many programs. So-called *context-sensitive help systems* now provide directed assistance. They take users not just to a table of contents for a reference manual but to a specific area that helps them solve their specific problems.

The very "look and feel" of most software is changing, as we explore in the next chapter. One feature is *windowing software,* in which you can work on several applications—word processing, database searching, and the like—*simultaneously*. Another important feature that is rapidly becoming popular is *graphical user interfaces,* in which the user issues commands through pull-down menus and symbols called icons.

Review Questions

1. What, in a phrase, is off-the-shelf software?
2. Describe some common features of applications software: the cursor, scrolling, menus, format, and special keys.
3. What is a Help screen?
4. What is word processing used for?
5. Describe the following word processing operations: word wrap, search and replace, and block move.
6. Describe the principal features of the worksheet area of an electronic spreadsheet.
7. What is a window? A page?
8. How do formulas and recalculation work in a spreadsheet?
9. What is a database?
10. Describe some of the features of a database manager: retrieve and display, sort, calculate, and format.
11. Explain the purpose of analytical graphics.

12. Name three common types of graphs and charts used in analytical graphics.
13. Describe the purpose of presentation graphics.
14. What does communications software do?
15. Describe some computer connections.
16. How does integrated software work?

Discussion Questions

1. Consider the tasks you spend most of your time doing, whether in school or at work. Do you spend more time on one task than on others—for example, writing or perhaps calculating? Do you use calculations in written reports? Do you send the same form letter to many different people?

    Integrated packages share information from one program with another. You can easily incorporate the address from a database manager, the calculations from a spreadsheet, and a graph of the results of the calculations in a letter. Separate or "stand-alone" programs—a word processing program all by itself, for example—usually perform their specific tasks much better. But generally they cannot share data with other programs.

    Would separate word processing, spreadsheet, and database management programs serve you best? Or would an integrated package that readily shares information among all three be better?

2. You're interested in basic applications software—say, word processing—for your microcomputer. How do you know what kind to buy? There are three paths to choose from.

    First, you can get the software free. This is known as *public domain software.* Someone writes a program and offers to share it without charge with everyone. Generally, you find these programs by belonging to a microcomputer users' group. You can also obtain such software by your telephone-linked microcomputer from an "electronic bulletin board." The software may be fine, but it also may be awful.

    Second, you can get the software as *shareware,* which may cost you perhaps $50 or less. Shareware operates on the honor system. It is distributed free, the same way as public domain software. After you have used it for a while and decide you like it, you're supposed to pay the author for it. Again, the quality varies, but some shareware is better than commercial software.

    Third, you can buy *commercial software,* such as the brand-name packages we mentioned in this chapter. Prices vary. They are generally higher in computer stores (say, $500 for a new word processing program) and lower with mail-order software houses. Features also vary, and vary tremendously. However, there are several periodicals that provide ratings and guides. For instance, *PC World* is a periodical that specializes in IBM and IBM-compatible microcomputers. For the last several years *PC World* has polled its readers to find out the best brands of software in various categories. It has released the results in its October issue. Other periodicals (*PC/Computing, MacWorld, InfoWorld*) also have surveys, reviews, and ratings.

    The following exercise can be extremely useful for you: Concentrate on your category of commercial software—say, word processing. Go to the library and look in every computer magazine you can find for reviews and ratings. What program seems to be the best? Which is right for you?

CHAPTER 2
Applications Software: Basic Tools

VISUAL SUMMARY

Applications software does "useful work." The five basic tools or types of general-purpose applications programs are used by many people for different kinds of tasks.

Word Processing

Word processing software is used to create, manipulate, and print **documents**—any kind of text material. Especially useful for deleting, inserting, and replacing. Principal features:

Word Wrap and Enter Key

Word wrap automatically carries cursor to new line. **Enter key** enters new paragraph or blank line.

Search and Replace

Search command allows user to quickly find a word or number in a document. **Replace** command allows user to replace word with another word.

Block and Move

A **block** is a portion of text that may be identified by **highlighting** (band of light). Moving the block to new location is done with **block move** command.

Other Features

- **Justifying,** underlining, boldfacing, and centering.
- **Spelling-checker** programs check spelling automatically.
- **Thesaurus** programs find alternative words.
- **Mail-merge** allows merging of names and addresses to personalize letters.

Examples of Packages

WordPerfect, Word, MacWrite.

Spreadsheets

An **electronic spreadsheet**, consisting of rows and columns, is used to present and analyze numeric data. The **worksheet area** is bounded by **column headings** across the top and **row headings** down the left-hand side. The **cell** is the intersection of column and row; position of the cell is called **cell address**. The **cell pointer (spreadsheet cursor)** indicates where data is to be entered. Principal features:

Format

Labels (column and row headings) and **values** (numbers in cells) can be displayed in different ways (e.g., with dollar signs and decimal points).

Formulas

Formulas, instructions for calculations, may be used to manipulate data.

Recalculation

Recalculation, automatic recomputation, is an important feature.

Windows

A **window**, the screen-sized area of a spreadsheet, may be moved to show a different part of a spreadsheet.

Examples of Packages

Lotus 1-2-3, Excel, Quattro Pro, SuperCalc.

Database Managers

A **database manager** (or **database management system, DBMS**) is used to structure a database, a large collection of computerized data. Data is organized as fields and records for easy retrieval. Principal features:

Retrieve and Display

Records can be easily located and displayed on the screen for viewing or updating.

Sort

Users can sort through records and rearrange them in different ways.

Calculate and Format

Math formulas may be used to manipulate data. Data may be printed out in different report formats.

Examples of Packages

dBASE, Paradox, R:base.

35
Visual Summary

Features Common to All Applications Software

- **Cursor**, blinking symbol on screen, shows where data is entered.
- **Scrolling** allows user to move ("scroll") through text.
- **Menu** lists commands (e.g., "Delete"). **Help menu** presents on-screen explanations.
- **Format**, or "look," can be altered (e.g., line spacing).
- **Special-purpose keys** (e.g., *Esc*, *Ctrl*) and **function keys** (e.g., *F1*, *F2*) allow entering and editing of data and execution of commands.
- **Macro** commands combine many keystrokes in time-saving fewer strokes.

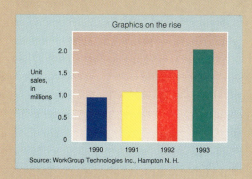

Graphics	Communications	Integrated Packages

Graphics programs display results of data manipulation for easier analysis and presentation. Two types of graphics programs are analytical and presentation.

Analytical Graphics

Analytical graphics programs put data in a form easier to analyze (e.g., bar charts, line graphs).

Presentation Graphics

Presentation graphics help communicate results or persuade, using color and titles.

Examples of Packages

Most analytical graphics come as part of spreadsheet programs. Examples of presentation graphics: Harvard Graphics, Freelance Plus, Draw Applause, Graph Plus.

Communications software enables a microcomputer user with modem to send and receive data over telephone or other communications line. Communications programs permit *connectivity*—allow microcomputers to connect with other information resources. Principal features:

Data Banks

Large computerized databases (e.g., electronic encyclopedias) are available.

Message Exchanges

Electronic bulletin boards and **electronic mail services** are available.

Financial Services

Users may look up stock quotations and airline reservations, order discount merchandise, and do home banking.

Examples of Packages

ProComm, Smartcom, Crosstalk.

An **integrated package** is an all-in-one software package. It includes spreadsheet, database manager, graphics, and perhaps word processing and communications programs.

Some Features

- Most important, it enables programs to work together and share the same data.
- Selected data may be retrieved by the database manager, analyzed by the spreadsheet, viewed graphically, report prepared by word processor, and sent over telephone by the communications program.

Examples of Packages

Works, First Choice, Symphony, Enable, Framework, Smart Ware.

CHAPTER 3
Systems Software

COMPETENCIES

After you have read this chapter, you should be able to:

1. Understand the importance of learning about systems software.

2. Distinguish among four kinds of systems software.

3. Explain the advantages and disadvantages of DOS.

4. Describe the pluses and minuses of Windows.

5. Discuss the benefits and drawbacks of OS/2.

6. Describe what's good and bad about Macintosh systems software.

7. Explain the advantages and disadvantages of Unix for microcomputers.

Becoming a microcomputer end user is like becoming the driver of a car. You can learn just enough to start up the car, take it out on the street, and pass a driver's license test. Or you can learn more about how cars work. That way you can drive any number of vehicles, know their limitations, and compare performance. Indeed, you could go so far as to learn to be a mechanic. Similarly, by expanding your knowledge about microcomputers, you extend what you can do with them. You don't have to be the equivalent of a mechanic—a computer technician. But the more you know, the more you expand your computer competency and productivity.

Cars all do the same thing—take you somewhere. But there was a time when you could choose between different automotive power systems: steam, electricity, or gasoline. Some systems were better for some purposes than others. You could have a car that was quiet or cheap to run, for instance. However, that same car perhaps took too long to start or wouldn't take you very far.

Microcomputers are in a comparable phase of evolution. Some computers do some things better than others do—are easier to learn, for instance, or run more kinds of applications software. Why is this? One important reason is the *systems software*, the "background" software that acts as an interface between the microcomputer and the user. Systems software also acts as an interface between the applications program and the input, output, and processing devices (see Figure 3-1). The most important microcomputer systems software are *DOS, OS/2, Macintosh,* and *Unix.* Which of these you can use depends in part on what kind of computer you have.

Why Learn About Systems Software?

Because Standards Are Changing, Users Need to Know More About Systems Software Than Was Previously Required.

Are you buying a pricey racing machine that you don't really need? Or are you buying an inexpensive, practical vehicle that may nonetheless soon become obsolete? These are the kinds of things many people think about when buying cars. Similar considerations apply

37
Why Learn About Systems Software?

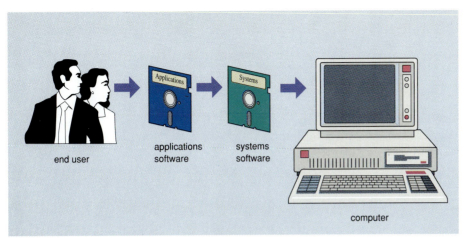

FIGURE 3-1
End users interact with applications software. Systems software interacts with the computer.

in buying microcomputers and software. If you are paying several thousand dollars for a computer system, it's important to know what it can and can't do (see Figure 3-2). Moreover, you hope the buying decision you make will be good for the next several years.

If the study of systems software seems to be remote from your concerns, it shouldn't be. Here's why.

■ *Competing systems software:* In earlier editions of this book there might not have been a need for this chapter. The kind of microcomputer systems software that predominated was the one for IBM and **IBM-compatibles** known as DOS. The other popular one was the one designed for the Apple Macintosh. Even then, Macintosh programs wouldn't run on IBM computers, and DOS programs wouldn't run on Macintosh computers. Today's very powerful microcomputers are demanding more and more from last year's systems

FIGURE 3-2
The IBM PS/2 Model 90XP 486 and the Apple Macintosh IIfx use different systems software. Although similar in many ways, these systems also have significant differences.

software. Now there are four competing forms of systems software, leading to the lack of a standard. Some observers have called this "a crisis in the microcomputer industry."

- *DOS limitations:* If DOS was so popular, why didn't the microcomputer industry just stay with it? The answer is that it has some practical limitations, as we shall discuss. Because it is so widespread, DOS will probably continue to be used for the next several years. Thus, it is well worth learning. However, as more powerful microcomputers become commonplace, other systems software will replace DOS. In sum, DOS is popular today but may fade in a few years.

- *One computer, many kinds of systems software:* Even now there are microcomputers that run more than one kind of systems software. Employers may require that you know more than one kind. For instance, many office workers may need to know how to work with both DOS and the new operating system known as OS/2. These two systems may run on the same computer.

- *More sophisticated users:* Previously, microcomputer users were satisfied with the performance offered by DOS. However, users are becoming more sophisticated, and they want to be able to fully exploit the power of these newer microcomputers. They are beginning to demand that microcomputers run programs that previously could run only on minicomputers and mainframes. To do this, more powerful systems software is required.

Even if you study only *one* kind of systems software, such as DOS, it's important to realize that such software is frequently revised. Revisions are made in order to handle new technology such as newly developed input and output devices. As systems software changes, you need to know what the effects are on your old applications software—and on your way of doing business.

Now let us see what, precisely, systems software is.

Four Kinds of Programs

Systems Software Consists of the Bootstrap Loader, Diagnostic Routines, Basic Input Output System, and Operating System.

Systems software deals with the physical complexities of how the hardware works. Systems software consists of four kinds of programs: bootstrap loader, diagnostic routines, basic input output system, and operating system. The last one, the operating system, is the one we are most concerned with in this chapter. However, we will briefly mention the others, which operate automatically.

- The **bootstrap loader** is the program that is stored permanently in the computer's electronic circuitry. It starts up the computer when you turn it on. It obtains the operating system from your diskette (or hard disk, if you have one) and loads it into primary storage in your computer. An instruction manual will usually tell you to "boot your diskette." This means you should put the operating system diskette in the disk drive and turn on the power. Or, if the operating system is on a hard disk, simply turn the power on.

- The **diagnostic routines** are also programs stored in the computer's electronic circuitry. They start up when you turn the machine on. They test the primary storage, the central processing unit (CPU), and other parts of the system. Their purpose is to make sure the computer is running properly. On some computers, the screen may say "Testing RAM" (a form of computer memory) while these routines are running.

- The **basic input output system** consists of service programs stored in primary storage. These programs enable the computer to interpret keyboard characters or transmit characters to the monitor or to a diskette.
- The **operating system,** the collection of programs of greatest interest to us, helps the computer manage its resources. The operating system takes care of a lot of internal matters so that you, the user, don't have to. For instance, it interprets the commands you give to run programs and enables you to interact with the programs while they are running.

One set of programs within the operating system is called **utility programs.** These programs perform common repetitious tasks, "housekeeping tasks." One important utility program is used for **formatting** (or **initializing**) blank diskettes. This program is very important. Before you can use a new diskette out of the box you buy in a store, you must *format* (initialize) it. Formatting prepares the diskette so that it will accept data or programs in your computer. After formatting a diskette, you can use a utility program to **copy** or duplicate files and programs from one diskette to another. You can **erase** or remove old files from a diskette. You can make a **backup** or duplicate copy of a diskette. You can **rename** the files on a diskette—that is, give them new filenames.

Every computer has to have an operating system. Two popular operating systems for IBM's mainframes, for example, are MVS and OS/VS. Digital Equipment Corporation (DEC) uses VAX/MVS as the operating system for its minicomputers. For end users, the most important operating systems are those for microcomputers. To achieve computer competency, it is essential that you know something about the four main operating systems on the market for microcomputers today. These are *DOS, OS/2, Macintosh,* and *Unix.*

DOS: The IBM Personal Computer Standard

DOS Is the Standard for IBM PCs, XTs, ATs, and Compatibles. It Is Very Popular, Runs Thousands of Applications, and Is Easy to Use.

DOS stands for *Disk Operating System.* Its developer, Microsoft Corporation, sells it under the name *MS-DOS.* (The "MS," of course, stands for Microsoft.) Microsoft licenses a version called *PC-DOS* to International Business Machines for its IBM personal computers (such as models PC, XT, and AT). A great many other microcomputer manufacturers have also been licensed to use DOS. DOS is the standard operating system for all microcomputers advertising themselves as "IBM-compatible," such as Compaq. Whatever machine it is used with, it is usually referred to simply as *DOS.*

There have been several upgrades since DOS was introduced. The 1981 original was labeled version 1.0 (see Figure 3-3). Since then there have been DOS 2.0, 2.1, 3.0, 3.1, 3.2,

DOS Version	Features
1.0	Original operating system for IBM PC and compatibles. Supported only flexible-disk drives.
2.0	Developed for IBM XT microcomputer. First version to support hard-disk drives.
3.0	Appeared about the same time as IBM AT microcomputer. Starting with 3.2 release, supported networking and 3½-inch disk drives.
4.0	Included pull-down menus and other sophisticated modifications.
5.0	Allows access to more memory.

FIGURE 3-3
Different versions of DOS.

3.3, 4.0, 4.1, and 5.0. (The first number refers to a "version," the second to a "release," which contains fewer refinements than a version.) An important characteristic of later DOS versions (the newer versions) is that they are "backward compatible." That is, you can still run applications programs with them that you could run on the earlier versions. The newest versions feature pull-down menus, as shown in Figure 3-4. With a pull-down menu, you use your mouse-directed cursor to unfold ("pull down") a menu from the top of your display screen.

Advantages There is no question that DOS has many advantages. The reasons for learning it are very compelling.

- *Popularity:* DOS is the most popular microcomputer operating system ever sold. In 1990, an estimated 14 million copies of the program were sold worldwide.
- *Number of applications:* An enormous number of applications programs have been written for DOS—more than 35,000. Indeed, more specialized software is available for DOS than for any other operating system. This software includes not just the "basic tools" we mentioned in Chapter 2 but many others as well.
- *Runs on inexpensive hardware:* As PC-DOS, the operating system runs on many IBM computers—the PC, XT, and AT—that are reasonably priced (in the $800 range, depending on the components of the hardware). In addition, MS-DOS is available for all kinds of domestic- and foreign-made IBM-compatible machines. The IBM Personal Computer set the standard for the business market. However, the appearance of similarly designed competitors has driven prices down, making microcomputers available to more people.
- *Ease of use:* Some operating systems are difficult to install on computers. With adequate accompanying instructions, DOS is not hard to install—and many publications and books are available. The operating system is also reasonably easy for novices to use.

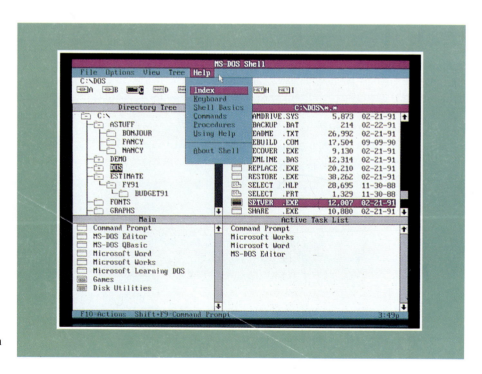

FIGURE 3-4
Example of pull-down menu from DOS 5.0.

Industry observers who have predicted the "death of DOS" may be acting prematurely. The system has some drawbacks, which we describe next. However, there is no doubt that we will continue to see DOS used in the 1990s. It will then slowly be replaced as the dominant operating system.

Disadvantages DOS is software, but software can only perform as well as the hardware for which it was designed. However, the hardware has evolved in significant ways. New microcomputers have more primary storage capacity and faster electronics than the old IBM PC, XT, and AT models. Let us see what these changes mean for DOS.

- *Limited primary storage:* Before an application program can be used, it must be stored in the computer's primary storage. An application program running with DOS has direct access to only 640 kilobytes (about 640,000 characters) of primary storage. With the newest version of DOS, 5.0, an additional 540 kilobytes can be accessed. However, much of the new software available for spreadsheets, database management, and graphics requires more primary storage. New microcomputers have much more primary storage. However, DOS by itself as the operating system cannot access all of this available primary storage. This restriction is an inherent limitation of DOS.
- *"Single tasking" only:* **Multitasking** is the term given to operating systems that can run several applications programs at the same time. We discuss multitasking further in the next section. Unfortunately, DOS by itself can only do *single tasking:* It can support only one user and one applications program at the same time.
- *Character-based interface:* In DOS, users issue commands by typing or by selecting items from a menu. This approach is called a **character-based interface.** Many users find another arrangement for issuing commands, the graphical user interface (described below), much easier.

The long-term future of DOS is not clear. By adding new windowing programs—such as Windows, discussed next—users are able to eliminate some of the previous disadvantages of DOS.

Most industry observers feel that over the next five years many of the newest generations of IBM computers will still be running DOS with windowing programs. This applies particularly to the less powerful models in the PS/2 line. The more powerful PS/2 computers, they feel, will probably be running OS/2 or some version of Unix. By the end of the decade, OS/2 or Unix may well begin to take over more of the business market.

DOS with Windows

DOS with Windows Can Run Several Programs at Once (Multitasking), Share Data Between Programs (Dynamic Data Exchange), Offers a Graphical User Interface, and Access More Primary Storage.

The WINDOW command is available with several different kinds of programs. For example, using this command in a spreadsheet enables you to split the screen. That way you can look at two sections of the worksheet at the same time.

Integrated packages extend your capabilities by allowing you to work on more than one application. For instance, you can work on a word processing document or on a spreadsheet. You can even copy a section of the spreadsheet to the word processing document. However—and this is the important point—*with an integrated package you cannot work on both applications simultaneously.*

Windowing software, however, is much more. When run with DOS, these programs create an **operating environment** that actually extends the capability of DOS. For

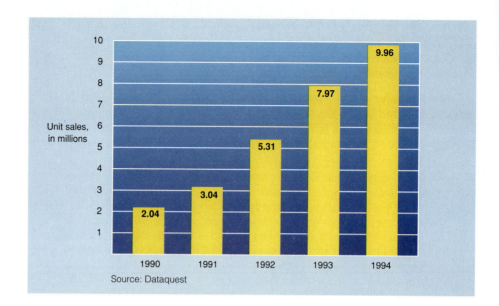

FIGURE 3-5
Sales of Microsoft's Windows.

example, windowing software allows you to work on a number of applications programs *simultaneously*. The most popular windowing program is Microsoft Corporation's Windows, with sales in the millions (see Figure 3-5). Others are Quarterdeck Office Systems' Desqview and Hewlett-Packard Company's NewWave.

Advantages   Windows extends the capabilities of DOS in four ways:

- *Multitasking:* Allows you to do multitasking—to work on a number of applications ("multiple tasks") simultaneously. For instance, you could be running a word processing program and a database management program at the same time. The word processing program would appear on your screen until you opened up a window to access the database management program. While you were writing a report using the word processing program, the other program could be searching a database for more information. You could also simultaneously open up another window for a graphics program to draw a picture. Thus, you can be viewing more than one program side by side at the same time.

- *Dynamic data exchange:* A system called the dynamic data exchange will enable one program to broadcast a request for certain information to other programs currently running and to receive an automatic response. For example, a spreadsheet program could be analyzing the salaries of middle managers. At the same time, a database management program could be updating all employee data. With both programs running, you could use the spreadsheet to request and receive the most recent salary data from the database management program.

- *Graphical user interface:* Windows (and other windowing programs available for DOS) offers a **graphical user interface (GUI).** (See Figure 3-6.) A graphical user interface allows the user to move a mouse (or use keyboard commands) to move a pointer or cursor on the screen. The user positions the pointer on graphic symbols called **icons** or on pull-down menus and then "clicks" (presses a button on) the mouse. For example, to specify printer commands using Windows, the user could move the pointer to the icon just above Print Manager and click the mouse. Most users have found this approach to issuing commands easier to learn than the character-based approach.

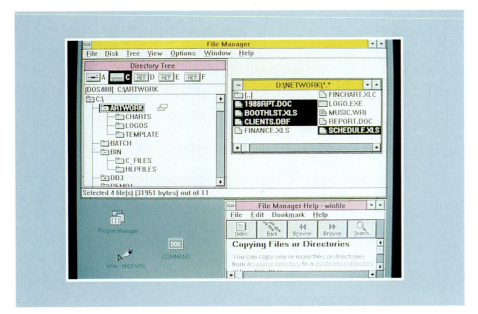

FIGURE 3-6
Windows 3.0 screen with graphical user interface.

- *More primary storage:* As mentioned before, DOS by itself has limited access to primary storage, thereby severely limiting software and hardware capabilities. Windows, however, has a **memory manager** that allows access well beyond 640 kilobytes. DOS with Windows can access billions of characters of primary storage.

Disadvantages Windows has dramatically increased the capabilities of DOS to include multitasking, sharing data, and more. Of course, DOS with Windows has some limitations.

- *Technological limitations:* DOS and multitasking programs—particularly Windows—will continue to find more applications and more users. However, at some time in the future, the software will likely reach its inherent limitations. That is, DOS will not be able to be enhanced beyond a certain level. Then more powerful, newer operating systems will likely prevail.
- *Limited applications:* One reason for the present popularity of Microsoft's Windows is that a great many applications programs are being designed to run specifically for Windows. In time, however, business users will likely require applications programs that exceed the capabilities of these present DOS-based programs.
- *Network capabilities:* In many business environments, software is shared among computers using a network. That way, several copies of the same application program are not required. Rather, a single copy is shared. This sharing is made possible and is controlled by systems software. Although network versions are being developed, Windows was not originally intended for networks and is not very efficient in that environment.

OS/2

OS/2 Was Developed for Powerful Microcomputers and Networking.

OS/2, which stands for *Operating System/2,* is one of the newest operating systems for microcomputers (see Figure 3-7, p. 44). Developed jointly by IBM and Microsoft

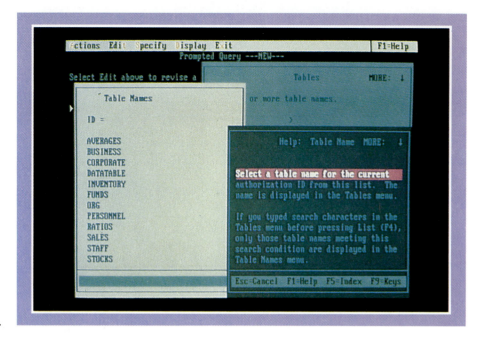

FIGURE 3-7
OS/2 with Help screen.

Corporation, the first version of OS/2 was released in December 1987. Since then there have been other versions (see Figure 3-8).

OS/2 was announced almost at the same time IBM announced its new generation of powerful microcomputers—the PS/2 line. The "PS" stands for *Personal System*. However, you should not assume that every model in this line can run OS/2—some cannot. Yet OS/2 *does* run on some older IBM machines. (They are the IBM PC-AT and the IBM PC-XT Model 286.)

The ability to run OS/2 depends on the kind of central processing unit you have in the computer. The *central processing unit (CPU)*, let us recall from Chapter 1, performs manipulations on the data that is input. The CPU is contained on a tiny **microprocessor,** or "microscopic processor," made out of a sandlike material called *silicon*. Microprocessors can be as small as ⅛-inch square and are often called **chips.**

OS/2 Version and Edition	Features
Standard Edition 1.0	IBM's first version. The minimum acceptable version. Runs on IBM PC-AT, PC-XT Model 286, and PS/2 Models 50, 60, and 80. Does multitasking.
Standard Edition 1.1	An upgrade of the Standard Edition. Includes Presentation Manager, the graphical user interface.
Extended Edition	Separately priced product, not an upgrade. Includes a built-in database manager and communications manager.
Standard Edition 1.2	Enhanced Presentation Manager, the graphical user interface. Handles files of up to 2 billion characters of data.
Extended Edition 1.2	Includes database for multiple users and sophisticated communications.
Standard Edition 1.3	Requires less primary storage than earlier editions. Includes type fonts for desktop publishing.

FIGURE 3-8
Different versions of OS/2.

OS/2 is designed to run on IBM and compatible microcomputers with particular kinds of microprocessors. They are the Intel 80286 (called a "'286" chip), 80386 ("'386" chip), and 80486 ("'486" chip). Early versions of OS/2 did not use the '386 and '486 microprocessors to best advantage, but future versions promise to do so.

Let us consider both the advantages and the disadvantages of this operating system.

Advantages   OS/2 offers some advantages that are simply not available with DOS without Windows. These advantages include multitasking, dynamic data exchange, graphical user interface, and more primary storage. OS/2 also has the following advantages over DOS with Windows.

- *Common User Interface:* Microcomputer applications programs written specifically for OS/2 have a consistent graphics interface. Across applications, the user is provided with similar screen displays, menus, and operations. This is also true for Windows' programs. Additionally, however, OS/2 offers a consistent interface with mainframes, minicomputers, and microcomputers.
- *Networking:* Unlike DOS with Windows, OS/2 was designed for network applications. OS/2's Extended Edition was initially developed and later enhanced to assist in the sharing of data and programs among several microcomputers.
- *Flexibility:* Unlike Windows, OS/2 is not constrained by an older operating system (DOS). OS/2 was designed specifically to maximize the performance of the newest, most powerful microcomputers. Therefore, it generally processes more efficiently and is better able to be modified to meet future needs of networked users.

Disadvantages   OS/2 also has some disadvantages compared to DOS with Windows.

- *Expense:* The purchase cost of OS/2 is much greater than the combined cost of DOS and Windows. Although prices vary, the cost of OS/2 is nearly 3 times greater.
- *Fewer applications:* Like Windows, OS/2 suffers because there are few applications programs developed specifically for it. Applications software developers state that it is not easy to write programs for OS/2. Although over 2,500 applications packages have been promised, very few have been completed. Furthermore, many software developers have delayed further OS/2-specific program development in order to focus on Windows programs.

Which operating system is more popular—Windows or OS/2? There is no doubt: Windows has sold over four million copies compared to only 600,000 for OS/2. It is interesting to note that almost all of the OS/2 sales have been to large corporations. Some industry observers have noted that the choice today for most users is pretty easy. Windows has more application programs, is powerful enough, and is less expensive. These observers also add that the choice tomorrow will likely not be so easy.

Macintosh Operating Systems

The Macintosh Software, Which Runs Only on Macintosh Computers, Offers a High-Quality Graphical User Interface and Is Very Easy to Use.

What can you do with OS/2 or DOS with Windows that you can't already do if you have an Apple Macintosh computer? That's what many people are asking. If it's a graphical user interface you want, that's been available for some time with the Mac. In the opinion of many industry observers, OS/2 and DOS with Windows look very similar to the Macintosh operating system. To appreciate the differences, let us look at how the Macintosh works.

The Macintosh operating system is contained in two primary files—the System file and the Finder. These two files work together to perform the standard operating system procedures. These procedures include tasks such as formatting disks, copying files, erasing files, and running applications programs. These system files also manage the user interface, displaying menus and activating tasks that are chosen from the menus by the user.

Apple has introduced numerous versions of its operating system. A recent version is the Apple Macintosh System 7. This version allows applications programs to exchange both data and instructions. There are also improvements in multitasking—more than one program can be run simultaneously, each one sharing the computer's CPU. In addition, there are improvements in the user's ability to gain access over telephone lines to databases in distant locations.

We mentioned that the advantages and disadvantages of microcomputer operating systems are associated with the microprocessors for which they were originally designed. IBM microcomputers have used microprocessor chips built by Intel, most recently the '286, '386, and '486 chips. Macintoshes, on the other hand, are built around Motorola 68000, 68020, and 68030 microprocessors. These Motorola chips cannot run DOS applications programs, and the Intel chips cannot run Macintosh applications programs. In the beginning, Apple found its Macintoshes hard to sell to corporations because nearly all business applications programs—such as Lotus 1-2-3—were written to run on DOS machines. It is possible now, however, to run IBM applications on a Macintosh. Users can install a '286 electronic circuit board in their Macs or can use special applications software that permits DOS applications to run on a Macintosh.

Advantages The Apple Macintosh popularized the graphical user interface (see Figure 3-9), including the use of windows, pull-down menus, and the mouse. The graphical user interface has several advantages:

FIGURE 3-9
The Macintosh graphical user interface.

- *Ease of use:* The graphical user interface has made the Macintosh popular with many newcomers to computing. This is because it is easy to learn. In fact, studies show that user training costs are *half* as much for Macintoshes as for DOS-based computers.
- *Quality graphics:* Macintosh has established a high standard for graphics processing. This is a principal reason why the Macintosh is popular for desktop publishing. Users are easily able to merge pictorial and text materials to produce nearly professional-looking newsletters, advertisements, and the like.
- *Consistent interfaces:* Macintosh applications have a consistent graphics interface. Across all applications, the user is provided with similar screen displays, menus, and operations.
- *Multitasking:* Like OS/2, the Macintosh System 7 enables you to do multitasking. That is, multiple programs can run simultaneously, each one sharing the CPU.
- *Communications between programs:* System 7 allows applications programs to share data and commands with other applications programs.

Disadvantages Many characteristics that were previously considered disadvantages may no longer prove to be so. Nevertheless, let us consider what these disadvantages are.

- *A "business" machine?* Apple has had to struggle against the corporate perception that its products are not for "serious business users." Corporate buyers have had a history of purchasing from IBM and other vendors of large computers. Many have viewed Apple from the beginning as a producer of microcomputers for game players and hobbyists.
- *Compatibility difficulties:* The incompatibility of DOS with Macintosh microprocessors made Macintoshes less attractive to corporate users interested in compatibility and connectivity. However, as noted above, hardware and software are now available for the Mac to allow it to run DOS applications. In addition, inexpensive communications networks are available to connect Macintoshes to other computers that use DOS. Apple has cooperated with Digital Equipment Corporation (DEC) to produce communications links between Macintoshes, IBM PCs, and mainframe computers.

Unix: The "Portable" Operating System

Unix Can Run on Many Different Microcomputers (Is "Portable"). It Is Not Limited by Primary Storage, Can Perform Multitasking, and Can Be Shared by Several Users at Once.

Unix has been around for some time. It was originally developed by AT&T for minicomputers and is very good for multitasking. It is also good for networking between computers. It has been, and continues to be, popular on workstations.

Unix initially became popular in industry because for many years AT&T licensed the system to universities for a nominal fee. The effect of this was that Unix was carried by recent computer science and engineering graduates to their new places of employment.

One important consequence of its scientific and technical orientation is that Unix has remained popular with engineers and technical people. It is less well known with businesspeople. All that, however, is probably about to change. The reason: With the arrival of very powerful microcomputers using the '386 chip and '486 chip, Unix has become a major player in the microcomputer world.

Let us consider the advantages and disadvantages of Unix.

Advantages Unix has the advantage of being a **portable** operating system. That means that it is able to be used with ("is portable to") many different computer systems. The other operating systems we have described are not nearly as portable. Having said this, however, we must hastily state that there are *different versions* of Unix, as we will describe. Let us first consider the advantages.

- *Multitasking:* Unix enables you to do multitasking. Assuming your microcomputer has the capability, Unix allows you to run multiple programs simultaneously, each one sharing the CPU.
- *Multiuser:* Unix not only shares the CPU among several simultaneous programs. It also shares it among multiple users, which OS/2 does not. At one point, the ability of several users to use one CPU simultaneously was considered a very significant cost advantage. Now, as hardware costs have come down, this advantage for microcomputers is not nearly as significant.
- *Not limited by primary storage:* Unix is not restricted by the hardware as the DOS and OS/2 systems are. Moreover, it can do a great many operations that were previously available only on minicomputers or mainframes. This means that, using Unix, a company can achieve the same performance and benefits using a microcomputer that previously required a large computer.
- *Networking:* Unix is able to share files over electronic networks with several different kinds of equipment. Although OS/2 promises to perform this same service, Unix systems have been successfully sharing across networks for years.

Disadvantages Unix was a minicomputer operating system used by programmers and computer science professionals some time before the rise of the microcomputer. This means it has certain qualities that make it useful to programmers—a lot of supporting utility programs and documentation, for instance. However, some of its features make it difficult for end users. Let us consider the disadvantages.

- *Limited applications software:* This is a great barrier at the moment. There are many engineering applications programs. Unfortunately, there are very few business applications programs, and businesses that are dependent on off-the-shelf programs for microcomputers will find offerings very limited. Moreover, many of those business programs that do exist require customization. However, most end users knowledgeable in DOS don't have the experience to customize Unix programs. This situation may change as more DOS offerings are rewritten for Unix.
- *No Unix standard:* This may be *the* biggest stumbling block. There is no Unix standard at any level. The principal microcomputer versions are the AT&T Unix System V, the University of California/Berkeley 4.2 Unix, and the Sun Microsystems SunOS. Microsoft has written a microcomputer version called Xenix, and Microsoft and AT&T are attempting to merge their versions to provide one standard. In addition, an organization called the Open Software Foundation is also trying to create a standard. This organization is a consortium of seven major computer suppliers led by IBM and DEC. All this means that whenever an applications program is written for one version of Unix, it may not run on other versions.
- *No standard graphical user interface:* Just as there is no Unix standard, there is also no standard graphical user interface. For instance, an attempt has been made to combine the Sun, AT&T, and U.C. Berkeley versions of Unix to produce a graphical user interface called Open Look or Sun/Open Windows. However, the Open Software Foundation has defined its own graphical user interface called OSF/Motif (see Figure 3-10). OSF Motif offers a single, consistent graphical user interface across both OS/2 and many Unix applications.

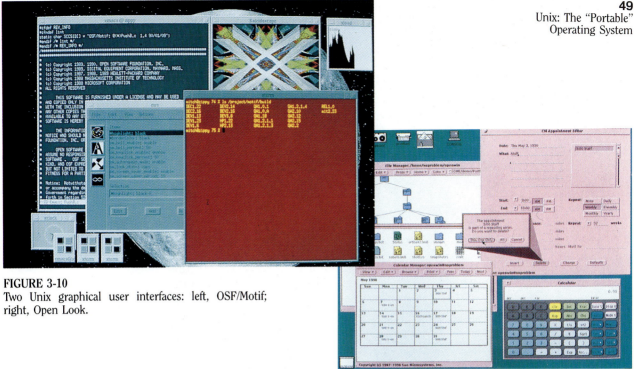

FIGURE 3-10
Two Unix graphical user interfaces: left, OSF/Motif; right, Open Look.

Although Unix can do many things, it can be difficult for novice microcomputer users to understand. This is one reason why it has had a limited impact to date. Some observers think it could yet become a leader among microcomputer operating systems. However, at least one industry watcher, Dataquest, thinks its share of the market will not expand appreciably beyond what it is now. (See Figure 3-11.)

Figure 3-12 on p. 50 summarizes some of the principal advantages and disadvantages of the present microcomputer operating systems.

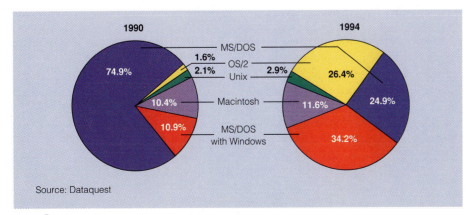

FIGURE 3-11
Worldwide unit sales of microcomputing operating systems—past and future.

Operating System	Pluses	Minuses
DOS	Many existing users, microcomputers, and applications	Limited memory; single tasking only; character-based interface
DOS with Windows	Multitasking; dynamic data exchange; graphical user interface; more primary storage	Technical limitations; limited applications available; limited network capabilities
OS/2	Multitasking; dynamic data exchange; graphical user interface; network capabilities; flexibility	Very limited applications available; expensive
Macintosh	Ease of use; quality graphics; graphical user interface; multitasking; communication among programs	Market perception; compatibility
Unix	Multitasking, multiuser; unlimited primary storage; networking capabilities	Limited business applications; no standard version; no standard graphical user interface

FIGURE 3-12
Pluses and minuses of present microcomputer operating systems.

A Look at the Future

The Popularity of Multitasking Software, Particularly Windows, May Keep DOS Strong, but Other Operating Systems May Be Adopted by Users in Large Organizations.

We continually read that this or that operating system is going to overturn DOS as the most popular microcomputer system software on the market. In fact, however, DOS remains strong and, when coupled with Windows, will very likely stay strong through the next several years. Many industry observers think OS/2 *may* eventually replace DOS (or DOS with Windows), but not anytime soon. The Macintosh operating system probably will not replace DOS, although it might grow slightly in its share of number of users. Unix supporters are in conflict as to which standard will prevail. Will it be Open Look from AT&T/Sun, or Motif from the Open Software Foundation? Anyone considering buying a sophisticated new microcomputer must think about these matters.

It appears that DOS and Macintosh will continue to serve people such as students, those with home microcomputers, and those running small businesses. DOS with Windows will also begin to pervade this group as people move up to more sophisticated computers. DOS with Windows will probably also rapidly move in the other direction—to "power users" such as businesspeople, academics, and local government officials. However, people in large organizations—corporations, universities, and major government departments—will probably find DOS with Windows insufficient after a while. As powerful microcomputers replace the old and as networking between computers becomes more important, these users will gradually change over to more powerful systems software. This will probably be a new version of OS/2 but also possibly some form of Unix.

Review Questions

1. What, in a phrase, is the difference between applications software and systems software?
2. What are four reasons for learning about systems software?
3. Describe what a bootstrap loader does.
4. What do diagnostic routines do?
5. What is the basic input output system?
6. What are utility programs?
7. What is another name for initializing a blank disk?
8. What is an "IBM-compatible" microcomputer?
9. Name two principal limitations of DOS.
10. What are the principal differences between DOS and DOS with Windows?
11. What is meant by *multitasking?*
12. What is a *graphical user interface?*
13. What is a microprocessor? Will OS/2 run on Intel 80286 and 80386 microprocessors?
14. Give three advantages of OS/2 over DOS with Windows.
15. What are two advantages of the Macintosh systems software?
16. What are two disadvantages of the Macintosh when used in a business environment?
17. Unix is said to be *portable.* What does this mean?
18. What is meant by the term *multiuser?*
19. What are four advantages of Unix?
20. What are three disadvantages of Unix?

Discussion Questions

1. Suppose you are buying a microcomputer just for yourself, without regard to cost. You want to be able to learn it quickly in order to do school-related projects. Such projects might include writing papers, perhaps some spreadsheet calculations, and occasionally some graphics. You will not be using it for communications. Given what you have read about operating systems, what kind of computer and operating system would you get, and why?

2. You are working for the business department of a college that teaches applications programs and the use of computers in business. Every four years the department receives an authorization to buy 50 new microcomputers—but it must spend the money *that year.* Consider the uncertainty about which operating system will prevail. Also, consider that the department will not be allowed to buy more hardware for another four years. What kind of microcomputers would you recommend purchasing, and why?

CHAPTER 3
Systems Software

VISUAL SUMMARY

Systems software does "background work" (like helping the computer do internal tasks).

Why Learn About Systems Software?
Users need to learn more about microcomputer systems software than was previously required because:
- There are four competing forms of systems software.
- DOS has limitations.
- Microcomputers may run more than one kind of systems software.
- Microcomputers now run systems software that used to run only on minicomputers and mainframes.

Four Kinds of Programs

Systems software is a collection of **programs** that help end users and applications programs to operate and to control a computer. There are four basic kinds of systems software programs.

- **Bootstrap loader**—starts computer when turned on and loads program into primary storage.
- **Diagnostic routines**—test parts of system to be sure computer is running properly.
- **Basic input output system**—transmits characters from the keyboard or to a monitor or diskette.
- **Operating system**—helps computer manage resources (e.g., interprets commands user gives to run programs). Includes **utility programs** for performing repetitive tasks—e.g., for **formatting** (or **initializing**) blank diskettes, to prepare it to accept data or programs from a particular computer. The most important microcomputer operating systems are DOS, OS/2, Macintosh, and Unix.

DOS

DOS, for Disk Operating System, is standard for IBM PC, XT, and AT computers and those calling themselves "IBM-compatible" (e.g., Compaq). DOS is developed in five versions: 1.0, 2.0, 3.0, 4.0, 5.0. All are "backward compatible"—applications programs can run on newer versions of DOS.

Advantages
- Most popular microcomputer operating system ever sold.
- Enormous number of applications.
- Runs on inexpensive microcomputers.
- Is relatively easy to install and use.

Disadvantages
- An applications program running on DOS has direct access to only 640 kilobytes of primary storage.
- Can only do *single tasking*—support only one user and one applications program at the same time.
- Character based user interface.

DOS with Windows

Windows is a program that runs with DOS. It creates an operating environment that significantly extends the capabilities of DOS.

Advantages
- Multitasking is possible—several applications can be run at the same time.
- Dynamic Data Exchange is available. With two or more applications running at the same time, data and results can be shared back and forth.
- Graphical user interface is provided. Commands can be executed by manipulating graphic symbols called icons.
- More primary storage access.

Disadvantages
- Technological limitations will likely be reached.
- Limited number of specialized applications programs available.
- Limited networking capabilities to link users.

52

53
Visual Summary

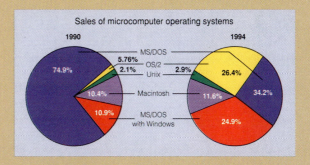

Sales of microcomputer operating systems

OS/2

OS/2 is an operating system that has been developed to support the most advanced microcomputers.

Advantages

Like DOS with Windows, it supports multitasking, dynamic data exchange, graphical user interface, and more primary storage. Additionally:

- Common user interface across mainframes, minicomputers, and microcomputers.
- Networking capabilities to link users sharing information.
- Flexibility to adjust to changing demands and processing efficiency.

Disadvantages

- More expensive than DOS with Windows.
- Fewer specialized applications programs available.

Macintosh Operating Systems

Several operating systems have been designed for Apple's **Macintosh**. New versions have been developed as new versions of the Macintosh have been developed.

Advantages

- Offers a high standard for graphics processing.
- Consistent graphics interface with all applications.
- Can do multitasking—running of multiple programs simultaneously.
- Can share data with other applications programs.
- Easy to use.

Disadvantages

- Some corporate buyers do not view Macintosh as a serious business machine.
- Equipment is somewhat expensive.

Unix

Unix, originally developed for minicomputers, is able to run on more powerful models of microcomputers. Unix is available in a number of different versions, many of which are not compatible.

Advantages

- Allows multitasking—running of multiple programs simultaneously.
- Allows multiple users to share computer simultaneously.
- Not limited by primary storage capacity.
- Able to share files over electronic networks with different equipment.

Disadvantages

- Few business applications programs are presently available.
- No one Unix standard exists; there are several versions (principal ones: Unix System V, Berkeley 4.2 Unix, SunOS).
- No standard graphical user interface exists.

CHAPTER 4
The Central Processing Unit

COMPETENCIES

After you have read this chapter, you should be able to:

1. Describe four classes of computer systems: microcomputer, minicomputer, mainframe, and supercomputer.

2. Explain the two main parts of the processor part of the central processing unit—the control unit and the arithmetic-logic unit.

3. Understand the workings and the functions of primary storage.

4. Describe how a computer uses binary codes to represent data in electrical form.

5. Describe the components of the system unit in a microcomputer.

How is the data in "data processing" actually *processed?* That is the subject of this chapter. Why do you need to know anything about it? The answer lies in three words: *speed, capacity,* and *flexibility.* After reading this chapter, you will be able to judge how fast, powerful, and versatile a particular microcomputer is. This knowledge should be valuable whenever you need to buy a computer or computer programs for yourself or for your employer.

Some time you may get the chance to watch when a technician opens up a microcomputer to fix it. You will see that it is basically a collection of electronic circuitry, as shown in Figure 4-1 on p. 55. The parts will be explained in this chapter. There is no need for you to understand how all these components work. However, it is important to understand the principles because you will then be able to determine how powerful a particular microcomputer is. This will help you judge whether it can run particular kinds of programs and can meet your needs as a user.

The Four Types of Computer Systems
Computer Systems Are Classified as Microcomputers, Minicomputers, Mainframes, and Supercomputers.

You have probably already begun learning how to use a microcomputer. Do you think the day might come when you will be dealing with larger computers?

The answer is: No doubt you will—even if you never see them. The reason is that microcomputers, as we have said, are often linked by communications lines to large computers. These large computers process great quantities of information. Thus, it is worth learning about the various categories of computers and what function each category serves. We will describe them in order from smallest to largest: *microcomputers, minicomputers, mainframes,* and *supercomputers.*

Microcomputers The most familiar kind of computer is the *microcomputer.* Microcomputers cost between $200 and $15,000 and, in the past, have been consid-

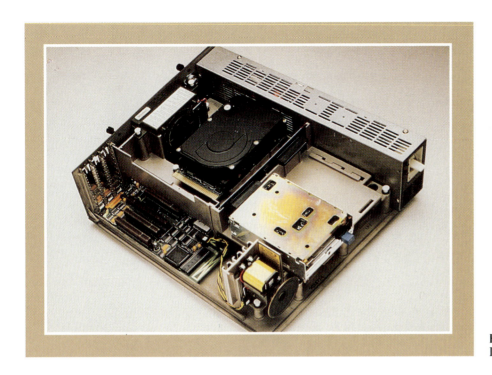

FIGURE 4-1
Inside a microcomputer.

ered to be of two types—*personal computers* and *workstations*. Let's see what these are.

- *Personal computers:* Until recently, **personal computers** were desktop or portable machines that ran comparatively easy-to-use applications software, such as the general-purpose "basic tools" we described in Chapter 2. They were usually easier to use and more affordable than workstations, but they had less sophisticated video display screens, operating systems, and networking capabilities. Most important, they did not have the processing power that workstations did.

    Examples of personal computers are Apple's Macintosh and IBM's various PS/2 models (see Figure 4-2).

FIGURE 4-2
A microcomputer: the IBM PS/2 Model 55SX desktop.

FIGURE 4-3
A workstation: the Sun386i workstation.

- *Workstations:* **Workstations** were—again, until recently—expensive, powerful machines used by engineers, scientists, and others who wanted to process a lot of data or run complex programs and display both work in progress and results graphically. Workstations used sophisticated display screens featuring high-resolution color graphics, operating systems such as Unix that permitted multitasking, and powerful networking links to other computers. The most significant distinguishing factor, however, was the powerful processor, which could churn out results much faster than personal computers.

  Examples of well-known workstations are those made by Sun, Apollo, and Hewlett-Packard. The Sun386i workstation (see Figure 4-3) is able to run both Unix and DOS applications. The number of workstations is expected to triple between 1990 and 1994 (see Figure 4-4).

However, the distinction between personal computer and workstation is now blurring. The principal reason is that the microprocessors used in personal computers are now as powerful as many of those used in workstations. More powerful microprocessors and increased graphics and communications capabilities now allow end users to run applications software that previously could run only on mainframes.

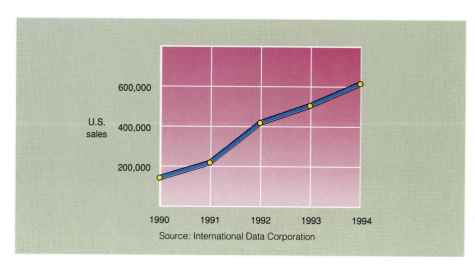

FIGURE 4-4
Expected surge in growth of technical workstations.

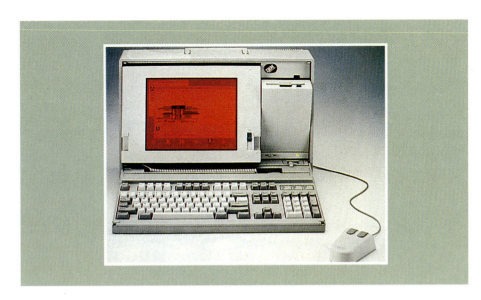

FIGURE 4-5
Transportable: the IBM PS/2 Model P75.

More powerful has also often meant smaller. One type of personal computer that is growing in popularity is the **portable computer,** which is easily carried around. There are four categories of portable computers.

- *Transportables:* **Transportables,** or **luggables,** weigh between 18 and 25 pounds. They generally offer greater computing power and screens that are easier to read than those on lighter-weight portables. However, because they must be plugged into a wall socket, they are inconvenient for travelers unable to find an AC power source.
  Typical users of transportables are construction engineers, who travel around with their computers and plug them in at different field offices. One transportable, the IBM PS/2 Model P75, is shown in Figure 4-5.

- *Laptops:* **Laptops,** which weigh between 10 to 16 pounds, may be either AC-powered, battery-powered, or both. The AC-powered laptop weighs 12 to 16 pounds. The battery-powered laptop weighs 10 to 15 pounds, batteries included, and can be carried on a shoulder strap.
  The user of a laptop might be an accountant or financial person who needs to work on a computer on an airplane. An example of a laptop is the 13-pound NEC ProSpeed 386SX-20 (see Figure 4-6).

FIGURE 4-6
Laptop: the 13-pound NEC ProSpeed 386SX.

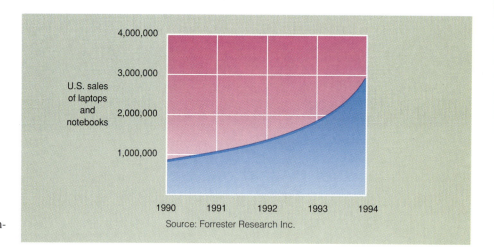

FIGURE 4-7
Growth of laptop and notebook computers.

- *Notebook PCs:* **Notebook personal computers** weigh between 5 and 10 pounds and can fit comfortably into most briefcases. Notebooks and laptops are among the fastest-growing categories of computers (see Figure 4-7).

    The user of a notebook PC might be a student, salesperson, or journalist, who uses the computer for note-taking. It is especially valuable in locations where electrical connections are not available. An example of a notebook computer is the battery-powered 7.5-pound Compaq LTE 386s/20 model 20 (see Figure 4-8).

- *Pocket PCs:* **Pocket personal computers** (sometimes called **palmtops**) are hand-held or pocket-size portables. Weighing 1 or 2 pounds, they are too small to fit on one's lap. Moreover, their keyboards are so tiny that two-handed typing is impossible. Pocket PCs are intended as complements to personal computers, not replacements. They allow you to connect with desktop computers or networks and exchange data with them. An example of a pocket PC is the 11-ounce Hewlett-Packard 95LX, nicknamed Jaguar (see Figure 4-9), which comes with Lotus 1-2-3 built in.

FIGURE 4-8
Notebook: the 7.5-pound Compaq LTE 386s/20 model 20.

59
The Four Types of Computer Systems

FIGURE 4-9
Pocket PC: The 11-ounce Hewlett-Packard Jaguar.

The user of a pocket PC might be a beverage-delivery driver who uses one to manage orders and feed daily inventory and sales to management. Or it might be a police officer who enters license numbers in a central computer through a radio hand-held computer, to detect stolen cars.

Minicomputers Costing from several thousand to half a million dollars, *minicomputers* were first developed as special-purpose mainframe computers. They were used, for instance, to control a machine tool in a factory. However, now they are widely used as general-purpose computers. Thus, the line between minis and mainframes has blurred and is constantly changing. Indeed, the more powerful models are called *superminis*. Figure 4-10 shows one of the more popular minicomputer systems, the VAX made by Digital Equipment Corporation (DEC).

FIGURE 4-10
Minicomputer: the VAX by DEC.

The Central Processing Unit

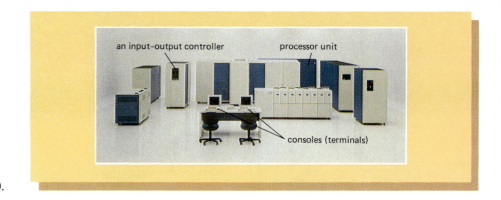

FIGURE 4-11
Mainframe: the IBM model 3090.

FIGURE 4-12
Supercomputer: the Cray Y-MP.

millisecond: thousandth of a second

microsecond: millionth of a second

nanosecond: billionth of a second

picosecond: trillionth of a second

FIGURE 4-13
Processing speeds.

Minicomputers work well in what are known as **distributed data processing** or **decentralized** systems. That is, a company's headquarters or central office may have a mainframe computer, known as the **host** computer. It may be linked by communication lines to minicomputers in branch offices that handle work at the local sites.

Mainframes Ranging in price from several hundred thousand dollars up to $10 million, *mainframe* computers can process millions of program instructions per second. Virtually all large organizations rely on these room-size systems to handle large programs with lots of data. Mainframes are used by insurance companies, banks, airline reservation systems, and large mail-order houses, among many others.

Figure 4-11 shows an advanced mainframe made by International Business Machines called the IBM Model 3090. IBM, the world's biggest computer company, is the dominant mainframe manufacturer, controlling roughly three-quarters of this market. If you peer into the computer room of any large organization, you will probably find one of the IBM 370 series of mainframe computers. Sales of these computers account for more than half of IBM's revenue.

Supercomputers *Supercomputers* are multimillion-dollar machines that are the fastest calculating devices ever invented. For example, the Y-MP (Figure 4-12), made by Cray Research Inc., costs $20 million and can perform as many as 4 billion arithmetic calculations per second. When it becomes available, the Cray 3, at 16 billion calculations per second, will be four times as powerful.

On the horizon are even more powerful supercomputers using a type of technology called **massively parallel processing.** These supercomputers consist of thousands of interconnected microprocessors. One massively parallel computer under development by Intel Corporation promises to be able to perform 32 billion calculations per second.

A desktop microcomputer processes data and instructions in millionths of a second, or **microseconds.** A supercomputer, by contrast, can operate at speeds measured in nanoseconds and even picoseconds—1 thousand to 1 million times as fast as microcomputers. (The definitions of such speeds appear in Figure 4-13.) Most supercomputers are used by government agencies. These machines are for applications requiring very large programs and large amounts of data that must be processed quickly. Examples are such tasks as worldwide weather forecasting, oil exploration, and weapons research.

The CPU

The Central Processing Unit Has Two Components—the Control Unit and the Arithmetic-Logic Unit.

The part of the computer that runs the program (executes program instructions) is known as the **processor** or *central processing unit (CPU)*. In a microcomputer, the CPU is on a single electronic component, a microprocessor chip, within the *system unit* or *system cabinet*. The system unit also includes circuit boards, memory chips, ports, and other components. A microcomputer's system cabinet may also house the monitor and disk drives, but these are considered separate from the CPU.

In Chapter 1 we said the system unit consists of electronic circuitry with two main parts, the processor (the CPU) and primary storage. Let us refine this further by stating that the CPU itself has two parts: the control unit and the arithmetic-logic unit. In a microcomputer, these are both on the microprocessor chip.

The Control Unit The **control unit** tells the rest of the computer system how to carry out a program's instructions. It directs the movement of electronic signals between *primary storage*—which temporarily holds data, instructions, and processed information—and the arithmetic-logic unit. It also directs these control signals between the CPU and input and output devices.

The Arithmetic-Logic Unit The **arithmetic-logic unit,** usually called the **ALU,** performs two types of operations—arithmetic and logical. *Arithmetic* operations are, as you might expect, the fundamental math operations: addition, subtraction, multiplication, and division. *Logical* operations consist of comparison. That is, two pieces of data are compared to see whether one is equal to (=), less than (<), or greater than (>) the other.

Primary Storage

Primary Storage Temporarily Holds Data, Program Instructions, and Information

Primary storage—also known as **internal storage, main memory,** or simply *"memory"*—is the part of the microcomputer that holds:

- Data for processing
- Instructions for processing the data—that is, the *program*
- Information—that is, processed data—waiting to be output or sent to secondary storage such as a diskette in a disk drive

Perhaps the most important fact to know about primary storage is that it holds its contents only temporarily—only as long as the microcomputer is turned on. When you turn the machine off, all the stored contents immediately vanish. We have said this before, but it bears repeating: The stored contents in primary storage can vanish very quickly, as during a power failure, for example. It is therefore a good practice repeatedly to save your work in progress to a secondary storage medium such as a diskette. For instance, if you are writing a report on a word processor, every 10 to 15 minutes you should stop and save your work.

The next important fact to know about primary storage is that its capacity varies in different computers. The original IBM Personal Computer, for example, can hold up to approximately 640,000 characters of data or instructions. By contrast, the IBM Personal System/2 Model 80 can hold 16 *million* characters, or over 24 times as much. If you are using an older computer with small primary storage, it may not be able to run such powerful programs as Lotus 1-2-3. Thus, you need to look at the software package before you buy and see how much primary storage it requires.

Registers Computers also have several additional storage locations called **registers,** which appear in the control unit and ALU and make processing more efficient. Registers are sort of special high-speed staging areas that hold data and instructions temporarily during processing. They are parts of the control unit and ALU rather than primary storage. Their contents can therefore be handled much faster than can the contents of primary storage.

The Processing Cycle To locate the characters of data or instructions in main memory, the computer stores them at locations known as **addresses.** Each address is designated by a unique number. Addresses may be compared to post office mailboxes. Their numbers stay the same, but the contents continually change.

Figure 4-14 gives an example of how primary storage and the CPU work to process information. Note that the various components of the CPU are linked by special electrical

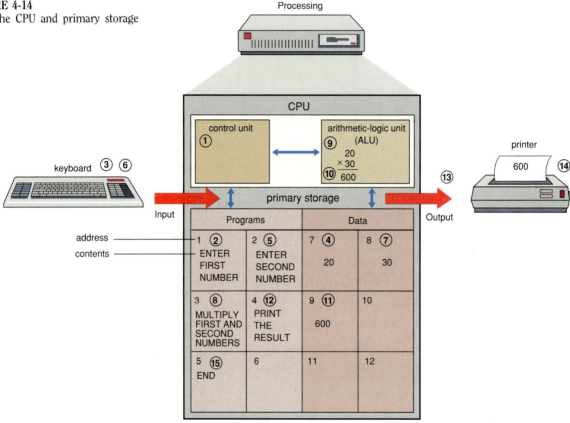

FIGURE 4-14
How the CPU and primary storage work.

1. The control unit recognizes that the entire program has been loaded into primary storage. It begins to execute the first step in the program.

2. The program tells the user, ENTER FIRST NUMBER.

3. The user presses the number *20* on the keyboard. An electronic signal is sent to the CPU.

4. The control unit recognizes this signal and routes the signal to an address in primary storage—address 7.

5. After completing the above program instruction, the control unit executes the next program instruction: ENTER SECOND NUMBER.

6. The user presses the number *30* on the keyboard. An electronic signal is sent to the CPU.

7. The control unit recognizes this signal and routes it to primary storage address 8.

8. The control unit now executes the next program AND SECOND NUMBERS.

9. To execute this instruction, the control unit informs the arithmetic-logic unit (ALU) that two numbers are coming and that the ALU is to multiply them. The control unit next sends the ALU a copy of the contents of address 7 (*20*) and then sends a copy of the contents of address 8 (*30*).

10. The ALU performs the multiplication: *20 × 30 = 600*.

11. The control unit sends a copy of the multiplied results (*600*) back to primary storage, to address 9.

12. The control unit executes the next program instruction: PRINT THE RESULT.

13. To execute this instruction, the control unit sends the contents of address 9 (*600*) to the printer.

14. The printer prints the value *600*.

15. The control unit executes the final instruction: END. The program is complete.

connections. In this example, the program will multiply two numbers—20 × 30, yielding 600. Let us assume the program to multiply these two numbers has been loaded into primary storage. The program asks the user to enter two values (20 and 30). It then multiplies the two values together (20 × 30). Finally, it prints out the result (600) on a printer. Figure 4-14 describes the process just after the program has been loaded into primary storage. Follow the steps in the figure to walk yourself through the diagram.

Note: This figure is a simplification of the actual processing activity in order to demonstrate the essential operations of the CPU. For instance, there are actually many more primary storage addresses—thousands or millions—than are shown here. In addition, the addresses are in a form the computer can interpret—electronic signals rather than the numbers and letters shown here.

The Binary System

Data and Instructions Are Represented Electronically with a Binary, or Two-State, Numbering System. The Two Principal Binary Coding Schemes Are EBCDIC and ASCII.

We have described the storage and processing of data in terms of *characters*. How, in fact, are these characters represented inside the computer?

We said that when you open up the system cabinet of a microcomputer, you see mainly electronic circuitry. And what is the most fundamental statement you can make about electricity? It is simply this: It can be either *on* or *off*.

Indeed, there are many forms of technology that can make use of this two-state on/off, yes/no, present/absent arrangement. For instance, a light switch may be on or off, or an electric circuit open or closed. A magnetized spot on a tape or disk may have a positive charge or a negative charge. This is the reason, then, that the binary system is used to represent data and instructions.

The decimal system that we are all used to has 10 digits (0, 1, 2, 3, 4, 5, 6, 7, 8, 9). The **binary system,** however, consists of only two digits—0 and 1. In the computer, the 0 can be represented by electricity's being off, and the 1 by electricity's being on. Everything that goes into a computer is converted into these binary numbers (see Figure 4-15). For example, the letter *W* corresponds to the electronic signal 01010111.

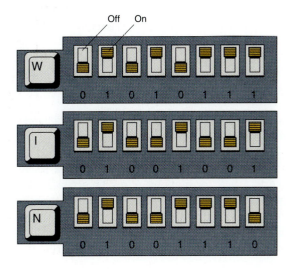

FIGURE 4-15
How the letters W-I-N are represented in on/off, zero/one binary code (ASCII).

64
The Central Processing Unit

8 bits = 1 byte (handwritten note)

Units of Measure for Capacity Each 0 or 1 in the binary system is called a **bit**—short for *bi*nary dig*it*. In order to represent numbers, letters, and special characters, bits are combined into groups of eight bits called **bytes.** Each byte typically represents one character—in many computers, one addressable storage location. The capacity of main memory, then, is expressed in numbers of bytes.

- One **kilobyte**—abbreviated **K, KB,** or **K-byte**—is equivalent to approximately 1000 bytes. (More precisely, 1 kilobyte is equal to 1024 bytes. However, the figure is commonly rounded to 1000 bytes.) This is a common unit of measure for memory or storage capacity of microcomputers. The older IBM PCs, for example, had a top capacity of 640K, or about 640,000 characters of data.
- One **megabyte**—**MB** or **M-byte**—represents 1 million bytes. Thus, a microcomputer system listed with a "16MB main memory" has primary storage capacity of about 16 million bytes. An example of such a microcomputer system is the IBM PS/2 Model 70.
- One **gigabyte**—**GB** or **G-byte**—represents about 1 billion bytes—a measure used with mainframe computers and supercomputers.
- One **terabyte** (**TB** or **T-byte**) represents about 1 trillion bytes.

Binary Coding Schemes Now let us consider an important question. How are characters represented as 0s and 1s ("off" and "on" electrical states) in the computer? The answer is in the use of *binary coding schemes*.

Two of the most popular binary coding schemes use eight bits to form each byte. These two codes are *EBCDIC* and *ASCII* (see Figure 4-16).

- **EBCDIC,** pronounced "*eb-see-dick*," stands for *E*xtended *B*inary *C*oded *D*ecimal *I*nterchange *C*ode. It was developed by IBM and is used on many IBM and other kinds of computers. As a result, EBCDIC is almost an industry standard for minicomputers and mainframe computers.
- **ASCII,** pronounced "*as*-key," stands for *A*merican *S*tandard *C*ode for *I*nformation *I*nterchange. This is the most widely used binary code for microcomputers.

When you press a key on the keyboard, a character is automatically converted into a series of electronic pulses that the CPU can recognize. For example, pressing the letter *W* on an IBM PS/2 keyboard causes an electronic signal to be sent to the CPU, which converts it to the ASCII value of 01010111.

The Parity Bit Just as you sometimes hear static on the radio, so there can also be "static," or electronic interference, in a circuit or communications line transmitting a byte. When you are typing the letter *W*, for example, the *W* should be represented in the CPU (in ASCII) as:

01010111

However, if the last 1 is garbled and becomes a 0, the byte will be read as 01010110—*V* instead of *W*. Is there a way, then, for the CPU to detect whether it is receiving erroneous data?

Indeed there is. Detection is accomplished by using a **parity bit**—an extra bit automatically added to a byte for purposes of testing accuracy. There are even-parity systems and odd-parity systems. In a computer using an even-parity system, the parity bit is set to either 0 or 1 to ensure that the number of 1s is even (see Figure 4-17). For instance, when the letter *W* is pressed on the keyboard, the signal 01010111 is emitted. Before the signal is sent to the CPU, the number of 1s is counted—in this case, 5. A parity

Character	EBCDIC	ASCII
A	1100 0001	0100 0001
B	1100 0010	0100 0010
C	1100 0011	0100 0011
D	1100 0100	0100 0100
E	1100 0101	0100 0101
F	1100 0110	0100 0110
G	1100 0111	0100 0111
H	1100 1000	0100 1000
I	1100 1001	0100 1001
J	1101 0001	0100 1010
K	1101 0010	0100 1011
L	1101 0011	0100 1100
M	1101 0100	0100 1101
N	1101 0101	0100 1110
O	1101 0110	0100 1111
P	1101 0111	0101 0000
Q	1101 1000	0101 0001
R	1101 1001	0101 0010
S	1110 0010	0101 0011
T	1110 0011	0101 0100
U	1110 0100	0101 0101
V	1110 0101	0101 0110
W	1110 0110	0101 0111
X	1110 0111	0101 1000
Y	1110 1000	0101 1001
Z	1110 1001	0101 1010
0	1111 0000	0011 0000
1	1111 0001	0011 0001
2	1111 0010	0011 0010
3	1111 0011	0011 0011
4	1111 0100	0011 0100
5	1111 0101	0011 0101
6	1111 0110	0011 0110
7	1111 0111	0011 0111
8	1111 1000	0011 1000
9	1111 1001	0011 1001

FIGURE 4-16
EBCDIC and ASCII binary coding schemes for representing data.

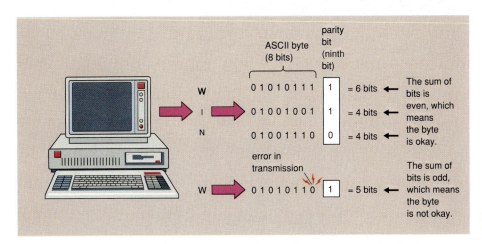

FIGURE 4-17
Example of parity bit.

bit is added to the front and set to 1, thereby making the number of 1s even. The signal 101010111 is sent. When the signal is received by the CPU, the number of 1s is checked again. If it is odd, it means an error has occurred. This is called a *parity error*. When a parity error occurs, the CPU requests that the signal be sent again. If the parity error occurs again, the message "parity error" will appear on your display. (Odd-parity systems act just the reverse of even-parity systems.)

Of course, the system does not guarantee accuracy. For example, if *two* erroneous 0s were introduced in the byte for *W,* the computer would accept the byte as correct. This is because the two erroneous 0s would add to an even 4 bits.

We have explained the principles by which a computer stores and processes data. We can now open up the system unit and take a look at some of the parts.

The System Unit

It's Important to Understand What's Inside the System Unit, So That You Can Talk Intelligently to Computer Specialists.

As mentioned, the part of the microcomputer that contains the CPU is called the *system unit* and is housed within the system cabinet. If you take off the cabinet, you will find that many parts can be easily removed for replacement. The IBM PS/2, for example, is modular. That is, entire sections can be replaced, as one would the parts of a car. In addition, many microcomputers are *expandable*. That is, more primary storage (main memory) may be added, as well as certain other devices.

Let us consider the following components of the system unit:

- System board
- Microprocessor chips
- Memory chips—RAM and ROM
- System clock
- Expansion slots and boards
- Bus lines
- Ports

System Board The **system board** is also called the **motherboard** (see Figure 4-18 on p. 66). It consists of a flat board that usually contains the CPU and some primary storage

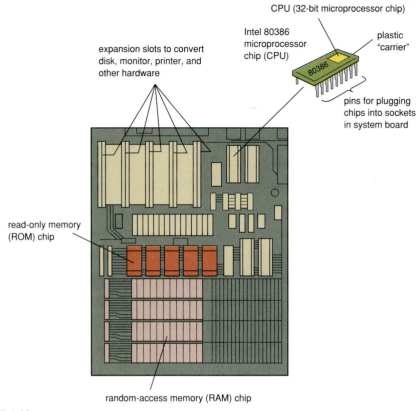

FIGURE 4-18
A microcomputer system board. The CPU is on a tiny microprocessor chip less than ⅛-inch square.

(main memory) *chips*. A chip consists of a tiny circuit board etched into a ⅛-inch square of sandlike material called silicon. A chip is also called a **silicon chip, semiconductor,** or **integrated circuit.** Chips are mounted on carrier packages, which then plug into sockets on the system board. In addition, system boards usually contain expansion slots, as we describe in another few paragraphs.

Microprocessor Chips   In a microcomputer, the CPU is contained on a single silicon chip called the *microprocessor*—"microscopic processor." Different microprocessors have different capabilities.

Chip capacities are often expressed in word sizes. A **word** is the number of bits (such as 8, 16, or 32) that can be accessed at one time by the CPU. The more bits in a word, the more powerful—and the faster—the computer. A 32-bit-word computer can access 4 bytes at a time. An 8-bit-word computer can access only 1 byte at a time. Therefore, the 32-bit computer is faster.

Some chips or "families" of chips have become famous as the basis for several important lines of microcomputers. (However, they are known by distinctly undramatic names: just product numbers.) Examples are shown in Figure 4-19. Their estimated market shares are shown in Figure 4-20.

As we mentioned, the growing power of microprocessor chips is what is changing everything about microcomputers. Motorola's 68030 chip, for example, is the basis for the Macintosh IIsi (see Figure 4-21). This machine can scroll through documents the length of *War and Peace* up to four times faster than the Macintosh SE. Motorola's next generation of microprocessor, the 68040 chip, is used in the NeXTstation (Figure 4-22, p. 68).

Word size	Manufacturer	Chip number	Personal computers using the chip
16-bit	Intel	8088	IBM Personal Computer
		8086	AT&T Personal Computer 6300
		80286	IBM PC/AT, Compaq Portable II
32-bit	Motorola	68000	Apple Macintosh
		68010	AT&T Personal Computer 7300
		68020	Apple Macintosh II
		68030	Apple Macintosh IIcx, IIsi
			NeXT computer
		68040	Hewlett-Packard MP900 workstations
			NeXT NeXTstation
	Intel	80386	IBM Personal System/2 Model 80, Compaq Deskpro 386
		80486	IBM PS/2 Model 70

FIGURE 4-19
Famous microprocessor chips.

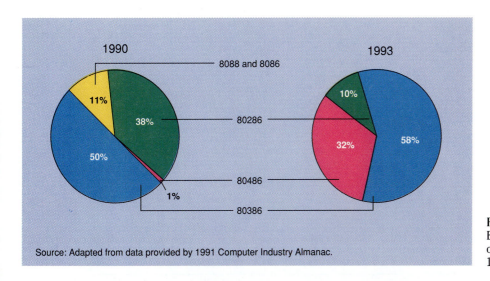

FIGURE 4-20
Estimated market share (percentage) of new microprocessors, 1990 and 1993.

FIGURE 4-21
The Macintosh IIsi, which uses Motorola's 68030 microprocessor.

68
The Central Processing Unit

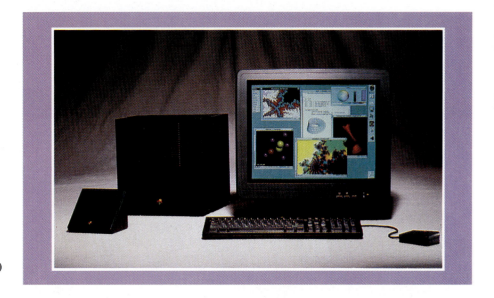

FIGURE 4-22
The NeXTstation, using the 68040 microprocessor.

FIGURE 4-23
The PS/2 486/25 "power platform" for the IBM PS/2 Model 70; it contains the Intel '486 chip.

The NeXTstation runs four times faster than the first NeXT computer. NeXT, Inc. was started by former Apple cofounder Steve Jobs. Intel's most recent offering, the 80486 chip, is four times faster than its predecessor, the '386 chip (see Figure 4-23).

However, even more powerful microprocessors are now available. **RISC chips** (RISC stands for "reduced instruction set computer"), such as the Motorola 88000 chip, are commonly found in workstations. RISC chips are beginning to supplant the present form of chip design (now known as *CISC,* for "complex instruction set computer"). Currently, workstations with RISC chips are being produced by Data General and IBM (see Figure 4-24). These machines are being used by scientists, engineers, designers, and other professionals. You should not assume that suddenly you will find these extraordinarily powerful machines on every desktop. Because of the cost of manufacturing and availability, it will probably be some time before these microcomputers become commonplace.

FIGURE 4-24
This IBM RISC System/6000 is one of several IBM workstations using the fast RISC chip.

Some specialized processor chips are also available. One example is a mathematics **coprocessor chip**—a chip that assists the main processor—that can help a CPU do very fast mathematical computations. The coprocessor is controlled by the main microprocessor, which sends it data and instructions.

RAM Chips The kind of internal storage we have been calling primary storage or main memory is of a type known as **random-access memory.** This is abbreviated **RAM** (pronounced "ram"). RAM is a term frequently used in conversations about microcomputers. Random-access memory holds the program and data that the CPU is presently processing. That is, it is *temporary* storage. (Secondary storage, which we shall describe in Chapter 6, is permanent storage, such as the data stored on diskettes. Data from this kind of storage must be loaded into RAM before it can be used.)

RAM is called temporary because as soon as the microcomputer is turned off, everything in RAM is lost. It is also lost if there is a power failure that disrupts the electric current going to the microcomputer. For this reason, as we mentioned earlier, it is a good idea to save your work in progress. That is, if you are writing on your word processor, every few minutes you should save, or store, the material.

In addition, when programs or data are written, or encoded, to RAM, the previous contents of RAM are lost. This is called the *destructive write process.* However, when programs and data are read, or retrieved, from RAM, their contents are not destroyed. Rather, the read process simply makes a copy of those contents. Consequently, this activity is called the *nondestructive read process.*

RAM storage is frequently expressed in kilobytes. Thus, a microcomputer with 640K RAM has primary storage that will hold about 640,000 characters of data and programs. The IBM PS/2 Model 50 has considerably more—up to 7MB RAM, or 7 million characters.

Knowing the amount of RAM is important! Some software programs may require more primary storage capacity than a particular microcomputer offers. For instance,

Lotus 1-2-3 Release 3.0 requires 1MB of RAM to run with DOS. Additional RAM is needed to hold any data. However, most IBM PC microcomputers have only 640K of RAM. This is not enough primary storage to hold the program, much less work with it.

As time goes on, users will probably not have to worry about whether their computers have enough RAM to handle programs and data. The reason is simple: RAM chips have been getting cheaper. Thus, computer manufacturers can afford to build microcomputers with a great deal of random access memory capacity.

ROM Chips Another type of memory, **read-only memory,** describes chips that have programs built into them at the factory. Read-only memory is abbreviated **ROM** (pronounced "rahm"). Unlike RAM chips, ROM chips cannot be changed by the user. "Read only" means that the CPU can read, or retrieve, the programs written on the ROM chip. However, the computer cannot write—encode or change—the information or instructions in ROM.

ROM chips typically contain special instructions for detailed computer operations. For example, ROM instructions may start the computer, give keyboard keys their special control capabilities, and put characters on the screen. ROMs are also called **firmware** because the programs are "firm" and cannot be easily altered.

Two important variations on the ROM chip are the following.

- **PROM (programmable read-only memory).** This means that a software manufacturer can write instructions onto the chip using special equipment. However, once it is written, it cannot be changed.
- **EPROM (erasable programmable read-only memory).** This is a PROM chip that can be erased with a special ultraviolet light. New instructions can then be written on it. (There are also some electrically erasable chips—EEPROM.)

System Clock The **system clock** controls how fast all the operations within a computer take place. The speed is expressed in **megahertz** (abbreviated **MHz**). One megahertz equals 1 million beats (cycles) per second. The faster the clock speed, the faster the computer can process information. In computer ads, you may see that an older IBM Personal Computer has a clock frequency of 4.77 MHz. Microcomputers built with the Intel '386 chips, by contrast, typically have a 20 MHz speed. They are so fast that manufacturers have had to devise special ways to enable RAM chips to keep up.

Expansion Slots and Boards Computers are known for having different kinds of "architectures." Machines that have **closed architecture** are those manufactured in such a way that users cannot easily add new devices. Most microcomputers have **open architecture.** They allow users to expand their systems by inserting optional devices known as **expansion boards.** Expansion boards are also called **plug-in boards, controller cards, adapter cards,** or **interface cards.**

The expansion boards plug into slots inside the system unit. Ports on the boards allow cables to be connected from the expansion boards to devices outside the system unit. Among the kinds of expansion boards available are the following:

- *Expanded primary storage:* These circuit boards consist of several additional RAM chips, which increase the capacity of the computer's primary storage. Early microcomputer users found that additional primary storage was their first requirement for handling newer, more sophisticated programs, such as integrated software. (See Figure 4-25.)
- *Display adapter cards:* These cards can be used to adapt a variety of color video display monitors to your computer.
- *Additional secondary storage:* Expansion cards may be used to add more flexible- or hard-disk storage capacity.

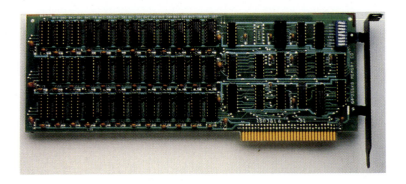

FIGURE 4-25
Expansion board.

- *Other "add-ons":* Expansion cards can be inserted to connect printers, communications devices, and other hardware.

Most computers have only a limited number of expansion slots. Thus, **multifunction boards** have been made available that combine several expansion activities on a single card. For example, a multifunction board may offer additional RAM and a display adapter of some sort.

Bus Lines A **bus line**—or simply **bus**—connects the parts of the CPU to each other. It also links the CPU with other important hardware. Examples are RAM and ROM chips and ports connecting with outside devices. A bus is a data roadway along which bits travel. Such data pathways resemble a multilane highway. The more lanes there are, the faster traffic can go through. Similarly, the greater the capacity of a bus, the more powerful and faster the operation. A 32-bit bus has greater capacity than a 16-bit bus, for example.

Why should you even have to care about what a bus line is? The answer is that, as microprocessor chips have changed, so have bus lines. Thus, the things you used to be able to do on some computers you may no longer be able to do on new ones.

The three principal bus lines (or "architectures") are the following:

- **Industry Standard Architecture (ISA):** This bus was developed for the IBM Personal Computer. First it was an 8-bit-wide data path, then (when the IBM AT was introduced) 16 bits wide. The '286 microprocessors and add-on expansion boards were able to satisfactorily move data along this 16-bit roadway. But then along came the '386 chip—which requires data paths that are *32* bits wide. And suddenly there was a competition between two 32-bit standards.

- **Micro Channel Architecture (MCA):** IBM decided to support the new '386 chip with a 32-bit bus line that was entirely new. You cannot simply remove your expansion boards from an IBM PC, XT, or AT and put them into an IBM PS/2 Model 80. With Micro Channel, they simply won't work. If you are not concerned about transferring boards, IBM's new standard is not a problem. You can take full advantage of the faster processor.

- **Extended Industry Standard Architecture (EISA):** This 32-bit bus standard was proposed in September 1988 by nine manufacturers of IBM compatibles, led by Compaq Computer Corporation. The purpose of EISA is to extend and amend the old ISA standard, so that all existing expansion boards can work with the new architecture.

As of the moment, it remains to be seen which 32-bit standard will prevail. (Apple also has a 32-bit bus standard, but it is completely incompatible with the ISA.) In making

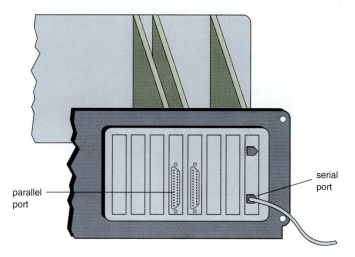

FIGURE 4-26
The ports in the back of a microcomputer.

a choice, users will have to decide how their performance will be improved. They will have to decide how much it will cost and what it will do to their previous investments in hardware.

Ports A **port** is a connecting socket on the outside of the system unit. This allows you to plug in other devices, such as video display monitors and printers. Figure 4-26 shows two types of ports.

- **Parallel ports** allow lines to be connected that will enable several bits to be transmitted simultaneously. An example might be an entire eight-bit ASCII character from the CPU to certain printers. Parallel lines move information faster than serial lines do. They are used for equipment, such as a printer, that is physically located close to the computer.
- **Serial ports** are for connecting lines that transmit bits one after the other on a single communications line. Serial lines frequently are used to link equipment that is not located close by. Thus, they are used, for example, to send information via a modem from the computer over a telephone line.

Ports are used to connect input and output devices to the system unit. It is customary to refer to all hardware outside the system unit—but not necessarily outside the system *cabinet*—as **peripheral devices.** In many microcomputers, disk drives are built into the system cabinet. In some laptop computers, the keyboard and monitor are also an integral part of the system cabinet.

A Look at the Future

Four New Technologies Could Make Computing Faster: RISC, Superconducting, Optical Computing, and Neural Networking. The Result Will Be "Downsizing Applications."

We already mentioned RISC (reduced instruction set computer) microprocessors. Some observers think the RISC chip will triple performance of the desktop processor every 1½ to 2 years.

Another technological improvement may come in the form of the materials used for microprocessors. At present, microprocessor chips are made out of silicon. Such chips are called *semiconductors* because electricity flows through the material with some resistance. *Superconducting* material, on the other hand, conducts electricity without resistance. Until recently, superconduction was considered impractical because the materials had to be at extremely low, subzero temperatures. However, research is now being done on "warm" superconductors, which offer the promise of faster on-and-off processing to give us lightning-quick computers.

A third area being explored is that known as *optical computing.* In this technology, a machine consisting of lasers, lenses, and mirrors uses pulses of light rather than currents of electricity to represent the on-and-off codes of data. Light is much faster than electricity. An experimental optical computer was introduced by Bell Laboratories in January 1990.

A fourth area, *neural networks,* is not a different kind of technology so much as a new arrangement using existing technology. Present computers—even supercomputers—are relatively slow because of a built-in structural limitation: the processor and the primary storage are physically separated. Although joined by a communications link, the processor must spend most of its time waiting for data to come from or go to memory. (The arrangement is known as the *von Neumann architecture,* after its originator, John von Neumann.) A neural network, however, consists of layers of processors interconnected somewhat like the neurons of biological nervous systems. One such computer developed by TRW has 250,000 processors and 5.5 million connections. As a result, data is transmitted to and from a processor at many times the speed of the old arrangements.

With these kinds of developments, it's clear that we are on the road to "downsizing applications." That is, computers will not only get smaller, as we are seeing with the newer portables, but also more powerful. Indeed, it is very easy to believe, as some industry observers suggest, that by the year 2000 desktop computers will be as powerful as the first supercomputer.

Review Questions

1. Distinguish among the four kinds of computer systems.
2. What are the three parts of the CPU, and what purpose does each serve?
3. What is the purpose of primary storage?
4. What are registers?
5. Describe how the control unit, arithmetic-logic unit, and primary storage work to process information (five steps).
6. What is the difference between the decimal system and the binary system? Why is the binary system used in the computer to represent data and instructions?
7. What is a bit? A byte?
8. What is a kilobyte? A megabyte? A gigabyte? A terabyte? What are their abbreviations?
9. What are the names (abbreviations) of the two primary coding schemes for representing letters, numbers, and special characters in binary form?
10. What kind of chips are usually contained on the system board?
11. What does *word* mean as a measure of the power of a microprocessor?
12. Distinguish between the RAM and ROM forms of memory.
13. Why is it important to know the amount of RAM in a microcomputer?
14. Why are ROM chips also called *firmware?*
15. What is the purpose of the system clock? How fast is a megahertz?
16. What is an expansion board?
17. What kinds of expansion boards are available for what purposes?

CHAPTER 4
The Central Processing Unit

VISUAL SUMMARY

The central processing unit (CPU) and primary storage are two major parts of a microcomputer system unit.

Four Types of Computers

From smallest to largest:
- Microcomputers
- Minicomputers
- Mainframes
- Supercomputers

Types of Computer Systems

From smallest to largest:

Microcomputers

Microcomputers cost $200–$15,000. Two principal categories are:
- *Personal computers*—desktop or portable computers, running easy-to-use applications software. **Portable computers** may be **transportables** or **luggables** (18–30 pounds), **laptops** (10–16 pounds), **notebook PCs** (5–10 pounds), or **pocket PCs** (1–2 pounds).
- *Workstations*—machines typically used by scientists and engineers, running complex programs and with powerful processors and sophisticated display screens.

Minicomputers

Minicomputers cost from several thousand to a half-million dollars and were first used as special-purpose mainframes. They work well in **distributed data processing** or **decentralized** systems, in which a **host** (central) computer is linked by communication lines to distant minicomputers.

Mainframes

Mainframes cost from several hundred thousand dollars up to $10 million and process millions of instructions per second. These are room-sized systems and are used by large organizations to handle large programs with lots of data.

Supercomputers

Supercomputers cost several million dollars and process billions of operations per second. They are used for very large programs and very large amounts of data requiring processing in a short period of time, as in weather forecasting. Supercomputers with **massively parallel processing** use thousands of interconnected microprocessors.

The CPU and Primary Storage

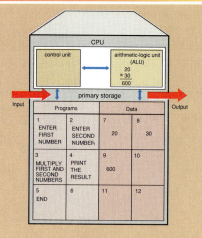

Central Processing Unit

The central processing unit (CPU) is the **processor**, the part of the computer that runs the program. The CPU has two parts:
- The **control unit** directs electronic signals between primary storage and the ALU, and between the CPU and input/output devices.
- The **arithmetic-logic unit (ALU)** performs *arithmetic* (math) operations and *logical* (comparison) operations.

Primary Storage

Primary storage **(internal storage, main memory)** holds data, instructions for processing data (the program), and information (processed data). The contents are held in primary storage only temporarily. Capacity varies with different computers.
- Additional storage units (in control unit and ALU) called **registers** help make processing more efficient.
- Characters of data or instructions are stored in primary storage locations called **addresses**.

Visual Summary

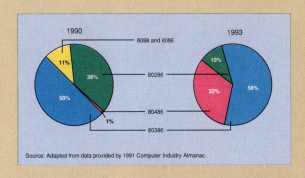

The Binary System

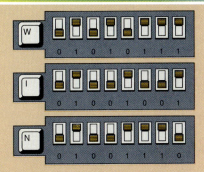

Data and instructions are represented electronically with a two-state **binary system** of numbers (0 and 1).

Measure of Capacity

- **Bit** (*bi*nary digi*t*)—0 or 1, corresponding to electricity being *on* or *off*.
- **Byte**—eight bits. Each byte represents one character. The primary storage capacity of a computer is measured in bytes.
- **Kilobyte (K)**—about 1000 bytes.
- **Megabyte (MB)**—about 1 million bytes.
- **Gigabyte (GB)**—about 1 billion bytes.
- **Terabyte (TB)**—about 1 trillion bytes.

Binary Coding Schemes

Two popular schemes for representing bytes are:
- **EBCDIC**—used in mini- and mainframe computers.
- **ASCII**—used in microcomputers.

Parity Bit

A **parity bit** is an extra bit added to a byte for error detection purposes.

The System Unit

In a microcomputer, the system unit consists of the following:

System Board

The **system board** contains the CPU and primary storage on **chips** (also called **silicon chips, semi-conductors, integrated circuits**).

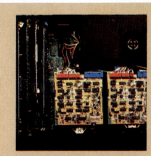

Microprocessor Chips

The *microprocessor chip* contains the CPU. Capacities are expressed in word sizes. A **word** is the number of bits (e.g., 16 or 32) that can be accessed at one time by the CPU.

RAM Chips

RAM (for **random-access memory**) **chips** temporarily hold data and instructions in primary storage.

ROM Chips

ROM (for **read-only memory**) **chips** (**firmware**) have programs built into them for operating important system devices. Variations on the ROM chip are:
- **PROM** (programmable read-only memory)
- **EPROM** (erasable programmable read-only memory)

System Clock

The **system clock** controls the speed of computer operations. Speed is expressed in **megahertz**—millions of beats per second.

Expansion Slots and Boards

Open architecture machines allow users to easily expand their systems (**closed architecture** machines do not). Users may add **expansion** (or **plug-in**) **boards** to:
- Expand primary storage capacity.
- Adapt color display monitors.
- Add flexible- or hard-disk storage capacity.

Bus Lines

A **bus line** (or **bus**) is a data roadway connecting parts of the CPU to each other.

Ports

A **port** is a connecting socket on the outside of the system unit for plugging in other devices.
- **Parallel ports** allow several bits to be transmitted simultaneously.
- **Serial ports** transmit one bit at a time.

18. What do bus lines do?
19. Name the three alternative bus architectures.
20. What are two types of ports, and what are they used for?

Discussion Questions

1. Look through a computer magazine or newspaper (*PC World, PC Magazine, Infoworld,* or some other periodical). Based on advertisements, what is the *least expensive* computer system you could assemble with system unit, monitor, keyboard, disk drive, and printer? It can be either new or used. (Don't worry for now whether the devices are necessarily compatible with one another.) Note the capacity of the main memory (in kilobytes). Discuss with classmates whether it would be large enough. What could you do to expand it with the kind of equipment you've selected?

2. The word *compatible* is sometimes used to describe a microcomputer that copies or closely resembles the microcomputers made by a well-known manufacturer, usually International Business Machines. Many such microcomputers are made overseas and are available at considerably less cost than IBM's models. Again look through a computer newspaper and list some computers advertised as "IBM-compatible." How do the prices compare from what you can find out? Do they have sufficient memory capacity? What are some of the risks of buying a compatible?

CHAPTER 5
Input and Output

How do you get data to the CPU? How do you get information out? Here we describe the two most important places where the computer interfaces with people. The first half of the chapter covers input devices; the second half covers output devices.

People understand language, which is constructed of letters, numbers, and punctuation marks. However, computers can understand only the binary machine language of 0s and 1s. Input and output devices are essentially *converters*. Input devices convert symbols that people understand into symbols that computers can process. Output devices do the reverse: They convert machine output to output people can comprehend. Let us, then, look at the devices that perform these conversions.

COMPETENCIES

After you have read this chapter, you should be able to:

1. Explain the difference between keyboard and direct-entry input devices and the POS terminal.

2. Describe the features of keyboards and differentiate among keyboard entry devices used with larger computer systems. These include dumb, smart, and intelligent terminals.

3. Describe direct-entry devices used with microcomputers. These include the mouse, touch screen, digitizer, light pen, image scanner, fax, bar-code reader, MICR, OCR, OMR, and voice-input devices.

4. Explain output devices, including monochrome monitors, graphics monitors, and flat-panel displays.

5. Describe printers—dot-matrix, daisy-wheel, laser, ink-jet, chain—and flatbed and drum plotters.

6. Describe voice-output devices.

7. Describe ergonomics.

Input

Input: Keyboard Versus Direct Entry

Input Devices Convert People-Readable Data into Machine-Readable Form. Input May Be Keyboard or Direct Entry.

Input devices take data and programs that people can read or understand and convert them to a form the computer can process. This is the machine-readable electronic signals of 0s and 1s that we described in the last chapter. Input devices are of two kinds: keyboard entry and direct entry.

- *Keyboard entry:* Data is input to the computer through a *keyboard* that looks like a typewriter keyboard but has additional keys. In this method, the user typically reads from an original document—called the **source document**—and enters that document by typing on the keyboard.

- *Direct entry:* Data is made into machine-readable form as it is entered into the computer; no keyboard is used.

78
Input and Output

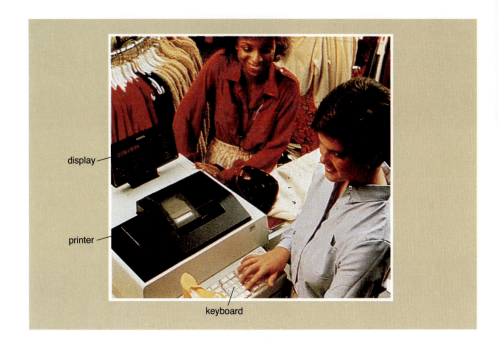

FIGURE 5-1
A point-of-sale terminal.

An example of an input device that uses both is a **point-of-sale** (**POS**) **terminal.** This is the sort of "electronic cash register" you see in department stores (see Figure 5-1). When clerks sell you a sweater, for example, they can type in the information (product code, purchase amount, tax) on the keyboard. Or they can use a hand-held **wand reader** to read special characters on the price tags as direct entry. The wand reflects light on the characters. The reflection is then changed by photoelectric cells to machine-readable code. Whether keyboard entry or direct entry, the results will appear on the POS terminal's digital display (see Figure 5-1).

Keyboard Entry

In Keyboard Entry, People Type Input. The Input Usually Appears on a Monitor.

Probably the most common way in which you will input data, at least at the beginning, is through a keyboard.

Keyboards Figure 5-2 shows two typical keyboards. Note the different kinds of keys:

- *Typewriter keys:* The keys that resemble the regular letters, numbers, and punctuation marks on a typewriter keyboard are called **typewriter keys.** Note the position of the **Enter** key, which is used to enter commands into the computer. The Enter key is sometimes also called the **Return** key.
- *Function keys:* The keys labeled *F1, F2,* and so on, are the *function keys.* These keys are used for tasks that occur frequently (such as underlining in word processing). They save you keystrokes.
- *Numeric keys:* The keys 0 to 9, called the **numeric keys** or **numeric keypad,** are used for tasks principally involving numbers. These may be useful when you are working with spreadsheets.
- *Special-purpose and directional arrow keys:* Examples of *special-purpose keys* are *Esc* (for "Escape"), *Ctrl* (for "Control"), *Del* (for "Delete"), and *Ins*

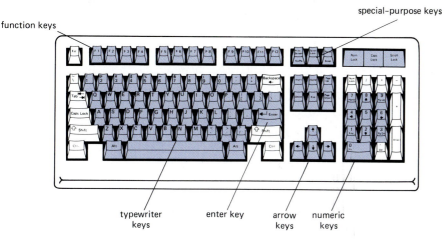

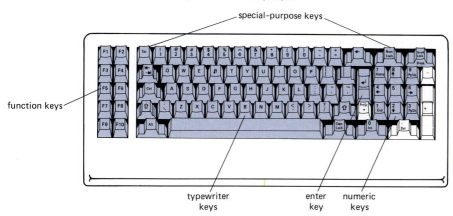

FIGURE 5-2
Two IBM keyboards.

(for "Insert"). These are used to help enter and edit data and execute commands. **Directional arrow keys** are used to move the cursor.

As we mentioned in Chapter 4, these keys convert letters, numbers, and other characters into electrical signals that are machine readable. These signals are sent to the computer's CPU.

Terminals A **terminal** is a form of input (and output) device that consists of a keyboard, a monitor, and a communications link. Terminals are of three types:

- A **dumb terminal** can be used to input and receive data, but it cannot process data independently. It is used only to gain access to information from a computer. Such a terminal may be used by an airline reservations clerk to access a mainframe computer for flight information.

- A **smart terminal** has some memory. It allows users to perform some editing or verification of data before it is sent to a large computer. A bank loan officer might do some calculations associated with making a loan on the smart terminal before this information is then stored in the bank's mainframe.

- An **intelligent terminal** includes processing unit, primary storage, and secondary storage such as magnetic disk. Essentially, an intelligent terminal is a microcomputer with some communications software and a telephone hookup (modem) or other communications link. These connect the terminal to the larger computer.

Nearly all large organizations have terminals connected to their minicomputers and mainframe computers. A clear recent trend, however, has been the use of microcomputers as terminals. As prices of microcomputers have dropped and their power and flexibility have climbed, companies have tended to buy these instead of terminals. Moreover, with the appropriate software and communications links, microcomputers can communicate exactly like specialized (dedicated) terminals.

Direct Entry

Direct Entry Creates Machine-Readable Data That Can Go Directly to the CPU. Direct Entry Includes Pointing, Scanning, and Voice-Input Devices.

Direct entry is a form of input that does not require data to be keyed by someone sitting at a keyboard. Direct-entry devices create machine-readable data on paper or magnetic media or feed it directly into the computer's CPU. This reduces the possibility of human error being introduced (as often happens when data is being entered through a keyboard) and is an economical means of data entry.

Direct-entry devices may be categorized into three areas:

- Pointing devices
- Scanning devices
- Voice-input devices

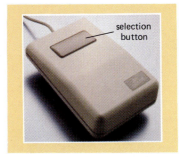

FIGURE 5-3
A mouse.

Pointing Devices Pointing, of course, is one of the most natural of all human gestures. There are a number of devices that use this method as a form of direct-entry input, as follows.

- *Mouse:* A *mouse* has a ball on the bottom and is attached with a cord to the system unit (see Figure 5-3). When rolled on the table top, the mouse directs the location of the cursor or pointer on the computer screen. The pointer can then be used to draw pictures or point to a particular instruction. Selection buttons on the mouse can be used to issue commands.

    At one time, the mouse was identified only with Apple microcomputers, but now it is becoming a standard for IBM's line of PS/2 models. Many people like the mouse because it reduces the need to input commands through a keyboard.

    A mouse is operated by rolling the ball beneath it along a flat surface. Sometimes no flat surface is available, as when one is on an airplane. In such cases, other pointing devices may be more convenient. An example is a mouse-like device with a ball that is attached to the side of the computer (see Figure 5-4). The device stays in one place, but the user can operate the ball with his or her thumb to guide the cursor.

FIGURE 5-4
This mouse-like device, Microsoft's Ballpoint Mouse, attaches to the side of a portable computer.

- *Touch screen:* A **touch screen** is a particular kind of monitor screen covered with a plastic layer. Behind this layer are crisscrossed invisible beams of infrared light. This arrangement enables someone to select actions or commands by touching the screen with a finger (Figure 5-5). Touch screens are easy to use, especially when people need information quickly. You are apt to see touch screen input devices used to convey visitor information in airports and hotels. However, they also have military and industrial applications.

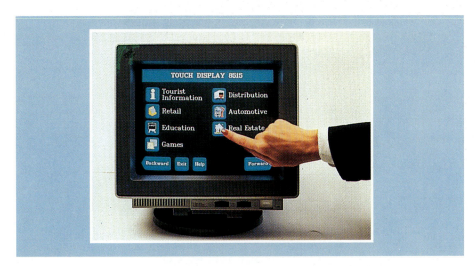

FIGURE 5-5
A touch screen.

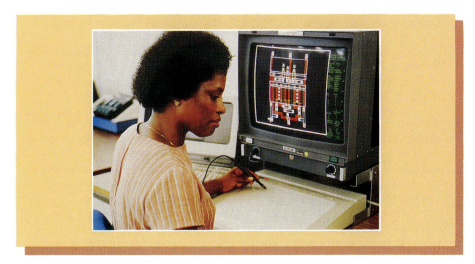

FIGURE 5-6
A digitizing tablet.

More recently, they are being used with microcomputers in applications that formerly used a mouse.

- *Digitizer:* A **digitizer** is a device that can be used to trace or copy a drawing or photograph. The shape is converted to digital data. A computer can then represent the data on the screen or print it out on paper. A **digitizing tablet** (see Figure 5-6) enables you to create your own images using a special stylus. The images are then converted to digital data that can be processed by the computer. Digitizers are often used by designers and architects.
- *Light pen:* A **light pen** (see Figure 5-7) is a light-sensitive penlike device. The light pen is placed against the monitor. This closes a photoelectric circuit and identifies the spot for entering or modifying data. Light pens are used by engineers, for example, in designing anything from microprocessor chips to airplane parts.

  The light pen will probably become a more important kind of input device because of the development of what are called "pen-based systems." (This technology is touched on in Chapter 12.)

Scanning Devices Direct-entry scanning devices record images of text, drawings, or special symbols. The images are converted to digital data that can be processed by a computer or displayed on a monitor. Scanning devices include the following:

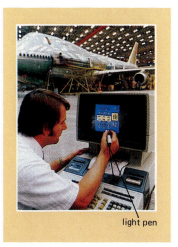

FIGURE 5-7
A light pen.

FIGURE 5-8
An image scanner.

- *Image scanner:* An **image scanner** (see Figure 5-8) identifies images on a page. It automatically converts them to electronic signals that can be stored in a computer. The process identifies pictures or different typefaces by scanning each image with light and breaking it into light and dark dots. The dots are then converted into digital code for storage. Image scanners are becoming widely used input devices, as the sales in Figure 5-9 indicate. Image scanners are commonly used in desktop publishing to scan graphic images that can then be placed in a page of text.

- *Fax machines:* **Facsimile transmission machines** have become extremely popular office machines, so much so that people often ask each other, "What's your fax number?" They are commonly called **fax machines.** Fax machines (see Figure 5-10) scan the image of a document and encode it as a series of instructions representing black-and-white image areas. They convert the instructions into a format (using a built-in modem) to send them electronically over telephone lines to a receiving fax machine. The receiving fax machine converts the signals back to an image and re-creates it on paper. The machine uses a process much like those used by office photocopiers. Fax machines are useful to anyone who needs to send images rather than text. Examples are engineering drawings, legal documents with signatures, and sales promotional materials.

    Most people use **dedicated fax machines.** These are specialized devices that do nothing else except send and receive documents from one place to another. Indeed, these are found not only in offices and print shops but even alongside phone booths in hotel lobbies and airports.

    However, for many microcomputers, an optional circuit board is available that may be inserted into one of the machine's expansion slots. Called **virtual fax,** this board, with appropriate software, allows you to create a document using your microcomputer. You can then convert it to a fax image and send it to a regular fax machine (or another similarly equipped microcomputer), which will print it. If you want to fax graphic images (pictures, not just text), you need a scanner to copy images into the computer.

    A fax-equipped microcomputer can also receive fax documents. These can be printed, if you have the right kind of printer (dot-matrix or laser), or viewed on your monitor screen. There is a limitation, however. You can't edit or change the content of the incoming fax messages on your computer unless you have a special kind of software.

FIGURE 5-9
Desktop scanners: sales are expected to increase.

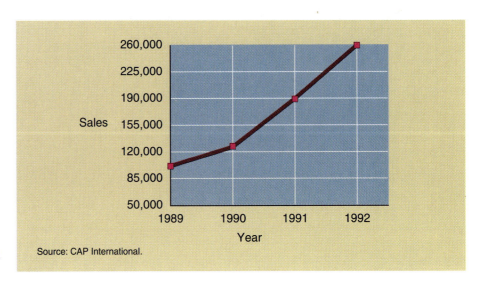

- *Bar-code readers:* You are probably principally familiar with bar-code readers from grocery stores. **Bar-code readers** (see Figure 5-11) are photoelectric scanners that read the **bar codes,** or vertical zebra-striped marks, printed on product containers. Supermarkets use a bar code system called the Universal Product Code (UPC). The bar code identifies the product to the supermarket's computer, which has a description and the latest price for the product. The computer automatically tells the POS terminal what the price is and prints the price and the product name on the customer's receipt.

- *Character and mark recognition devices:* There are three kinds of scanning devices formerly used only with mainframes that are now being found in connection with the more powerful microcomputers.

  Magnetic-ink character recognition (MICR) is a direct-entry method used in banks. This technology is used to automatically read those futuristic-looking numbers on the bottom of checks. A special-purpose machine known as a **reader/sorter** reads characters made of ink containing magnetized particles.

  Optical-character recognition (OCR) uses special preprinted characters, such as those printed on utility and telephone bills. They can be read by a light source and changed into machine-readable code. A common OCR device is the hand-held *wand reader* (see Figure 5-12). These are used in department stores to read retail price tags by reflecting light on the printed characters.

  Optical-mark recognition (OMR) is also called mark sensing. An OMR device senses the presence or absence of a mark, such as a pencil mark. OMR is used in tests such as the College Board's Scholastic Aptitude Test and the Graduate Record Examination.

Voice-Input Devices **Voice-input devices** (see Figure 5-13) convert a person's speech into a digital code. Most such systems must be "trained" to the particular user's voice. This is done by matching his or her spoken words to patterns previously stored in the computer. Some systems have been devised that can recognize the same word as

FIGURE 5-10
A fax machine.

FIGURE 5-11
A bar-code reader.

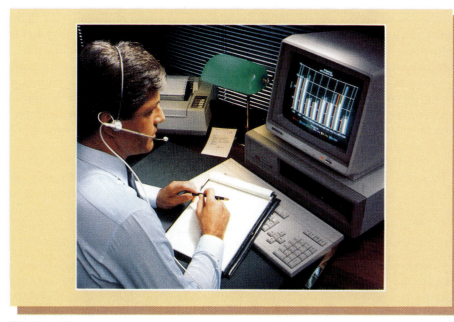
FIGURE 5-13
A voice-input device.

FIGURE 5-12
A wand reader.

spoken by many different people. However, until recently the list of words has been limited. A recently developed voice-activated system, the Dragon Dictate, recognizes over 30,000 words and adapts to individual voices. There are even systems that will translate from one language to another, as from English to Japanese.

Voice-input systems enable users to keep their hands free for other tasks. Thus, they are an obvious advantage for disabled people. But they are also used by people performing quality-control testing, package sorting, and baggage handling; by radiologists dictating reports; and by stockbrokers sending orders for stocks they want to buy and sell. A product called VoiceFont enables office workers to attach voice memos to their word processing, spreadsheet, and database files. All these systems are also called **speech-recognition devices** or **voice-recognition systems.**

Output

Output: Monitors, Printers, Plotters, Voice

Output Devices Convert Machine-Readable Information into People-Readable Form.

Data that is input to and then processed by the computer remains in machine-readable form until it is made people-readable by output devices.

The output devices we shall describe for microcomputers are monitors, printers, plotters, and voice-output.

Types of Monitors

Monitors May Be Single Color, or Monochrome, for Use with Text or Multicolor for Use with Graphics.

Monitors are also called **display screens** or *video display terminals (VDTs)*. The kinds of monitors seem divided into two categories according to **screen resolution**—the clarity of the images on the screen. Images are represented on monitors by individual dots or "picture elements" called **pixels.** A pixel is the smallest unit on the screen that can be turned on and off or made different shades. The *density* of the dots—that is, the number of rows and columns of dots—determines the clarity of the images, the resolution.

In general, monitors with extremely high resolution are needed for such purposes as engineering workstations and computer-aided design. Monitors with lower resolution are considered suitable for general business use. However, the differences are closing fast. Thus, you should be prepared to view your work in all kinds of displays.

How many colors and how good the resolution is depend in part on the technology of the monitor. Most of those that sit on desks are built in the same way as television sets. These are called **cathode-ray tubes** and are often referred to by their abbreviation, **CRTs.** Another technology, used in portable computers, which can't fit the long tube required of the CRT, is the **flat-panel display.** Here the monitor lies flat instead of standing upright.

We will distinguish between monochrome monitors and graphics monitors.

Monochrome Monitors   In the early days of the microcomputer, you could buy a monitor that provided easily readable text or a monitor that provided color—but not both. Some people needed monitors that would mainly show words and numbers—for example, secretaries, stockbrokers, travel agents, and the like. Their preferred form of display was **monochrome monitors,** those showing one color on a dark background. The text could be viewed in white, green, or amber. (The Apple Macintosh monitor duplicated the ink-on-paper look of black on a white background.) Today monochrome monitors are used principally in portable computers, where size is a major consideration. They are able to display both text and graphics.

Because CRTs are too bulky to be transported, the flat-panel display was devised for portable computers. These monitors are more compact and consume less power than CRTs but unfortunately do not typically show color.

Portable machines use several kinds of flat-panel technology:

- **Liquid-crystal display (LCD)** was one of the first kinds of displays (see Figure 5-14, which shows a Toshiba portable). An LCD does not emit light of its own. Rather, it consists of crystal molecules. An electric field causes the molecules to line up in a way that alters their optical properties. Unfortunately, many LCDs are difficult to read in sunlight or other strong light. Many portable computers now use backlit LCDs, which are brighter and easier to read.

- The **electroluminescent (EL) display** type of flat panel is better. It actively emits light when it is electrically charged (see Figure 5-15, which shows a Hewlett-Packard portable).

- The **gas-plasma display** is the best type of flat screen, because it is almost as good as a CRT-type screen. Like a neon light bulb, the plasma display uses a gas that emits light in the presence of an electric current. However, gas-plasma displays cannot be battery operated, which restricts their portability. They must be plugged into a regular wall plug offering AC current. In addition, they cannot show sharp contrast. The gas is either energized or it's not. Unlike a CRT, a gas-plasma display cannot be partially lit. Figure 5-16 shows the gas-plasma screen on a Toshiba portable.

FIGURE 5-14
Liquid-crystal display.

FIGURE 5-15
Electroluminescent display.

Graphics Monitors Graphics monitors (see Figure 5-17) display both alphanumeric characters and visual or graphic images. Graphics monitors have gone through the following stages:

- **CGA** stands for *C*olor *G*raphics *A*dapter. This was a circuit board introduced by IBM that could be inserted into the computer. It was a way of giving a monitor a color display (provided the monitor was itself designed for color, not monochrome). The monochrome resolution was 640 by 350 pixels and made text easily readable. The CGA resolution for four colors was only 320 by 200 pixels. This made text display grainier and harder to read than on a monochrome monitor.

- **EGA** stands for *E*nhanced *G*raphics *A*dapter. This board, which had a resolution of 640 by 350 pixels, was designed to support 16 colors, rather than just four. It was a significant step up in quality, offering resolution nearly like that

FIGURE 5-16
Gas-plasma display.

Monitor type	Pixels	Colors
CGA	320 × 200	4
EGA	640 × 350	16
VGA	640 × 480	16
	or 320 × 200	256
Super VGA	800 × 600	256
	or 1024 × 768	256
XGA	1024 × 768	65,536

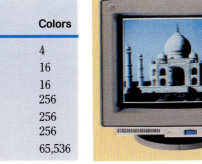
FIGURE 5-17
Types of graphics monitors.

in monochrome. Anyone upgrading to EGA from CGA, however, also had to buy a new monitor. The EGA monitor is still very popular today.

- **VGA** stands for *Video Graphics Array*. When used just for text, the resolution of this board is 720 by 400 pixels. The VGA is far superior to the CGA and EGA boards in its handling of color. You can get 16 colors at a resolution of 640 by 480 pixels. Or you can get 16 times as many colors—256 colors—with a resolution of 320 by 200. It is useful in many applications, such as industrial design, in which precise measurements must be taken directly from the screen.

- **Super VGA** is the name given to a very high resolution standard that displays up to 256 colors. Super VGA has a minimum of 800 by 600 resolution; some high-priced models have a 1024 by 768 resolution. The technology is used by highly skilled graphic designers and others who need the sharpest resolution and most color available.

- **XGA** stands for *Ex*tended *G*raphics *A*rray and has a resolution of up to 1024 by 768 pixels. Under normal circumstances, it displays up to 256 colors. However, with special equipment, it can handle up to 65,536 colors. XGA is becoming a standard for some very powerful microcomputer systems, such as the IBM 486 PS/2 models.

Printers

Five Kinds of Printers Used with Microcomputer Systems Are Dot-Matrix, Daisy-Wheel, Laser, Ink-Jet, and Chain.

The images output on a monitor screen are often referred to as **soft copy.** Information output on paper—whether by a printer or by a plotter—is called **hard copy.**

Five popular kinds of printers used with microcomputers are dot-matrix, daisy-wheel, laser, ink-jet, and chain (see Figure 5-18).

Dot-Matrix Printer **Dot-matrix printers** can produce a page of text in less than 10 seconds and are highly reliable. These inexpensive printers are the most popular machines used with microcomputers. Indeed, two-thirds of all printers sold are dot-matrix. In general, they are used for tasks where a high-quality image is not essential. Thus, they are often used for documents that are circulated within an organization rather than

FIGURE 5-18
Types of printers.

Printer	Characteristics	Typical use
Dot-matrix	Reliable, inexpensive; forms text and graphics by pixels; some color printing	In-house communications
Daisy-wheel	Letter-quality; prints text only; being replaced by other technology	External documents
Laser	Very high quality; forms text and graphics by pixels, using photocopying process	Desktop publishing
Ink-jet	High color quality; sprays drops of ink on paper	Advertising pieces
Chain	Extremely fast; can change type styles; shared by networks of microcomputers	High-quality text documents

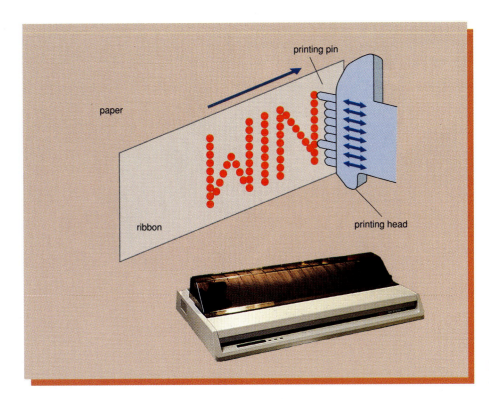

FIGURE 5-19
A dot-matrix printer.

shown to clients and the public. However, some dot-matrix printers print color and *are* used for advertising and promotional purposes.

The dot-matrix printer (see Figure 5-19) forms characters or images using a series of small pins on a print head. The pins strike an inked ribbon and create an image on paper. Printers are available with print heads of 9, 18, or 24 pins. The pins print a character in a manner that resembles the way individual lights spell out a number on a basketball scoreboard.

On some printers, the number of pins in the print head can be varied. This way, for example, just 9 pins can be used to rapidly print a draft-quality letter. This letter would be clear enough to read. However, it would not be as attractive as one you would want to send, say, to a customer. If the printer is set at 18 pins, it will print a near-letter-quality document, although more slowly. In 24-pin mode, the printer will print out a document that, to most people, is indistinguishable from letter-quality printing—almost as crisp as that produced by standard office typewriters.

Dot-matrix printers are especially useful because they can print any black-and-white image that the software is capable of creating. This means they will print not just letters and numbers but also shapes and graphics. As mentioned, some dot-matrix printers also print in color, using multicolored ribbons.

Daisy-Wheel Printer The **daisy-wheel printer** is a form of letter-quality printer. In this printer, the print mechanism, the **daisy wheel**, consists of a removable wheel with a set of spokes. At the end of each spoke is a raised character. After the wheel is turned to align the correct character, it is then struck with a hammer.

These printers produce very high quality, professional-looking correspondence. However, they are slower and less reliable than dot-matrix printers. Their sales have declined dramatically as a result of the appearance of better dot-matrix printers and relatively inexpensive laser printers.

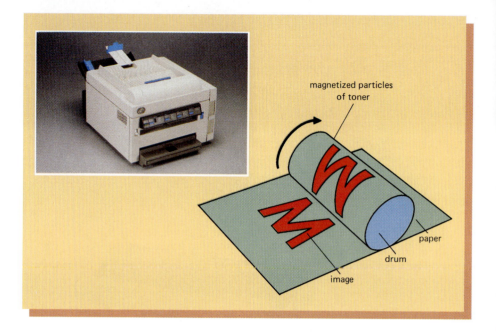

FIGURE 5-20
A laser printer.

FIGURE 5-21
An ink-jet printer.

Laser Printer The **laser printer** (see Figure 5-20) creates dotlike images (like a dot-matrix printer) on a drum, using a laser beam light source. The characters are treated with a magnetically charged inklike toner and then are transferred from drum to paper. A heat process is used to make the characters adhere. This technology is similar to that of a photocopying machine.

The laser printer produces images with excellent letter and graphics quality. It is widely used in applications requiring high-quality output. This has made possible the whole new industry of desktop publishing. As we've mentioned earlier, desktop publishing software enables people to merge text and graphics. The publications produced have a polish that rivals the work of some professional typesetters and graphic artists. Moreover, the laser printer can produce eight pages of text in about a minute. This printer is therefore frequently used for brochures, promotion pieces, and other tasks for which appearance is especially important.

Ink-Jet Printer An **ink-jet printer** sprays small droplets of ink at high speed onto the surface of the paper. This process not only produces a letter-quality image but also permits printing to be done in a variety of colors. Ink-jet printers are often used to duplicate color graphics from a monitor onto the printed page (see Figure 5-21). Ink-jet printers are used wherever color and appearance are important, as in advertising and public relations.

Chain Printer You probably won't find a **chain printer** on a desk next to a microcomputer standing alone by itself. This is because a chain printer is an expensive, high-speed machine designed originally to serve mainframes and minicomputers. However, you may see it in organizations that link several microcomputers together by a communications network. When several users share this resource, then the expense of serving microcomputers becomes justified.

A chain printer consists of several sets of characters connected together on a printing chain. Like a bicycle chain (see Figure 5-22), the chain revolves in front of the paper. Hammers are aligned with each position. When a character passes by, the hammer in that position strikes the paper and ribbon against it.

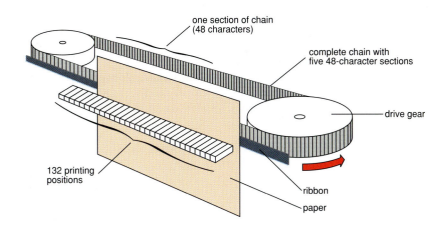

FIGURE 5-22
A chain printer.

Chain printers can reach speeds of up to 3000 lines per minute—extremely fast. They are also very reliable. A further advantage is that the chains can be changed for different type fonts or styles.

Printer Features   Some general qualities to note about microcomputer printers are as follows:

- *Bidirectional:* Many of the faster printers are **bidirectional.** That is, they print in two directions. One line is printed as the print element moves to the right. The following line is printed as the print head moves to the left. This saves the time of making a carriage return, as on a typewriter.
- *Tractor feed:* Most microcomputer users buy continuous-form printer paper, the pages of which can be separated after printing. In a typewriter the paper is gripped by the roller (platen). In most microcomputer printers the paper is held in place by a **tractor feed** mechanism. This reduces the chance of the paper's getting out of alignment. The tractor feed has sprockets that advance the paper, using holes on the edges of continuous-form paper.
- *Type styles:* Some printers allow you to change type styles by changing the printing element. Others require you to do something with the software. Still others do not allow a change in type style.
- *Shared use:* Dot-matrix and daisy-wheel printers are quite often used to serve individual microcomputers. Ink-jet and laser printers, and chain printers particularly, can be quite expensive. Thus, in organizations they are often found linked to several microcomputers through a communications network.
- *Portability:* Some people (travelers, for instance) require not only a portable computer but also a portable printer. Rugged printers are available that are battery-powered and weigh less than 7 pounds. These printers typically are either dot-matrix or ink-jet. Such printers are recharged using a special connection that can be plugged into an AC outlet. Some can even be recharged through a car's cigarette lighter.

Plotters

Plotters Are Special-Purpose Drawing Devices.

Plotters are special-purpose output devices for producing bar charts, maps, architectural drawings, and even three-dimensional illustrations. Plotters can produce high-quality multicolor documents and also documents that are larger in size than most printers can handle.

Plotters are of three types: flatbed, drum, and electrostatic.

Flatbed Plotter The **flatbed plotter** is also called a **table plotter** (see Figure 5-23). It holds paper stable while a pen or pens of different colors, directed by the software, move around on the paper. This type of plotter is useful for producing large drawings, such as architectural drawings.

Drum Plotter In the **drum plotter** (see Figure 5-24), the pen or pens move across the paper. The paper is rolled on a drum. Drum plotters are used for smaller drawings, such as graphs.

Electrostatic Plotter Flatbed plotters and drum plotters use pens. Electrostatic plotters do not. **Electrostatic plotters** use electrostatic charges to create images made up of tiny dots on specially treated paper. The image is produced when the paper is run through a developer. Electrostatic plotters produce high-resolution images and are faster than pen plotters.

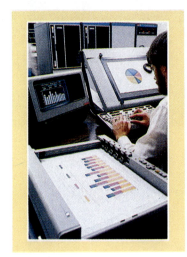
FIGURE 5-23
A flatbed plotter.

Voice-Output Devices

Voice-Output Devices Vocalize Prerecorded Sounds.

Voice-output devices make sounds that resemble human speech but actually are prerecorded vocalized sounds. With one Macintosh program, the computer speaks the synthesized words "We'll be right back" if you type in certain letters and numbers. (The characters are *Wiyl biy ray5t bae5k*—the numbers elongate the sounds.) Voice output is not anywhere near as difficult to create as voice input. In fact, there are many occasions when you will hear synthesized speech being used. Examples are found in soft-drink machines, on the telephone, and in cars.

Voice-output can be used as a reinforcement tool for learning, such as to help students study a foreign language. Or it can help a user double-check numbers being keyed into a spreadsheet.

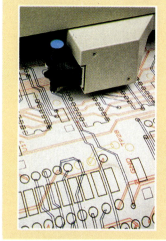
FIGURE 5-24
A drum plotter.

A Look at the Future

Developers Are Trying to Overcome Difficulties in Improving Handwritten and Voice Input. We May See Display Screens That Are Larger, Smaller, and with Lifelike Graphics. Microcomputers May Merge with Television.

We can expect some startling developments in input and output in the future. Already, some companies are trying to avoid the keyboard altogether by developing pen-based computers that *convert handwritten text* into electronic data. Some are also giving hand-held computers *wireless communications* with more powerful, stationary computers. (We describe communications in Chapter 7.)

There are many reports that *voice-recognition technology* is rapidly progressing. However, it probably will be a few years before it is sophisticated enough to record many pages of uninterrupted speech. Still, there are many companies that say they are working on devising dictation devices that accept continuing, rather than halting, speech.

On the output side, as computers continue to shrink we may see some hand-held, special-purpose versions sporting *1-inch display screens.* Alternatively, *screens may become larger,* with high-quality resolution. We will also probably begin to see *flat-panel,* full-color screens replace the old video-display tubes everywhere. Finally, screens may show *graphics as lifelike,* and images may be automated in ways we have not seen before. For instance, someday, technology will allow for *computerized three-dimensional video holograms,* such as might provide pictures of a patient's brain during neurosurgery.

Perhaps one of the most exciting future developments is the expected *merger of microcomputers and television.* This may come about in part through the establishment of all-digital *high definition television (HDTV).* HDTV will deliver a much clearer and more detailed wide-screen picture. The purpose of this technology is not to allow microcomputer users to watch TV as they work, although they can indeed do that. Rather, it will enable them to freeze video sequences to create still images. These images can then be digitized and output as artwork or stored on videodisks. This technology could be useful to graphic artists, publishers, and educators.

Review Questions

1. What are the differences between keyboard entry and direct entry as forms of input?
2. What is a POS terminal? What are two input devices on it that represent the two methods of inputting data?
3. What are the four kinds of keys on a keyboard?
4. Distinguish among the three kinds of terminals: dumb, smart, and intelligent.
5. List some direct-entry input devices.
6. How does a mouse work?
7. What input device recognizes images and converts them into electronic signals?
8. How does an image scanner work?
9. Which direct-entry input device is particularly helpful to certain disabled people?
10. List four output devices.
11. What uses are monochrome monitors best suited for?
12. What are three kinds of flat-panel displays used with portable computers?
13. What are pixels? What do they have to do with screen resolution?
14. Explain how a dot-matrix printer works.
15. Explain how a daisy-wheel printer works.
16. Describe how an ink-jet printer operates.
17. State how a laser printer works.
18. What can a plotter do that a printer cannot?
19. What is the difference between a flatbed plotter and a drum plotter?
20. Is voice output more difficult to engineer than voice input?

Discussion Questions

1. The mouse is a wonderful input device. You can use it to move a cursor on the screen to the exact location you want, like pointing with a finger. Then you can press a button on the mouse to make something happen, like deleting some text. Yet the mouse isn't the answer to everything. If you type a lot of text, it is easier to delete characters using the keys on the keyboard. With a mouse, you must take your hands off the keys, find the mouse, and use it to make the deletion.

    Which do you think you would feel more comfortable with if you had never typed a letter before—deleting through the keyboard or deleting using a mouse?

CHAPTER 5
Input and Output

VISUAL SUMMARY

Input devices convert symbols that people understand into symbols the computer can process. Two kinds of input are keyboard and direct entry.

A **point-of-sale (POS) terminal**, or electronic cash register, is both keyboard and direct entry. Data may be typed in or may be read from characters on price tags with a hand-held **wand reader**.

Input

Keyboard Entry

Keyboard entry may be categorized as keyboards and terminals.

Keyboards

In keyboard entry, data is typed into the CPU. A keyboard consists of:
- **Typewriter keys**, for regular letters, numbers, etc., and **Enter (Return)** key to enter commands.
- **Function keys** (*F1*, *F2*, etc.), for special tasks.
- **Numeric keys**, for typing in numbers.
- **Special-purpose keys** (e.g., *Del* for "Delete") and **directional arrow keys** (to move cursor).

Terminals

A **terminal** is an input/output device with keyboard, monitor, and communications link. Terminals are of three types:
- **Dumb**—sends and receives only; does no processing.
- **Smart**—allows some editing of data.
- **Intelligent**—has processing and primary and secondary storage and software for processing data.

Direct Entry

Direct-entry devices may be categorized as pointing, scanning, or voice-input devices.

Pointing Devices

- **Mouse**—directs cursor on screen.
- **Touch screen**—touching your finger to the screen selects actions.
- **Digitizer**—converts image to digital data. A **digitizing tablet** converts images using a stylus.
- **Light pen**—recognizes a spot on the screen as input.

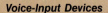

Scanning Devices

- **Image scanner (bit-mapping device)**—converts an image to digital code.
- **Facsimile transmission (fax) machine**—converts images to electronic signals for sending over telephone lines. **Dedicated fax machines** are specialized devices. **Virtual fax** boards may be inserted in microcomputers to send and receive images.
- **Bar-code reader**—scans zebra-striped **bar codes** on products to reveal their prices.
- Character and mark recognition devices include: **magnetic-ink character recognition (MICR)**, used by banks to read magnetized-ink numbers on checks, which are sorted by a **reader/sorter** machine; **optical-character recognition (OCR)**, used to read special preprinted characters (e.g., on utility bills); **optical-mark recognition (OMR)**, which senses pencil marks (e.g., on College Board tests).

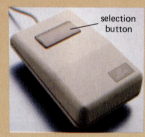

Voice-Input Devices

Also called **speech-recognition devices** or **voice-recognition systems, voice-input devices** convert a person's spoken words to digital code.

Visual Summary

Output devices convert machine output to output people can understand.

Output devices include monitors, printers, plotters, and voice-output.

Output

Monitors

Monitors **(display screens)** vary:
- They may be monochrome (single-color) or multicolor.
- The **screen resolution**—the clarity of images on the screen—may differ. Images are represented by individual dots or **pixels** (picture elements).
- They may be television-like **CRTs (cathode-ray tubes)**, as in most desktop models, or **flat-panel displays**, as in portable computers.

Monochrome Monitors

Monochrome monitors show one color on a dark background. Portable microcomputers are typically monochrome and use several kinds of flat-panel displays:
- **Liquid-crystal display (LCD)**—uses crystal molecules.
- **Electroluminescent (EL) display**—actively emits light.
- **Gas-plasma display**—uses gas that emits light.

Graphics Monitors

Graphics monitors display both alphanumeric characters and graphic images. Five types are:
- **CGA** (**C**olor **G**raphics **A**dapter)—4 colors, grainy text.
- **EGA** (**E**nhanced **G**raphics **A**dapter)—16 colors, clearer text.
- **VGA** (**V**ideo **G**raphics **A**rray)—16 or 256 colors, superior resolution.
- **Super-VGA**—256 colors, very high resolution.
- **XGA** (**Ex**tended **G**raphics **A**rray)—256 or 65,536 colors.

Printers

Output from display screens is called **soft copy**. Output from a printer is called **hard copy**. Five types of printers are:

- **Dot-matrix**—forms text and graphic images with a matrix of pins; it is the most popular form today.
- **Daisy-wheel**—prints office-quality correspondence from a revolving wheel; it is declining in use.
- **Laser**—prints with light beam and magnetically charged toner. Lasers print high-quality text and graphics; they are becoming very popular (e.g., in desktop publishing).
- **Ink-jet**—sprays droplets of ink on paper; it is good for color and provides very good quality.
- **Chain**—characters on printing chain are hit with hammer, striking paper and ribbon; it prints at very high speeds.

Plotters

Plotters produce multicolor bar charts, maps, architectural drawings. Three types are:
- **Flatbed (table plotter),** in which paper is held steady.

- **Drum,** in which paper revolves on a drum.

- **Electrostatic,** in which electrostatic charges create images.

Voice-Output Devices

Voice-output devices make sounds resembling human speech.

2. Some printers are expensive; some are not. Different printers may be used for different purposes, and appearances matter more for some activities than for others. Suppose you are going to rent a printer, and you do not want to spend too much money. Yet you still want the printer that will be most effective for the job. The printers you have to choose from are dot-matrix, daisy-wheel, and laser. State which one you would rent for each of the following tasks:
   (a) Publishing a brochure to advertise your new business
   (b) Printing out memos with figures and bar graphs for use among managers and employees in your office but not to be seen by the public
   (c) Printing out several copies of a letter to be individually signed by you and sent to people who might be able to contribute money to a cause you represent

CHAPTER 6
Secondary Storage

Data may be input, processed, and output as information. But one of the best features about using a computer is the ability to save—that is, store—information permanently, after you turn off the computer. This way, you can save your work for future use, share information with others, or modify information already available. Permanent storage holds information external from the CPU. Permanent storage is also called *secondary* storage, to distinguish it from the temporary *primary* storage inside the computer. Secondary storage allows you to store programs, such as WordPerfect and Lotus 1-2-3. It also allows you to store the data processed by programs, such as text or the numbers in a spreadsheet.

What if you could buy a microcomputer and use your portable audiotape recorder to store programs and data? Actually, this was once advertised as a feature. In the early 1980s there were over 150 kinds of microcomputers being offered. Some inexpensive computers were advertised at that time that could store information on the tape in one's audiotape recorder.

To find a particular song on an audiotape, you may have to play several inches of tape. Finding a song on an LP record on a turntable, in contrast, can be much faster. You can simply lift up the record arm and quickly move it to the song of your choice. That, in brief, represents the two different approaches to external storage. These two approaches are called *sequential access* and *direct access*.

Tape storage falls in the category of **sequential access storage.** Information is stored in sequence, such as alphabetically. You may have to search a tape past all the information from A to P, say, before you get to Q. This may involve searching several inches or feet, which takes time.

Generally speaking, disk storage falls in the category of **direct access storage.** That is, it is like moving the arm on a turntable directly to the song you want. This form of storage allows you to directly access information. Therefore, retrieving data and programs is much faster with disks than with tape.

Now let us consider in detail how data is organized.

COMPETENCIES

After you have read this chapter, you should be able to:

1. Contrast direct access and sequential access storage.

2. Describe how data is organized: characters, fields, records, files, and databases.

3. Describe how diskettes and disk drives work and how to take care of them.

4. Describe the following kinds of disks: internal hard disk, hard-disk cartridge, and hard-disk packs.

5. Discuss optical disks.

6. Describe magnetic tape streamers and magnetic tape reels.

Data Organization

Data Is Organized into Characters, Fields, Records, Files, and Databases.

Computers encode data with "on" and "off" electrical states or "present" and "absent" electromagnetic charges or impulses. We saw this in Chapter 4. Individual data items are represented by 0 (off) and 1 (on) and are called *bits*. Collections of eight bits are organized into **bytes,** representing characters. Characters can be letters, numbers, or special signs such as $, ?, and !.

To be processed by the computer or stored in secondary storage, data is organized into groups or categories. Each group is more complex than the one before (see Figure 6-1):

- *Character:* A *character* can be a single letter, number, or special character such as a punctuation mark or $.
- *Field:* A *field* contains a set of related characters. On a college registration form or a driver's license, a person's first name is a field. Last name is another field, street address another field, city yet another field, and so on.
- *Record:* A *record* is a collection of related fields. Everything on a person's driver's license, including number and expiration date, forms a record.
- *File:* A *file* is a collection of related records. All the driver's licenses issued in one county could be a file.
- *Database:* A *database* is a collection of related files. The department of motor vehicles in your state has a database of all vehicles registered in the state. The database consists of all files from each county and may be used in many different ways. For example, a car manufacturer might need to recall a particular car model because of a manufacturing defect. The manufacturer might ask the database for a list of all owners of that car model. The manufacturer could then notify those owners about the recall. A police department might have a partial license number (say, beginning with "ROB") of a car involved in a crime. They could ask for a list of all cars with license numbers with that beginning.

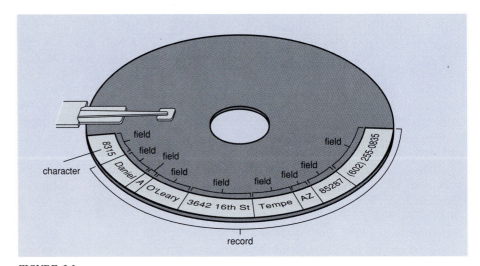

FIGURE 6-1
How data is organized. All these pieces would make up one file. A database is made up of a great many files.

Four Kinds of Secondary Storage

Microcomputer Secondary Storage May Be on Diskette, Hard Disk, Optical Disk, or Tape.

We described random-access memory (RAM) in Chapter 4. This is the *internal* and *temporary* storage of data and programs in the computer's memory. Once the power is turned off or interrupted, everything in internal storage disappears. Such storage is therefore said to be **volatile.** Thus, we need *external, more permanent,* or **nonvolatile,** ways of storing data and programs. We also need external storage because users need much more capacity than is possessed by a computer's primary memory.

The most widely used external storage media include the following:

- Diskette
- Hard disk
- Optical disk
- Magnetic tape

Magnetic tape is *not* the most popular form of storage—for microcomputers or for larger computers. This is true despite all those movies you've seen that show computer rooms with reels of magnetic tape turning. For computers of all types, magnetic tape is mainly used as *backup.* That is, tape is used to make a copy in case other forms of storage are lost or damaged. The advantage of disk storage is speed.

Diskettes

Diskettes Are Removable Storage Media That Are Inserted into Disk Drives.

Diskettes, often called simply **disks,** are flat, circular pieces of mylar plastic that rotate within a jacket. Data and programs are stored as electromagnetic charges on a metal oxide film coating the mylar plastic. Data and programs are represented by the presence or absence of these electromagnetic charges, using the ASCII or EBCDIC data representation codes. The two most popular sizes of diskettes are 5¼-inch diameter and 3½-inch diameter. Larger and smaller sizes are also available, although they are not standard for most microcomputers.

Diskettes are also called *flexible disks,* **floppy disks,** and **floppies.** This is because the plastic disk inside the diskette covers is flexible, not rigid. The 5¼-inch size comes encased in a flexible plastic jacket (see Figure 6-2). The 3½-inch standard is encased in a hard plastic jacket (see Figure 6-3). Both have a flexible disk inside and therefore both are called "floppy."

The Disk Drive The *disk drive* obtains stored data and programs from a diskette. It is also used to store data and programs on a diskette.

A disk drive consists of a box with a slot into which you insert the diskette. Often the slot is covered by a door, called the **drive gate.** A motor inside the drive rotates the diskette. As the diskette rotates, electronic heads can "read" data from and "write" data to the diskette. As we stated earlier, *read* means the disk drive *copies* data (stored as magnetic impulses) from the diskette. *Write* means the disk drive *transfers* data, the electronic signals in the computer's memory, onto the diskette.

It's important to realize that reading makes a copy from the original data; it does not alter the original. Writing, on the other hand, *writes over*—and replaces—any data that is already there. This is like recording a new song over an old one on a tape recorder. The same is true of data or programs on a diskette.

Cutout area exposes magnetic suface of diskettes

FIGURE 6-2
A 5¼-inch diskette.

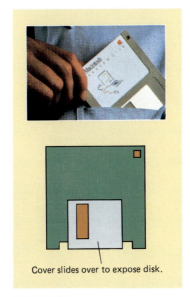

Cover slides over to expose disk.

FIGURE 6-3
A 3½-inch diskette.

98
Secondary Storage

FIGURE 6-4
Disk drives built in to system cabinet.

FIGURE 6-5
External disk drive (3½-inch), outside of system cabinet.

Microcomputer disk drives are usually built into the computer system cabinet along with the processor unit, as shown in Figure 6-4. Sometimes the disk drive is external, a separate component outside the system cabinet (see Figure 6-5).

Except for a few special-purpose machines, all microcomputers have at least *one* disk drive for flexible diskettes. This is the only way most software programs (such as word processors) initially can be entered into the computer's primary storage.

How a Disk Drive Works A diskette is inserted into the slot in the front of the disk drive, and the drive gate is closed (see Figure 6-6). Closing the gate positions the diskette around a spindle and holds it so that it can revolve without slipping. When the drive is in motion, the diskette can turn at about 300 revolutions per minute, depending on the drive.

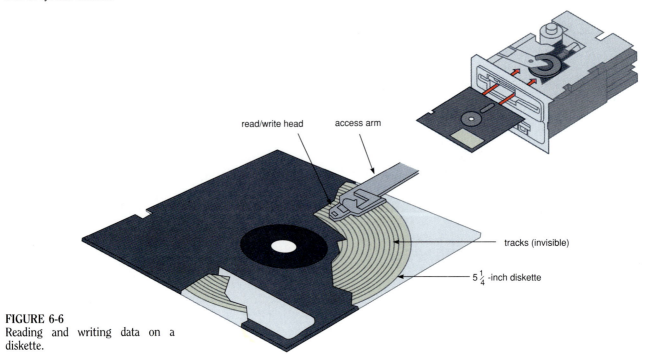

FIGURE 6-6
Reading and writing data on a diskette.

The magnetic data signals are transferred from diskette to computer (and computer to diskette) through **read-write heads** (see Figure 6-6). The read-write head is on an **access arm,** which moves back and forth over the diskette. To read or write on a particular part of the diskette, the access arm moves the read-write head on the diskette. This is called the **seek** operation. The drive then rotates the diskette to the proper position. This is called the **search** operation.

Drive A and Drive B A microcomputer may operate with just one disk drive, but it involves some extra complications. (For instance, when copying from one diskette to another, you have to constantly switch the two diskettes in the drive.) Most microcomputers have two disk drives. One may be a *hard-disk drive,* as we describe later, but here we are concerned with two flexible-disk drives.

Normally the drive into which you put your **program disk**—the software program such as a word processor—is **drive A.** On many microcomputers, drive A is the left-hand or upper drive, either on the front of the machine or on the side (see Figure 6-7). The drive into which you put the *data disk* is normally **drive B.** This drive is on the right or lower side on many computers. The data disk is the disk that will store the information you are creating, such as a report. (*Note:* The reference to "A" and "B" drives is used with many computer systems, notably IBM and IBM-compatibles. Even systems that do not use these terms, however, usually still have program disks and data disks.)

The Parts of a Diskette Figure 6-8 shows the parts of a 5¼-inch diskette. Figure 6-9 (on p. 100) shows the parts of a 3½-inch diskette. Both kinds of diskettes work the same way in principle, although there are some differences.

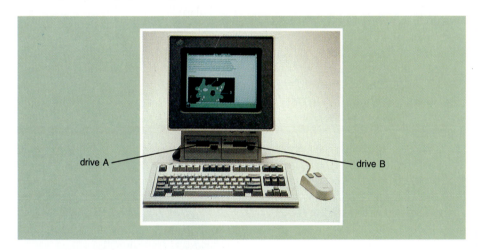

FIGURE 6-7
Two disk drives: A and B.

FIGURE 6-8
The parts of a 5¼-inch disk.

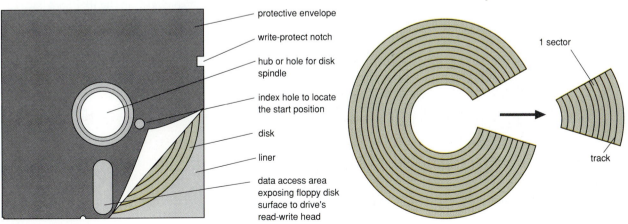

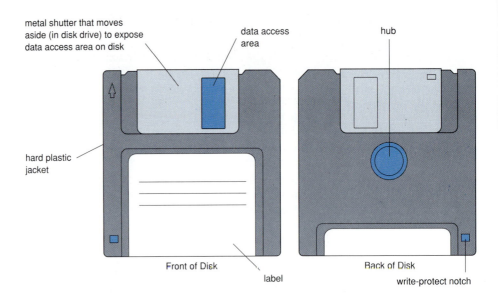

FIGURE 6-9
The parts of a 3½-inch disk.

As Figure 6-8 shows, data is recorded on a diskette in rings called **tracks.** These tracks are closed concentric circles, not a single spiral as on a phonograph record. Unlike a phonograph record, these tracks have no visible grooves. Looking at an exposed diskette, you would see just a smooth surface. Each track is divided into invisible wedge-shaped sections known as **sectors.** The fields of data within a particular record are organized according to tracks and sectors on a diskette.

Almost all diskettes are manufactured without tracks and sectors in place. These are called **soft-sectored diskettes,** and they must be adapted to the particular brand of microcomputer and disk drive you are using. Thus, you must put the tracks and sectors on yourself, using a process called *formatting,* or *initializing.*

Figure 6-10 shows the storage capacity of different 5¼-inch diskettes. Often you will see boxes of such diskettes labeled "DS,DD" (or "2S/2D"), which means "double-sided, double-density." A diskette of this sort (in the case of DOS) is usually formatted to have 40 tracks on each side. Each side contains nine sectors of 512 bytes each. This adds up to 368,640 bytes, or 360K—the equivalent of 260 typewritten pages. However, as we mentioned earlier, a 3½-inch diskette typically has twice the capacity—720K. Along with their more efficient size, this high storage capacity is a major reason more microcomputers now use the 3½-inch diskettes. (A recent entry by IBM is a 2.88 megabyte "super" floppy.)

Special note: A not uncommon problem today is that some diskettes can be read by one microcomputer but *not* by another. Consider two models in the IBM PS/2 line. The Model 50 might be able to read a particular 3½-inch disk. The Model 30, however, might not be able to read that same 3½-inch disk. Most likely the reason is that the data disk was originally formatted to hold 1.44 megabytes of data. The Model 50 has a high-capacity disk

Description	Bytes
5¼-inch	
Double-sided, double density	360 KB
High-capacity	1.2 MB
3½-inch	
Double-sided, double-density	720 KB
Double-sided, high-density	1.44 MB

FIGURE 6-10
Common capacities of 5¼-inch and 3½-inch flexible diskettes.

drive. It is able to read such a high-density disk, as well as the standard density data disks (720K). Model 30s and most other microcomputer systems don't have high-capacity drives and thus can't read such high-density disks. A similar situation may occur with IBM PCs and XTs not being able to read high-density disks formatted to run on IBM ATs. Suggestion: If you are using more than one type of disk drive—high-capacity and standard—*format all diskettes to be standard density.* That way your disks will run on both types of drives (even though storage capacity on the disks won't be as great).

The two most popular sizes of diskettes have distinct differences in the ways the jacket and the write-protect notch are handled:

- *5¼-inch:* On the 5¼-inch version, the **jacket,** or liner—the protective outer covering—is made of flexible plastic or cardboard (refer to Figure 6-8, p. 99). The diskette is protected by a paper envelope, or sleeve, when it is not in the disk drive. The **write-protect notch** can be covered with a removable tab, which comes with the diskette when you buy it. This prevents the computer from accidentally writing (overlaying) data over information on the diskette that you want to keep.
- *3½-inch:* The 3½-inch version is the sturdier of the two (refer to Figure 6-9). The jacket is made of hard plastic rather than flexible plastic or cardboard. The write-protect notch is covered by a sliding shutter. When you open the shutter, the write-protect notch prevents the computer from accidentally writing over information already on the diskette.

Taking Care of Diskettes   Taking care of diskettes boils down to three rules:

1. *Don't bend the diskettes or put heavy weights on them.* For 5¼-inch diskettes, do not write on them with ballpoint pens. Use a felt-tip pen when writing on the index label.
2. *Don't touch anything visible through the protective jacket* (such as the data access area).
3. *Keep diskettes away from strong magnetic fields* (like motors or telephones). Also *keep them away from extreme heat* (like a car trunk) *and chemicals* (such as alcohol and solvents). Keep 5¼-inch diskettes in their paper envelopes and store them in a file box when they are not in use.

Of course, the best protection is to make a *backup,* or duplicate, copy of your diskette.

Despite these cautions, you will find diskettes are actually quite hardy. For instance, you can send them through the mail if you enclose them in cardboard or use special rigid mailing envelopes. They usually can also be put through the x-ray machines at airport security checkpoints without loss of data.

Hard Disks

Hard Disks Are of Three Types: Internal Hard Disk, Hard-Disk Cartridge, and Hard-Disk Pack.

Hard disks consist of metallic rather than plastic platters. They are also tightly sealed to prevent any foreign matter from getting inside. Hard disks come in three forms: *internal hard disk, hard-disk cartridge,* and *hard-disk pack.*

Internal Hard Disk   An **internal hard disk** consists of one or more metallic platters sealed inside a container. The container includes the motor for rotating the disks. It also contains an access arm and read-write heads for writing data to and reading data from the

102
Secondary Storage

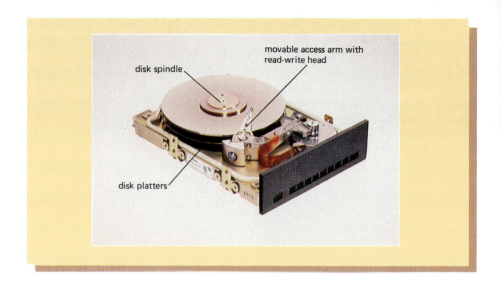

FIGURE 6-11
The inside of a hard disk drive.

disks. The operation is much the same as it is for flexible-disk drives. That is, the disk drive has a seek operation and a search operation for reading and writing data in tracks and sectors.

From the outside of a microcomputer, an internal hard disk looks merely like part of a front panel on the system cabinet. Figure 6-11 shows the inside of an internal hard disk. This is a 5¼-inch metallic platter with an access arm that moves back and forth. Drives with 3½-inch-diameter hard disks are also available. These provide faster access times because the access arm and read-write heads travel shorter distances across the diameter of the disk.

Internal hard disks have two advantages over flexible disks: capacity and speed. A hard disk can hold many times the information of a similar size flexible disk. One 20-megabyte internal hard disk, for instance, can hold the same amount of information as 56 double-sided, double-density flexible disks. Some *external* hard-disk drives for microcomputers (drives that are not built into the system cabinet) can store as many as 1000 megabytes. Moreover, access is faster: A hard disk spins 10 times faster than a flexible disk.

Sometimes adding an internal hard disk to a microcomputer can be a problem. An internal hard-disk drive might displace one of the two flexible-disk drives. An external hard-disk drive might take up too much space on your desk. However, an alternative is to buy a 1-inch-thick **hardcard.** This is a circuit board with a disk that plugs into an expansion slot in the computer. A 50- and a 105-megabyte hardcard available for IBM PCs and IBM-compatibles are shown in Figure 6-12. There is also a 40-megabyte hardcard.

FIGURE 6-12
Two hardcards, 50 and 105 megabytes, which fit into an expansion slot in the system unit.

Hard-Disk Cartridges The disadvantage of hard disks or hardcards is that they have only a fixed amount of storage and cannot be easily removed. Hard-disk cartridges (see Figure 6-13) have the advantage of being as easy to remove as a cassette from a videocassette recorder. They can give microcomputer systems fast access to very large quantities of data. The amount of storage available is limited only by the number of cartridges. The Tandon Personal Data Pac, for instance, is a self-contained removable hard-disk cartridge that has a storage capacity of 40 megabytes. While a regular hard-disk system has a fixed storage capacity, a removable hard-disk cartridge system is unlimited—you can just buy more removable cartridges. A removable 20 megabyte palm-sized hard disk called the Discte weighs only 7 ounces and may be moved easily from laptop to laptop.

Hard-Disk Packs Microcomputers that are connected to other microcomputers, minicomputers, or mainframes often have access to external hard-disk packs (see Figure 6-14). Microcomputer hard-disk drives typically have only one or two disk platters and one or two access arms. In contrast, **hard-disk packs** consist of *several* platters aligned one above the other, thereby offering much greater storage capacity. These hard-disk packs resemble a stack of phonograph records. The difference is that there is space between the disks to allow the access arms to move in and out (Figure 6-15, p. 104). Each access arm has two read-write heads. One reads the disk surface above it; the other reads the disk surface below it. A disk pack with 11 disks provides 20 recording surfaces. This is because the top and bottom outside surfaces of the pack are not used.

All the access arms move in and out together. However, only *one* of the read-write heads is activated at a given moment. **Access time** is the time between when the com-

FIGURE 6-13
Removable 40-megabyte hard disk.

FIGURE 6-14
A disk pack being removed from a disk drive.

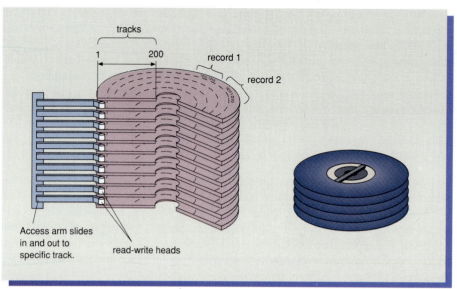

FIGURE 6-15
How a disk pack operates.

puter requests data from secondary storage and when the transfer of data is completed. Access time—which for most disk drives is under 25 milliseconds—depends on four things:

- How quickly the access arm can get into position over a particular track. This is known as **seek time**.
- How fast a particular read-write head can be activated. This is called **head switching time**.
- How long it takes the disk to rotate under the read-write head. This is called **rotational delay time**.
- How long it takes for data to transfer from the disk track to primary storage. This is called **data transfer time**.

You may well use your microcomputer to gain access to information over a telephone or other communications line. (We show this in the next chapter.) Such information is apt to be stored on disk packs. One large information service (named Dialog), for example, has over 300 databases. These databases cover all areas of science, technology, business, medicine, social science, current affairs, and humanities. All of these are available through a telephone link with your desktop computer. With more than 100 million items of information, including references to books, patents, directories, journals, and newspaper articles, such an information resource may be of great value to you in your work.

The reason a hard disk is enclosed in a tightly sealed container is to prevent any foreign material from getting inside. The hard disk is an extremely sensitive instrument. The read-write head rides on a cushion of air about 0.000001 inch thick. It is so thin that a smoke particle, fingerprint, or human hair could cause what is known as a head crash. A **head crash** happens when the surface of the read-write head or particles on its surface contact the magnetic disk surface. A head crash is a disaster for a hard disk. It means that some or all of the data on the disk is destroyed. Hard disks are assembled under sterile conditions and sealed from impurities within their permanent containers.

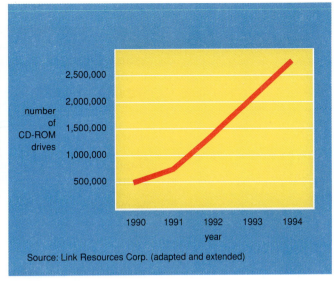

FIGURE 6-16
Optical disk, and past and estimated sales of CD-ROM drives.

Optical Disks

Optical Disks Are Used for Storing Great Quantities of Data.

An **optical disk** (see Figure 6-16) may hold more than 700 megabytes of data—the equivalent of hundreds of floppy disks. Moreover, an optical disk makes an immense amount of information available even on a microcomputer. Optical disks are having a great impact on storage technology today, but we are probably only just beginning to see their effects.

In optical disk technology, a laser beam burns tiny pits representing data into the surface of a plastic or metallic disk. To read the data, a laser scans these areas and sends the data to a computer chip for conversion. Optical disks are made in diameters of 3½, 4¾, 5¼, 8, 12, and 14 inches.

There are three kinds of optical disks available: *CD-ROM, WORM,* and *Erasable Optical Disks* (see Figure 6-17).

Technology	Storage space
CD-ROM	540–748 MB
WORM	122–6400 MB
Erasable	281–3200 MB

FIGURE 6-17
Comparison of optical disks.

CD-ROM **CD-ROM** stands for *compact disk–read-only memory.* Like the commercial CD found in music stores, a CD-ROM is a "read-only" disk. **Read-only** means it cannot be written on or erased by the user. Thus, you as a user have access only to the data imprinted by the manufacturer. CD-ROM disks are used to distribute large databases and references. An example is Computer Library, a CD-ROM containing over 50,000 computer, technical, and business articles and abstracts. A CD-ROM disk can store 540 to 748 megabytes of data.

WORM **WORM** stands for *write once, read many.* **Write-once** means that a disk can be written on just once. After that, it can be read many times without deterioration and cannot be written on or erased by the user. Because the data cannot be erased, WORM disks are ideal for use as archives. A WORM disk can store between 122 and 6400 megabytes of data.

Erasable Optical Disks An **erasable optical disk** has a great deal of data capacity, but it resembles a microcomputer diskette in that the drive can both write and rewrite information. That is, a disk that has been written on can be erased and used over and over again. An example is the NeXT computer system's optical disk, which can hold pictures and sounds, as well as 100,000 pages of text. An erasable optical disk can store 281 to 3200 megabytes (or even 1 gigabyte) of data.

Magnetic Tape

Magnetic Tape Streamers and Magnetic Tape Reels Are Used Primarily for Backup Purposes.

We mentioned the alarming consequences that can happen if a hard disk suffers a head crash. You will lose some or all of your data or programs. Of course, you can always make copies of your hard-disk files on flexible diskettes. However, this can be time consuming and may require many diskettes. Here is where magnetic tape storage becomes important. Magnetic tape falls in the category of sequential access storage and is therefore slower than direct access storage. However, it is an effective way of making a *backup,* or duplicate, copy of your programs and data.

There are two forms of tape storage. These are *magnetic tape streamers,* for use with microcomputers, and *magnetic tape reels,* for use with minicomputers and mainframes.

Magnetic Tape Streamers Many microcomputer users with hard disks use a device called a **magnetic tape streamer** or a **backup tape cartridge unit** (see Figure 6-18). This machine enables you to duplicate or make a backup of the data on your hard disk onto a tape cartridge. The capacities of such tape cartridges vary from 10 to 60 megabytes. Advanced forms of backup technology known as **digital audiotape (DAT) drives,** which use 2- by 3-inch cassettes, store 1.3 gigabytes or more. The copying from hard disk varies in speed from 1 to 5 megabytes per minute. On a 20-megabyte hard disk, it might take you only 5 to 20 minutes to back up the entire contents. Compare this to, say, 2 hours with 48 diskettes. If later your internal hard disk fails, you can have it repaired (or get another hard disk). You can restore all your lost data and programs in a matter of minutes.

Magnetic Tape Reels The kind of cassette tapes you get for an audiotape recorder are only about 200 feet long. They record 200 characters to the inch. A reel of magnetic tape used with minicomputer and mainframe systems, by contrast, is ½ inch wide and ½

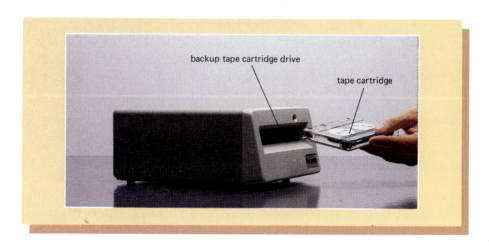

FIGURE 6-18
Backup tape cartridge and drive in system unit.

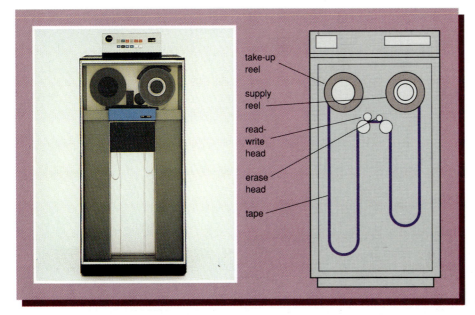

FIGURE 6-19
Data is recorded on magnetic tape on tape reels.

mile long. It stores 1600 to 6400 characters to the inch. Such tapes are run on **magnetic tape drives** or **magnetic tape units** (see Figure 6-19). You may never actually see these devices yourself. However, as a microcomputer user sharing storage devices with other users, you may have access to them through a minicomputer or mainframe.

A magnetic tape drive consists of two reels—a **supply reel** and a **take-up reel.** It also has a read-write head and an erase head. The read-write head reads (retrieves) magnetized areas on the tape, which represent data. It then converts them to electrical signals and sends them to the CPU. The read-write head also writes (records) data from the CPU onto the tape. During the writing process, any previous data on the tape is automatically erased.

Magnetic tape moves through the drive in a "start and stop" manner. The reason for this is that once a record is read, the CPU and program must process it. If the tape continues moving, the next record might pass the read-write head before the CPU and program were ready for it. Thus, the tape must pause after a record has been read and start when the computer is ready for the next record.

However, allowance must be made for the tape to "get up to speed" when it starts again. Otherwise, the data will be distorted when it is read. Consequently, some ½-inch gaps must be built into the tape between the records. These gaps give the tape enough time to gain the proper speed. These gaps are called **interrecord gaps** (**IRGs**) (see Figure 6-20).

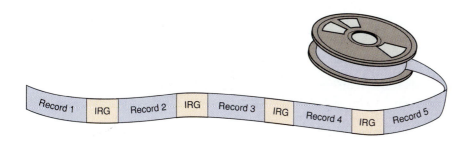

FIGURE 6-20
Magnetic tape with interrecord gaps.

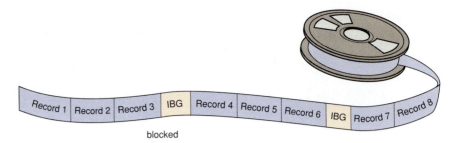

FIGURE 6-21
Magnetic tape with interblock gaps.

This ½ inch of space between records could add up to a lot of unused tape. It might otherwise be used for storing data. Consequently, records are often grouped together as **blocks.** These blocks are called **physical records.** The term "physical records" is used to distinguish them from the actual records, which are called **logical records.** The blocks are then separated from each other by a ½-inch gap called an **interblock gap** (**IBG**) (see Figure 6-21).

Companies often store reels of magnetic tape in **tape libraries.** This demonstrates an important advantage of tapes: a lot of data can be stored in compact space. In addition, tapes have a feature that helps keep them reasonably secure. Before a tape can be used, a **write-enable ring** must be placed over the hub as it is mounted on the tape drive. This prevents tapes from accidentally being written over.

A Look at the Future

Flexible Diskettes and Hard Disks Will Continue to Increase in Capacity. Disk Arrays and Data-Compression Technology Will Also Add Storage Room. Image Processing Promises to Be a Growing Field.

The principal trend now in evidence—namely, that of packing more and more data in less and less space—will doubtless continue. For instance, 3½-inch floppy diskettes, which are surpassing 5¼-inch diskettes as the dominant storage format, can now store 1.44 megabytes of information. Other diskettes may become available that will store 20 megabytes or more—some say *100* megabytes or more.

Hard disks will also have greater capacity. Whereas a conventional optical disk can hold perhaps 600 megabytes (about 270,000 typewritten pages), a 12-inch optical disk being developed will hold a terabyte. That's nearly 450 million pages, about 18,000 *Encyclopedia Britannicas.*

Two other steps are being taken to improve storage efficiency. Companies are connecting groups of small, inexpensive hard-disk drives together in a form known as *disk arrays.* These can outperform single drives of comparable capacity. A technology known as *data-compression technology* eliminates redundant patterns that appear in data by identifying repeating patterns and assigning a token to them. It then replaces all similar patterns with these tokens.

Some new storage developments are becoming particularly important for storing pictures as well as text. Presently, conventional optical disks can store large amounts of text, but pictures take up a great deal of space. One 8½-by-11-inch color photo, for instance, consumes about 25 megabytes of data—about half the capacity of a typical microcomputer hard disk. But even now the makers of *Compton's Encyclopedia* are marketing all 26 volumes on a single CD-ROM disk—including 15,000 pictures. In the future, such giant storage capacity will permit the development of *multimedia*. This is a way in which computers (as we discuss in Chapter 12) can combine all sorts of media, such as video, graphics, and audio.

A particularly important development in coming years is a whole field known as *image processing*. In word processing, just the text of documents is stored. In image processing, a kind of "electronic snapshot" of a document is taken with a device resembling a copying machine. The image is then transformed into computer code and may be stored on an optical disk. Imaging technology is now used by credit card companies to make paper-based reproductions of credit card receipts. Image processing promises to be a burgeoning field in the years ahead.

Review Questions

1. Explain the difference between direct access storage and sequential access storage. Which is more apt to be identified with magnetic disk and which with magnetic tape?
2. Describe the five levels of data organization, beginning with character (byte).
3. What are four kinds of secondary storage?
4. What is meant by the terms *volatile* and *nonvolatile?*
5. What are the various names given to *diskettes?*
6. Describe how a flexible-disk drive works.
7. What is a seek operation? a search operation?
8. What are drive A and drive B used for in a microcomputer?
9. What are tracks? sectors?
10. Explain the difference between a hard-sectored disk and a soft-sectored disk.
11. State the three primary rules about taking care of flexible diskettes.
12. How does an internal hard-disk drive work?
13. What is the advantage of hard disks over flexible diskettes?
14. Explain the advantage of a hardcard.
15. Explain what a hard-disk cartridge is.
16. How are hard-disk packs for mainframe computers different from hard disks for microcomputers?
17. Identify the following: access time; seek time; head switching time; rotational delay time; data transfer time.
18. What is so disastrous about a head crash?
19. Explain what an optical disk is.
20. What is the purpose of a tape streamer or tape backup unit for microcomputers?
21. How does a magnetic tape drive work?
22. Distinguish between an interrecord gap and an interblock gap.
23. Describe the difference between physical records and logical records.

Discussion Questions

1. We are presently in a transitional stage with flexible diskettes. The older 5¼-inch diskettes, such as those used with the IBM PC, AT, and XT and IBM clones, are

CHAPTER 6
Secondary Storage

V I S U A L   S U M M A R Y

Primary storage in microcomputers is **volatile;** everything in it disappears when the power is turned off. Secondary storage is **nonvolatile;** it stores data and programs even after the power is turned off.

Data Organization

Access

Two different approaches to secondary storage are:
- **Sequential access storage**—information is stored in sequence (e.g., alphabetically), a characteristic of tape storage.
- **Direct access storage**—information may be stored in any order and accessed directly, a characteristic of disk storage.

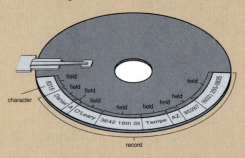

- **Character**—letter, number, special character (e.g., A, 1, %).
- **Field**—set of related characters (e.g., person's last name).
- **Record**—collection of related fields (e.g., name and address).
- **File**—collection of related records (e.g., all driver's licenses issued in one city on one day).
- **Database**—collection of related files (e.g., all driver's licenses issued in one state).

Diskette

Diskettes **(disks, floppy disks)** are circular plastic disks. Two principal types are:
- *5¼-inch*—these hold about 360 KB.
- *3½-inch*—these hold about 720 KB.

The Disk Drive

- A diskette is inserted through a **drive gate** into a *disk drive,* which has an **access arm** equipped with **read-write heads** that move on the diskette (**seek** operation), which is rotated to the proper position (**search** operation).
- The read-write head *reads* (obtains) data or programs from the diskette and sends it to the CPU or *writes* (transfers) data from the CPU to the diskette.

Parts of Diskette

- Data is recorded on a diskette's **tracks** (rings) and **sectors** (sections). In **soft-sectored diskettes,** tracks and sectors must be adapted to particular microcomputers by *formatting (initializing).*
- A diskette is protected by the **jacket** (liner), paper envelope, and **write-protect notch** (covered by tab or shutter).

110

111
Visual Summary

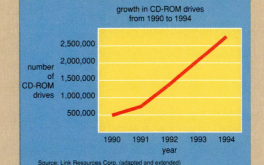

Four Most Widely Used Secondary Storage Media
- Diskette
- Hard disk
- Optical disk
- Magnetic tape

Hard Disk

A *hard disk* is an enclosed disk drive that contains one or more metallic disks. Enclosing the disk in a sealed container prevents material entering that causes a **head crash**, failure of the disk and destruction of data on it. Hard disks come in three forms:

Internal Hard Disk

An **internal hard disk** has one or more metallic platters sealed inside a container. A motor rotates the disk, and an access arm reads and writes data to and from the hard disk.
- Hard disks have far more capacity than a flexible disk does (e.g., a 20 MB hard disk = 56 flexible disks).
- A particular form of internal hard disk is the **hardcard**, a circuit board that plugs into an expansion slot.

Hard-Disk Cartridges

Hard-disk cartridges can be removed when they are filled or are to be transported.

Hard-Disk Packs

Mini- and mainframe computers use **hard-disk packs,** which are hard disks consisting of several platters in a stack, accessible by multiple access arms and read-write heads.

Optical Disks

An **optical disk** is a metallic disk that, using a laser beam for reading and writing, may hold more than 700 MB. Three kinds of optical disks are:
- **CD-ROM** (Compact Disk–Read-Only Memory)—cannot be written on or erased by user **(read-only).**
- **WORM** (Write Once, Read Many)— **write once** can be written to one time, after which it cannot be erased by users but can be read many times without deterioration.
- **Erasable optical disks**—can be written on and erased and reused.

Magnetic Tape

Magnetic tape storage is mainly used to back up (duplicate) programs and data on disks. Two forms are:

Magnetic Tape Streamers

Magnetic tape streamers **(backup tape cartridge units)** consist of tape cartridges used to back up microcomputer hard disks.

Magnetic Tape Reels

Magnetic tape reels, used to back up mini- and mainframe computer storage, run on **magnetic drives (magnetic tape units).**
- Drives have a **supply reel** and a **take-up reel.**
- Tape moves in "start and stop" manner. Thus, ½-inch **interrecord gaps (IRGs)** may be present to give computer take-up room.
- Records on tape may be grouped as **blocks,** with ½-inch **interblock gaps (IBGs)** between them.
- Tapes are stored in **tape libraries.** For security, before a tape can be used, a **write-enable ring** must be put over the hub.

widespread. Your school or workplace no doubt has many of its programs and much of its data on disks of this size. However, the newer 3½-inch diskettes are much hardier, have more capacity, and will probably become more popular in the future. These first became popular with the Apple Macintosh but now are standard with the IBM PS/2 line of microcomputers.

Suppose most of the people with whom you might exchange programs and information have IBM-compatibles with the older 5¼-inch disk drives. Suppose also you have a chance to buy an inexpensive IBM clone (under $1,500) with this type of drive. Should you buy it, or should you wait and get a more expensive machine with 3½-inch drives?

2. So many choices! The volume of your work has become quite large. You decide that you can no longer handle the several file boxes full of floppy diskettes you now use. You have to get serious and get a hard-disk drive. However, if a hard-disk drive suffers a head crash, you can lose all the programs and data on it. Moreover, you have *lots* of data you need to save.

What kind of storage system would you get—hard disk, hardcard, hard disk and magnetic tape backup (tape streamer), hard-disk cartridge, or optical disk? Discuss.

CHAPTER 7
Communications

A familiar instrument—the telephone—has extended our uses for the microcomputer enormously. With the telephone or other kind of communications equipment, you can connect your microcomputer to other people and other, larger computers. As we've mentioned earlier, this *connectivity* puts the power of a mainframe on your desk. The result is increased productivity—for you as an individual and for the groups and organizations of which you are a member. Connectivity has become particularly important in business, where individuals now find themselves connected in networks to other individuals and departments.

Imagine: You are a real estate salesperson, and the telephone in your car rings. It is a client, who is on the phone in his car across town. He asks you about a certain property, and you agree to meet him there. After you go back to look at the property, you connect your laptop computer to your car phone. You then dial the multiple listing service and get information on the property. This is an example of the use of communications to expand computer capabilities.

In Chapter 2, you learned about communications software. In this chapter, you will learn about communications systems. **Data communications systems** are the electronic systems that transmit data over communications lines from one location to another. You might use data communications through your microcomputer to send information to a friend using another computer. You might work for an organization whose large computer system is spread all over a building or even all over the country. That is, all the parts—input and output units, processor, and storage devices—are in different places and linked by communications. Or you might use *telecommunications* lines—telephone lines—to tap into information located in an outside data bank. You could then transmit it to your microcomputer for your own reworking and analysis.

Data communications is now considered essential in business. As we will see, an important part of communications is the *network,* a system connecting two or more

COMPETENCIES

After you have read this chapter, you should be able to:

1. Describe communications resources available: fax machines, electronic bulletin boards, electronic mail, voice-messaging systems, shared resources, databases, commercial services, and groupware.

2. Describe communications hardware, such as types of modems.

3. Describe the cable and air communications channels—telephone, coaxial, and fiber-optic cables; microwave relays; and satellites.

4. Discuss bandwidth, serial versus parallel transmission, direction of flow, modes of transmission, and protocols.

5. Explain four communications network arrangements: star, bus, ring, and hierarchical.

6. Describe local area, metropolitan area, and wide area networks.

computers. A popular form of network is the *local area network (LAN),* in which computers are connected together within a limited area, such as within the same building. In one survey, 82 percent of the respondents said there was a local area network within their company or organization. There are many occasions when you and coworkers need a network to gain access to one another's information. Such information may be on sales, customers, prices, schedules, or products. The list is nearly endless.

Communications and Connectivity

With Communications Capability, Microcomputer Users Can Transmit and Receive Data and Gain Access to Electronic Information Resources.

You may have a desktop microcomputer next to a telephone. You may (or may someday) have a laptop microcomputer and a cellular phone in your car. Or you may have a microcomputer that is directly connected to other computers without telephone lines at all. Whatever the case, communications systems present many opportunities for transmitting and receiving information, giving you access to many resources. This brings up the important revolution represented by this chapter, that of connectivity.

Connectivity means that you can connect your microcomputer by telephone or other telecommunications lines to other computers and sources of information anywhere. With this connection, you are linked to the world of larger computers. This includes minicomputers and mainframes and their large storage devices, such as disk packs, and their enormous volumes of information. Thus, computer competence becomes a matter of knowing not only about microcomputers. You should also know something about larger computer systems and their information resources. We describe these resources in greater detail in the next two chapters.

Let us consider the options that connectivity makes available to you. These include *fax machines, electronic bulletin boards, electronic mail, voice-messaging systems, shared resources, databases, commercial services,* and *groupware* (see Figure 7-1).

Fax Machines   As we stated in Chapter 5, *fax machines*—facsimile transmission machines—are now extremely popular in offices (see Figure 7-2). Indeed, they have become essential machines in many workplaces. These devices, you'll recall, scan the image of a document. They convert the image to signals that can be sent over a telephone line to a receiving machine. This machine prints the image out on paper. Microcomputers, using virtual fax—built-in facsimile circuit boards—also can be used to send and receive fax messages. Fax circuit boards require scanners to read in hardcopy documents because the material must be put into primary storage before it can be transmitted.

Sending a document by fax is certainly faster—it arrives immediately—than any delivery service. It also is often cheaper than overnight delivery, unless you're sending more than 50 pages of a document. Almost every fax machine can exchange messages with every other fax machine, and all you need is the receiving machine's phone number. It can transmit photographs and other artwork, as well as text in various typefaces.

If you are in the business of meeting deadlines—as most people are—a fax machine can be invaluable. Construction engineers can get cost estimates to major contractors. Lawyers can get contracts to other lawyers. Advertising people can get prospective ad layouts to their clients. Just as important, because people often respond better to pictures than to text, fax can get a picture to them quickly.

Electronic Bulletin Boards   This is an activity you can begin to discover yourself if you have access to a microcomputer and the necessary telephone links. **Electronic bulle-**

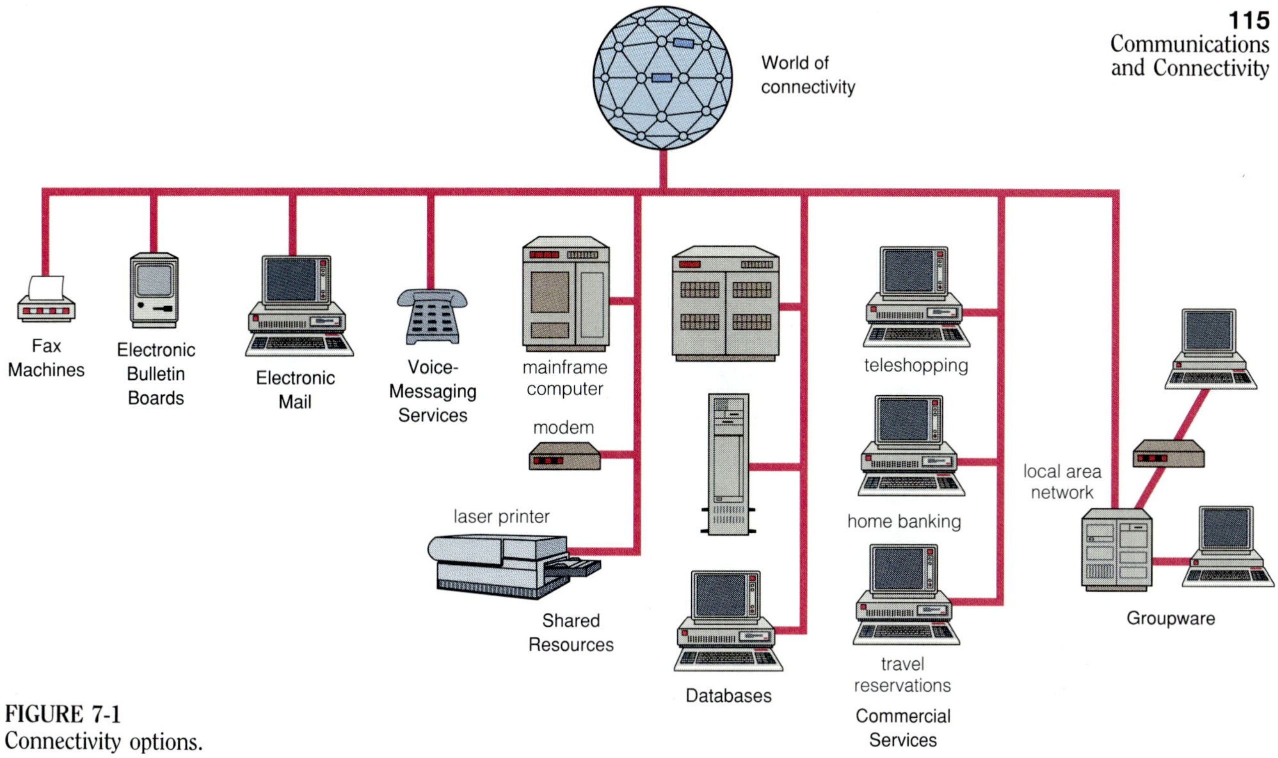

FIGURE 7-1
Connectivity options.

tin boards** are like public bulletin boards, usually open to everybody. The difference is that you need a microcomputer, a telephone connection, and the board's telephone number. Such bulletin boards have been popular with microcomputer hobbyists and enthusiasts for many years. They are rapidly gaining favor with other people, too.

Bulletin boards exist for almost any subject. Many are concerned with new developments and problems related to particular brands of microcomputers. Others have to do with hobbies, such as rock music, science fiction, or genealogy. Still others serve special interests, such as political causes, or professional groups, such as lawyers. Finally, some companies offer bulletin boards as a means by which customers can get advice from other customers. They can also get advice from the company itself regarding a particular service or product.

Electronic Mail Also called **E-mail, electronic mail** (Figure 7-3, p. 116) resembles bulletin boards. But often it uses a special communications line rather than a telephone line. In addition, electronic mail offers confidentiality. A **password**—a special sequence of numbers or letters that limits access—is required in order to get into the "mailbox." The mailbox is simply a file stored on a computer system.

To send a message, you dial the special number, specify the password and number of the mailbox, and type in the message. You can also put the same message in several mailboxes at the same time. To gain access to your own mailbox, you dial the number of the electronic mail system and type in your password. You can look through the list of file names and transmission times of the messages. You then transfer to your own computer the messages you want to keep.

Electronic mail is used within companies to help employees exchange memos, set up meetings, and the like. It may also be used between companies. Sometimes outside electronic bulletin board services are used for these business purposes.

Voice-Messaging Systems **Voice-messaging systems** are computer systems linked to telephones that convert the human voice into digital bits. They resemble conventional

FIGURE 7-2
A fax machine.

FIGURE 7-3
Electronic mail.

answering machines and also resemble electronic mail systems. However, they can receive large numbers of incoming calls and route them to the appropriate "voice mailboxes." They can deliver the same message to many people. They allow callers to leave "voice mail"—recorded voice messages. They can forward calls to your home or hotel, if you wish. When you check for your messages, you can speed through them or slow them down. You can dictate replies into the phone, and the system will send them out.

Sharing Resources An extremely important option that connectivity gives microcomputer users is that it lets them share expensive resources. We have mentioned many of these: laser printers, chain printers, disk packs, and magnetic tape storage. Only in rare instances would a single microcomputer user need the use of, say, a disk pack. However, several microcomputers linked in a network make this option not only feasible but in many cases even essential.

Communications networks also permit microcomputer users to share workstations, minicomputers, and mainframes. This is why we have stressed that it's important to know what these machines are. Finally, connectivity makes incompatible microcomputers compatible. For a long time, corporations were baffled about how to make Macintoshes and IBM PCs work with each other. Now, however, the use of local area networks to link Macintoshes and IBM microcomputers is a reality, and more and more such networks are coming into use.

Databases As we saw in Chapter 2, with a microcomputer you can have your own personal database. An example of such a database might be a collection of names and addresses. A *database,* as we mentioned, is a collection of integrated data. By "integrated," we mean the data consists of logically related files and records.

Your personal database might consist of data that only you use. However, it may also be data you share with others. The data might be stored on your microcomputer's hard disk. Or it might be located somewhere else. That is, you might use a shared database, such as one a company might provide its employees so they can share information. This could be information stored on disk packs and accessible from the company's mainframe. You could gain access by using your microcomputer linked to your telephone and **downloading** selected data. That is, you could transfer the data from the larger computer to your microcomputer. Then you could process and manipulate the data as you chose. The reverse is **uploading**—transferring from your microcomputer to a mainframe or minicomputer.

Commercial Services Several businesses offer services specifically for microcomputer users. For example:

- *Teleshopping:* You dial into a database listing prices and descriptions of products such as appliances and clothes. You then order what you want and charge the purchase to a credit card number. The merchandise is delivered later by a package delivery service.
- *Home banking:* If you arrange it with your bank, you may be able to use your microcomputer to pay some bills (such as to big department stores and utilities). You can also make loan payments and transfer money between accounts.
- *Investing:* You can get access to current prices of stocks and bonds and enter buy and sell orders.
- *Travel reservations:* Just like a travel agent, you can get information on airline schedules and fares. You can also order tickets, charging the purchase to your credit card.

Groupware As more and more networks become established, a new kind of software may become popular. Known as **groupware** or *collaboration technology,* this software allows two or more people on a network to work on the same information at the same time.

With older technology, two people on a network working on the same document must take turns sending it back and forth. With groupware, people can work on the same document at the same time. For instance, people in a group could sit at a table in a meeting room, each person with a microcomputer. They could all watch a single large screen on the wall. They could make tentative additions and deletions on the document until everyone agrees.

Groupware can also be used to send forms throughout a corporation. The computer system can automatically remind participants of deadlines and track progress. Other groupware can be used to enable a contractor to keep track of its suppliers, who receive and acknowledge orders electronically. Perhaps the best-known groupware is Lotus Notes, which combines a database with electronic-mail and word-processing features.

User Interface

Microcomputers Require Modems to Send and Receive Messages Over Telephone Lines.

A great deal of computer communications is over telephone lines. However, because the telephone was originally designed for voice transmission, telephones typically send and receive **analog signals** (see Figure 7-4). Computers, in contrast, send and receive **digital signals.** These represent the presence or absence of an electronic pulse—the on/off binary signals we mentioned in Chapter 4. To convert the digital signals of your microcomputer to analog and vice versa, you need a modem.

Modems and Communications Speeds The word *modem* is short for "*mo*dulator-*dem*odulator." **Modulation** is the name of the process of converting from digital to analog. **Demodulation** is the process of converting from analog to digital. The modem enables digital microcomputers to communicate across analog telephone lines. Both voice communications and data communications can be carried over the same telephone line.

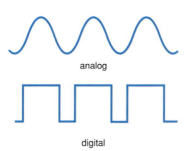

FIGURE 7-4
Analog versus digital signals.

The speed with which modems transmit data varies. Communications speeds are expressed in *bits per second (bps)*. The most popular microcomputer speeds are 300, 1200, and 2400 bps. The higher the speed, the faster you can transmit a document—and therefore the cheaper your line costs. For example, transmitting a 10-page single-spaced report takes 20 minutes at 300 bps. It takes 5 minutes at 1200 bps and 2½ minutes at 2400 bps.

Types of Modems The two types of modems are external and internal.

- The **external modem** stands apart from the computer and is connected by a cable to the computer's serial port. Another cable connects the modem to the telephone wall jack (see Figure 7-5). Some modems weigh as little as 3 ounces, making them practical for use with portable computers.
- The **internal modem** consists of a plug-in circuit board inside the system unit (see Figure 7-6).

Not all computer communications must be converted from digital to analog and back. Computer systems connected by coaxial or fiber-optic cables can transmit digital data directly through these channels.

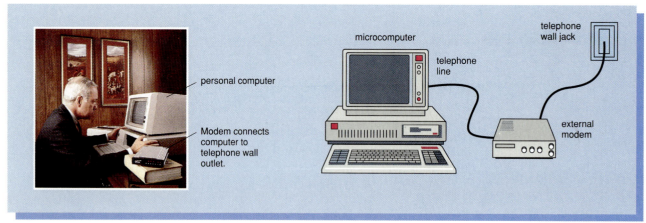

FIGURE 7-5
An external direct-connect modem.

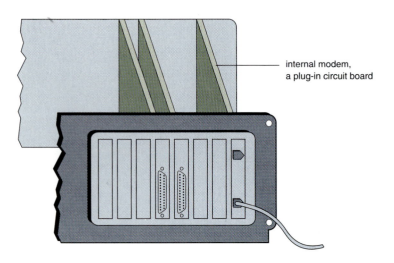

FIGURE 7-6
An internal modem, viewed as a plug in the back of a microcomputer.

Communications Channels

Data May Flow Through Five Kinds of Communications Channels: Telephone Lines, Coaxial Cable, Fiber-Optic Cable, Microwave, and Satellite.

The two ways of connecting microcomputers with each other and with other equipment are through the cable and through the air. Specifically, five kinds of technology are used to transmit data. These are telephone lines (twisted pair), coaxial cable, fiber-optic cable, microwave, and satellite. The diameters and transmission capacities of the three kinds of cable are compared in Figure 7-7.

Telephone Lines Most telephone lines that you see strung on poles consist of cables made up of hundreds of copper wires, called **twisted pairs.** A single twisted pair culminates in a wall jack into which you can plug your phone. Telephone lines have been the standard transmission medium for years for both voice and data. However, they are now being phased out by more technically advanced and reliable media.

Coaxial Cable **Coaxial cable,** a high-frequency transmission cable, replaces the multiple wires of telephone lines with a single solid copper core. In terms of number of telephone connections, a coaxial cable has 80 times the transmission capacity of twisted pair. Coaxial cable is often used to link parts of a computer system in one building. It is also used for undersea telephone lines.

Fiber-Optic Cable In **fiber-optic cable,** data is transmitted as pulses of light through tubes of glass. In terms of number of telephone connections, fiber-optic cable has 26,000 times the transmission capacity of twisted pair (see Figure 7-7). However, it is significantly smaller. Indeed, a fiber-optic tube can be half the diameter of a human hair. Although limited in the distance they can carry information, fiber-optic cables have several advantages. Such cables are immune to electronic interference, which makes them more secure. They are also lighter and less expensive than coaxial cable and are more reliable at transmitting data. They transmit information using beams of light at

FIGURE 7-7
Comparing cable size and capacity: twisted pair, coaxial cable, and fiber-optic cable.

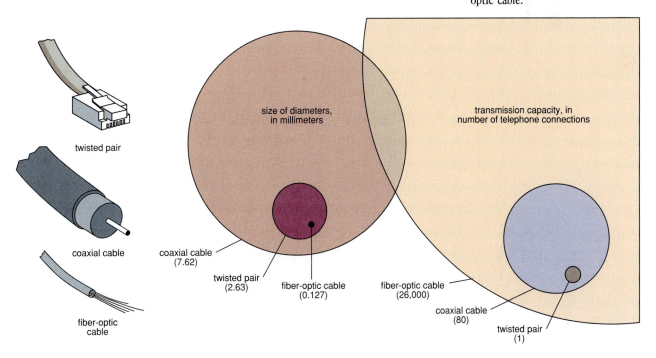

light speeds instead of pulses of electricity, making them far faster than copper cable. Fiber-optic cable is rapidly replacing twisted-pair telephone lines.

Microwave In this communications channel the medium is not a solid substance but rather the air itself. **Microwaves** are high-frequency radio waves that travel in straight lines through the air. Because the waves cannot bend with the curvature of the earth, they can be transmitted only over short distances. Thus, microwave is a good medium for sending data between buildings in a city or on a large college campus. For longer distances, the waves must be relayed by means of "dishes," or antennas. These can be installed on towers, high buildings, and mountaintops, for example (see Figure 7-8).

Satellites Orbiting about 22,000 miles above the earth, **satellites** are also used as microwave relay stations. Many of these are offered by Intelsat, the *In*ternational *Te*lecommunications *Sat*ellite Consortium, which is owned by 114 governments and forms a worldwide communications system. Satellites rotate at a precise point and speed above the earth. This makes them appear stationary so that they can amplify and relay microwave signals from one transmitter on the ground to another (see Figure 7-9). Thus, satellites can be used to send large volumes of data. Their only drawback is that bad weather can sometimes interrupt the flow of data.

Data Transmission

Several Technical Matters Affect Data Communications. They Are Bandwidth, Serial Versus Parallel Transmission, Direction of Flow, Modes of Transmission, and Protocols.

Several factors affect how data is transmitted. They include speed or bandwidth, serial or parallel transmission, direction of data flow, modes of transmitting data, and protocols.

Bandwidth The different communications channels have different data transmission speeds. This bits-per-second transmission capability of a channel is called its **bandwidth.** Bandwidth may be of three types:

- *Voiceband:* **Voiceband** is the bandwidth of a standard telephone line and used often for microcomputer transmission; the bps is 110–9600 bps.

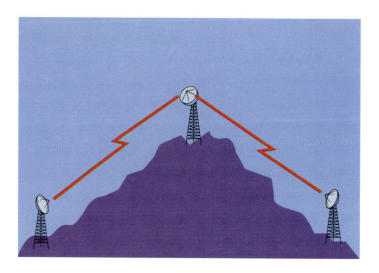

FIGURE 7-8
Microwave transmission.

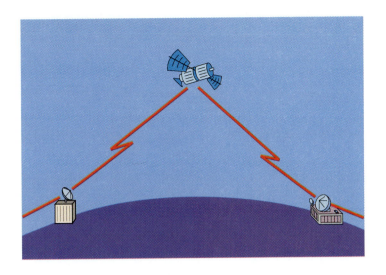

FIGURE 7-9
Satellite relaying microwave signals from earth.

- *Medium band:* The **medium band** is the bandwidth of special leased lines used mainly with minicomputers and mainframe computers; the bps is 9600–256,000.
- *Broadband:* The **broadband** is the bandwidth that includes microwave, satellite, coaxial cable, and fiber-optic channels. It is used for very high-speed computers whose processors communicate directly with each other. It is in the range of 256,000–1 million bps.

Serial and Parallel Transmission Data travels in two ways: serially and in parallel. These are represented in Figure 7-10.

- In **serial data transmission,** bits flow in a series or continuous stream, like cars crossing a one-lane bridge. Each bit travels on its own communications line. Serial transmission is the way most data is sent over telephone lines. Thus, the plug-in board making up the serial connector in a microcomputer's modem is usually called a *serial port.* More technical names for the serial port are **RS-232C connector** and **asynchronous communications port.**
- With **parallel data transmission,** bits flow through separate lines simultaneously. In other words, they resemble cars moving together at the same speed on a multilane freeway. Parallel transmission is not used for communications over telephone lines. It is, however, a standard method of sending data from a computer's CPU to a printer.

Direction of Data Transmission There are three directions or modes of data flow in a data communications system (see Figure 7-11, p. 122).

- **Simplex communication** resembles the movement of cars on a one-way street. Data travels in one direction only. It is not frequently used in data communications systems today. One instance in which it is used may be in point-of-sale (POS) terminals in which data is being entered only.
- In **half-duplex communication,** data flows in both directions, but not simultaneously. That is, data flows in only one direction at any one time. This resembles traffic on a one-lane bridge. Half-duplex is very common and is frequently used for linking microcomputers by telephone lines to other microcomputers, minicomputers, and mainframes. Thus, when you dial into an

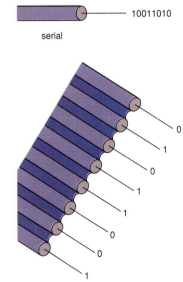

FIGURE 7-10
Serial versus parallel kinds of transmission.

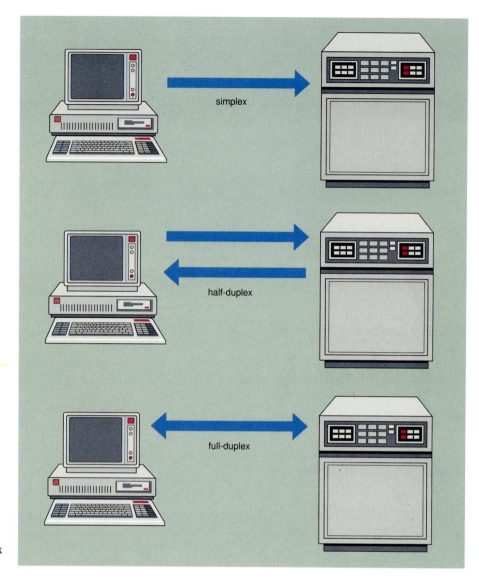

FIGURE 7-11
Simplex, half-duplex, and full-duplex communication.

electronic bulletin board through your microcomputer, you may well be using half-duplex communication.

- In **full-duplex communication,** data is transmitted back and forth at the same time, like traffic on a two-way street. It is clearly the fastest and most efficient form of two-way communication. However, it requires very special equipment and is used primarily for mainframe communications. An example might be the weekly sales figures that a supermarket or regional office sends to its corporate headquarters in another state.

Modes of Transmitting Data Data may be sent by asynchronous or synchronous transmission (see Figure 7-12).

- In **asynchronous transmission,** the method used with most microcomputers, data is sent and received one byte at a time. Asynchronous transmission is often used for terminals with slow speeds. Its advantage is that the data can be transmitted whenever convenient for the sender.

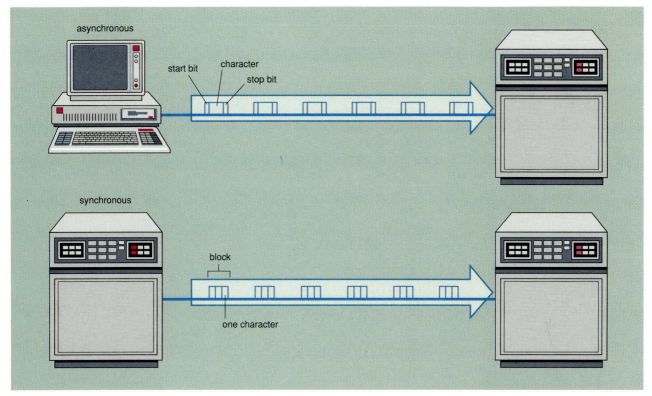

FIGURE 7-12
Asynchronous and synchronous communication.

- **Synchronous transmission** is used to transfer great quantities of information by sending several bytes or a block at a time. For the data transmission to take place, the sending and receiving of the blocks of bytes must occur at carefully timed intervals. Thus, the system requires a synchronized clock. Although the equipment for this type of transmission is much more expensive, data is transmitted faster, and so transmission is often cheaper.

Protocols For data transmission to be successful, sender and receiver must follow a set of communication rules for the exchange of information. These rules for exchanging data between computers are known as the line **protocol.** A communications software package such as Crosstalk will help define the protocol, such as speeds and modes, for connecting with another microcomputer.

When different types of microcomputers are connected in a network, the protocols can become very complex. Obviously, for the connections to work, these network protocols must adhere to certain standards. The first commercially available set of standards was IBM's Systems Network Architecture (SNA). This works for IBM's own equipment, but other machines won't necessarily communicate with them. The International Standards Organization has defined a set of communications protocols called the Open Systems Interconnection (OSI). The purpose of the OSI model is to identify functions provided by any network, whether it be NetWare for Macintosh or LAN Manager for IBM. The OSI model separates each network's functions into seven "layers" of protocols, or communication rules. When two network systems communicate, their corresponding layers may exchange data. This assumes that the microcomputers and other equipment on each network have implemented the same functions and interfaces.

Network Configurations

A Computer Network May Have One of Four Basic Configurations: Star, Bus, Ring, or Hierarchical.

Communications channels can be connected in different arrangements, or *networks,* to suit different users' needs. A *computer network* is a communications system connecting two or more computers. This arrangement allows users to exchange information and share resources (software and hardware). A network may consist only of microcomputers, or it may integrate microcomputers (or other terminals) with larger computers. Networks may be simple or complex, self-contained or dispersed over a large geographical area.

The four principal configurations of networks are *star, bus, ring,* and *hierarchical.*

Star Network In a **star network,** a number of small computers or peripheral devices are linked to a central unit (see Figure 7-13). This central unit may be a *host computer* or a *file server.* You may encounter these terms frequently.

- A *host computer* is a large centralized computer, usually a minicomputer or a mainframe.
- A **file server** is a large-capacity hard-disk storage device. It stores data and programs.

All communications pass through this central unit. Control is maintained by **polling.** That is, each connecting device is asked ("polled") whether it has a message to send. Each device is then in turn allowed to send its message.

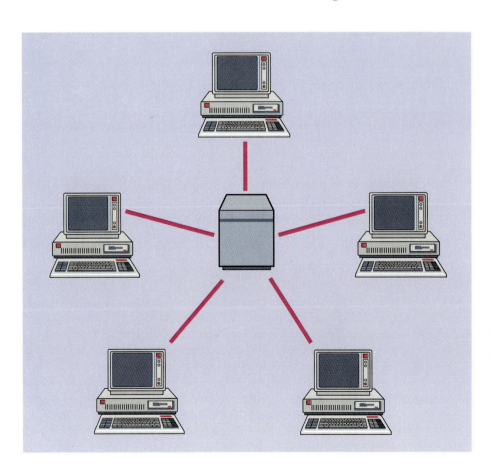

FIGURE 7-13
Star network.

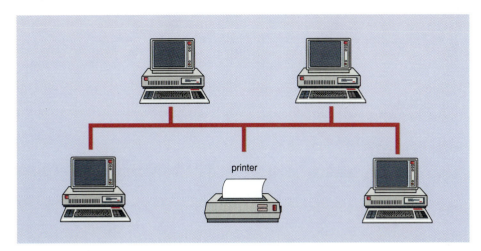

FIGURE 7-14
Bus network.

One particular advantage of the star form of network is that it can be used to provide a **time-sharing system.** That is, several users can share resources ("time") on a central computer. The star is a common arrangement for linking several microcomputers to a mainframe that allows access to an organization's database.

Bus Network In a **bus network,** each device in the network handles its own communications control. There is no host computer or file server. All communications travel along a common connecting cable called a **bus** (see Figure 7-14). As the information passes along the bus, it is examined by each device to see if the information is intended for it.

The bus network is frequently used when only a few microcomputers are to be linked together. This arrangement is common in systems for electronic mail or for sharing data stored on different microcomputers. The bus network is not as efficient as the star network for sharing common resources. (This is because the bus network is not a direct link to the resource.) However, a bus network is less expensive and is in very common use.

Ring Network In a **ring network,** each device is connected to two other devices, forming a ring (see Figure 7-15, p. 126). There is no central file server or computer. Messages are passed around the ring until they reach the correct destination. With microcomputers, the ring arrangement is the least frequently used of the four networks. However, it often is used to link mainframes, especially over wide geographical areas. These mainframes tend to operate fairly autonomously. They perform most or all of their own processing and only occasionally share data and programs with other mainframes.

A ring network is useful in a decentralized organization because it makes possible a *distributed data processing system.* That is, computers can perform processing tasks at their own dispersed locations. However, they can also share programs, data, and other resources with each other.

Hierarchical Network The **hierarchical network** consists of several computers linked to a central host computer, just like a star network. However, these other computers are also hosts to other, smaller computers or to peripheral devices (Figure 7-16).

Thus, the host at the top of the hierarchy could be a mainframe. The computers below the mainframe could be minicomputers, and those below, microcomputers. The hierarchical network—also called a **hybrid network**—thus allows various computers to share databases, processing power, and different output devices.

A hierarchical network is useful in centralized organizations. For example, different departments within an organization may have individual microcomputers connected to

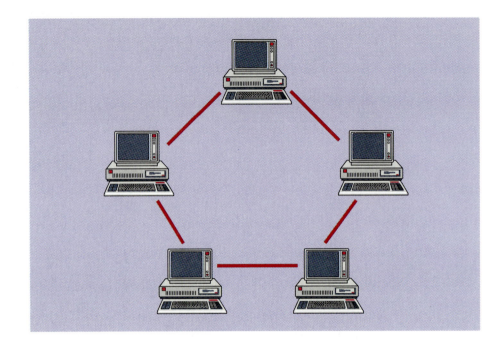

FIGURE 7-15
Ring network.

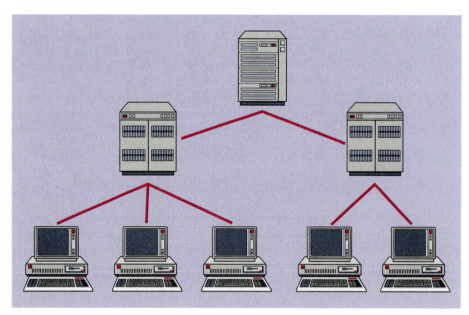

FIGURE 7-16
Hierarchical network.

departmental minicomputers. The minicomputers in turn may be connected to the corporation's mainframe, which contains data and programs accessible to all.

Network Types

Communications Networks Differ in Geographical Size. Three Important Types Are LANs, MANs, and WANs.

Clearly different types of channel—cable or air—allow different kinds of networks to be formed. Telephone lines, for instance, may connect communications equipment within the same building. In fact, many new buildings—called "*smart buildings*"—have coaxial or fiber-optic cable installed inside the walls. This makes it easy to form communications networks.

Networks may also be citywide and even international, using both cable and air connections. Here let us distinguish between three types: *local area networks, metropolitan area networks,* and *wide area networks.*

Local Area Networks Networks with computers and peripheral devices in close physical proximity—within the same building, for instance—are called **local area networks (LANs).** Linked by cable—telephone, coaxial, or fiber-optic—LANs often use a bus form of organization.

Figure 7-17 shows an example of a LAN. This typical arrangement has two benefits. People can share different equipment, which lowers the cost of equipment. For instance, here the four microcomputers share the laser printer and the file server, which are expensive pieces of hardware. (Individual microcomputers many times also have their own less expensive printers, such as the dot-matrix printer shown here.) Other equipment may also be added to the LAN—for instance, mini- or mainframe computers or optical disk storage devices.

Note that the LAN shown in Figure 7-17 also features a **network gateway.** A LAN may be linked to other LANs or to larger networks in this manner. With the gateway, one LAN may be connected to the LAN of another office group or to others in the wider world.

Experts predict great growth of microcomputer LANs. Figure 7-18 on p. 128 shows that LANs installed throughout the United States are expected to double between 1990 and 1993.

Metropolitan Area Networks The next step up from the LAN might be the **MAN**—the **metropolitan area network.** Such networks have been around for some time as links between office buildings in a city. The latest innovation, however, is the *cellular phone system,* which permits car phones.

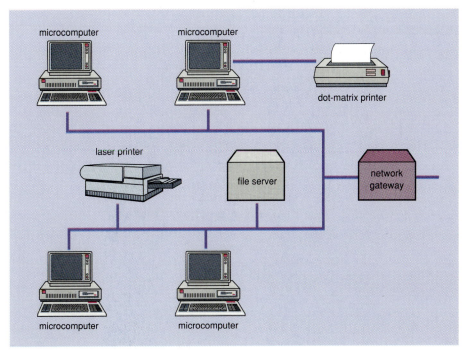

FIGURE 7-17
A local area network that includes a file server and network gateway.

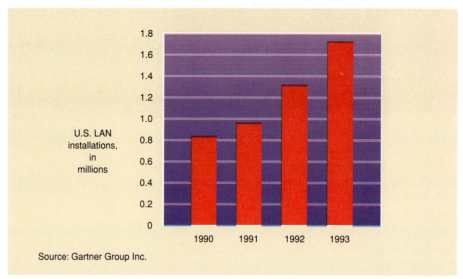

FIGURE 7-18
Estimated growth of local area networks installed in the U.S.

Wide Area Networks   **Wide area networks (WANs)** are countrywide networks. Among other kinds of channels, they use microwave relays and satellites to reach users over long distances—for example, from Los Angeles to New York (see Figure 7-19). In the United States, some important WANs are Tymnet, Telenet, and Uninet.

The difference between a LAN and a WAN is the geographical range. Both may have various combinations of hardware, such as microcomputers, minicomputers, mainframes, and various peripheral devices.

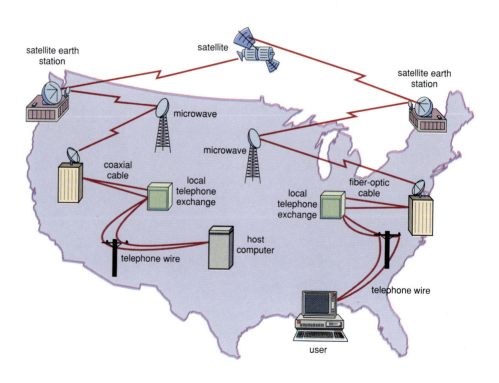

FIGURE 7-19
Example of a wide area network.

A Look at the Future

New Developments in Hardware, the Telephone System, and Radio Networks Suggest New Trends: Fewer "Standalone Computers," the Era of the Portable Office, and Downsized Applications.

The next decade will see phenomenal changes in the area of communications. Consider just some improvements in hardware. *Fax machines* are no fad. It is expected that the number installed in the United States will jump to about 30 million by the end of the century. *File servers* have been introduced for microcomputers, making them more useful in networks. These file servers have a much greater storage capacity and can get access to data more quickly than ordinary desktop computers can. *Modems* will also improve, becoming easier to use and faster at sending data. *Fiber-optic cables* will become cheaper to install, opening up more and faster communication lines. *Cellular phones* are providing mobile phone service in more parts of the nation, enabling people to do computer and fax communications directly from modems in their cars.

One of the most important developments will be the expansion of the *Integrated Services Digital Network (ISDN).* In use in the United States since 1988, ISDN consists of a set of technologies and international-exchange standards that will make today's telephone system completely digital. It is estimated there are 4 million digital phone lines in the United States and likely to increase to 30 million by the year 2000. This opens up the possibility of a worldwide computer network. At that point, modems could be replaced by so-called *terminal adapters,* linking computers to the telephone network and enabling the sending of data at phenomenal speeds. ISDN also allows everything to be transmitted at once: not only data and fax but also voice and video information.

Already, however, computer networks are moving away from telephone lines. IBM and Motorola have developed a nationwide *radio network* that allows users of hand-held computers to communicate from almost anywhere. This would allow people working in the field, such as real estate brokers, package-delivery workers, and police officers, to easily tie into a central computer. Indeed, the developers think this technology might well supplant cellular phone networks.

What do all these trends suggest? First, the "standalone" computer—the type that is not connected to any network—will in the 1990s become mostly a thing of the past. Second, we have arrived at the era of the *portable office.* Hooking a portable computer or fax machine to a cellular phone line or radio network while one is traveling makes workers more efficient. Third, we are clearly at the point of so-called *downsized applications.* That is, more and more applications that were once available only on mainframes and minicomputers are now possible on network-linked microcomputers.

Review Questions

1. Define the term *data communications systems.*
2. What are electronic bulletin boards?
3. Describe how electronic mail differs from electronic bulletin boards.
4. What is a database?
5. Describe what is meant by *downloading* information.
6. What is a password?
7. List four kinds of commercial services available for microcomputer users with communications hookups.
8. List the five kinds of communications channels.
9. What is the difference between an analog signal and a digital signal?

CHAPTER 7
Communications

V I S U A L   S U M M A R Y

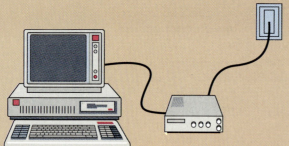

Data communications systems are the electronic systems that transmit data over communications lines from one location to another.

Communications and Connectivity

When a microcomputer is linked by a communications line, it provides the user with *connectivity*—connection to the world of larger computers and secondary storage. Options that connectivity makes available are:

Fax Machines

Fax (facsimile transmission) machines convert images to signals and send them over telephone lines to receiving fax machines.

Electronic Bulletin Boards

Electronic bulletin boards are forums on a variety of subjects available to telephone-linked microcomputer users.

Electronic Mail

Electronic mail systems resemble bulletin boards but are restricted in access. Users must use a **password** (special code) in order to read messages waiting for them.

Voice-Messaging Systems

Voice-messaging systems are telephone-linked computer systems that convert a voice message to digital bits and distribute it to many locations.

Sharing Resources

Microcomputer users may share expensive resources (e.g., laser and chain printers, disk packs, workstations, large computers).

User Interface

For voice transmission, telephones use **analog signals,** which represent a range of frequencies. Computers send **digital signals,** the presence or absence of an electronic pulse (corresponding to binary 0 or 1).

Modems and Communications Speeds

- A *modem* ("*mo*dulator *dem*odulator") converts digital to analog and vice versa. **Modulation** = digital to analog. **Demodulation** = analog to digital.
- Speeds are 300, 1200, 2400 bits per second.

Types of Modems

- **External modem**—outside system cabinet and connected by cable.
- **Internal modem**—plug-in circuit board inside system unit.

Databases

Individuals may share their databases with others and vice versa. They may **download** (transfer) information from storage devices on large computers.

Commercial Services

Examples of commercial services are: *teleshopping* (for ordering discount merchandise), *home banking* (for transferring between accounts and paying bills), *investment services,* and *travel reservations* services.

Groupware

Groupware, or *collaboration technology,* allows users on a network to work on same document at same time.

Communications Channels

Data may be transmitted by:

Telephone Lines

Most phone lines have consisted of copper wires called **twisted pairs.**

Coaxial Cable

Coaxial cable is high-frequency, solid-core cable.

Fiber-Optic Cable

Fiber-optic cable transmits data as pulses of light through tubes of glass.

Microwave

Microwaves are high-frequency radio waves that travel in a straight line.

Satellites

Satellites act as microwave relay stations rotating above the earth.

131
Visual Summary

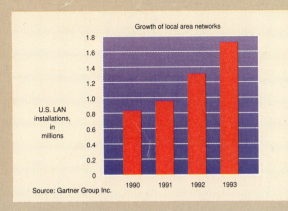

Data Transmission

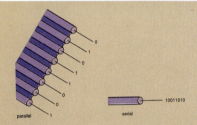

Factors affecting data transmission are:

Bandwidth

Bandwidth, bits-per-second transmission capacity of a channel, may be **voiceband**—telephone line, 110–9600 bps; **medium band**—mainframe leased lines, 9600–256,000 bps; **broadband**—coaxial, fiber optic, microwave, satellite channels, 256,000–1 million bps.

Serial and Parallel Transmission

The two ways data travels are **serial data transmission**—bits flow in continuous stream, and **parallel data transmission**—bits flow through separate lines simultaneously.

Direction of Data Transmission

Three directions of data flow are **simplex communication**—data travels in one direction only; **half-duplex communication**—data flows in both directions, but not simultaneously; **full-duplex communication**—data is transmitted back and forth at the same time.

Modes of Transmitting Data

Two modes are **asynchronous transmission**—data is sent and received one byte at a time, and **synchronous transmission**—several bytes (a block) are sent at one time.

Protocols

A **protocol** defines rules by which senders and receivers may exchange information.

Network Configurations

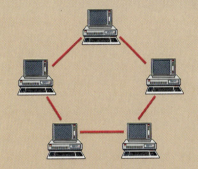

A *network* is a communications system connecting two or more computers. Four principal configurations are:

Star Network

In a **star network,** a number of small computers or peripheral devices are linked to a central unit. It is useful in a **time-sharing system,** in which several users share resources or a central computer.

Bus Network

In a **bus network,** there is no central unit. Each network device handles its own communications, which travel along the **bus,** or connecting cable.

Ring Network

In a **ring network,** there is no central unit. Each device is connected to two other devices. It is useful in decentralized organizations as a *distributed data processing system.*

Hierarchical Network

The **hierarchical network (hybrid network)** consists of several computers linked to a central host, and other computers are hosts to smaller computers or peripheral devices. It is useful in centralized organizations.

Network Types

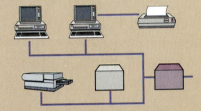

Three types of geographical networks are:

Local Area Networks

Local Area Networks (LANs) are computers and peripheral devices close together (e.g., in same building). Linked by telephone, coaxial, or fiber-optic cable, LANs often take bus form. LANs may be linked to other LANs or networks by a **network gateway.**

Metropolitan Area Networks

A **metropolitan area network (MAN)** consists of citywide networks, often using cellular phones.

Wide Area Networks

Wide area networks (WANs) are countrywide networks, often using microwave relays and satellites.

10. What is the purpose of a modem?
11. Describe the two types of modems.
12. Distinguish serial from parallel transmission.
13. Describe the difference between simplex, half-duplex, and full-duplex communication.
14. Distinguish synchronous from asynchronous transmission.
15. Discuss the four basic arrangements microcomputer communications networks may take.
16. What is a file server?
17. Describe the concept of time sharing.
18. Describe what a distributed data processing system is.
19. What is a local area network? A wide area network?
20. Describe what groupware does.

Discussion Questions

1. What is an electronic bulletin board? See if you can find out what's available in your area. Local microcomputer publications often print the telephone numbers of bulletin boards. They often list the principal subject of interest, the kinds of microcomputers served, and the baud rate of the modems. Identify a bulletin board you think might interest you.

    If you can't find a printed list of bulletin boards, try contacting a microcomputer users' group for help. Users' groups are clubs or volunteer organizations. Their members meet to help each other solve problems or share interests regarding particular personal computers.

2. Using the same sources as above, find out what kind of commercial services are in your area. Examples might be home banking, teleshopping, and travel services. Do you think you would find any of these truly of value?

CHAPTER 8
Files and Databases

Like a library, the purpose of secondary storage is to store information. How is such information organized? What are files and databases, and why know anything about them? Perhaps the answer is: To become competent at making use of information in the Information Age, you have to know how to *find* that information.

At one time, it was not important for microcomputer users to have to know much about files and databases. However, the recent arrival of very powerful microcomputer chips and their availability to communications networks has changed that. To attain true computer competency, you need to know how to gain access to the files and databases on your own personal computer. You also need to be able to access those available from other sources. Communications lines extend the reach of your microcomputer well beyond the desktop.

Files

Understanding How Files Work Means Understanding Data Organization, Key Fields, Batch Versus Real-Time Processing, Master Versus Transaction Files, and File Organization.

You want to know if you're going to be able to graduate in June. You call your school's registrar after your last semester exams to find out your grade point average. Perhaps you are told, "Sorry, that's not in the computer yet." Why can't they tell you? How is the school's computer system any different from, say, your bank's, where deposits and withdrawals seem to be recorded right away?

Data Organization From Chapter 6 we learned that data is organized as follows:

- *Character:* A character is a single letter, number, or special character such as a punctuation mark or $.
- *Field:* A field contains a set of related characters. On a college registration form or a driver's license, a person's first name is a field. Last name is another field, street address another field, city yet another field, and so on.

COMPETENCIES

After you have read this chapter, you should be able to:

1. Understand the difference between batch processing and real-time processing.

2. Describe the difference between master files and transaction files.

3. Define and describe the three types of file organization: sequential, direct, and index sequential.

4. Describe the advantages of a database.

5. Describe the essentials of a database management system (DBMS).

6. Describe three ways of organizing a DBMS: hierarchical, network, and relational.

7. Distinguish among individual, company, distributed, and proprietary databases.

8. Discuss some issues of productivity and security.

- *Record:* A record is a collection of related fields. Everything on a person's driver's license, including number and expiration date, is a record.
- *File:* A file is a collection of related records. All the driver's licenses issued in one county could be a file.

An example of how data is organized is shown in Figure 8-1 (which appeared in Chapter 6). Note that a student's name is not one field, it is three: first name, middle initial, and last name.

The Key Field Figure 8-1 also shows the student's identification number. Is such a number really necessary? Certainly most people's names are different enough that at a small college, say, you might think identification numbers wouldn't be necessary. However, as anyone named Robert Smith or Susan Williams knows, there are plenty of other people around with the same name. Sometimes they even have the same middle initial. This is the reason for the student identification number: The number is unique, whereas the name may not be.

This distinctive number is called a *key field*. A **key field** is the particular field of a record that is chosen to uniquely identify each record. The key may be social security number, employee identification number, or part number.

Batch Versus Real-Time Processing Traditionally data is processed in two ways. These are (1) *batch processing,* what we might call "later"; and (2) *real-time processing,* what we might call "right away." These two methods have been used to handle common record-keeping activities such as payroll and sales orders.

- *Batch processing:* In **batch processing,** data is collected over several days or weeks. It is then processed all at once—as a "batch." If you have a gasoline credit card, your bill probably reflects batch processing. That is, during the month, you buy gas and charge it to your credit card. Each time, the gasoline dealer sends a copy of the transaction to the oil company. At some point in the month, the company's data processing department puts all those transactions (and those of many other customers) together. It then processes them at one time. The oil company then sends you a single bill totaling the amount you owe.
- *Real-time processing:* Totaling up the sales charged to your gasoline credit card is an example of batch processing. You might use another kind of card— your card for your bank's automatic teller machine (ATM)—for the second

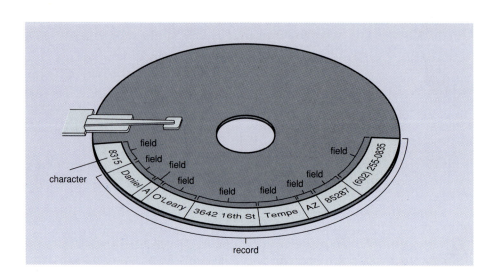

FIGURE 8-1
How data is organized.

kind of processing. **Real-time processing** occurs when data is processed at the same time the transaction occurs. As you use your ATM card to withdraw cash, the system automatically computes the balance remaining in your account.

At one time, only tape storage, and therefore only sequential access storage (as we discussed in Chapter 6), was available. All processing then was batch processing and was done on mainframe computers. Even today, a great deal of mainframe time is dedicated to this kind of processing. Many smaller organizations, however, use microcomputers for this purpose.

Real-time processing is made possible by the availability of disk packs and direct access storage (as we described in Chapter 6). Direct access storage enables the user to quickly go directly to a particular record. (In sequential access storage, by contrast, the user must wait for the computer to scan several records one at a time. It continues scanning until it comes to the one that's needed.) Not long ago, specialized terminals were used to enter data and perform real-time processing. Today, however, more and more microcomputers are being used for this purpose. In addition, because microcomputers have become so powerful, smaller companies and departments of large companies use these machines by themselves for many real-time processing needs. That is, they use them without connecting to a mainframe.

Master Versus Transaction Files Two types of files are commonly used to update data—a *master file* and a *transaction file*.

- The **master file** is a complete file containing all records current up to the last update. An example is the data file used to prepare your last month's telephone bill or bank statement.

- The **transaction file** contains *recent* changes to records that will be used to update the master file. An example could be a temporary "holding" file that accumulates telephone charges or bank deposits and withdrawals through the present month.

File Organization File organization may be of three types: *sequential, direct,* and *index sequential.*

- *Sequential file organization:* In a **sequential file,** records are physically stored one after another in some order. This order is determined by the *key field* on each record, such as the student identification number shown in Figure 8-1. In this arrangement, to find the record about a particular student, the registrar's office would sequentially search through the records. It would search them one at a time until the student's number was found. If your number is 8315, the computer will start with record number 0000. It will go through 0001, 0002, and so on, until it reaches your number.

  Sequential files are often stored on tape, although disk packs may also be used.

- *Direct file organization:* For **direct file organization,** records are not stored physically one after another. Rather, they are stored on a disk in a particular location that can be determined by their key field. Knowing the key field allows the computer to access the record directly; no sequential search is necessary.

  In direct file organization, data must be stored on disks. Also, a method must exist for going directly to the key fields of all records.

- *Index sequential file organization:* **Index sequential file organization** is a compromise between sequential and direct file organizations. It stores records in a file in sequential order. However, an index sequential file also contains an index. The index lists the key to each group of records stored and the corresponding disk address for that group. When the user seeks a particular record, the computer starts searching sequentially by looking at the beginning of the group of records.

For example, the college registrar could index certain *ranges* of student identification numbers—0000 to 2000, 2001 to 4000, and so on. For the computer to find your number (e.g., 8315), it would first go to the index. The index would give the location of the range in which your number appears on the disk (e.g., 8001 to 10,000). The computer would then search sequentially (from 8001) to find your number.

Index sequential file organization requires disks or other direct access storage device.

All three kinds of file organization have their advantages and disadvantages.

The advantage of *sequential files* is that they are useful when all or a large part of the records need to be accessed—for example, when the next term's course offerings are being mailed out. They also have a cost advantage, since they can be stored on magnetic tape, which is less expensive than disk. The disadvantage of sequential files is that records must be ordered in a certain way and be searched one at a time.

The advantage of *direct file organization* is that it is much faster than sequential for locating a specific record. For example, if your grades were stored in a direct file, the registrar could access them very quickly. They could be accessed just by your student identification number. The disadvantage of this form of organization is cost: It needs more storage on a hard disk. It also is not as good as sequential file organization for large numbers of updates or for listing large numbers of records.

Index sequential file organization is faster than sequential but not as fast as direct access. This kind is best used when large batches of transactions must occasionally be updated, yet users also want frequent, quick access to records. For example, every month a bank will update bank statements to send to its customers. However, customers and bank tellers need to be able to have up-to-the-minute information about checking accounts.

Database

A Database Consolidates Multiple Files of Duplicate Information.

Many organizations have multiple files on the same subject or person. For example, records for the same customer may appear in different files in the sales department, billing department, and credit department. If the customer changes her or his name or moves, every file must be updated. If one file is overlooked, it can cause embarrassments. For example, a product ordered might be sent to the new address, but the bill might be sent to the old address.

Moreover, data spread around in different files is not as useful as it can be if many users have access to it. The marketing department, for instance, might want to do special promotions to customers who order large quantities of merchandise. However, they may be unable to do so because that information is in the billing department. A database can make the needed information available.

A *database* is defined as a collection of integrated data. By "integrated," we mean the data consists of logically related files and records.

The Need for Databases For both individuals and organizations, there are many advantages to having databases:

- *Sharing:* In organizations, information from one department can be readily shared with others, as we saw in the example above.
- *Security:* Users are given passwords or access only to the kind of information they need to know. Thus, the payroll department may have access to employees' pay rates, but other departments would not.
- *Fewer files:* With several departments having access to one file, there are fewer files. Excess storage, or what is called "data redundancy," is reduced. Microcomputers linked by a network to a file server, for example, could replace the hard disks located in several individual microcomputers.
- *Data integrity:* Older filing systems many times did not have "integrity." That is, a change made in the file in one department might not be made in the file in another department.

Software for a Database Management System   In order to create, modify, and gain access to the database, special software is required. This software is called a *database management system,* which is commonly abbreviated *DBMS.*

Some DBMSs, such as dBASE, are designed specifically for microcomputers. Other DBMSs are designed for minicomputers and mainframes. Once again, increased processing power and the wide use of communications networks linked to file servers are changing everything. Now microcomputer DBMSs have become more like the ones used for mainframes—and vice versa.

DBMS software is made up of a data dictionary and a query language.

The Data Dictionary   The **data dictionary** contains a description of the structure of the data used in the database. For a particular item of data, it defines the names used for a particular field. It defines what type of data that field is (alphabetic, numeric, or alphanumeric). It also specifies the number of characters in each field and whether that field is a key field. An example of a data dictionary appears in Figure 8-2.

Query Language   Access to most databases is accomplished with a **query language.** This is an easy-to-use language understandable to most users. Examples of microcomputer query languages are found in dBASE and R:Base.

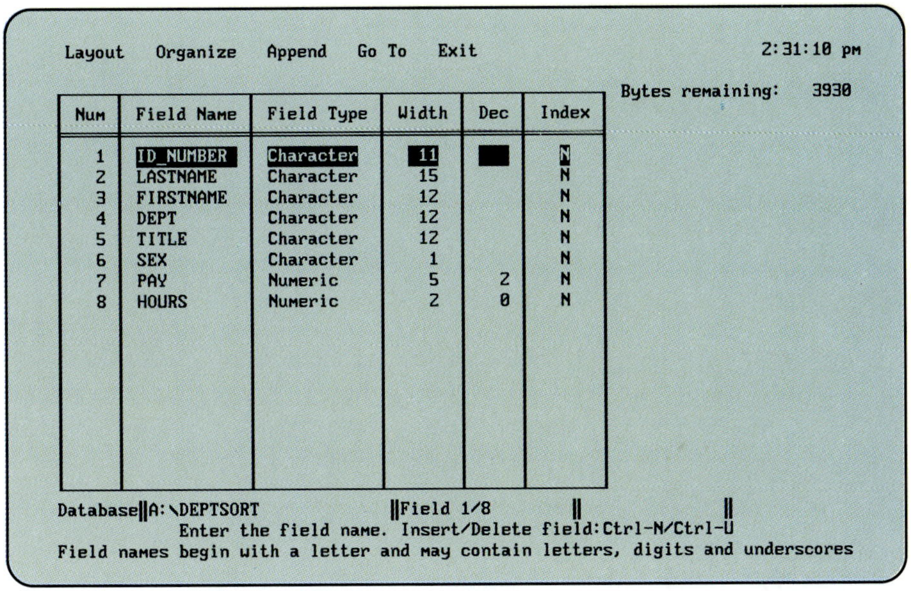

FIGURE 8-2
The data dictionary for dBASE IV. This screen defines the structure for records in an employee payroll file.

Query languages have commands such as DISPLAY, ADD, COMPARE, LIST, and UPDATE. For example, imagine you wanted the names of all salespeople in an organization whose sales were greater than their sales quotas. You might type the statement "DISPLAY ALL FOR SALES > QUOTA."

DBMS Organization

The Three Principal DBMS Organizations Are Hierarchical, Network, and Relational.

The purpose of a database is to integrate individual items of data—that is, to transform isolated facts into useful information. We saw that files can be organized in various ways (sequentially, for example) to best suit their use. Similarly, databases can also be organized in different ways to best fit their use. Although other arrangements have been tried, the three most common formats are *hierarchical, network,* and *relational.*

The Hierarchical Database   In a **hierarchical database,** fields or records are structured in **nodes.** Nodes are points connected like the branches of a tree (an upside-down tree). The nodes farther down the system are subordinate to the ones above, like the hierarchy of managers in a corporation. An example of a hierarchical database for part of a nationwide airline reservations system is shown in Figure 8-3. Each entry has one **parent node,** although a parent may have several **child nodes.** To find a particular field you have to start at the top with a parent and trace down the tree to a child.

In the airline reservations system example, the parent nodes are those labeled "Departure," the airports from which planes are leaving. The first child is any of the airports labeled "Arrival," various flights' destinations. The third child is "Flight number." The fourth child is "Passenger."

The problem with a hierarchical database is that if one parent node is deleted, so are all the subordinate child nodes. Moreover, a child node cannot be added unless a parent

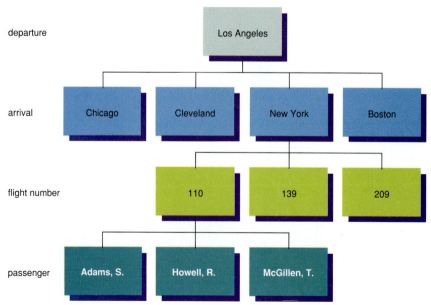

FIGURE 8-3
Example of a hierarchical database.

node is added first. The most significant limitation is the rigid structure: one parent only per child, and no relationships between the child nodes themselves.

The Network Database A **network database** also has a hierarchical arrangement of nodes. However, each child node may have more than one parent node. That is, there are additional connections—called **pointers**—between parent nodes and child nodes (see Figure 8-4). Thus, a node may be reached through more than one path. It may be traced down through different branches.

An example of the use of a network organization is that shown in Figure 8-4 for students taking courses. If you trace through the logic of this organization, you can see that each student can have more than one teacher. Each teacher can also teach more than one course. Students may take more than a single course. This is an example of how the network arrangement is more flexible and in many cases more efficient than the hierarchical arrangement.

The Relational Database The most flexible organization is the **relational database.** In this structure, there are no access paths down a hierarchy to an item of data. Rather, the data elements are stored in different tables, each of which consists of rows and columns (see Figure 8-5, p. 140). A table is called a **relation.**

An example of a relational database is shown in Figure 8-5. The second table consists of all car license plate numbers issued within a particular state. Within the table, a row resembles a record—for example, the license plate number of a car and the owner of that car. A column entry resembles a field. The car license number is one field; the owner's name and address are another field. All related tables must have a *common data item* (a key field). Thus, any piece of information stored on one table can be linked with any piece of information stored on another table. One key field might be a car license number. Another might be a person's name. Another might be a driver's license number.

Thus, police officers who stop a speeding car can radio the license plate number to the department of motor vehicles. They can use the license number as the key field. With it they can find out about any traffic violations (such as parking tickets) for which the car has been cited. Also using the license plate number as a key field, they can obtain the

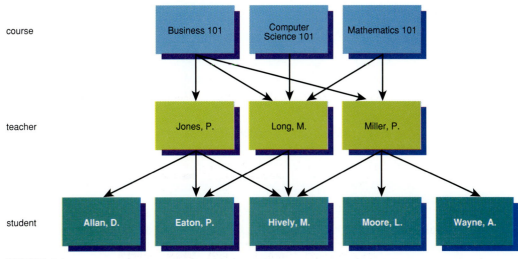

FIGURE 8-4
Example of a network database.

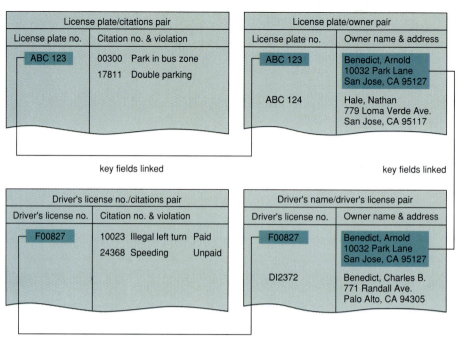

FIGURE 8-5
Example of a relational database.

name and address of the car's owner. Using the car owner's name as another key field, they can obtain his or her driver's license number. With the driver's license number as another key field, they can learn if that driver has been cited for other traffic violations. They can also learn whether any fines were paid. They can do this even if the driver has been driving a dozen other cars.

The most valuable feature of relational databases is that entries can be easily added, deleted, and modified. The hierarchy and network databases are more rigid. The relational organization is common for microcomputer DBMSs, such as dBASE and R:Base. Relational databases are also becoming more popular for mainframe- and minicomputer-based systems.

Types of Databases

There Are Four Kinds of Databases: Individual, Company, Distributed, and Proprietary.

Databases may be small or large, limited in accessibility or widely accessible. Databases may be classified into four types: *individual, company* (or shared), *distributed,* and *proprietary.*

The Individual Database   The **individual database** is also called a **microcomputer database.** It is a collection of integrated files useful mainly to just one person. Typically, the data and the DBMS are under the direct control of the user. They are stored either on the user's hard-disk drive or on a LAN file server. This is the kind of database that we described in Chapter 2.

There may be many times in your life when you will find this kind of database valuable. If you are in sales, for instance, a microcomputer database can be used to keep track of customers. If you are a sales manager, you can keep track of your salespeople and their performance. If you are an advertising account executive, you can keep track of what work and how many hours to charge to which client.

The Company, or Shared, Database Companies, of course, create databases for their own use. The **company database** may be stored on a mainframe and managed by a computer professional (known as a database administrator). Users throughout the company have access to the database through their microcomputers linked to local area networks or wide area networks.

Company databases are of two types:

- The **common operational database** contains details about the operations of the company, such as sales or production information.

- The **common user database** contains selected information both from the common operational database and from outside private (proprietary) databases. Managers can tap into this information on their microcomputers or terminals and use it for decision making.

As we will see in the next chapter, company databases are the foundation for management information systems. For instance, a department store can record all sales transactions in the database. A sales manager can use this information to see which salespeople are selling the most products and thereby determine year-end sales bonuses. Or the store's buyer can learn which products are selling well or not selling and make adjustments when reordering. A top executive might combine overall store sales trends with information from outside databases about consumer and population trends. This information could be used to change the whole merchandising strategy of the store.

The Distributed Database Many times the data in a company is stored not in just one location but in several locations. It is made accessible through a variety of communications networks. The database, then, is a **distributed database.** That is, it is located in a place or places other than where users are located. The hard-disk drives are connected by a communications network to a mainframe.

For instance, some database information can be at regional offices. Some can be at company headquarters, some down the hall from you, and some even overseas. Sales figures for a chain of department stores, then, could be located at the various stores, but executives at district offices or at the chain's headquarters could have access to these figures.

The Proprietary Database A **proprietary database** is generally an enormous database that an organization develops to cover certain particular subjects. It offers access to this database to the public or selected outside individuals for a fee. Sometimes proprietary databases are also called *information utilities* or *data banks*. An example is CompuServe, which sells a variety of consumer and business services to microcomputer users (see Figure 8-6).

Some important proprietary databases are the following:

- *CompuServe:* Offers consumer and business services, including electronic mail.

- *Dialog Information Services:* Offers business, technical, and scientific information.

- *Dow Jones News/Retrieval:* Provides world news and information on business, investments, and stocks.

- *Mead Data Central:* Offers news and information on business and law.

There are also specialized proprietary databases for investors and financial analysts, such as Chase Econometric Associates.

FIGURE 8-6
Proprietary database: CompuServe's opening screens.

Costs If you have a microcomputer, modem, and phone at home, many of these proprietary databases are available to you. Usually you pay a start-up fee, an hourly charge for searching the database, and the phone company or telecommunications line charges.

As you might expect, fees and charges are high during the normal nine-to-five business hours. However, proprietary databases often offer cheaper after-hours rates. Dialog Information Services, for example, offers Knowledge Index nights and weekends for (as of this writing) a start-up fee of $35. An online search charge (which includes telecommunications line costs) is $24 an hour. This service offers comprehensive coverage of journals, abstracts, research reports, reviews, news, tax information, and bibliographies. Fields covered range from agriculture to social science.

Database Uses and Issues

Databases Help Users Keep Current and Plan for the Future, but Keeping Them Secure Is Important. Databases May Be Supervised by a Database Administrator.

Databases offer great opportunities for productivity. In fact, in corporate libraries, electronic databases are now considered more valuable than books and journals. However, maintaining databases means users must make constant efforts to keep them from being tampered with or used for the wrong purposes.

Data for Strategic Uses Databases help users keep up to date and plan for the future. Among the hundreds of databases available to help users with both general and specific business purposes are the following.

- *Business directories* providing addresses, financial and marketing information, products, and trade and brand names.
- *Demographic data,* such as county and city statistics, current estimates on population and income, employment statistics, census data, and so on.
- *Business statistical information,* such as financial information on publicly traded companies, market potential of certain retail stores, and other business information.
- *Text databases* providing articles from business publications, press releases, reviews on companies and products, and so on.

Importance of Security Precisely because databases are so valuable, their security has become a vital issue. One concern is that personal and private information about people stored in databases will be used for the wrong purposes. For instance, a person's credit or medical records might be used to make hiring or promotion decisions.

Another concern is with preventing unauthorized users from gaining access to a database. For example, there have been numerous instances in which a **computer virus** has been launched into a database or network. Computer viruses are hidden instructions that "migrate" through networks and operating systems and become embedded in different programs and databases. Some are relatively harmless, but others may destroy data. Certus International, which sells software to combat viruses, polled more than a thousand corporations. It found that a majority had suffered at least one virus attack (see Figure 8-7).

Security can require putting guards on company computer rooms and checking the identification of everyone admitted (see Figure 8-8). It can also include storing back-up tapes or disks of all valuable information in another location. We describe these and other security issues in detail in Chapter 13.

143
Database Uses and Issues

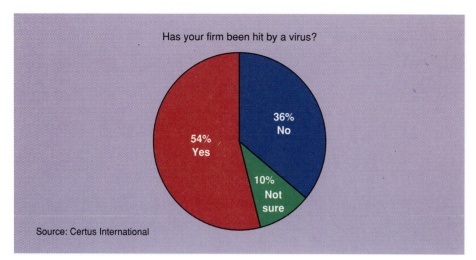

FIGURE 8-7
Firms reporting at least one computer virus attack.

FIGURE 8-8
Guards are one way of ensuring computer security.

The Database Administrator Librarians have had to be trained in the use of electronic databases so that they can help their corporate users. However, corporate databases of all sorts—not just those in the library—have become so important that many large organizations now employ a **database administrator (DBA).** He or she helps determine what kind of structure the large databases should take and evaluates the performance of the DBMS. For shared databases, the DBA also determines which people have access to what kind of data; these are called **processing rights.** In addition, the DBA is concerned with such significant issues as security, privacy, and ethics (described in Chapter 13).

A Look at the Future

Large Databases Give Us Everything from Specialty Phone Books to Census Maps. Risks Are Increased Compromises of Privacy and Security. Products Are Available to Sift Information.

Data collection and its uses are sure to get more and more sophisticated. Microcomputer users now, for instance, can get computerized *specialty phone books* loaded with corporate names, telephone numbers, and other data. A database project of awesome proportions is the huge national computer map being developed by the U.S. Census Bureau. Known as *TIGER* (for Topologically Integrated Geographic Encoding and Reference system), it will have 23 million street intersections and can be coupled with statistics that provide a numerical or income profile of every block in the United States.

Big databases not only have great potential payoffs in productivity but also great risks for privacy and security. One worry is that corporations and governments may use them to create unnecessary or dangerous confidential files (dossiers) about private citizens. Another is that a fire, earthquake, computer virus, sabotage, or other disaster that disrupts a local communications or computer system can have nationwide or worldwide effects.

Finally, the mountains of information generated by databases have now created a new industry: products that sift the information to give us what we really want to know. These products range from personal newsletters to filtering technology that scans data for key words specified by the user.

Review Questions

1. What is the difference between batch processing and real-time processing? Give an example of each.
2. What is a master file?
3. What is a transaction file?
4. Define what is meant by *key field*.
5. Describe sequential file organization.
6. Explain direct file organization.
7. Describe index sequential file organization.
8. Why are databases needed?
9. Define what is meant by a database.
10. State four advantages of databases.
11. What is a database management system (DBMS)?
12. Describe what a data dictionary is.
13. Describe the purpose of a query language.

14. Discuss the three principal ways of organizing a database.
15. What is an individual database?
16. What is a company database?
17. What is a distributed database?
18. What is a proprietary database?
19. What is a computer virus?
20. Describe the role of the database administrator.

Discussion Questions

1. When you are establishing the structure of a database, the first requirement is to indicate what fields you will have. You must also determine the maximum number of characters (bytes) each may occupy. And you must decide which fields are alphanumeric (both letters and numbers) and which fields are numeric only (which means they can be used for arithmetic operations). Finally, you need to decide which fields are the key fields. That is, which are important enough to do sorting on, so that, for instance, you can produce lists in alphabetical order or sequential order? Suppose you are setting up an individual database on your microcomputer that will contain facts about friends, coworkers, or prospective employees. Such facts might include names, addresses, telephone numbers, social security numbers, and "special characteristics" (e.g., birth dates, spouse's names). Make a list of the fields you want to include. List their length, whether alphanumeric or numeric, and which will be key fields. Discuss the reasons for your decisions.

2. Let us assume you have decided on a specialized field of study (your major). Take a few minutes to list the kinds of information you are required to research for papers, projects, and assignments. For example, as a business marketing student, you might need to know about sales techniques, advertising budgets, telemarketing campaigns, and the like. With this list in hand, go to the library. Find out which information utilities or data banks would be most valuable to you (e.g., CompuServe, Dialog, Dow Jones/News Retrieval, Mead Data Central).

CHAPTER 8
Files and Databases

V I S U A L S U M M A R Y

Through communication lines, users can gain access to files and databases.

Files

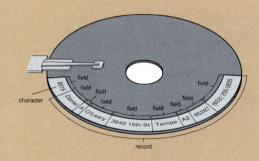

Understanding how files work means understanding the following:

Data Organization

- *Character*—letter, number, special character.
- *Field*—set of related characters.
- *Record*—collection of related fields.
- *File*—collection of related records.
- *Key field*—field of a record that uniquely identifies a record in a file.

Batch Versus Real-Time Processing

Two methods of processing:
- **Batch processing**—transactions are collected over time, then processed all at once.
- **Real-time processing**—data is processed at the same time transactions occur.

Master Versus Transaction Files

- **Master file**—a complete file containing all records current to the last update.
- **Transaction file**—a temporary "holding file" containing recent changes that will be used to update the master file.

File Organization

Three types of file organization are:
- **Sequential**—records are stored one after the other in ascending or descending order. Order is determined by the *key field* on each record (e.g., alphabetically by person's last name). This method is often used with magnetic tape.
- **Direct**—records are stored in order by a key field such as a special number. This method is often used with magnetic disk.
- **Index sequential**—records are stored in a file in sequential order, but the file also has an index listing the key to each group of records stored. This method is used with magnetic disk storage.

Database

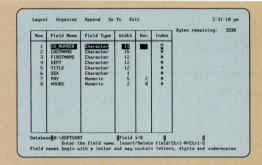

A *database* is a collection of integrated data—logically related files and records.

The Need for Databases

Advantages of databases:
- Sharing—users may share with others.
- Security—access is restricted to authorized people.
- Fewer files—a company avoids multiple files on the same subject.
- Data integrity—changes in one file are made in other files as well.

Software for a DBMS

A **database management system (DBMS)** is the software for creating, modifying, and gaining access to the database. A DBMS consists of:
- **Data dictionary**—describes the structure of the data used in the database (e.g., if data is alphabetic, numeric, alphanumeric).
- **Query language**—easy-to-use language to get access to the database.

147
Visual Summary

Has your firm been hit by a virus?

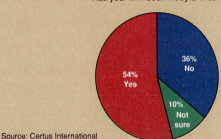

54% Yes
36% No
10% Not sure

Source: Certus International

DBMS Organization

Three principal DBMS organizations are:

Hierarchical Database

In a **hierarchical database,** fields and records are structured in **nodes,** points connected like tree branches. An entry may have a **parent** node with several **child** nodes. A node may be reached by only one path.

Network Database

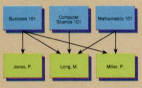

In a **network database,** nodes are arranged hierarchically, but a child node may have more than one parent. There are additional connections called **pointers.** A node may be reached by several paths.

Relational Database

| Driver's name/driver's license pair ||
Driver's license no.	Owner name & address
F00827	Benedict, Arnold 10032 Park Lane San Jose, CA 95127
DI2372	Benedict, Charles B. 771 Randall Ave. Palo Alto, CA 94305

In a **relational database,** data is stored in pairs on tables (called **relations**) of rows and columns; data items are found by means of an index. Entries may be easily modified in a relational DBMS.

Types of Database

Four types of databases are:

Individual Database

The **individual database** (or **microcomputer database**) is a collection of integrated files useful mainly to just one person.

Company, or Shared, Database

The **company (shared) database** may be stored on a mainframe and managed by a computer professional (database administrator). Users have access through microcomputers. Two types of company databases are:
- **Common operational database**—contains details about company operations.
- **Common user database**—contains selected information from the common operational database and from outside private databases.

Distributed Database

The **distributed database** is spread out geographically and is accessible by communications links.

Proprietary Database

A **proprietary database** is available by subscription to customers (e.g., offering business, technical, or scientific information).

Database Uses and Issues

Databases offer increased productivity but also risks to security.

Data for Strategic Uses

Databases help users keep current and plan for the future. Among databases available are business directories, demographic data, business statistical information, and text databases.

Importance of Security

Two security concerns are that private information in databases will be used for wrong purposes and that unauthorized users will gain access. An example of a threat to databases is a **computer virus,** hidden instructions that "migrate" into programs and databases and destroy them.

The Database Administrator

The **database administrator (DBA)** is a specialist in large organizations who sets up and manages the database and determines **processing rights**—which people have access to what kind of data.

CHAPTER 9
Information Systems

COMPETENCIES
After you have read this chapter, you should be able to:

1. Explain how changing technology has made the microcomputer a resource that can use information systems.

2. Explain how organizations can be structured according to five functions and three management levels.

3. Describe how information flows in an organization.

4. Distinguish among a transaction processing system, a management information system, and a decision support system.

5. Describe what an executive information system is.

Communications links and databases connect you with information resources far beyond the surface of your desk. The microcomputer offers you access to a greater quantity of information than was possible a few years ago. In addition, you also have access to a better *quality* of information. As we show in this chapter, when you tap into a computer-based information system, you not only get information—you also get help in *making decisions.*

Give two reasons why computers are used in organizations. No doubt you can easily state one of them: to keep records of events. However, the second reason might be less obvious: to help make decisions. For example, as we showed earlier, point-of-sale terminals, those computerized cash registers in department stores, are used not only to record sales. They also record which salespeople made which sales. This information can be used for decision making. For instance, it can help the sales manager decide which salespeople will get year-end bonuses for doing exceptional work.

Keeping accurate records and making good decisions are extremely important in running any successful organization, small or large. Let us begin to see how information systems can help you with this.

The Information Revolution

Technology Advances Are Making Database Storage and Retrieval Available to Microcomputers Everywhere.

The first kind of microcomputer to which you are introduced may do just about everything you want—for the moment. Indeed, this may be so even though it is one of the less powerful models. You can use it to handle all the kinds of programs we have called "basic tools," such as word processing and spreadsheets.

However, the situation in the workplace is rapidly changing. Now technology has made microcomputers so powerful that the word *micro* is almost no longer meaningful. Indeed, people even talk about *supermicros.* If you have access to a newer microcomputer, then you practically have the power of a mainframe sitting on your desk.

As a result, a new term has come into the language: "down-sizing." **Down-sizing** means moving applications from larger computers to smaller ones—usually from mainframes and minicomputers to microcomputers. This trend corresponds to another significant development—the down-sizing of *management staffs*. In recent years, many companies have scaled down their staffs, in the process reducing the number of middle-level managers. Since much of the company's work still remains, the microcomputer has become more important. It allows one person, typically a manager, to perform more of these tasks.

Here is what the down-sizing of computers means to you.

- *Faster processing and more primary storage:* Many older microcomputers have only 640K or even just 256K of primary storage (main memory). Their processing capacities are limited and their speeds are relatively slow. The most recent microcomputer generation, however, has enormous power. Processing speeds and primary storage capacities approach those previously reserved for minicomputers and mainframes. As a result, a microcomputer can run not only such DBMS programs as dBASE and R:base. They can also run some even more powerful programs. These include not only more sophisticated operating systems but also high-powered applications programs, such as desktop publishing programs.

- *More powerful secondary storage:* In large organizations, databases have always required storage devices that can hold a lot of data. This meant that company databases required disk packs in order to create and retrieve large amounts of data. The cost and the processing speeds of these disk packs could be handled only by mainframes and minis. Today two changes are taking place. (1) High-volume storage such as optical disks is available for microcomputer users. (2) In addition, when linked to communications networks, microcomputer users have access to databases stored on disk packs.

- *Microcomputers offer easier access to large databases:* Until recently, in many large organizations, only people who could use terminals connected to a mainframe could get access to large databases. Now, however, terminals are being replaced by microcomputers connected by local area networks or other communications networks to mainframes and databases.

   Today nearly everyone who needs access can readily obtain it. In fact, the role of the mainframe is changing. More and more mainframe time is being used to handle database operations. More and more processing of the data, on the other hand, is being done by microcomputers.

In short, the capabilities of the desktop computer have been dramatically expanded (see Figure 9-1). In the future, you will be able to call upon it for an enormous quantity of information for help in making decisions. Let us see how this would work. To understand this, we need to understand how an organization is structured and how information flows within it.

How Information Flows in an Organization

Information Flows Up and Down Among Managers and Sideways Among Departments.

An **information system** (like the microcomputer system we discussed in Chapter 1) is a collection of *hardware, software, people, procedures,* and *data*. These work together to provide information essential to running an organization. This is information that will successfully produce a product or service and, for profit-oriented enterprises, derive a profit.

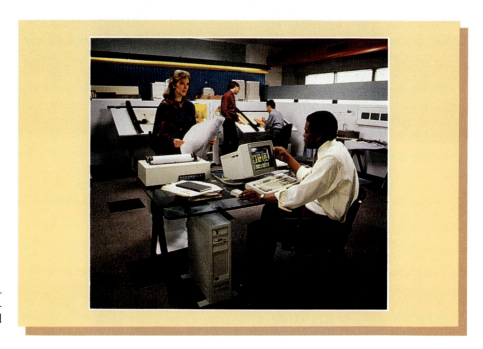

FIGURE 9-1
The capabilities of the microcomputer have been dramatically expanded, as with this IBM PS/2 Model 80.

In large and medium-sized organizations, computerized information systems don't just keep track of transactions and day-to-day business operations. They also support the flow of information within the organization. This information flows both vertically and horizontally. In order to understand this, we need to understand how an organization is structured. One way to examine an organization's structure is to view it from a functional perspective. That is, you can study the different basic functional areas in organizations and the different types of people within these functional areas.

As we describe these, you might consider how they apply to any organization you are familiar with. Or consider how they apply to a hypothetical manufacturer of sporting goods, The HealthWise Group. Think of this as a large company that manufactures equipment for sports and physical activities, including those that interest you. These goods range from every type of ball imaginable (from golf to soccer to bowling) to hockey pads, leotards, and exercise bicycles.

Functions Depending on the services or products they provide, most organizations have departments that perform five basic functions. These are *accounting, production, marketing, personnel,* and *research* (see Figure 9-2). Their purposes are as follows:

- *Accounting:* This department keeps track of all financial activities. It pays bills, records payments, issues paychecks, and compiles periodic financial

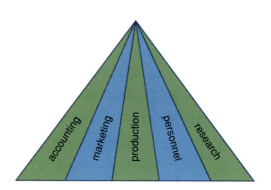

FIGURE 9-2
The five functions of an organization.

FIGURE 9-3
Production: This department is responsible for making products—in this case, running shoes.

statements. At HealthWise, for example, this department performs two major activities. First, it records bills and other financial transactions with sporting goods stores and produces financial statements. Second, it produces financial budgets and forecasts of projected financial performance to help managers run the business.

- *Production:* This department makes the product (see Figure 9-3). It takes in raw materials and puts people to work to turn out finished goods (or services). The department may be a manufacturing activity or, in the case of a retail store, for example, an operations activity. It manages purchases, inventories, and flows of goods and services. At HealthWise, this department is a big purchaser of steel and aluminum, materials that go into weight-lifting and exercise machines.

- *Marketing:* Advertising, promotion, and sales are handled by this department (see Figure 9-4). The people in this department plan, price, promote, sell, and

FIGURE 9-4
Marketing: This department handles advertising, promotion, and sales.

152
Information Systems

distribute goods and services to customers. At HealthWise they even get involved in what colors to put on the equipment that is sold.

- *Personnel:* This department finds and hires people and handles matters such as sick leave and retirement benefits. In addition, it is concerned with evaluation, compensation, and professional development. As you might imagine, HealthWise has rather good health benefits.

- *Research:* The Research (or Research and Development) Department has two tasks. First, it does product research. That is, it does basic research and relates new discoveries to the firm's current or new products. For instance, research people at HealthWise might look into new ideas from exercise physiologists about muscle development. They might use this knowledge in designing new physical fitness machines. Second, it does product development. That is, it develops and tests new products created by research people. It also monitors and troubleshoots new products as they are being produced.

Whatever your job in an organization, it is likely to be in one of these departments. Within the department, you may also be at one of the management levels.

Management Levels Most people who work in an organization are not managers, of course. At the base of the organizational pyramid are the secretaries, clerks, welders, drivers, and so on. These people produce goods and services. Above them, however, are various levels of managers—people with titles such as supervisor, director, regional manager, and vice president. These are the people who do the planning, organizing, and controlling necessary to see that the work gets done. At HealthWise, for example, the district sales manager for Oregon directs salespeople promoting exercise-related equipment to stores, gyms, and health clubs in that state. Other job titles might be vice president of marketing, director of personnel, or production manager.

Management in many organizations is divided into three levels: top-level, middle-level, and supervisors (see Figure 9-5). They may be described as follows:

- *Top management:* **Top-level managers** are concerned with *long-range planning* (also called *strategic planning*). They need information that will help them to plan the future growth and direction of the organization. For example, the HealthWise vice president of marketing might need to determine the demand and the sales strategy for a new product. Such a product might be a stationary exercise bicycle with a biometric feedback mechanism.

- *Middle management:* Top managers supervise **middle-level managers,** who deal with *control and planning* (also called *tactical planning*). Middle management implements the long-term goals of the organization. For example, the HealthWise regional sales manager for the Northwest sets sales goals for

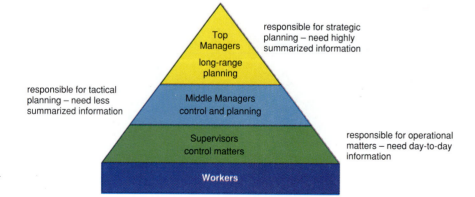

FIGURE 9-5
The concerns and tasks of management.

district sales managers in Washington, Oregon, and Idaho. He or she also monitors their sales performance.

- *Supervisors:* **Supervisors** manage and monitor the employees or workers, those who actually produce the goods and services. Thus, these managers have the responsibility relating to *operational matters.* They monitor day-to-day events and immediately take corrective action, if necessary. For example, at HealthWise, a production supervisor monitors the materials needed to build exercise bicycles. If parts begin to run low, the supervisor must take action immediately.

The concerns of the three levels of managers are represented in Figure 9-5.

Information Flow   Each level of management has different information needs. Top-level managers need information that is summarized in capsule form to reveal the overall condition of the business. They also need information from outside the organization, because top-level managers need to try to forecast and plan for long-range events. Middle-level managers need summarized information—weekly or monthly reports. They need to develop budget projections as well as to evaluate the performance of supervisors. Supervisors need detailed, very current day-to-day information on their units so that they can keep operations running smoothly.

To support these different needs, information *flows* in different directions (see Figure 9-6). The top-level managers, such as the chief executive officer (CEO), need information not only from below and from all departments. They also need information from outside the organization. For example, at HealthWise, they are deciding whether to introduce a line of hockey equipment in the southwestern United States. The vice president of marketing must look at relevant data. Such data might include availability of ice rinks and census data about the number of young people. It might also include sales histories on related cold-weather sports equipment.

For middle-level managers, the information flow is both horizontal and vertical across functional lines within the organization. For example, the regional sales managers at HealthWise set their sales goals by coordinating with their middle-manager counterparts in the production department. They are able to tell sales managers how many products will be produced, of what kind (expensive versus inexpensive), and when. An example of a product might be exercise bicycles. The regional sales managers also must coordinate with the strategic goals set by the top managers. They must set and monitor the sales goals for the supervisors beneath them.

For supervisory managers, information flow is primarily vertical. That is, they communicate mainly with their middle managers and with the workers beneath them. For instance, at HealthWise, production supervisors rarely communicate with people in the

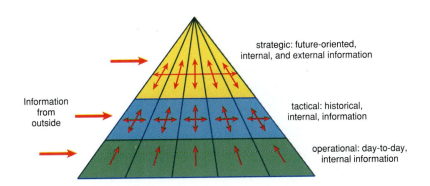

FIGURE 9-6
The flow of information within an organization.

FIGURE 9-7
For supervisory managers, information flow is vertical, from managers to workers beneath them.

accounting department. However, they are constantly communicating with production-line workers and with their own managers (see Figure 9-7).

Now we know how a large organization is usually structured and how information flows within the organization. But how is a computer-based information system likely to be set up to support its needs? And what do you, as a microcomputer user, need to know to use it?

The Levels of Computer-Based Information Systems

Computer-Based Information Systems Have Three Levels: Transaction Processing System, Management Information System, and Decision Support System.

All large organizations maintain a computerized database. This database records all routine activities: employees hired, materials purchased, products produced, and the like. Such recorded events are called **transactions.** From this database of transactions, large organizations develop two kinds of computerized information systems. As Figure 9-8

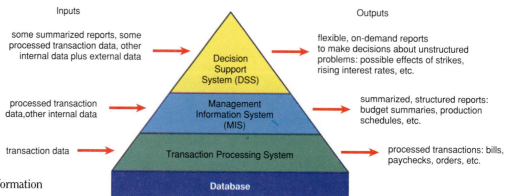

FIGURE 9-8
The three levels of information systems.

shows, these systems may be thought of as forming a three-level pyramid, each primarily (but not exclusively) supporting one of the three levels of management:

- *Transaction processing system:* The **transaction processing system** records day-to-day transactions such as customer orders, bills, inventory levels, and production output. The transaction processing system generates the database that acts as the foundation for the other two information systems.
- *Management information system:* The **management information system** (**MIS**) summarizes the detailed data of the transaction processing system in standard reports. Such reports might include production schedules and budget summaries.
- *Decision support system:* The **decision support system** (**DSS**) provides a flexible tool for analysis. The DSS helps managers make decisions about unstructured problems, such as the effect of events and trends outside the organization. Like the MIS, the DSS draws on the detailed data of the transaction processing system.

Let us describe these three kinds of information systems in more detail.

Transaction Processing Systems

A Transaction Processing System Records Routine Operations.

The purpose of a *transaction processing system* is to help an organization keep track of routine operations and to record these events in a database. The data from operations—for example, customer orders for HealthWise's products—makes up a database that records the transactions of the company. This database of transactions is used to support an MIS and a DSS.

One of the most essential transaction processing systems for any organization is in the accounting area (see Figure 9-9). Every accounting department handles six basic activities. Five of these are sales order processing, accounts receivable, inventory and purchasing, accounts payable, and payroll. All of these are recorded in the general ledger, the sixth activity. We explain these below.

Let us take a look at these six activities. They will make up the basis of the accounting system for almost any office you might work in.

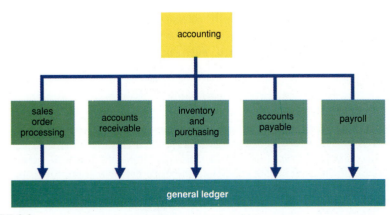

FIGURE 9-9
Transaction processing system for accounting.

FIGURE 9-10
Sales order processing records the demands for the company's product.

- The **sales order processing** activity records the customer requests for the company's product or service (see Figure 9-10). When an order comes in—a request for a set of barbells, for example—the warehouse is alerted to ship a product.

- The **accounts receivable** activity records money received from or owed by customers. HealthWise keeps track of bills paid by sporting goods stores and also by gyms and health clubs to which it sells directly.

- The parts and finished goods that the company has in stock are called **inventory**—all exercise machines in the warehouse, for example. An *inventory control system* keeps records of the number of each kind of part or finished good in the warehouse or company storage. **Purchasing** is the buying of materials and services. Often a *purchase order* is used. This is a form that shows the name of the company supplying the material or service and what is being purchased.

- **Accounts payable** refers to money the company owes its suppliers for materials and services it has received—steel and aluminum, for example.

- The **payroll** activity is concerned with calculating employee paychecks. Amounts are generally determined by the kind of job, hours worked, and kinds of deductions (such as taxes, social security, medical insurance). Paychecks may be calculated from employee time cards or, in some cases, supervisors' time sheets.

- The **general ledger** keeps track of all summaries of all the foregoing transactions. A typical general ledger system can produce income statements and balance sheets. *Income statements* show a company's financial performance—income, expenses, and the difference between them for a specific time period. *Balance sheets* list the overall financial condition of an organization. They include assets (for example, buildings and property owned), liabilities (debts), and how much of the organization (the equity) is owned by the owners.

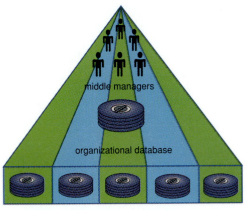

FIGURE 9-11
An MIS draws on the databases of more than one department.

Management Information Systems

A Management Information System Produces Summarized, Structured Reports.

A *management information system (MIS)* is a computer-based information system that produces standardized reports in summarized, structured form. It is used to support middle managers. An MIS differs from a transaction processing system in a significant way. Whereas a transaction processing system *creates* databases, an MIS *uses* databases. Indeed, an MIS can draw from the databases of *several* departments (see Figure 9-11). Thus, an MIS requires a *database management system* that integrates the databases of the different departments. Middle managers need summary data often drawn from across different functional areas.

An MIS produces reports that are *predetermined*. That is, they follow a predetermined format and always show the same kinds of content. Although reports may differ from one industry to another, there are three common categories of reports:

- **Periodic reports** are produced at regular intervals—weekly, monthly, or quarterly, for instance (see Figure 9-12). Examples are HealthWise's monthly sales or production report. The sales reports from district sales managers are combined into a monthly report for the regional sales managers. For comparison purposes, a regional manager is also able to see the sales reports of other regional managers.
- **Exception reports** call attention to unusual events. An example is a sales report that shows that certain items are selling significantly above or below marketing department forecasts. For instance, if fewer exercise bicycles are selling than were predicted for the Northwest sales region, the regional manager will receive an exception report. That report may be used to alert the district managers and salespeople to give this product more attention.
- The opposite of a periodic report, a **demand report** is produced on request. An example is a report on the numbers of, and jobs held by, women and minorities. Such a report is not needed periodically, but it may be required when requested by the U.S. government. At HealthWise, many government contracts require this information. It's used to certify that HealthWise is achieving certain government equal-opportunity guidelines.

FIGURE 9-12
Periodic reports may be produced weekly, monthly, or quarterly.

Decision Support Systems

A DSS Helps Decision Makers Analyze Unanticipated Situations.

Managers often must deal with unanticipated questions. For example, the HealthWise vice president in charge of manufacturing might ask, how would a strike affect production schedules? A *decision support system (DSS)* enables managers to get answers to unexpected and generally nonrecurring kinds of problems. They do this using interactive terminals (or microcomputers) and software. **Interactive** means that there is immediate communication between the user and the computer system. That is, when input data is entered into the computer, it is processed immediately. The output results are promptly displayed on the screen.

A DSS, then, is quite different from a transaction processing system, which simply records data. It is also different from a management information system, which summarizes data in predetermined reports. A DSS is used to *analyze* data. Moreover, it produces reports that do not have a fixed format. This makes the DSS a flexible tool for analysis.

Many DSSs are designed for large computer systems. However, microcomputers, with their increased power and sophisticated software, such as spreadsheet and database programs, are being used for DSS. Users of a DSS are managers, not computer programmers. Thus, a DSS must be easy to use—or most likely it will not be used at all. Commands need to be in language like English: "SEARCH" or "FIND," for instance. A HealthWise marketing executive might want to know which territories are not meeting their sales quotas and need additional advertising support. To find out, the executive might type "FIND ALL FOR SALES < QUOTA."

How does a decision support system work? Essentially, it consists of four parts: the user, system software, data, and what are called *decision models*.

The User The user could be you. In general, the user is someone who has to make decisions—a manager, and often a top-level manager.

System Software The system software is essentially the operating system—programs designed to work behind the scenes to handle detailed operating procedures. In order to give the user a good, comfortable interface, the software typically is "menu-driven." That is, the screen presents easily understood lists of commands, giving the user several options.

The Data The data in a DSS is stored in a database and consists of two kinds: *Internal* data—data from within the organization—consists principally of transactions from the transaction processing system. *External* data is data gathered from outside the organization. Examples are data provided by marketing research firms, trade associations, and the U.S. government (such as customer profiles, census data, and economic forecasts).

The Decision Models The **decision models** give the DSS its analytical capabilities. There are three basic types of models: strategic, tactical, and operational. *Strategic models* assist top-level managers in long-range planning, such as stating company objectives or planning plant locations. *Tactical models* help middle-level managers control the work of the organization, such as financial planning and sales promotion planning. Such models help middle-level managers implement top managers' long-range plans. *Operational models* help lower-level managers accomplish the day-to-day activities of the organization, such as evaluating and maintaining quality control.

Executive Information Systems

Executive Information Systems Are Specially Designed, Simplified Systems for Top Executives.

A DSS requires some training. Many top managers have other people in their offices running DSSs for them and reporting their findings. Top-level executives also want something more concise than an MIS—something that produces very focused, short status reports.

Executive information systems (EISs) are also known as **executive support systems (ESSs)**. They consist of sophisticated software that, like an MIS or a DSS, can draw together data from an organization's databases in meaningful patterns. However, an EIS is specifically designed to be easy to use. This is so that a top executive with little spare time can obtain essential information without extensive training. Thus, information is often displayed in very condensed form and in bold graphics.

Consider an executive information system used by the president of HealthWise. It is available on his IBM PS/2 Model 70. The first thing each morning, the president calls up the EIS on his display screen, as shown in Figure 9-13. Note that the screen gives a condensed account of activities in the five different areas of the company. (These are Accounting, Marketing, Production, Personnel, and Research.) On one particular morning, the EIS shows business in four areas proceeding smoothly. However, in the first area, Accounting, the percentage of late-paying customers—past due accounts—has increased 3 percent. Three percent may not seem like much. But HealthWise has had a history of problems with late payers, which has left the company at times strapped for cash. The president decides to find out the details. To do so, he presses *1* (corresponding to Accounting) on his keyboard.

The second screen shows information about past due accounts expressed in graphic form (see Figure 9-14, p. 160). The status of today's late payers is shown in red. The status of late payers at this time a year ago is shown in blue. The differences between today and a year ago are not appreciable for customers making their payments 11 or more days late. However, there is a significant difference between now and then for customers paying 1–10 days late. As a result, HealthWise has $180,653 in past due accounts today, compared to $175,391 a year ago. The president thus knows that he must take some

```
                 THE ALAMEX CORPORATION
              EXECUTIVE INFORMATION SUMMARY

     1. Accounting:  Past due accounts up 3%

     2. Marketing:   Total sales 5% over goal

     3. Production:  Production on schedule

     4. Personnel:   Labor negotiations progressing smoothly

     5. Research:    New steel alloy tested positively


     To obtain additional details, enter appropriate number
```

FIGURE 9-13
Example of first screen of an executive information system, showing information in condensed text form.

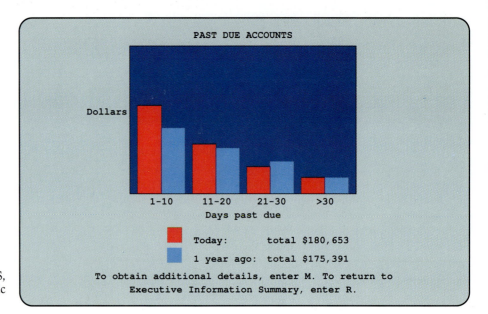

FIGURE 9-14
Example of second screen of EIS, showing details expressed in graphic form.

action to speed up customer payments. (For example, he might call this to the attention of the vice-president of Accounting. The vice-president might decide to offer discounts to early payers or charge more interest to late payers.)

EISs not only permit a firm's top executives to gain more direct access to information about the company's performance. Some of them also have electronic mail setups that allow managers to communicate directly with other executives. Some systems even have structured forms to help managers streamline their thoughts before sending electronic memos. In addition, an EIS may be organized to retrieve information from databases outside the company, such as business-news services. This enables a firm to watch for stories on competitors and stay current on relevant news events that could affect its business. For example, news of increased sports injuries caused by running and aerobic dancing, and the consequent lessened interest by people in these activities, might cause HealthWise to alter its sales and production goals for its line of fitness-related shoes.

A Look at the Future

Information from Executive Information Systems Will Be Made Available in Conference-Room Microcomputers and Eventually in Laptops.

Executive information systems, still being developed in many companies, are definitely the wave of the future. By the mid-1990s, some observers think, executives will use *laptops* to get EIS information while they are traveling. For that to happen, however, laptops will routinely need to weigh less than 2 pounds, startup must be instant, and updating of information must be automatic.

Before use of laptop EISs becomes popular, experts think, large companies will equip their *conference rooms* with microcomputers that have speedy communications with corporate computers around the world. These meeting-room computers will become part of management presentations, as well as serve executives visiting from elsewhere.

As executive information systems become more a part of corporate life, something else will happen. Competent computer end users (perhaps like yourself) who have risen through the management ranks will begin to demand more from their EISs. Thus, the relatively simple kinds of EISs often seen in use today will be replaced by systems that offer much more power and many more options.

Review Questions

1. Define what an *information system* is.
2. Name five departments often found in medium-sized and large organizations.
3. What is the purpose of each department?
4. Name three levels of management common within organizations.
5. What are the responsibilities of managers on each level?
6. What are differences in the kinds of information that managers at each level need?
7. Name the three levels of computer-based information systems.
8. What does a transaction processing system do?
9. What does a management information system do?
10. What does a decision support system do?
11. Describe the six activities of an accounting department.
12. What is the general ledger, and what purpose does it serve?
13. Distinguish among the three different reports produced by a management information system.
14. What is the principal difference between a management information system and a decision support system in the kind of reports produced?
15. Distinguish between the two kinds of data used in a DSS.
16. What is a decision model?
17. Distinguish among the three types of decision models used in a DSS.
18. Explain what an executive information system is.

Discussion Questions

1. The five functions or departments of an organization we described are accounting, production, marketing, personnel, and research. Clearly these departments would be found in, say, an automobile company. They would not be found—at least in the same form—in a department store, an employment agency, a hospital, or a college. Nevertheless, these organizations do offer products and/or services, and they probably (if large enough) have three management levels.

    How do you think these organizations would differ from the five-function structure we described in this chapter? Choose an organization and interview someone within it to find out. For example, what is the equivalent of "production" in a hotel or "marketing" in a hospital?

2. If you are presently attending school, you might want to learn what kinds of transactions are used in the database of a particular office or department. In this chapter, we described the transactions in the transaction processing system of an accounting department. See if you can discover the transactions that go into the database of some other department. Some departments you might consider are registrar, housing, fund raising, financial aid, and alumni affairs.

CHAPTER 9
Information Systems

VISUAL SUMMARY

Technology advances are making database storage and retrieval available to microcomputers everywhere. Microcomputers now have faster processing and more primary storage, more powerful secondary storage, and easier access to large databases. Computer-based information systems stored on these databases can be accessed by microcomputers. Thus, applications are being **down-sized** from mainframes to microcomputers.

How Information Flows

Information flows up and down among managers and sideways among departments.

Functions

Most organizations have departments that perform five functions:
- *Accounting*—manages finances, including orders, bills, paychecks.
- *Production*—makes the product (or service).
- *Marketing*—promotes and sells the product (or service).
- *Personnel*—hires people, manages employee benefits.
- *Research*—develops new products (or services).

Management Levels

Management in many organizations has three levels:
- **Top-level managers** are concerned with long-range planning, forecasting future events.
- **Middle-level managers** are concerned with control and planning, implementing long-term goals.
- **Supervisors** are concerned with control of operational matters, monitoring day-to-day events and supervising workers.

Information Flow

Information flows in different directions:
- For top-level managers—flow is up within the organization and into the organization from outside.
- For middle-level managers—flow is horizontally across and vertically within departments.
- For supervisors—flow is primarily vertical.

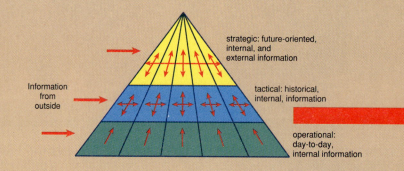

Visual Summary

```
        THE ALAMEX CORPORATION
        EXECUTIVE INFORMATION SYSTEM

1. Accounting:  Past due accounts up 3%
2. Marketing:   Total sales 5% over goal
3. Production:  Production on schedule
4. Personnel:   Labor negotiations progressing smoothly
5. Research:    New steel alloy tested positively

To obtain additional details, enter appropriate number
```

Executive Information System

An **executive information system (EIS)** or **executive support system (ESS)** draws data together from an organization's databases but is designed to be easier to use than MISs or DSSs. Information is displayed in condensed form and in bold graphics.

Levels of Information Systems

All organizations have computerized databases holding records of routine activities called **transactions**. Three levels of computerized information systems are: **transaction processing systems, management information systems,** and **decision support systems.**

Transaction Processing System

Records day-to-day transactions. An example is in accounting, which handles six activities:
- **Sales order processing**—records customer orders.
- **Accounts receivable**—shows money received from or owed by customers.
- **Inventory** and **purchasing**—shows availability of parts and finished goods and what supplies and services have been purchased.
- **Accounts payable**—shows money owed suppliers.
- **Payroll**—shows paychecks, deductions, benefits.
- **General ledger**—summarizes all of the above transactions.

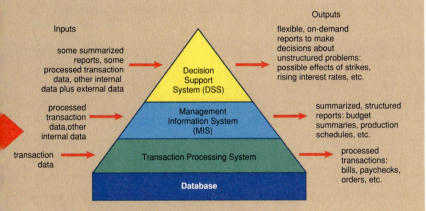

Management Information System (MIS)

Requires database management system to integrate the databases of different departments. An MIS produces *predetermined* reports:
- **Periodic reports**—produced at regular intervals.
- **Exception reports**—show unusual events.
- **Demand reports**—produced on request.

Decision Support System (DSS)

Enables managers to get answers for unanticipated questions. A DSS consists of:
- The *user*—usually a manager.
- The *software system*—contains easily understood list of commands ("menu-driven").
- The *data*—both internal data (transactions) from the organization and external data.
- A **decision model**—gives the DSS its analytical capabilities. It may be a *strategic model* to assist top managers in long-range planning; a *tactical model* to help middle-level managers control the work of the organization; or an *operational model* to help supervisors do day-to-day activities.

CHAPTER
Systems Analysis and Design

10

COMPETENCIES

After you have read this chapter, you should be able to:

1. Describe the six phases of the systems life cycle.

2. Discuss how problems or needs are identified during Phase 1, preliminary investigation.

3. Explain how the current system is studied and new requirements are specified in Phase 2, systems analysis.

4. Describe how a new or alternative information system is designed in Phase 3, systems design.

5. Explain how new hardware and software are acquired, developed, and tested in Phase 4, systems development.

6. Discuss how a new information system is installed and users are trained in Phase 5, systems implementation.

7. Describe Phase 6, systems maintenance, the systems audit and ongoing evaluation, to see if a new system is doing what it's supposed to.

8. Understand prototyping.

Most people in an organization are involved with an information system of some kind, as we saw in the previous chapter. Assuredly, most microcomputer users in the future will not only have access to such a system. They will also be part of one. For an organization to *establish* a system, and for users to make it truly useful, requires considerable thought and effort. Fortunately, there is a six-step problem-solving process for accomplishing this. It is known as *systems analysis and design*.

Big organizations can make big mistakes. For example, General Motors spent $40 billion putting in factory robots and other high technology in its automaking plants. It then removed much of this equipment and reinstalled that basic part of the assembly line—the conveyor belt. Why did the high-tech production systems fail? The probable reason was that GM didn't devote enough energy to training its work force in how to use the new systems.

The government also can make big mistakes. In one year, the new Internal Revenue Service computer system was so overwhelmed it could not deliver many tax refunds on time. The reason? Despite extensive testing of much of the system, a great deal of testing was *not* done. Thus, when the new system was phased in, the IRS found it could not process tax returns as quickly as it had hoped. Many tax refunds were delayed.

Both of these examples show the necessity for thorough planning—especially when an organization is trying to implement a new kind of system. Despite the spectacular failures above, there *is* a way to avoid such mistakes. It is called *systems analysis and design*.

Why should you, as a computer end user rather than a computer professional, know anything about this procedure? There are three reasons:

- Especially if you work for a large organization, a systems analysis and design study will sometime undoubtedly focus on your job. Knowing how the procedure works will enable you to deal with it better.

- You can use the steps in systems analysis and design to improve your own productivity within the organization. That is, you can use the procedure to solve problems within your own corner of the organization. Or you can use it to assist professionals in solving larger problems within the organization.

- You can use this procedure to reduce the risk of a new project's failing. Many new information systems fail or do not work well for a variety of reasons. If you use systems analysis and design, you can minimize the chances of these flaws occurring.

Systems Analysis and Design

Systems Analysis and Design Is a Six-Phase Problem-Solving Procedure for Examining an Information System and Improving It.

We described three types of information systems in the last chapter. Now let us consider: What, exactly, is a **system?** We can define it as a collection of activities and elements organized to accomplish a goal. As we saw in the last chapter, an *information system* is a collection of hardware, software, people, procedures, and data. These work together to provide information essential to running an organization. This information helps to produce a product or service and, for profit-oriented businesses, derive a profit.

Information—about orders received, products shipped, money owed, and so on—flows into an organization from the outside. Information—about what supplies have been received, which customers have paid their bills, and so on—also flows inside the organization. In order to avoid confusion, these flows of information must follow some system. However, from time to time, organizations need to change their information systems. Reasons may be organizational growth, mergers and acquisitions, new marketing opportunities, revisions in governmental regulations, availability of new technology, or other changes.

Systems analysis and design is a six-phase problem-solving procedure for examining an information system and improving it.

The six phases, known as the **systems life cycle** (see Figure 10-1), are as follows:

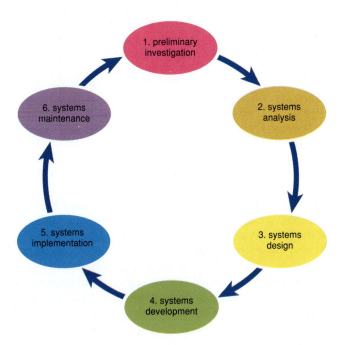

FIGURE 10-1
The six-phase systems life cycle.

1. *Preliminary investigation:* The information problems or needs are identified.
2. *Systems analysis:* The present system is studied in depth. New requirements are specified.
3. *Systems design:* A new or alternative information system is designed.
4. *Systems development:* New hardware and software are acquired, developed, and tested.
5. *Systems implementation:* The new information system is installed and adapted to the new system, and people are trained to use it.
6. *Systems maintenance:* In this ongoing phase, the system is periodically evaluated and updated as needed.

In organizations, the six-phase systems life cycle is used by computer professionals known as **systems analysts.** These people study an organization's systems to determine what actions to take and how to use computer technology to assist them. You may well find yourself working with such professionals in evaluating and changing parts of an organization with which you are involved. It's important that you understand how the six phases work. After all, you better than anyone should understand what is needed in your part of the organization. And you should be best able to express that need. Developing a large computer-based information system requires the close collaboration of end users and systems analysts.

The procedure is also one that *you* as an end user can perform, working on your own or with a systems analyst. In fact, you may *have* to use the procedure. More and more end users are developing their own systems. This is because in many organizations there is a three-year backlog of work for systems analysts. For instance, suppose you recognize that there is a need for certain information within your organization. Obtaining this information will require the introduction of new hardware and software. You go to seek expert help from systems analysts in studying these information needs. At that point you discover they are so overworked it will take them three years to get to your request! You can see, then, why many managers are learning to do these activities themselves. In any case, learning these six steps will give you skills that raise your computer competency. And they can also make you more valuable to an organization.

Let us now describe each phase in the systems life cycle.

Phase 1: Preliminary Investigation

In the Preliminary Investigation Phase, the Problems Are Briefly Identified and a Few Solutions Are Suggested.

The first phase is a **preliminary investigation** of a proposed project to determine the need for a new information system (see Figure 10-2, p. 167). This usually is requested by an end user or a manager who wants something done that is not presently being done. For example, suppose you work for Advantage Advertising, a fast-growing advertising agency. Advantage Advertising produces a variety of different ads for a wide range of different clients. The agency employs both regular staff people and on-call freelancers. One of your responsibilities is to keep track of the work performed for each client and the employees who performed the work. In addition, you are responsible for tabulating the final bill for each project.

How do you figure out how to charge which clients for which work done by which employees? This kind of problem is common not only in advertising agencies. It is found in many other service organizations (such as lawyers' and contractors' offices). Indeed, it is a problem in any organization where people charge for their "time" and clients need proof of hours worked.

FIGURE 10-2
Phase 1: preliminary investigation.

In Phase 1, the systems analyst—or the end user—is concerned with three tasks. These are (1) briefly defining the problem, (2) suggesting alternative solutions, and (3) preparing a short report. This report will help management decide whether to pursue the project further. (If you are an end user employing this procedure for yourself, you may not produce a written report. Rather, you would report your findings directly to your supervisor.)

Defining the Problem Defining the problem means examining whatever current information system is in use. Determining what information is needed, by whom, when, and why, is accomplished by interviewing and making observations. If the information system is large, this survey is done by a systems analyst. If the system is small, the survey can be done by the end user.

For example, suppose at Advantage Advertising account executives, copywriters, and graphic artists at present simply keep track of the time they spend on different jobs by making notations on their desk calendars. (Examples might be: "Client A, telephone conference, 15 minutes"; "Client B, design layout, 2 hours.") This approach is somewhat helter-skelter. Written calendar entries look somewhat unprofessional to be shown to clients. Moreover, often a large job has many people working on it. It is difficult to pull together all their notations to make up a bill for the client. Some freelancers work at home, and their time slips are not readily available. These matters constitute a statement of the problem: The company has a manual time-and-billing system that is slow and difficult to implement.

As an end user, you might experience difficulties with this system yourself. You're in someone else's office, and a telephone call comes in for you from a client. Your desk calendar is back in your own office. You have two choices. You can always carry your calendar with you. As an alternative, you can remember to note the time you spent on various tasks when you return to your office. The secretary to the account executive is continually after you (and everyone else at Advantage) to provide photocopies of your calendar. This is so that various clients can be billed for the work done on various jobs. Surely, you think, there must be a better way to handle time and billing.

Suggesting Alternative Systems This step is simply to suggest some possible plans as alternatives to the present arrangement. For instance, Advantage could hire more secretaries to collect the information from everyone's calendars (including telephoning those working at home). Or it could use the existing system of network-linked microcomputers that staffers and freelancers presently use. Perhaps, you think, there is already some off-the-shelf packaged software available that could be used for a time-and-billing system. At least there might be one that would make your own job easier.

Suppose you take this notion to your boss—that you find some way to automate your time-and-billing procedures, using your own microcomputer. Your boss feels that's a fine idea but points out that whatever you do will affect other people inside and outside Advantage Advertising. The thing to do, your manager says, is to check out your suggestion with the company's systems analyst.

The systems analyst, you find, is extremely busy—so much so that this individual's current work backlog amounts to three years' worth. You might wonder how an organization could stay in business with problems piling up for this long. That is precisely the reason for learning how to do systems analysis and design yourself. This, in fact, is what the systems analyst suggests you do. You do the work yourself; the analyst will help you wherever possible.

Preparing a Short Report For large projects, the systems analyst would write a short report summarizing the results of the preliminary investigation and suggesting alternative systems. The report may also include schedules for further development of the project. This document is presented to higher management, along with a recommendation to continue or discontinue the project. Management then decides whether to finance the second phase, the systems analysis.

For Advantage Advertising, your report might point out that billing is frequently delayed. It could say that some tasks may even "slip through the cracks" and not get charged at all. Thus, as the analyst has pointed out, you suggest the project might pay for itself merely by eliminating lost or forgotten charges.

Phase 2: Analysis

In the Systems Analysis Phase, the Present System Is Studied in Depth, and New Requirements Are Specified.

In Phase 2, **systems analysis,** data is collected about the present system (see Figure 10-3). This data is then analyzed, and new requirements are determined. We are not concerned with a new design here, only with determining the *requirements* for a new system. The design itself will be done in Phase 3. Systems analysis is concerned with gathering data and analyzing the data. It usually is completed with summarizing documentation.

Gathering Data Here the systems analyst—or the end user doing systems analysis—expands on the data gathered during Phase 1. She or he adds details about how the current system works. Data is obtained from observation and interviews. It is also obtained from studying documents that describe the formal lines of authority and standard operating procedures. One document is the **organization chart,** which shows levels of management and formal lines of authority (see Figure 10-4, top). You might note that an organization chart resembles the hierarchy of three levels of management we described in Chapter 9. The levels are top managers, middle managers, and supervisors (see Figure 10-4, bottom). In addition, data may be obtained from questionnaires given to people using the system.

Note in Figure 10-4 (top) that we have preserved the department labeled "Production." (However, the name in an advertising agency might be something like "Creative

169
Phase 2: Analysis

FIGURE 10-3
Phase 2: analysis.

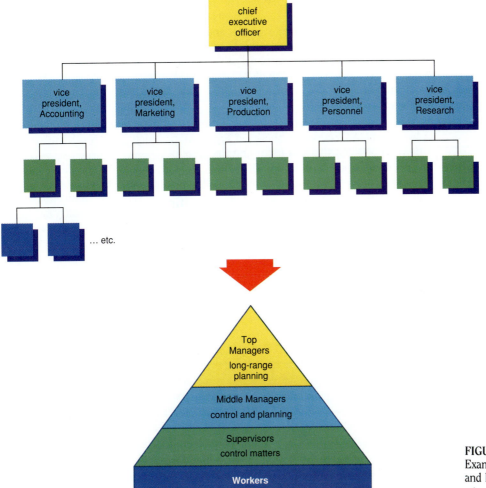

FIGURE 10-4
Example of an organization chart—and how it corresponds to the management pyramid.

Services.") Obviously, the products an advertising agency produces are ads: radio and television commercials, magazine and newspaper ads, billboard ads, and so on. In any case, if the agency is working on a major advertising campaign, people from several departments might be involved. There might also be people from different management levels within the departments. Their time charges will vary depending on how much they are paid.

Analyzing the Data In this step, the data is analyzed to learn how information currently flows and to pinpoint why it is not flowing appropriately. The whole point of this step is to apply *logic* to the existing arrangement to see how workable it is. Many times the current system is not operating correctly because prescribed procedures are not being followed. That is, the system may not really need to be redesigned. Rather, the people in it may need to be shown how to follow correct procedures.

Many different tools are available to assist systems analysts and end users in the analysis phase. Some of the principal ones are as follows:

- *Checklists:* Numerous checklists are available to assist in this stage. A **checklist** is a list of questions. It is helpful in guiding the systems analyst and end user through key issues for the present system.

    For example, one question might be "Can reports be easily prepared from the files and documents currently in use?" Another might be "How easily can the present time-and-billing system adapt to change and growth?"

- *Top-down analysis methodology:* The **top-down analysis methodology** is used to identify the top-level components of a complex system. Each component is then broken down into smaller and smaller components. This kind of tool makes each component easier to analyze and deal with.

    For instance, the systems analyst might look at the present kind of bill submitted to a client for a complex advertising campaign. The analyst might note the categories of costs—employee salaries, telephone and mailing charges, travel, supplies, and so on.

- *Grid charts:* A **grid chart** shows the relationship between input and output documents. An example is shown in Figure 10-5, which indicates the relationship between the data input and the outputs.

    For instance, a time card form is one of many inputs that produces a particular report, such as a client's bill. (Other inputs might be forms having to do with supplies, travel, and other costs of an advertising campaign.) Horizontal rows represent inputs, such as time card forms. Vertical rows represent output documents, such as different clients' bills. A checkmark at the intersection of a row and column means that the input document is used to create the output document.

Forms (Input)	Reports (output)		
	Report A	Report B	Report C
form 1	✓		✓
form 2	✓	✓	
form 3			✓
form 4			✓

FIGURE 10-5
Example of a grid chart.

Phase 2: Analysis

	Decision rules						
	1	2	3	4	5	6	7
Conditions If …	Y	Y	Y	Y	N	N	N
And if …	Y	N	Y	N	Y	Y	N
And if …	Y	Y	N	N	Y	N	N
Actions Then do …	✓						
Then do …		✓	✓		✓		
Then do …				✓		✓	✓

FIGURE 10-6
Example of a decision table.

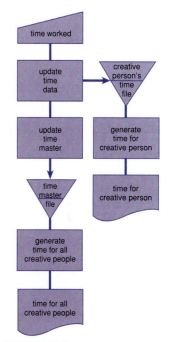

FIGURE 10-7
Example of a system flowchart.

- *Decision tables:* A **decision table** (see Figure 10-6) shows the decision rules that apply when certain conditions occur. It also shows what action should take place as a result. One rule might be "*If* creative time spent on account was by a freelance employee *and if* that employee worked overtime, *then* charge the client XXX amount." There might be different types of decision rules for different kinds of employees.
- *System flowcharts:* **System flowcharts** show the flow or input of data, processing and output, or distribution of information. An example of a system flowchart keeping track of time for advertising "creative people" is shown in Figure 10-7. The explanation of the symbols used (and others not used) appears in Figure 10-8. Note this describes the present manual, or noncomputerized, system. (A *system* flowchart is not the same as a *program* flowchart, which is very detailed. Program flowcharts are discussed in the next chapter.)
- *Data flow diagrams:* **Data flow diagrams** show the data or information flow within an information system. The data is traced from its origination through processing, storage, and output. An example of a data flow diagram is shown in Figure 10-9.
- *Automated design tools:* **Automated design tools** are software packages that evaluate hardware and software alternatives according to requirements given by the systems analyst. They are also called **computer-aided software engineering tools,** or **CASE tools.** They enable several systems analysts and programmers to automate and to coordinate their efforts on a project.

Documenting the Systems Analysis Stage In larger organizations, the systems analysis stage is typically documented in a report for higher management. The systems analysis report describes the current information system, the requirements for a new system, and a possible development schedule. For example, at Advantage Advertising, the system flowcharts will show the present flow of information in a manual time-and-billing system. Some of the boxes in the system flowchart might be replaced with symbols showing where a computerized information system could work better. For example, in

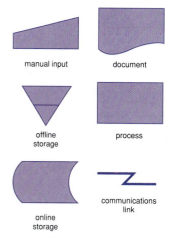

FIGURE 10-8
Guide to system flowchart symbols.

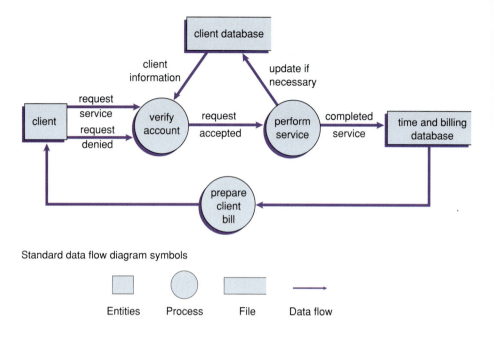

FIGURE 10-9
Example of a data flow diagram.

Figure 10-7, the offline storage symbol ("time master file") might be replaced by an online storage symbol. That is, the information in the file would be instantly accessible.

Management studies the report and decides whether to continue with the project. Let us assume your boss and higher management have decided to continue. You now move on to Phase 3, systems design.

Phase 3: Design

In the Systems Design Phase, a New or Alternative Information System Is Designed.

Phase 3, **systems design** (see Figure 10-10), consists of three tasks. They are (1) designing alternative systems, (2) selecting the best system, and (3) writing a systems design report.

FIGURE 10-10
Phase 3: design.

Designing Alternative Systems In almost all instances, more than one design can be developed to meet the information needs. Systems designers evaluate each alternative system for feasibility. By "feasibility" we mean three things:

- *Economic feasibility:* Will the costs of the new system be justified by the benefits it promises?
- *Technical feasibility:* Are reliable hardware, software, and trained people available to make the system work?
- *Operational feasibility:* Can the system actually be made to operate in the organization, or will people—employees, managers, clients—resist it?

Selecting the Best System When choosing the best design, managers must consider these four questions. (1) Will the system fit in with the organization's overall information system? (2) Will the system be flexible enough so it can be modified in the future? (3) Can it be made secure against unauthorized use? (4) Are the benefits worth the costs?

For example, one aspect you have to consider at Advantage Advertising is security. Should freelancers and outside vendors enter data directly into a computerized time-and-billing system, or should they continue to submit time slips manually? In allowing these people outside your organization to directly input information, are you also allowing them access to files they should not see? Do these files contain confidential information, perhaps information of value to rival advertising agencies?

Writing the Systems Design Report The report is prepared for higher management and describes the alternative designs. It presents the costs versus the benefits and outlines the effect of alternative designs on the organization. It usually concludes by recommending one of the alternatives.

Phase 4: Development

In the Systems Development Phase, New Hardware and Software Are Developed, Acquired, and Tested.

Phase 4, **systems development**, has three steps. They are: (1) developing software, (2) acquiring hardware, and (3) testing the new system (see Figure 10-11).

FIGURE 10-11
Phase 4: development.

Developing Software Applications software for the new information system can be obtained in two ways. It can be purchased as off-the-shelf packaged software and possibly modified, or it can be custom designed. If any of the software is to be specially created, the steps we will outline on programming (in Chapter 11) should be followed.

With the systems analyst's help, you have looked at time-and-billing packaged software designed for service organizations. Such organizations might include advertising agencies, law firms, and building contractors. The systems analyst points out that it is important that the time-and-billing data be collected in an appropriate manner so that it can be used for a variety of purposes. Such a system will not only help supervisory and middle managers do their jobs but also help top managers make decisions.

Unfortunately, you find that none of the packaged software will do. Most of the packages seem to work well for one person (you). However, none seem to be designed for many people working together. It appears, then, that software will have to be custom designed. (We discuss the process of developing software in Chapter 11 on programming.)

Acquiring Hardware Some new systems may not require new computer equipment, but others will. The kinds needed and the places they are to be installed must be determined. This is a very critical area. Switching or upgrading equipment can be a tremendously expensive proposition. Will a microcomputer system be sufficient as a company grows? Are networks expandable? Will microcomputers easily communicate with one another? Will people have to undergo costly training?

The systems analyst tells you that there are several different makes and models of microcomputers currently in use at Advantage Advertising. Fortunately, all are connected by a local area network to a file server that can hold the time-and-billing data. To maintain security, the systems analyst suggests that an electronic mailbox can be installed for freelancers and others outside the company to use to post their time charges. Thus, it appears that existing hardware will work just fine.

Testing the New System After the software and equipment have been installed, the system should be tested. Sample data is fed into the system. The processed information is then evaluated to see whether results are correct. Testing may take several months if the new system is complex.

For this step, you take some time and expense charges from an ad campaign that Advantage ran the previous year. You then ask some people in Creative Services to test it on the system. You observe that time is often charged in fractions of minutes and that the software ignores these fractions of time. You also see that some of the people in Creative Services have problems knowing where to enter their times. To solve the first problem, you must see that the software is corrected to allow for fractional minutes. To solve the second problem, you must see that the software is modified so that an improved user entry screen is displayed. After the system has been thoroughly tested and revised as necessary, you are ready to put it into use.

Phase 5: Implementation

In the Systems Implementation Phase, the New Information System Is Installed, and People Are Trained to Use It.

Another name for **systems implementation** (see Figure 10-12) is **conversion.** It is the process of changing—converting—from the old system to the new.

Types of Conversion There are four approaches to conversion: *direct, parallel, pilot,* and *phased.*

- In the **direct approach,** the conversion is done simply by abandoning the old and starting up the new. This can be risky. If anything is still wrong with the

FIGURE 10-12
Phase 5: implementation.

new system, the old system is no longer available to fall back on.

The direct approach is not recommended precisely because it is so risky. Problems, big or small, invariably crop up in a new system. In a large system, a problem might just mean catastrophe.

- In the **parallel approach,** old and new systems are operated side by side until the new one has shown it is reliable.

    This approach is low-risk. If the new system fails, the organization can just switch to the old system to keep going. However, keeping enough equipment and people active to manage two systems at the same time can be very expensive. Thus, the parallel approach is used only in cases in which the cost of failure or of interrupted operation is great.

- In the **pilot approach,** the new system is tried out in only one part of the organization. Later it is implemented throughout the rest of the organization.

    The pilot approach is certainly less expensive than the parallel approach. It also is somewhat riskier. However, the risks can be controlled because problems will be confined to only certain areas of the organization. Difficulties will not affect the entire organization.

- In the **phased approach,** the new system is implemented gradually over a period of time.

    This is an expensive proposition, because the implementation is done slowly. However, it is certainly one of the least risky approaches.

In general, the pilot and phased approaches are the most favored methods. Pilot is preferred when there are many people in an organization performing similar operations—for instance, all sales clerks in a department store. Phased is more appropriate for organizations in which people are performing different operations.

You and the systems analyst succeed in convincing the top managers of Advantage Advertising to take a pilot approach. The reason is that it is easy to select one trial group—the group of which you are a member. Moreover, this group is eager to try the new system. Thus, the new time-and-billing system is tried first with a handful of people in your particular department.

Training Training people is important, of course. Some people may begin training early, even before the equipment is delivered, so that they can adjust more easily. In some cases, a professional software trainer may be brought in to show people how to operate the system. However, at Advantage Advertising the time-and-billing software is simple enough that the systems analyst can act as the trainer.

Phase 6: Maintenance

Systems Maintenance Is First a Systems Audit and Then an Ongoing Evaluation to See Whether a System Is Performing Productively.

After implementation comes **systems maintenance,** the last step in the systems life cycle (see Figure 10-13). Maintenance has two parts—a *systems audit* and *periodic evaluation.*

In the **systems audit,** the system's performance is compared to the original design specifications. This is to determine if the new procedures are actually furthering productivity. If they are not, some further redesign may be necessary.

After the systems audit, the new information system is periodically evaluated and further modified, if necessary. All systems should be evaluated from time to time to see whether they are meeting the goals and providing the service they are supposed to.

For example, over time the transaction database at Advantage Advertising is expanded. After a year or two, the systems analyst might suggest that the time-and-billing part of it be reevaluated. For instance, the analyst might discover that telephone and mailing charges need to be separated. This might be because, with more people using the electronic mailbox and more people sharing data, telephone charges are now higher.

Figure 10-14 summarizes the six-step systems life cycle.

FIGURE 10-13
Phase 6: maintenance.

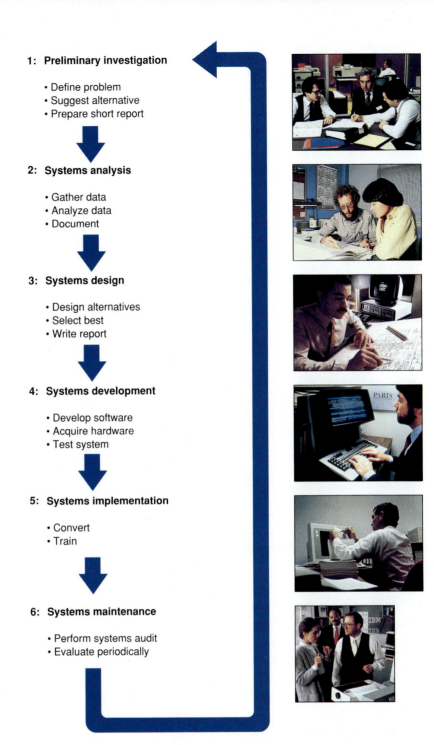

FIGURE 10-14
Summary of the systems life cycle.

Prototyping

Prototyping Consists of Devising a Model of a New System for Users to Try Out.

Is it necessary to follow every phase of the six phases of systems analysis and design? It may be desirable, but often there is no time to do so. For instance, hardware may change so fast that there is no opportunity for the evaluation, design, and testing just described.

A faster alternative is prototyping. **Prototyping** means to build a model, or prototype (pronounced "*proh*-toh-type"), that can be modified before the actual system is installed. For instance, the systems analyst for Advantage Advertising might develop a menu as a possible screen display for the time-and-billing system. Users could try it before the system is put into place.

Prototyping is considered a "quickie" way of building a system. It allows users to find out right away how a change in the system can help their work. However, relying on prototyping alone can be risky. It might lead to a system's being changed or installed without all costs and other matters being considered.

A Look at the Future

The Systems Life Cycle Will be Shortened Using a Method Called Rapid Applications Development.

The traditional systems life cycle can take a long time—sometimes years, in the case of large projects for large organizations. Because the pace of business is increasing, to stay competitive, corporations must shorten development life cycles so that products can be produced more quickly.

In the future, we will probably see increasing use of a new method called *rapid applications development (RAD),* which is intended to reduce development to months instead of years. RAD uses powerful development software (such as CASE), small teams, and highly trained people to produce applications much faster and with higher-quality results than traditional methods do.

Review Questions

1. What is a system?
2. What is the purpose of systems analysis and design?
3. What is the six-phase problem-solving procedure called?
4. List the six phases.
5. What do systems analysts do?
6. Describe the three steps required in Phase 1, preliminary investigation.
7. Describe the three steps required in Phase 2, systems analysis.
8. What is a checklist?
9. Describe top-down analysis methodology.
10. What is a grid chart?
11. Describe a decision table.
12. What is a system flowchart?
13. Explain the three steps in Phase 4, systems development.
14. Describe the four possible ways of carrying out Phase 5, systems implementation.
15. What is systems maintenance?
16. Describe prototyping.

Discussion Questions

1. Pick an activity in school or at work that you find inefficient or irritating. Is the preregistration system too confusing? Are the deadlines unrealistic for financial aid?

Is it hard to find a parking space? Is there a way to put Phase 1, preliminary investigation, of the systems life cycle into effect now to remedy this problem? This is the stage in which you would briefly identify problems and suggest a few possible solutions. You might then write a short report to help higher management decide whether to go ahead with Phase 2. See whether you can pose a few solutions and find out who is in a position of authority to make possible changes.

2. Interview a systems analyst at the computer center of your school or information systems or data processing department at work. Find out the analyst's opinion of the systems life cycle approach as used in the real world.

CHAPTER 10
Systems Analysis and Design

V I S U A L   S U M M A R Y

Systems analysis and design is a six-phase problem-solving procedure for examining an information system and improving it. The six phases are called the **systems life cycle.**

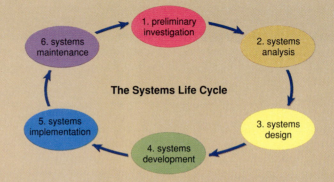

The Systems Life Cycle

1. preliminary investigation
2. systems analysis
3. systems design
4. systems development
5. systems implementation
6. systems maintenance

Phase 1: Preliminary Investigation

The **preliminary investigation** determines the need for a new information system. The tasks of this phase are:

— *Defining the problem*—what information is needed, by whom, when, and why.

— *Suggesting alternative systems.*

— *Preparing a short report*—a presentation to management.

Phase 2: Analysis

In **systems analysis** data is collected about the present system. The tasks of this phase are:

— *Gathering data*—using observation, interviews, and questionnaires and looking at documents such as the **organization chart,** which shows a company's functions and levels of management.

— *Analyzing the data*—using several analytical tools:
  • **Checklists** show what key issues to evaluate.
  • **Topdown analysis methodology** shows what are important and lesser components.
  • **Grid charts** show relationship between input and output documents.
  • **Decision tables** show what decision rules apply when certain conditions occur and what action should result.
  • **System flowcharts** show flow or input of data, processing and output, or distribution.
  • **Data flow diagrams** show data flow within an organization.

Phase 3: Design

Systems design consists of the following three tasks:

Designing alternative systems—using programming tools. Systems are evaluated for feasibility—economic, technical, and operational.

Selecting the best system—considering if the system will fit, is flexible, can be made secure, and is cost-effective.

Writing the systems design report—describing this phase for higher management.

— • **Automated design tools** are software packages to evaluate hardware and software alternatives. They are called **computer-aided software engineering (CASE) tools.**

— *Documenting systems analysis stage*—describing results for higher management.

181
Visual Summary

Prototyping, a faster alternative to the systems life cycle, consists of building a model of a new system for users to try out (e.g., possible screen display).

| Phase 4: Development | Phase 5: Implementation | Phase 6: Maintenance |

The **systems development** phase has three steps:

- **Developing software**—determining whether packaged or custom software is needed.
- **Acquiring hardware**—obtaining new computer equipment, if necessary.
- **Testing the new system**—using made-up data.

Systems implementation (conversion) is the process of changing from the old system to the new.

Types of Conversion

Four ways to convert are:
- **Direct approach**—abandoning the old and starting up the new.
- **Parallel approach**—operating the old and new side by side until the new one proves its worth.
- **Pilot approach**—trying out the new system in only one part of an organization.
- **Phased approach**—implementing the new system gradually.

Training

A software trainer may be used to train end users on the new system.

Systems maintenance has two parts:

Systems audit—in which a systems analyst compares the new system to design specifications to see if it is productive.

Periodic evaluation—the new system is periodically evaluated and revised, if necessary.

CHAPTER 11
Programming and Languages

COMPETENCIES

After you have read this chapter, you should be able to:

1. Understand the six steps of programming.

2. Describe Step 1, problem definition.

3. Discuss Step 2, the make-or-buy decision, whether to write a custom program or buy a prewritten program.

4. Describe Step 3, program design, and the program design tools of top-down program design, pseudocode, flowcharts, and logic structures.

5. Explain Step 4, coding the program.

6. Describe Step 5, debugging, and the tools for correcting programs.

7. Discuss Step 6, documenting the program.

8. Explain the five generations of programming languages.

How do you go about getting a job? You look through newspaper classified ads, check with employment services, write to prospective employers, and so on. In other words, you do some *general problem solving* to come up with a broad plan. This is similar to what you do in systems analysis and design. Once you have determined a *particular* job you would like to have, you then do some *specific problem solving*. That is what you do in programming. In this chapter, we describe programming in two parts. They are (1) the steps in the programming process and (2) some of the programming languages available.

Why should you need to know anything about programming? The answer is simple. You might need to deal with programmers in the course of your work. You may also be required to do some programming yourself in the future. A new field has emerged known as *end-user application development*. In this field, users like you create their own business application programs, without the assistance of a programmer. Thus, organizations avoid paying high software development costs. You and other end users avoid waiting months for programmers to get around to projects important to you.

In the last chapter, we described the six phases of the system life cycle. They are (1) preliminary investigation, (2) systems analysis, (3) systems design, (4) systems development, (5) systems implementation, and (6) systems maintenance. Programming is a part of Phase 4, as illustrated in Figure 11-1. Note that the bottom part of that figure constitutes an outline of the steps in programming. We follow that outline in this chapter.

Programs and Programming

Programming Is a Six-Step Procedure for Producing a Program—a List of Instructions—for the Computer.

What exactly *is* programming? Many people think of it as simply typing words into a computer. That may be part of it—but certainly not all of it. Programming, as we've hinted, is actually a *problem-solving procedure*.

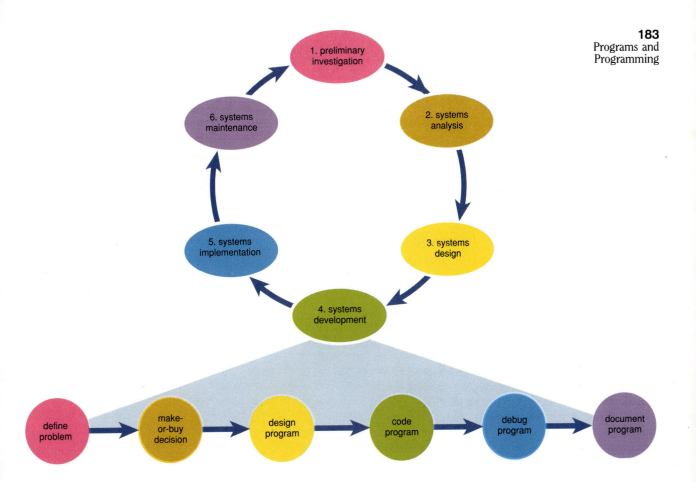

FIGURE 11-1
Where programming fits in the system life cycle.

What Is a Program? To see how programming works, think what a program is. A *program* is a list of instructions for the computer to follow to accomplish the task of processing data into information. The instructions are made up of statements used in a programming language, such as BASIC, Pascal, or C.

Applications software or *applications programs,* as we said in Chapter 1, are the kind of programs that do "end-user work." These are things such as word processing and accounting tasks. *Systems software,* we said, is concerned with "background" tasks such as housekeeping chores involving computer operations. In this chapter we are concerned with applications programs.

By now you are probably familiar with one kind of applications program—the *purchased, prewritten* programs. These are so-called off-the-shelf programs such as word processors, spreadsheets, and database managers, which may be purchased on diskettes. However, applications programs may also be *created* or *custom-made*—either by a professional programmer or by you, the end user. In Chapter 10, we saw that the systems analyst looked into the availability of time-and-billing software for Advantage Advertising. Will off-the-shelf software do the job, or should it be custom written? This is one of the first things that needs to be decided in programming.

What Is Programming? A program is a list of instructions for the computer to follow to process data. **Programming** is a six-step procedure for creating that list of instructions. Only *one* of those steps consists of typing (keying) words into a computer.

The six steps, as shown in the bottom part of Figure 11-1, are as follows:

1. Define the problem.
2. Decide whether to make or buy software.
3. Design the program.
4. Code—that is, write—the program; this is the "typing in" part.
5. Test—that is, debug—the program.
6. Document the program.

Step 1: Define the Problem

In the Definition Step, the Program's Objectives, Outputs, Inputs, and Processing Requirements Are Determined.

Program definition is also called **program analysis.** It requires that the programmer—or you, the end user, if you are following this procedure—specify four tasks. They are (1) the program's objectives, (2) the desired output, (3) the input data required, and (4) the processing requirements. Let us consider these.

Determining Program Objectives You solve all kinds of problems every day. A problem might be deciding how to commute to school or work or which homework or report to do first. Thus, every day you determine your *objectives*—the problems you are trying to solve. Programming is the same. You need to make a clear statement of the problem you are trying to solve (see Figure 11-2). An example would be "I want a time-and-billing system to keep track of the time I spend on different jobs for different clients of Advantage Advertising."

Determining the Desired Output It is best always to specify outputs before inputs. That is, you should list what you want to *get out of* the computer system. Then you should determine what will *go into* it. The best way to do this is to draw a picture. You—the end user, not the programmer—should sketch or write what you want the output to look like in its final form. It might be printed out or displayed on the monitor.

For example, if you want a time-and-billing report, you might write out or draw something like that shown in Figure 11-3. Another form of output from the program might be bills to clients.

FIGURE 11-2
Problem definition: write a clear statement of the problem.

Client name: Allan Realty Month and year: Jan '92

Date	Worker	Regular Hours & Rate	Overtime Hours & Rate	Bill
1/2	M. Jones	5 @ $10	1 @ $15	$65.00
	K. Williams	4 @ $30	2 @ $45	$210.00
Total				

FIGURE 11-3
End user's handwritten example of printed output desired.

Determining the Input Data Once you know the output you want, you can determine the input data and the source of this data. For example, for a time-and-billing report, you can specify that one source of data to be processed should be time cards. These are usually logs or statements of hours worked submitted on paper forms. The log shown in Figure 11-4 is an example of the kind of input data used in Advantage Advertising's manual system. (Note that military time is used. For example, instead of writing "5:45 P.M.," people would write "1745.")

Determining the Processing Requirements Here you define the processing tasks that must happen for input data to be processed into output. For Advantage, one of the tasks for the program will be to add the hours worked for different jobs for different clients.

First you must determine all the processing requirements. Then you can find out whether you need to create a special program to handle them or if you can buy an existing program. This leads to the next step, the make-or-buy decision.

Daily Log

Worker:
Date:

Client	Job	Time in	Time out
A	TV commercial	800	915
B	Billboard ad	935	1200
C	Brochure	1315	1545
A	Magazine ad	1600	1745

FIGURE 11-4
Example of statement of hours worked—manual system. Hours are expressed in military time.

FIGURE 11-5
Make-or-buy: test software to decide if purchasing packaged software will solve the problem or if the software must be custom-made.

Step 2: Make-or-Buy Decision

In the Make-or-Buy Step, You Must Determine Whether Applications Software Must Be Custom Written or May Be Prewritten.

After the problem definition step, you have a **make-or-buy decision** to make. Will you have to *make* the software—have the program custom written by a programmer—or can you *buy* it as a prewritten program? (See Figure 11-5.) Obviously, just being able to use off-the-shelf purchased software can save you time. Many such programs exist. However, you may not find anything quite meets your needs. This means a programmer may have to adapt a commercially available program or create one from scratch.

Thus, you need to evaluate the feasibility of the program. You need to see whether the potential improvements of a custom-made program will outweigh the costs and time needed to write it. You should analyze the pluses and minuses.

Can you buy an existing time-and-billing program that will meet your needs? This is, in fact, a common requirement. Indeed, you find in your search with the systems analyst that several time-and-billing systems are available. Unfortunately, none of them exactly meets your needs. The systems analyst points out that if others in your organization will use the time-and-billing system, that will justify the cost of developing your own system. This system would be used for everyone working for Advantage Advertising. All workers must report their total hours. They must also state which hours (or portions) were spent working on particular projects so that clients can be billed correctly. You and the systems analyst therefore decide that you will *make* rather than *buy* the software.

Step 3: Design the Program

In the Design Step, a Solution Is Created Using Programming Techniques Such as Top-Down Program Design, Pseudocode, Flowcharts, and Logic Structures.

If you decide that the software must be custom-made, you then take the **program design** step (see Figure 11-6). Here you plan a solution, preferably using **structured**

Step 3:
Design the Program

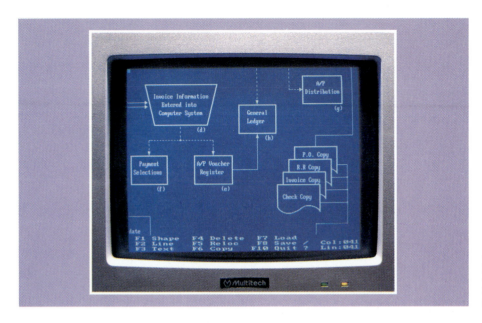

FIGURE 11-6
Design: in custom-made programs, flowcharts are drawn to map out a solution.

programming techniques. These techniques consist of the following: (1) top-down program design, (2) pseudocode, (3) flowcharts, and (4) logic structures.

Top-Down Program Design First you determine the outputs and inputs of the computer program you will create. Then you can use **top-down program design** to identify the program's processing steps. Such steps are called **program modules** (or just **modules**). Each module is made up of logically related program statements.

Figure 11-7 shows an example of a top-down program design for a time-and-billing

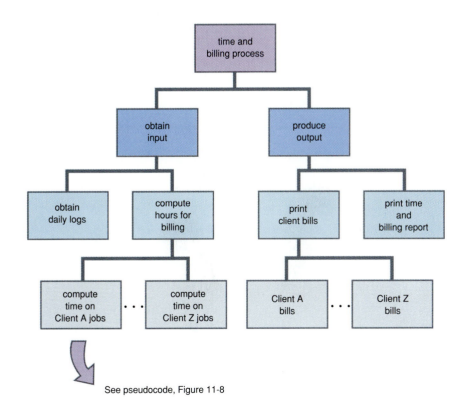

FIGURE 11-7
Example of top-down program design.

FIGURE 11-8
Example of pseudocode.

> **Compute time for Client A**
>
> Set total regular hours and total overtime hours to zero.
> Get time in and time out for a job.
> If worked past 1700 hours, then compute overtime hours.
> Compute regular hours.
> Add regular hours to total regular hours.
> Add overtime hours to total overtime hours.
> If there are more jobs for that client, go back and compute time
>   for that job as well.

See flowchart, Figure 11-9

report. Each of the boxes shown is a module. Under the rules of top-down design, each module should have a single function. The program must pass in sequence from one module to the next until all modules have been processed by the computer. Three of the boxes—"Obtain input," "Compute hours for billing," and "Produce output"—correspond to the three principal computer system operations. These operations are *input, process,* and *output.*

Pseudocode **Pseudocode** ("*soo*-doh-code") is a narrative form of the logic of the program you will write. It is like doing a summary or an outline form of the program. Figure 11-8 shows the pseudocode you might write for one module in the time-and-billing program. This shows the reasoning behind determining hours—including overtime hours—worked for different jobs for one client, Client A. Again, note this expresses the *logic* of what you want the program to do.

Flowcharts We mentioned system flowcharts in the previous chapter. Here we are concerned with **program flowcharts.** These graphically present the detailed sequence of steps needed to solve a programming problem. Figure 11-9 explains the standard flowcharting symbols and gives an example of a program flowchart. This flowchart expresses all the logic for just *one* module—"Compute time on Client A jobs"—in the top-down program design.

Let us proceed to explain the steps in the flowchart. The numbers below correspond to those in Figure 11-9.

① Initialize total regular hours and total overtime hours to be zero.
② Read in information about when the job was started and completed.
③ Check to see if there was any overtime on the job.
④ If there was overtime, compute how much.
⑤ Compute the number of regular hours.
⑥ Add the number of regular hours to a running total of regular hours for this client.
⑦ Add the number of overtime hours to a running total of overtime hours for this client.
⑧ If there are more jobs for this client, go back to step 1 for the next job.
⑨ Stop if no more jobs for this client.

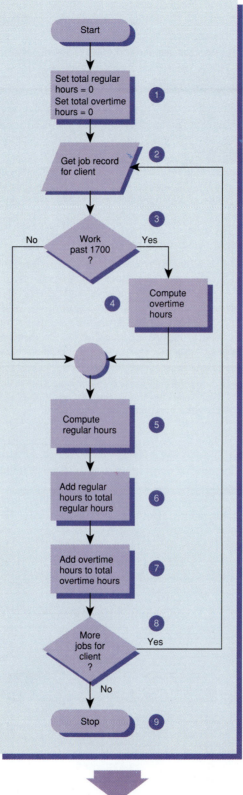

FIGURE 11-9
Flowchart symbols and example of a program flowchart for computing time worked.

Perhaps you can see from this why a computer is a computer, and not just a fancy adding machine. A computer not only does arithmetic. It can also *make comparisons*—whether something is greater than or less than, equal to or not equal to.

But have we skipped something? How do we *know* which kind of twists and turns to put in a flowchart so that it will logically work? The answer is the use of logic structures.

Logic Structures How do you link the various parts of the flowchart? The best way is a combination of three **logic structures** called *sequence, selection,* and *loop.* Using these arrangements enables you to write so-called *structured programs,* which take much of the guesswork out of programming. Let us look at the logic structures.

- In the **sequence structure,** one program statement follows another (see Figure 11-10). Consider, for example, the "compute time" flowchart (Figure 11-9 on p. 189). The two "add" boxes are "Add regular hours to total regular hours" and "Add overtime hours to total overtime hours." They logically follow each other. There is no question of "yes" or "no," of a decision suggesting other consequences.

- The **selection structure** occurs when a decision must be made. The outcome of the decision determines which of two paths to follow (see Figure 11-11). This structure is also known as an **IF-THEN-ELSE structure,** because that is how you can formulate the decision.

  Consider, for example, the selection structure in the "compute time" flowchart (Figure 11-9), which is concerned about computing overtime hours. It might be expressed in detail as follows:

  **IF hour finished for this job is later than or equal to 1700 hours (5:00 P.M.),
  THEN overtime hours equals the number of hours past 1700 hours.
  ELSE the overtime hours equal zero.**

- The **loop structure** describes the activity in which a process may be repeated as long as a certain condition remains true. The structure is called a "loop" or "iteration" because the program loops around (iterates or repeats) again and again.

  The loop structure has two variations: *DO UNTIL* and *DO WHILE* (see Figure 11-12). The **DO UNTIL structure** is the most used form. An example is as follows.

  DO read in job information UNTIL there are no more jobs.

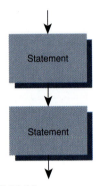

FIGURE 11-10
Sequence logic structure.

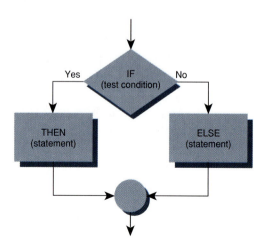

FIGURE 11-11
Selection (IF-THEN-ELSE) logic structure.

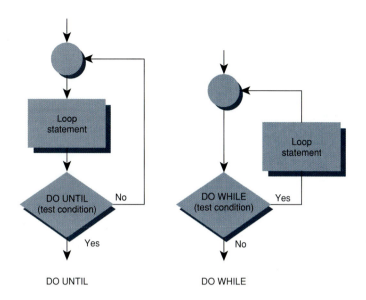

FIGURE 11-12
Loop logic structures: DO UNTIL and DO WHILE.

An example of the **DO WHILE structure** is:

DO read in job information WHILE (that is, as long as) there are more jobs.

There is a difference between the two loop structures. If you have several statements that need to be repeated, the decision when to *stop* repeating them can appear at the *beginning* of the loop (DO WHILE). Or, it can appear at the *end* of the loop (DO UNTIL). The DO UNTIL loop means that the loop statements will be executed at least once. This is because the loop statements are executed *before* you are asked whether to stop.

Step 4: Code the Program
"Coding" Is the Actual Writing of the Program, Using a Programming Language.

Writing the program is called **coding** (see Figure 11-13, p. 192). Here you use the logic you developed in the program design step to actually write the program. That is, you write out—using pencil and paper or typing on a computer keyboard—the letters, numbers, and symbols that make up the program. An example of the handwritten code for the "compute time" module is shown in Figure 11-14 on p. 192. This is the "program code" that instructs the computer what to do. Coding is what many people think of when they think of programming. As we've pointed out, however, it is only one of the six steps in the programming process.

The Good Program What are the qualities of a good program? Above all, it should be reliable; that is, it works under most conditions. It should catch obvious and common input errors. It should also be understandable by programmers other than the person who wrote it. After all, someone may need to make changes in the program in the future. The best way to code effective programs is to write so-called *structured programs,* using the logic structures described in Step 3.

Which Language? An important decision is which language to write the program in. There are hundreds of programming languages, but for microcomputers the most popular have been BASIC and Pascal. We describe programming languages later in this

192
Programming
and Languages

FIGURE 11-13
Coding: the written program is typed into a computer.

```
begin
total_regular := 0;
total_overtime := 0;
while not eof(input_file) do
    begin
    readln (input_file, hour_in, minute_in, hour_out, minute_out);
    if (hour_out >= 17) then
        overtime := (hour_out - 17) + (minute_out/60)
    else
        overtime := P;
    regular := (hour_out - hour_in) + (minute_out - minute_in)/60) - overtime;

    total_regular := total_regular + regular;
    total_overtime := total_overtime = overtime;
    end;
end.
```

FIGURE 11-14
Handwritten code of "compute time" module. (The number "17" stands for "1700 hours," or 5 P.M.)

See Figure 11-15

chapter. First you must determine the program's logic. Then you can write (code) it in whatever language you choose that is available on your computer. Figure 11-15 presents a Pascal program for the "compute time" module. The next step is debugging, or testing, the program.

```
Program compute_time:

var
   input_file : text;
   total_regular,
   total_overtime,
   regular,
   overtime : real;
   hour_in,
   minute_in,
   hour_out,
   minute_out : integer;

begin
assign(input_file,'time.txt');
reset(input_file);

total_regular := 0;
total_overtime := 0;
while not eof(input_file) do
   begin
   readln(input_file,hour_in,minute_in,hour_out,minute_out);
   if (hour_out >= 17)then
      overtime := (hour_out - 17) + (minute_out/60)
   else
      overtime := 0;
   regular := (hour_out - hour_in) + ((minute_out - minute_in)/60) - overtime;
   total_regular := total_regular + regular;
   total_overtime := total_overtime + overtime;
   end;

writeln('regular = ',total_regular);
writeln('overtime = ',total_overtime);
end.
```

FIGURE 11-15
The "compute time" program written in Pascal.

Step 5: Debug the Program

"Debugging" Is Testing a Program and Correcting Syntax and Logic Errors.

Debugging is a programmer's word for *testing* and then *eliminating* errors ("getting the bugs out"). It means running the program you have written on a computer and then fixing the parts that do not work (see Figure 11-16, p. 194). Programming errors are of two sorts: *syntax errors* and *logic errors*.

Syntax Errors A **syntax error** is a violation of the rules of whatever language the program is being written in. For example, in the programming language called Pascal, the instruction "write ln" is wrong. It is supposed to be "writeln." That is an example of a syntax error.

Logic Errors A **logic error** is when the programmer has used an incorrect calculation or left out a programming procedure. For instance, if you give the wrong rate for overtime hours, this is an example of a logic error.

FIGURE 11-16
Debugging: the program is tested for errors, using sample data.

The Debugging Process Several methods have been devised for finding and removing both types of errors, as follows.

- *Desk checking:* In **desk checking,** a programmer sitting at a desk checks (proofreads) a printout of the program. The programmer goes through the listing line by line looking for syntax and logic errors.
- *Manual testing with sample data:* Both correct and incorrect data is run through the program—manually, not with a computer—to test for correct processing results.
- *Attempt at translation:* The program is run through a computer, using a translator program. The translator attempts to translate the written program from the programming language (such as Pascal) into the machine language. Before the program will run, it must be free of syntax errors. Such errors will be identified by the translating program.
- *Testing sample data on the computer:* After all syntax errors have been corrected, the program is tested for logic errors. Sample data is used to test the correct execution of each program statement.

Step 6: Document the Program

"Documenting" Means Writing a Description of the Purpose and Process of the Program.

Documentation consists of written descriptions and procedures about a program and how to use it. Actually, documentation is not something done just at the end of the programming process. It should be carried on throughout all the programming steps. Documentation is important for people who may be involved with the program in the future (see Figure 11-17), as follows:

- *For users:* End users need to know how to use the software. Some organizations may offer training courses to guide users through the program. However, other organizations may expect users to be able to learn a package just from the written documentation. An example of this sort of documentation is the manuals that accompany purchased software.

FIGURE 11-17
Documentation is needed so that others may understand the program.

- *For operators:* Documentation must be provided for computer operators. If the program sends them error messages, for instance, they need to know what to do about them.
- *For programmers:* Even the creator of the original program may not remember much about it. Other programmers wishing to update and modify it—that is, perform **program maintenance**—may find themselves frustrated without adequate documentation. This kind of documentation should include text and program flowcharts, program listings, and sample output. It might also include system flowcharts to show how the particular program relates to other programs within an information system.

This completes the six steps of the programming process. However, we need to return to Step 4, coding, and briefly discuss programming languages.

Five Generations of Programming Languages

Languages Are Described as Occurring in "Generations," from Machine Languages to Natural Languages.

Computer professionals talk about **levels** or **generations of programming languages,** ranging from "low" to "high." Programming languages are called *lower level* when they are closer to the language the computer itself uses. The computer understands the 0s and 1s that make up bits and bytes. They are called *higher level* when they are closer to the language humans use—that is, for English speakers, more like English.

There are five generations of programming languages. These are (1) machine languages, (2) assembly languages, (3) procedural languages, (4) problem-oriented languages, and (5) natural languages. Let us briefly consider these.

Machine Languages: The First Generation We mentioned earlier that data starts with a *byte.* A byte is made up of *bits,* consisting of 1s and 0s. These 1s and 0s may correspond to electricity's being on or off in the computer. They may also correspond to a magnetic pulse's being present or absent on storage media such as disk or tape. From this two-state system have been built coding schemes that allow us to construct letters, numbers, punctuation marks, and other special characters. Examples of these coding schemes, as we saw, are ASCII and EBCDIC.

Data represented in 1s and 0s is said to be written in **machine language.** To see how hard this is to understand, imagine if you had to code this:

$$11110010011100111010010000100000111000000101011$$

Machine languages also vary according to make of computer—another characteristic that makes them hard to work with.

Assembly Languages: The Second Generation **Assembly languages** have a clear advantage over the 1s and 0s of machine language because they use abbreviations. Abbreviations are easier for human beings to remember. The machine language code we gave above could be expressed in assembly language as

$$\text{PACK 210(8,13),02B(4,7)}$$

This is still pretty obscure, of course, and so assembly language is also considered low-level.

Assembly languages also vary from computer to computer. With the third generation, we advance to high-level languages, many of which are considered **portable.** That is, they can be run on more than one kind of computer—they are "portable" from one machine to another.

Procedural Languages: The Third Generation People are able to understand languages that are more like their own language (e.g., English) than machine languages or assembly languages. However, most people require some training in order to use higher-level languages. This is particularly true of procedural languages.

Procedural languages are programming languages with names like BASIC, Pascal, C, COBOL, and FORTRAN. They are called "procedural" because they are designed to express the logic—the procedures—that can solve general problems. Procedural languages, then, are intended to solve *general* problems. COBOL, for instance, is used in all kinds of business applications, such as payroll and inventory control. It is fourth-generation languages, discussed next, that are intended to solve *specific* problems.

For a procedural language to work on a computer, it must be translated into machine language so the computer can understand it. Depending on the language, this translation is performed by either a *compiler* or an *interpreter*.

- A **compiler** converts the programmer's procedural language program, called the *source code,* into a machine language code, called the *object code*. This object code can then be saved and run later. Examples of procedural languages using compilers are Pascal, COBOL, and FORTRAN.
- An **interpreter** converts the procedural language one statement at a time into machine code just before it is to be executed. No object code is saved. An example of a procedural language using an interpreter is BASIC.

What is the difference between using a compiler and using an interpreter? When a program is run, the compiler requires two steps before the program can be executed. These two steps are source code and object code. The interpreter, in contrast, requires only one step. The advantage of a compiler language is that once the object code has been obtained, the program executes faster. The advantage of an interpreter language is that programs are easier to develop.

The principal procedural languages with which you may come in contact are as follows:

- *BASIC:* Short for *B*eginner's *A*ll-purpose *S*ymbolic *I*nstruction *C*ode, **BASIC** is the most popular microcomputer language. Widely used on microcomputers and easy to learn, it is suited to both beginning and experienced programmers. It is also interactive—user and computer communicate with each other directly during the writing and running of programs.

- *Pascal:* Another language that is widely used on microcomputers and easy to learn is **Pascal.** It is named after Blaise Pascal, a seventeenth-century French mathematician. Pascal has become quite popular in computer science educational programs. One advantage is that it encourages programmers to follow structured coding procedures. It also works well for graphics. We showed an example of Pascal in Figure 11-15.

- *C:* **C** is a general-purpose language that also works well with microcomputers. It is useful for writing operating systems, database programs, and some scientific applications. Programs are portable: They can be run without change on a variety of computers.

- *COBOL:* **COBOL**—which stands for *CO*mmon *B*usiness-*O*riented *L*anguage—is the most frequently used programming language in business. Until recently, COBOL was available only for use with large computers. Now, however, versions exist that run on microcomputers. Though harder to learn than BASIC, its logic is easier for a person who is not a trained programmer to understand.

    Writing a COBOL program is sort of like writing the outline for a term paper. The program is divided into four divisions. The divisions in turn are divided into sections, which are divided into paragraphs, then into statements. The *Identification Division* gives the name of the program, author, and other identifying information. The *Environment Division* describes the computer or computers to be used. The *Data Division* describes the data to be used in the program. The *Procedure Division* describes the actual processing procedures.

- *FORTRAN:* Short for *FOR*mula *TRAN*slation, **FORTRAN** is the most widely used scientific and mathematical language in the world. It is very useful for processing complex formulas. Thus, many scientific and engineering programs have been written in this language.

- *Ada:* **Ada** is named after an English countess regarded as the first programmer. It was developed under the sponsorship of the U.S. Department of Defense. Originally designed for weapons systems, it has commercial uses as well. Because of its structured design, modules (sections) of a large program can be written, compiled, and tested separately before the entire program is put together.

- *RPG:* **RPG,** short for *R*eport *P*rogram *G*enerator, enables people to prepare business reports quickly and easily. A user need not be concerned with solution procedures so much as with the input and output. Users can easily learn to fill out specifications in detailed coding forms for common business applications like accounts receivable and accounts payable. A report will then be produced with little effort.

Problem-Oriented Languages: The Fourth Generation

Third-generation languages are valuable, but they require training in programming. Problem-oriented languages require little special training on the part of the user.

Unlike general-purpose languages, **problem-oriented languages** are designed to solve specific problems. Some of these fourth-generation languages are used for very specific applications. For example, IFPS (interactive financial planning system) is used to develop financial models. Many consider Lotus 1-2-3 and dBASE to be flexible fourth-generation languages. This group also includes query languages and applications generators:

- *Query languages:* **Query languages** enable nonprogrammers to use certain easily understood commands to search and generate reports from a database. An example is the commands used on an airline reservations system by clerks needing flight information.
- *Applications generators:* An **applications generator** is software with numbers of modules—logically related program statements—that have been preprogrammed to accomplish various tasks. An example would be a module that calculates overtime pay. The programmer can simply state which task is needed for a particular application. The applications generator will select the appropriate modules and run a program to meet the user's needs.

Natural Languages: The Fifth Generation **Natural languages** are still being developed. They are designed to give people a more human ("natural") connection with computers. The languages are human languages: English, French, Japanese, or whatever. Researchers also hope that natural languages will enable a computer to *learn*—to "remember" information, as people do, and to improve upon it. Clearly, this area is extremely challenging.

Figure 11-18 summarizes the five generations of languages.

A Look at the Future

Ways of Making Program Development More Efficient Include Computer-Aided Software Engineering (CASE) and Object-Oriented Programming.

Ten years ago, a computer program of a few thousand lines was considered long. Today a word processing program may contain 50,000 lines. Programs needed to run modern aircraft, medical equipment, or financial institutions can run to millions of lines. Thus, in the future, programming will become only more important, not less. To appreciate this, consider that in early 1990 *one* software error (bug) plunged American Telephone & Telegraph's long-distance telephone network into chaos for nine hours. During this time, AT&T was able to put through only about half of all long-distance calls attempted, severely affecting airline reservations systems, among other businesses.

Professional programmers are constantly looking for ways to make their work easier, faster, and more reliable. One tool that holds promise is one we mentioned in the last chapter: *CASE*. CASE (computer-aided software engineering) tools provide some automation and assistance in one or more phases of the programming process: designing, coding, and debugging.

Another tool is *object-oriented programming* languages. These languages differ from conventional programming languages in that they use and manipulate "objects." These objects can be graphic symbols, modules or blocks of programming code, or data. These languages promise to play a significant role in program development for two primary reasons. First, they are well suited for designing and using graphical user interfaces like those used in the Macintosh, OS/2, and Unix operating systems. Second, the languages are highly modular, allowing programmers to isolate, combine, and reuse programming code very efficiently.

Generation and name	Characteristics
1st—Machine languages	Uses 0s and 1s (bits and bytes).
2nd—Assembly languages	Uses abbreviations.
3rd—Procedural languages	Intended to solve *general* problems. Two widely used languages are COBOL for business programs and FORTRAN for scientific and engineering programs. Other procedural languages include BASIC, Pascal, C, Ada, and RPG.
4th—Problem-oriented languages	Intended to solve *specific* problems. Two types are (1) very specific, such as IFPS for financial models, and (2) flexible, such as Lotus 1-2-3, dBASE, query languages, and applications generators.
5th—Natural languages	Still being developed, they are intended to more closely resemble human languages.

FIGURE 11-18
Five generations, or levels, of programming languages.

Review Questions

1. What is the definition of a *program?*
2. What is the difference between a prewritten program and a custom-made program?
3. What is the definition of *programming?*
4. Describe the six steps involved in programming.
5. What are the four tasks involved in Step 1, problem definition?
6. Explain Step 2, the make-or-buy decision.
7. What is the tool known as top-down program design, used in Step 3, program design?
8. What are program modules?
9. What is a program flowchart?
10. What are the three logic structures used?
11. Explain the difference between the two loop (iteration) structures, DO UNTIL and DO WHILE.
12. What is pseudocode?
13. Explain the differences between syntax errors and logic errors in Step 5, debugging.
14. Explain some of the debugging tools, such as desk checking.
15. Who are three kinds of people that need good documentation, Step 6?
16. What are the five generations of programming languages?
17. Explain the difference between a compiler and an interpreter.
18. Name the seven procedural languages with which you may come in contact.
19. Under problem-oriented languages, explain what query languages and applications generators are.
20. What will be the principal advantage of natural languages if researchers are successful in developing them?

CHAPTER 11
Programming and Languages

VISUAL SUMMARY

A *program* is a list of instructions for the computer to follow to do a task. The instructions are made up of statements written in a programming language (e.g., BASIC). *Programming* is a six-step procedure for producing that list.

Step 1: Define the Problem

Program definition, also called **program analysis,** consists of specifying four tasks:

- Determining program objectives.
- Determining the desired output.
- Determining the input data.
- Determining the processing requirements.

Step 2: Make-or-Buy Decision

The **make-or-buy decision** is a choice between having the program custom written by a programmer or buying it as a prewritten software package.

Step 3: Design the Program

If the program is to be custom-made, in **program design** a solution is designed, using **structured programming techniques,** consisting of the following:

- **Top-down program design**—major processing steps, called **program modules,** are identified.
- **Pseudocode**—a narrative expression of the logic of the program is written.
- **Program flowcharts**—graphic representations of the steps needed to solve the programming problem are drawn.
- **Logic structures**—three arrangements are used in program flowcharts to write so-called structured programs.

Logic Structures

The three logic structures consist of:

- **Sequence**—one program statement followed by another.
- **Selection** (or **IF-THEN-ELSE**)—when a decision must be made.
- **Loop**—when process is repeated as long as a condition is true. May be either **DO UNTIL** or **DO WHILE.**

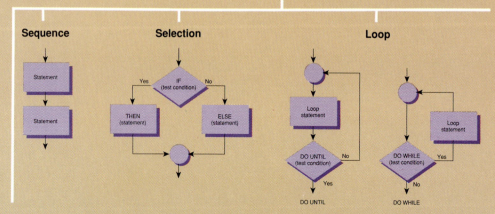

200

Visual Summary

Generation and name	Characteristics
1st—Machine languages	Uses 0s and 1s (bits and bytes).
2nd—Assembly languages	Uses abbreviations.
3rd—Procedural languages	Intended to solve *general* problems. Two widely used languages are COBOL for business programs and FORTRAN for scientific and engineering programs. Other procedural languages include BASIC, Pascal, C, Ada, and RPG.
4th—Problem-oriented languages	Intended to solve *specific* problems. Two types are (1) very specific, such as IFPS for financial models, and (2) flexible, such as Lotus 1-2-3, dBASE, query languages, and applications generators.
5th—Natural languages	Still being developed, they are intended to more closely resemble human languages.

Step 4: Code the Program

- **Coding** consists of writing the program.
- **Good programs** should be structured programs, using logic structures.
- A **programming language** should be chosen that is appropriate for the programming problem and the computer. (See *Languages,* top of this page.)

Step 5: Debug the Program

Debugging consists of testing the program to eliminate **syntax errors** (violation of rules of programming language) and **logic errors** (incorrect calculations or solution procedures). Debugging methods consist of:

- **Desk checking**—careful reading of a printout of the program.
- **Manual testing**—using sample data to test for correct processing results.
- **Attempt at translation**—running the program through a computer, using a translator program.
- **Testing sample data**—testing the program for logic errors on a computer, using sample data.

Step 6: Document the Program

Documentation consists of a written description of the program and the procedures for running it for users, operators, and programmers during **program maintenance**—modifying or updating of the program.

Discussion Questions

1. Programming, you'll recall, is a six-step procedure for creating a computer program. A program is the list of instructions that the computer must follow to accomplish its task. Using just pencil and paper, can you devise the steps in a program that will do all of the following? (1) Pay a sales bonus of 1 percent of total sales to salespeople who sell $100,000 worth of goods in a year. (2) Pay a bonus of 5 percent for those who sell $500,000 worth. (3) Pay a bonus of 10 percent for those who sell $1,000,000 worth.

2. Look at the section on procedural languages (third generation). If you were going to take a course on a programming language, which one would you choose first, and why?

CHAPTER 12
Emerging Applications: Power Tools

Expect surprises—exciting ones, positive ones. This is the view to take in achieving computer competency. If at first the surprises worry you, that's normal. Most people wonder how well they can handle something new. But the latest technological developments also offer you new opportunities to vastly extend your range. As we show in this chapter, for example, software that for many years was available only for mainframes has recently become available for microcomputers. Here's a chance to join the computer-competent of tomorrow.

Power tools: This is the characterization we have given to a whole new generation of software and hardware only recently available for microcomputers. Desktop managers. Project management software. Desktop publishing software. Hypertext and multimedia. CAD/CAM programs. Artificial intelligence, including robotics, knowledge-based and expert systems, and artificial reality. Is there really a need to know anything about these new developments? There is if you want to be like those professionals in every area who are at the forefront of their disciplines. They are there because they have found more efficient ways to use their talents and time. You owe it to yourself, therefore, to at least be aware of what this software and hardware can do.

COMPETENCIES

After you have read this chapter, you should be able to:

1. Describe desktop managers.

2. Discuss project management software.

3. Explain what desktop publishing is.

4. Describe new media: hypertext and multimedia.

5. Describe CAD/CAM software.

6. Explain artificial intelligence: robotics, knowledge-based and expert systems, artificial reality.

Desktop Managers

A Desktop Manager Is a Program That Stays in the Computer's Primary Storage and Provides Desktop "Accessories," Such as Notepad and Calculator.

Desktop managers are programs that can be held in primary storage at the same time you are running other programs. Such other programs might include a word processor, spreadsheet, or database manager. While you are working, without having to abandon these other programs, you may call upon a desktop manager to give you the kind of "desktop accessories" that help you get your job done. Such accessories might include an appointment calendar, calculator, notepad, personal telephone directory, and automatic

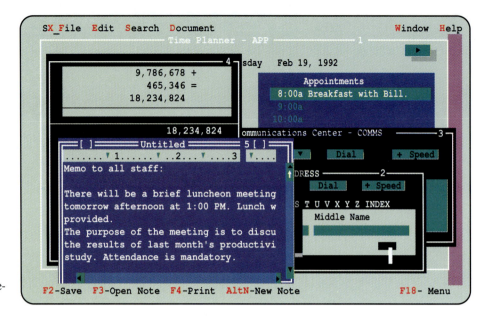

FIGURE 12-1
Example of desktop manager, Sidekick 2.0.

telephone dialer. They appear on your video display screen on top of whatever you are working on. Figure 12-1 shows an example of Sidekick, one of the most popular desktop managers. Here an appointment calendar and a phone directory are displayed as windows in a word processing program.

Desktop managers are quite handy. You may become among the thousands of managers who begin their working day by reviewing their electronic calendars to see what appointments they have. Later, while you're working on a spreadsheet, say, someone calls to schedule an important business meeting. You can simply type a command that "pops up" the desktop manager on the screen, type in the meeting time on your calendar, and then save the information on your diskette. With another command, you make the desktop manager disappear from the screen and return to your word processing task. After you are finished for the day, you can remove the diskette, which will store all the information.

Desktop managers are called **memory-resident programs.** This is because they stay in the computer's memory (primary storage) all the time, until the computer is turned off. The value of a desktop manager is that it enables you to keep your desk free of notepads, phone directories, and calculators.

Project Management Software

Project Management Software Allows You to Plan, Schedule, and Control the People, Resources, and Costs of a Project.

There are many occasions in business where projects need to be watched to avoid delays and cost overruns. A **project** may be defined as a one-time operation composed of several tasks that must be completed during a stated period of time. Examples of large projects are found in construction, aerospace, or political campaigns. Examples of smaller jobs might occur in advertising agencies, corporate marketing departments, or management information systems departments.

Project management software enables users to plan, schedule, and control the people, resources, and costs needed to complete a project on time. For instance, the contractor building a housing development might use it to keep track of the materials,

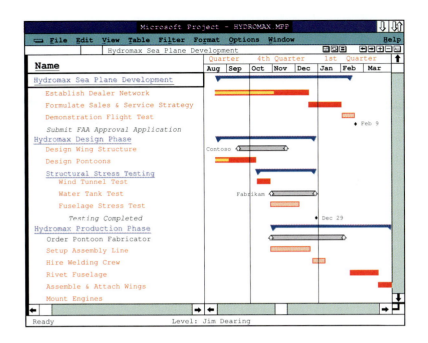

FIGURE 12-2
Gantt chart from Microsoft Project for Windows project management software.

dollars, and people required for success. Examples of project management software are Harvard Project Manager, Microsoft Project for Windows, Project Scheduler 4, SuperProject, and Time Line.

A typical use of project management software is to show the scheduled beginning and ending dates for a particular task. It then shows the dates when the task was completed. Two important tools found in project management software are Gantt charts and PERT charts.

Gantt Charts A **Gantt chart** uses bars and lines to indicate the time scale of a series of tasks. You can see whether the tasks are being completed on schedule. The time scale may range from minutes to years. An example of a Gantt chart is shown in Figure 12-2.

PERT Charts A **PERT chart** shows not only the timing of a project but also the relationships among its tasks. (PERT stands for Program Evaluation Review Technique.) The relationships are represented by lines that connect boxes stating the tasks. With project management software, these boxes can be easily moved around. You can see how changes in the schedule will affect various tasks. Figure 12-3 on p. 206 shows an instance of a PERT chart.

Desktop Publishing

A Desktop Publishing Program Allows You to Mix Text and Graphics to Create Publications of Nearly Professional Quality.

How would you like to generate a report that combined text and graphics and *really* impressed people with its looks? Suppose you wanted to create a report that looked like an article in a newsmagazine? When you present a report prepared on a word processing program, you are basically concerned with content; the appearance is secondary. When you do that same report with a desktop publishing program, the looks can be outstanding. An example of a page prepared by desktop publishing is shown in Figure 12-4, p. 206.

Many publications—most books and magazines, for instance—are created by professionals trained in graphic arts and typesetting. They use equipment that often costs

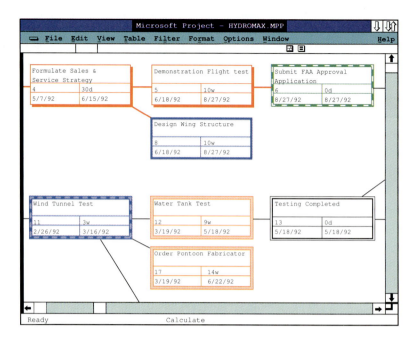

FIGURE 12-3
PERT chart from Microsoft Project for Windows project management software.

FIGURE 12-4
Page produced by desktop publishing software.

several thousand dollars. However, there are many publications where such experience and expense are not necessary. Examples are newsletters, forms, catalogs, brochures, posters, menus, and advertisements. These are all candidates for desktop publishing. Real estate agents may use desktop publishing for sales sheets. Travel agents may use it for advertisements, architects for proposals, and government officials for presentations.

Desktop publishing is the process of using a microcomputer, a laser printer, and the necessary software to mix text and graphics (see Figure 12-5). Some word processing programs are being developed with this capability. However, here we are concerned with specialized software that allows you to create publications that are of almost professional quality. The software enables you to select a variety of typestyles, just like those that commercial printers use. It also allows you to create and select graphic images. The laser

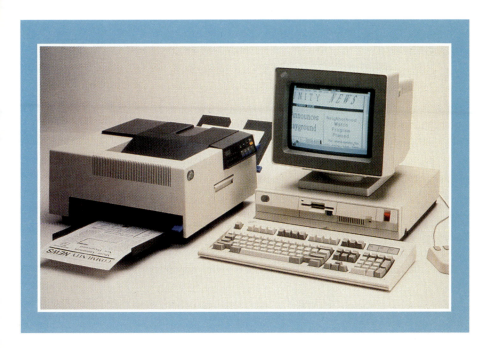

FIGURE 12-5
Desktop publishing: microcomputer, laser printer, and mouse.

printer produces a higher-quality printed result than is possible with other microcomputer printers. An example of a display screen of material produced using the desktop publishing program Ventura Publisher is shown in Figure 12-6. Other popular programs are PageMaker and First Publisher.

Desktop publishing lets you place various kinds of text and graphics together in a publication designed almost any way you want. For instance, imagine you are a marketing manager for an airplane manufacturer and you are preparing a presentation on a new aircraft. You could use a word processing program to type the text. You could then use other software to create graphics. Or you might use graphics that have already been created from a graphics program. You can even get photographs that have been copied

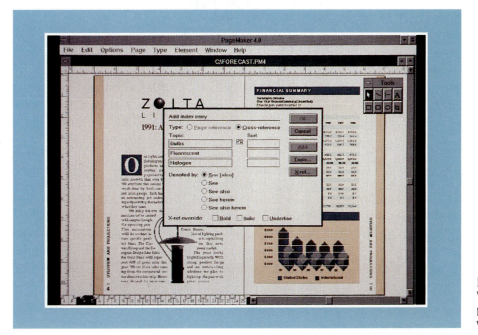

FIGURE 12-6
Video display screen showing a page produced by desktop publishing software from PageMaker.

into a computer by a special scanning device. The desktop publishing program allows you to integrate all of these and look at your work on the display screen as one page. You can also look at two facing pages in reduced size or an enlarged view of a partial page. You can rearrange text and columns. You can enlarge or reduce any element and choose from all kinds of typestyles and sizes.

In Ventura Publisher, something called a **style sheet** enables you to determine the basic appearance of single or multiple pages. You can decide how many columns of type will be on a page. You can choose the size and typestyle of both text and headings. You can even select the width of lines and boxes that separate text and pictures. You can place an image anywhere on a page simply by putting a cursor at the point you wish. If a graphic image is positioned on top of text, the text will automatically realign around the image.

If you are not trained as a graphic designer, Ventura offers 25 sample style sheets. These can be used for brochures, newsletters, books, and so on. As you become more experienced, you can modify these style sheets or even create your own.

Once a document is composed on the screen, it must be transmitted to an output device that can print it out. This task is accomplished by what are known as **page description languages.** A page description language describes the shape and position of letters and graphics to the printer. An example is Adobe's PostScript, which is used in the PageMaker product. Other examples are Interpress from Xerox and Document Description Language (DDL) from Imagen.

New Media: Hypertext and Multimedia

New Media Include Hypertext and Multimedia. Hypertext Is Software That Can Connect Any Text or Picture with Any Other. Multimedia Can Link Text, Graphics, Video, and Sounds.

Where is the next area in which a revolution will happen in microcomputing? Many observers think it will be in something called "new media." *Media* refers to the formats in which information is communicated or expressed. For example, a medium may be text, graphics, animation, music, voice, or video. *New media* refers to delivery systems that combine media, using a microcomputer as the controlling framework. The two principal kinds of new media are *hypertext* and *multimedia*.

Hypertext **Hypertext** is sophisticated software that allows users to organize and access information in creative ways. It is designed to work the way people think. It enables people to link facts into sequences of information in ways that parallel the methods people use to discover knowledge. Hypertext encourages you to follow your natural train of thought as you seek information, rather than follow the restrictive search-and-retrieval methods of traditional database systems.

Much of the interest in hypertext has been generated by HyperCard, which runs on Apple's Macintosh computer. IBM's version, which runs on IBM PCs, PC-compatibles, and the IBM PS/2 line of computers, is called LinkWay. HyperCard is based on the concept of card files, just like note cards, only these are electronic. Information is recorded on basic filing units that Apple calls *cards*. A card is a computer screen filled with data comprising a single record. Cards in turn are organized into related files (bodies of information) called *stacks*. Cards and stacks are easily created and edited by the user through the use of Macintosh's typing and drawing tools.

You can create various connections between cards and stacks, and by fields of information on the cards, by means of *buttons*. A button is an area of the screen that is sensitive to the "click" of a mouse. Using your mouse to guide the cursor, you move to one of these buttons on the screen. You then press ("click") the selection button on top of the mouse, and you will be connected to another card or stack.

By clicking buttons, you can "navigate" through the cards and stacks to locate information or to discover connections between ideas contained in the stacks. For example, suppose an electronic "encyclopedia" or "textbook" has been developed containing information about Native Americans. Figure 12-7 shows how you might do research in this subject. Each stack contains pertinent data: text, statistics, maps, charts, or pictures. You can define buttons to link the information. The links may be sequential, going from one card to another in a stack. Or the links may be hierarchical, so that you can go from a summary to detailed information about a particular topic. Whatever the method, the links are varied so that you can sort through and gain access to related information in whatever ways are convenient to you.

Clearly, what is interesting about hypertext is that it enables users to search for and to link information in many different ways. Users can follow their own methods of discovery, using intuition and idea association to gain knowledge.

Multimedia Multimedia, also called **hypermedia,** is much more than hypertext. While hypertext focuses primarily on linking textual information, **multimedia** can link all sorts of media into one form of presentation. These media may include text, graphics, animation, video, music, and voice.

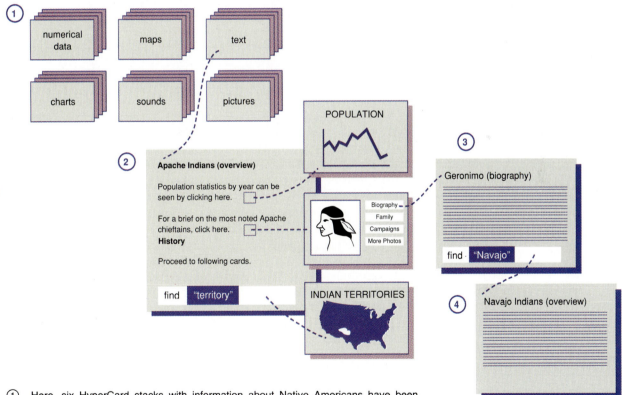

① Here, six HyperCard stacks with information about Native Americans have been developed.

② You navigate through the information by "pressing" ("clicking") on buttons that appear on the screen. Buttons call up linked data on other cards and promote self-paced, self-guided study. Information can also be accessed using the HyperCard "Find" feature.

③ Linking data is not a one-way street. From any card, you can access other cards to probe deeper into a line of thought.

④ Or you can embark on an entirely new course of investigation.

FIGURE 12-7
Hypertext: how HyperCard works.

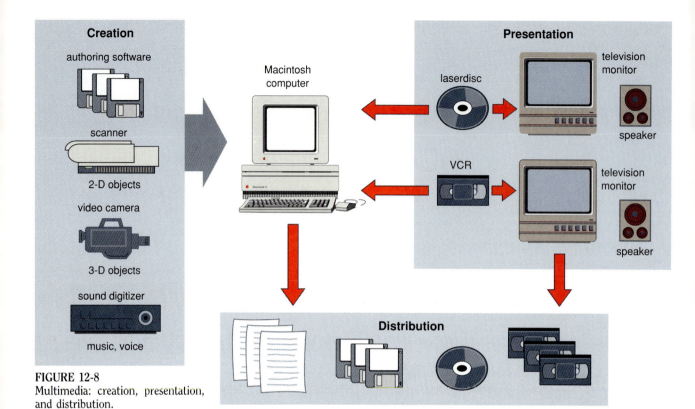

FIGURE 12-8
Multimedia: creation, presentation, and distribution.

An example of how these can be put together was demonstrated by a music professor as follows. Using an application written with HyperCard, the professor presented a multimedia lesson about a particular symphony. For hardware, he attached a Macintosh and a CD-ROM disk drive to a speaker system and a television monitor. The demonstration showed there were many ways to navigate through the program. For instance, the professor could call up biographical anecdotes about the composer. Or, he could present an outline of the symphony's major themes which had music attached. When the Macintosh's mouse was clicked on the items in the outline, the audience could hear how a theme was restated as the symphony progressed. Or program notes could be made to appear that would provide a running commentary. Or, by clicking the mouse on an obscure term, the professor could call up a definition from the program's glossary.

Figure 12-8 shows what might be involved in developing a multimedia presentation about events leading up to the Civil War. In the creation stage, one could use a Macintosh and HyperCard as authoring software to integrate information. This information could come in the form of text through a scanner, graphics and animation through a video camera, and sound through a sound digitizer. The multimedia lesson could be packaged on a CD-ROM disk or videocassette tape and presented through a television monitor and speaker. The lesson could be stored and distributed on several types of media: hardcopy (text), flexible diskettes, CD-ROM disks, or videocassette tapes.

Figure 12-9 shows the dramatic projected rise in multimedia systems in the United States over the next few years. There are four primary business areas in which multimedia is expected to be used. The first is training, in which workers are taught new skills. The second is sales and information, in which multimedia "catalogs" are used to reach customers. The third area is desktop applications. Here multimedia may be used to enhance presentations or company communications. The fourth area is industrial and scientific operations. Here voice commands may be used to direct remote computers removed from human contact.

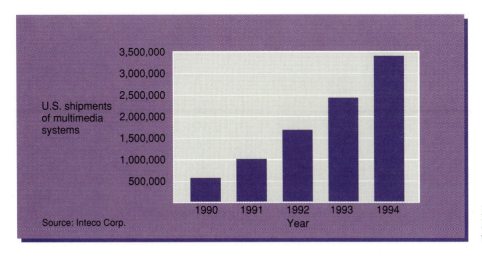

FIGURE 12-9
Expected sales in multimedia systems.

CAD/CAM

CAD Is Computer-Aided Design. CAM Is Computer-Aided Manufacturing.

Computers have revolutionized systems for designing and manufacturing products. These are sometimes mentioned together as *CAD/CAM*—for *computer-aided design/computer-aided manufacturing*. However, they are really two separate applications.

The *really* radical change in this area is that only recently have these systems become available for microcomputer users. Just five years ago, for example, CAD work required computer systems costing over $100,000. Today much of that same kind of work can be done on microcomputer systems costing only $6,000. This means that many applications are now cost effective—which gives you the opportunity to do creative work previously reserved for specialists.

Computer-Aided Design A product must first be designed. This is true whether it is as large as an airplane, as small as a computer chip, or as ordinary as a shoe. Until recently, industrial designers and engineers sat at drawing boards and drew rough sketches. Then they produced more refined sketches. Then they built and tested scale models. Then they made production drawings for manufacturing the product.

Some engineers and designers, however, did not design products this old-fashioned way. Rather they prepared their sketches and drawings on an expensive computer, using expensive software called **computer-aided design (CAD)** software. CAD software is a type of program that manipulates images on a screen (see Figure 12-10). One advantage of this kind of program is that the product can be drawn in three dimensions and then rotated on the screen so the viewer can see all sides.

Today, just as desktop publishing has made graphic arts and publications available to everyone, CAD is also accessible to microcomputer users (see Figure 12-11). With software known as VersaCAD, for example, you can design an entire house by yourself. Or you can create clothes, furniture, industrial products, whatever your design interest—all on screen. Similar CAD software is also available for IBM microcomputers, such as AutoCAD 386 or AutoCAD for OS/2.

A variation on CAD are **computer-aided design and drafting (CADD)** systems. CADplan is one such program that is available for microcomputers. Such programs cannot really teach you to design—that is, conceptualize a drawing. However, they can help you do drafting or drawing. CADD programs come equipped with such symbols as

212
Emerging Applications:
Power Tools

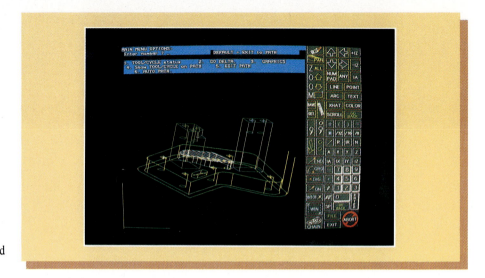

FIGURE 12-10
CAD: example of computer-aided design.

FIGURE 12-11
Architectural plan drawn with CAD for Orlando, Florida, airport.

straight lines, arcs, circles, and points. These help you put together graphic elements. You can edit drawings by moving portions around, changing shapes, and rotating objects. An architect, for example, can change room dimensions and shapes, even the entire floor plan of a house. Some CADD programs also enable you to do drawings in layers, as though you were using clear plastic overlays. Another feature is that images can be stored on disk and then inserted into other drawings. Although most CADD programs perform only two-dimensional design, a few can work in three dimensions.

Computer-Aided Manufacturing Abbreviated **CAM, computer-aided manufacturing** is a term that describes programs that control automated factory equipment, including machine tools and robots. Examples are systems that regulate production in an oil refinery, that monitor nuclear power plants, and that manufacture textiles. As with CAD programs, previously CAM software was expensive and available only with mainframes. Now microcomputer CAM systems are showing up everywhere. They are used to handle communications and to route information from manufacturing equipment. They are also used to generate data and programs to run tools on the factory floor.

An instance in which both CAD and CAM have been used together on a microcomputer is found in a steel mill. A designer draws an I-beam shape with the CAD program on the computer's screen. The program then calculates the CAM instructions. It determines the exact specifications for securing clamps to a steel roll. It indicates the type of cutting needed to make the I-beam out of the steel roll. It determines where the cutting tools will start and stop and how many tool passes are required. CAD/CAM software is also used in making cars and other manufacturing applications. CAD is used to design cars; CAM is used to control factory robots and coordinate other areas of production.

As we've stated, the availability of CAD/CAM software on microcomputers is a recent and potentially far-reaching development. As others have observed, today's unfathomable is tomorrow's mundane. Whatever field you are in, as CAD/CAM applications become available, you should make it a point to become familiar with them.

Artificial Intelligence

Artificial Intelligence Attempts to Develop Computer Systems That Simulate Human Thought Processes and Actions. Three Areas Are Robotics, Knowledge-Based and Expert Systems, and Artificial Reality.

Does human intelligence really need the presence of "artificial intelligence," whatever that is? Indeed, you might worry, do we need the competition? Actually, the goal of artificial intelligence is not to replace human intelligence, which is probably not replaceable. Rather it is to help people be more productive. Let us describe how this might work.

In the past, computers used calculating power to solve *structured* problems, the kinds of tasks described throughout this book. People—using intuition, reasoning, and memory—were better at solving *unstructured* problems, whether building a product or approving a loan. Most organizations have been able to computerize the tasks once performed by clerks. However, knowledge-intensive work, such as that performed by many managers, is only beginning to be automated.

Now the field of computer science known as **artificial intelligence** (**AI**) is moving into the mainstream of data processing. AI attempts to develop computer systems that can mimic or simulate human thought processes and actions. These include reasoning, learning from past actions, and simulation of human senses such as vision and touch. True artificial intelligence that corresponds to human intelligence is still a long way off. However, several tools that emulate human problem solving and information processing have been developed. Many of these tools have practical applications for business, medicine, law, and many other fields.

Let us now consider three areas in which human talents and abilities have been enhanced with "computerized intelligence":

- Robotics
- Knowledge-based and expert systems
- Artificial reality

Robotics **Robotics** is the field of study concerned with developing and using robots. Some toylike household robots (such as the Androbots) have been made for entertainment purposes. However, these are not the kind we are interested in here. **Robots** are machines used in factories and elsewhere. They differ from most assembly-line machines

FIGURE 12-12
Industrial robot: using claw to pick up objects—in this case, an egg.

in that they can be reprogrammed to do more than one task. Among the kinds of robots are the following.

- *Industrial robots:* Industrial robots are used in factories to perform certain assembly-line tasks. Examples are machines used in automobile plants to do welding, painting, and loading. In the garment industry, robot pattern cutters create pieces of fabric for clothing. Some types of robots have claws for picking up objects (see Figure 12-12).
- *Perception systems:* Some robots imitate some of the human senses. For example, robots with television-camera vision systems are particularly useful. They can be used for guiding machine tools, for inspecting products, and for identifying and sorting parts (see Figure 12-13). Other kinds of perception systems rely on a sense of touch, such as those used on microcomputer assembly lines to put parts into place.
- *Mobile robots:* Some robots act as transporters, such as "mailmobiles." They carry mail through an office, following a preprogrammed route. Office workers can leave their desks to exchange mail when the robot comes by. Others act as computerized carts to deliver supplies and equipment at medical centers.

Knowledge-Based and Expert Systems People who are expert in a particular area—certain kinds of law, medicine, accounting, engineering, and so on—are generally well paid for their specialized knowledge. Unfortunately for their clients and customers, they are expensive, not always available, and hard to replace when they move on.

What if you were to somehow *capture* the knowledge of a human expert? What if you then made it accessible to everyone through a computer program? This knowledge could be not only reasonably priced but also always available. Indeed, if you were an expert

FIGURE 12-13
Perception system: vision-system robot, used for welding.

yourself, you could use such a program to double-check your own judgments. Moreover, as an expert yourself, you could create your own computer program containing much of what you know.

All this is exactly what is being done with so-called *knowledge-based* and *expert systems*. And again, the good news is that these programs, previously available only for mainframe computers, are now rapidly being developed for microcomputers.

Computer professionals make a distinction between two types of specialized software.

- *Knowledge-based systems:* **Knowledge-based systems** are programs that are based on "surface knowledge." This consists of facts and widely accepted rules, such as those that might be found in a firm's procedures manual. This kind of knowledge is also called "textbook knowledge"—it includes facts and rules you might find in a textbook. Such systems tell how certain decisions should be made or tasks accomplished. An example is the kind of automatic check-in machine some airlines offer. Using this machine allows passengers to avoid waiting in lines for a ticketing agent. Rather they interact with a knowledge-based system. It assigns them seats according to their preferences for window versus aisle or other seat, and so on. The system then automatically issues passengers their boarding passes.

- *Expert systems:* **Expert systems** are programs based on both "surface knowledge" and "deep knowledge." Essentially they emulate the knowledge of human experts skilled in a particular field—for instance, that of a geologist, tax lawyer, or medical doctor. These programs incorporate both textbook knowledge and "tricks of the trade" that an expert acquires after years of experience. As a result, the programs can be exceedingly complex. For example, ExperTAX, which helps accountants figure out a client's tax options, consists of over 2000 rules.

Over the past decade, expert systems have been developed in areas such as medicine, geology, chemistry, and military science. There are expert systems with such names as Oil Spill Advisor, Bird Species Identification, and even Midwives Assistant. A system called Grain Marketing Advisor helps farmers select the best way to market their grain. Another, called Senex, shows how to treat breast cancer based on advanced treatment techniques.

Personal Machinist is an expert system designed to help the maintenance staff repair robots used in car-manufacturing operations. A typical screen from this expert system is shown in Figure 12-14. Personal Machinist consists of 120 rules covering the majority of the problems encountered with a particular kind of factory robot.

Expert systems are created using a programming language or a shell. **Shells** are special kinds of software that allow a person to custom-build a particular kind of expert system. For instance, the shell called VP-Expert has a database and can work with Lotus 1-2-3 and dBASE. This shell can then be used to build different kinds of expert systems. For example, VP-Expert has helped gardeners to assemble information about the most effective natural pest controls to use for specific purposes. Texas Instruments has developed an entire line of microcomputer-based shells called the Personal Consultant Series. These shells have been used to build Senex and Grain Marketing Advisor, among others we mentioned.

Artificial Reality   Suppose you could create and virtually experience any new form of reality you wish. You could see the world through the eyes of a child, a robot—or even a lobster. You could explore faraway resorts, the moon, or inside a nuclear waste dump, without leaving your chair. This simulated experience is rapidly becoming possible with a form of AI known as *artificial reality*.

Also known as **virtual reality** or **virtual environments, artificial reality** consists of headgear and gloves that you wear and software that translates data into images. The headgear (one type is called Eyephones) has earphones and three-dimensional stereoscopic screens. The glove (DataGlove) has sensors that collect data about your hand movements. When coupled with the software (such as a program called Body Electric), this interactive sensory equipment allows you to experience alternative realities to the physical world.

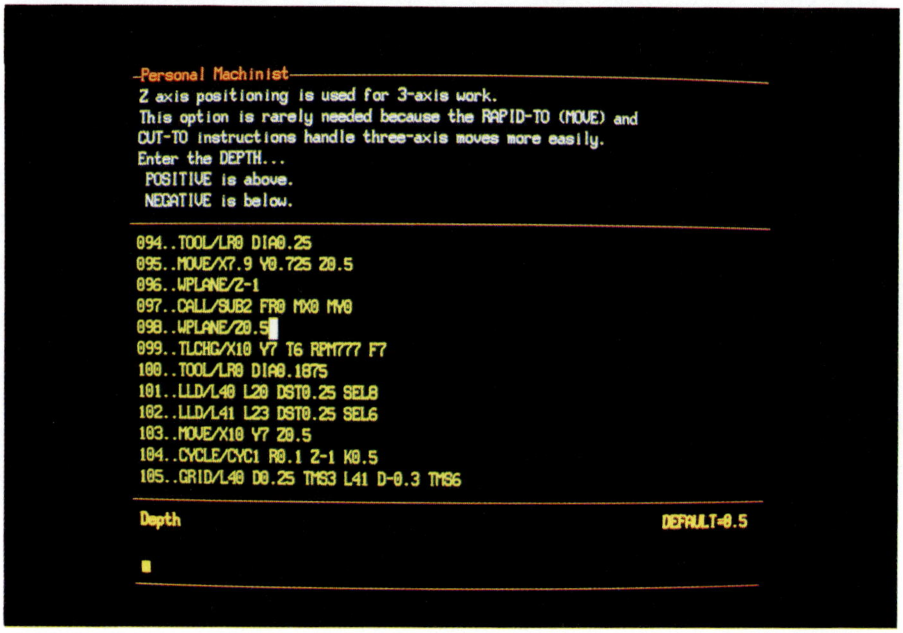

FIGURE 12-14
Expert system: Personal Machinist aids technicians in diagnosing problems with robots.

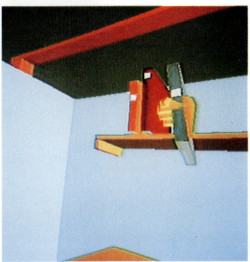

An example of artificial reality is shown in the three photos of Figure 12-15. The first picture shows a man wearing interactive sensory headset and glove. When the man moves his head, the stereoscopic views change. The second picture shows what the man is looking at—a simulation of an office. The third picture shows how the view changes as the user "goes" over to a bookshelf and "reaches" up for a book.

There are several possible applications for artificial reality. The ultimate recreational use might be something resembling a "giant virtual amusement park." More seriously, we can simulate important experiences or training environments such as flying, surgical operations, spaceship repair, or nuclear disaster cleanup.

FIGURE 12-15
Artificial reality: sensory headset and glove, view of simulated office, reaching for a book.

A Look at the Future

The "Downsizing" of Computer Applications Will Continue. So Will the Broadening of the Scope of Applications, as in Current Research into "Artificial Life."

As we have pointed out elsewhere in the book, we can expect the trend of *"downsizing" of applications* to continue. That is, tasks that could once be performed only by mainframes will increasingly be done with microcomputers. Computer networks will link mainframes, microcomputers, workstations, and servers of all kinds—file servers, database servers, and communications servers. These developments will have an effect on the kinds of resources available to you in your career.

Just as important, we will probably also see a *broadening of the scope of applications.* Already well along in development, for instance, are *pen-based computers.* These are portable computers with handwriting-recognition capabilities that can identify printed letters, digits, and punctuation. They can even be modified to accept particular handwriting styles. Also presently being marketed are compact disk players that display audio and video programs on a TV set. These enable viewers to navigate by sight and sound through encyclopedias and atlases. These and similar devices may be forerunners to so-called *information appliances.* Such an appliance would bundle a computer, telephone, fax machine, photocopier, color printer, and laser discs or CDs into one intelligent machine.

In the 21st century, the concepts applied in artificial intelligence, such as robotics, will be applied to all sorts of things. Even now, for instance, an experimental house in Japan, known as the "TRON House," has microprocessors and sensors built into everything. Windows open and close to maintain optimum ventilation. Background music reduces in volume when the telephone rings. Kitchen computers take the guesswork out of cooking. Bathroom computers monitor one's health. No doubt we will see similar extension of computer technology to the workplace.

Most spectacularly, there are already attempts to go beyond artificial intelligence to something called *artificial life.* In this field, researchers are trying to develop programs that learn and develop on their own. For instance, computers are used to simulate living systems and to make computerized environments in which simulations of organisms eat, reproduce, and die. The outcome of these investigations may produce defenses against the computer viruses that have damaged networks and databases. They may also further our understanding of how human urban communities work.

Review Questions

1. What does a desktop manager do?
2. What is meant by the term *memory-resident program?*
3. Explain what project management software does.
4. Describe what Gantt charts and PERT charts are?
5. What does a desktop publishing program let you do?
6. Describe what a page description language does.
7. What does a hypertext program do?
8. Explain how multimedia works.
9. What does CAD/CAM stand for?
10. Give an example of how CAD is used.
11. Explain what CADD does.
12. Give an example of how CAM is used.
13. What are three categories of artificial intelligence?
14. Explain the different areas of robotics.
15. Define knowledge-based systems.
16. Explain what an expert system is.
17. What is a shell?
18. Explain how artificial reality works.

Discussion Questions

1. Some word processing programs seem to be evolving into important desktop publishing programs. Indeed, WordPerfect's latest versions have desktop publishing features. If so, is there any point in your learning word processing alone? Discuss.

2. There are some areas in which it is very difficult to create an expert system. For example, one developer started out to build a program that would be used to pick stocks for investors. However, he found out there *are* no true experts on the stock market. (There are just many theorists and educated guessers.) Bearing this in mind, what areas would you like to see an expert system developed for? Perhaps one already exists, or perhaps you may hit on a new idea.

CHAPTER 12
Emerging Applications: Power Tools

VISUAL SUMMARY

Some recent important microcomputer applications are desktop managers, project management software, desktop publishing, hypertext and multimedia, CAD/CAM, and artificial intelligence—robotics, knowledge-based and expert systems, and artificial reality.

Desktop Managers

Desktop managers (also called **memory resident programs**) stay in primary storage at the same time other programs are running and provide "pop-up" assistance of such "desktop accessories" as appointment calendar, calculator, notepad, personal telephone directory, and automatic telephone dialer.

Example of Package

Sidekick.

Project Management Software

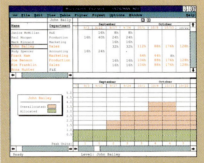

Project management software allows you to plan, schedule, and control the people, resources, and costs of a project. A **project** is a one-time operation composed of several tasks that must be completed during a stated period of time.

Two important tools found in project management software are:

Gantt Charts

A **Gantt chart** uses bars and lines to indicate the time scale of a series of tasks so you can see whether the tasks are being completed on schedule.

PERT Charts

A **PERT chart** shows not only the timing of a project but also the relationships among its tasks.

Examples of Packages

Harvard Project Manager, Microsoft Project for Windows, Project Scheduler 4, SuperProject, Time Line

Desktop Publishing

Desktop publishing is the process of using a microcomputer, laser printer, and necessary software to mix text and graphics and create publications of almost professional quality. Once a document is composed on the monitor screen, it is transmitted by a **page description language,** which describes the shape and position of letters and graphics, to a printer for printing out.

Examples of Packages

Ventura Publisher, PageMaker, First Publisher

Visual Summary

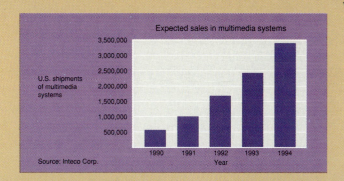

New Media

New media refers to ways of combining and controlling information in a variety of forms. These forms include text, graphics, animation, music, voice, and video. Two principal kinds of new media are **hypertext** and **multimedia**.

Hypertext

Hypertext is software that stores information in **cards** and **stacks** and allows users to navigate this information in creative and useful ways through **buttons**.

Multimedia

While hypertext relates primarily to textual information, multimedia includes much more: graphics, animation, music, voice, and video. The use of multimedia is dramatically increasing. Four primary business uses are:
- training
- sales and information
- desktop applications
- industrial and scientific applications

Examples of Packages

Apple's HyperCard and IBM's LinkWay.

CAD/CAM

CAD/CAM software is used for designing and manufacturing products.

Computer-Aided Design

Computer-aided design (CAD)—or **computer-aided design and drafting (CADD)**—software allows images to be manipulated on screen (e.g., in three dimensions).

Computer-Aided Manufacturing

Computer-aided manufacturing (CAM) software controls automated factory equipment (e.g., machine tools and robots).

Examples of Packages

VersaCAD, AutoCAD, CADplan.

Artificial Intelligence

Artificial intelligence is a research field to develop computer systems simulating human thought processes and actions. Three areas include:

Robotics

Robotics is a research field to develop machines that can be reprogrammed to do more than one task. Some types are industrial robots, perception systems, and mobile robots.

Knowledge-Based and Expert Systems

These are computer programs that duplicate the knowledge humans have for performing specialized tasks.
- **Knowledge-based systems** use "surface knowledge"—facts and widely accepted rules.
- **Expert systems** use "deep knowledge," both surface knowledge and "tricks of the trade" of human experts (e.g., geologist).

Artificial Reality

Also known as **virtual reality** or **virtual environments,** this consists of interactive sensory equipment to simulate alternative realities to the physical world.

CHAPTER

Workplace Issues, Privacy, and Security

13

The tools and products of the information age do not exist in a world by themselves. As we said in Chapter 1, a computer system consists not only of software, hardware, data, and procedures but also of *people*. Because of people, computer systems may be used for both good and bad purposes. In this chapter we examine what some of the people issues are.

More than 10 million American workers now use video display terminals (VDTs) every day. About 3 million more VDTs are being added each year. Indeed, about one-third of Americans used a computer at work in 1989, according to the U.S. Census Bureau. More of these are women than men (see Figure 13-1), and most of them are in clerical or administrative support jobs. What are the consequences of the widespread presence of this technology? We consider some of the effects below.

COMPETENCIES

After you have read this chapter, you should be able to:

1. Describe health and other workplace issues.

2. Discuss privacy issues raised by the presence of large databases and electronic networks.

3. List the major laws on privacy.

4. Explain the effects of computer crimes, including the spreading of computer viruses.

5. Describe other hazards to the computer.

6. Discuss security measures that may be taken.

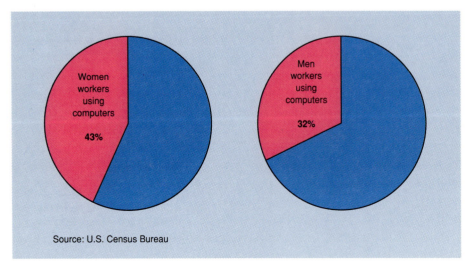

FIGURE 13-1
Percentage of men and women users of computers at work.

Workplace Issues

Computer Users Should Take Steps to Avoid Physical and Mental Health Risks and to Increase Productivity.

Even though the cost of computers has decreased significantly, they are still expensive. Why have them, then, unless they can make workers more effective? Ironically, however, there are certain ways in which computers may actually make people *less* productive. Many of these problems are most apt to affect those working in data-entry-intensive positions, such as clerks and word-processor operators. However, they may also happen to anyone whose job involves heavy use of the computer. As a result, there has been great interest in a field known as ergonomics.

Ergonomics (pronounced "er-guh-*nom*-ix") is defined as the study of human factors related to computers. It is concerned with fitting the job to the worker rather than forcing the worker to contort to fit the job. As computer use has increased, so has interest in ergonomics. People are devising ways that computers can be designed and used to increase productivity and avoid health risks.

Physical Health Matters Sitting in front of a screen in awkward positions for long periods may lead to physical problems. These can include eyestrain, headaches, back pain, and other problems. Users can alleviate these by taking frequent rest breaks and by using well-designed computer furniture. Some recommendations by ergonomic experts for the ideal setup for a microcomputer or workstation are shown in Figure 13-2.

The physical health matters related to computers that have received the most attention recently are the following.

- *Avoiding eyestrain and headache:* Our eyes were made for most efficient seeing at a distance. However, VDTs require using the eyes at closer range for a long time, which can create eyestrain, headaches, and double vision.

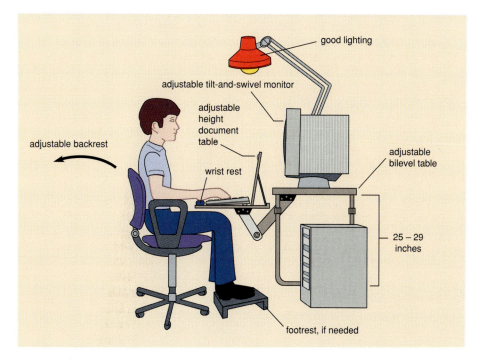

FIGURE 13-2
Recommendations for the ideal workstation.

To make the computer easier on the eyes, take a 15-minute break every hour or two. Keep computer screens away from windows and other sources of bright light to minimize reflected glare on the screen. Special anti-glare screen coatings and "glare shields" are also available. Make sure the screen is three to four times brighter than room light. Keep everything you're focusing on at about the same distance. For example, the computer screen, keyboard, and a document holder containing your work might be positioned about 20 inches away. Clean the screen of dust from time to time.

- *Avoiding back and neck pains:* Many people work at VDT screens and keyboards that are in improper positions. The result can be pains in the back and neck.

   To avoid such problems, make sure equipment is adjustable. You should be able to adjust your chair for height and angle, and the chair should have good back support. The table on which the monitor stands should also be adjustable, and the monitor itself should be of the tilt-and-swivel kind. Keyboards should be detachable. Document holders should be adjustable.

- *Avoiding effects of electromagnetic fields:* Like many household appliances, video display terminals generate invisible electromagnetic field (EMF) emissions, which can pass through the human body. Some observers feel that there could be a connection between these EMF emissions and possible miscarriages (and even some cancers). A study by the government's National Institute of Occupational Safety and Health found no statistical relationship between VDTs and miscarriages. Even so, several companies have introduced low-emission monitors. They state that no health or safety problems exist with older monitors; rather, they are merely responding to market demands.

   One recommendation is that computer users should follow a policy of "prudent avoidance" in reducing their exposure to EMF emissions. They should try to sit about 2 feet or more from the computer screen and 3 feet from neighboring terminals. The strongest fields are emitted from the sides and backs of terminals.

- *Avoiding repetitive strain injury:* Data-entry operators in some companies may make as many as 23,000 keystrokes a day. Some of these workers and other heavy keyboard users have fallen victim to a disorder known as repetitive strain injury.

   Repetitive strain injury (RSI)—also called **repetitive motion injury** and **cumulative trauma disorders**—is the name given to a number of injuries. These result from fast, repetitive work that can cause neck, wrist, hand, and arm pains. In 1988, RSI accounted for nearly half of all workplace illnesses in private industry, compared to only 18 percent in 1981. Some RSI sufferers are slaughterhouse, textile, and automobile workers, who have long been susceptible to the disorder. However, the large increase was mainly caused by the addition of so many more computer users in the intervening years. One particular RSI, **carpal tunnel syndrome,** found among heavy computer users, consists of damage to nerves and tendons in the hands. Some victims report the pain is so intense that they cannot open doors or shake hands.

   Before the computer, typists would stop to change paper or make corrections, thus giving themselves tiny but frequent rest periods. Because RSI is caused by repetition and a fast work pace, avoidance consists in finding ways to take frequent short rest breaks. Experts also advise getting plenty of sleep and exercise, losing weight, sitting up straight, and learning stress-management techniques.

Mental Health Matters Computer technology offers not only ways of improving productivity but also some irritants that may be counterproductive.

- *Avoiding noise:* Computers can be quite noisy. Working next to an impact printer for several hours, for instance, can leave one with ringing ears. Also, users may develop headaches and tension from being continually exposed to the high-frequency, barely audible squeal produced by computer monitors. This is particularly true for women, who hear high-frequency sounds better than men do. They may be affected by the noise even when they are not conscious of hearing it.

    Sound-muffling covers are available for reducing the noise from impact printers. However, there appears to be no immediate solution for abating the noise from monitors.

- *Avoiding stress from excessive monitoring:* Research shows that workers whose performance is monitored electronically suffer more health problems than do those watched by human supervisors. For instance, a computer may monitor the number of keystrokes a data-entry clerk completes in a day. It might tally the time a customer-service person takes to handle a call. The company might then decide to shorten the time allowed and to continue monitoring the employees electronically. By so doing, it may force a pace leading to physical, RSI-type problems and mental health difficulties. For example, one study found that electronically monitored employees reported more boredom, higher tension, extreme anxiety, depression, anger, and severe fatigue.

    Recently it has been shown that electronic monitoring actually is not necessary. For instance, both Federal Express and Bell Canada replaced electronic monitoring with occasional monitoring by human managers. They found that employee productivity stayed up and even increased.

A new word—*"technostress"*—has been proposed to describe the stress associated with computer use that is harmful to people. Technostress is the tension that arises when we have to unnaturally adapt to computers rather than having computers adapt to us.

Design with People in Mind   Electronic products from microwave ovens to VCRs to microcomputers offer the promise of more efficiency and speed. Often, however, the products are so overloaded with features that users cannot figure them out. Because a microprocessor chip will handle not just one operation but several, manufacturers feel obliged to pile on the "bells and whistles." Thus, many home and office products, while being fancy technology platforms, are difficult for humans to use.

A recent trend among manufacturers has been to deliberately strip down the features offered rather than to constantly do all that is possible. In appliances, this restraint is shown among certain types of "high-end" audio equipment, which come with fewer buttons and lights. In computers, there are similar trends. Surveys show that consumers want "plug and play" equipment—machines that they can simply turn on and quickly start working. Thus, computers are being made easier to use, with more menus, windows, and use of icons and pictures. For instance, the menus and pictures made popular by Macintosh are now being used with great success in Microsoft Corporation's Windows.

Similar attempts at designing computers for ease in human use are found in other areas. For example, psychologists have found that workers regard expert systems—the complex programs that emulate human experts—much as they would human expertise. To be trusted by humans, the programs must contain procedures that are very close to the logic processes used by experts. That is, they must appear to think like humans in order to be acceptable.

Computers and Privacy

Every Computer User Should Be Aware of Privacy Matters, Including How Databases and Online Networks Are Used and the Major Privacy Laws.

We are all entitled to the right of **privacy.** This includes the right to keep personal information, such as credit ratings and medical histories, from getting into the wrong hands. Many people worry that this right is severely threatened. Let us see what some of the concerns are.

Use of Large Databases Large organizations are constantly compiling information about us (see Figure 13-3). For instance, our social security numbers are now used routinely as key fields in databases for organizing our employment, credit, and tax records. Indeed, even children are now required to have social security numbers. Shouldn't we be concerned that cross-referenced information might be used for the wrong purposes?

Every day, data is gathered about us and stored in large databases. For example, for billing purposes, telephone companies compile lists of the calls we make, the numbers called, and so on. A special telephone directory (called a reverse directory) lists telephone numbers followed by subscriber names. Using it, governmental authorities and others could easily get the names, addresses, and other details about the persons we call. Credit card companies keep similar records. Supermarket scanners in the grocery checkout counters record what we buy, when we buy it, how much we buy, and the price. So do publishers of magazines and newspapers and mail-order catalogs.

A vast industry of data gatherers or "information resellers" now exists that collects such personal data. They then sell it to direct marketers, fund-raisers, and others. Even government agencies contribute; some state motor vehicle departments sell the car registration data they collect. Database concerns have been able to collect names, ad-

FIGURE 13-3
Large organizations are constantly compiling information about us, such as the kinds of products we buy.

dresses, and other information for about 80 percent of American households. The average person is on 100 mailing lists and 50 databases, according to some privacy experts.

In such ways, your personal preferences and habits become marketable commodities. This raises two questions.

- *Spreading information without personal consent:* How would you feel if your name and your taste in movies were made available nationwide? For a while, Blockbuster, a large video rental company, considered doing just this. What if a great deal of information about your shopping habits—collected about you without your consent—was made available to any microcomputer user who wanted it? Until it dropped the project, Lotus Development Corporation and Equifax Inc. were preparing to market disks containing information on 120 million American consumers. (Lotus claimed it was only providing small businesses with the same information currently available to larger organizations.) Finally, how would you feel if your employer was using your *medical* records to make decisions about placement, promotion, and firing? A 1988 University of Illinois survey found that half of the Fortune 500 companies were using employee medical records for that purpose.

- *Spreading inaccurate information:* How *accurate* is the information being circulated? Mistakes that creep into one computer file may find their way into other computer files. For example, credit records may be in error. Moreover, even if you correct an error in one file, the correction may not be made in other files. Indeed, erroneous information may stay in computer files for years. It's important to know, therefore, that you have some recourse. The law allows you to gain access to those records about you that are held by credit bureaus. Under the Freedom of Information Act (described below), you are also entitled to look at your records held by government agencies. (Portions may be deleted for national security reasons.)

Use of Electronic Networks   Suppose you use your company's electronic mail system to send a coworker an unflattering message about your supervisor. Later you find the boss has been spying on your exchange. Or suppose you are a subscriber to an online electronic bulletin board. You discover that the company that owns the bulletin board screens all your messages and rejects those it deems inappropriate.

Both these cases have actually happened. The first instance, of firms eavesdropping on employees, has inspired attempts at federal legislation. One proposed law would not prohibit electronic monitoring but would require employers to provide prior written notice. They would also have to alert employees during the monitoring with some sort of audible or visual signal. The second instance, in which online information services have restrictions against libelous, obscene, or otherwise offensive material, exists with most commercial services. In one case, the Prodigy Information Service terminated the accounts of eight members who were using the electronic-mail system to protest Prodigy's rate hikes.

Prodigy executives argued that the U.S. Constitution does not give members of someone else's private network the right to express their views without restrictions. Opponents say that the United States is becoming a nation linked by electronic mail. Therefore, there has to be fundamental protection for users against other people reading or censoring their messages.

The Major Laws on Privacy   Some federal laws governing privacy matters are as follows:

- *Fair Credit Reporting Act:* The **Fair Credit Reporting Act of 1970** is intended to keep inaccuracies out of credit bureau files. Credit agencies are barred from sharing credit information with anyone but authorized customers. Consumers have the right to review and correct their records and to be notified of credit investigations for insurance and employment.

Drawbacks: Credit agencies may share information with anyone they reasonably believe has a "legitimate business need." Legitimate is not defined.

- *Freedom of Information Act:* The **Freedom of Information Act of 1970** gives you the right to look at data concerning you that is stored by the federal government.

    Drawback: Sometimes a lawsuit is necessary to pry data loose.

- *Privacy Act:* The **Privacy Act of 1974** is designed to restrict federal agencies in the way they share information about American citizens. It prohibits federal information collected for one purpose from being used for a different purpose.

    Drawbacks: Exceptions written into the law permit federal agencies to share information anyway.

- *Right to Financial Privacy Act:* The **Right to Financial Privacy Act of 1979** sets strict procedures that federal agencies must follow when seeking to examine customer records in banks.

    Drawback: The law does not cover state and local governments.

- *Computer Fraud and Abuse Act:* The **Computer Fraud and Abuse Act of 1986** was passed to allow prosecution of unauthorized access to computers and databases.

    Drawbacks: The act is limited in scope. People with legitimate access can still get into computer systems and create mischief without penalty.

- *Video Privacy Protection Act:* The **Video Privacy Protection Act of 1988** prevents retailers from selling or disclosing video-rental records without the customer's consent or a court order.

    Drawbacks: The same restrictions do not apply to even more important files, such as medical and insurance records.

- *Computer Matching and Privacy Protection Act:* The **Computer Matching and Privacy Protection Act of 1988** sets procedures for computer matching of federal data. Such matching can be for verifying a person's eligibility for federal benefits or for recovering delinquent debts. Individuals are given a chance to respond before the government takes any adverse action against them.

    Drawbacks: Many possible computer matches are not affected, including those done for law-enforcement or tax reasons.

Currently, privacy is primarily an *ethical* issue, for many records stored by nongovernment organizations are not covered by existing laws. Yet individuals have shown that they are concerned about controlling who has the right to personal information and how it is used. Figure 13-4 summarizes a Code of Fair Information Practice. The code was recommended in 1977 by a committee established by former Secretary of Health, Education and Welfare Elliott Richardson. It has been adopted by many information-collecting businesses, but privacy advocates would like to see it written into law.

Threats to Computers

Threats to Computer Security Are Computer Crimes, Including Electronic Break-ins, and Natural and Other Hazards.

Keeping information private in part depends on keeping computer systems safe from criminal acts, natural hazards, and other threats.

1. *No secret databases:* There must be no record-keeping systems containing personal data whose very existence is kept secret.
2. *Right of individual access:* Individuals must be able to find out what information about them is in a record and how it is used.
3. *Right of consent:* Information about individuals obtained for one purpose cannot be used for other purposes without their consent.
4. *Right to correct:* Individuals must be able to correct or amend records of identifiable information about them.
5. *Assurance of reliability and proper use:* Organizations creating, maintaining, using, or disseminating records of identifiable personal data must make sure the data is reliable for its intended use. They must take precautions to prevent such data from being misused.

FIGURE 13-4
Principles of the Code of Fair Information Practice.

Computer Criminals A **computer crime** is an illegal action in which the perpetrator uses special knowledge of computer technology. Computer criminals are of four types:

- *Employees:* The largest category of computer criminals consists of those with the easiest access to computers—namely, employees (see Figure 13-5, p. 230). Sometimes the employee is simply trying to steal something from the employer—equipment, software, electronic funds, proprietary information, or computer time. Sometimes the employee may be acting out of resentment and is trying to "get back" at the company.
- *Outside users:* Not only employees but also some suppliers or clients may have access to a company's computer system. Examples are bank customers who use an automatic teller machine. Like employees, these authorized users may obtain confidential passwords or find other ways of committing computer crimes.

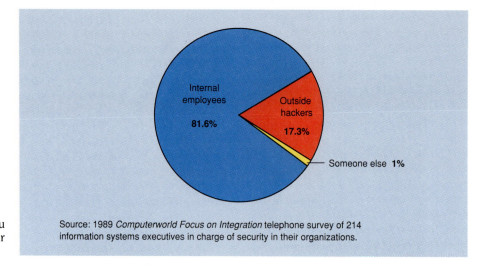

FIGURE 13-5
The experts reply: Whom do you consider to be a threat against your network?

Source: 1989 *Computerworld Focus on Integration* telephone survey of 214 information systems executives in charge of security in their organizations.

- *"Hackers" and "crackers":* Some people think of these two groups as being the same, but they are not. **Hackers** are people who gain unauthorized access to a computer system for the fun and challenge of it. **Crackers** do the same thing but for malicious purposes. They may intend to steal technical information or to introduce what they call a "bomb"—a destructive computer program—into the system. (A similar illegal user is the "phone phreak," who explores the phone system, often with the intent of making free phone calls.)

- *Organized crime:* Organized crime has discovered that computers can be used just like legitimate business people use them but for illegal purposes. For example, they are useful for keeping track of stolen goods or illegal gambling debts. In addition, counterfeiters and forgers use microcomputers and printers to produce sophisticated-looking documents, such as checks and driver's licenses.

Computer Crime   Computer crime can take various forms, as follows.

- *Damage:* Disgruntled employees sometimes attempt to destroy computers, programs, or files. For example, in a crime known as the **Trojan horse program** instructions can be written to destroy or modify software or data.
  In recent years, computer viruses have gained wide notoriety. **Viruses** are programs that "migrate" through networks and operating systems and attach themselves to different programs and databases (see Figure 13-6). A variant on the virus is the **worm,** also called **bacteria.** This destructive program fills a computer system with self-replicating information, clogging the system so that its operations are slowed or stopped. Viruses typically find their way into microcomputers through copied diskettes or programs downloaded from electronic bulletin boards. Because viruses can be so serious—certain "disk-killer" viruses can destroy all the information on one's system—computer users are advised to exercise care in accepting new programs and data from other sources (see Figure 13-7). Detection programs are available to alert users when certain kinds of viruses enter the system. Unfortunately, new viruses are being developed all the time and not all viruses can be detected.

- *Theft:* Theft can take many forms—of hardware, of software, of data, of computer time. Thieves steal equipment, of course, but there are also "white-collar crimes." Thieves steal data in the form of confidential information such as preferred client lists or use (steal) their company's computer time to run another business.

231
Threats to Computers

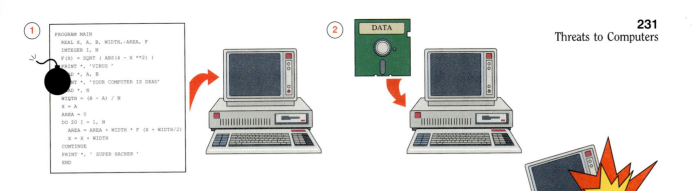

① A virus begins when a "cracker" or programmer writes a program that attaches itself to an operating system, another program, or piece of data.

② The virus travels via floppy disk or downloading from networks or bulletin boards anywhere that the operating system, program, or data travels.

③ The virus is set off. A nondestructive virus may simply print a message ("Surprise!"). A destructive virus may erase data, destroy programs, and even (through repeated reading and writing to one location) wear out a hard disk. The virus may be set off either by a time limit or by a sequence of operations by the user.

FIGURE 13-6
How a computer virus can spread.

1. Make back-up copies of your data on a frequent basis.
2. Protect data on your floppy disks by using write/protect tabs.
3. Turn off your microcomputer when you're not using it.
4. Don't use master disks. Make a working copy and store the master.
5. Avoid downloading computer games from electronic bulletin boards.
6. Limit your use of "shareware" programs.
7. Do not loan out your utility or other software programs.

FIGURE 13-7
How to prevent computer viruses and minimize damage.

Unauthorized copying—a form of theft—of programs for personal gain is called **software piracy.** According to the **Software Copyright Act of 1980,** it is legal for the owner of a program to make copies of that program for backup purposes. However, none of them can be resold or given away. A user may also modify a program to make it useful—again, provided it is not for purposes of resale. Penalties for violation of this law are payment of monetary damages to the developer of the program and even prison terms for offenders.

- *Manipulation:* Finding entry into someone's computer network and leaving a prankster's message may seem like fun, which is why hackers do it. It is still against the law. Moreover, even if the manipulation seems harmless, it may cause a great deal of anxiety and wasted time among network users.

    The **Computer Fraud and Abuse Act of 1986** makes it a crime for unauthorized persons even to *view* (let alone copy or damage) data using any computer across state lines. It also prohibits unauthorized use of any government computer or computer used by any federally insured financial institution. Offenders can be sentenced to up to 20 years in prison and fined up to $100,000.

    Of course, using a computer in the course of performing some other crime, such as selling fraudulent products, is also illegal.

Other Hazards   There are plenty of other hazards to computer systems and data besides criminals. They include the following:

- *Natural hazards:* Natural forces include fires, floods, wind, hurricanes, tornadoes, and earthquakes. Even home computer users should store back-up disks of programs and data in safe locations in case of fire or storm damage.

- *Civil strife and terrorism:* Wars, insurrections, and other forms of political unrest are real risks in some parts of the world. Even developed countries, however, must be mindful that acts of sabotage are possible.

- *Technological failures:* Hardware and software don't always do what they are supposed to do. For instance, too little electricity, caused by a brownout or blackout, may cause the loss of data in primary storage. Too much electricity, as when lightning or other electrical disturbance affects a power line, may cause a **voltage surge,** or **spike.** This excess of electricity may destroy chips or other electronic components of a computer.

    Many microcomputer users buy a low-cost **surge protector,** a device that separates the computer from the power source of the wall outlet. When a voltage surge occurs, it activates a circuit breaker in the surge protector, protecting the computer system.

    Another technological catastrophe is when a hard disk drive suddenly "crashes," or fails, perhaps because it has been bumped inadvertently. If the user has forgotten to make back-up copies of data on the hard disk, it may be lost.

- *Human errors:* Human mistakes are inevitable. Data-entry errors are probably the most commonplace. Programmer errors also occur frequently. Some mistakes may result from faulty design, as when a software manufacturer makes a deletion command closely resemble another command. Some may be the result of sloppy procedures, as when office workers keep important correspondence under filenames that no one else in the office knows.

Security

Security Measures Consist of Restricting Access, Anticipating Disasters, and Making Back-up Copies of Data.

Security is concerned with protecting information, hardware, and software. They must be protected from unauthorized use as well as from damage from intrusions, sabotage, and

FIGURE 13-8
Natural disasters such as fires can play havoc with computers as well as with other business assets.

natural disasters (see Figure 13-8). Considering the numerous ways in which computer systems and data can be compromised, we can see why security is a growing field. Some of the principal aspects are as follows.

Restricting Access Security experts are constantly devising ways to protect computer systems from access by unauthorized persons. Sometimes security is a matter of putting guards on company computer rooms and checking the identification of everyone admitted. Oftentimes it is a matter of being careful about assigning passwords to people and of changing them when people leave a company. *Passwords,* let us recall, are the secret words or numbers that must be keyed into a computer system before it will operate. In some "dial-back" computer systems, the user telephones the computer, punches in the correct password, and hangs up. The computer then calls back at a certain pre-authorized number.

Some security systems use **biometrics,** the science of measuring individual body characteristics. This may consist of using machines that can recognize one's fingerprints, signature, voice, or even photograph.

Anticipating Disasters Companies (and even individuals) that do not make preparations for disasters are not acting wisely. **Physical security** is concerned with protecting hardware from possible human and natural disasters. **Data security** is concerned with protecting software and data from unauthorized tampering or damage. Most large organizations have a **disaster recovery plan** describing ways to continue operating until normal computer operations can be restored.

Hardware can be kept behind locked doors, but often employees find this restriction a hindrance, and so security is lax. Fire and water (including the water from ceiling sprinkler systems) can do great damage to equipment. Many companies therefore will form a cooperative arrangement to share equipment with other companies in the event of catastrophe. Special emergency facilities may be created called **hot sites** if they are fully equipped computer centers. They are called **cold sites** if they are empty shells in which hardware must be installed.

Backing Up Data   Equipment can always be replaced. A company's *data,* however, may be irreplaceable. Most companies have ways of trying to keep software and data from being tampered with in the first place. They include careful screening of job applicants, guarding passwords, and auditing data and programs from time to time. The safest procedure, however, is to make frequent backups of data and to store them in remote locations.

Security for Microcomputers   If you own a microcomputer system, there are several procedures to follow to keep it safe:

- *Avoid extreme conditions:* Don't expose the computer to extreme conditions. Rain or sun from an open window, extreme temperatures, cigarette smoke, and spilled drinks or food are harmful to microcomputers. Clean your equipment regularly. Use a surge protector.
- *Guard the computer:* Put a cable lock on the computer. If you subscribe or belong to an online information service, do not leave passwords nearby. Etch your driver's license number or social security number into your equipment so that it can be identified in the event it is recovered after theft.
- *Guard programs and data:* Store disks properly, preferably in a locked container. Make backup copies of all your important files and programs. Store copies of your files in a different—and safe—location from the site of your computer.

A Look at the Future

New Legislation Will Be Needed to Define Access to Government Files and to Regulate Government Interference in Free Speech in the New Electronic World.

Technology often has a way of outracing existing social and political institutions. For instance, citizens have a right to request government records under the Freedom of Information Act. But even in its most recent amendment, in 1986, the act does not mention "computer" or define the word "record." Can the government therefore legally deny, as one agency did, a legitimate request for data on corporate compliance with occupational safety and health laws? *Access laws lag* behind even as the government collects more information than ever.

In addition, there has been a rise in computer-related crimes, such as bank and credit-card fraud, viruses, and electronic break-ins of government and private computer systems. As law-enforcement agencies crack down on these computer operators, they may also be jeopardizing the rights of computer users who are not breaking the law. Such users may be suffering illegal searches and violation of constitutional guarantees of free speech. However, it is not clear how the First Amendment protects speech and the Fourth Amendment protects against searches and seizures in this electronic world. One professor of constitutional law has proposed a *27th Amendment to the Constitution.* This amendment would extend the other freedoms in the Bill of Rights, such as those on free speech and restrictions on search and seizure, to cover all new technology and mediums for generating, storing, and altering information.

Review Questions

1. Define *ergonomics*.
2. What kind of activities can you take to avoid computer-related eyestrain, headaches, and back and neck pains?
3. What can you do to minimize the possible effects of electromagnetic field emissions?
4. What are *repetitive strain injuries* and how can they be avoided?
5. Describe some mental health problems associated with frequent computer use.
6. What are two major problems associated with the computer-related collection of personal data about you?
7. Discuss some of the privacy problems related to use of electronic networks.
8. Name and describe four of the seven major laws on privacy discussed in the chapter.
9. What four types of people are likely to be computer criminals?
10. How does a *computer virus* do damage?
11. What is *software piracy*?
12. What does the Computer Fraud and Abuse Act prohibit?
13. Name some of the principal hazards to computers other than computer crimes.
14. Define what is meant by *security*.
15. Name three ways of protecting the security of computers.
16. Discuss three ways of keeping microcomputers safe.

Discussion Questions

1. It used to be that only people who held jobs (or whose spouses had jobs) had credit cards. In recent years, however, banks have decided that some college students are good credit risks and have extended them Visa, MasterCard, gasoline, and other credit cards. If you are currently a credit-card holder, you might be curious what your credit rating is. As we stated in this chapter, the law permits you access to your credit records and allows you to correct any errors you see. Because errors may affect your credit rating itself (determining whether you will be eligible for loans in the future), this is an important right.

    The three major credit bureaus in the United States are as follows: (a) TRW, Box 749029, Dallas, TX 75374; (b) CBI/Equifax Credit Information Services, Box 720516, Atlanta, GA 30358; (c) Trans Union Corp., 212 South Market St., Wichita, KS 67202. To get a copy of your credit report, send a signed letter that includes your name, address (for the past five years, with dates), social security number, date of birth, and your spouse's name (if married). There may or may not be a fee (usually from $2 to $15). Once you have your report, look it over and let the bureau know of any inaccuracies.

2. What, exactly, *can* you find out about yourself from government files? What government files is your name apt to be in? (Some possibilities: Internal Revenue Service, Social Security Administration, Veterans Administration.) The Freedom of Information Act allows you access to government files, although portions may be deleted for national security reasons.

    For this exercise, go to the library and read up on the Freedom of Information Act. Determine what government agency or agencies probably have files that include facts about you. Find out where to write to get access to your file, then compose a letter to that agency or agencies. (Chances are you will not get a response within this semester or quarter, let alone access to your file, but at least you can start the process.)

CHAPTER 13
Workplace Issues, Privacy, and Security

V I S U A L   S U M M A R Y

One-third of Americans use a computer at work. Thus, there are many "people issues" connected with computers.

Workplace Issues

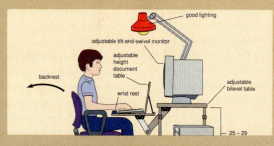

Users should take steps to increase productivity and avoid physical and mental health risks. **Ergonomics** is the study of human factors related to computers.

Physical Health Matters

Some computer-associated physical health matters that can be avoided:
- Eyestrain and headache: Take frequent breaks, avoid glare on monitor screen.
- Back and neck pains: Use adjustable chairs, tables, keyboards.
- Electromagnetic fields: May lead to miscarriages, but not proven. Sit 2 feet from screen, 3 feet from adjacent computers.
- **Repetitive strain injury (RSI):** Also known as **repetitive motion injury** and **cumulative trauma disorders,** RSIs are neck, wrist, hand, and arm injuries resulting from fast, repetitive work. **Carpal tunnel syndrome,** damage to nerves and tendons in hands, afflicts heavy keyboard users. Avoidance consists of frequent short rest breaks.

Mental Health Matters

Irritations consist of:
- Noise from clattering printers and high-frequency squeal from monitors.
- Stress from excessive monitoring.

Design with People in Mind

Computers are being designed for easier use.

Computers and Privacy

Privacy is the right to keep personal information about us from getting into the wrong hands.

Use of Large Databases

Large databases are constantly compiling information about us. A vast industry of data gatherers or "information resellers" collects data about us and sells it to direct marketers and others. This raises two questions:
- Information about you may be spread without your consent.
- Inaccurate information may be circulated from one computer file to another.

Use of Electronic Networks

Some information networks have been used to eavesdrop on employees or to restrict members' messages.

Major Laws on Privacy

Some federal laws governing privacy are:
- **Fair Credit Reporting Act (1970),** restricting sharing of credit information.
- **Freedom of Information Act (1970),** giving citizens right to see federal files about them.
- **Privacy Act (1974),** restricting federal information collected for one purpose from being used for another.
- **Right to Financial Privacy Act (1979),** setting procedures government must follow in seeking banks' customer records.
- **Computer Fraud and Abuse Act (1986),** prosecuting unauthorized access to computers and databases.
- **Video Privacy Protection Act (1988),** preventing retailers from disclosing customers' video-rental records.
- **Computer Matching and Privacy Protection Act (1988),** setting procedures for government's matching of federal data.

Visual Summary

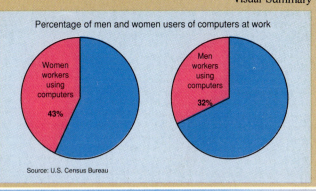

Threats to Computers

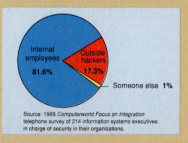

Threats to computers include the following:

Computer Criminals

Computer criminals are of four types:
- Employees—the largest category of computer criminals.
- Outside users—suppliers or clients.
- **Hackers,** who gain unauthorized access to computer systems for fun, and crackers, who do the same thing for malicious purposes.
- Organized crime figures, who use computers to assist illegal businesses or do forgeries and counterfeiting.

Computer Crime

Computer crime takes the following forms:
- Damage, as when criminals destroy files. The **Trojan horse program** is used to tamper with files or data. **Viruses** are programs that migrate through networks and operating systems and attach themselves to programs and databases, perhaps disabling them. A variant on the virus is a **worm (bacteria),** which fills the computer system until it stops.
- Theft, of hardware, software, data, or computer time. **Software piracy** is unauthorized copying of programs. The **Software Copyright Act (1980)** allows making copies for backup purposes only for personal use.
- Manipulation, as in unauthorized entry to a computer system for fun. The **Computer Fraud and Abuse Act (1986)** prohibits unauthorized persons from viewing data in computers used in crossing state lines.

Other Hazards

Other hazards to computer systems are:
- Natural hazards, such as fires and floods.
- Civil strife and terrorism.
- Technological failures, as when an electrical disturbance causes a **voltage surge (spike),** which may be avoided with a **surge protector** or circuit breaker.
- Human error, as in data-entry and programming mistakes, faulty hardware design, and sloppy procedures.

Security

Security is concerned with protecting information, hardware, and software from unauthorized use and from damage.

Restricting Access

Computer systems are protected by screening users, such as by asking them to type in correct passwords. Systems using **biometrics,** the science of measuring individual body characteristics, may recognize fingerprints or voices.

Anticipating Disasters

Physical security is concerned with protecting hardware from disasters. **Data security** is concerned with protecting software and data. Many organizations have a **disaster recovery plan** prescribing ways for computer systems to operate after a disaster. **Hot sites** are alternate computer centers. **Cold sites** are sites in which hardware must be installed.

Backing Up Data

Data must be frequently backed up and stored in safe places.

Security for Microcomputers

Procedures for safeguarding microcomputers are:
- Avoid extreme conditions, such as heat and smoke.
- Guard the computer, using locks.
- Guard programs and data, putting backup copies in a safe place.

CHAPTER 14
Your Future: Using Information Technology

COMPETENCIES

After you have read this chapter, you should be able to:

1. Explain why it's important to have an individual strategy in order to be a "winner" in the information age.

2. Describe how technology is changing the nature of competition.

3. Discuss three ways people may react to new technology.

4. Describe how you can use your computer competence to stay current and to take charge of your career.

Throughout this book, we have emphasized practical subjects that are useful to you now or will be very soon. Accordingly, this final chapter is not about the far future of, say, 10 years from now. Rather, it is about the near future—about developments whose outlines we can already see. It is about how organizations adapt to technological change. It is also about what you as an individual can do to keep your computer competency up to date.

Are the times changing any faster now than they ever have? It's hard to say. People who were alive when radios, cars, and airplanes were being introduced certainly lived through some dramatic changes. Has technology made our own times even more dynamic? Whatever the answer, it is clear we live in a fast-paced age. The challenge for you as an individual is to devise ways to stay current.

Being a Winner

To Be a Winner in the Information Revolution, You Need an *Individual* Strategy.

Most businesses have become aware that they must adapt to changing technology or be left behind. Many organizations are now making formal plans to keep track of technology and implement it in their competitive strategies. For example, banks have found that automated teller machines (ATMs) are vital to retail banking (see Figure 14-1). Not only do they require fewer human tellers, but they can also be made available 24 hours a day. More and more banks are also trying to go electronic, doing away with paper transactions wherever possible. Thus, ATM cards can now be used in certain places to buy gas or groceries. Many banks are also trying to popularize home banking, so that customers can use microcomputers for certain financial tasks. In addition, banks are exploring the use of some very sophisticated applications programs. These programs will accept and analyze cursive writing (the handwriting on checks) directly as input.

Clearly, such changes do away with some jobs—those of many bank tellers and cashiers, for example. However, they create opportunities for other people. New

FIGURE 14-1
Automatic teller machines are examples of technology used in business strategy.

technology requires people who are truly capable of working with it. These are not the people who think every piece of equipment is so simple they can just turn it on and use it. Nor are they those who think each new machine is a potential disaster. In other words, new technology needs people who are not afraid to learn it and are able to manage it. The real issue, then, is not how to make technology better. Rather, it is how to integrate the technology with people.

You are in a very favorable position compared with many other people in industry today. After reading the previous 13 chapters, you have learned not only the basics of hardware, software, and connectivity. You have also learned the most *current* technology. You are therefore able to use these tools to your advantage—to be a winner.

How do you become and stay a winner? In brief, the answer is: You must form your own individual strategy for dealing with change. First let us look at how businesses are handling technological change. Then let us look at how people are reacting to these changes. Finally, we will offer a few suggestions that will enable you to keep up with—and profit by—the information revolution.

Technology and Organizations

Technology Changes the Nature of Competition by Introducing New Products, New Enterprises, and New Relationships Among Customers and Suppliers.

Technology can introduce new ways businesses compete with each other. Some of the principal changes are as follows.

New Products Technology creates products that operate faster, are priced cheaper, are often of better quality, or are wholly new. Indeed, new products can be custom tailored to a particular customer's needs. For example, financial services company Merrill Lynch took advantage of technology to launch a Cash Management Account. This ac-

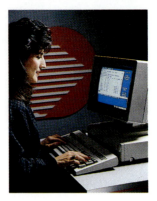

FIGURE 14-2
The Sabre reservations system used by American Airlines.

count combines information on a person's checking, savings, credit card, and securities accounts into a single monthly statement. It automatically sets aside "idle" funds into interest-bearing money market funds. The result is that customers can get a complete picture of their financial condition at one time. However, even if they don't pay much attention to their statements, their surplus funds are invested automatically.

New Enterprises Information technology can build entire new businesses. An example is the availability of facsimile (fax) machine business. Now chains of quick-print and photocopying shops offer fax services. For a few dollars you can send a fax message to, or receive one from, nearly anywhere in the United States.

A company may use its extra information systems capability to develop new services for customers outside the area it serves directly. For example, American Airlines has a reservations system called Sabre that lists the flight schedules of every major airline in the world. Travel agents with online access to Sabre pay American a fee for every reservation made on Sabre for other airlines (see Figure 14-2).

New Customer and Supplier Relationships Businesses that make their information systems easily available may make their customers less likely to take their business elsewhere. For instance, Federal Express, the overnight package delivery service, does everything possible to make its customers dependent on it. Airbills are given to the customer with the customer's name, address, and account number preprinted on them, making shipping and billing easier. Package numbers are scanned into the company's information system, so that they can be tracked from pickup point to destination (see Figure 14-3). Thus, apprehensive customers can be informed very quickly of the exact location of their packages as they travel toward their destination.

Technology and People

People May Be Cynical, Naïve, or Frustrated by Technology.

Clearly, recent technological changes, and those sure to come in the near future, will produce some upheavals in the years ahead. How should we be prepared for them?

People have different coping styles when it comes to technology. It has been suggested, for instance, that people react to the notion of microcomputers in business in three ways. These ways are *cynicism, naïveté,* and *frustration.*

FIGURE 14-3
Federal Express tries to make its customers dependent on it by using its information systems to make package delivery reliable.

241
Technology and People

FIGURE 14-4
The cynic: "These gadgets are overrated."

Cynicism The cynic feels that, for a manager at least, the idea of using a microcomputer is overrated (see Figure 14-4). Learning and using it take too much time, time that could be delegated to someone else. Doing spreadsheets and word processing, according to the cynic, are tasks that managers should understand. However, their real job is to develop plans and set goals for the people being supervised.

Cynics may express their doubts openly, especially if they are top managers. Or they may only pretend to be interested in microcomputers, when actually they are not interested at all.

Naïveté Naïve people may be unfamiliar with computers. Thus, they may think computers are magic boxes capable of solving all kinds of problems that they are really unable to handle (see Figure 14-5). In contrast, some naïve persons are actually quite familiar with computers. However, such people underestimate the difficulty of changing computer systems or of generating information.

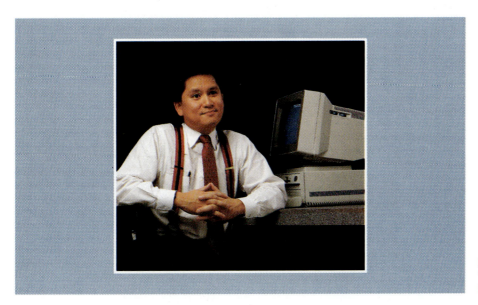

FIGURE 14-5
The naïve: "Let the computer make the decision."

FIGURE 14-6
The frustrated: "This stuff doesn't make sense half the time."

Frustration The frustrated person may already be quite busy and may hate having to take time to learn about microcomputers. Such a person feels imposed on at having to learn to keep up. Often she or he is too impatient to try to understand the manuals explaining what hardware and software are supposed to do. The result, therefore, is continual frustration (see Figure 14-6). Some people are frustrated because they try to do too much. Or they're frustrated because they find manuals difficult to understand. Oftentimes, they feel stupid, when actually the manuals are at fault.

Cynicism, naïveté, and frustration are not just confined to microcomputers, of course. They apply to all new technology. Do you see yourself reacting in any of these ways? They are actually commonplace responses—part of just being human. Knowing which, if any, of these reactions characterize you or your superiors may help you survive and react in positive ways in organizational life.

How You Can Be a Winner

Individuals Need to Stay Current, Develop Specialties, and Be Alert to Organizational Changes and Opportunities for Innovation.

So far we have described how progressive organizations are using technology in the information age. Now let's concentrate on you as an individual. How can you stay ahead? Here are some ideas.

Stay Current Whatever their particular line of work, successful professionals keep up both with their own fields and with the times. We don't mean you should try to become a computer expert and read a lot of technical magazines. Rather, you should concentrate on your profession and learn how computer technology is being used within it.

Every field has trade journals, whether the field is interior design, personnel management, advertising, or whatever. Most such journals regularly present articles about the uses of computers. It's important that you also belong to a trade or industry association and go to its meetings. Many associations sponsor seminars and conferences that describe the latest information and techniques.

Maintain Your Computer Competence Actually, you should try to stay *ahead* of the technology. Books (see Figure 14-7), journals, and trade associations are the best source

FIGURE 14-7
Some books covering computers.

FIGURE 14-8
Professional organizations and contacts help you keep up in your field.

of information about new technology that applies to your field. The general business press—*Business Week, Fortune, Inc., The Wall Street Journal,* and the business section of your local newspaper—also carries computer-related articles.

However, if you wish, you can subscribe to a magazine that covers microcomputers and information more specifically. Examples are *InfoWorld, PC World,* and *MacWorld.* You may also find it useful to look at newspapers and magazines that cover the computer industry as a whole. An example of such a periodical is *ComputerWorld.*

Develop Professional Contacts Besides being members of professional associations, successful people make it a point to maintain contact with others in their field. They stay in touch by telephone and letter and go to lunch with others in their line of work. Doing this lets them learn what other people are doing in their jobs. It tells them what other firms are doing and what tasks are being automated. Developing professional contacts can keep you abreast not only of new information but also of new job possibilities (see Figure 14-8). It also offers social benefits. An example of a professional organization that is found in many areas is the local association of realtors.

Develop Specialties Develop specific as well as general skills. You want to be well rounded within your field, but certainly not a "jack of all trades, master of none." Master a trade or two *within* your profession. At the same time, don't become identified with a specific technological skill that might very well become obsolete.

The best advice is to specialize to some extent. However, don't make your specialty so tied to technology that you'll be in trouble if the technology shifts. For example, if your career is in marketing or graphics design, it makes sense to learn about desktop publishing (see Figure 14-9). That way you can learn to make high-quality, inexpensive graphics layouts. It would not make as much sense for you to become an expert on, say, the various types of monitors used to display the graphics layouts because such monitors are continually changing.

Expect to take classes during your working life to keep up with developments in your field. Some professions require more keeping up than others—that of a computer spe-

FIGURE 14-9
Desktop publishing: a good specialty to develop for certain careers.

FIGURE 14-10
Informal communication can alert you to important organizational changes.

cialist, for example, compared to that of a personnel manager. Whatever the training required, always look for ways to adapt and improve your skills to become more productive and marketable. There may be times when you are tempted to start all over again and learn completely new skills. However, a better course of action is to use emerging technology to improve your present base of skills. This way you can build on your current strong points and then branch out to other fields from a position of strength.

Be Alert for Organizational Change Every organization has formal lines of communication—for example, supervisor to middle manager to top manager. However, there is also the grapevine—informal lines of communication (see Figure 14-10). Some service departments will serve many layers of management and be abreast of the news on all levels. For instance, the art director for advertising may be aware of several aspects of a companywide marketing campaign. Secretaries and administrative assistants know what is going on in more than one area.

Being part of the office grapevine can alert you to important changes—for instance, new job openings—that can benefit you. However, you always have to assess the validity of what you hear on the grapevine. Moreover, it's not advisable to be a contributor to "office gossip." Behind-the-back criticisms of other people can have a way of getting back to the person criticized.

Be especially alert for new trends within the organization—about future hiring, layoffs, automation, mergers with other companies, and the like. Be alert for areas receiving the greatest attention from top management. One tip-off is to see what kind of outside consultants are being brought in. Independent consultants are usually invited in because a company believes it needs advice in an area with which it has insufficient experience.

Look for Innovative Opportunities You may understand your job better than anyone—even if you've only been there a few months. Look for ways to make it more efficient. How can present procedures be automated? How can new technology make your tasks easier? Discuss your ideas with your supervisor, the training director, or the head of the information systems department. Or discuss them with someone else who can see that you get the recognition you deserve. (Coworkers may or may not be receptive and may or may not try to take credit themselves.)

FIGURE 14-11
Present your ideas as saving money rather than "improving information."

A good approach is to present your ideas in terms of *saving money* rather than "improving information" (see Figure 14-11). Managers are generally more impressed with ideas that can save dollars than with ideas that seem like potential breakthroughs in the quality of decisions.

In general, it's best to concentrate on the business and organizational problems that need solving. Then look for a technological way of solving them. That is, avoid becoming too enthusiastic about a particular technology and then trying to make it fit the work situation.

A Look at the Future: The Rest of Your Life
Being Computer-Competent Means Always Taking Positive Control.

This is not the end; it is the beginning. Being a skilled computer end user—being computer-competent—is not a matter of thinking "Some day I'll . . . " ("Some day I'll have to learn all about that."). It is a matter of living in the present and keeping an eye on the future. It is also a matter of having the discipline to keep up with the prevailing technology. It is not a matter of focusing on vague "what-ifs." It is a matter of concentrating on your goals and learning how the computer can help you achieve them. Being an end user, in short, is not about trying to avoid failure. Rather, it is about always going toward success—about taking control over the exciting new tools available to you.

Review Questions

1. How do you become and stay a winner in the information age?
2. Give an example of how technology can change the nature of competition.

CHAPTER 14
**Your Future:
Using Information Technology**

VISUAL SUMMARY

Being a winner in the Information Revolution means devising an individual strategy for dealing with change.

Technology and Organizations

Technology can introduce new ways businesses compete with each other.

New Products

Technology creates products that operate faster, are priced more cheaply, are often of better quality, or are wholly new. New products can be custom tailored to a particular customer's needs.

New Enterprises

Technology can build entire new businesses (e.g., an airline charges travel agents for using its reservations system for making reservations on other airlines).

New Customer and Supplier Relationships

Businesses that make their information systems easily available may make their customers less likely to take their business elsewhere (e.g., overnight delivery services closely track packages and bills).

Technology and People

Three common reactions to the prospect of new technology are:

Cynicism

The cynics feel that new technology is overrated and too troublesome to learn.

Naïveté

The naïve believe that technology can solve problems it cannot.

Frustration

The frustrated are impatient and irritated about taking time to learn new technology.

247
Visual Summary

Being a skilled computer end user—being computer-competent—is a matter of living in the present and keeping an eye on the future. It is a matter of concentrating on your goals and learning how the computer can help you achieve them.

How You Can Be a Winner

Six ongoing activities that can help you be successful are as follows:

Stay Current

Stay current in your field—by reading trade journals and the general business press and by joining professional associations.

Maintain Your Computer Competence

Stay current with technology—by being alert for computer-related articles in trade journals in your field, general computer magazines, and books.

Develop Professional Contacts

Develop professional contacts with others in your field.

Develop Specialties

Develop some specialties within your field, mastering a trade or two within your profession.

Be Alert for Organizational Change

Use informal lines of communication—the "grapevine"—to be alert for organizational changes.

Look for Innovative Opportunities

Improve your prospects by looking for ways to make your job more efficient—e.g., by finding ways to save money.

3. What are three responses or attitudes that people are apt to have when confronted by new technology?
4. Name six strategies individuals should follow in order to be successful in the information age.
5. What periodicals might you read in order to keep current on changes in microcomputer technology?

Discussion Questions

1. We have discussed the future. What about the past? What about all those obsolete but still useful ("orphaned") microcomputers and related equipment? One solution is offered by groups that collect donated hardware and software for nonprofit organizations. (Examples are organizations concerned with conservation, veterans, child care, arts, and so on.) These groups also offer "mentors," volunteers with some experience in microcomputers who assist the nonprofit organizations in learning to use their new systems.

    Two examples are CompuMentor (89 Stillman St., San Francisco, CA 94107), and Connect (c/o Technical Development Corporation, 11 Beacon St., Suite 1100, Boston, MA 02108). Are you aware of anyone with equipment or skills to donate? Try contacting these or similar organizations (you may learn about them through local computer users' groups) to see how you can help.

2. If you were to take another course on computers or information science, what would probably interest (or benefit) you most?

GLOSSARY

Access Arm: The arm that holds the read-write head and moves back and forth over the surface of a diskette.

Access Time: The period between the time that the computer requests data from a secondary storage device and the time that the transfer of data is completed.

Accounts Payable: The activity that shows the money a company owes to its suppliers for the materials and services it has received.

Accounts Receivable: The activity that shows what money has been received from or is owed by customers.

Ada: A procedural language named after Ada Augusta, daughter of the nineteenth-century English poet Lord Byron. She is considered to be the first programmer. Originally designed for weapons systems, Ada has commercial uses as well.

Adapter Card: *See* Expansion Board.

Address: Location in primary storage in which character of data or instruction is stored during processing.

AI: *See* Artificial Intelligence.

ALU (Arithmetic-Logic Unit): The part of the CPU that performs arithmetic and logical operations.

Analog Signal: A signal that represents a range of frequencies, such as the human voice.

Analytical Graphics: A form of graphics used to put numeric data into forms that are easier to analyze, such as bar charts, line graphs, and pie charts.

Applications Generator: Software with modules that have been preprogrammed to accomplish various tasks, such as calculation of overtime pay.

Applications Software: Software that can perform useful work such as word processing, cost estimating, or accounting tasks.

Artificial Intelligence (AI): A field of computer science that attempts to develop computer systems that can mimic or simulate human thought processes and actions.

Artificial Reality: Interactive sensory equipment (headgear and gloves) that allows user to experience alternative realities to the physical world.

ASCII (American Standard Code for Information Interchange): A binary coding scheme widely used on all computers, including microcomputers.

Assembly Languages: The second generation of programming languages. These languages use abbreviations for program instructions.

Asynchronous Communications Port: *See* Serial Port.

Asynchronous Transmission: The method whereby data is sent and received one byte at a time.

Automated Design Tool: Software package that evaluates hardware and software alternatives according to requirements given by the systems analyst.

Backup Diskette: Duplicate copy of program or data diskette.

Backup Tape Cartridge Unit: *See* Magnetic Tape Streamer.

Bacteria: *See* Worm.

Bandwidth: The bit-per-second transmission capability of a channel.

Bar Code: A code consisting of vertical zebra-striped marks printed on cans, boxes, and other containers, read with a bar-code reader.

Bar-Code Reader: Input device consisting of photoelectric scanner that reads bar codes for processing.

BASIC (Beginner's All-purpose Symbolic Instruction Code): An easy-to-learn procedural programming language widely used on microcomputers.

Basic Input Output System: *See* BIOS.

Batch Processing: Processing performed all at once on data that has been collected over several days.

Bidirectional: Characteristic of printer, in which print element moves first to the right on one line, then to the left on the following line.

Binary System: A numbering system in which all numbers consist of only two digits—0 and 1.

Biometrics: Science of measuring individual body characteristics. Some security systems use biometric machines that can recognize a person's fingerprints, signature, or voice.

BIOS (Basic Input Output System): Type of systems software. Consists of programs that interpret keyboard characters or transmit characters to monitor or diskette.

Bit (Binary Digit): A 0 or 1 in the binary system.

Block: A portion of text that is marked before being processed further.

Block (of records): Group of records on magnetic tape.

Block Move: The process of moving a unit of text that has been marked (blocked).

Boldface: Printing consisting of extra dark lettering.

Bootstrap Loader: Systems software that starts up computer when the machine is turned on and loads operating system into primary storage.

bps: Acronym for bits per second.

Broadband: The bandwidth that includes microwave, satellite, coaxial cable, and fiber-optic channels. It is used for very high speed computers.

Bus Line (Bus): An electronic data roadway that connects parts of the CPU with each other and the CPU with other important devices. Also a connecting cable in a bus network.

Bus Network: A network where all communications travel along a common path. Each device in the network handles its own communications control. There is no host computer or file server.

Byte: A unit consisting of eight bits. There are 256 possible bit combinations in a byte.

C: A general-purpose procedural language originally designed for writing operating systems. Widely used and portable.

CAD (Computer-Aided Design): A type of computer program that manipulates images such as three-dimensional objects on the screen.

CAD/CAM: Acronym for Computer-Aided Design/Computer-Aided Manufacturing.

CADD (Computer-Aided Design and Drafting): Programs that come equipped with straight lines, arcs, circles, and other elements for making graphic designs.

CAM (Computer-Aided Manufacturing): A type of program that controls automated factory equipment, including machine tools and robots.

Carpal Tunnel Syndrome: A disorder found among heavy computer users, consisting of damage to nerves and tendons in the hands. *See also* Repetitive Strain Injury.

CASE (Computer-Aided Software Engineering) Tool: *See* Automated Design Tool.

CD–ROM (Compact Disk–Read-Only Memory): A form of optical disk that allows data to be read but not recorded.

Cell: The intersection of a row and a column in a spreadsheet.

Cell Address: The position of a cell in a spreadsheet.

Cell Pointer: An indicator for the place where data is to be entered or changed in a spreadsheet.

CGA (Color Graphics Adapter): Circuit board that may be inserted into a microcomputer that changes some monitors from monochrome to color display. It offers four colors.

Chain Printer: Printer used mainly with mainframes and microcomputers. It consists of a printing chain with several sets of characters that moves at high speed in front of the paper. A hammer strikes paper and ribbon against the character.

Character: A letter, number, or other symbol.

Character-Based Interface: Arrangement for issuing commands, in which users type commands or select items from a menu. *Compare* Graphical User Interface.

Checklist: List of questions that helps show whether key elements are being evaluated in the present system.

Child Node: A node one level below the node being considered in a hierarchical database or network.

Chip: Integrated electronic circuit consisting of a tiny (1/8-inch square) circuit board etched on silicon. Examples are CPU and memory chips.

Closed Architecture: Computer designed so that users cannot get inside to add any new devices.

Coaxial Cable: A high-frequency transmission cable that replaces the multiple wires of telephone lines with a single solid copper core.

COBOL (COmmon Business-Oriented Language): A procedural language most frequently used in business, originally developed by Admiral Grace Hopper.

Coding: The fourth step of the programming procedure, during which the actual program is written in a programming language.

Cold Site: Special emergency facility in which hardware must be installed but which is available to a company in the event of disaster to its computer system. *Compare* Hot Site.

Column Headings: The labels across the top of the worksheet area of a spreadsheet.

Common Operational Database: An integrated collection of records that contains details about the operations of a company.

Common User Database: A type of company database that contains selected information both from the common operational database and from outside proprietary databases.

Common User Interface: Similar software screen that can be used to access different hardware.

Communications System: *See* Data Communications System.

Company Database: A collection of integrated records shared throughout a company or other organization.

Compatible: Low-cost microcomputer made by a competitor that is compatible with microcomputers made by a major manufacturer, such as International Business Machines. "Compatible" means it will run most of the same software as will run on IBM machines.

Competency: *See* Computer Competency.

Compiler: Software that converts the programmer's procedural-language program (source code) into machine language (object code).

Computer Competency: Achievement of sufficient knowledge about and skill with computers so that end users can meet their information needs and improve their productivity.

Computer Crime: Illegal action in which the perpetrator uses special knowledge of computer technology. Criminals may be employees, outside users, hackers and crackers, and organized crime members.

Computer Fraud and Abuse Act (1986): Law allowing prosecution of unauthorized access to computers and databases.

Computer Matching and Privacy Protection Act (1988): Law setting procedures for computer matching of federal data for verifying eligibility for federal benefits or for recovering delinquent debts.

Computer Network: A communications system connecting two or more computers and their peripheral devices.

Computer Program: *See* Program.

Computer System: A system consisting of people, procedures, software, hardware, and data.

Computer Virus: Hidden instructions that migrate through networks and operating systems and become embedded in different programs. They may be designed to destroy data or simply to display messages.

Connectivity: The electronic connections between computers and information resources and the resulting connections between people that such technology allows.

Control Unit: The section of the CPU that tells the rest of the computer how to carry out program instructions.

Controller Card: *See* Expansion Board.

Conversion: *See* Systems Implementation.

Coprocessor Chip: A chip that is subordinate to the main processor (CPU). It assists the main processor in performing very fast mathematical computations.

Copy: Duplicate.

CPU (Central Processing Unit): Part of the computer that consists of the control unit, arithmetic-logic unit, and primary storage. It executes program instructions.

Cracker: Person who gains unauthorized access to a computer system for malicious purposes. *Compare* Hacker.

CRT (Cathode-Ray Tube): An output display device that resembles a television screen.

Cumulative Trauma Disorders: *See* Repetitive Strain Injury.

Cursor: A blinking symbol on the screen that shows where data may be entered next.

Custom-Made Software (Custom Program): Software designed by a professional programmer for a particular purpose.

Daisy Wheel: A wheel consisting of spokes, with each spoke ending in a raised character.

Daisy-Wheel Printer: Letter-quality printer that uses a daisy wheel. When a spoke on the wheel is struck with a hammer against an inked ribbon, the character image is transferred to paper.

Data: The raw, unprocessed facts that are input to a computer system.

Data Bank: *See* Proprietary Database.

Data Communications System: An electronic system that transmits data over communications lines from one location to another.

Data Dictionary: A dictionary that contains a description of the structure of data used in a database.

Data Flow Diagram: Diagram used by systems analyst to show data or information flow within an information system.

Data Processing System: *See* Transaction Processing Information System.

Data Security: Activity concerned with protecting software and data from unauthorized tampering or damage.

Data Transfer Time: The time taken for data to be transferred from the disk track to primary storage.

Database: A collection of integrated data that gives different people access to the same data to use for different purposes.

Database Manager: *See* DBMS.

DBA (Database Administrator): The person who helps determine the structure of, performance of, and access to databases in a company.

DBMS (Database Management System): A program for setting up a database and retrieving information from it later. Consists of a data dictionary and a query language.

Debugging: The fifth step of the programming procedure. A programmer's word for testing the program and then eliminating errors.

Decentralized System: *See* Distributed Data Processing System.

Decision Model: A model that is based on statistical packages, simulations, long-range plans, and other concepts. It gives the decision support system its analytical capabilities.

Decision Table: Shows the decision rules that apply when certain conditions occur and what action should take place as a result.

Dedicated Fax Machine: Specialized machine for sending and receiving images of documents over telephone lines.

Demand Report: The opposite of a scheduled report. A demand report—for example, a revised sales forecast—is produced on request.

Demodulation: The process performed by modems in converting analog signals to digital signals.

Desk Checking: The process of checking out a computer program by studying the program listing while sitting at a desk.

Desktop Manager: Program that stays in microcomputer's memory (primary storage) at the same time other programs are being run. The desktop manager allows the user to interrupt the other program and gain access to "desktop accessories" such as appointment calendar, notepad, and calculator.

Desktop Publishing: The process of using a microcomputer, laser printer, and the necessary software to mix text and graphics to produce final, composed pages.

Diagnostic Routine: Program in systems software that starts up when a microcomputer is turned on. Diagnostic routines test the primary storage, CPU, and other parts of the system to make sure the computer is running properly.

Digital Signal: A signal that represents the presence or absence of an electronic pulse.

Digitizer: Input device that can be used to trace a copy of a drawing or photograph. The shape is converted to digital data, which can then be represented on a monitor screen or printed out on paper.

Digitizing Tablet: A tablet that can be used to create images by moving a special stylus over its surface. The image is then converted to electronic signals that can be processed by a computer.

Direct Access Storage: A form of storage that allows any particular piece of information to be retrieved directly.

Direct Approach: The approach for systems implementation whereby the old system is simply abandoned for the new.

Direct Entry: Form of input that does not require data to be keyed by someone sitting at a keyboard. Direct-entry devices create machine-readable data on paper or magnetic media or feed it directly into the computer's CPU.

Direct File Organization: A file organization that makes use of key fields to go directly to the record being sought rather than reading records one after another.

Directional Arrow Keys: The keys labeled with arrows, used to move the cursor.

Disaster Recovery Plan: Plan used by large organizations describing ways to continue operating following disaster until normal computer operations can be restored.

Disk Address: The identifiable location on a disk where data is stored.

Disk Drive: Input mechanism that obtains stored data and programs from a diskette. It also stores data and programs on a diskette.

Disk Pack (Hard-Disk Pack): A disk pack that uses the same basic technology as hard disks but resembles a stack of phonograph records with multiple recording surfaces and read-write heads.

Diskette (Disk): A flat, circular piece of magnetically treated mylar plastic that rotates within a jacket.

Display Screen: *See* Monitor.

Distributed Data Processing System: A data processing system that consists of a mainframe and minicomputers that are geographically separated but linked together by communications.

Distributed Database: A database that can be made accessible through a variety of communications networks. That allows portions of the database to be located in different places.

DO UNTIL and DO WHILE Structures: Two particular forms of loop structures.

Document: Any kind of text material, such as a letter or a report.

Documentation: The sixth (and final) step of the programming procedure. Consists of written descriptions and procedures about a program and how to use it. Should be carried on throughout all steps of the programming procedure.

DOS (Disk Operating System): The standard operating system for all computers advertised as "IBM-compatible."

Dot-Matrix Printer: A printer that forms characters or images using a matrix of pins that strike an inked ribbon.

Downloading: The process of transferring information from a remote computer to the computer that you are operating.

Down-sizing: Describes applications being moved from larger computers to smaller ones, as from mainframes and minicomputers to microcomputers.

Drive A: Normally the disk drive into which a microcomputer user inserts the program diskette. On many microcomputers, drive A is the left-hand or upper drive.

Drive B: Normally the disk drive into which a microcomputer user inserts the data diskette. It is often the right-hand or lower drive.

Drive Gate: The door covering the slot in a disk drive into which a diskette is inserted.

Drum Plotter: A plotter that produces images by moving a pen linearly as the paper is rolled on a drum.

DSS (Decision Support System): A system that draws on an organization's MIS and outside databases to produce flexible, on-demand reports for managers.

Dumb Terminal: A terminal that can be used to input and receive data, but cannot process the data independently.

EBCDIC (Extended Binary Coded Decimal Interchange Code): A binary coding scheme that is a standard for minicomputers and mainframe computers.

EGA (Enhanced Graphics Adapter): Circuit board that may be inserted into a microcomputer producing 16 colors on a monitor. It offers higher-quality resolution than CGA.

EIS (Executive Information System): Software that draws data from an organization's databases together in patterns meaningful to top executives.

EISA: *See* Extended Industry Standard Architecture.

EL (Electroluminescent) Display: A display that actively emits light when electrically charged.

Electronic Bulletin Board: Electronically posted information on a computer that can be accessed by other computers using telephone lines.

Electronic Spreadsheet: A form based on the traditional accounting worksheet that can be used to present and analyze numeric data.

E-Mail (Electronic Mail): Similar to an electronic bulletin board, but provides confidentiality and may use special communications rather than telephone lines.

End User: A person who uses microcomputers or has access to large computers.

Enter Key: The key used to enter a command into the computer after it has been typed.

EPROM (Erasable Programmable Read-Only Memory): A

chip that contains instructions that can be written and then erased with ultraviolet light so that the instructions can be changed.

Erasable Optical Disk: An optical disk on which the disk drive can write information and also erase and rewrite information.

Erase: Remove, as in removing obsolete electronic files from a diskette.

Ergonomics: The study of human factors related to computers.

ESS (Executive Support System): *See* EIS.

Exception Report: Report that calls attention to unusual events, such as problems with a production schedule.

Expansion Board: Optional device board that is usually added inside the system cabinet.

Expert System: Sophisticated knowledge-based system that essentially emulates the knowledge of human experts skilled in a particular field.

Exporting: Feature that allows file to be saved in a form so that it can be inserted into another program, as from a word processing program into a spreadsheet. *Compare* Importing.

Extended Industry Standard Architecture (EISA): Standard for bus line developed by nine manufacturers of IBM-compatible microcomputers. This bus line has a 32-bit-wide data path, but it is designed to extend the old ISA (Industry Standard Architecture) bus standard.

External Modem: A modem that stands apart from the computer and is connected by a cable to the computer's serial port.

Facsimile Transmission (Fax) Machine: Device that scans an image and sends it electronically over telephone lines to receiving fax machine, which converts electronic signals back to an image and re-creates it on paper.

Fair Credit Reporting Act (1970): Law prohibiting credit agencies from sharing credit information with anyone but authorized customers and giving consumers right to review and correct their credit records.

Fiber-Optic Cable: A special transmission cable made of glass tubes that are immune to electronic interference. Data is transmitted through fiber-optic cables in the form of pulses of light.

Field: An item consisting of one or more logically related characters.

File: A collection of logically related records.

File Server: A hard-disk storage device with large capacity.

Firmware: *See* ROM.

Flatbed Plotter: Plotter that holds the paper stable while a pen moves around the paper.

Flat-Panel Display: Display that uses technologies that allow the screen to be a flat panel instead of a bulky tube such as that used in television receivers.

Flat Tension Mask: A new technology that produces a much more brilliant video image than other conventional graphics monitors.

Flexible Disk (Flexible Diskette): *See* Diskette.

Flexible-Disk Drive: The device used to retrieve information from and store information on a diskette.

Floppy Disk (Floppy): *See* Diskette.

Flowchart: *See* Program Flowchart; System Flowchart.

Format: Appearance of a text document, such as spacing or margins.

Formatting: The process of placing tracks and sectors on a disk before using it to record data and programs.

Form-Letter Feature: *See* Mail-Merge Feature.

Formula: The instructions for a calculation in a spreadsheet.

FORTRAN (FORmula TRANslation): The most widely used scientific and mathematical procedural language.

Freedom of Information Act (1970): Law giving citizens right to examine data about them in federal government files, except for that restricted for national security reasons.

Front-End Processor: A specialized computer that helps handle the input data from other devices. This leaves the mainframe computer free for other tasks.

Full-Duplex Communications: A mode of communications in which data is transmitted back and forth at the same time.

Function Keys: Keys labeled *F1, F2,* and so on, used for tasks that occur frequently, such as underlining in word processing.

Gantt Chart: Chart using bars and lines to indicate the time scale of a series of tasks.

Gas-Plasma Display: Form of technology used in some flat screens for portable computers. Like a neon light bulb, the monitor uses a gas that emits light in the presence of an electric current.

Gate: *See* Drive Gate.

Gateway: *See* Network Gateway.

GB or G-byte (Gigabyte): A unit of capacity equal to 1,073,741,824 bytes (about one billion bytes).

General Ledger: The activity that produces income statements and balance sheets based on all transactions in a company.

Generations of Programming Languages: The five generations are machine languages, assembly languages, procedural languages, problem-oriented languages, and natural languages.

Graphical User Interface (GUI): Special screen that allows software commands to be issued through the use of graphic symbols (icons) or pull-down menus.

Graphics Monitor: Monitor that displays both alphanumeric characters and visual or graphic images.

Grid Chart: Chart that shows the relationship between input and output documents.

Groupware: Software that allows two or more people on a communications network to work on the same document at the same time.

Hacker: Person who gains unauthorized access to a computer system for the fun and challenge of it. *Compare* Cracker.

Half-Duplex Communications: A mode of communications in which data flows in both directions, but not simultaneously.

Hardcard: Circuit board with hard disk drive that plugs into an expansion slot in a microcomputer.

Hard Copy: Images output on paper by a printer or plotter.

Hard Disk: Enclosed disk drive that contains one or more metallic disks. A hard disk has many times the capacity of a diskette.

Hard-Disk Cartridge: A device containing a hard disk, which can be removed from and inserted into a drive as easily as a cassette in a videotape recorder.

Hard-Disk Drive: A nonremovable, enclosed disk drive that reads data from and writes data to a hard disk.

Hardware: Equipment that includes a keyboard, monitor, printer, the computer itself, and other devices.

Head Crash: A hard-disk disaster that happens when the surface of the read-write head itself or particles on the surface of the head come into contact with the magnetic disk surface. A head crash causes the loss of some or all of the data on the disk.

Head Switching Time: The time required for a particular read-write head to be activated.

Help Menu (Help Screen): Explanations of how to perform various tasks presented on the screen.

Hierarchical Database: A database in which the fields or records are structured in nodes, like the hierarchy of managers in a corporation.

Hierarchical Network: A network consisting of several computers linked to a host computer, just like a star network. However, the computers linked to the host are themselves hosts to other computers.

Highlighting: Special lighting of a block of text or data displayed on the screen.

Host Computer: A central computer, such as a mainframe computer at a company's headquarters or central office. The central computer in a star network.

Hot Site: Special emergency facility consisting of fully equipped computer center, available to a company in the event of disaster to its computer system. *Compare* Cold Site.

Hybrid Network: *See* Hierarchical Network.

Hypermedia: *See* Multimedia.

Hypertext: Software that enables users to organize and access information so that any file can be connected with any other file.

IBG (Interblock Gap): The separation between blocks of records on magnetic tape.

IBM-Compatible: *See* Compatible.

Icon: Graphic symbol on a screen representing a command (e.g., a trash can for a deletion command).

IF-THEN-ELSE Structure: A logical selection structure whereby one of two paths is followed according to IF, THEN, and ELSE statements in a program.

Image Scanner: A direct-entry device that identifies images on paper and automatically converts them to electronic signals that can be stored in a computer.

Importing: Feature that allows file to be retrieved from one program and inserted into the program the user is working on, as from a spreadsheet to a word processing program. *Compare* Exporting.

Index Sequential File Organization: A compromise between sequential and direct file organizations. Records are stored sequentially, but an index is used to access a group of records directly.

Individual Database: A collection of integrated records useful mainly to just one person.

Industry Standard Architecture (ISA): Standard for bus line developed for IBM Personal Computer. It first consisted of an 8-bit-wide data path, then a 16-bit-wide data path.

Information: Data that has been processed by a computer system.

Information System: A collection of hardware, software, people, data, and procedures that work together to provide information essential to running an organization.

Initializing: *See* Formatting.

Ink-Jet Printer: Printer that forms characters by spraying small droplets of ink at high speed onto the surface of the paper.

Input Device: Piece of equipment that takes data and puts it into a form that a computer can process.

Integrated Circuit: *See* Chip.

Integrated Package: A collection of computer programs that work together and share information.

Intelligent Terminal: A terminal that includes a processing unit, primary storage, secondary storage, and software for processing data.

Interactive: Describes activity in which there is immediate communication between the user and the computer system.

Interface Card: *See* Expansion Board.

Internal Hard Disk: Storage device consisting of one or more metallic platters stored inside a container. Internal hard disks are installed inside the system cabinet of a microcomputer.

Internal Modem: A modem that is a plug-in circuit board located inside the computer.

Internal Storage: *See* Primary Storage.

Interpreter: Software that converts a procedural language one statement at a time into machine language just before the statement is executed.

Inventory: The material or products that a company has in stock.

IRG (Interrecord Gap): Gap between records on magnetic tape required to give the tape enough time to gain the proper speed.

ISA: *See* Industry Standard Architecture.

Jacket: The protective outer covering for a diskette.

Justification (Justified Margins): The process of evening up margins, such as the right margin in a printed book.

K, KB, or K-byte (Kilobyte): A unit of capacity equal to 1024 bytes (about one thousand bytes).

Keyboard: Input device that looks like a typewriter keyboard but has additional keys.

Key Field: A group of logically related characters in a file record used for sorting purposes.

Knowledge-Based System: Program that is based on facts and widely accepted rules about how certain decisions should be made or tasks accomplished.

Labels: The column and row headings in spreadsheets.

LAN (Local Area Network): Network that consists of computers and other devices that are physically near each other, such as within the same building.

Laptop: Portable computer weighing 10–16 pounds.

Laser Printer: Printer that creates dotlike images on a drum using a laser beam. The characters are then treated with magnetically charged inklike toner and transferred from the drum to the paper.

LCD (Liquid-Crystal Display): Display that consists of liquid crystal molecules whose optical properties can be altered by an applied electric field. Does not emit light of its own.

Letter-Quality Printer: Printer that produces output with the quality of that produced by an office typewriter. Used for formal correspondence and reports.

Light Pen: A light-sensitive penlike device used with a special monitor to enter commands by touching the monitor with the pen.

Logic Error: Error that occurs when a programmer has used an incorrect calculation or left out a programming procedure.

Logic Structure: Structure that controls the logical sequence in which computer program instructions are executed. The three structures are sequence, selection, and loop.

Logical Record: The actual record on magnetic tape.

Loop Structure: A logic structure in which a process may be repeated as long as a certain condition remains true.

Luggable: *See* Transportable.

Machine Languages: The first generation of programming languages. In them only the binary digits (0 and 1) are used to express program statements and data.

Macro: A keyboard command that enables users to consolidate several keystrokes for a command into only one or two keystrokes.

Magnetic Tape: Tape used to store data or programs.

Magnetic Tape Drive (Magnetic Tape Unit): Device used to read data from and store data on magnetic tape.

Magnetic Tape Streamer: Device that allows duplication (backup) of the data stored on a hard disk.

Mail-Merge Feature: A word processing feature that allows names, addresses, and other material to be inserted into documents from other files.

Mainframe Computer: Computer that can process millions of program instructions per second. Mainframes usually occupy a special room to accommodate special wiring and air conditioning. They are used by large companies.

Main Memory: *See* Primary Storage.

Make-or-Buy Decision: The second step in the programming procedure when a decision is made to buy a prewritten program or have it custom-written by a programmer.

MAN (Metropolitan Area Network): This type of network serves customers in the same city or region and can be accessed by mobile (cellular) telephone. Often created by a local telephone company.

Mark Sensing: *See* OMR.

Massively Parallel Processing: Technology used in form of supercomputers that consists of thousands of interconnected microprocessors. *See also* Supercomputer.

Master File: A complete file containing all records current up to the last update.

MB or M-byte (Megabyte): A unit of capacity equal to 1,048,576 bytes (about one million bytes).

MCA: *See* Micro Channel Architecture.

Medium Band: The bandwidth of special leased lines, used mainly with minicomputers and mainframe computers.

Memory: *See* Primary Storage.

Memory-Resident Program: *See* Desktop Manager.

Menu: A list of available commands presented on the screen.

Menu Bar: Line or two across the top or bottom of screen listing available software commands.

MHz (Megahertz): A unit of frequency equal to one million cycles (beats) per second.

MICR (Magnetic-Ink Character Recognition): A direct-entry method used in banks to read the stylized numbers on the bottoms of checks.

Micro Channel Architecture (MCA): Standard for a bus line developed to support IBM's line of PS/2 microcomputers based on the 80386 microprocessor. The MCA bus has a data path that is 32 bits wide.

Microcomputer: A small, low-cost computer designed for individual users.

Microcomputer Database: *See* Individual Database.

Microcomputer System: System involving a microcomputer that has five parts: people, procedures, software, hardware, and data.

Microprocessor: A CPU for a microcomputer contained on a single sliver of silicon. *See* Chip.

Microsecond: One-millionth of a second.

Microwave: Radio wave that travels in straight line through the air. Microwaves are relayed by means of antennas installed on high buildings, mountaintops, or satellites.

Middle-Level Manager: Person who oversees the supervisory (lower-level) managers and deals with control and planning. Middle-level managers implement the goals of the organization.

Millisecond: One-thousandth of a second.

Minicomputer: Computer that is larger than desktop in size. First developed as special-purpose mainframe computers, minicomputers have capabilities between those of microcomputers and those of mainframe computers.

MIS (Management Information System): System that expresses the transactions of a data processing system in a summarized, structured form.

Modem (MOdulator-DEModulator): A device that changes the digital electronic signals of the computer into the analog electronic signals that can travel over a telephone line and vice versa.

Modulation: The process performed by modems in converting digital signals to analog signals.

Module: *See* Program Module.

Monitor: An output device like a television screen that displays data processed by the computer.

Monochrome Monitor: Monitor that displays characters in only one color, such as amber or green.

Motherboard: *See* System Board.

Mouse: An input device that can be rolled on a tabletop to direct the position of the cursor on the screen. Has selection buttons for entering commands.

MS-DOS (Microsoft Disk Operating System): *See* DOS.

Multifunction Board: Expansion board that combines several functions on a single card.

Multimedia: Technology that presents information on more than one delivery medium, including text, graphics, animation, video, music, and voice.

Multitasking Software: Term given to operating systems that can run several applications programs at the same time. *See also* Windowing Software.

Nanosecond: One-billionth of a second.

Natural Languages: The fifth generation of programming languages. These languages use human languages such as English to give people a more natural connection with computers.

Network: *See* Computer Network.

Network Database: Database that is similar to a hierarchical database, except that each child node may have more than one parent node.

Network Gateway: Connection by which a local area network may be linked to other LANs or to larger networks.

New Media: Information delivery systems that combine media, such as text, graphics, voice, and video, using a microcomputer as the controlling framework.

Nodes: Points connected in a database or network like the branches of a tree.

Nonvolatile Storage: Permanent storage used to preserve data and programs.

Notebook PC: Portable computer weighing 5–10 pounds.

Numeric Keypad: The keys 0 to 9, located on separate keys adjacent to the typewriter keyboard.

OCR (Optical-Character Recognition): A direct-entry method that uses special preprinted characters that can be read by a light source.

Offline Storage: Data that is not directly accessible to the CPU until the tape or disk has been loaded onto an input device.

Off-the-Shelf Software: *See* Packaged Software.

OMR (Optical-Mark Recognition): A direct-entry method that senses the presence or absence of a mark, such as a pencil mark.

Online Storage: Data that is directly accessible to the CPU.

Open Architecture: Computer that contains expansion slots inside that anyone can use for adding extra memory chips or other accessories.

Operating Environment: *See* Windowing Software.

Operating System: System that consists of several programs that help the computer manage its own resources, such as manipulating files, running programs, and controlling the keyboard and screen.

Optical Disk: A device that can hold as much as 500 megabytes of data. Lasers are used to record and read data on the disk.

Organization Chart: Chart that shows an organization's functions and levels of management.

OS/2 (Operating System/2): A multitasking operating system for microcomputers developed jointly by IBM and Microsoft Corporation.

Outlining Program: Program that allows users to use Roman numerals, then capital letters, then Arabic numbers, etc., to write an outline. To organize ideas, the user puts in the main topic head, then the subtopics, sub-subtopics, etc. When the placement of an idea is changed, the outline is resequenced automatically.

Output Device: Device that displays the information processed by the computer.

Packaged Software: Any program for sale that has been prewritten by professional programmers.

Page: *See* Window.

Page Description Language: Language that describes the format of a page to a printer in a standard way.

Palmtop: *See* Pocket PC.

Parallel Approach: The approach for systems implementation whereby the old and new systems are operated side by side until the new one has been shown to be reliable.

Parallel Data Transmission: The method of transmission whereby each bit in a character (byte) flows through a separate line simultaneously.

Parallel Port: A type of port that allows lines to be connected so that bits can be transmitted simultaneously.

Parent Node: A node one level above the node being considered in a hierarchical database or network.

Parity Bit: An extra bit automatically added to a byte during keyboarding to test accuracy.

Pascal: A procedural programming language widely used on microcomputers. It is named after Blaise Pascal, a seventeenth-century mathematician.

Password: Secret word or numbers that limits access to information such as electronic mail.

Payroll: The activity concerned with calculating employee paychecks.

Periodic Report: Report produced at regular intervals such as weekly, monthly, or yearly.

Peripheral Device: Hardware that is outside of the system unit, such as disk drive or printer.

Personal Computer: *See* Microcomputer.

PERT (Program Evaluation Review Technique) Chart: Chart using lines and boxes that shows the time scale of a series of tasks for a project and the relationships among the tasks.

Phased Approach: The approach for systems implementation whereby the new system is implemented gradually over a period of time.

Physical Record: A block of records on magnetic tape.

Physical Security: Activity concerned with protecting hardware from possible human and natural disasters.

Picosecond: One-trillionth of a second.

Pilot Approach: The approach for systems implementation whereby the new system is tried out in only one part of the organization before it is implemented throughout the organization.

Piracy: *See* Software Piracy.

Pixel (Picture Element): The smallest area on a screen that can be turned on and off or be made different shades of gray or different colors.

Plotter: Special-purpose output device for producing high-quality graphical images such as architectural drawings.

Plug-In Board: *See* Expansion Board.

Pocket PC: Hand-held or pocket-size portable computer, weighing 1–2 pounds.

Pointers: The additional connections in a network database between parent nodes and child nodes.

Pointing Device: Direct-entry device that uses pointing to input data.

Polling: The process whereby a host computer or file server asks each connecting device whether it has a message to send and then allows the message to be sent.

Port: A connecting socket on the outside of the system unit for devices such as video displays and printers.

Portable Computer: Microcomputer that can be carried around. *See also* Laptop, Notebook PC, Transportable, Pocket PC.

Portable Programming Language: Language that results in programs that can be run on more than one kind of computer.

POS (Point-of-Sale) Terminal: Terminal that consists of a keyboard, screen, and printer. It is used like a cash register.

Preliminary Investigation: The first phase of the systems life cycle. It involves defining the problem, suggesting alternative systems, and preparing a short report.

Presentation Graphics: Graphics used to communicate a message through the use of color, dimensionality, titles, and so on. Presentation graphics may make use of analytical graphics.

Primary Storage: The part of a microcomputer that temporarily holds data for processing, instructions for processing the data, and information (processed data) waiting to be output.

Printer: A device that produces printed paper output.

Privacy: Right to keep personal information from being used for purpose for which it was not intended.

Privacy Act (1974): Law restricting federal agencies in the way they share information about citizens. It prohibits federal information collected for one purpose from being used for a different purpose.

Problem-Oriented Languages: The fourth generation of programming languages. Designed to solve specific problems by allowing end users simply to describe what they want.

Procedural Languages: The third generation of programming languages, designed to express the logic that can solve general problems using English-like statements.

Procedures: The rules or guidelines to follow when using hardware, software, and data.

Processing Rights: The determination of which people have access to what kinds of data in databases.

Processor: *See* CPU.

Program: A set of step-by-step instructions that tell a computer how to accomplish a task.

Program Definition (Program Analysis): The first step in

257

the programming process. During this phase, the program's objectives, desired output, input data required, and processing requirements are specified.

Program Design: The third step of the programming procedure. During this phase, custom software is designed, preferably using structured programming techniques.

Program Flowchart: Chart that graphically presents the detailed sequence of steps needed to solve a programming problem.

Program Maintenance: The process of updating and modifying a completed program that has been through the six-step programming process.

Program Module: A processing step of a program made up of logically related program statements.

Programming: A six-step procedure for creating a program.

Programming Language: A set of rules that tell a computer what operations to perform. Usually written in a form resembling English for ease of use.

Project: A one-time operation composed of several tasks that must be completed during a stated period to time.

Project Management Software: Program used to plan, schedule, and control the people, resources, and costs needed to complete a project on time.

PROM (Programmable Read-Only Memory): Chips that contain instructions that can be written but not changed.

Proprietary Database: Generally, an enormous database that an organization develops to cover certain particular subjects. Access to this type of database is usually offered for a fee.

Protocols: A set of rules for the exchange of information, such as those used for successful data transmission.

Prototyping: Building a model (prototype) that can be modified before the actual system is installed. Should be used along with careful system analysis and design procedures.

Pseudocode: A narrative form of the logic of a computer program.

Pull-Down Menu: List of software commands that "drops down" from a menu bar at the top of the screen.

Purchasing: The buying of raw materials and services.

Query Language: An easy-to-use language understandable to most users that is used to generate reports from databases.

RAM (Random-Access Memory): Temporary storage that holds the program and data that the CPU is processing.

Read: *See* Reading Data.

Reader/Sorter: A special-purpose machine that reads characters made of ink containing magnetized particles.

Reading Data: For diskettes, the process of taking the magnetized spots from the diskette, converting them to electronic signals, and transmitting them to primary storage inside the computer.

Read-Only Disk: Optical disk, such as CD-ROM, on which data is imprinted by the manufacturer and cannot be altered by the user.

Read-Write Head: Electronic head that can read data from and write data onto a disk.

Real-Time Processing: Processing performed at the same time that data is collected.

Recalculation: The process of recomputing values in electronic spreadsheets automatically.

Record: A collection of logically related fields.

Register: High-speed staging area that holds data and instructions temporarily during processing.

Relation: A table in a relational database that contains information on a specified subject.

Relational Database: The most flexible database organization, where data elements are stored in tables and there is no hierarchical structure imposed.

Rename: Give new filename to file on a diskette.

Repetitive Strain Injury (RSI, Repetitive Motion Injury, Cumulative Trauma Disorders): Category of injuries resulting from fast, repetitive work that cause neck, wrist, hand, and arm pains. *See also* Carpal Tunnel Syndrome.

Replace: In word processing, command that enables user to search for a word and replace it with another one.

Return Key: *See* Enter Key.

RGB (Red-Green-Blue) Monitor: Monitor that allows the results of graphics software to be presented in a variety of different color designs.

Right to Financial Privacy Act (1979): Law setting strict procedures that federal agencies must follow when seeking to examine customer records in banks.

Ring Network: A network in which each device is connected to two other devices, forming a ring. There is no host computer, and messages are passed around the ring until they reach the correct destination.

RISC (Reduced Instruction Set Computer) Chip: Powerful microprocessor chip, such as the Motorola 88000, found in workstations.

Robot: Machine used in factories and elsewhere that can be preprogrammed to do more than one task.

Robotics: The field of study concerned with developing and using robots.

ROM (Read-Only Memory): Chips containing programs that are built into the system board at the factory. The instructions on these chips cannot be changed.

Rotational Delay Time: The time taken for the disk to rotate under the read-write head.

Row Headings: The labels down the left-hand side of the worksheet area of a spreadsheet.

RPG (Report Program Generator): A procedural language that enables people to prepare business reports quickly and easily.

RS-232C Connector: *See* Serial Port.

Sales Order Processing: The activity that records the demands of customers for the company's product or service.

Satellite: A satellite is often placed in orbit so that it appears to remain in a fixed position with respect to the earth (that is, it is geostationary). Geostationary satellites are often used to relay microwave transmissions.

Scanning Device: Direct-entry device that converts images to digital data that can be processed by a computer or displayed on a screen.

Scheduled Report: *See* Periodic Report.

Screen: *See* Monitor.

Screen Resolution: A measure of the crispness of images and characters on a screen, usually specified in terms of the number of pixels in a row or column.

Scrolling: A feature that enables the user to move quickly through the text forward or backward.

Search: In word processing, command that enables user to find a particular term in a document.

Search Operation: Activity in which a disk drive rotates diskette to proper position so that the read-write head can find the appropriate data on the diskette.

Secondary Storage: Permanent storage used to preserve programs and data, including diskettes, hard disks, and magnetic tape.

Sectors: Sections shaped like pie wedges which divide the tracks on disks.

Security: Activity of protecting information, hardware, and software from harm and from unauthorized use.

Seek Operation: Activity in which the access arm in a disk drive moves back and forth over the diskette to read data from, or write data to, the diskette.

Seek Time: The time required for the access arm to get into position over a particular track.

Selection Structure: A logic structure that determines which of two paths will be followed when a decision must be made by a program.

Semiconductor: *See* Chip.

Sequence Structure: A logic structure in which one program statement follows another.

Sequential Access Storage: A method of storage where information is stored in sequence, and all information preceding the desired information must be read first.

Sequential Files: Files in which records are stored one after another in ascending or descending order.

Serial Data Transmission: The method of transmission in which bits flow in a series, one after another.

Serial Port: A port set up for serial data transmission.

Shared Database: *See* Company Database.

Shell: Special-purpose program that allows a person to custom-build a particular kind of expert system.

Silicon: Sandlike material used for making tiny circuit boards called chips.

Silicon Chip: *See* Chip.

Simplex Communications: A mode of communications in which data travels in one direction only.

Smart Terminal: A terminal that has some memory and allows users to perform some data editing or verification before the data is sent to the host computer.

Soft Copy: Images or characters output on a monitor screen.

Soft-Sectored Diskette: Diskette that must be initialized (formatted) to place tracks and sectors on the surface.

Software: Another name for computer programs.

Software Copyright Act (1980): Law allowing owners of programs to make copies for backup purposes, and to modify them to make them useful, provided they are not resold or given away.

Software Piracy: Unauthorized copying of programs for personal gain.

Source Document: The original version of a document before any processing has been performed on it.

Special-Purpose Keys: Keys labeled *Ctrl, Del, Ins,* and so on, used to help enter and edit data and execute commands.

Speech-Recognition Device: *See* Voice-Input Device.

Spelling-Checker Program: A program used with a word processor to check the spelling of typed text against an electronic dictionary.

Spike: *See* Voltage Surge.

Spreadsheet: *See* Electronic Spreadsheet.

Spreadsheet Cursor: *See* Cell Pointer.

Star Network: A network of computers or peripheral devices linked to a central computer through which all communications pass. Control is maintained by polling.

Structured Programming Techniques: Techniques that consist of top-down program design, pseudocode, flowcharts, and logic structures.

Structured Walkthrough: A process in which several programmers, including the creator of the program, review the program, analyzing it for completeness, accuracy, and quality of design.

Supercomputer: Multimillion-dollar computers that are the fastest calculating devices made, processing over one billion program instructions per second. *See also* Massively Parallel Processing.

Supervisor: Lower-level manager responsible for managing and monitoring workers. Supervisors are concerned with operational matters—monitoring day-to-day events.

Supply Reel: The reel from which magnetic tape is being drawn into a tape drive.

Surge Protector: Device separating computer from power source of wall outlet, which protects computer system by activating circuit breaker when excess electricity appears.

Synchronous Transmission: The method whereby data is transmitted several bytes or a block at a time.

Syntax Error: Violation of the rules of whatever language a computer program is written in.

System: A collection of activities and elements designed to accomplish a goal.

System Board: A flat board that usually contains the CPU and some primary storage (main memory).

System Cabinet: The cabinet that houses the CPU.

System Clock: The clock that controls how fast the operations within a computer can take place.

System Flowchart: Chart that shows the kinds of equipment used to handle the data or information flow.

System Unit: The part of a microcomputer that contains the CPU.

Systems Analysis: The second phase in the systems life cycle. During this phase, data is gathered and analyzed and a systems analysis report is produced.

Systems Analysis and Design: A six-phase problem-solving procedure for examining an organization's information system and improving it.

Systems Analyst: Computer professional who studies systems in an organization to determine what actions to take and how to use computer technology to assist in taking them.

Systems Audit: Part of maintenance phase of systems analysis and design in which systems analyst compares new system to the design specifications to see if new procedures are furthering productivity.

Systems Design: The third phase of the systems life cycle. It consists of designing alternative systems, selecting the best system, and writing a systems design report.

Systems Development: The fourth phase of the systems life cycle. It consists of developing software, acquiring hardware, and testing the new system.

Systems Implementation: The fifth phase of the systems life cycle. It is the process of changing (converting) from the old system to the new and training people to use it.

Systems Life Cycle: The six phases of systems analysis and design.

Systems Maintenance: The sixth (final) phase of the systems life cycle. It involves evaluating the new information system from time to time and modifying it if necessary.

Systems Software: "Background software" that includes programs that help the computer manage its own internal resources. The most important part of systems software is the operating system.

Table Plotter: *See* Flatbed Plotter.

Take-Up Reel: The reel used to wind magnetic tape that has been drawn through a tape drive.

Tape Backup Unit: *See* Magnetic Tape Streamer.

Tape Library: Group of magnetic tapes stored by companies and other institutions.

Tape Streamer: *See* Magnetic Tape Streamer.

TB or T-byte (Terabyte): A unit of capacity equal to 1,099,511,627,776 bytes (about one trillion bytes).

Terminal: A form of input (and output) device that consists of a keyboard, monitor, and communications link.

Thesaurus Program: A program used with word processing to find suitable alternatives for a typed word by presenting choices from an electronic thesaurus.

Time-Sharing System: A system that allows several users to share resources in the host computer.

Top-Down Analysis Methodology: The method used to identify the top-level component of a system and break this component down into smaller components for analysis.

Top-Down Program Design: The process of identifying the top element (module) for a program and then breaking the top element down into smaller pieces in a hierarchical fashion.

Top-Level Manager: Manager concerned with long-range (strategic) planning. Top-level managers supervise middle-level managers.

Touch Screen: A monitor screen that allows actions or commands to be entered by the touch of a finger.

Touch-Tone Device: A direct-entry device that sends data over telephone lines to a central computer.

Tracks: Closed, concentric rings on a disk on which data is recorded.

Tractor Feed: Printer mechanism with sprockets that advance printer paper, using holes on edges of continuous-form paper.

Transaction File: A file containing recent changes to records that will be used to update the master file.

Transaction-Oriented Processing: *See* Real-Time Processing.

Transaction Processing Information System: Records day-to-day transactions.

Transactions: Events recorded in a database, such as employees hired or materials and products produced.

Transportable: Portable computer weighing 18–25 pounds.

Trojan Horse Program: Type of computer crime in which someone writes instructions that will destroy or modify someone else's software or data.

Twisted Pair: Copper-wire telephone line.

Typewriter Keys: The keys on a keyboard that resemble the regular letters, numbers, punctuation marks, and so on, on a typewriter.

Unix: An operating system originally developed by AT&T which has been adapted to run on a wide variety of computers, including microcomputers.

Unjustification (Unjustified Margins): The process of having uneven or "ragged right" margins, such as the right margin in a typewritten letter.

Uploading: The process of transferring information from the computer you are operating to a remote computer.

Utility Program: Program that performs common repetitious tasks, such as keeping files orderly, merging, and sorting.

Value: The number contained in a cell of a spreadsheet.

VDT (Video Display Terminal): An output display device that resembles a television screen.

VGA (Video Graphics Array): Circuit board that may be inserted into microcomputer and offers up to 256 colors. It is superior in quality to CGA and EGA.

Video Privacy Protection Act (1988): Law preventing retailers from selling or disclosing video-rental records without the customer's consent or a court order.

Virtual Environment: *See* Artificial Reality.

Virtual Fax Board: Expansion board that fits into microcomputer that enables user to write a document, which is then converted to a facsimile image and is sent electronically over telephone lines to a receiving fax machine, which re-creates the image on paper.

Virtual Reality: *See* Artificial Reality.

Virus: *See* Computer Virus.

Voiceband: The bandwidth of a standard telephone line.

Voice-Input Device (Voice-Recognition System): A direct-entry device that converts a person's speech into a numeric code that can be processed by a computer.

Voice-Messaging System: Computer system linked to telephones that convert human voice into digital bits and store telephoned messages in "voice mailboxes" for retrieval later.

Voice-Output Device: Device that makes sounds resembling human speech which are actually prerecorded vocalized sounds.

Volatile Storage: Temporary storage that destroys the current data when power is lost or new data is read.

Voltage Surge (Spike): Excess of electricity, which may destroy chips or other computer electronic components. *See also* Surge Protector.

Walkthrough: *See* Structured Walkthrough.

WAN (Wide Area Network): A countrywide network that uses microwave relays and satellites to reach users over long distances.

Wand Reader: A special-purpose hand-held device used to read OCR characters, such as that used in department stores to read price tags.

Window: An area defined on the screen for viewing data from a program.

Windowing Software: Software that allows a number of applications programs ("multiple tasks") to be used simultaneously.

Word: A unit that describes the number of bits (such as 8, 16, or 32) in a common unit of information.

Word Processing: The use of a computer to create, manipulate, and print documents comprised of text, such as letters, reports, and contracts.

Word Wrap: A feature of word processing that automatically moves the cursor from the end of one line to the beginning of the next.

Worksheet Area: The area of a spreadsheet consisting of rows and columns that intersect in cells.

Workstation: A more sophisticated microcomputer which can communicate with more powerful computers and sources of information.

Worm (Bacteria): Variant on computer virus, a destructive program that fills a computer system with self-replicating information, clogging the system so that its operations are slowed or stopped.

WORM (Write Once, Read Many) Drive: A form of optical disk that allows data to be written only once but read many times without deterioration.

Write: *See* Writing Data.

Write-Enable Ring: A ring that must be placed over the hub of a magnetic tape to allow data to be written to the tape.

Write-Once Disk: Optical disk on which data is recorded by lasers and cannot be erased by the user.

Write-Protect Notch: A notch on a diskette used to prevent the computer from destroying data or information on the diskette.

Writing Data: For diskettes, the process of taking the electronic information processed by the computer and recording it magnetically onto the diskette.

XGA (Extended Graphics Array): Circuit board that can be inserted into a microcomputer and offers up to 256 colors under normal circumstances and 65,536 colors with special equipment.

INDEX

Access arm, on disk drives, 99
Access time, for hard disks, 103–104
Ada programming language, 197
Adapter cards, 70
Addresses in primary storage, 62
ALU (arithmetic-logic unit), 61
American Standard Code for Information Interchange (ASCII), 64–65, 196
Analog and digital signals, 117
Analytical graphics programs, 27–28
Apple computers. See Macintosh microcomputers
Applications generators, 198
Applications software, 6, 13, 14, 17–32
    artificial intelligence (AI), 13, 213–217, 221
    artificial reality, 13, 216–217
    CAD/CAM, 211–213, 221
    CADD, 211–212, 221
    CASE, 171, 198
    communications software, 6, 14, 29–31, 35
    custom vs. off-the-shelf, 174, 183, 186
    database management systems, 6, 14, 25–27, 34
    desktop managers, 13, 203–204, 220
    desktop publishing, 13, 205–208, 220
    developed by end users, 182
    for DOS with Windows, 43
    downsizing, 129, 149, 217–218
    expert systems, 13, 214–216
    features common to, 17–20, 35
    file managers, 6
    graphics programs, 6, 14, 27–29, 34
    hypertext, 13, 208–209
    integrated packages, 6, 14, 31, 35
    knowledge-based systems, 13, 214–216
    make-or-buy decision, 186
    multimedia, 13, 109, 209–210
    new media, 208–210, 221
    and OS/2, 45
    power tools, 203
    and problem-oriented languages, 198
    project management, 13, 204–205, 220
    robotics, 13, 213–214
    spreadsheets, 6, 14, 23–25, 34
    and Unix, 48
    windowing, 34, 41–43
    word processors, 6, 14, 20–23, 34
    See also Software
Apollo workstations, 56
Architecture, computer:
    and bus lines, 71
    open and closed, 70
    von Neumann, 73
Arithmetic-logic unit (ALU), 61
Artificial intelligence (AI), 13, 213–217, 221
    artificial reality, 13, 216–217
    expert systems, 13, 214–216
    knowledge-based systems, 13, 214–216
    robotics, 13, 213–214
Artificial life, 218
Artificial reality, 13, 216–217
ASCII (American Standard Code for Information Interchange), 64–65, 196
Ashton-Tate, 17
Assembly languages, 196
Asynchronous communications port, 121
Asynchronous transmission, 122–123
AT&T:
    and Open Look, 50
    and Unix, 47
Audit, systems, 176
AutoCAD, 211
Automated design tools, 171

Backing up:
    diskettes, 39
    with magnetic tape, 106–108
    and security, 142, 236
Bacteria, computer, 230
Bandwidth, 120–121
Banking by microcomputer, 117
Bar charts, 28
Bar-code readers, 83
Basic input/output system, 39
BASIC programming language, 191, 197
Batch processing, 134–135
Bidirectional printers, 89
Binary system, 63–65, 75
Biometrics, and security, 233
Bits, defined, 64
Blocks:
    moving, in word processing, 21
    of records, on tape, 108
Boards:
    adapter cards, 70
    controller cards, 70
    expansion, 70–71
    hardcards, 102
    interface cards, 70
    motherboards, 65
    multifunction, 71
    system, 65–66
    virtual fax, 88
Body Electric, 216
Bootstrap loader, 38
Broadband transmission, 121
Bulletin boards, electronic, 30, 227
Bus lines, 71
Bus networks, 125
Bytes, defined, 64

C programming language, 197
Cable, for communications systems, 119, 129
CAD (computer-aided design), 211–212, 221
CADD (computer-aided design and drafting), 211–212, 221
CAM (computer-aided manufacturing), 212–213, 221

Car phones, 127
Cards. *See* Boards
Cards in Hypercard, 208–209
Carpal tunnel syndrome, 224
Cartridges, magnetic tape, 106
CASE (computer-aided software engineering) tools, 171, 198
Cathode-ray tubes (CRTs), 84
CD-ROM (compact disk–read-only memory), 105
 and multimedia, 109
Cells, in spreadsheets, 24
Cellular phone systems, 127, 129
Census Bureau, 144
Central processing unit (CPU), 8, 15, 44, 60–61
 and primary storage, 62–63, 74
 on system board, 66
 See also Multitasking, Multiuser operating systems
CGA (Color Graphics Adapter) boards, 85
Chain printers, 88
Character-based interface, 41
Character recognition devices, 83
Characters, defined, 11, 15, 96, 133
Chart (Microsoft), 28
Chase Econometric Associates, 141
Chips. *See* Microprocessors, Primary Storage
CISC (complex instruction set computer) chips, 68
Closed architectures, 70
Coaxial cable, 119
COBOL programming language, 197
Code of Fair Information Practice, 228–229
Collaboration technology, 117
Communications, 113–131
 channels for, 119–120, 130
 devices, 11, 15
 full-duplex, 122
 half-duplex, 121
 microwave, 120
 simplex, 121
 software, 6, 14, 29–31, 35
 systems, 113
 See also Networks
Compaq LTE/386 laptop, 58
Compilers, 196
CompuServe proprietary database, 141
Computer-aided software engineering (CASE) tools, 171, 198
Computer competency, 1–2, 12–13, 238–245
Computer crime, 13, 229–231, 235
Computer Fraud and Abuse Act, 228, 232
Computer Matching and Privacy Protection Act, 228
Computer viruses, 142–143, 230–231
Computers:
 design of, 225

four kinds of, 3–4, 54–60, 74
pen-based, 218
portable, 57–59
and security, 228–236
using, to be a winner, 238–239
and the workplace, 13, 222–236
Connectivity, 12–13, 15, 113–117, 130
Control unit of CPU, 61
Controller cards, 70
Conversion to new computer systems, 174–175
Coprocessors, math, 69
Copying files, 39
CPU (central processing unit), 8, 15, 44, 60–61
 and primary storage, 62–63, 74
 on system board, 66
 See also Multitasking, Multiuser operating systems
Crackers, and computer crime, 230
Cray Y-MP supercomputer, 60
Crime, and computers, 13, 229–231, 235
Crosstalk Mk.4 2.0, 29, 30
CRTs (cathode-ray tubes), 84
Cursors, 18, 24, 79
Cutting and pasting, 21

Daisy-wheel printers, 87
Data, 5, 11, 15
 backing up, 236
 downloading and uploading, 116–117
 integrity of, 137
 organization of, 11, 15, 96, 110, 133–134, 146
 privacy for, 13, 226–228, 234
 reading/writing by disk drives, 9, 97
 redundancy of, 137
 security of, 228–236
 See also Databases
Data banks, 30, 141
Data communications systems, 113
Data compression, 108
Data dictionaries, 137
Data disks, 99
Data entry, in databases, 27
Data flow diagrams, 171–172
Data General, 68
Data processing, distributed, 125
Data transfer time, 104
Data transmission, 120–123, 131
 asynchronous/synchronous, 122–123
 and bandwidth, 120–121
 protocols for, 123
 serial and parallel, 121
Database administrators (DBAs), 144
Database management systems (DBMSs), 6, 14, 25–27, 34, 137–140

calculating in, 26
custom data entry forms in, 27
data dictionaries for, 137
formats of, 138–140, 147
hierarchical, 138
network, 139
query languages for, 27, 137–138, 198
relational, 139–140
reports in, 26, 27
retrieve and display in, 26
sorting in, 26
structure of, 25
See also Integrated Packages
Databases, 11, 15, 25, 96, 136–144, 146–147
 company (shared), 141
 distributed, 141
 fields in, 25
 files in, 25
 individual, 140
 microcomputer access to, 149
 and privacy, 13, 226–228, 234
 proprietary, 141–142
 security of, 137, 142, 228–230
 shared, 116, 137
 types of, 140–142, 147
 uses for, 142
 See also Information systems
DataGlove, 216–217
Dataquest, 49
dBASE IV, 25, 26, 27, 137
 and VP-Expert, 216
Debugging programs, 193–194
Decision models, 158
Decision support systems (DSSs), 144–155, 158
Decision tables, 171
Demand reports, 157
Demodulation, 117
Density, high-capacity and standard, 100–101
Design tools, automated, 171
Desk checking programs, 194
Desktop managers, 13, 203–204, 220
Desktop publishing, 13, 88, 205–208, 220
 and word processing, 23
DesqView (Quarterdeck), 42
Destructive write process, 69
Diagnostic routines, 38
Dialog Information Services, 141–142
Digital and analog signals, 117
Digital audio tape (DAT) drives, 106
Digital Equipment Corporation (DEC), 39, 47, 59
Digitizers, 81
Direct access storage, 95
Direct entry, 80–84, 92
 vs. keyboarding, 77–79
 with pointing devices, 80–81, 92
 with scanning devices, 81–83
 with voice-input devices, 83–84

263
Index

Direct file organization, 135–136
Disaster recovery plans, 122
Disk arrays, 108
Disk drives, 97–99, 110
  access arm, 99
  external, 98
  function of, 9
  hard disk, 9, 101–104
  two, usage of, 9, 99
Disk packs, 103–104
Diskettes:
  backing up, 39
  capacities of, 100
  care of, 101
  compatibility of, 100–101
  density of, 100–101
  formatting, 39
  parts of, 99–100, 110
  reading and writing to, 9, 97–98
  soft-sectored, 100
  as storage, 8–9, 15, 100
  two common sizes of, 8–9, 97, 99–100, 110
  write-protect notch on, 101
Disks. *See* CD-ROM; Diskettes; Hard disks; Optical disks
Display adapter cards, 70
Display screens. *See* Monitors
Distributed data processing, 125
Distributed databases, 141
Document Description Language (DDL), 208
Documentation:
  of programs, 194–195
  of systems analysis, 171–172
Documents:
  source, 77
  in word processing, 20–21
DOS operating system, 7, 39–43, 50, 52
  compatibility with OS/2, 45
  future of, 38, 41
  versions of, 39–40
  with Windows, 41–43, 50, 52
Dot-matrix printers, 86
Dow Jones News/Retrieval proprietary database, 141
Downloading data, 116
Downsizing applications, 129, 149, 217–218
Draw Applause, 29
Drive gate, 97
Drum plotters, 90
Dumb terminals, 79
Dynamic Data Exchange:
  and OS/2, 45
  and DOS with Windows, 42
Dynamic file links, in spreadsheets, 25

EBCDIC (Extended Binary Coded Decimal Interchange Code), 64, 196
EEPROM (electronically erasable programmable read-only memory), 70
EGA (Enhanced Graphics Adapter) boards, 85
Electroluminescent (EL) displays, 85
Electromagnetic field (EMF) emissions, 224
Electronic bulletin boards, 30, 114–115, 227
Electronic mail (E-mail) services, 30, 115–116, 227
Electronic spreadsheets. *See* Spreadsheets
Electrostatic plotters, 90
Enable (integrated package), 31
End users, 2
  as application developers, 182
Enter key, 21, 78
EPROM (erasable programmable read-only memory), 70
Erasable optical disks, 106
Erasing files, 39
Ergonomics, 223
Error checking:
  and parity bits, 64–65
  in programs, 193–194
Excel (Microsoft), 24
Exception reports, 157
Executive information systems (EISs), 159–160
Expansion boards, 70–71
Expert systems, 13, 214–216
Extended Binary Coded Decimal Interchange Code (EBCDIC), 64, 196
Extended Graphics Array (XGA) monitors, 86
Extended Industry Standard Architecture (EISA), 71
Eyephones, 216

Fair Credit Reporting Act of 1970, 227–228
Fax (facsimile transmission) machines, 82, 114, 129
Fiber-optic cable, 119, 129
Fields, 11, 15, 96, 133–134
  in databases, 25
  key, 134, 139
File managers, 6, 14
File servers, 124, 129
Files, 11, 15, 96, 134
  backing up, 39
  copying, 39
  database, 25
  erasing, 39
  master vs. transaction, 135
  organization of, 135–136
  renaming, 39
  spreadsheet, linking, 25

Financial services, and communications software, 31
First Choice (integrated package), 31
First Publishers, 207
Flatbed plotters, 90
Flat-panel displays, 84–85
Floppy disks (*see* Diskettes)
Flowcharts:
  program, 188–191
  system, 171
Form-letter feature, 23
Formatting:
  database reports, 26
  diskettes, 39
  documents, 18, 21–22
  in spreadsheets, 24
Formulas, in spreadsheets, 24
FORTRAN programming language, 197
Framework (integrated package), 31
Freedom of Information Act, 228
Freelance Plus, 29
Full-duplex communication, 122
Function keys, 20, 78

Gantt charts, 205
Gas-plasma displays, 85
Gateways, in networks, 127
Gigabytes (GBs or G-bytes), 64
Graph Plus, 29
Graphical user interfaces (GUI), 34
  DOS with Windows, 41–43
  for Macintosh, 45–47
  for OS/2, 45
  for Unix, 48–49
Graphics monitors, 85–86
Graphics:
  analytical, 27–28
  presentation, 27
  programs, 6, 27–28, 33
  in spreadsheets, 25
Grid charts, 170
Groupware, 117

Hackers, and computer crime, 230
Half-duplex communication, 121
Hard copy output, 86
Hard disks, 9, 15, 101–104, 111
  access time for, 103–104
  expansion cards as, 70
  external, 98
  hardcards as, 102
  head crashes of, 104
  internal, 101–102
  packs of, 103–104
  removable, 103
  seek time for, 104
Hardcards, 102
Hardware, 5, 7–11, 12, 15
  acquiring, 174
  communications devices, 11, 15

input devices, 7–8, 15
output devices, 10, 15
storage devices. *See* Primary storage; Secondary storage
system unit, 8, 15
Harvard Graphics, 29
Head crashes, 104
Health issues, and computers, 222–225
Help systems:
 content-sensitive, 34
 menus and screens, 18
Hewlett-Packard, 42, 56
Hierarchical databases, 138
Hierarchical networks, 124–126
High definition television (HDTV), 91
Host computers, 124
Hybrid networks, 124
Hypercard, 208–209
Hypermedia, 209
Hypertext, 13, 208–209

IBM mainframe computers:
 model 3090, 60
 MVS operating system, 39
 OS/VS operating system, 39
 370 series, 60
IBM microcomputers:
 linked to Macintoshes, 47
 PCs, XTs, ATs, 40, 44, 61
 PS series, 37, 44, 55, 57, 61
 systems software for, 37, 38
Icons, 42
Idea processors, 23
Image processing, 109
Image scanners, 82
Index sequential file organization, 134–135
Industry Standard Architecture (ISA), 71
Information, defined, 5
Information appliances, 218
Information systems, 148–161
 decision support systems, 155, 163
 executive information systems (EISs), 159–160
 and functional departments, 150–152
 information flow in, 153–154, 162
 management information system (MIS), 155, 163
 and management levels, 152–153, 163
 transaction processing systems, 155, 163
Information technology, 238–245
 individual strategy for managing, 242–245
Information utilities, 141
Initializing diskettes, 39
Ink-jet printers, 88

Input:
 direct entry, 77, 80–84
 by keyboard, 77–79
Input devices, 7–8, 15, 92
 bar code readers, 83
 character recognition devices, 83
 digitizers, 81
 fax machines, 82, 129
 image scanners, 82
 keyboards, 7, 77–79
 light pens, 81
 mouse, 8, 80
 point-of-sale (POS) terminals, 78, 92
 reader/sorter machines, 83
 terminals, 79–80, 92
 touch screens, 80–81
 voice-input, 83–84
 wand readers, 78, 83
Integrated circuits, 8, 66
Integrated Services Digital Network (ISDN), 129
Integrated software packages, 6, 31
Intel microprocessors, 45, 67, 68
Intelligent terminals, 79
Intelsat (International Telecommunications Satellite Consortium), 120
Interactive processing, 158
Interblock gaps (IBGs), 108
Interface cards, 70
Internal storage (*see* Primary storage)
International Standards Organization, 123
Interpress page description language, 208
Interpreters, for program translation, 196
Interrecord gaps (IRGs), 107
Investing, by microcomputer, 117

Jackets, on diskettes, 101
Justifying text, 21

Key fields, 134, 139
Keyboards, 7, 92
 directional arrow keys on, 79
 Enter key on, 21, 78
 Esc key on, 20
 function keys on, 20, 78
 input by, 7, 77–79
 numeric keys on, 78
 special-purpose keys on, 18–20, 78–79
 typewriter keys on, 78
Kilobytes (Ks, KBs, or K-bytes), 64
Knowledge-based systems, 13, 214–216
Knowledge Index, 142

Labels, in spreadsheets, 24
LAN Manager, 123
Languages:
 object-oriented (OOPS), 198
 page description, 4, 208
 problem-oriented, 198
 programming, 191, 195–198
 query, 27, 137–138, 198
Laptop computers, 57
 for executive information systems, 160
 monitors for, 85
Laser printers, 88
Legislation:
 for computer crime, 232, 236
 for data privacy, 227–228, 236
Light pens, 81
Line graphs, 28
Linking spreadsheet files, 25
Liquid-crystal displays (LCDs), 85
Local area networks (LANs), 12, 114, 127
Logic errors, in programs, 193
Logic structures, for programming, 190–191
Logical operations, 61
Logical records, on tape, 108
Loop structure, 190
Lotus Corporation, 17
Lotus Notes, 117
Lotus 1-2-3, 23, 24
 and VP-Expert, 216
Luggable computers, 57

Machine languages, 195–196
Macintosh microcomputers:
 and business applications, 47
 and Hypercard, 208–209
 linked with IBM micros, 47
 Macintosh II, 37, 68
 monitor for, 84
Macintosh operating system, 7, 14, 45–47, 51, 52
 and multitasking, 47
 running DOS applications on, 47
 System 7, 46–47
Macros, in software applications, 20
MacWrite, 21
Magnetic-ink character recognition (MICR), 83
Magnetic tape, for backup, 106–108, 111
Mail-merge, 23
Mai services, electronic, 30, 115–116, 227
Main memory (*see* Primary storage)
Mainframe computers, 4, 60
Maintenance:
 of programs, 195
 of systems, 176–177
Management information systems (MISs), 154–155, 157

Massively parallel processing, 60
Master files, 135
Math coprocessor chips, 69
Mead Data Central database, 141
Medium band transmission, 121
Megabytes (MBs or M-bytes), 64
Memory:
   electronically erasable read-only memory (EEPROM), 70
   erasable programmable read-only memory (EPROM), 70
   measurements of capacity, 64
   primary storage, 8, 15
   programmable read-only (PROM), 70
   random-access (RAM), 69–70
   read-only (ROM), 70
   secondary storage, 8–9, 15
Memory manager, in Windows, 42
Menus, 18
Message exchanges, 30
Metropolitan area networks (MANs), 127
Micro Channel Architecture (MCA), 71
Microcomputer systems, 1, 3, 54–55
   for desktop publishing, 207
   down-sizing to, 149
   five parts of, 4–5, 14–15
   portable, 57–59
   security for, 236
   and television, 91
   as terminals, 80
   See also Hardware, Workstations
Microprocessors, 8, 44–45, 66–67
   coprocessors, 69
   market shares of, 67
   RISC chips, 68
Microseconds, 60
Microsoft Corporation, 17, 39
Microwave communications, 120
Milliseconds, 60
Minicomputers, 3–4, 59–60
Models, decision, 158
Modems, 11, 15, 129
   as communications devices, 11
   and communications speeds, 117–118
   external and internal, 118
Modulation, 117
Modules, in programs, 187
Monitors, 10, 15, 84–86, 93
   display adapter cards for, 70
   graphics, 85–86
   and health issues, 222–225
   monochrome, 84–85
   and screen resolution, 84–86
Motherboards, 65
Motif operating system, 50
Motorola microprocessors, 46, 66–67
Mouse, 8, 80
MS-DOS (*see* DOS operating system)
Multifunction boards, 71
Multimedia software, 13, 209–210

Multimedia storage, 109
Multitasking, 41
   and DOS with Windows, 42
   on Macintosh systems, 46–47
   and Unix, 48
Multiuser operating systems, 48
MVS, IBM operating system, 39

Nanoseconds, 60
Natural programming languages, 198
NEC ProSpeed laptop, 57
NetWare, 123
Network databases, 139
Networks, 12, 15, 113, 131
   bus, 125
   configurations for, 124–126, 131
   connecting different operating systems, 47
   and DOS with Windows, 43
   gateways in, 127
   hierarchical (hybrid), 124, 126
   hybrid, 124
   Integrated Services Digital Network (ISDN), 129
   local area (LANs), 12, 127
   metropolitan area (MANs), 127
   neural, 73
   and OS/2, 45
   polling and, 124
   radio, 129
   ring, 125, 126
   star, 124–125
   time sharing on, 124
   and Unix, 48
   wide-area (WANs), 128
Neural networks, 73
New media systems, 208–210, 221
NewWave (HP), 42
NeXT computers, 66–68
Nodes, in databases, 139
Nondestructive read process, 69
Nonvolatile storage, 70
Notebook computers, 58

Object-oriented programming (OOPS) languages, 198
Off-the-shelf software, 17, 174, 183, 186
Open architectures, 70
Open Look operating system, 50
Open Software Foundation, 50
Open System Interconnection (OSI), 123
Operating environments, 41
Operating systems, 7, 14, 36–50
   comparison of, 49, 52–53
   compatibility between, 46
   DOS, 7, 14, 39–41, 52
   DOS with Windows, 41–43, 50, 52
   future of, 50
   Macintosh, 7, 14, 45–47, 53

   multiuser, 48
   OS/2, 7, 14, 43–45, 53
   sales of, 49
   Unix, 7, 14, 47–49, 50, 53
   utility programs within, 39
Operational models, 158
Optical character recognition (OCR), 83
Optical computing, 73
Optical disks, 105–106, 108, 111
Optical mark recognition, (OMR), 83
Organizational charts, 168–169
OS/2 operating system, 7, 14, 43–45, 50, 53
OS/VS, IBM operating system, 39
Outlining programs, 23
Output devices, 10, 15, 84–90, 93
   monitors, 10, 15, 84–86
   plotters, 89–90
   printers, 10, 15, 86–89, 93
   soft copy, 86
   voice-output devices, 90

Page description languages, 4, 208
PageMaker (Aldus), 207
Palmtop computers, 58–59
Paradox DBMS, 25
Parallel conversion of systems, 175
Parallel data transmission, 121
Parallel ports, 72
Parallel processing, 60
Parity bits, 64–65
Parity errors, 64–65
Pascal programming language, 191, 193, 197
Passwords, 115, 233, 236
PC-DOS. *See* DOS
Pen-based computers, 218
Perception systems, 214
Periodic reports, 157
Peripheral devices, defined, 72
Personal computers. *See* Microcomputer systems
Personal Consultant Series (Texas Instruments), 216
Personal Machinist, 216
PERT charts, 205, 206
Phased conversion of systems, 175
Physical records, on tape, 108
Picoseconds, 60
Pie charts, 28
Pilot testing systems, 175
Piracy, software, 232
Pixels, defined, 84
Plotters, 89–90, 93
Plug-in boards, 70
Pocket computers, 58
Point-of-sale (POS) terminals, 78, 92
Pointing devices, for direct entry, 80–81, 92
Polling, in networks, 124

Portable computers, 57–59, 129
　monitors for, 85
　printers for, 89
Ports:
　asynchronous communication, 121
　parallel and serial, 72, 121
PostScript page description language, 208
Presentation graphics programs, 27–29
Primary storage, 8, 15, 61–63, 95, 149
　addresses in, 62
　and the CPU, 62–63, 74
　and DOS, 41
　expanding, 65, 70
　RAM chips for, 69–70
　and Unix, 48
Printers, 10, 15, 86–89, 93
　bidirectional, 89
　chain, 88
　daisy-wheel, 87
　dot-matrix, 86
　ink-jet, 88
　laser, 88
　portable, 89
　shared use of, 89
　tractor feeds on, 89
　and type styles, 89
Privacy Act of 1974, 228
Privacy of personal data, 13, 226–228, 234
Problem-oriented languages, 198
Procedural languages, 196–198
Procedures, as part of a system, 4–5, 14
Processing:
　batch vs. real-time, 134–135
　cycle, 62–63
　distributed, 125
　interactive, 158
　rights, 1
　speed of, 60, 149
　transaction, 155–156, 163
Processor chips. *See* Microprocessors
ProComm, 30
Prodigy Information Service, 227
Program disks, 99
Programming, 182–195, 200–201
　coding the program, 191–193
　in DBMSs, 27
　debugging the program, 193–194
　defining the problem, 184–185
　designing the program, 186–191
　desk checking programs, 194
　documenting the program, 194–195
　errors in, 193–194
　flowcharts, 188–191
　language, choosing, 191, 195–198
　logic structures in, 190–191
　maintenance, 195
　make-or-buy decision, 186
　and pseudocode, 188
　top-down, 187

Programming languages:
　Ada, 197
　application generators, 198
　assembly languages, 196
　BASIC, 191, 197
　C, 197
　COBOL, 197
　compilers for, 196
　five generations of, 195–199
　FORTRAN, 197
　interpreters for, 196
　machine languages, 196–197
　natural languages, 198
　object-oriented (OOPS), 198
　Pascal, 191, 193, 197
　portable languages, 197
　problem-oriented languages, 197–198
　procedural languages, 196–198
　query languages, 27, 137–138, 198
　RPG, 197
　SQL, 27
Programs. *See* Software
Project for Windows, 205
Project management software, 13, 204–205, 220
PROM (programmable read-only memory), 70
Proprietary databases, 141–142
Protocols, for data transmission, 123
Prototyping computer systems, 177–178
Pseudocode, 188
Pull-down menus, 18

Quarterdeck Office Systems, 42
Quattro Pro, 24
Query languages, 27, 137–138, 198

Radio network, 129
Ragged-right text, 21
RAM (random-access memory) chips, 69–70
Rapid applications development (RAD), 178
R:base DBMS, 25, 137
Read/write heads, 99
Reader/sorter machine, 83
Reading/writing data, 9, 97
Real-time processing, 134–135
Recalculation, in spreadsheets, 4, 24
Records, 11, 15, 96, 134
　in databases, 25
　logical and physical, 108
　on magnetic tapes, 108
Registers, 61
Relational databases, 139–140
Renaming files, 39
Repetitive strain injury (RSI), 224
Reports:
　categories of, 157
　systems design, 173

Right to Financial Privacy Act, 228
Ring networks, 125, 126
RISC (reduced instruction set computer) chips, 68
Robotics, 13, 213–214
ROM (read-only memory), 70
Rotational delay time, 104
RPG (Report Program Generator), 197
RS-232C connector, 121

Satellite transmission, 120
Scanning devices, 81–83, 92
Screen resolution, 84–86
Scrolling, defined, 18
Security, computer, 228–236
Search and replace function, 21
Secondary storage, 8–9, 95–111, 149
　diskettes, 8–9, 97–101
　expansion boards for, 70–71
　hard disks, 9, 15, 101–104, 111
　magnetic tape, 106–108, 111
　optical disks, 105–106, 108, 111
Sectors, on diskettes, 100
Security of databases, 137, 142, 228–230
Seek time, for hard disks, 104
Seek/search operations, 99
Selection structure, 190
Semiconductors, 66, 72
Sequential access storage, 95
Sequential file organization, 135–136
Serial ports, 72, 121
Serial data transmission, 121
Shell software for expert systems, 216
Signals, analog and digital, 117
Silicon, and microprocessors, 66
Simplex communication, 121
Simplifier, The, 32
SmartCom, 30
SmartWare II (integrated package), 31
Smart terminals, 79
Soft copy output, 86
Soft-sectored diskettes, 100
Software, 5–7, 12, 14
　applications. *See* Applications software
　automated design tools, 171
　basic tools, 2, 6
　communications, 6, 14, 29–31, 35
　custom, 6, 14, 174, 183, 186
　integrated packages, 6, 31
　memory-resident programs, 204
　multitasking, 41, 42, 46–48
　off-the-shelf, 17, 174, 183, 186
　packaged, 6, 14
　piracy of, 232
　systems, 6–7
　windowing, 34, 41–43
Software Copyright Act of 1980, 232
Source documents, 77
Speech-recognition devices, 84

268
Index

Speed:
    access time, on hard disks, 103–104
    modem, 117–118
    processing, 60, 149
Spelling-checker programs, 22
Spikes, in voltage, 232
Spreadsheets, 6, 14, 23–25, 34
    cells in, 24
    consolidation of worksheets, 25
    formulas in, 24
    graphics in, 25
    linking files in, 25
    parts of, 24
    and "what-if" analysis, 24
    windows in, 24
    See also Integrated Packages
SQL (Structured Query Language), 27
Star networks, 124–125
Storage:
    on digital audio tape, 106
    direct access, 95
    on magnetic tape, 106–108
    multimedia, 109
    on optical disks, 105–106, 108, 111
    primary, 8, 15, 41, 61–63, 74
    secondary, 8–9, 15, 95–111, 149
    sequential access, 95
    volatile and nonvolatile, 69–70
    See also CD-ROM; Diskettes; Hard disks
Strategic models, 158
Streamers, magnetic tape, 106
Stress, and computers, 225
Style sheets, in DTP, 208
Sun Microsystems:
    and Open Look, 50
    workstations, 56
SuperCalc, 24
Supercomputers, 4, 60
Superconducting material, 72
Superminicomputers, 59
SuperVGA boards, 86
Surges, in voltage, 232
Switching time, of hard disks, 104
Symphony (integrated package), 31
Synchronous transmission, 122–123
Syntax errors in programs, 193
System boards, 65–66
System flowcharts, 171
System 7 (Macintosh), 46–47
System unit, 8, 15, 61, 65–72, 75
Systems analysis and design, 13, 164–178
    analysis phase, 168–172
    design phase, 172–173
    development phase, 173–174
    documenting, 171–172
    implementation phase, 174–176
    maintenance phase, 176
    preliminary investigation phase, 166–168
    prototyping in, 177–178
    testing the system, 174

Systems analysts, role of, 166
Systems audit, 176
Systems life cycle, 165–166, 177, 180–181
Systems Network Architecture (SNA), 123
Systems software, 6–7, 14, 36–50

Table plotters, 90
Tactical models, 158
Tape, magnetic, 106–108
Tape drives:
    digital audio (DAT), 106
    magnetic, 107
Technostress, 225
Telecommunications, 113, 119
Telenet, 128
Teleshopping, 117
Television, and microcomputers, 91
Terabytes (TBs or T-bytes), 64
Terminal adapters, 129
Terminals, 79–80, 92
    dumb, 79
    intelligent, 79
    microcomputers as, 80
    POS, 78
    smart, 79
Thesaurus programs, 23
TIGER (Topologically Integrated Geographic Encoding and Reference system), 144
Time sharing, on networks, 125
Top-down analysis, 170
Top-down program design, 187
Touch screens, 80–81
Tracks, on diskettes, 99–100
Tractor feeds, on printers, 89
Training, for new systems, 176
Transaction files, 135
Transaction processing systems, 154–156
Transmission:
    asynchronous/synchronous, 122–123
    data, 120–123, 131
    fax, 82, 129
    microwave and satellite, 120
    serial and parallel, 121
Transportable computers, 57
Travel reservations by microcomputer, 117
Trojan horse programs, 230
Twisted-pairs cable, 119
Tymnet, 128
Type styles, and printers, 89

Uninet, 128
Universal Product Code (UPC), 83
Unix operating system, 7, 14, 47–49, 50, 53
    and networking, 48
    versions of, 48

Unjustified text, 21
Uploading data, 117
U.S. Census Bureau, 144
User interfaces:
    for DOS, 41
    for DOS with Windows, 42
    graphical, 32, 45–47
    for the Macintosh, 45–47
    and modems, 117–118, 130
    for OS/2, 45
    for Unix, 48–49
Utility programs, 39

Values, in spreadsheets, 24
VAX minicomputers, 59
VAX/MVS, DEC operating system, 39
Ventura Publisher, 207
VersaCAD, 211
VGA (Video Graphics Array) boards, 86
Video display screens. *See* Monitors
Video Privacy Protection Act, 228
Virtual fax boards, 82
Virtual reality, 216–217
Viruses, computer, 142–143, 230–231
Voiceband, 120
Voice-input devices, 83–84
Voice-messaging systems, 115–116
Voice-output devices, 90
Voice-recognition devices, 84, 90
Volatile storage, 70
Voltage surges, 232
von Neumann, John, 73
VP-Expert shell, 216

Wand readers, 78, 83
"What-if" analysis, 24
Wide area networks (WANs), 128
Windowing software, 32, 41–43
Windows (Microsoft), 41–43, 52
Windows, in spreadsheets, 24
Word, defined, 66
Word (Microsoft), 21
Word processing, 6, 14, 20–23, 34
    See also Integrated packages
Word wrap, 21
Wordbench, 32
WordPerfect, 17, 18, 20, 21
Workplace, and computers, 13, 222–236
Works (integrated package), 31
Workstations:
    defined, 56
    and RISC chips, 68
    Sun386i, 56
WORM (write once, read many), 105
Worms, computer, 230–231
Write-protect notch, 101
Writing/reading data, 9, 97

XGA (Extended Graphics Array), 86

ILLUSTRATION CREDITS

Figures 1-1, 9-10, and 10-11: Courtesy of AT&T.

Figures 1-4 (top), 1-7, 1-9, 1-11, 3-2 (left), 3-7, 4-1, 4-2, 4-5, 4-11, 4-23, 4-24, 4-25, 5-1, 5-5, 5-8, 5-17, 5-21, 5-22, 6-2, 6-4, 6-5, 6-7, 6-15, 6-19 (left), 9-1, 9-3, 10-12, 10-13, 11-2, 11-5, 11-13, 11-16, 11-17, 12-5, 13-7 (left), 13-8, 14-1, 14-8, 14-10, 14-11: Courtesy of IBM.

Figures 1-4 (bottom), 1-10, 3-2 (right), 3-9, 4-21, 6-3, 6-17, and 9-4: Courtesy of Apple Computer, Inc.

Figures 1-6 and 5-3: Courtesy of Mouse Systems.

Figures 1-8, 4-19, 5-11, 5-12, 6-14, 9-12, and 13-3: Courtesy of NCR.

Figures 1-13, 1-14, 4-9, 5-6, 5-7, 5-15, 5-24, 5-25, 7-3, and 9-7: Courtesy of Hewlett-Packard.

Figure 1-15: Courtesy of Multitech Systems.

Figure 2-4: Courtesy of WordPerfect Corp.

Figure 2-9: Bar chart adapted from a photo courtesy of Ashton-Tate.

Figure 2-9: Line graph and pie chart adapted from photos courtesy of Lotus Development Corp.

Figure 2-10: Courtesy of Zenographics.

Figure 2-11: Based on a photo of Crosstalk Mk.420 screen, *PC World*, April 1991, p. 142.

Figures 3-2 (right), 3-9, and 4-21: Courtesy of Will Mosgrove/Apple Computer, Inc.

Figures 3-4, 3-6, 5-4, 12-2, and 12-3: Courtesy of Microsoft Corp.

Figure 3-10 (left): Courtesy of Open Software Foundation.

Figures 3-10 (right) and 4-3: Courtesy of Sun Microsystems.

Figure 4-6: Courtesy of NEC.

Figure 4-8: Courtesy of Compaq.

Figure 4-10: Courtesy of Digital Equipment Corp.

Figure 4-12: Courtesy of Cray Research, Inc.

Figure 4-23: Courtesy of NeXT.

Figures 5-10 and 7-2: Courtesy of Lanier Worldwide, Inc.

Figures 5-13 and 8-8: Courtesy of Texas Instruments.

Figures 5-14, 5-16, and 6-16: Courtesy of Toshiba.

Figure 5-18: From *Personal Computing*, December 1987, pp. 121 and 123.

Figures 5-19 and 14-7: Courtesy of Radio Shack / A Division of Tandy Corp.

Figures 5-20 (bottom) and 5-21 (top): Courtesy of Okidata.

Figure 6-11: Courtesy of Seagate.

Figure 6-12: Courtesy of Plus Development Corp.

Figure 6-13: Courtesy of Tandon.

Figure 6-18: Courtesy of Archive Corp.

Figure 7-5 (left): Courtesy of Hayes Microcomputer Products, Inc.

Figure 7-7: Reprinted with permission of Arthur Andersen & Co. and adapted from *Trends in Information Technology*. © copyright 1987, Arthur Andersen & Co. All rights reserved.

Figure 10-2: Courtesy of Sperry Corporation.

Figure 10-3: Courtesy of Los Alamos National Laboratory.

Figure 10-10: Courtesy of Honeywell, Inc.

Figure 11-6: Courtesy of Patton & Patton.

Figure 12-1: Based on a photo of Sidekick 2.0 screen, *PC Magazine*, April 16, 1991, p. 38.

Figures 12-4 and 12-6: Courtesy of Aldus Corp.

Figure 12-7: Adapted from illustration on pp. 6–7, *Syllabus*, published quarterly by Apple Computer, Inc. © Apple Computer, Inc. Permission courtesy of *Syllabus*, an Apple Higher Education Publication.

Figure 12-8: Adapted from illustration on p. 2 of October–November 1989 *Syllabus*, P.O. Box 2716, Sunnyvale, CA 94087.

Illustration Credits

Figures 12-10 and 12-14: Courtesy of Computer Vision.

Figures 12-11 and 12-15: Courtesy of Autodesk.

Figure 12-12: Courtesy of Hitachi, Ltd.

Figure 12-13: Courtesy of GMF Robotics.

Figure 13-4: Courtesy of BASF.

Figure 14-2: Courtesy of American Airlines.

Figure 14-3: Courtesy of Federal Express.

Figure 14-4, 14-5, and 14-6: Copyright 1990 Bill Delzell.

Figure 14-9: Courtesy of Xerox Corp.

Microcomputer Disk Operating System
with Introduction to the Labs

Copyright © 1991 by McGraw-Hill, Inc. All rights reserved. Printed in the United States of America. Except as permitted under the United States Copyright Act of 1976, no part of this publication may be reproduced or distributed in any form or by any means, or stored in a database or retrieval system, without the prior written permission of the publisher.

2 3 4 5 6 7 8 9 0   KGP KGP   9 0 9 8 7 6 5 4 3 2 1

P/N 048805-3

ORDER INFORMATION:
ISBN 0-07-048805-3

MS DOS is a registered trademark of Microsoft, Inc.
IBM, IBM PC, and PC DOS are registered trademarks of International Business Machines, Inc.

CONTENTS

Introduction to the Labs   **L1**
Organization of the Labs   L1
How the Case Study Explains Software   L2
Directions and Commands   L3
General Systems Requirements   L4
Installation   L5

Overview   **Getting Started with Your Microcomputer**   **DOS3**
Computer Hardware   DOS3
Computer Software   DOS7
Naming a File   DOS8

Lab 1   **Using the Disk Operating System (DOS)**   **DOS9**
Before You Begin   DOS9
Loading DOS   DOS10
Displaying a Directory (DIR)   DOS13
Clearing the Screen (CLS)   DOS15
Formatting a Diskette (FORMAT) and Assigning a Volume Label (/V)   DOS16
Formatting a Diskette (FORMAT) and Copying the Operating System (/S)   DOS19
Copying Files (COPY)   DOS20
Renaming Files (RENAME)   DOS25
Erasing Files (ERASE)   DOS26
Key Terms   DOS27
Matching   DOS27

Lab 2   **Managing Your Hard Disk**   **DOS28**
Subdirectories   DOS28
Making Directories   DOS29
Changing Directories   DOS32
Changing the DOS Prompt   DOS33
Using the TREE command   DOS36
Displaying the Contents of a File   DOS38
Removing Directories   DOS38
Creating a Batch File   DOS40
Key Terms   DOS42
Matching   DOS42
Practice Exercises   DOS43

Summary   **DOS**   **DOS44**
Glossary of Key Terms   DOS44
Functional Summary of Selected DOS Commands   DOS46

Index   **DOS47**

INTRODUCTION TO THE LABS

The labs in the *McGraw-Hill Microcomputing* series each require about one hour to complete. They are designed to provide you with practical skills in using the following kinds of software, which are the most widely used in business and industry:

- Disk operating system
- Word processing
- Spreadsheet
- Database
- Local area network

The labs describe not only the most important commands and concepts, but also explain why and under what circumstances you will use them. That is, by presenting an ongoing case study—The Sports Club, which is based on input from actual health-club managers—we show how such software is used in a real business setting.

Organization of the Labs

The Labs Are Organized in the Following Categories: Overview, Objectives, Case Study, Lab Activities, Key Terms, Matching and Practice Exercises, Glossary of Key Terms, and Functional Summary of Selected Commands, and Index.

Overview The overview, which appears in the first of the succession of labs, describes (1) what the program can do for you, (2) what the program is, (3) the generic terms that this and all similar programs use (e.g., all word processing programs, regardless of brand name), and (4) the case study to be presented in the labs covered by the program.

Objectives The objectives list the concepts and commands to be learned in that particular lab.

Case Study The case study introduces the specific case covered by the particular lab—the general problems that the software activities will help you solve.

Lab Activities   The lab activities consist of detailed, step-by-step directions for you to follow in order to solve the problems of the case. Display screens show how a command or procedure is supposed to look. Labs should be followed in sequence, because each succeeding lab builds on the ones preceding it. In addition, screen displays and directions become less specific. This feature allows you to think about what you have learned, avoids simple rote learning, and reinforces earlier concepts and commands, helping you to gain confidence.

Key Terms   Terms that appeared in **boldfaced (dark) type** throughout the lab are also listed at the end of each lab.

Matching and Practice Exercises   Each lab concludes with a matching exercise and with several practice problems. The practice problems, which require use of a microcomputer, are designed to reinforce concepts and commands presented in the lab.

Glossary of Key Terms   The glossary, which appears at the end of each lab section, defines all the key terms that appeared in bold throughout the labs for that particular kind of software.

Functional Summary of Selected Commands   Each section of labs also concludes with a quick-reference source for selected commands for that particular software. The commands are categorized by the type of function performed.

Index   Each section of labs contains an index for quick reference back to specific items within that section.

How the Case Study Explains Software

The Sports Club Ongoing Case Study Shows How to Solve Real-World Business Problems Using a Word Processor, a Spreadsheet, and a Database Program.

The ongoing case study of the Sports Club, a health and athletic club offering many activities (swimming, tennis, weight room, sauna, and so on), was written with the help of experience contributed by actual health-club managers. In our scenario, the club has recently had great growth in membership and is trying to update its facility and management procedures, using newly purchased software with their microcomputer system.

The reader follows Sports Club employees as they perform their jobs with this software, as follows:

Section I: Microcomputer Disk Operating System—Labs 1–2   This section first describes the hardware of a microcomputer system. It then shows you how to use the Disk Operating System (DOS) to start the computer system, format diskettes, make back-up copies of program and data diskettes, and perform other tasks. The second DOS Lab covers directories, paths, and batch files.

Section II: Word Processing—Labs 1–4   The word processing program is explained by showing how a letter welcoming new club members is created, revised, formatted, saved, and printed.

Section III: Spreadsheets—Labs 1–5 Use of the spreadsheet program is shown by depicting how the operating budget for the Courtside Cafe is created and modified. A proposal to expand services that will produce a 20-percent profit margin in one year is analyzed. Growth in club membership over five years is graphed.

Section IV: Database—Labs 1–4 Creation, modication, updating, and making a report of a database of member information is demonstrated. The software is also used to sort and index data about club employees and summarize the information in a professional report.

Section V: Local Area Network—Lab 1 A local area network connecting five microcomputers and two printers is used by club employees to produce documents using the application software and shared data files. The local area network is also used to send and receive electronic mail.

Directions and Commands

Commands and Directions Are Expressed Through Certain Standard Conventions.

We have followed certain conventions in the labs for indicating keys, key combinations, commands, command sequences, and other directions.

Keys Computer keys are expressed in abbreviated form, as follows:

Computer Keys	Display in Text
Alt (Alternate)	ALT
← or Bksp (Backspace)	Bksp
Caps Lock (Capital Lock)	CAPS LOCK
Ctrl (Control)	CTRL
Cursor Movement:	
↑ (Up)	↑
↓ (Down)	↓
← (Left)	←
→ (Right)	→
Del (Delete)	DEL
End	END
ESC (Escape)	ESC
↵ (Enter/Return)	↵
Function Keys:	
F1 through F10	F1 through F10
Home	HOME
Ins (Insert)	INS
Num Lock (Number Lock)	NUM LOCK
PgDn (Page Down)	PGDN
PgUp (Page Up)	PGUP
PrtSc (Print Screen)	PrtScr
Scroll Lock	SCROLL LOCK
⇧ (Shift)	SHIFT
⇆ or Tab	TAB

Key Combinations Many programs require that you use a combination of keys for a particular command: for example, the pair of keys CTRL and F4. You should press them in the order in which they appear, from left to right, holding down the first key while pressing the second. In the labs, commands that are used in this manner are separated by a hyphen—for example: CTRL - F4.

Directions The principal directions in the labs are "Press," "Move to," "Type," and "Select." These directions appear on a separate line beginning at the left margin, as follows:

- *Press:* This means press or strike a key. Usually a command key will follow the direction (such as DEL for "Delete"). For example:

    Press: DEL

- *Move to:* This means you should move your cursor or cell pointer to the location indicated. For example, the direction to move to line 4, position 12, would appear as:

    Move to: Ln 4 Pos 12

- *Type:* This means you should type or key in certain letters or numbers, just as you would on a typewriter keyboard. Whatever is to be typed will appear in **boldface (dark) type.** For example:

    Type: January

- *Select:* Many programs use a sequence of selections to complete a command. In the beginning, we will introduce these commands separately. Later, as you become more familiar with the software, we will combine the commands on a single line. Each command may be separated by a "slash" /. The command sequences will follow the word (Select*.*) If the first letter of a command appears in **boldface**, you can select that command by typing the letter. Other parts of the command sequence that are to be typed will also appear in **boldface.** For example, the command to open a database file will appear as:

    Select: **S**et Up / Database file / B: / MEMBERS.DBF / **N**

This means you should type the letter "S," select "Database file" as the type of file you want to use, select "B:" as the disk drive, select "MEMBERS.DBF" from a list of database files, and then type the letter "N."

General System Requirements

To complete the labs, the following hardware and software are needed:

Hardware

- An IBM or IBM-compatible computer system with two disk drives and a minimum of 256K RAM memory.
- A monochrome or color monitor and a keyboard.
- A printer

Operating System Software

- DOS 2.0 version or higher.

Applications Software

- *Applications software program diskettes as selected by your instructor.* These diskettes may be purchased as a package or will be supplied by your instructor. The McGraw-Hill Microcomputing Labs are available in the following versions: Lotus 1-2-3 Releases 2.01 and 2.2, VP-Planner, VP-Planner Plus, SuperCalc4, WordPerfect 4.2, WordPerfect 5.0, WordPerfect 5.1, WordStar 4.0, dBASE III PLUS, and dBASE IV. Additionally, a complete series of 12 labs using Microsoft Works 2.0 is available. The following educational versions of the software programs are available through McGraw-Hill to accompany this manual: WordPerfect 4.2, WordStar 4.0, SuperCalc4, and dBASE III PLUS.

- *User data diskette.* The files needed to perform the labs and to complete the practice exercises are included on a separate diskette that is supplied by your instructor.

Hardware/Software Assumptions

The directions and figures in the book assume the use of an IBM or IBM-compatible computer system with two disk drives. If you have a computer system with one disk drive, a hard-disk drive, or a system that is networked, your instructor will provide you with alternative directions.

Installation

Programs Must Be "Installed" in Order to Run on Certain Equipment. Consult Your Instructor.

Most software has to be installed or "custom-tailored" to run with specific computers and printers. The documentation accompanying the software gives details. If you find that, for some reason, your software will not print out correctly and won't run on your microcomputer, ask your instructor for assistance.

OVERVIEW
Getting Started with Your Microcomputer

A microcomputer system is composed of five essential parts: the user, hardware, software, storage, and data. All parts of the system are closely linked: one part of the system cannot operate without the others. The user needs to know how to operate the computer hardware and use the software programs to input and analyze data or information.

Computer Hardware

The physical part of the computer system, called **hardware,** consists of four components: input devices, the system unit, secondary storage devices, and output devices.

The **input devices** allow you to enter information or data into the processor. The most common input device is a keyboard. Other types of input devices are a mouse and a scanner. The **system,** or **processing, unit** consists of the disk drive(s), memory, and the microprocessor, or CPU. The system unit executes the software program instructions, performs calculations, and temporarily stores data and programs. The most common form of **secondary storage** is a diskette. It provides a place to permanently store information or data that is input into the computer. The **output devices** allow you to see the results of your work. A monitor is used for temporary display. A printer is used to make a permanent copy of your data. A typical computer system is shown in Figure 1.

Input Devices The **keyboard** is the most common type of input device. It allows you to communicate with the computer. It consists of four main areas: the

FIGURE 1

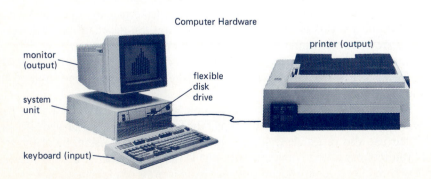

DOS4
Getting Started with Your
Microcomputer

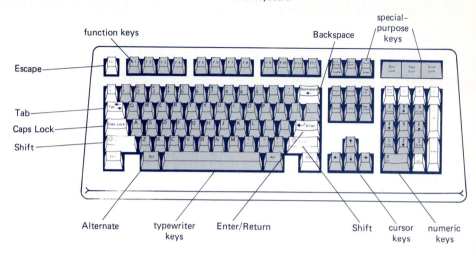

FIGURE 2

function keys, the typewriter keys, the numeric keypad, and special-purpose keys. Figure 2 shows a typical IBM PC keyboard.

The central area of the keyboard contains the typing keys. They are letters, numbers, and special characters such as the semicolon and the dollar sign, as they appear on a standard typewriter. You use these keys just like you would a normal typewriter.

The other typing keys and their uses are described below.

KEY	ACTION
(SHIFT)-letter	Types uppercase letter
(SHIFT)-number	Types symbol shown above number on that key
(CAPS LOCK)	Allows entry of all uppercase alphabetic characters without using (SHIFT)
(TAB)	Moves cursor preset number of spaces to the right
(SHIFT)-(TAB)	Moves cursor preset number of spaces to the left
⏎ (return or enter)	Moves the cursor to the next line (same as a typewriter); Allows the user to enter data or command sequences

At the right side of the keyboard is the numeric keypad. It consists of nine keys with arrows and numbers on them. Generally these keys are used to direct the movement of the cursor on the display screen. The cursor is a flashing bar that the computer uses to tell you its present location on the display. Use of these keys moves the cursor in the direction of the arrow. The numeric-keypad area can also be used to enter numbers. This is accomplished by pressing the (NUM LOCK) key. However, numbers are more often entered using the top row of the typing keys.

There are also some keys in the numeric keypad with words on them: (HOME), (END), (PGUP), and (PGDN). These keys will have different meanings depending on the software program you are using.

Depending on the type of keyboard, you will find a series of function keys either along the left side or across the top of the keyboard. They are labeled (F1), (F2), etc. Their use also varies depending on the program you are using. Basically, they allow you to enter a long command with one keystroke. Instead of using 10 keys to give the computer a command, all you need to do is press one function key.

Scattered throughout the keyboard are special-purpose keys. The uses of these keys change with the type of work you are doing. Generally they have the following uses:

Key	Action
ESC (escape)	Quits or goes back one step in a program command
CTRL (control)	Used in combination with another key to perform a special task
ALT (alternate)	Assigns another function to a given key
PrtScr (print screen)	Prints a hard copy of whatever is on the display screen when pressed along with the SHIFT key
SCROLL LOCK	When pressed with the ↑ and ↓ keys, moves the document up or down on the screen
Pause/Break	May let you stop a program for a short time
INS (insert)	Allows you to insert characters between other characters
DEL (delete)	Erases the character that the cursor is on
Bksp (backspace)	Erases character to the left of cursor (this key may also appear as a left-facing arrow, ⟵)

System Unit The **system unit** is housed inside the system cabinet. Within the system unit are several components. The most important are the microprocessor, main memory, and the disk drives. Figure 3 displays the parts of a system unit, and the following describes these parts.

The **microprocessor,** also called the **central processing unit (CPU),** is the part of the system unit that does the actual computing. It contains the circuitry through which data is processed and instructions are executed. In a microcomputer the microprocessor consists of a single silicon chip, such as the model shown in Figure 3 made by Intel Corporation.

The **main memory,** or **primary storage** component, of the system unit is where data and instructions are stored during processing by the microprocessor. Depending on the amount of memory your computer system has, the number of storage chips within the system unit will vary.

As Figure 3 shows, there are two types of main memory, **read-only memory (ROM)** and **random-access memory (RAM).** The ROM area contains built-in instructions that direct the operations of the computer. ROM is not accessible to the user. The other type of memory, RAM, is accessible to the user. It is the computer's workplace. The RAM area holds the software programs and data that are loaded from the diskette. RAM is also referred to as **temporary memory** because whatever is in RAM is lost if the power is turned off. The data in temporary memory can be permanently saved, however, on computer diskettes that are inserted into the disk drive.

The **disk drive** provides the means for you to retrieve and save your data and programs onto a diskette. There are two types of drives: a **flexible-disk** drive and a **fixed,** or **hard-disk, drive.** The flexible-disk drive reads (obtains) information stored on a removable diskette into RAM or writes (transfers) information onto the diskette from RAM. It allows the user to load instructions into the computer from program diskettes and to save data onto and retrieve data from the data diskettes.

The drive is housed in the front of the computer as shown in Figure 4. A slot allows you to insert a diskette into the drive. The data is read from or written to the diskette by the read-write head mechanism inside each drive.

If there are two disk drives, they are referred to as the A drive and the B drive. If the drives are positioned side by side, the A drive is on the left. If your drives are

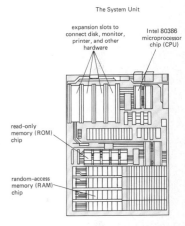

FIGURE 3

located one above the other, the A drive is the one on top. Usually the A drive contains the program diskette and the B drive, the data diskette.

If you have one disk drive, it can act as both the A and B drives, depending on the diskette inserted into the drive. Some computers have a hard disk drive in place of or in addition to the B drive. It is a permanent fixture containing one or more metallic disks that are used to store data files and software programs. It is usually referred to as the C drive. More information can be stored on the hard disk, and it is more quickly accessed than the information from a flexible disk.

Secondary Storage A **diskette** is the permanent storage medium for either data (e.g., a business letter) or a software program (e.g., a word processor, to edit that letter). The data and program information are stored on a circular plastic diskette as a series of electromagnetic spots. By inserting these diskettes in the disk drive, you provide the system with the directions and the data to work with. Diskettes come in several sizes. The most common sizes are 5 1/4 inch and 3 1/2 inch. The type of diskette you will use will depend on your computer hardware requirements. Figure 4 shows the 5 1/4- and 3 1/2-inch diskettes.

Since the diskettes contain a permanent copy of your work, it is very important that this data not be lost or destroyed. If it is, you could lose a lot of time and effort. To help preserve your diskettes, there are some things you should know about their care and handling:

1. Excessive heat can melt or warp the diskette. Do not, for example, expose your diskette to excessive sunlight through the window of your car or to excessive heat by placing it on your heater.

2. Diskettes use magnetism to store your data. Do not expose the disk to magnetic fields such as your telephone receiver, a loudspeaker, or a television. The magnetic fields from these machines can alter the data on your diskette.

3. Do not touch the surface of the diskette through the oval opening. Always handle the case only. The oils from your skin can damage the surface of the diskette.

4. Store your diskettes standing up or in a vertical position. This way they will not bend or warp. Always place the 5 1/4 diskette in its protective sleeve.

5. Do not bend diskettes or place heavy objects on them.

6. Do not write on a 5 1/4 diskette with a ballpoint pen. The pressure from the pen can crease the diskette and damage it. If you must write on your diskette, use a felt-tip pen. It is best, however, to write the label before you place it on the diskette.

7. Be careful when inserting the diskette into the drive. Make sure the label side is up. The label end goes into the drive last. Close the drive door gently.

Output Devices The **monitor, or video display screen,** is how the computer communicates with you. The computer prints messages on the video display screen to tell you what it is doing. In our case, it will relay program messages or instructions called **prompts.** It will also display results of calculations, graphs, and text input.

The video display screen can be either a monochrome screen display or a color screen display. A monochrome screen can display only one color — usually white, green, or amber on a black background screen. The color screen can usually display between 2 and 16 colors, depending on the quality of the monitor. If you have a

FIGURE 4

color monitor or a monochrome monitor with a graphics board, you can view all of your work, including graphs, on your display screen.

Along with the video display screen, a **printer** serves as a way for the computer to tell you what you have input and what it has done. The difference is that the printer generates a permanent hard copy of your work. Some printers can print both text and graphics. Others can print only text. If you have a printer that prints only text, you would need a device called a **plotter** to generate graphs. Figure 5 shows a picture of a printer (left) and a plotter (right).

Printers can produce hard copy that is either near letter (draft) quality or letter quality. Draft-quality print is formed by a series of dots and consequently may not appear solid. Letter-quality print is solid, like that produced by a typewriter.

The most popular type of printer that produces draft-quality print is the dot-matrix printer. Dot-matrix printers produce letters by a series of pins that produce dots in the form of the letter on the paper in ink. These printers are fast and economical.

Letter-quality print is produced by daisy-wheel, ink-jet, and laser printers. The daisy-wheel printer produces letters in ink from a thimble containing the characters (much like an electronic typewriter). The ink-jet printer sprays ink in the pattern of the character. The most recent type of printer used with microcomputers is the laser printer. It creates characters by means of an electronic charge. The laser printer is a high-resolution printer that produces typeset-quality text and graphics.

Although most printers can also print graphs, you may want to use a plotter to draw pictures and graphs. Most plotters use several pens of different colors to produce a multicolor drawing. The graphs and drawings produced by a plotter have much better line resolution and precision than graphs produced by a dot-matrix printer. A plotter produces professional presentation-quality graphs.

Computer Software

Software is the set of instructions that directs the computer to process information. These instructions are called **programs.** Without software, the computer cannot work. A commonly used analogy is that the computer hardware is the engine, while the software is the fuel that allows the engine to operate. Without software the hardware would be useless.

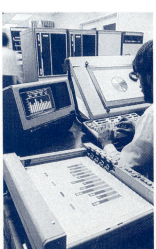

FIGURE 5

There are two types of software available for computers: systems software and applications software.

Systems Software **Systems software** programs coordinate the operation of the various hardware components of the computer. The systems software or operating system program helps the user to actually operate the computer systems. They are effectively an interface between the user and the computer.

The operating system oversees the processing of the application programs and all input and output of the system. Without the operating system, you cannot use the applications software programs provided with this book. The operating system controls computer system resources and coordinates the flow of data to and from the microprocessor and to and from input and output devices such as the keyboard and the monitor.

Systems software is usually provided by the computer manufacturer. The various types of computers require different systems software programs to operate. Some of the most popular are MS-DOS, Apple-DOS, and UNIX.

Applications Software **Applications software** is a set of programs designed for specific uses or "applications", such as word processing, graphics, or spreadsheet analysis. Applications software can be either custom-written or purchased ready-made.

Normally, to use an application program like Lotus 1-2-3, you insert the program diskette; load the program into the computers main memory; execute (run) the program; and then create, edit, or update a file. When you have finished, you need to save the work you have done on a diskette. If you don't save your work and you turn off the computer or load another software program, it is erased from memory and everything you have done will be lost.

The operating system acts as the mediator between the hardware and the application program. It is responsible for loading the applications software into memory and then starting the program. When you have finished using the applications software you are returned to the operating system.

Naming a File

In order to save your work as a file on the diskette, you must assign it a name. Each **filename** must be unique to that particular diskette. For example, if you give a new file the same filename as a file already on the diskette, the contents of the original file will be replaced by the contents of the new file. Many software programs have safeguards to prevent accidentally overwriting one file with another.

Filenames consist of two parts: the name the user creates, and a **file extension,** which is usually assigned by the software program. The two parts of a filename are separated by a period. They are shown in Figure 6.

A filename can be no longer than eight characters. It can have no spaces, commas, or periods. It should be descriptive of the contents of the file. For example, the filename CHECKBK would be a good name for a file that contains your checking account information.

The file extension can be up to three characters long. Application programs use different extensions so that you can distinguish among them. For instance, Lotus 1-2-3 files have a file extension of "WK1." Thus, when you see a file with that extension, you will know that it is used with Lotus 1-2-3. The filename above would now read CHECKBK.WK1 if it had been created using Lotus 1-2-3.

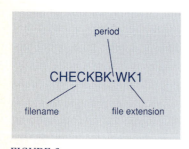

FIGURE 6

LAB 1
Using the Disk Operating System (DOS)

This lab provides instructions for starting your computer and loading and using the operating system used by the IBM PC's called DOS (Disk Operating System). You will learn how to display the directory of files on a diskette and how to prepare a new diskette for use. You will make duplicate or backup copies of the applications software diskettes and of the data diskette, which contains the program files needed to run the labs in this book. Finally, you will learn how to rename and erase files from a diskette.

OBJECTIVES

In this lab you will learn how to:

1. Start the computer system using DOS.
2. Display a diskette directory.
3. Clear the display screen.
4. Format a diskette.
5. Copy files.
6. Rename files.
7. Erase files.

Before You Begin

The procedure you will follow in this lab varies with the type of computer system you have: one disk, two disk, or hard disk drives. These directions are written for computer systems having two drives. In a two-disk-drive system, the first drive (upper or left) is called the A drive. The second (lower or right) is the B drive. If you have a one-drive or hard-drive system, your instructor will give you additional directions.

Before you begin this lab, you will need the following:

- **Hardware:** An IBM or IBM-compatible computer system with two disk drives and a minimum of 256K RAM memory

  Note: If you have an IBM or IBM-compatible computer with one disk drive or a hard-disk drive, ask your instructor for directions.

- **Operating Systems Software:** DOS version 2.0 or higher

  Note: Depending on the version of DOS you are using, your screen displays may differ slightly from the figures shown in this lab which use DOS version 3.30. These differences are minor and do not affect the lab instructions.

- **Applications Software:** The applications software program diskettes selected by your instructor

- **User Data Diskette:** The data diskette containing files you will use while completing the labs

In addition, you will need a supply of blank diskettes with sleeves, labels, and write-protect tabs equal to the total of the number of applications software program diskettes plus the data diskette.

Loading DOS

The operating system program controls computer system resources. It also coordinates the flow of data to and from the system unit and to and from input and output devices like the keyboard and the monitor. It allows you to create files and run applications programs.

The operating system used for the IBM PC is DOS, which stands for disk operating system. DOS consists of three files—COMMAND.COM, IBMDOS.COM, and IBMBIO.COM. COMMAND.COM is the program that reads whatever is typed at the keyboard and processes the commands given to the computer. The last two files handle input and output to and from the computer and manage the files on the diskette.

To start your computer and load DOS:

1. Take the DOS diskette out of its protective sleeve and insert it into drive A of your computer. Make sure the label side is up. Close the drive door.
2. Turn the computer on by moving the power switch to the "up" position.
3. If necessary, turn your monitor on and adjust the contrast and brightness.

After a few seconds you will hear the whirring sound of the diskette in the drive. This is followed by a beep, and the light near the A drive will blink on and off. When the disk drive light is on, it tells you the computer is either reading from or writing to the diskette in that drive.

Caution: Do not remove or insert a diskette into the drive when the light is on. This can result in damage to the files on the diskette.

When you turn the computer on, it performs a memory check to determine whether all the RAM locations are able to receive and store data correctly. It also initializes the equipment for use. Then it accesses the disk drive and reads the three DOS files into RAM.

Your display screen should look like Figure 1-1.

FIGURE 1-1

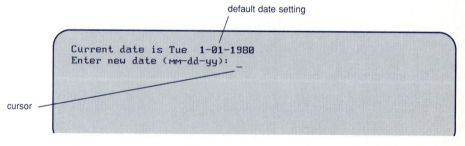

In the figure, DOS displays the current day of the week and date as Tue 1-01-1980. The date display on your screen may be slightly different. This is the default date. A **default** setting is the initial setting that is used by the program if it is not directed to use another. If you do not enter a different date, the program assumes that you want to use the default date setting.

The second line of the message displayed on the screen, "Enter new date (mm-dd-yy):" asks you to enter a new date. The flashing line or bar following this message is called the **cursor.** The cursor shows you where the next character you type will appear. If the default date is correct, to enter it as displayed,

Press: ⏎

If the default date is not correct, you will want to enter the correct date. The date is entered in the form month-day-year (mm-dd-yy). The three parts of the date can be separated by hyphens (-), slashes (/), or periods (.).

The correct date is entered by typing:

1 or 2 numbers between 1 and 12 for the month.

1 or 2 numbers between 1 and 31 for the day.

2 numbers between 80 and 99 or 4 numbers between 1980 and 1999 for the year.

Use the number keys above the alphabet keys to enter the current date. The figures in this lab will display the date 9-22-91. To enter the current date, replace the date below (9-22-91) with the current date,

Type: 9-22-91 (enter the current date)

If you make a mistake while typing, use the (Bksp) (backspace) key to erase the characters back to the error. Then retype it correctly.

To indicate you have completed the date and want to enter it into the program,

Press: ⏎

Your display screen should be similar to Figure 1-2.

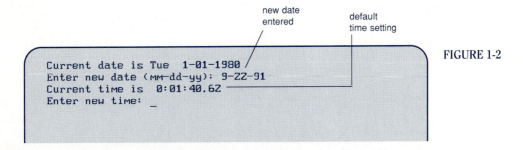

FIGURE 1-2

Note: If your display screen is still prompting you to enter the date, it may be that you entered the date incorrectly. Try again.

The next message on the screen displays the current time. Again, DOS displays a default time. The format for the time is hours:minutes:seconds.hundredths of a second. The default time starts with 0 hours, 0 minutes, 0 seconds, and 0 one-hundredths of a second each time the computer is turned on.

The current time displayed on your screen will reflect the amount of time that has lapsed since the computer was turned on. If the default time is correct, to enter it,

Press: ⏎

If the default time is not correct, the correct time can be entered. DOS uses a 24-hour clock that is similar to a military clock. 1:00 A.M. is the first hour on the 24-hour clock and 1:00 P.M. is the thirteenth hour. You add 12 to the afternoon hour to enter the correct time.

The correct time is entered by typing:

1 or 2 numbers between 0 and 23 for the hour.

1 or 2 numbers between 0 and 59 for the minutes.

1 or 2 numbers between 0 and 59 for the seconds.

1 or 2 numbers between 0 and 99 for the hundredths of seconds.

It is not necessary to enter all four parts of the time. You can simply enter the hour, or the hour and minutes, or the hour, minutes, and seconds.

The hour, minutes, and seconds are separated by a colon (:). The hundredths of a second are separated from seconds by a period (.).

Use the number keys above the alphabet keys to enter the hour and minutes only for the current time. The figures in this lab will display the time as 10:15. To respond to the prompt to enter the current time, replace the time below (10:15) with your current time,

Type: **10:15** (enter the current time)

If you make a mistake while typing, use the (Bksp) key to erase the characters back to the error. Then retype it correctly.

To indicate you have completed the time and want to enter it into the program,

Press: ⏎

Your display screen should look like Figure 1-3.

FIGURE 1-3

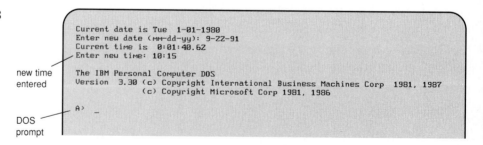

new time entered

DOS prompt

Entering the current date and time sets the date and time for the system clock. If you leave your computer system on, the clock will continue to run.

It is not necessary to enter the current date and time in reponse to the DOS date and time prompts. You can simply accept the defaults by pressing ⏎. However, it is not a good practice to do so. This is because whenever you create or update a file, the date and time are recorded in the directory next to the filename when the file is saved. This information can help you find the most recent version of a file.

That's all there is to it: you have just completed the loading of your operating system. Starting the computer and loading DOS is often called **booting** the system. The operating system can also be reloaded after the computer is already on. This is called a **warm boot.** To reload DOS, you would hold down the (CTRL) (control) and (ALT) (alternate) keys together and then press the (DEL) (delete) key once. This causes the computer to start over. Everything that was in main memory is erased. Either type of booting will do the same thing—enable you to use DOS to control the operation of the computer and the applications software programs.

Immediately after DOS is loaded, the version of DOS in use and the copyright information are displayed. The version of DOS used in this lab is 3.3. If you are using a different version of DOS, some of the figures in this lab may not match your display screen exactly. However, they will be similar.

Following the copyright information, the DOS **prompt,** A>, followed by the cursor appears on the display. The letter A tells you the **default drive** is the A drive. This is the drive that DOS will search to get a file or to execute a program unless you instruct it otherwise. It is the current drive because it is the drive DOS will use.

The > is known as the **prompt character.** It lets you know DOS is waiting for instructions from the user. The A > sign then is known as the "A prompt."

DOS commands can be entered following the prompt in either upper- or lowercase characters. A space is used to separate parts of a command and ⏎ is pressed to enter the command into the central processing unit when you are finished typing it. For example, suppose you want to change the current drive to B. Following the A>, you would type B: and press ⏎. The DOS prompt would change to B>. The current drive would be the B drive. So DOS would read from and write to files on the diskette in the B drive.

DOS Commands

Displaying a Directory (DIR)

Often you will want to see a list of all the files on the diskette. A portion of each diskette is devoted to maintaining a listing of all filenames. This listing is called a **directory.** To display a list of the filenames, the DIR (**DIRECTORY**) command is used.

This command can be issued with or without the DOS diskette in the drive. This is because the program statements to display a directory have been copied into RAM when DOS was loaded. This type of DOS command is called an **internal command** because it stays in RAM until you turn off the system unit or load DOS again.

Other DOS commands require that the DOS diskette be in the drive when the command is issued. These are **external commands** because they are not read into RAM when DOS is loaded. Instead, the program statements to perform the DOS command are read from the DOS diskette whenever the command is used.

The following DOS commands used in this lab are internal commands: DIR, CLS, COPY, RENAME, and ERASE. The only command used in this lab that is an external command is FORMAT.

DOS commands can be entered in either upper- or lowercase characters. Or you can use a combination of the two. To display the directory of files on the DOS diskette in the A drive, at the A>,

Type: **DIR**
Press: ⏎

Watch your display screen carefully. The information and filenames listed at the beginning of the directory scroll off the top of the screen to allow the filenames at the bottom of the directory to be seen. This is because there are more files in the directory than can be displayed on the screen at one time. Your display screen should look similar to Figure 1-4.

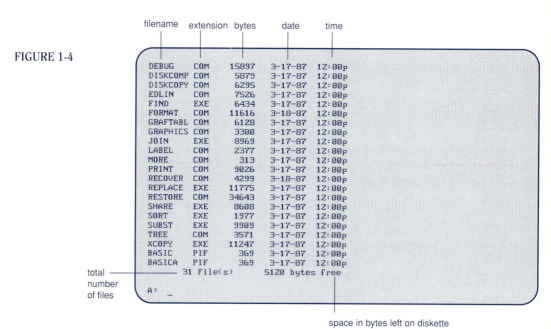

FIGURE 1-4

The DIR command displays the filename, the file extension, the size of the file in bytes, and the date and time the file was created or last updated. By entering the correct date and time when loading DOS, you can quickly determine when a file was created or updated.

Note: The filenames displayed on your screen may differ from the filenames shown in Figure 1-4. This is a function of the version of DOS you are using.

The total number of files on the diskette and the number of bytes of remaining space on the diskette are displayed at the bottom of the list of filenames.

The A> is displayed again, indicating that DOS is now ready to accept another command.

As you noticed, when the screen was filled with filenames, the files listed at the beginning of the directory scrolled off the screen to allow the rest of the directory to be seen. This may be unsatisfactory. The DIR command can be altered so that it will pause, or stop the scrolling of the filenames, when the display screen is full. The command to do this is DIR/P **(DIR**ECTORY/**P**AUSE). The / is a **switch character** that is entered following the DIR command. It tells the command to handle a task in a different manner. A switch can be used in many DOS commands. The switch character is then followed by the appropriate switch letter, in this case P for pause.

Type: `DIR/P`
Press: `⏎`

When the screen is filled, the filenames do not continue to scroll off the top of the screen. Instead, the DIR command pauses the display of filenames. To continue viewing the rest of the filenames, following the directions on the bottom of the screen,

Press: `any key`

Continue viewing the files on the DOS diskette. When there are no more filenames on the diskette, the A> will appear on the screen again.

Another way to view a directory of filenames allows more files to be viewed on the display at one time. This is done by displaying the filenames across the width of the display screen. This command is DIR/W (**DIR**ECTORY/**W**IDE).

Type: `DIR/W`
Press: `⏎`

Your display screen should be similar to Figure 1-5.

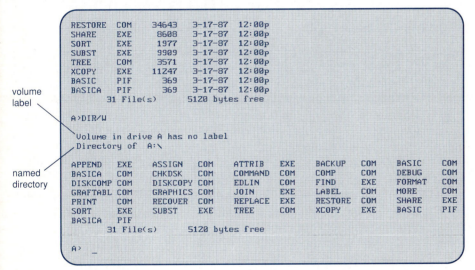

FIGURE 1-5

The files are listed across the screen. Notice that the file size, date, and time information are omitted. The two lines of information above the list of filenames tell you whether the diskette has been assigned a volume label and the name of the directory being viewed. We will discuss volume labels in more detail shortly.

Clearing the Screen (CLS)

At times the display screen can get cluttered. This makes reading the screen difficult. For example, your display currently shows the end of the listing of files from the DIR/P command and all the files in response to the DIR/W command. Although there is room at the bottom of the screen to enter further commands, it would be easier to read if the screen was erased or cleared first. The DOS command to erase the display screen is CLS (**CLEAR SCREEN**). This is an internal DOS command.

Type: CLS
Press: ⏎

Your display screen should be similar to Figure 1-6.

FIGURE 1-6

home position

All information on the display is erased. The DOS prompt and cursor moves into the upper left-hand corner (**home** position) of the display screen. Now when you issue the next command, the screen will be much easier to read.

Formatting a Diskette (FORMAT) and Assigning a Volume Label (/V)

Before a new diskette can be used, it must be **formatted** or converted from a generic state into a form that can be used by your computer. Diskettes are shipped from the manufacturer in a blank form so that they can be used by a variety of computers.

The DOS command to format a new diskette is FORMAT. The FORMAT command initializes or prepares a new diskette to accept DOS information and files. Specifically, it sets up and labels the tracks and sectors on the diskette to accept data. It checks the tracks for any bad spots that cannot be used to store data. It marks off these areas so they cannot be used. The FORMAT command also sets up the area on the diskette where the directory of files will be maintained.

While formatting the diskette, you can also specify that you want to assign the diskette a volume name or identification. To tell the FORMAT command to perform the extra task of assigning a volume label to the diskette, the switch /V is entered following the FORMAT command.

The volume label switch will allow you to enter an identifying label on the diskette. The volume label could identify the contents of the diskette or, as we will use it, the name of the diskette's owner.

As discussed earlier, DOS commands such as DIR and CLS can be issued without the DOS diskette in the drive. These internal commands are stored in RAM. Commands such as FORMAT require that the DOS diskette be in the drive when the command is issued. They are called external commands because their program statements are not transferred into main memory when the system is booted. The program to perform the command must be read from the diskette into memory every time the command is used. When you are finished using the command, the FORMAT program is cleared from memory.

DOS17

You are now ready to format your first new diskette. We will format the diskette and assign it a volume label. You will enter your last name as the volume label.

Your DOS diskette should be in the A drive. Check to see if your DOS diskette has a write-protect tab over the write-protect notch. If it does not, cover the write-protect notch with a write-protect tab to prevent your accidentally erasing or writing on the DOS diskette.

We will tell DOS to format the blank diskette which will be located in the B drive and to assign it a volume label. The command to format a diskette in the B drive and assign it a volume label is FORMAT B:/V.

Immediately following the A >,

Type: **FORMAT B:/V**
Press: ⏎

Notice that the A-drive light goes on as the program to format a diskette is read into memory.

Your display screen should look similar to Figure 1-7.

```
A>FORMAT B:/V
Insert new diskette for drive B:
and strike ENTER when ready_
```

FIGURE 1-7

Following the directions on the display, take a new diskette out of its protective sleeve. Insert the new diskette, label side up, in the B drive. Close the drive door.

Press: ⏎

While the diskette is being formatted, a message is displayed on the screen. Depending on your version of DOS, it will either say "Head: 0 Cylinder: 0" or "Formatting . . .". Both messages are telling you that the blank diskette is in the process of being formatted.

Any diskette, old or new, can be formatted. If you format a used diskette, any files or information on it will be erased during formatting. Be careful only to format diskettes that do not contain information that you may want. When formatting is complete, your display screen should look similar to Figure 1-8.

```
A>FORMAT B:/V
Insert new diskette for drive B:
and strike ENTER when ready

Format complete

Volume label (11 characters, ENTER for none)? _
```

FIGURE 1-8

The message "Format complete" is displayed. DOS is now prompting you to enter the volume label. As you can see from the prompt, a volume label cannot be longer than 11 characters. If you did not want to enter a volume label after all, you could simply presse ⏎ to leave the volume label blank.

To enter your last name as the volume label (in place of O'LEARY, type your last name), in either upper- or lowercase characters,

Type: O'LEARY (type your last name)
Press: ⏎

Your display screen should be similar to Figure 1-9.

FIGURE 1-9

```
A>FORMAT B:/V
Insert new diskette for drive B:
and strike ENTER when ready

Format complete

Volume label (11 characters, ENTER for none)? O'LEARY          ──── volumn label

    362496 bytes total disk space
    362496 bytes available on disk

Format another (Y/N)?_
```

The volume label, your last name, is entered on the diskette. The total number of bytes on the diskette and bytes available for use are displayed.

Next DOS asks whether you want to format another diskette. If you wanted to format another diskette, you would type "Y" for "Yes." Although we need to format several more new diskettes, we will format them later, using an additional FORMAT switch. To end formatting, respond "N" for "No" as follows,

Type: N
Press: ⏎

The A> is displayed again. You have formatted your first diskette, and it is now ready to use. Remove the diskette from the B drive. To show that this diskette has been formatted, we will label it. Before placing a label on the diskette, write the words "Backup Data" on the label. This diskette will be used to hold your duplicate or backup copy of the files on the data diskette. Then, place the label on the diskette.

Caution: If you need to write on a label that is already on a diskette, use a felt-tip pen only.

Formatting a Diskette (FORMAT) and Copying the Operating System (/S)

DOS19

Your other new diskettes will be used to hold backup copies of the applications software programs you will be using to run the labs in this book. The FORMAT command can be used both to format the diskette and to copy the operating system files onto the diskette. The /S (**s**ystem) switch copies the DOS files to the diskette during the FORMAT command.

Copying the DOS files to your diskette during formatting will make your diskette bootable. That is, you will not need the DOS diskette when starting the system. As a convenience in working with applications software, it is desireable to have a copy of DOS on your program diskettes whenever possible.

We will now format your remaining blank diskettes using both the /V and /S switches.

First, clear the screen,

Type: CLS
Press: ⏎

With the DOS diskette in the A drive,

Type: FORMAT B:/V/S
Press: ⏎

Follow the directions on the screen. Take a new diskette out of its protective sleeve, insert it in the B drive, and close the drive door.

Press: ⏎

The formatting message appears on the screen while the diskette is formatted. After a minute or so, formatting is complete and your display screen will be similar to Figure 1-10.

```
A>FORMAT B:/V/S
Insert new diskette for drive B:
and strike ENTER when ready

Format complete
System transferred

Volume label (11 characters, ENTER for none)? _
```

FIGURE 1-10

Notice the message "System transferred." This tells you that the DOS files have been copied to your diskette.

Complete the volume label information by entering your last name.

The number of bytes used by the system file is displayed along with the total number of bytes of disk space and available disk space. Note that sometimes the applications software program is too large and there is not enough diskette space to have both the DOS programs and the applications software programs on one diskette. If this happens, you would need to boot DOS using the DOS diskette each time you used that program.

Next DOS asks whether you want to format another diskette. Since you need to format the remaining new diskettes,

Type: Y
Press: ⏎

Remove the formatted diskette and place it in its sleeve. Put your name on a label and place it on the diskette so that you know it is formatted.

Following the directions on the screen, insert the next new diskette in the B drive and press ⏎.

In the same manner, use the FORMAT B:/V/S command to format your remaining diskettes. When all the diskettes are formatted, to end the FORMAT command, at the prompt "Format another?",

Type: N
Press: ⏎

Copying Files (COPY)

Now that all your new diskettes have been formatted, they are ready to be used to store information. The information we will store on the diskette that you formatted with /V only and labeled "Backup Data" will be a duplicate copy of the files on the original data diskette. The other diskettes which were formatted with both /V and /S will be used to hold backup copies of the applications software programs that were supplied to you.

A **backup** diskette holds a duplicate copy of the files from another diskette. You can back up an entire diskette or as many files on the diskettes as you want. You should always make a backup copy of your data diskette, the diskette containing the files you create and use with the applications software programs. You never know when a diskette could go bad and you could lose your files.

The COPY command lets you copy a single file or all the files from one diskette to another. It is an internal command and does not require that the DOS diskette be in the drive. First, you will make a backup copy of the original data diskette. This diskette contains all the files you will need to run the labs in this book.

To clear the screen,

Type: CLS
Press: ⏎

The diskette you want to copy files from is called the **source** diskette by DOS. The diskette that you want to copy files to is called the **target** diskette. Remove the DOS diskette from the A drive. Place the source diskette — the original data diskette — in the A drive and close the door.

First, let's take a look at the files on the original data diskette in the A drive. The A> should be on the screen. If it is not, change the default drive to the A drive. At the A>,

Type: **DIR/W**
Press: ⏎

DOS21

The files on the data diskette are listed. The files on your data diskette may not match exactly or be in the same order as the files in Figure 1-12. The files on your data diskette are the files you need to run the applications software programs selected by your instructor. Notice that some files do not have a file extension. Some software programs automatically assign a file extension to the filename you enter; others do not. If there is a filename extension, it must be used when issuing a DOS command that requires a filename as part of the command.

To copy the file, ARTICLE.DOC, from the diskette in the A drive (source) to the diskette in the B drive (target) using the same filename, the full DOS command would be written as shown in the first example in Figure 1-11 on the next page.

The space after the DOS command (COPY) and before the drive to copy TO (B:) are the only spaces entered in the command. The filename and extension are separated by a period.

The same command can be entered without specifying the drive to copy FROM (A:). The default (current) drive would be assumed by DOS. The command then would appear as in the second example in Figure 1-11.

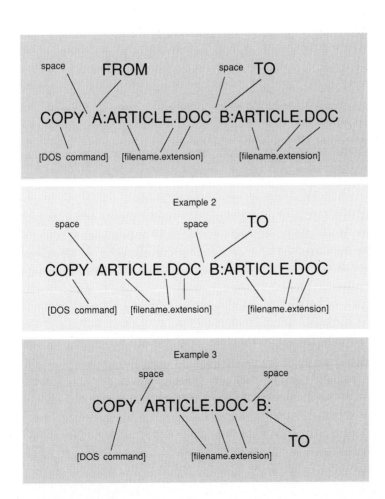

FIGURE 1-11

The command can be shortened even more by omitting the filename and extension following the TO drive designation. DOS assumes then that you want to copy the file using the same filename as in the FROM designation. The command then is written as in the third example in Figure 1-11.

Place the formatted diskette labeled "Backup Data" in the B drive.
Enter the copy command exactly as shown below:

Type: **COPY ARTICLE.DOC B:**
Press: ⏎

When the file is read from the diskette in the A drive into memory, the A drive light goes on. When the light on the B drive goes on, the file is being written from memory onto the diskette in the B drive.

Your display screen should look similar to Figure 1-12.

```
A>DIR/W

 Volume in drive A has no label
 Directory of  A:\

BLANK      EXT      LETTER             LETTER2            EDIT               EDIT2
CASE                LETTER3            DEF-WP             ZOOFARI            WELCOME
ARTICLE  DOC        TEXT-WP            ROWS     WK1       SURVEY   WK1       CAFE1     WK1
CAFE2    WK1        PETSHOP  WK1       FOOD     WK1       GROWTH   WK1       MEMBERS2  DBF
TILES30  DBF        STAFF    DBF       EMPLOYEE DBF       EMPLOYE2 DBF       EMPZNAME  NDX
EMPZDEPT NDX        NETWORK  COM       NETWORK  SCR
       28 File(s)     231424 bytes free

A>COPY ARTICLE.DOC B:
       1 File(s) copied

A>  _
```

FIGURE 1-12

DOS tells you that one file has been copied and you are returned to the DOS prompt.

We could continue to copy each file individually from the diskette in the A drive to the diskette in the B drive. But that would take a lot of time. A quicker way to copy all the files from one diskette to another is to use the DOS global filename characters, called **wildcards,** as part or all of the filename. Wildcard characters can be used in any DOS command that requires a filename as part of the command. The two wildcard characters are * and ?. They are interpreted as follows:

    ?   Match any one character in the filename
    *   Match any number of characters in the filename

For example, to copy a file with the filename ARTICLE.DOC, any character can be replaced with a ?. If the I in the filename is replaced with a ? (ART?CLE.DOC), the command to copy this file is then written as COPY ART?CLE.DOC B: This command tells DOS to copy all filenames on the diskette beginning with ART, having any next character (?), and ending with CLE and the file extension .DOC from the default drive (A) to the diskette in the B drive. If there were another file on the diskette with the filename ARTOCLE.DOC, it would also be copied since the ? stands for any character.

To copy all the files with a filename extension of .DOC, the filename is replaced by an *. The command is then written as COPY *.DOC B: This command tells DOS to copy any filename (*) with a file extension of .DOC from the diskette in the default drive (A) to the diskette in the B drive.

Since we need to copy all the files from the diskette in drive A to the diskette in drive B we can use a wildcard character in place of both the filename and the extension (*.*). The command to copy all the files is written as COPY *.* B:. This command tells DOS to copy every file (any filename and any filename extension) on the diskette in the default drive (A) to the diskette in the B drive.

Clear the display screen (CLS).

Type: COPY *.* B:
Press: ⏎

As each file is copied, the drive lights go on and off as the file is read from one drive and copied to the other. The name of each file is displayed after it is copied. After all the files are copied, your display screen should look similar to Figure 1-13.

```
LETTER3
DEF-WP
ZOOFARI
WELCOME
ARTICLE.DOC
TEXT-WP
ROWS.WK1
SURVEY.WK1
CAFE1.WK1
CAFE2.WK1
PETSHOP.WK1
FOOD.WK1
GROWTH.WK1
MEMBERS2.DBF
TILES30.DBF
STAFF.DBF
EMPLOYEE.DBF
EMPLOYE2.DBF
EMP2NAME.NDX
EMP2DEPT.NDX
NETWORK.COM
NETWORK.SCR
        28 File(s) copied

A> _
```

FIGURE 1-13

When all the files are copied, a message tells you the number of files copied and the DOS prompt appears again.

Once copying is complete, let's check to see whether the files have actually been transferred to your backup data diskette.

Clear the display screen (CLS).
With the original data diskette in A,

Type: DIR/W
Press: ⏎

The directory of the files in the original data diskette is displayed.

To compare the listing of files on the original data diskette with the files on the backup data diskette in the B drive,

Type: **DIR B:/W**
Press: ⏎

Your display screen should be similar to Figure 1-14.

```
Volume in drive A has no label
Directory of  A:\

BLANK     EXT    LETTER           LETTER2         EDIT           EDITZ
CASE             LETTER3          DEF-WP          ZOOFARI        WELCOME
ARTICLE   DOC    TEXT-WP          ROWS      WK1   SURVEY    WK1  CAFE1     WK1
CAFE2     WK1    PETSHOP   WK1    FOOD      WK1   GROWTH    WK1  MEMBERS2  DBF
TILES30   DBF    STAFF     DBF    EMPLOYEE  DBF   EMPLOYEZ  DBF  EMPZNAME  NDX
EMPZDEPT  NDX    NETWORK   COM    NETWORK   SCR
         28 File(s)     231424 bytes free

A>DIR B:/W

Volume in drive B is O'LEARY
Directory of  B:\

ARTICLE   DOC    BLANK     EXT    LETTER           LETTER2        EDIT
EDITZ            CASE             LETTER3          DEF-WP         ZOOFARI
WELCOME          TEXT-WP          ROWS      WK1    SURVEY    WK1  CAFE1     WK1
CAFE2     WK1    PETSHOP   WK1    FOOD      WK1    GROWTH    WK1  MEMBERS2  DBF
TILES30   DBF    STAFF     DBF    EMPLOYEE  DBF    EMPLOYEZ  DBF  EMPZNAME  NDX
EMPZDEPT  NDX    NETWORK   COM    NETWORK   SCR
         28 File(s)     231424 bytes free

A>
```

FIGURE 1-14

All the files that were on the original data diskette are now on the previously blank diskette in the B drive. Notice that the volume label on the backup data diskette displays your last name where O'LEARY appears in Figure 1-14. This is the result of the FORMAT/V command.

Notice the file named BLANK.EXT on both diskettes (the second filename). We will be using this file shortly to demonstrate other DOS commands.

Now you are ready to make backup copies of the applications software programs you will be using to run the labs in this book.

You should have the same number of formatted blank diskettes left as you have applications software program diskettes. The formatted blank diskettes have been formatted using both the /S (system files copied) and /V (volume label assigned) switches.

Note: Whenever possible, make copies of your applications software program diskettes. Some program diskettes are copy-protected, however, and a backup copy cannot be made.

To make a copy of the first applications program diskette:

Place the original software program diskette in A drive.
Place one of the blank formatted diskettes in the B drive.

Type: **COPY *.* B:**
Press: ⏎

The files on the original applications software program diskette are copied onto the diskette in the B drive. To display a directory of the files on the original diskette in the A drive,

Type: DIR/W
Press: ⏎

To compare this directory to your directory of files on the backup diskette in drive B,

Type DIR B:/W
Press: ⏎

You will see that there is an extra file on the backup diskette. It is the COMMAND.COM file that was copied to the diskette when it was formatted with /S. The other two DOS files, IBMDOS.COM and IBMBIO.COM, were also copied to the backup disk. However, they do not appear in the file directory because they are **hidden files.** You will also notice that the number of bytes free on the two diskettes is different because of the space the DOS files take up on the diskette in drive B.

Remove the diskette from the B drive. Using a felt-tip pen only, label the diskette with the applications software program name and the word "backup," to show that this is a backup diskette.

Using the same procedure, make backup copies of the other applications software program diskettes. Label the backup copies appropriately.

Renaming Files (RENAME)

Sometimes a filename may be confusing to you or it may no longer be descriptive of the file contents. So you may want to rename it. DOS makes this easy for you to do. To change the name of a file, the RENAME command is used.

Recall the file named BLANK.EXT on your data diskette. This is a filename only. It does not contain information you will need to run the labs. It is a dummy or empty file.

Clear the display screen.
Place your backup data diskette in drive A. We will change the filename BLANK.EXT to DUMMY.EXT.

At the A >,

Type: RENAME BLANK.EXT DUMMY.EXT
Press: ⏎

To make sure the filename was changed, let's obtain a directory.

Type: DIR/W
Press: ⏎

Your display screen should be similar to Figure 1-15.

```
A>RENAME BLANK.EXT DUMMY.EXT

A>DIR/W

 Volume in drive A is O'LEARY
 Directory of  A:\

DUMMY    EXT      LETTER           LETTER2         EDIT             EDIT2
CASE              LETTER3          DEF-WP          ZOOFARI          WELCOME
ARTICLE  DOC      TEXT-WP          ROWS     WK1    SURVEY   WK1     CAFE1    WK1
CAFE2    WK1      PETSHOP  WK1     FOOD     WK1    GROWTH   WK1     MEMBERS2 DBF
TILES30  DBF      STAFF    DBF     EMPLOYEE DBF    EMPLOYE2 DBF     EMPZNAME NDX
EMPZDEPT NDX      NETWORK  COM     NETWORK  SCR
       28 File(s)     231424 bytes free

A>_
```

FIGURE 1-15

As you can see, the filename has been changed.

Erasing Files (ERASE)

A file can easily be erased from a diskette if you no longer need it, using the ERASE command. We really do not need the file DUMMY.EXT.

To erase this file from the backup data diskette in the A drive, at the A>,

Type: **ERASE DUMMY.EXT**
Press: ⏎

To verify that the file was erased,

Type: **DIR/W**
Press: ⏎

Your display screen should look similar to Figure 1-16.

FIGURE 1-16

```
DUMMY    EXT      LETTER           LETTER2         EDIT             EDIT2
CASE              LETTER3          DEF-WP          ZOOFARI          WELCOME
ARTICLE  DOC      TEXT-WP          ROWS     WK1    SURVEY   WK1     CAFE1    WK1
CAFE2    WK1      PETSHOP  WK1     FOOD     WK1    GROWTH   WK1     MEMBERS2 DBF
TILES30  DBF      STAFF    DBF     EMPLOYEE DBF    EMPLOYE2 DBF     EMPZNAME NDX
EMPZDEPT NDX      NETWORK  COM     NETWORK  SCR
       28 File(s)     231424 bytes free

A>ERASE DUMMY.EXT

A>DIR/W

 Volume in drive A is O'LEARY
 Directory of  A:\

LETTER            LETTER2          EDIT             EDIT2            CASE
LETTER3           DEF-WP           ZOOFARI          WELCOME          ARTICLE  DOC
TEXT-WP           ROWS     WK1     SURVEY   WK1     CAFE1    WK1     CAFE2    WK1
PETSHOP  WK1      FOOD     WK1     GROWTH   WK1     MEMBERS2 DBF     TILES30  DBF
STAFF    DBF      EMPLOYEE DBF     EMPLOYE2 DBF     EMPZNAME NDX     EMPZDEPT NDX
NETWORK  COM      NETWORK  SCR
       27 File(s)     232448 bytes free

A>_
```

The file is no longer listed in the directory.

You have been introduced to many of the most basic and important DOS commands during this lab. Place write-protect tabs over the notch on the original diskettes. Store them in a safe place. Use the backup copies while working on the labs in this book. If you damage or erase one of the backup diskettes, make another copy from the original diskette.

Key Terms

DOS	external command
default	switch character
cursor	home
booting	formatted
warm boot	unformatted
prompt	backup
default drive	source
prompt character	target
directory	wildcard
internal command	hidden files

Matching

1. A>   _____   a. displays a listing of the files on a diskette, pausing when the screen is full
2. DOS   _____   b. an external command
3. /S   _____   c. clears the display screen
4. RENAME   _____   d. the default drive is A
5. ERASE   _____   e. the disk operating system
6. DIR/P   _____   f. the diskette whose files you want to copy
7. CLS   _____   g. assigns a new name to a file
8. *.*   _____   h. any filename and any file extension
9. source   _____   i. removes a file from the diskette
10. FORMAT   _____   j. copies the DOS files to the diskette

LAB 2
Managing Your Hard Disk

Objectives

In this lab you will learn how to:

1. Create and remove directories.
2. Specify paths to files.
3. Change directories.
4. Change the DOS prompt.
5. Display the contents of a file.
6. Create a batch file.

In the first DOS lab you learned many of the basic DOS commands which allow you to manage the files on your disk. In this lab you will learn about several more complex DOS commands. Specifically, you will learn how to create and use subdirectories and batch files.

Subdirectories

In DOS Lab 1 you accessed many DOS commands from the "A prompt." When you did this, you were in the **root directory,** or main DOS directory. When you used the DIR command to see a list of the files on the disk, you were looking at the contents of the root directory. Generally, the root directory contains your DOS files: COMMAND.COM, IBMDOS.COM, and IBMBIO.COM.

As you add more files to the root directory it gets very crowded and disorganized. This is especially true of hard disks, which can hold large amounts of data. To help organize files into like categories, you can create subdirectories. A **subdirectory** is a subdivision of the root directory.

For example, you may want to store software programs, and the files you create using these programs, by the type of program. Alternatively, you might want to store your programs and information by project. Let's say that while you are taking this course you want to keep all of the files you will be using with the spreadsheet program in one subdirectory and the files you will be using with the word processing program in another subdirectory. Furthermore, you want to separate the files you will be using in each lab by creating another subdirectory for each lab. You could do this in the following manner:

Root Directory: DOS files

Subdirectory 1: Spreadsheet Program Files

    Subdirectory A: Lab 1 data files
    Subdirectory B: Lab 2 data files

Subdirectory 2: Word Processing Program Files

    Subdirectory A: Lab 1 Data files
    Subdirectory B: Lab 2 data files

Rather than keeping all of your files in the root directory and then wondering how all of them relate to each other, the use of subdirectories allows you to organize your files.

This kind of a directory system is known as a **tree-structured directory**, since a root directory can have many subdirectories, each of which in turn can have many subdirectories, and so on.

Graphically, the tree-structured directory would look like this:

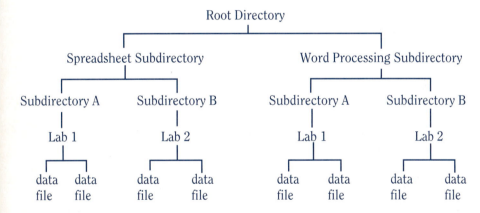

Imagine the directory as an upside-down family tree with the original parents (root) as the base of the tree. Their children are branches (subdirectories) on the tree, and then their grandchildren are branches (more subdirectories) under the children.

Making Directories

Put the DOS System Disk in drive A and the data diskette you created in Lab 1 in drive B. Boot the system and respond to the date and time prompts if necessary.

The A> should be on your screen.

Note: The instructions in this lab assume you are using a two-disk-drive computer system that does not have a hard disk. If you have a hard disk system, DOS should be on your hard disk. Insert your data disk in the A drive. Substitute drive A

DOS30
Managing Your Hard Disk

for drive B and drive C (or the drive containing DOS on your hard disk) for drive A in the instructions in this lab.

To see a listing of files on the disk in the B drive,

Type: DIR B:
Press: ⏎

All the files on your data disk are located in the root directory. Notice that there is no directory actually called by the name "root." The root directory is denoted by the backslash (\), in this case B:\.

The A> should be displayed below the listing of filenames. When you specified the drive (B:) as part of the DIR command, you told DOS to access the drive and to perform the command on the disk in that drive; but it did not change the current drive to B. The current drive is still A.

To create a subdirectory, you use the MKDIR (**MAKE DIRECTORY**) command. This command can also be abbreviated as MD. You will try this command by creating a subdirectory for the spreadsheet files. A subdirectory, like a file, must be assigned a name. The same rules apply for subdirectory names as applied for filenames. Generally, however a file extension is not added to a subdirectory name. You will name this subdirectory SS.

Clear the screen.

The command to make a directory on the B drive from the current drive (A) is MD B:\SS.

At the A>,

Type: MD B:\SS
Press: ⏎

Drive B runs for a second while it records the information for the subdirectory on the disk. To look at the directory,

Type: DIR B:
Press: ⏎

Your screen should be similar to Figure 2-1.

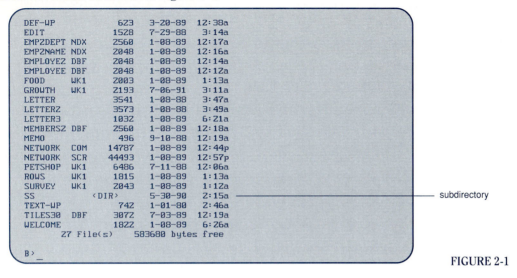

FIGURE 2-1

The original files are listed along with a new file. This is the file you created as a subdirectory. You can tell it is a subdirectory file by the <DIR> message (abbreviation for directory) which is displayed in place of the file extension and size data.

Rather than create the next subdirectory on the B drive from the A drive, you will change the current drive to B. To do this,

Type: B:
Press: ⏎

The B> should be displayed. Now the current drive is B, and any DOS commands you enter which do not include a drive designation will affect the disk in the B drive. To create another subdirectory on the disk in the B drive and name it WP,

Type: MD WP
Press: ⏎

You did not need to include the drive (B:\) in the command this time because you had changed the current drive to B first. If you do not include a drive as part of the command, the command affects the current drive. If you include the drive (B:\), then the command affects the specified drive.

Including the drive as part of the command helps avoid unexpected surprises. For example, it is easy to forget that you changed the current drive and find you have accidentally created a subdirectory or used a command accidentally on the wrong drive. Using the drive as part of the command is particularly important when you are erasing files on a disk using the wildcard characters "*.*". This way you can avoid accidentally erasing files from the disk in a drive you were not expecting DOS to access.

To display a listing of the files in the B drive,

Type: DIR
Press: ⏎

You should now have two subdirectories on your disk, SS and WP in the root directory. In the subdirectory SS you could store your spreadsheet program files, and in the subdirectory WP you could store your word processing program files.

Changing Directories

Even though you have created two subdirectories, you are still in the root directory. The directory you are in is called the **current directory**. By default, when you first access a disk you are in the root directory, which is also the current directory.

The method DOS uses to let you access files in a subdirectory is through the use of **paths**. A path is a chain of directory names that tells DOS how to maneuver through the subdirectories to find the subdirectory containing the files you are looking for.

To get from the root directory to a subdirectory, or from a subdirectory to another subdirectory, you use the CHDIR (**CH**ANGE **DIR**ECTORY) command. This command can also be abbreviated as CD.

You are now in the root directory of the disk in drive B. To enter the path command to move into the SS subdirectory, you could type CD SS or CD B:\SS. Since the current drive is B,

Type: CD SS
Press: ⏎

The current directory is now SS. But how do you know that you are in this subdirectory? To verify that you are in the SS subdirectory,

Type: DIR
Press: ⏎

Your screen should be similar to Figure 2-2.

FIGURE 2-2

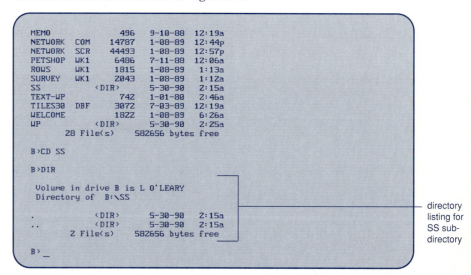

directory listing for SS subdirectory

The second line of the directory listing displays "Directory of B:\SS." This tells you that you are in the subdirectory SS immediately below the root directory (\). Below this information, two subdirectories are listed as "." and "..". The "." subdirectory represents the subdirectory you are currently viewing. The ".." subdirectory represents the parent directory of the SS subdirectory, or the directory one level above the current directory. In this case the parent directory is the root directory. That is:

    Root .. (parent directory)
    SS   . (current directory)

To instruct DOS to start with the directory you are currently using, use the "." as the first character in the path. If you want DOS to access one level up, use "..". For instance, to display a directory listing of the root directory files from the current subdirectory, SS,

Type: **DIR..**
Press: ⏎

You are now viewing the contents of the root directory. You have not, however, moved back into the root directory. The current directory is still SS. Subdirectories are stored just like files on a disk, so they appear in the root directory.

The root directory can also be accessed by typing a \ instead of the .. symbols.

Type: **DIR**
Press: ⏎

The list of files in the root directory is displayed.

Changing the DOS Prompt

Another way to keep track of the subdirectory you are in is to change the DOS prompt to display the subdirectory information. The standard DOS prompt (A>,B>) does not tell you if you are in a subdirectory or in the root directory.

Note: Your computer may already display the subdirectory information. If it does, you can skip to the paragraph below Figure 2-3.

This can be changed using the PROMPT command. This is shorthand for the SET PROMPT command. It will allow you to customize the DOS prompt using symbols called **prompt codes**. All prompt codes begin with a $ and are immediately followed by the symbol or character. (Your DOS manual provides a listing of all prompt code symbols.) The initial DOS prompt uses the prompt codes NG. The $N symbol makes DOS display the current drive letter and the $G symbol displays the greater-than (>) character. The prompt code symbol that will display the current path is $P. To change the default DOS prompt to display the current path and the greater-than symbol, the prompt codes PG are used.

Clear the screen.

Type: **PROMPT PG**
Press: ⏎

Your screen should be similar to Figure 2-3.

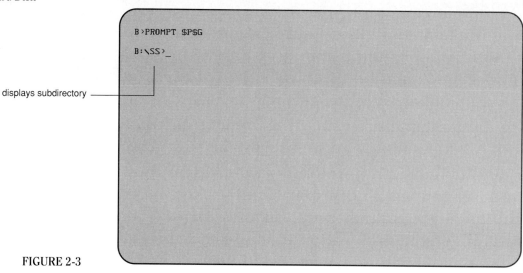

displays subdirectory

FIGURE 2-3

Your DOS prompt should now appear as B:\SS>. The \ signifies the root directory and the SS tells you the name of the subdirectory you are in. This is helpful as you do not need to use the DIR command to confirm which subdirectory you are in each time you change directories.

Next you will create another subdirectory within the SS subdirectory to hold the data files used in Lab 1. This subdirectory will be named LAB1 and will be subordinate to the SS subdirectory.

Type: MD LAB1
Press: ⏎

Type: DIR
Press: ⏎

The directory listing now displays "LAB1 <DIR>" within the subdirectory SS. You are still in the SS directory, however, and it is still the current directory. Not until you change directories (CD) does the current directory change.

Type: CD LAB1
Press: ⏎

LAB1 is now the current directory. You are two subdirectory levels below the root directory. The DOS prompt should show the path you have taken as B:\SS\LAB1>. From the root directory you went to the SS subdirectory, and from there to the LAB1 subdirectory.

Now that you have "pathed" your way through to the appropriate subdirectory, you will return to the root directory. To return to the root directory, the CD command is used again. If you type CD followed by two periods (CD..), you will move from the current directory to the directory immediately above it (SS).

Type: CD..
Press: ⏎

You are now in the SS subdirectory, and the DOS prompt should be B:\SS>. To move to the subdirectory one level up, in this case the root directory,

Type: CD..
Press: ⏎

You are now in the root directory, and the DOS prompt should be B:\>. Next, you want to move back into the LAB1 subdirectory. Graphically, you want to flow through the directory as follows:

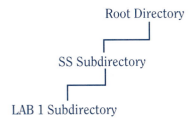

To do this you could enter the command CD SS and then the command CD LAB1. A faster way, however, is to specify a complete path as part of the CD command.

Type: CD\SS\LAB1
Press: ⏎

You instructed DOS to move from the root directory to the SS subdirectory and, finally, to the LAB1 subdirectory. The DOS prompt should display B:\SS\LAB1>.

A faster way to move back to the root directory is to type CD followed by a \. This command will return you directly to the root directory from any subdirectory level. To return directly to the root directory,

Type: CD\
Press: ⏎

Your screen should be similar to Figure 2-4.

FIGURE 2-4

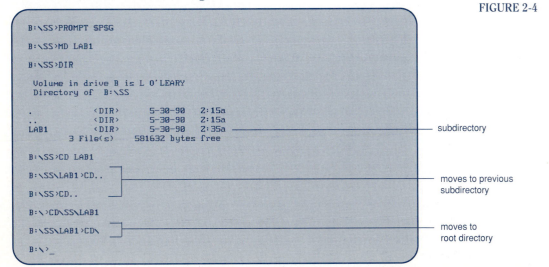

Using the TREE command

In Lab 1 you learned how to copy files using the COPY command. To copy a file from the root directory into a subdirectory, you must specify the path as part of the COPY command. You will copy the spreadsheet file SSFILE from the root directory to the subdirectory LAB1. To do this,

Type: COPY SSFILE \SS\LAB1
Press: ⏎

The path \SS\LAB1 instructed DOS to copy the file from the current directory (the current directory is assumed by DOS unless another is specified) to the subdirectory LAB1. If the current directory is not the directory containing the file you wanted to copy, you would also need to tell DOS where to locate the file. For example, if the file you wanted to copy was in the root directory of the disk in drive A, and the current directory was the root directory of drive B, the command to copy the file would be COPY A:SSFILE B:\SS\LAB1.

To verify that the file was copied into the correct subdirectory, you could view a directory listing (DIR). Another way is to use the TREE command. The TREE command is an external DOS command; therefore, if you are using a two-disk system, make sure the DOS disk is in drive A.

Clear the screen.

Type: A:TREE B:
Press: ⏎

Your screen should be similar to Figure 2-5.

FIGURE 2-5

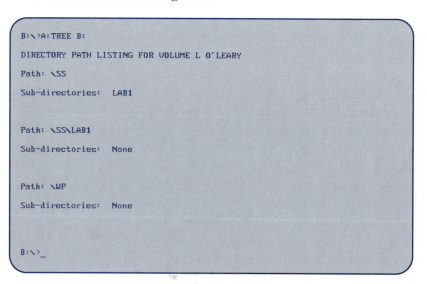

All the directory paths for the disk in drive B are displayed. As you can see, each of the subdirectories is listed, along with the path used to access each one.

However, the files in the directories are not displayed. To list any files in the subdirectories in addition to the directories, the /F (Files) switch is used.

Clear the screen.

Type: A:TREE/F B:
Press: ⏎

You can use CTRL - S to stop the scrolling of the screen.

Your screen should be similar to Figure 2-6.

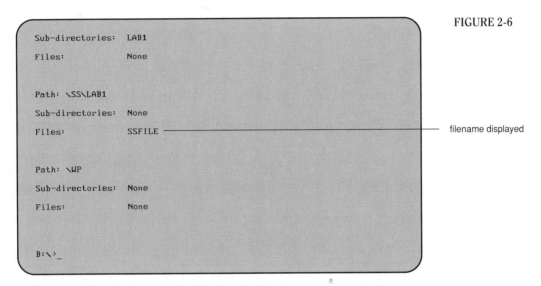

FIGURE 2-6

filename displayed

First, all files in the root directory are listed. Then the subdirectory paths and all files saved in each subdirectory are listed. The next to last path listed on your screen states the following:

        Path: \SS\LAB1

        Sub-directories: None

        Files: SSFILE

This shows you the path taken to access the LAB1 subdirectory. DOS also tells you that there are no more subdirectories that can be accessed from LAB1, and that the file SSFILE resides in the subdirectory LAB1.

The TREE command gives you a good look at how the subdirectories are organized, and what files are located in the different subdirectories. Whenever you are unfamiliar with the contents of a disk, using this command will let you quickly determine how it is organized.

Next you want to move into the LAB1 subdirectory to access the file SSFILE.

Clear the screen.

Type: CD \SS\LAB1
Press: ⏎

The DOS prompt shows that you have changed directories and that the current directory is LAB1.

Displaying the Contents of a File

If you want to display the contents of a file while in DOS, you can use the TYPE command. This is an internal DOS command. Although the TYPE command will display the contents of a file on the screen, some files may not be readable. However, most text can be displayed in a legible format. To use this command to display the contents of SSFILE,

Type: TYPE SSFILE
Press: ⏎

Your screen should be similar to Figure 2-7.

FIGURE 2-7

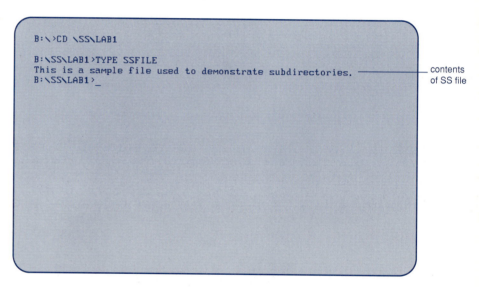

contents of SS file

The contents of this file consist of the sentence: "This is a sample file used to demonstrate subdirectories."

Removing Directories

At some point you may no longer need the subdirectories you have created, and you will want to remove them from the disk to save space. (Each subdirectory requires a minimum of 1K, or 1024 characters, of storage.)

You learned how to erase files with the ERASE command. However, this command cannot be used to remove a subdirectory from a disk. The command which will do this is RMDIR (**REMOVE DIRECTORY**) or RD. Before removing a directory, all files within the directory must first be erased. Thus to remove the subdirectory LAB 1, you must first erase the file SSFILE. To do this,

Type: ERASE SSFILE
Press: ⏎

When you remove a directory the current directory cannot be the directory you want to remove. To move out of the LAB 1 subdirectory into the directory one level above,

Type: CD..
Press: ⏎

You should now be in the SS subdirectory.
To remove the subdirectory LAB1,

Type: RD LAB1
Press: ⏎

To verify that the subdirectory LAB1 no longer exists on the disk,

Type: DIR
Press: ⏎

Your screen should be similar to Figure 2-8.

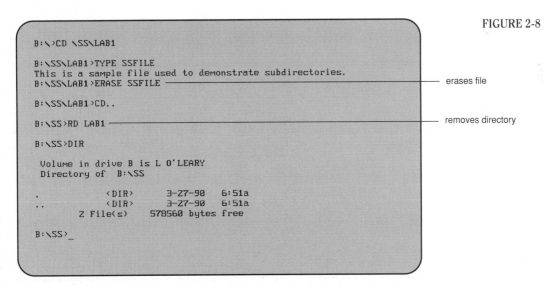

FIGURE 2-8

As you can see, the subdirectory LAB1 has been removed.

Remove the subdirectories SS and WP. To do this, change to the root directory first, then issue the RD command. Display a directory. There should no longer be any subdirectories on your disk. You should be in the root directory.
Clear the screen.

Creating a Batch File

Up to this point you have learned how to use DOS. Now you are going to learn how to make DOS use *itself*. You can do this through the use of batch files.

A **batch file** consists of a series of DOS commands that are stored in a file. When instructed to do so, DOS will execute the commands in the batch file, one line at a time. These commands are executed just as they would be if they were typed in at the keyboard.

So what's the advantage of having a batch file? If you have a task that you will repeat over and over again, such as loading a program, it's better to put the commands in a batch file. This way you won't misspell one of the commands or make some other kind of mistake. You can just type the commands once, save them, and then execute them as a batch file.

A batch file can be created using the DOS command, COPY CON. This command copies the commands entered at the keyboard, or CONsole, to a file. The filename of a batch file consists of one to eight allowable characters. The file extension is .BAT.

You will use the COPY CON command to create a batch file named SAMPLE.BAT. This file will execute the following four DOS commands: clear the screen (CLS), prompt you to enter the date (DATE), change the DOS prompt back to the original format (PROMPT NG), and display a directory (DIR).

To direct DOS to copy the commands you will enter next from the keyboard (console) into a batch file named SAMPLE.BAT,

Type: `COPY CON SAMPLE.BAT`
Press: ⏎

The cursor moves down to the next line. Now you can start typing the DOS commands you want to record in the batch file. The first command you want your batch file to perform is to clear the screen (CLS).

Type: `CLS`

Make sure you entered this command correctly. Once you press ⏎ you cannot go back and correct the error in the line.

Press: ⏎

Next you want the batch file to prompt you to enter the date. The DATE command will display this prompt.

Type: `DATE`

Again, check your entry carefully.

Press: ⏎

Next, you want the batch file to change the DOS prompt to display the current drive and greater-than symbol (>) only. To do this,

Type: `PROMPT $N$G`
Press: ⏎

Finally, you want the batch file to display a directory of drive B.

Type: DIR B:

You have entered the entire batch file. To tell DOS that this is the end of the batch file,

Press: F6

The F6 key enters a ^Z character at the end of the batch file. This tells DOS that this is the end of the file and to save the file to disk under the filename specified in the COPY CON command (SAMPLE.BAT.)

Press: ⏎

Your screen should be similar to Figure 2-9.

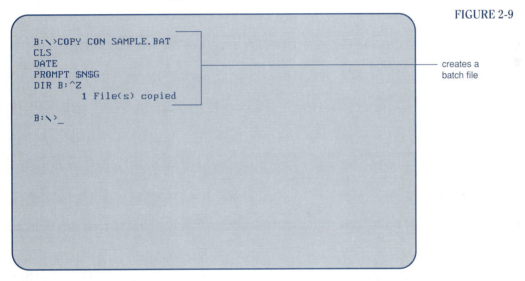

FIGURE 2-9

creates a batch file

The message "1 File(s) copied" is displayed. The batch file SAMPLE.BAT has been written to the data disk.
    To check the contents of this file,

Type: TYPE SAMPLE.BAT
Press: ⏎

If you see an error in the batch file commands, start over again by recreating the file. A batch file can also be entered using the non-document mode of a word processing program. With this method errors can be easily corrected.
    To tell DOS to execute the commands in the batch file, simply type the filename following the prompt. You do not need to enter the .BAT file extension. If you were not in the directory containing the batch file, you would need to include the path before the filename. At the B:\>,

Type: SAMPLE
Press: ⏎

Once DOS locates the file, it is executed one line at a time. The SAMPLE.BAT file should have cleared your screen, and the DOS DATE prompt should be displayed. DOS has executed the first two commands in the batch file. In response to the date prompt, enter the current date. When you press ⏎, DOS will execute the third batch file command NG. Finally, a directory of the disk in drive B should be displayed on your screen.

Notice that the directory contains the batch file you created and the DOS prompt is back to its original format (B>).

Note: If your batch file contains an error, DOS will display a " syntax error" message. This means that DOS was unable to understand the command because it was entered incorrectly. To correct the batch file, recreate the file, following the directions exactly. Check each line of the file for accuracy before pressing ⏎. Then execute the batch file again.

Although this was a simple example of a batch file, you can see how batch files can save you time by executing frequently used sequences of DOS commands.

Key Terms

root directory
subdirectory
tree-structured directory
current directory

path
prompt code
batch file

Matching

1. path
2. MKDIR
3. DIR B:\SS
4. CD
5. DIR.
6. DIR\
7. PG
8. COPY CON filename
9. TREE
10. RD

_____ a. DOS command to create a directory
_____ b. displays directory paths
_____ c. displays a directory listing of current directory
_____ d. chain of directory names used to move through subdirectories
_____ e. removes a directory
_____ f. prompt codes
_____ g. copies entries from keyboard to a file
_____ h. displays directory listing of root directory
_____ i. makes another directory the current directory
_____ j. displays a directory listing of the SS directory on the disk in the B drive

Practice Exercises

The following problems have been designed to reinforce many of the key concepts and techniques presented in this module. Do each problem carefully and completely, referring back only when necessary.

1. Create the following hierarchical directory on your data disk.

   Once you've created this directory, use the TREE command to verify all of your subdirectory relationships.

2. Create and execute a batch file that will copy the file SSFILE into the Product Analysis subdirectory you created in problem 1. Then have it display the file contents and finally erase the file.

SUMMARY
DOS

Glossary of Key Terms

Applications software: A set of programs that tells the computer how to manipulate data and text.

Backup: A duplicate copy of a file or files on a diskette.

Batch file: A series of DOS commands that are stored in a file with a .BAT file extension. When instructed, DOS will execute the commands in the batch file, one line at a time.

Boot: To start the computer by turning on the system unit and loading the systems software program.

Computer system: The user, hardware, software, secondary storage, and data.

Current directory: The active directory or the last directory you accessed using a CD command.

Cursor: A blinking line or rectangle showing where the next character you type will be.

Default drive: The letter appearing in the DOS prompt that tells you which drive DOS will use.

Default settings: The settings assumed by the program if no other setting is specified.

Directory: The location of the list of filenames maintained on the diskette.

Diskette: A plastic disk which stores data and program instructions as electromagnetic spots. The data on the diskette can be read from the diskette by the disk drive and loaded into RAM. Conversely, data in RAM can be written to the diskette.

Disk drive: The mechanical device in the system unit which reads from and writes to a diskette.

Disk Operating System (DOS): The systems software for IBM and IBM-compatibles.

External DOS command: A DOS command that requires that the DOS diskette be in the drive when the command is used. This is because the program statements to perform the command must be read from the diskette and loaded into RAM.

Filename: A unique and descriptive name assigned to each file on a diskette.

Format: To prepare a new diskette for use by your computer system.

Hard-disk drive: A permanent fixture of the system unit that contains one or more magnetic disks used to store data and programs. Also called a fixed disk drive.

Hardware: The physical components and electronics of the computer. It consists of input devices, the system unit, secondary storage devices, and output devices.

Hidden files: Files that are on the diskette but do not appear when a directory of filenames is displayed.

Home: The upper left-hand corner of the display screen.

Input devices: Devices (such as a keyboard) that allow the user to enter data or information into the computer in a form that the computer can process.

Internal DOS command: A DOS command that can be used without the DOS diskette in the drive. This is because the program statements to perform the command have been copied into RAM when DOS was loaded.

Keyboard: An input device, very similar to a typewriter keyboard, that allows you to communicate with the computer.

Main memory: The temporary storage area of the system unit that holds data and instructions for use by the microprocessor during processing.

Microprocessor: The electronic circuitry through which data is processed and instructions are executed.

Monitor: The output device which displays messages on the monitor for temporary viewing by the user.

Output devices: Devices (such as a printer or monitor) that allow the computer to inform the user to see what has been input and what the program has done.

Path: A chain of directory names that tells DOS how to maneuver through the directories and subdirectories.

Plotter: A high-quality output device used mainly for graphics, although it can also be used for text.

Primary storage: The part of the system unit that temporarily holds data and programs. It is also called main memory.

Printer: An output device that gives you a printed copy of your work.

Prompt: The characters displayed by DOS to indicate that the computer is ready to accept commands. The prompt consists of the default-drive letter followed by the > character (e.g., A>).

Prompt codes: Special DOS symbols that begin with a $ character. They are used with the PROMPT command to allow you to customize the DOS prompt.

Random-access memory (RAM): The part of main memory that holds the data and instructions while the computer is on.

Read-only memory (ROM): The part of main memory that controls the operations of the computer system.

Root directory: The main directory of a disk. Subdirectories can be created below the root directory.

Secondary storage devices: Devices (such as a diskette) that permanently save the data and instructions held in RAM.

Source: The original diskette you want to copy.

Subdirectory: Additional directories or subdivisions of the root directory that are used to organize the files on a disk.

Switch: The / character followed by the appropriate letter. It is used to tell DOS to perform a command in a different manner.

System unit: The electronic circuitry that executes the software program instructions, performs calculations, and temporarily stores data and programs.

Target: The diskette that will hold the files copied from the source diskette. It becomes the backup diskette.

Tree-structured directory: The organization of a disk into directories and subdirectories that resemble an upside-down family tree.

Warm boot: Reloading DOS after the computer is already turned on, using (CTRL)-(ALT), (DEL).

Wildcard: DOS global filename characters, ? and *, that give you greater flexibility when referring to a filename in a DOS command.

Functional Summary of Selected DOS Commands

FUNCTION	COMMAND	ACTION
Clear Screen	CLS	Clears the display screen
Copy Files	COPY filename drive	Copies the contents of a file to another diskette
	COPY *.* drive	Copies all the files on one diskette to another
	COPY *.extension drive	Copies all the files with the same file extension to another diskette
	COPY filename.* drive	Copies all the files with the same file name to another diskette
Display Directory	DIR	Lists the files on a diskette
	DIR/P	Lists the files on a diskette, pausing when the display screen is full
	DIR/W	Lists the files on a diskette in a wide display format
Erase Files	ERASE filename	Removes a file from the diskette
	ERASE *.*	Removes all files from the diskette
Format Diskette	FORMAT drive	Prepares a new diskette for use
	FORMAT drive /S	Prepares a new diskette for use and copies DOS to the diskette
	FORMAT drive /V	Prepares a new diskette for use and assigns a volume name to it
Rename File	RENAME	Assigns a new name to a file
Display File	TYPE	Displays the contents of a file
Change Directory	CHDIR or CD	Accesses a new directory or subdirectory
Make Directory	MKDIR or MD	Makes a new directory or subdirectory
Remove Directory	RMDIR or RD	Removes or deletes a subdirectory
Display Tree	TREE	Shows all subdirectory relationships
	TREE/F	Shows all subdirectories and files
Create Batch File	COPY CON filename.BAT	Creates batch file from keyboard entry
	F6	Marks end of batch file

INDEX

Applications software, DOS8

Backing up files, DOS20
Backslash (\), DOS30, DOS33
Batch files, creating, DOS40-DOS42
Booting in DOS, DOS13

Central processing unit (CPU), DOS5
CHDIR command, DOS32
Clearing the screen, DOS15-DOS16
CLS command, DOS15-DOS16
Color plotters, DOS7
COMMAND.COM file, DOS10, DOS25, DOS28
Commands, DOS:
    CHDIR, DOS32
    CLS, DOS15-DOS16
    COPY, DOS20-DOS25, DOS36
    COPY CON, DOS40
    DIR, DOS13-DOS15
    entering, DOS13
    ERASE, DOS26-DOS27, DOS38
    external, DOS13, DOS16
    FORMAT, DOS16-DOS20
    internal, DOS13
    MKDIR, DOS30
    PROMPT, DOS33
    RENAME, DOS25-DOS26
    RMDIR, DOS38-DOS39
    TREE, DOS36-DOS38
    TYPE, DOS38
COPY command, DOS20-DOS25, DOS36
COPY CON command, DOS40
Copying files, DOS20-DOS25
    between drives keeping filename, DOS21-DOS22
    with wildcard characters, DOS22-DOS23, DOS24, DOS30
Current directory, DOS32
Cursor:
    defined, DOS4
    movement, DOS4

Data, protecting, DOS6, DOS27
Date, entering, DOS10-DOS11
Defaults:
    date settings, DOS10
    disk drive, DOS13
DIR command, DOS13-DOS15
    with /P, DOS14
    with /W, DOS15
Directories, disk:
    changing, DOS32-DOS33
    current, DOS32
    displaying, DOS13-DOS15, DOS36
    making, DOS29-DOS32
    paths in, DOS32, DOS36
    pause between screens, DOS15
    removing, DOS38-DOS39
    root directory, DOS28-DOS29, DOS33, DOS35
    subdirectories, DOS28-DOS29, DOS32
    tree-structured, DOS29
    wide-screen, DOS15
Disk drives:
    changing, DOS13
    default, DOS13
    letters for, DOS5
    lights on, DOS10
    types of, DOS5
Diskettes:
    backing up, DOS20
    defined, DOS6
    formatting, DOS16-DOS20
    inserting and removing, DOS10
    listing files on, DOS13-DOS15
    preserving, DOS6
    source and target, DOS20
    volume label on, DOS16-DOS18
DOS (disk operating system):
    booting, DOS13
    copying system files, DOS19-DOS20
    files for, DOS10, DOS19-DOS20, DOS25, DOS28

Index

loading, DOS10–DOS13
prompt, DOS6, DOS13, DOS33–DOS36, DOS40
reloading, DOS13
version of, DOS9, DOS13
(*See also* Commands, DOS)

ERASE command, DOS26–DOS27, DOS38
Erasing files, DOS26–DOS27, DOS39
Errors, syntax, DOS42
External commands, DOS13, DOS16

Filenames in DOS, DOS21
Files:
    backing up, DOS20
    batch, creating, DOS40–DOS42
    copying, DOS20–DOS25
    displaying contents of, DOS38
    for DOS, DOS10, DOS19–DOS20, DOS25, DOS28
    erasing, DOS26–DOS27, DOS39
    hidden DOS, DOS25
    renaming, DOS25–DOS26
Fixed-disk drives, DOS5
Flexible-disk drives, DOS5
FORMAT command, DOS16–DOS20
Formatting diskettes:
    and copy system files, DOS19–DOS20
    with volume label, DOS16–DOS18
Function keys:
    location on keyboard, DOS4
    F6 (end of file), DOS41

Hard-disk drive, DOS5
Hardware components, DOS3–DOS7
Home position, on screen, DOS16

IBMBIO.COM file, DOS10, DOS25, DOS28
IBMDOS.COM file, DOS10, DOS25, DOS28

Input devices, DOS3–DOS5
Internal commands, DOS13

Keyboard:
    function keys, DOS4
    kinds of keys, DOS4
    numeric keypad, DOS4
    special-purpose keys, DOS5
    typing keys, DOS4

Loading DOS, DOS10–DOS13

Memory, RAM and ROM, DOS5
Microprocessor, DOS5
Mistakes in typing, DOS12
MKDIR command, DOS30
Monitors, defined, DOS6

Numeric keypad, DOS4

Operating system (*see* DOS)
Output devices, DOS3, DOS6–DOS7

Paths, DOS32, DOS36
Plotters, DOS7
Primary storage, DOS5
Printers:
    draft and letter quality, DOS7
    types of, DOS7
Processing unit (*see* System unit)
Programs, software, DOS7
Prompt, DOS:
    changing, DOS33–DOS36, DOS40
    character for, DOS13
    codes for, DOS33
PROMPT command, DOS33
Prompts, DOS6

Random-access memory (RAM), DOS5
Read-only memory (ROM), DOS5

WordPerfect 5.1

Copyright © 1991 by McGraw-Hill, Inc. All rights reserved. Printed in the United States of America. Except as permitted under the United States Copyright Act of 1976, no part of this publication may be reproduced or distributed in any form or by any means, or stored in a database or retrieval system, without the prior written permission of the publisher.

234567890 KPKP 90987654321

P/N 048806-1

ORDER INFORMATION:
ISBN 0-07-048806-1

WordPerfect 5.1 is a registered trademark of WordPerfect Corporation.
IBM, IBM PC, and PC DOS are registered trademarks of International Business Machines, Inc.

CONTENTS

Overview Word Processing WP3
Definition of Word Processing WP3
Advantages of Using a Word Processor WP3
Word Processing Terminology WP4
Case Study for Labs 1–4 WP5

Lab 1 Editing a Document WP6
Loading the WordPerfect 5.1 Program WP6
    Starting WordPerfect on a Two-Disk System WP6
    Starting WordPerfect on a Hard-Disk System WP7
The Editing Screen WP8
Entering WordPerfect 5.1 Commands WP9
Using the Pull-Down Menu WP9
Using a Mouse WP13
Using the Function Keys WP15
Retrieving a File WP17
Moving the Cursor WP19
Using the Mouse to Move the Cursor WP27
Editing a Document WP28
    Exercise 1.1 Deleting Characters: (BKSP) WP29
    Exercise 1.2 Deleting Characters: (DEL) WP31
    Exercise 1.3 Inserting Characters: Insert Mode WP32
    Exercise 1.4 Inserting Characters: Typeover Mode WP33
    Exercise 1.5 Deleting Words: (CTRL)-(BKSP) WP35
    Exercise 1.6 Deleting from Cursor to End of Line: (CTRL)-(END) WP36
    Exercise 1.7 Deleting Several Lines of Text: (ESC), (CTRL)-(END) WP37
    Exercise 1.8 Inserting and Deleting Blank Lines WP38
    Exercise 1.9 Undeleting Text WP40
Clearing the Screen WP41
Listing File Names WP42
Editing the Welcome Letter WP44
Saving and Replacing an Existing File WP44
Printing a Document WP45
Exiting WordPerfect 5.1 WP48
Key Terms WP48
Matching WP48
Practice Exercises WP49

Lab 2 Creating and Formatting a Document WP50
Creating a Document WP50
Spell-Checking WP52
Saving a New File WP54
Combining Files WP56
Moving Text WP57
Using the Block Command WP59
Using the Date Command WP62
Aligning Text Flush with the Right Margin WP63
Setting Margins WP65
Using and Setting Tabs WP67
Displaying Hidden Codes WP70
Searching and Replacing Text WP73
Setting Justification WP75
Printing the Document WP76
Saving the Document in a New File WP77
Key Terms WP78
Matching WP78
Practice Exercises WP78

Lab 3 Merging and Refining Documents WP83
The Merge Feature WP83
Entering Merge Codes in the Primary File WP84
Creating the Secondary File WP89
Merging the Primary and Secondary Merge Files WP94
Centering and Boldfacing Text WP95
Using Two Document Files WP98
Creating a Split Screen WP99
Moving Text Between Documents WP100
Closing a Split Screen WP101
Underlining Text WP102
Defining Columns WP103
Reformatting the Screen Display WP106
Viewing the Document WP107
Changing Justification WP109
Using Hyphenation WP109
Saving and Exiting Two Document Files WP111
Key Terms WP111
Matching WP111
Practice Exercises WP112

Lab 4 Creating a Research Paper WP116
Creating an Outline WP116
Editing the Outline WP121
Creating Lines WP125
Creating a Table of Contents WP127
Creating Footnotes WP134
Editing a Footnote WP138
Numbering Pages WP139
Suppressing Page Numbers WP140
Centering Text Top to Bottom WP141
Using Block Protection WP142
Preventing Widows and Orphans WP144
Printing the Report WP146
Key Terms WP146
Matching WP147
Practice Exercises WP147

Summary WordPerfect 5.1 WP150
Glossary of Key Terms WP150
Functional Summary of Selected WordPerfect Commands WP153

Index WP157

OVERVIEW
Word Processing

The most popular applications software used on a microcomputer today is a word processor. To put your thoughts in writing, from the simplest note to the most complex book, is a time-consuming process. Even more time-consuming is the task of editing and retyping the document to make it perfect. There was a time that perfection in written communication was difficult, if not impossible, to achieve. With the introduction of word processing, errors should be nearly nonexistent—not because they are not made, but because they are easy to correct. Word processors let you throw away the correction fluid, scissors, paste, and erasers. Now, with a few keystrokes, you can correct errors, move paragraphs, and reprint your document easily.

Definition of Word Processing

Word processing applications software is a program that helps you create any type of written communication via a keyboard. A word processor can be used to manipulate text data to produce a letter, a report, a memo, or any other type of correspondence. Text data is any letter, number, or symbol that you can type on a keyboard. The grouping of the text data to form words, sentences, paragraphs, and pages of text results in the creation of a document. Through a word processor you can create, modify, store, retrieve, and print part or all of a document.

Advantages of Using a Word Processor

The speed of entering text data into the computer depends on the skill of the user. If you cannot type fast, a word processor will not improve your typing speed. However, a word processor will make it easier to correct and change your document. Consequently, your completed document will take less time to create.

Where a word processor excels is in its ability to change, modify, or edit a document. Editing involves correcting spelling, grammar, and sentence-structure errors. With a word processor, the text is stored on a diskette. As errors are found, they are electronically deleted and corrected. Once the document is the way you want it to appear, it is printed on paper. Good-bye, correction fluid!

In addition to editing a document, you can easily revise or update it through the insertion or deletion of text. For example, a document that lists prices can easily be updated to reflect new prices. A document that details procedures can be revised by deleting old procedures and inserting new ones. This is especially helpful when a document is used repeatedly. Rather than re-creating the whole document, only the parts that change need to be revised.

Revision also includes the rearrangement of pieces or blocks of text. For example, while writing a report, you may decide to change the location of a single word or several paragraphs or pages of text. You can do it easily by using Block and Move commands. Blocks of text can also be copied from one area of the document to another. This is a real advantage when the text includes many recurring phrases or words.

Combining text in another file with your document is another advantage of word processors. An example of this is a group term paper. Each person is responsible for writing a section of the paper. Before printing the document, the text for all sections, which is stored in different files, is combined to create the complete paper. The opposite is also true. Text that may not be appropriate in your document can easily be put in another file for later use.

Many word processors include special programs to further help you produce a perfect document. A spell-checker will check the spelling in a document by comparing each word to a dictionary of words. If an error is found, the program will suggest the correct spelling. A syntax checker electronically checks grammar, phrasing, capitalization, and other types of syntax errors in a document. A thesaurus will display different words, each with a meaning similar to the word you entered.

After changes are made and the document appears ready to be printed, the word processor also makes it easy to change the design or appearance of the document. For example, a word processor lets you set the line spacing of a document. You can decide how large you want the right, left, top, and bottom margins. The number of lines printed on each page can be specified. In addition, you can quickly specify whether the pages will or will not be numbered and where (top or bottom, centered or not) the number will appear. Further, a word processor will let you enter headers and footers on each page or specified pages.

If, after reading the printed copy, you find other errors or want to revise or reformat the document, it is easy to do. Simply reload the document file, make your changes, and reprint the text! Now that saves time!

Word Processing Terminology

The following list of terms and definitions are generic in nature and are associated with most word processing programs.

Block: Any group of characters, words, lines, paragraphs, or pages of text.

Boldface Produces dark or heavy print.

Center: Centers a line of text evenly between the margins.

Character string: Any combination of letters, numbers, symbols, and spaces.

Delete: To erase a character, word, paragraph, or block of text from the document.

Flush right: Aligns text on the right-hand margin.

Format: Defines how the printed document will appear; includes settings for underline, boldface, print size, margin settings, line spacing, etc.

Insert mode: Allows new text to be entered into a document between existing text.

Justified: The text has even left and right margins, produced by inserting extra spaces between words on each line.

Merge: Combine text in one document with text in another.

Overstrike: Causes the printer to print one character over another to make the type darker.

Search: Scans the document for all matching character strings.

Search and replace: Scans the document for all matching character strings and replaces them with others.

Template: A document, like a form letter, that contains blank spaces for automatic insertion of information that varies from one document to another.

Typeover mode: New text is entered in a document by typing over the existing text on the line.

Unjustified: The text has an even left margin and an uneven, or ragged, right margin.

Word wrap: Automatic adjustment of number of characters or words on a line while entering text; eliminates pressing the ↵ (return) key at the end of each line

Case Study for Labs 1–4

Karen Barnes is the membership assistant for the Sports Club. The club just purchased a word processing program. Her first assignment using the software package is to create a letter welcoming new members to the club.

In Lab 1, the rough draft of the letter entered by Karen is corrected. During this process, the basic cursor-movement keys and editing features are demonstrated.

Lab 2 continues with modifying the welcome letter by entering new text, combining files, and rearranging paragraphs and blocks of text. The print, line, and page formats are modified, and the completed document is printed.

In Lab 3, the welcome letter is changed to a form letter using the Merge feature. Next, another document is created using text taken from the welcome letter. The Split Screen feature lets the user view both documents on the screen at the same time, greatly simplifying the process. Finally, the document is changed to column format to be used in the club newsletter.

In the final wordprocessing lab, Peg, a student intern at the Sports Club, is writing a term paper. As part of this process you will learn how to create an outline, produce a table of contents, and enter footnotes. Several new format features are also demonstrated.

LAB
Editing a Document   1

OBJECTIVES

In this lab you will learn how to:

1. Load the WordPerfect 5.1 program.
2. Issue a WordPerfect 5.1 command.
3. Retrieve a file.
4. Move around a document.
5. Delete characters, words, and lines of text.
6. Undelete text.
7. Insert text in Insert and Typeover modes.
8. Insert and delete blank lines.
9. Clear the display.
10. List file names.
11. Save and replace a file.
12. Print a document.
13. Exit WordPerfect 5.1.

CASE STUDY

Karen Barnes, the membership assistant for the Sports Club, has been asked to create a letter welcoming new members to the club. The letter should briefly explain the services offered by the club. Karen has written a rough draft of the welcome letter using WordPerfect 5.1. However, it contains many errors. You will follow Karen as she uses WordPerfect 5.1 to correct and modify the letter.

Loading the WordPerfect 5.1 Program

Starting WordPerfect on a Two-Disk System

Boot the system by turning on the computer and loading DOS. After you have responded to the DOS date and time prompts, the A> should appear on your display screen.

Remove the DOS diskette and place the backup WordPerfect 1 diskette in the A drive and the backup data diskette in the B drive.

To load the WordPerfect 5.1 program, you will begin by changing the default disk drive to B. This tells the system that the diskette in the B drive will be used to save and retrieve files. At the A>,

Type: **B:**
Press: ⏎

To tell the system that the WordPerfect program diskette is in the A drive and to load the program into memory,

Type: A:WP
Press: ⏎

After a few moments, your display screen should provide copyright information, the version number of your copy, and the default drive that the system will use.

This screen also prompts you to insert the WordPerfect 2 disk. Follow these directions by removing the WordPerfect 1 disk from drive A, inserting the WordPerfect 2 disk, and pressing any key.

The editing screen is displayed. Skip to the section, "The Editing Screen," on the next page.

Starting WordPerfect on a Hard-Disk System

The WordPerfect program should have already been installed on your hard disk. It is assumed that the program files are on the C drive in the subdirectory \WP. If yours is in a different drive or subdirectory, substitute the appropriate drive and subdirectory name in the directions below.

The drive door(s) should be open. Turn on your computer and, if necessary, respond to the date and time prompts. The DOS C> should be displayed.

Put your data disk in drive A and, if necessary, close the door.

To load the WordPerfect 5.1 program, begin by changing the default disk drive to A. At the C>,

Type: A:
Press: ⏎

Drive A is now the default drive. This means that the diskette in the A drive will be used to save and retrieve files. Now you are ready to load the WordPerfect program. The command, WP, will load the program into memory. You must include the drive and subdirectory path as part of the command to tell the system where to find the WordPerfect files. To do this,

Type: C:\WP\WP
Press: ⏎

After a few moments, your screen should briefly display the opening screen. This screen contains copyright information, the version number of your copy, and the default drive that the system will use. This is quickly replaced with the Editing screen.

WP8
Editing a Document

The Editing Screen

Your display screen should be similar to Figure 1-1.

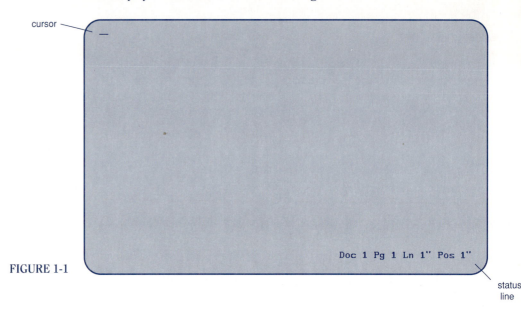

FIGURE 1-1

This is a blank WordPerfect 5.1 Editing screen. The blinking line or dash in the upper left corner is the **cursor**. It shows you where the next character you type will appear.

The line of information at the bottom of the screen is the **status line**. It displays four items of information about the current location of the cursor:

Doc 1 This shows which **document** window displays the cursor. A **window** is an area of the screen which displays the document. You can enter and edit text in two separate windows at a time. These windows are displayed as Doc 1 or Doc 2 in the status line. Currently, the cursor is in the document 1 window, and the window occupies the entire screen.

Pg 1 This shows the number of the **page** the cursor is located on. A page refers to the physical page when a document is printed. It is currently on page 1.

Ln 1" This tells you the vertical distance in inches between the cursor and the top of the page. This is the **line** on which the cursor rests. The cursor is currently 1 inch from the top of the page.

Pos 1" This tells you the horizontal location, or **position** of the cursor on the line. The position is displayed in inches from the left edge of the page. The cursor is currently 1 inch from the left edge of the page.

The line and position locations of the cursor you see on your screen are **default**, or initial, WordPerfect 5.1 settings. WordPerfect comes with many default settings. These are generally the most commonly used settings. For example, the current position of the cursor at 1 inch from the left edge of the page is the default left margin setting. The right margin default setting is 1 inch from the right edge of the page. When the document is printed, the printed page will have 1-inch left and right margins. Other default settings include a standard paper-size setting of 8-1/2 by 11 inches, tab settings every .5 inch, and single line spacing. If you do not specify different settings, WordPerfect uses the default settings.

Entering WordPerfect 5.1 Commands

The WordPerfect 5.1 editing screen is blank, except for the status line. Commands are entered using the pull-down menus or the function keys. Both methods produce the same result.

Using the Pull-Down Menu

A **pull down menu** displays a list of commands in a box that are available for selection when the menu is selected. Using the pull-down menu lets you see the various commands and options available. This is particularly helpful to people who are just learning to use the program.

To activate the pull-down menu,

Press: ALT - = (hold down ALT while pressing =)

Your display screen should be similar to Figure 1-2.

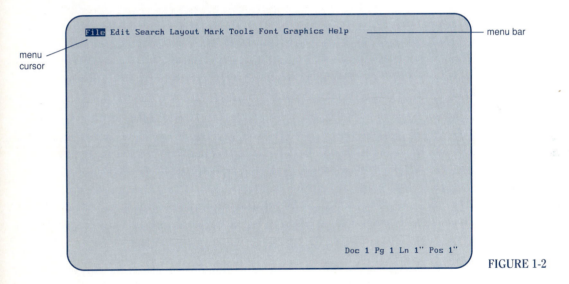

FIGURE 1-2

The top line of the screen displays the **menu bar**. It lists the names of nine menus which can be opened. The first menu name, File, is highlighted with the **menu cursor**. The → and ← keys are used to move the menu cursor in the direction of the arrow from one menu name to the next.

Press: →

The menu cursor is positioned on Edit.

Press: → (8 times)

The menu cursor has moved to each menu name and in a circular fashion has returned to the File menu.

To activate the pull-down menu of commands associated with the highlighted menu,

Press: ⏎

Your display screen should be similar to Figure 1-3.

FIGURE 1-3

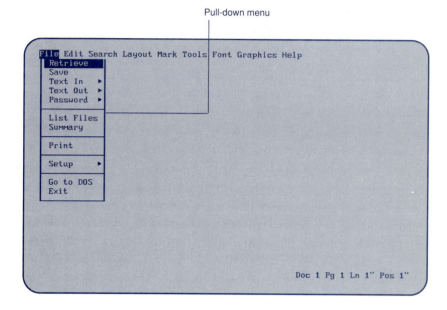

The pull-down menu of commands is displayed in a box below the File menu name, and the first pull-down menu command, Retrieve, is highlighted. Now pressing → will move the menu cursor to the next pull-down menu.

Press: →

The Edit pull-down menu is displayed. Notice that the menu cursor is not positioned on the first command, Move; instead it is positioned on the third command, Paste. This is because the first two commands are not available for selection at this time. Pull-down menu commands which cannot be selected are surrounded by brackets ([]). Additionally the menu cursor cannot be positioned on a command that is not available for selection.

The ↑ and ↓ keys are used to move the menu cursor within the pull-down menu.

Press: ↓

The menu cursor has moved to the next available command, Undelete.

Press: ↓ (2 times)

Your display screen should be similar to Figure 1-4.

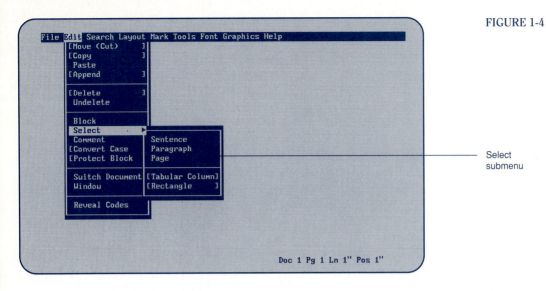

FIGURE 1-4

WP11
Using the
Pull-Down Menu

Select submenu

The menu cursor is positioned on Select. Notice the > symbol following the command name. This symbol tells you that a **submenu** of options will be displayed when the command is highlighted. In this case, the submenu consists of the options displayed in the box to the right.

Press: →

The menu cursor remains positioned on the pull-down command, Select, and another menu cursor highlights the first submenu option, Sentence. The ↑ and ↓ keys are used to move around the submenu.

Press: ↓

The submenu cursor is positioned on Paragraph.

Press: ←

The submenu cursor is cleared.

Press: (PGDN)

The menu cursor is positioned on the last command in the Edit menu, Reveal Codes. Pressing (PGDN) or (PGUP) in a pull-down menu or submenu will quickly move the menu cursor to the first or last command in the menu.

Press: (PGUP)

The menu cursor is positioned back on Paste. To see what commands are available in the other menus,

Press: → (9 times)

The File pull-down menu should be displayed. To remove the pull-down menu,

Press: `ESC`

Pressing `ESC` when a menu is displayed "backs up," or cancels, the previous selection.

When a pull-down menu is not displayed a quick way to move the menu cursor to the last menu name in the menu bar from any location on the bar is to press `END`.

Press: `END`

The menu cursor is positioned on Help. The same action could have been accomplished using `HOME`, `→`; however, it requires an extra keystroke.

Press: `←`

The menu cursor moved one menu to the left. To move quickly to the first menu, File,

Press: `HOME`, `←`

A quicker way to move to and activate a pull-down menu is to type the **mnemonic letter** (the highlighted letter associated with the menu name) of the menu you want to select. To select **Help**,

Type: `H`

The Help menu is selected, and the pull-down menu of commands is displayed.

So far you have moved the menu cursor to highlight many commands. However, you have not yet selected or executed a command. A command is selected by highlighting the command with the menu cursor and pressing `↵`, or by typing the mnemonic letter associated with the command.

Note: If you find that you have selected the wrong command, use Cancel (`F1`) to cancel the selection, or `ESC` to back out of a selected menu.

The menu cursor is over the first command, Help. Since this command is highlighted, it can be selected by pressing `↵`. It can also be selected by typing the mnemonic letter "h."

Select: Help

Your display screen should be similar to Figure 1-5.

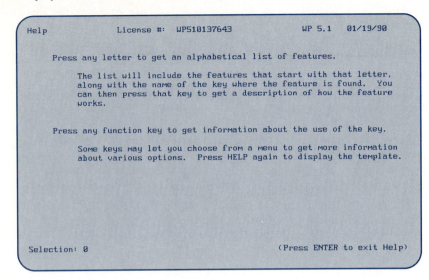

FIGURE 1-5

You have executed the Help menu's Help command. A full screen of information about how the Help system works is displayed. You will use Help shortly for more information. For now, following the directions on the screen to exit Help,

Press: ⏎

You are returned to the blank Editing screen. Once a command is executed and completed, you are returned to the Editing screen rather than to the menu.

Using a Mouse

If you have a mouse attached to your computer, follow the instructions below. If you do not have a mouse, skip to the next section, "Using the Function Keys."

The mouse controls a pointer on your screen. As soon as you move the mouse the pointer appears.

Move the mouse in any direction.

The pointer appears as a solid rectangle. You move the pointer on the screen by moving the mouse over the desk top in the direction you want the pointer to move.

Move the mouse in all directions (up, down, left, and right) and note the movement of the pointer on the screen.

If you pick up the mouse and move it to a different location on your desk top, the pointer will not move on the screen. This is because the pointer movement is controlled by the rubber-coated ball on the bottom of the mouse. This ball must move within its socket in order for the pointer to move on the screen. The ball's movement is translated into signals that tell the computer how to move the on-screen pointer.

On top of the mouse are two or three buttons. These buttons are used to enter user input instructions. Quickly pressing and releasing a mouse button is called clicking. To activate the WordPerfect 5.1 menu bar, click the right mouse button.

The menu bar appears at the top of the screen, just as if you had used the keyboard equivalent, ALT - =. (See Figure 1-2.)

Move the mouse so that the pointer is within the menu bar.
Move the mouse to the right and left to move the pointer from one menu name to the next. This has the same effect as using the (→) and (←) keys to move the menu cursor within the menu bar.

Position the pointer anywhere within File on the menu bar. To activate the pull-down menu,

Click: Left button

Note: If the pointer is not on a menu name when you click the left button, the menu will be cleared from the screen. If this happens, click the right button again to display the menu bar and try again.

The pull-down menu of commands is displayed below the File menu name, and the menu cursor is positioned on Retrieve. This is the same as if you had pressed (↵) using the keyboard (See Figure 1-3).

With the pointer still in the menu bar, hold down the left mouse button and move the mouse slowly to the right along the menu bar. Do not release the left button until the pointer is positioned over Tools.

Note: If, when you release the left button, the pointer is not on a menu name, the menu bar is cleared from the screen. If this happens, click the right button again to re-display the menu bar and try again.

Note: Developing the skill for moving the mouse and correctly positioning the pointer takes some time. If you accidentally find yourself in the wrong location or in a command that you did not intend to select, click the right button on a two-button mouse or the center button on a three-button mouse. This action will cancel most selected commands.

The process of holding down the left button as you move the mouse is called **dragging**. After dragging the mouse through the menu bar, releasing the left button selects the menu the pointer is on. Dragging the mouse along the menu bar while the pull-down menu is displayed has the same effect as using the (→) and (←) keys to move from one menu to another when the pull-down menu is displayed.

Note: If, while dragging the menu, you decide you do not want to select a menu, move the pointer to any area outside the menu bar or submenu box and release the left button. The menu is cleared. Also, at any point you can cancel the menu by clicking the right button.

Move the pointer to Help and click the left button. You have now selected the Help menu. This action has the same effect as typing the mnemonic letter of the menu.

Use the mouse to move the pointer to each of the three pull-down menu commands.

To select a pull-down menu command, move the pointer to the command (anywhere on the line within the menu box) and click the left button. You can also drag the mouse within the pull down-menu. This way you can see the submenu options associated with the highlighted pull-down menu command. When you release the left button the option is selected. Be careful when dragging the menus that you have the menu cursor on the correct menu item before releasing the left button.

Either method has the same effect as selecting the pull-down command using the arrow keys to highlight the command and pressing ⏎, or by typing the mnemonic letter.

To select the Help command, move the pointer to Help and press the left button. Your screen should look similar to Figure 1-5, shown earlier

Note: If the pointer is not on a pull-down menu command when you select it, the menu bar is cleared from the screen. If this happens, click the right button again to re-display the menu bar and try again.

You have executed the Help menu's Help command. To exit the Help screen,

Click: Right button

This has the same effect as pressing ⏎.

Using the Function Keys

The other way to issue a WordPerfect 5.1 command is to use the function keys. WordPerfect provides a function key template to place over the function keys to tell you what command each function key performs. If you have a function template place the appropriate template for your keyboard over the function keys.

Each function key, alone or in conjunction with other keys, can perform four different commands. The template lists the four commands associated with each function key. Notice that the commands are displayed in four colors. These colors tell you the key combinations to use to perform that specific task or activity. The color code and key combinations are explained below:

Color	Press
red	CTRL and function key
green	SHIFT and function key
blue	ALT and function key
black	function key alone

For example, F3 used alone or in combination with CTRL, SHIFT, or ALT, accesses four different WordPerfect commands, as shown below:

Key Combination	Command
CTRL - F3	Screen
SHIFT - F3	Switch
ALT - F3	Reveal Codes
F3	Help

The Help command, F3, accesses the Help system as if you had selected Help from the menu bar and then Help from the pull-down menu of commands. To show how you can access Help using the Function key,

Press: Help F3

The same screen of information (Figure 1-5) about how to use the WordPerfect Help system is displayed. This time you will use Help to display information about the function key template on the screen (in case you do not have a template or lose or forget your template in the future). Following the directions on the Help screen to display the template,

Press: Help (F3)

Your display screen should be similar to Figure 1-6.

FIGURE 1-6

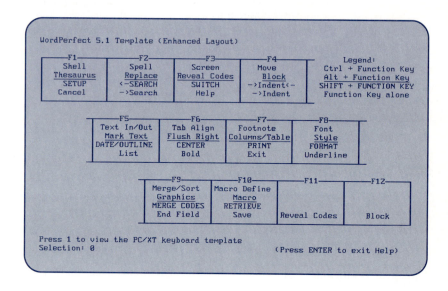

The Enhanced Layout template for keyboards whose function keys are above the typewriter keys is displayed.

If your function keys are located to the left of the typewriter section of the keyboard (PC/XT keyboard), following the directions on the screen,

Press: 1

The IBM PC/XT keyboard layout is displayed.

Depending upon your keyboard, the grid of 10 or 12 boxes displayed on the screen contains the WordPerfect commands that are associated with the function keys. Instead of a color code, the legend to the right lists the keys ((CTRL), (SHIFT) and (ALT)) that are used in combination with the function key, or the function key alone.

The function key template could also have been displayed using the pull-down menu by selecting Help and then Template.

To leave the Help screen,

Press: ⏎

You are returned to the blank WordPerfect screen.

Note: If your template is a black and white photocopy of the template provided by WordPerfect, then use red, green, and blue highlight pens to color code your template.

Retrieving a File

Karen worked on the first draft of the welcome letter yesterday and saved it on the diskette in a file named LETTER.

To open a file in WordPerfect, the Retrieve command is used. To use the pull-down menu to select the Retrieve command,

Press:

The Retrieve command is a command in the File menu. Because the menu cursor is already positioned over the File menu, to select it,

Press:

The pull-down menu of 11 commands associated with the File menu is displayed. The Retrieve command is highlighted. To select the Retrieve command,

Press:

Note: To cancel an incorrect menu selection, press (F1) (Cancel) to terminate the command, or (ESC) to back up one step in the command selection.

Your display screen should be similar to Figure 1-7.

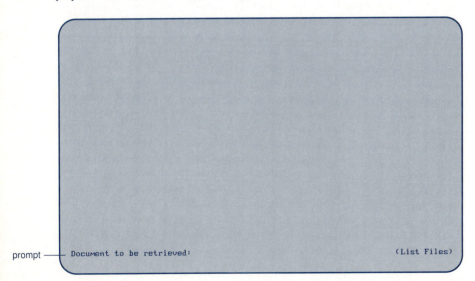

FIGURE 1-7

The cursor location information in the status line has been replaced by a WordPerfect prompt "Document to be retrieved." A **prompt** is the way the program tells you it needs more information. In this case the prompt wants you to enter the name of the file to be retrieved.

Before entering the file name, you will use Help for information about the Retrieve command. The WordPerfect Help system is **context-sensitive**. This means that whenever a command is in use, pressing Help ((F3)) will display information about that particular command.

Press: Help (F3)

Your display screen should be similar to Figure 1-8.

FIGURE 1-8

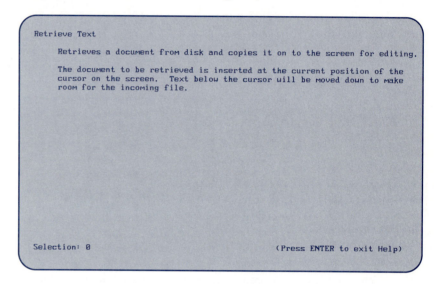

This screen tells you how the Retrieve command works. Most importantly it tells you that when you retrieve a file, a copy is displayed on the screen while the original file remains unchanged on the disk. The WordPerfect Help feature will provide specific information about the command you are using.

To leave the Help screen,

Press: ⏎

You are returned to the same place you were before using Help. You are now ready to enter the name of the file to retrieve. The file name can be entered in either upper- or lowercase letters. However, WordPerfect will always display a file name in uppercase.

Type: LETTER
Press: ⏎

After a few moments your display screen should be similar to Figure 1-9.

FIGURE 1-9

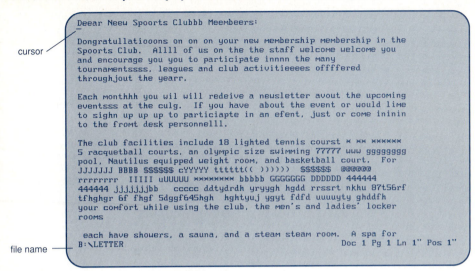

The Retrieve command loads a copy of the file from the diskette into memory. The original file remains on the diskette. The first three paragraphs of the rough draft of the welcome letter are displayed on the screen. As you can see, it contains many errors, which you will correct in this lab.

In addition to the cursor location information, the status line displays the file name of the file in use. This information will sometimes be replaced with other WordPerfect messages. Often a prompt (like the one you responded to when retrieving the file) or a menu of choices to select from will be displayed in the status line as part of the command sequence. Again, if you find that you have entered an incorrect command and are accidentally in the wrong menu, press Cancel (F1) or ESC. Then reenter the command correctly.

You could have also entered this command using the function key combination, SHIFT - F10. Look on your template next to the F10 key. The word "Retrieve" is printed in green letters. The top left-hand corner of the template displays the color code. Green means to use SHIFT in combination with the function key (hold down SHIFT and, while holding it down, press F10).

Moving the Cursor

The cursor can be moved around the screen by using the arrow keys or by using the mouse. The arrow keys, located on the numeric keypad or on the separate cursor key area, move the cursor one character space in the direction indicated by the arrow.

Note: Be careful to use only the keys specified as you are following the directions in this section. If you do, the instructions and figures in the text should be the same as what you see on your screen. Also, make sure the NUM LOCK (number lock) key is not on when using the numeric keypad area. If it is, numbers will be entered on the screen rather than the cursor moving through the text.

Press: → (6 times)

WP20
Editing a Document

Your display screen should be similar to Figure 1-10.

FIGURE 1-10

cursor

```
Deear Neew Spoorts Clubbb Meembeers:

Dongratullatiooons on on on your new membership membership in the
Spoorts Club.  Allll of us on the the staff welcome welcome you
and encourage you you to participate innnn the many
tournamentssss, leagues and club activitieeees offffered
throughjout the yearr.

Each monthhh you wil will redeive a newsletter avout the upcoming
eventsss at the culg.  If you have  about the event or would lime
to sighn up up up to particiapte in an efent, just or come ininin
to the fromt desk personnelll.

The club facilities include 18 lighted tennis courst * ** ******
5 racquetball courts, an olympic size swimming 77777 www ggggggg
pool, Nautilus equipped weight room, and basketball court.   For
JJJJJJ BBBB $$$$$$ cYYYYY tttttt(( )))))  $$$$$$  @@@@@@
rrrrrrrr  IIIII uUUUUU ******* bbbbb GGGGGGG DDDDDD 444444
444444 jjjjjjjbb   ccccc ddtydrdh yryygh hgdd rrssrt nkhu 87t56rf
tfhghgr 6f fhgf 5dggf645hgh  hghtyuj ygyt fdfd uuuuyty ghddfh
your comfort while using the club, the men's and ladies' locker
rooms

 each have showers, a sauna, and a steam steam room.   A spa for
B:\LETTER                                        Doc 1 Pg 1 Ln 1" Pos 1.6"
```

new position value

The cursor moved six character spaces to the right along the line. It should be positioned under the "N" in "Neew." Notice how the status line reflects the change in the horizontal location of the cursor on the line. The position value increased to 1.6" as the cursor moved to the right along the line. The position value is displayed as a decimal. The current cursor location then is 1-6/10 inch from the left edge of the page.

Press:

The cursor moved down one line. Since this is a blank line, the cursor moved back to the left margin on the line. The status line reflects the change in the location of the cursor by telling you that the new vertical or line location of the cursor is Ln 1.17", and the horizontal location of the cursor is Pos 1". Like the position value, the line value is displayed as a decimal. Line numbers increase as you move down the page. The current line location of the cursor is 1-17/100 inch from the top of the page.

Press: ↓

The cursor moved down to the next line and back to Pos 1.6". It should be on the "t" in "Dongratullatiooons." The cursor moved to position 1.6 because it was last located in a line containing text (line 1") at that position. The cursor will attempt to maintain its position in a line of text as you move up or down through the document.

By holding down either ← or →, the cursor will move quickly character by character along the line.

To see how this works, hold down → and move the cursor to the right along the line until it is under the "i" in the word "in."

The status line should show that the cursor is on Pos 6.9". If you moved too far to the right along the line of text, use ← to move back to the correct position.

This saves multiple presses of the arrow key. Many of the WordPerfect cursor movement keys can be held down to execute multiple moves.

Press: (2 times)

The cursor moved up two lines and should be positioned at the end of the first line.
Using the arrow keys and the status line for cursor location reference,

Move to: Ln 3.17" Pos 7.4" (end of first line of third paragraph)

Note: Throughout the WordPerfect 5.1 labs you will be instructed to move the cursor to specific line and position locations (for example, Move to: Ln 3.17" Pos 7.4"). To confirm the appropriate cursor position, the location of the cursor in the text is described in parentheses (for example, "end of first line of third paragraph"). If your cursor is not at the described location, move it there before continuing.

The default right margin setting is 1 inch from the right side of the paper (Pos 7.5".) To see what happens when the cursor reaches the right margin,

Press: →

The cursor automatically moved to the beginning of the next line. Unlike a typewriter, you did not need to press a return key to move from the end of one line to the beginning of the next. It is done automatically for you.
You can also move the cursor word by word in either direction on a line by using CTRL in combination with → or ←. CTRL is held down while pressing the arrow key.

Press: CTRL - → (5 times)

The cursor skipped to the beginning of each word and moved five words to the right along the line. It should be positioned on the "s" in the word "size."
To move back to the first word in this line,

Press: CTRL - ← (5 times)

The cursor should be positioned on "5," the first character in the line. If the cursor is positioned in the middle of a word, CTRL - → will move the cursor to the beginning of the next word; however, CTRL - ← will move the cursor to the beginning of the word it is on, rather than to the beginning of the preceding word.
The cursor can be moved quickly to the end of a line of text by pressing END. To move to the end of this line,

Press: END

Pressing HOME and then → will have the same effect. But it requires the use of two keys rather than one.
Unfortunately, simply pressing HOME will not take you to the beginning of a line of text. Because HOME is used in combination with several other keys, you must use it followed by ← to move to the beginning of a line.
To move back to the beginning of the line,

Press: HOME
Press: ←

The cursor should be back on the "5."

The letter is longer than what is currently displayed on the screen. To move to the bottom line of the screen, using ⬇,

Move to: Ln 4.83" Pos 1" (beginning of the first line of the fourth paragraph)

The screen can display only 24 lines of text at a time. If the cursor is positioned on either the top or bottom line of the screen, using ⬆ or ⬇ will move, or **scroll**, more lines of the document onto the screen. As you scroll up or down through the document, the lines at the top or bottom of the screen move out of view to allow more text to be displayed.

To scroll the rest of the letter into view on the screen,

Press: ⬇ (13 times)

The cursor should be at the beginning of the word "Sports" (Ln 7").

Your display screen should be similar to Figure 1-11.

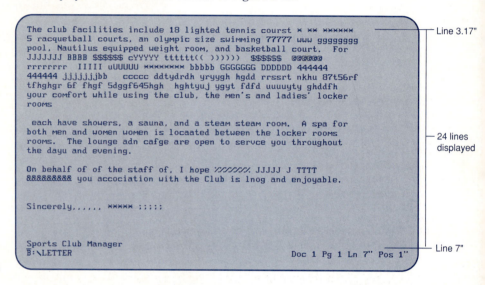

FIGURE 1-11

The first 13 lines of the letter are no longer visible on the screen. They scrolled off the top of the screen to allow the new lines at the bottom of the screen to be displayed.

Each time you pressed ⬇ a new line of text was brought into view at the bottom of the screen. At the same time a line of text scrolled out of view at the top of the screen.

The screen still displays only 24 lines of the letter. The cursor can be moved quickly to the top line of the screen by pressing (HOME) followed by ⬆. To move to the top line of the screen,

Press: (HOME)
Press: ⬆

The cursor should be at the beginning of Ln 3.17", on the "t" in "the."

HOME followed by **↓** will move the cursor to the last line of the screen.

Press: HOME
Press: ↓

The cursor should be positioned back at the beginning of "Sports" on the last line (Ln 7") of the screen.

You can also move to the top or bottom of the screen by using the minus (-) or plus (+) signs located to the right of the numeric keypad. (Do not use the plus or minus signs located in the upper row of the keyboard.) To move to the top of the screen,

Press: -

The cursor is positioned back on the first line of text on the screen.

Press: +

The cursor is positioned back on the last line of the screen.

Using the plus or minus keys to move to the bottom or top of the screen requires fewer keystrokes than using HOME and ↑ or ↓.

The screen is positioned over 24 lines of text on page 1 of the document (see Figure 1-11). WordPerfect differentiates between a screen and a page. A screen can display only 24 lines of text, whereas the printed page can display many more lines of text.

The cursor can be moved to the top or bottom line of a page using the CTRL - HOME key combination (while holding down CTRL press HOME). This is called the Go to key because of the prompt you will see displayed in status line.

Press: CTRL - HOME

Your display screen should be similar to Figure 1-12.

FIGURE 1-12

```
The club facilities include 18 lighted tennis courst × ×× ××××××
5 racquetball courts, an olympic size swimming 77777 www gggggggg
pool, Nautilus equipped weight room, and basketball court.  For
JJJJJJJ BBBB $$$$$$ cYYYYY tttttt(( )))))  $$$$$$ @@@@@@
rrrrrrr  IIIII uUUUUU ××××××× bbbbb GGGGGGG DDDDDD 444444
444444 jjjjjjjbb   ccccc ddtydrdh yryygh hgdd rrssrt nkhu 87t56rf
tfhghgr 6f fhgf 5dggf645hgh   hghtyuj ygyt fdfd uuuuyty ghddfh
your comfort while using the club, the men's and ladies' locker
rooms

 each have showers, a sauna, and a steam steam room.  A spa for
both men and women women is locaated between the locker rooms
rooms.  The lounge adn cafge are open to seruce you throughout
the dayu and evening.

On behalf of of the staff of, I hope ////// JJJJJ J TTTT
&&&&&&&& you accociation with the Club is lnog and enjoyable.

Sincerely,,,,,, ××××× ;;;;;


Sports Club Manager
Go to _
```

prompt

WP24
Editing a Document

The prompt "Go to" is displayed in the status line. A number, a character, ↑ or ↓ can be entered at this prompt.

To move to the top of the current page,

Press: ↑

The cursor should be positioned on the first line (1") of page 1. The screen is positioned over the first 24 lines of text on this page.

To move the cursor to the last line of page 1,

Press: CTRL - HOME
Press: ↓

The cursor should be positioned on the last line of page 1. The dashed line at the bottom of the screen shows the location of the end of page 1 and the beginning of page 2.

Press: ↓

Your display screen should be similar to Figure 1-13.

FIGURE 1-13

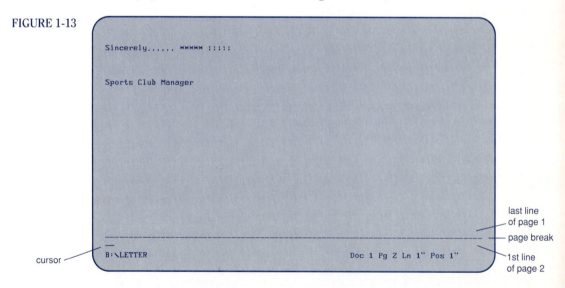

The cursor should be positioned on the last line of the screen. This is the first line of page 2 in the document.

The cursor can also be quickly moved from one page of text to another using the (PGUP) (page up) and (PGDN) (page down) keys. The message "Repositioning" will appear briefly in the status line while the cursor moves to the new location.

To move back to the top of the previous page,

Press: PGUP

The cursor is positioned on the first line of page 1.

To move to the top of page 2,

Press: PGDN

Your display screen should be similar to Figure 1-14.

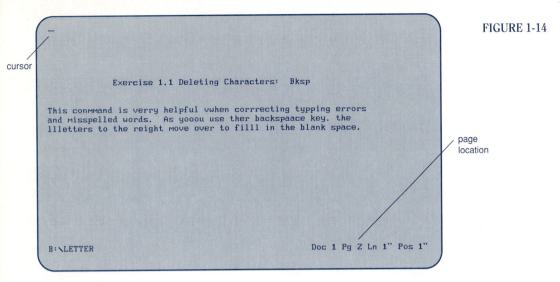

FIGURE 1-14

The cursor should be on the first line of page 2. The screen is positioned over the first 24 lines of page 2. Using (PGUP) or (PGDN) always positions the cursor on the left margin of the first line of the page.

To move through several pages of the document at once, you could press (PGDN) or (PGUP) multiple times. Or you can use the GoTo key combination again.

To move to page 5 of this document,

Press: (CTRL) - (HOME)

To respond to the "Go to" prompt, enter the page number. Use the number keys on the top line of the keyboard, above the alphabetic keys, as follows:

Type: 5
Press: ⏎

Your display screen should be similar to Figure 1-15.

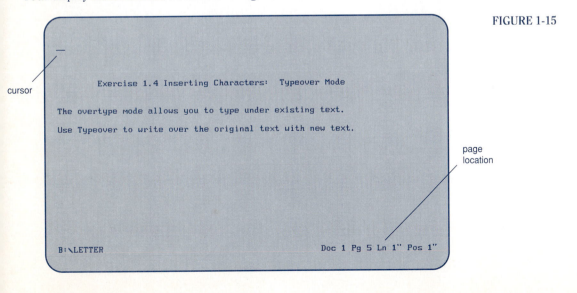

FIGURE 1-15

The cursor is positioned on the first line of page 5.
The biggest jump the cursor can make is to move to the beginning or end of a document. To move to the end of this document,

Press: (HOME)
Press: (HOME)
Press: ↓

Your display screen should be similar to Figure 1-16.

FIGURE 1-16

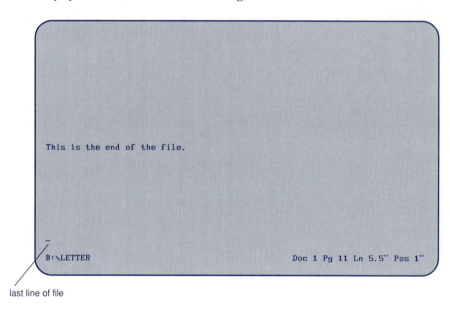

last line of file

The cursor should be positioned on a blank line. This line is the last line in the document.
To move quickly back to the first line of text in the document,

Press: (HOME)
Press: (HOME)
Press: ↑

The cursor should be positioned on the first line of page 1 of this document.

To review, the following cursor movement features have been covered:

Key	Action
→	One character to right
←	One character to left
↑	One line up
↓	One line down
CTRL - →	One word to right
CTRL - ←	One word to left
HOME - →	Right end of line
END	Right end of line
HOME, ←	Left edge of screen
HOME, ↑	Top of screen
- (minus sign)	Top of screen
HOME, ↓	Bottom of screen
[+] (plus sign)	Bottom of screen
CTRL - HOME, ↑	Top of current page
CTRL - HOME, ↓	Bottom of current page
CTRL - HOME page number	Top of page number specified
PGUP	Top of previous page
PGDN	Top of next page
HOME, HOME, ↑	Beginning of document
HOME, HOME, ↓	End of document

Using the Mouse to Move the Cursor

If you do not have a mouse, skip to the next section, "Editing a Document." If you have a mouse, you can use it to move the cursor to a specific location in a document. To do this, position the mouse pointer at the location in the text where you want to move the cursor and click the left button. Using the mouse,

Move to: "y" of "your" (first line of first paragraph)

Notice the cursor has not moved and the status line information has not changed.

Click: left button

The cursor is now positioned under the "y," and the status line reflects its new location in the document (Ln 1.33" Pos 3.8").
   Practice using the mouse to move the cursor by moving it to the following locations on the screen:

Move to: "E" in "Each" (first line of second paragraph)

Move to: "b" in "basketball" (third line of third paragraph)

Move to: "s" in "sauna" (last line on screen)

   Try moving the mouse pointer to the next line of text.
   It will not move beyond the displayed text on the screen. To scroll the text on the screen, with the mouse pointer positioned on either the top or bottom line of

the text on the screen, hold down the right button and move the mouse slightly up or down. The screen will continue to scroll until you release the button.

To try this, with the mouse positioned on the last line of text on the screen (not the status line) hold down the right button and move the mouse downward. Be careful that you do not quickly click the right button, as this will cause the menu to be displayed. If this happens, click the right button again to cancel the menu.

After a moment to stop the scrolling, release the right button.
Upon releasing the right button, the cursor also moves to the mouse pointer location. If there is no text on the line where you stopped scrolling, the cursor will be positioned at the beginning of the line.

Scroll the document upward until you are back on the first line of text on page 1.

To review, the following mouse features have been covered:

Mouse	Action
In Editing screen:	
Click right button	Displays menu.
Click left button	Positions cursor.
Dragging - right button	Scrolls screen.
In pull-down menus:	
Click right button	Backs out of all menus and removes menu bar from screen.
Click left button	Displays menu choices for menu-bar item positioned on or selects menu item.
Dragging	Moves across menu-bar and displays pull-down menu for each of the nine menus. Moves down a pull-down menu, highlights each choice and displays submenu if available. Releasing the button selects the highlighted command.

Editing a Document

Now that you have learned how to move the cursor around the document, you are ready to learn how to **edit**, or correct errors in a document.

The next part of this lab contains a series of exercises. Each exercise will show you a WordPerfect editing feature and allow you to practice using the feature. As you read the text in the book you will be directed to use the editing feature to correct the exercise on your display screen. When have completed the exercise, a figure in the book will show you how your display screen should appear. After completing each exercise press (PGDN) to go to the next exercise. To begin the exercise,

Press: (PGDN)

Exercise 1.1 Deleting Characters: BKSP

WP29
Editing a Document

Your display screen should be similar to Figure 1-17.

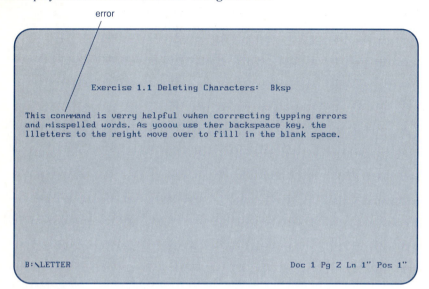

FIGURE 1-17

The first exercise, "Exercise 1.1 Deleting Characters: Bksp," should be on your display screen.

The BKSP (backspace) key will **delete,** or erase, a character to the left of the cursor. This key may be labeled with a left-facing arrow, the word "Backspace" or "Bksp," or a combination of the two. It is located above the ⏎ key.

The paragraph in the exercise on the display screen contains several errors that you will correct using the BKSP key. The first error on the screen is in the second word, "conmmand." The word should be "command." The "n" needs to be deleted.

To position the cursor to the right of the "n,"

Move to: Ln 2.33" Pos 1.8" (first "m" in "conmmand")

Note: If you are using the mouse to move the cursor, use the information in parentheses to tell you where to position the mouse pointer. Then verify the cursor position using the line and position information.

As a character is deleted, the text to the right will move over to fill in the space left by the deleted character. Watch your screen carefully as you

Press: BKSP

The character to the left of the cursor, in this case the "n", is deleted. The text to the right then moves over one space to fill in the space left by the character that was deleted.

There is now an extra space at the end of this line. As soon as you move the cursor to the right one space or down a line, WordPerfect will examine the line to see whether the word beginning on the next line ("and") can be moved up to fill in

WP30
Editing a Document

the space without exceeding the margin setting. This process of filling in the spaces is called **reformatting**. Watch your screen carefully as you correct the error in the word "verry."

Move to: Ln 2.33" Pos 2.9" (second "r" in "verry")
Press: BKSP
Press: → (1 time)

Your display screen should look similar to Figure 1-18.

FIGURE 1-18

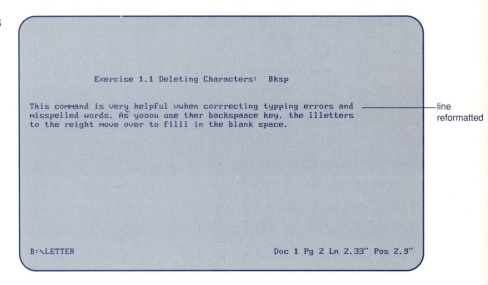

line reformatted

The word "and" from the beginning of the line below moved up to the end of the current line. The deletion of the extra characters created enough space for the whole word to move up a line. As you move the cursor through the text it will be automatically reformatted.

The automatic reformatting of text is the default setting in WordPerfect 5.1. As you move through the text the lines above the cursor will always display properly on the screen.

Continue this exercise by using BKSP to correct the text on the display. As you edit and move through the text, WordPerfect will constantly reexamine the margin space and reformat as needed.

When you are finished your display screen should be similar to Figure 1-19.

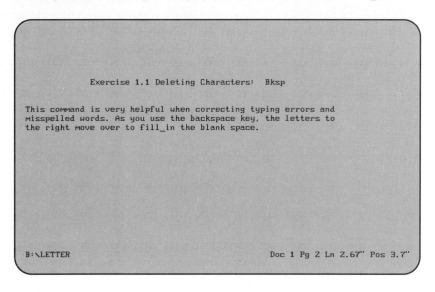

FIGURE 1-19

WP31
Editing a Document

As you can see, each time you press (BKSP) the cursor "backs up" through the text, deleting the character to the left of the cursor. The text is reformatted as needed.

Exercise 1.2 Deleting Characters: (DEL)

To move to the next exercise,

Press: (PGDN)

The second exercise, "Exercise 1.2 Deleting Characters: Del," should be on your screen.

A second way to delete a character is with (DEL). On most keyboards the (DEL) key is at the right side of the keyboard beneath the numeric keypad. This key will delete the character the cursor is positioned under.

The first error is in the second word in the first line of the exercise, "**u**you."

Move to: Ln 2.67" Pos 1.5" (under the first "u" in "uyou")

To delete the "u,"

Press: (DEL)

The "u" was removed, and the text to the right moved over to fill in the blank space. The paragraph will be reformatted as needed.

Complete the exercise by using (DEL) to correct the text on the screen. When you are done your display screen should be similar to Figure 1-20 on the next page.

WP32
Editing a Document

```
            Exercise 1.2 Deleting Characters:   Del

When you use the Del key, the character under the cursor is
deleted. This command is useful when you see an error in the text
several lines back. Instead of using the backspace key and
deleting all the correct text, use the arrow keys to move the
cursor to the location of the error, and press Del.

As the characters are deleted, the text from the right fills in
the blank space.




B:\LETTER                                       Doc 1 Pg 3 Ln 3.33" Pos 4.3"
```

FIGURE 1-20

Exercise 1.3 Inserting Characters: Insert Mode

Press: (PGDN)

Text can be entered into a document in either the **Insert** or **Typeover modes**. The default setting for WordPerfect is the Insert mode. As you type in Insert mode, new characters are inserted into the existing text. The existing text moves to the right to make space for the new characters.

The first sentence on the screen should read: "The **Insert** mode allows new text **to** be entered into **a** document." The three missing words, "Insert," "to" and "a" can be easily entered into the sentence without retyping it.

To enter the word "Insert" before the word "mode" in the first sentence,

Move to:	Ln 3" Pos 1.4" (under the "m" in "mode")
Type:	**Insert**
Press:	Space bar

The word "Insert" has been entered into the sentence by moving everything to the right to make space as each letter is typed.

Next, to enter the word "to" before the word "be,"

Move to:	Line 3" Pos 4.2" (under the "b" in "be")
Type:	**to**
Press:	Space bar

Finally, to enter the word "a" before the word "document,"

Move to:	Ln 3" Pos 6.1" (under the "d" in "document")
Type:	**a**
Press:	Space bar

Your display screen should be similar to Figure 1-21.

FIGURE 1-21

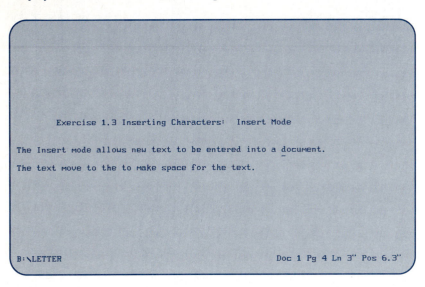

```
        Exercise 1.3 Inserting Characters:   Insert Mode

The Insert mode allows new text to be entered into a document.
The text move to the to make space for the text.




B:\LETTER                           Doc 1 Pg 4 Ln 3" Pos 6.3"
```

As each new character was entered into the existing text, the text to the right moved over to make space.

In a similar manner, correct the second sentence on the screen to read: "The **old** text move**s** to the **right** to make space for the **new** text". Your display screen should be similar to Figure 1-22.

FIGURE 1-22

```
        Exercise 1.3 Inserting Characters:   Insert Mode

The Insert mode allows new text to be entered into a document.
The old text moves to the right to make space for the new text.




B:\LETTER                           Doc 1 Pg 4 Ln 3.33" Pos 6.8"
```

Exercise 1.4 Inserting Characters: Typeover Mode

Press: (PGDN)

The second method of entering text in a document is to use the Typeover mode. In this mode, the new text types over the existing characters.

The (INS) (insert) key, located to the left of the (DEL) key, changes the mode from Insert to Typeover.

Press: (INS)

Your display screen should be similar to Figure 1-23.

FIGURE 1-23

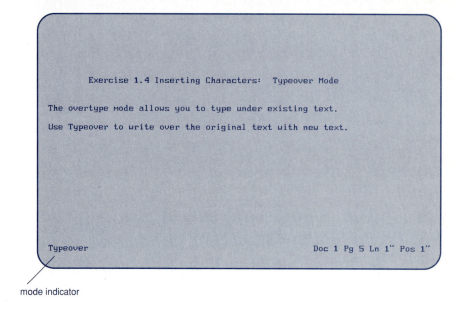

mode indicator

To tell you that the Typeover mode is on, the word "Typeover" appears on the left side of the status line.

The first sentence should read: "The **Typeover** mode allows you to type **over** existing text." To correct this sentence,

Move to: Ln 2.5" Pos 1.4" (beginning of "overtype")
Type: Typeover

As each character was typed, the character (or space) under it was replaced with the character being typed.

Next, to replace the word "under" with "over,"

Move to: Ln 2.5" Pos 4.7" (beginning of "under")
Type: over

Notice that there is still one extra character. To remove the extra "r,"

Press: (DEL)

Your display screen should be similar to Figure 1-24.

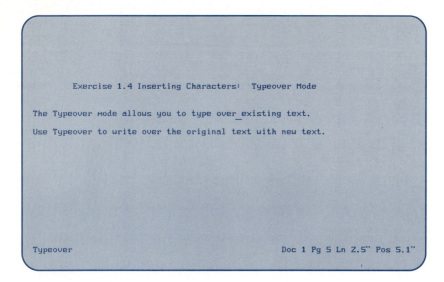

FIGURE 1-24

In a similar manner, correct the sentence to be: "**The** typeover **mode replaces** the original text with new text."

To turn off the Typeover mode,

Press: INS

Exercise 1.5 Deleting Words: CTRL - BKSP

Press: PGDN

The CTRL - BKSP key combination is used to delete entire words. The cursor can be positioned on any character of the word to be deleted, or one space to the left of the word to be deleted.

The first line on the screen contains several duplicate words. It should read: "This command is very helpful for deleting unnecessary words.

To remove the first duplicate word, "command,"

Move to: Ln 2.67" Pos 1.5" ("c" of "command")
Press: CTRL - BKSP

The word the cursor is positioned on is deleted. Notice also that one blank space was deleted, leaving the correct number of spaces between words.

If the cursor is placed on a blank space immediately after a word, then using CTRL - BKSP deletes the word to the left of the cursor and the blank space the cursor is on.

Use CTRL-BKSP to delete the other duplicate words in the sentences on the screen. After completing the exercise, your display screen should be similar to Figure 1-25.

FIGURE 1-25

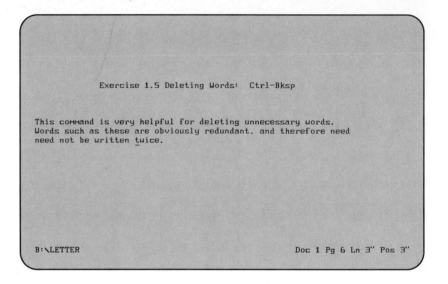

The text to the right filled in the blank space when you deleted a word. The paragraph was reformatted as needed. You may have also noticed that any punctuation following a word is considered part of the word and is deleted also.

Exercise 1.6 Deleting from Cursor to End of Line: CTRL - END

Press: PGDN

The CTRL - END key combination will delete everything on a line from the cursor to the right. If the cursor is placed at the beginning of a line, all the text on the line is deleted.

You will delete the unnecessary text following the word "cursor" in the first line in this exercise.

Move to: Ln 2.67" Pos 4.5" (first "8" immediately following "cursor")
Press: CTRL - END

The text from the cursor to the right is deleted.

Continue this exercise by deleting the unnecessary characters at the end of the next two lines.

Next, delete the entire contents of the fourth line by placing the cursor on the first character in the line.

Your display screen should be similar to Figure 1-26.

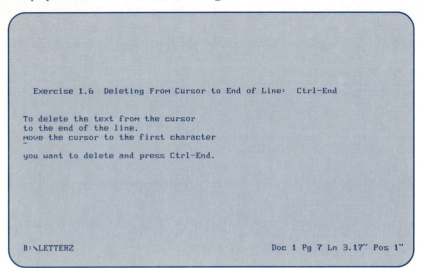

FIGURE 1-26

Exercise 1.7 Deleting Several Lines of Text: (ESC), (CTRL) - (END)

Press: (PGDN)

Several lines of text can be deleted at once by using (ESC) followed by the (CTRL) - (END) key combination. To delete several lines of text, first move the cursor to the beginning of the line of text to be deleted.

To erase the lines which are labeled as lines 13, 14, and 15 on the screen, first,

Move to: Ln 3" Pos 1" (beginning of line 13)

Next, count the number of lines you want to erase. You want to delete three lines. To do this, you could use the (CTRL) - (END) command three times to erase the contents of each line. Or you can use (ESC) to tell WordPerfect to repeat a function a specified number of times.

Press: (ESC)

The status line displays the prompt "Repeat Value = 8." The number 8 is the default setting.

(ESC) acts as a **repeater** to specify the number of times to repeat a specified function. The number you enter tells WordPerfect how many times to repeat the function you will enter next. Do not press ⏎ after typing in your response to the prompt.

To repeat the function three times,

Type: 3

There are many functions which can be repeated. To move through a document you can press (ESC) and the ↑ and ↓ keys to move up or down a specified number of lines, (PGUP) or (PGDN) to move forward or backward by pages, (→) or (←) to move right or left character by character along a line. To delete text you can press (ESC) and (CTRL)-(BKSP) to remove a specified number of words, (CTRL)-(END) to remove lines of text, or (CTRL)-(PGDN) to delete pages. In this case, to remove the three lines of text,

Press: (CTRL)-(END)

Your display screen should be similar to Figure 1-27.

FIGURE 1-27

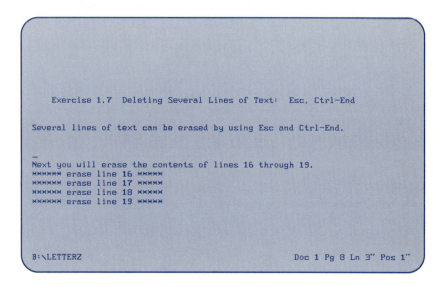

The contents of lines 13, 14, and 15 have been deleted.
In a similar manner, erase lines 16 through 19.
(ESC) can be entered before using the arrow and (DEL) keys, (PGUP), (PGDN), (HOME)-(↓) and (HOME)-(↑), and (CTRL)-(←) and (CTRL)-(→) to tell WordPerfect to repeat the procedure the specified number of times. It can also be used to enter the same character into the text a number of times.

Exercise 1.8 Inserting and Deleting Blank Lines

Press: (PGDN)

The (↵) key is used to insert a blank line into text or to mark the end of a paragraph. It is called a **hard carriage return**
If (↵) is pressed in the middle of a line of text, all text to the right of the cursor moves to the beginning of the next line. For example,

Move to: Ln 2.5" Pos 5.3 ("m" of "middle" in the first line of this exercise)
Press: (↵)

A hard carriage return is entered at the end of the first line, and the text from the cursor to the right moves down to the beginning of the next line.

If you press (BKSP) the hard carriage return at the end of the first line is deleted, and the text returns to its original location.

Press: (BKSP)

If ⏎ is pressed at the beginning of a line, a blank line is inserted into the document. To see how this works,

Move to: Ln 3" Pos 1" (beginning of "If" on the fourth line of this exercise)
Press: ⏎

A blank line is inserted into the text, forcing the line the cursor is on to move down one line.

If ⏎ is pressed at the end of a paragraph or line of text, the cursor moves to the beginning of the next line.

Move to: Ln 3.83" Pos 7.5" (end of last line in the exercise)
Press: ⏎

The cursor moves to the beginning of the next line.

To delete a blank line, position the cursor at the beginning of the blank line and press (DEL). To try this,

Move to: Ln 3.5" Pos 1" (beginning of blank line between second and third sentences)
Press: (DEL)

Your display screen should be similar to Figure 1-28.

FIGURE 1-28

```
          Exercise 1.8 Inserting and Deleting Blank Lines

     If you press the Enter (Return) key in the middle of a line of
     text, Wordperfect moves the text to the right down to the next
     line.

     If you press the Enter (Return) key at the beginning of a line,
     WordPerfect inserts a blank line.
     If you press the Enter (Return) key at the end of a paragraph or
     line of text, the cursor moves to the beginning of the next line.




     B:\LETTER                              Doc 1 Pg 9 Ln 3.5" Pos 1"
```

The blank line is deleted, and the text below moves up one line.

Exercise 1.9 Undeleting Text

Press: PGDN

It is easy to accidentally delete text you did not intend to delete. Fortunately the Edit>Undelete, or Undelete (F1), command lets you restore your deletions. To do this, each time you delete text WordPerfect stores it in a special file called a **buffer**. Only the last three deletions are stored.

To see how this works, delete the three sentences numbered 1, 2, and 3 by moving to the beginning of each line and pressing CTRL - END.

To restore the deleted text,

Select: Edit
Select: Undelete

Your screen should be similar to Figure 1-29.

FIGURE 1-29

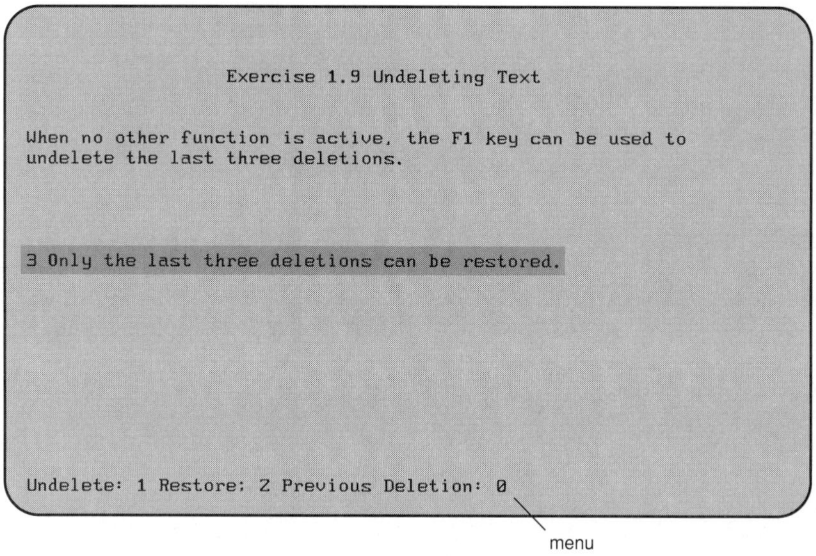

```
                    Exercise 1.9 Undeleting Text

When no other function is active, the F1 key can be used to
undelete the last three deletions.



3 Only the last three deletions can be restored.







Undelete: 1 Restore; 2 Previous Deletion: 0
```
— menu

The most recently deleted text (sentence 3) appears highlighted on the screen. The undelete menu appears in the status line. It lets you restore the highlighted text or see the previous deletions. To see the previous deletion,

Select: Previous

The second deletion is displayed. You can also use the up and down arrow keys to display the deletions.

Press: ↑

The first deletion is displayed.

Press: ↑

The third deletion is displayed again. To restore the highlighted text,

Select: Restore

The third deletion is reentered at the cursor position.
Restore the first and second deletions in numerical order above sentence 3. To do this, first position the cursor in the location where you want the text displayed. Then select the Edit>Undelete command, display the deleted text, and select Restore. When you are done the screen should appear as it did before you deleted the sentences.

To review, the following editing keys have been covered:

Key	Action
(BKSP)	Deletes character to left of cursor
(DEL)	Deletes character at cursor
(INS) on	Inserts character into text
(INS) off	Uses Typeover mode to insert text
(CTRL) - (BKSP)	Deletes word cursor is on
(↵)	Moves cursor to next line
	Inserts a blank line
(CTRL) - (END)	Deletes line of text from cursor to right
(ESC) # (function)	Repeats certain functions n times, where n= any number
Undelete (F1)	Restores the last three deletions

Clearing the Screen

Now that you know how to move around a document and how to use several different types of editing keys, you will correct the rough draft of the welcome letter Karen created. A copy of the rough draft is in another file named **LETTER2**.

Before retrieving a new file, you must clear the current document from the screen. If you do not clear the current document from the screen, the file you retrieve will combine with the document on the screen, creating a third document.

All WordPerfect 5.1 commands are issued by using the pull-down menu or the function key combination. As you use WordPerfect 5.1 commands throughout this series of labs, the command will be presented using both the function keys and the pull-down menus. The pull-down menu command sequence will be presented first. It will appear following the word "Select." Each menu command in the sequence will be separated with >, and the mnemonic letter will appear boldfaced. For example, the command to retrieve a file will appear as "Select: **F**ile>**R**etrieve."

The function key equivalent command will appear below the pull-down menu command sequence. It will be preceded with >> for example, the command to retrieve a file using the function key will appear as ">> Retrieve (SHIFT) - (F10)."

As you become familiar with the program you will probably rely less on the pull-down menus to issue commands and more on the function keys. This is because the function keys accomplish the same procedure with fewer keystrokes. Always have your function key template handy, as you will find is a very helpful reminder of the key combination to use.

To clear the current document from the screen, use the pull-down menu command, File Exit, or the function key Exit (F7) command,

Select: File>Exit
>> Exit (F7)

The prompt in the status line, "Save Document? Yes (No)," is asking whether you want to save the changes you made to the current file, LETTER, in memory to the diskette. In most cases, before you clear a document from the screen, you will want to save the work you have done onto a diskette. In this way you would be able to retrieve the file again and resume work on it if needed. Notice that following the prompt WordPerfect displays the response to the prompt as "Yes." This is the default response. To respond to the prompt, you can type the appropriate letter (Y or N) or you can position the mouse pointer on the option and click the left button. Additionally, you can simply press ⏎ to accept the default response.

You do not want to save the edited version of the document. By responding "N" (No) to the prompt, the changes you made to the document file LETTER will not be saved. The original version of the file LETTER remains on the diskette unchanged. You can retrieve the file LETTER again and repeat the exercises for practice. To indicate that you do not want to save the document as it appears on the screen,

Type: N

The next prompt, "Exit WP? No (Yes)," is asking if you want to exit the WordPerfect program. This time the default response is "No." If you select Yes the screen clears, and the operating system prompt will appear in the lower left-hand corner of the display screen. You could then turn your computer off, load another program, or reload the WordPerfect 5.1 program. If you accept the default (No), the display screen will clear and you can continue using the WordPerfect 5.1 program by creating a new document or, as you will do, retrieving another document file. Since you want to continue working in WordPerfect,

Press: ⏎

The document LETTER is cleared from the screen, and a blank WordPerfect screen is displayed.

Listing File Names

The new file you want to use is named LETTER2. A listing of the files on the disk can be displayed by using the List Files or List (F5) command.

Select: File>List Files
>> List (F5)

The name of the current directory (B or A) is displayed in the status line. If you wanted to see a display of the files on a diskette in another drive, you could enter the name of the new directory. A listing of the files in that directory would then be displayed. The current drive, however, would not change. If you wanted to actually change the current directory to another directory, you would type =, as the prompt in the status line indicates. The current directory name would disappear. You could then enter the name of the directory you wanted to use. Since you simply want to see a listing of the files on the diskette in the current (A or B) drive,

Press: ⏎

Your display screen should be similar to Figure 1-30.

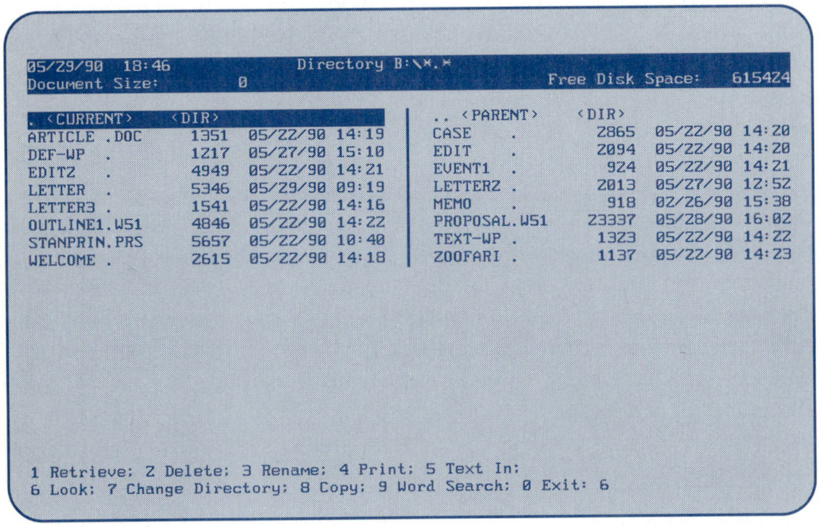

FIGURE 1-30

```
05/29/90  18:46              Directory B:\*.*
Document Size:       0                    Free Disk Space:    615424

.  <CURRENT>    <DIR>                 ..  <PARENT>    <DIR>
ARTICLE .DOC    1351  05/22/90 14:19    CASE    .     2865  05/22/90 14:20
DEF-WP  .       1217  05/27/90 15:10    EDIT    .     2094  05/22/90 14:20
EDIT2   .       4949  05/22/90 14:21    EVENT1  .      924  05/22/90 14:21
LETTER  .       5346  05/29/90 09:19    LETTER2 .     2013  05/27/90 12:52
LETTER3 .       1541  05/22/90 14:16    MEMO    .      918  02/26/90 15:38
OUTLINE1.WS1    4846  05/22/90 14:22    PROPOSAL.WS1 23337  05/28/90 16:02
STANPRIN.PRS    5657  05/22/90 10:40    TEXT-WP .     1323  05/22/90 14:22
WELCOME .       2615  05/22/90 14:18    ZOOFARI .     1137  05/22/90 14:23




1 Retrieve; 2 Delete; 3 Rename; 4 Print; 5 Text In;
6 Look; 7 Change Directory; 8 Copy; 9 Word Search; 0 Exit: 6
```

The top of the screen displays the current date and time, the name of the directory being viewed, the size of the document you are currently working on, and the remaining free diskette space. Beneath this information is an alphabetized list of the files in the directory in two columns. The file names are alphabetized from left to right across the column and then down the column. The directory includes files which are not WordPerfect files. The files listed on your screen may differ from the files in Figure 1-30 depending upon the software programs selected by your instructor.

The file you want to retrieve, LETTER2, appears in the directory. The menu of **options** in the status line allows you to organize and work with the files on the disk. An option is selected by typing the number to the left of the option name, or typing the highlighted letter, or positioning the mouse pointer on the option and clicking the left mouse button. Notice the first menu option, 1 Retrieve. By selecting this option you can retrieve the WordPerfect file you want to use. To do this, first you need to move the highlight bar, by using the arrow keys or by dragging the mouse, over the file name you want to retrieve.

Move to: LETTER2

With the highlight bar over the file name you want to retrieve, to retrieve the file,

Select: Retrieve

The document LETTER2 is displayed on the screen. Using the List Files (F5) command to display a file directory and retrieve a file is very helpful when you are not sure of the name of the file you want to use. The result, retrieval of a file, is the same as if you used the Retrieve ((SHIFT)-(F10)) command or selected File>Retrieve from the menu.

Editing the Welcome Letter

The rough draft of the welcome letter is displayed on the screen. Using the editing features presented above, correct the letter on your screen. Refer to Figure 1-31 for missing words. Use it as a guide to how your screen should appear when you are done. Check that there is only one blank space between words and following a period.

Saving and Replacing an Existing File

The file saved on the diskette as LETTER2 does not include the editing changes you have just made to the document on the screen. When you are entering text, it is stored temporary memory (RAM) only. Not until you **save** the document to the diskette are you safe from losing your work due to power failure or other mishap.

To save the document to disk and continue working on the file, use the File>Save or (F10) command.

Select: File>Save
    >>   Save (F10)

In response to the prompt to save the document,

Type: Y

Your display screen should be similar to Figure 1-31.

FIGURE 1-31

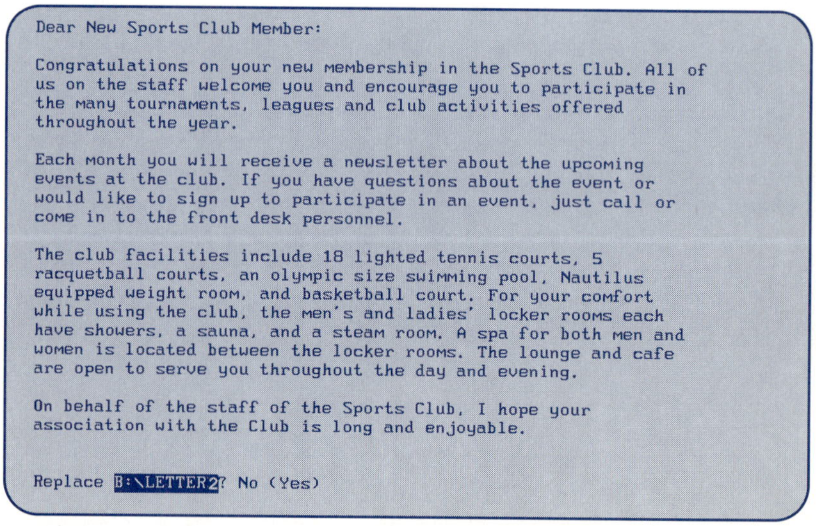

```
Dear New Sports Club Member:

Congratulations on your new membership in the Sports Club. All of
us on the staff welcome you and encourage you to participate in
the many tournaments, leagues and club activities offered
throughout the year.

Each month you will receive a newsletter about the upcoming
events at the club. If you have questions about the event or
would like to sign up to participate in an event, just call or
come in to the front desk personnel.

The club facilities include 18 lighted tennis courts, 5
racquetball courts, an olympic size swimming pool, Nautilus
equipped weight room, and basketball court. For your comfort
while using the club, the men's and ladies' locker rooms each
have showers, a sauna, and a steam room. A spa for both men and
women is located between the locker rooms. The lounge and cafe
are open to serve you throughout the day and evening.

On behalf of the staff of the Sports Club, I hope your
association with the Club is long and enjoyable.

Replace B:\LETTER2? No (Yes)
```

The prompt "Replace:" appears in the status line. The file disk drive location and name of the original file, LETTER2, are displayed after the prompt.

You could save both the original version of the document and the revised document as two separate files. To do this, you would enter a new file name for the revised version at this prompt. However, you do not want to keep the original version. Instead you will **replace,** or write over, it with the current version of the document on the screen. To save the current version of the document on the display screen over the version currently on the diskette, using the same file name,

Press: ⏎

The next prompt protects the user from accidentally writing over an existing file. It asks you to confirm that you want to replace the contents of the file on the diskette with the revised document on the display.

If you enter N (No), the "Document to be Saved:" prompt appears again to allow you to enter a new file name. Since you want to replace the original document on the diskette with the new document on the display,

Type: Y

The revised document writes over the original document saved on the diskette, and you are returned to the document.

Printing a Document

Karen wants to print a hard copy of the welcome letter to give to the Membership Coordinator. If you have printer capability you can print a copy of the document displayed on the screen.

Note: Please consult your instructor for printing procedures that may differ from the directions below.

The Print menu is accessed by selecting Print from the File menu or by pressing (SHIFT) - (F7) (Print).

Select: **File>Print**
>> Print (SHIFT) - (F7)

Your display screen should be similar to Figure 1-32.

FIGURE 1-32

```
Print

    1 - Full Document
    2 - Page
    3 - Document on Disk
    4 - Control Printer
    5 - Multiple Pages
    6 - View Document
    7 - Initialize Printer

Options

    S - Select Printer                      Standard Printer
    B - Binding Offset                      0"
    N - Number of Copies                    1
    U - Multiple Copies Generated by        WordPerfect
    G - Graphics Quality                    Medium
    T - Text Quality                        Draft




Selection: 0
```

The document has been temporarily removed from the screen to display the Print screen. This screen is divided into two menus, Print and Options. The Print menu lets you print a document from the screen or from a document stored on a disk. The Options menu lets you select the printer and make changes to the printer settings.

In the Options menu, notice that to the right of the menu options, the selected printer and printer settings are displayed. The selected printer is Standard Printer. This is the **active printer**, or the printer that WordPerfect 5.1 expects to use to print the document.

The active printer can be changed using the Select Printer option.

Select: Select Printer

The Select Printer screen is displayed. At the top of the screen is a list of printers your school has defined. If Standard Printer is listed here, it will be highlighted, and an asterisk (*) indicates that it is the active printer.

To select the appropriate printer, first move the highlight bar to the name of the printer you want to use. The Select option (1) in the menu in the status line lets you change the highlighted printer to the active printer.

Select: Select

You are returned to the Print screen, and the printer you selected should be displayed as the active printer.

Now you are ready to instruct WordPerfect to print the letter. If necessary turn the printer on and adjust the paper so that the perforation is just above the printer scale.

The first two Print menu options let you specify how much of the document you want printed. If you wanted to print the full document, then option 1 Full Document would be selected. If you wanted to print only the page the cursor is on, then you would select **P**age.

To print a copy of the entire document,

Select: ▸Full Document▸

Your printer should be printing out the document, and the letter is again displayed on your screen.

The printed copy of the welcome letter should be similar to Figure 1-33. It may not match exactly if you changed the active printer from Standard Printer to another printer. The number of words on a line in your printed document and the document on your screen may have changed. This is a result of the printer you selected.

FIGURE 1-33

```
Dear New Sports Club Member:

Congratulations on your new membership in the Sports Club. All of
us on the staff welcome you and encourage you to participate in
the many tournaments, leagues and club activities offered
throughout the year.

Each month you will receive a newsletter about the upcoming
events at the club. If you have questions about the event or
would like to sign up to participate in an event, just call or
come in to the front desk personnel.

The club facilities include 18 lighted tennis courts, 5
racquetball courts, an olympic size swimming pool, Nautilus
equipped weight room, and basketball court. For your comfort
while using the club, the men's and ladies' locker rooms each
have showers, a sauna, and a steam room. A spa for both men and
women is located between the locker rooms. The lounge and cafe
are open to serve you throughout the day and evening.

On behalf of the staff of the Sports Club, I hope your
association with the Club is long and enjoyable.

Sincerely,


Sports Club Manager
```

Notice that the right margins are even, rather than uneven or **ragged** as shown on the screen. This is one of WordPerfect's default print settings. You will look at several of these settings in the next lab.

Note: Documents created with WordPerfect 5.1 are printer-specific. That is, documents specify the active printer. All the document files supplied with the labs specify the Standard Printer as the active printer. To print any of these files, you may need to change the active printer to one appropriate for your particular microcomputer system.

Exiting WordPerfect 5.1

To leave WordPerfect 5.1 select File>Exit or Exit (F7).

Select: File>Exit
  >> Exit (F7)

In response to the prompt to save the file, you can respond No, since no changes were made to the document since you last saved it.

Select: No

To exit WordPerfect 5.1,

Select: Yes

You are returned to the DOS prompt.
   Always exit the WordPerfect 5.1 program using the File>Exit ((F7)) command. Never turn off your computer until you exit properly, or you may lose text.

KEY TERMS

cursor	scroll
status line	edit
document	delete
window	reformat
page	Insert mode
line	Typeover mode
position	repeater
default	hard carriage return
pull-down menu	buffer
menu bar	option
menu cursor	replace
submenu	save
mnemonic letter	active printer
prompt	ragged
context-sensitive	

MATCHING

1. (F7) _____ a. displays a menu of command choices that can be selected
2. (ESC) _____ b. cancels a command or exits a file
3. typeover _____ c. a question or indicator from the program that requires input from the user
4. status line _____ d. new text writes over old text in a document
5. (ALT) - = _____ e. creates a hard carriage return

6. prompt _____ f. retrieves a document file
7. ⏎ _____ g. deletes word cursor is on
8. SHIFT - F10 _____ h. displays cursor location information or menu and command prompts
9. CTRL - BKSP _____ i. deletes several lines of text
10. ESC CTRL - END _____ j. causes a command to repeat a specified number of times

PRACTICE EXERCISES

1. Retrieve the file EDIT. Follow the directions in the file to correct the sentences. Save the edited version of the file as EDIT. When you have completed the exercise print a copy of the file. Remember to select the appropriate printer for your microcomputer system.

2. Retrieve the file EDIT2. Follow the directions above the six paragraphs to correct the text in this file. Your corrected document should look like the text beginning on page WP3 in the section "Advantages of Using a Word Processor." Save the edited file as EDIT2. When you have completed the exercises print a copy of the file. Remember to select the appropriate printer for your microcomputer system.

3. Retrieve the file MEMO. This is a WordPerfect 5.1 document which is similar to the document you edited in Lab 1. It contains many errors. Edit the document using the commands you learned in this lab. Save the edited file as MEMO. Print a copy of the edited document. Remember to select the appropriate printer for your microcomputer system.

Your edited document should look like this:

TO: All Sports Club Employees

FROM: Ernie Powell, Sports Club Manager

DATE: December 1, 1992

The Sports Club will have the following holiday hours:

December 24, 1992	6:00 AM to 3:00 PM
December 25, 1992	closed all day
December 31, 1992	6:00 AM to 3:00 PM
January 1, 1993	closed all day

4. Retrieve the file CASE. Correct the text in this file using the commands you learned in this lab. Your corrected document should look like the text on page WP5, "Case Study for Labs 1-4." Save the corrected version of the file as CASE. Print the edited document. Remember to select the appropriate printer for your computer system.

LAB

Creating and Formatting a Document   2

OBJECTIVES

In this lab you will learn how to:

1. Create a new document.
2. Spell-check a document.
3. Save a document.
4. Combine files.
5. Move text.
6. Block text for copying and moving.
7. Enter the system date.
8. Align text flush with the right margin.
9. Set margins.
10. Use and set tabs.
11. Display hidden codes.
12. Search and replace text.
13. Set justification.

CASE STUDY

After editing the rough draft of the welcome letter, Karen showed it to the membership coordinator. The coordinator would like the letter to include information about monthly club fees and the new automatic fee payment program. We will follow Karen as she enters the new information into a file, combines it with the welcome letter, and adds some finishing touches to the letter.

Creating a Document

Boot the system by turning on the computer and loading DOS. Enter the current date when responding to the DOS date prompt. Load WordPerfect. If you are not sure of the procedure, refer to Lab 1, "Introduction to WordPerfect."

A blank WordPerfect screen is like a blank piece of paper you put into the typewriter. To create a new document, simply begin typing the text. When the cursor reaches the end of a line, however, do not press ⏎. WordPerfect will decide when to move the words down to next line based on the margin settings. This is called **word wrap**. The only time you need to press ⏎ is at the end of a paragraph or to insert blank lines.

As you type the text shown below, do not press ⏎ until you are directed to at the end of the paragraph. There should be one space following a period at the end of a sentence. If you make typing errors as you enter the text, use the editing features you learned in Lab 1 to correct your errors.

Type: **The Sports Club is offering a new program to all its members which will save you writing a check each month. Upon your authorization, the bank will send payment of your monthly charges directly to the club. You will receive a copy of your monthly statement to confirm the accuracy of your bill. If you are interested in the automatic fee payment program, please contact the accounting department to make the necessary arrangements (931-4285 ext. 33).**

Press: ↵

Your display screen should be similar to Figure 2-1.

FIGURE 2-1

```
The Sports Club is offering a new program to all its members
which will save you writing a check each month. Upon your
authorization, the bank will send payment of your monthly charges
directly to the club. You will receive a copy of your monthly
statement to confirm the accuracy of your bill. If you are
interested in the automatic fee payment program, please contact
the accounting department to make the necessary arrangements
(931-4285 ext. 33)._

                                        Doc 1 Pg 1 Ln 2.17" Pos 2.8"
```

The text on your screen may not exactly match the text in Figure 2-1. This is because the active printer your WordPerfect 5.1 program is using controls the font (print) size, which affects the number of characters WordPerfect can display on a line and where it will word wrap the line of text.

As you can see, the automatic word wrap feature makes entering text in a document much faster than typing. This is because a carriage return does not need to be pressed at the end of every line.

To insert a blank line,

Press: ↵

To enter the second paragraph,

Type: **The regular monthly membership fee is $45.00. Other expenses, such as league and lesson fees, pro-shop purchases, and charges at the Courtside Cafe can also be billed to your account. The charges will be itemized on your monthly statement and added to your regular monthly fee.**

To end the second paragraph,

Press: ⏎

Your display screen should be similar to Figure 2-2.

FIGURE 2-2

```
The Sports Club is offering a new program to all its members
which will save you writing a check each month. Upon your
authorization, the bank will send payment of your monthly charges
directly to the club. You will receive a copy of your monthly
statement to confirm the accuracy of your bill. If you are
interested in the automatic fee payment program, please contact
the accounting department to make the necessary arrangements
(931-4285 ext. 33).

The regular monthly membership fee is $45.00. Other expenses,
such as league and lesson fees, pro-shop purchases, and charges
at the Courtside Cafe can also be billed to your account. The
charges will be itemized on your monthly statement and added to
your regular monthly fee.
_
                                                Doc 1 Pg 1 Ln 3.33" Pos 1"
```

Check that you have entered the two paragraphs correctly. Do not be concerned if there is a difference in where WordPerfect decided to word wrap. If you find any errors, correct them using the editing features you learned in Lab 1.

Spell-Checking

It is always a good idea to check your spelling in a document when you are finished working on it. To help you do this quickly, WordPerfect has a built-in dictionary that checks for spelling errors. Additionally it will look for words which are incorrectly capitalized and duplicate words.

To enter several intentional errors in this document,

Change the spelling of "Sports" to "Sprots" in the first line.
Enter a second "new" after the word "new" in the first line.
Change the word "program" to "pROgram" in the first line.

Now you will check the spelling of your document. If you are running WordPerfect from a two-disk system, remove your data disk from drive B and insert the Speller disk. If you have a hard-disk system, WordPerfect will automatically access the spell-check program on your disk.

Begin by positioning the cursor at the top of the document so that the entire document will be checked.

Press: (PGUP)

To begin spell-checking,

Select: Tools>Spell
>> Spell (CTRL) - (F2)

The menu in the status line lets you specify how much of the document you want to check. You can spell-check a word, a page, or a whole document. To check the document,

Select: Document

Your screen should be similar to Figure 2-3.

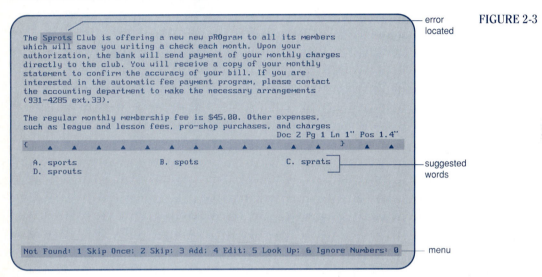

FIGURE 2-3

The Speller has encountered the first word which is not in its dictionary. The word "Sprots" is highlighted. The lower half of the screen lists four suggested replacements. The menu options in the status line have the following effect:

Skip Once   accepts the word as correct for this occurrence only

Skip   accepts the word as correct throughout the spell-check of this document

Add Word   adds the word to the **supplementary dictionary**. The Speller uses the supplementary dictionary as a secondary dictionary whenever it does not encounter the word in the main dictionary. When a word is added to the supplemental dictionary, the Speller will always accept the added word as correct.

Edit   positions the cursor on the word so you can change the spelling directly

Look Up   looks up words that match a pattern

Ignore Numbers   does not check the spelling of words containing numbers

To change the spelling of the word to one of the suggested spellings, press the letter corresponding to the correct word in the list.

Press: A

The Speller replaces the misspelled word with the selected replacement and moves on to locate the next error. The double word error has been located. The menu options in the status line have the following effect:

Skip	leaves the words as they are
Delete 2nd	deletes the second occurrence of the word
Edit	positions the cursor on the second duplicate word so you can edit it
Disable Double Word Checking	ignores double-occurring words for the rest of the document

To delete the second duplicate word,

Select: 3 Delete 2nd

The next error the Speller locates is the capitalization error. To edit the word,

Select: 4 Edit

Correct the word to "program."

To resume spell-checking,

Press: Exit (F7)

Finally the Speller stops on the word "Courtside." Although this is the correct spelling for the word, the Speller dictionary does not contain this word. To leave the word as it is in the document,

Select: 2 Skip

There should be no other misspelled words. However, if the speller encounters others in your file, correct them as needed. When no others are located the word count is displayed. To exit the spell-checker,

Press: Space bar

Note: Two-disk users: Remove the Speller disk from drive B and insert your data disk.

Saving a New File

Next Karen needs to retrieve the file containing the welcome letter and add the new paragraphs to it. But first she needs to save the current document to the diskette and clear the screen.

You could use the File>Save or (F10) command to save the revised document. But as you saw in the previous lab, this command returns you to the document. Since Karen does not want to keep working on the same file, she will save the file while clearing the screen by using the File>Exit or (F7) command.

The difference between the Save command and the Exit command is:

Save saves the document on the diskette and returns you to the current document.

Exit saves the document on the diskette, clears the document from the screen (and memory), and lets you either continue working with WordPerfect by retrieving or creating another document, or leave the program.

To save the two paragraphs on the screen to a file on the diskette, use the File>Exit or (F7) command.

Select: File>Exit
>> Exit (F7)

The prompt "Document to be saved:" appears in the status line. WordPerfect is prompting you to enter the name of the file. The file name should be descriptive of the contents of the file. It can consist of two parts.

The first part of the file name is required and can be up to eight characters long. There can be no spaces within it. If you want to use two words in the name, separate them with a hyphen or an underscore. You will use the file name AUTO-PAY.

The second part of the file name is the file extension. It can be up to three characters long and is separated from the first part of the file name by a period. It is not required. You will use the extension .DOC to show that this is a document file. The file name can be entered in either upper- or lowercase letters.

Type: AUTO-PAY.DOC
Press: ⏎

After a few moments the document is saved on the diskette and cleared from the screen. At this point you could leave the WordPerfect program by entering **Y** to the prompt, "Exit WP?." However, since you have a lot more to do, in response to the prompt,

Type: N

Next Karen will retrieve the welcome letter. A complete, corrected copy of the welcome letter is saved for you in a file named LETTER3.

Retrieve the file LETTER3 using either File>Retrieve (SHIFT) - (F10) or File>List Files (F5).

Combining Files

The welcome letter is displayed on the screen. After looking at the letter Karen decides she wants the two new paragraphs from the AUTO-PAY.DOC file to be entered following the third paragraph of the welcome letter.

Move to: Ln 4.17" Pos 1" (beginning of blank line separating paragraphs three and four)

The contents of two files can be combined easily be retrieving the second file without clearing the display screen of the current file. A copy of the contents of the retrieved file is entered at the location of the cursor into the document on the display screen.

To combine the text in the AUTO-PAY.DOC file with the current file (LETTER3) on the display, at the location of the cursor, retrieve the AUTO-PAY.DOC file using either File>Retrieve (SHIFT) - (F10) or File>List Files (F5). If you use List Files, respond Yes to the prompt in the status line to combine with the current document.

Your display screen should be similar to Figure 2-4.

FIGURE 2-4

```
Dear New Sports Club Member:

Congratulations on your new membership in the Sports Club. All of
us on the staff welcome you and encourage you to participate in
the many tournaments, leagues and club activities offered
throughout the year.

Each month you will receive a newsletter about the upcoming
events at the club. If you have questions about the event or
would like to sign up to participate in an event, just call or
come in to the front desk personnel.

The club facilities include 18 lighted tennis courts, 5
racquetball courts, an olympic size swimming pool, Nautilus
equipped weight room, and basketball court. For your comfort
while using the club, the men's and ladies' locker rooms each
have showers, a sauna, and a steam room. A spa for both men and
women is located between the locker rooms. The lounge and cafe
are open to serve you throughout the day and evening.
The Sports Club is offering a new program to all its members
which will save you writing a check each month. Upon your
authorization, the bank will send payment of your monthly charges
directly to the club. You will receive a copy of your monthly
statement to confirm the accuracy of your bill. If you are
B:\LETTER3                                    Doc 1 Pg 1 Ln 4.17" Pos 1"
```

AUTO-PAY.DOC text combined with LETTER3

The two paragraphs from the AUTO-PAY.DOC file have been inserted into the welcome letter at the location of the cursor.

To separate paragraphs 3 and 4 with a blank line,

Press: ⏎

To view the rest of the text, using the ↓ key,

Move to: Ln 8.17" Pos 1" (last line of letter)

Moving Text

After looking over the welcome letter Karen decides she would like to change the order of the paragraphs in the letter. She wants the paragraph about the automatic fee payment program (paragraph 4) to follow the paragraph about the monthly membership fees (paragraph 5).

A complete sentence, paragraph, or page of text can be moved by selecting Edit>Select from the menu or by using the Move (CTRL) - (F4) command. First the cursor must be positioned anywhere within the piece of text to be moved. You will place the cursor on the first character (T) of paragraph 4.

Move to: Ln 4.33" Pos 1" ("T" of "The" at beginning of paragraph 4)

Next, to use the pull-down menu to select the Move command,

Select: Edit>Select

There are three submenu options available for selection: Sentence, Paragraph, and Page. These options allow you to specify the area of text to be moved. To specify a paragraph,

Select: Paragraph

Your display screen should be similar to Figure 2-5.

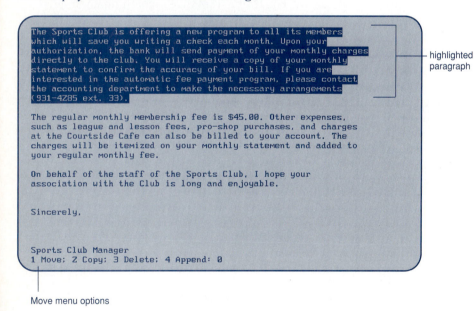

FIGURE 2-5

highlighted paragraph

Move menu options

The entire paragraph is highlighted. Only one sentence, paragraph, or page of text can be marked (highlighted) for moving at a time.

The status line now displays four more menu options: Move, Copy, Delete, and Append. They have the following meanings:

Move   allows you to remove the text from its present location so it can be moved to another location

Copy   leaves the original text and moves a duplicate to another location

Delete   permanently removes the text from the document

Append   lets you add the text to the end of a file on the disk

The default option, 0, displayed at the end of the menu, allows you to cancel the command. A menu option which appears in the status line is selected by typing the number to the left of the option you want to use or by typing the highlighted letter. Rather than select the Move option at this time, you will cancel your command selections. This will allow you to see how the Move command works when using the function key equivalent, (CTRL) - (F4).

Press: ⏎

To reposition the cursor within the paragraph to be moved,

Press: (↑) (2 times)

The cursor should be on Ln 5.55" Pos 1" (the "(" of the telephone number).
     To use the function key equivalent,

Press: (CTRL) - (F4)

The same three options, which let you specify the area of text to move (**S**entence, **P**aragraph, or Pa**g**e), appear in the status line.
     To specify the entire paragraph,

Select: Paragraph

Your screen should again look like Figure 2-5.

Now the same menu of four Move options appears in the status line. To continue the Move command by moving the paragraph from one location in the document to another, select Move as follows:

Select: **M**ove

The marked paragraph is removed from the document and is stored in temporary memory until needed. The text below the deleted paragraph moves up. The status line now directs you to move the cursor and press ⏎ to retrieve the text.
     You will reenter the paragraph below the paragraph on the monthly fees. To do this,

Move to: Ln 5.33" Pos 1" ("O" of "On")
Press: ⏎

Your display screen should be similar to Figure 2-6.

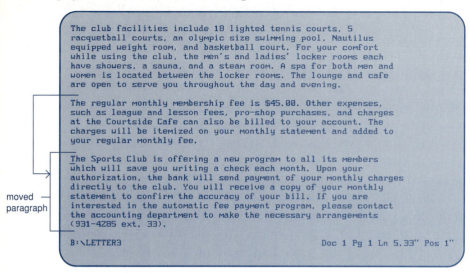

FIGURE 2-6

The marked paragraph is reentered into the document beginning at the cursor location. That was a lot quicker than retyping the whole paragraph!

Note: When the use of the function key command instruction requires a selection from a menu displayed in the status line, the instructions will appear separated by commas. For example: >> CTRL - F4, **2 P**aragraph, **1 M**ove.

Using the Block Command

Next Karen wants to move the telephone number of the accounting department. She wants it to follow the reference to the accounting department in the same sentence. Because the telephone number is not a complete sentence, paragraph, or page of text, the Move command cannot be used by itself. Instead it is used along with the Block command.

The Block (Edit>Block or ALT - F4) command is used to mark an area, or **block**, of text. A block of text can be as short as a single letter or as long as several pages of text. The marked text can then be acted upon by the Move command.

Before using the Block command, the cursor must be placed on the first character in the block of text to be moved. In this case it is the opening parenthesis surrounding the telephone number.

Move to: Ln 6.5" Pos 1" ("(" at beginning of telephone number)

To access the Block command,

Select: Edit>Block
 >> Block (ALT - F4)

Note: Dragging the mouse across text automatically turns on the Block feature. Therefore, if you use the mouse to specify a block of text, you do not need to select Edit>Block or press ALT - F4 first.

The message "Block on" flashes in the status line. This shows that the Block command is active. Next, the area of text to be moved must be identified. To do this the text is highlighted by moving the cursor using the cursor movement keys or dragging the mouse (hold down the left button while moving the mouse) to the end of the area of text to be moved. To highlight the telephone number, using → or dragging the mouse,

Move to: Ln 6.5" Pos 2.7" (")" of telephone number)

The highlight should cover the phone number through the closing parenthesis. The text to be moved is now defined. Once a block of text is defined many different WordPerfect commands can be used to manipulate the block. For example, it can be underlined, deleted, copied, or centered on the page.

Karen wants to move this block of text to another location in the document. To do this the Move (**E**dit>**M**ove or CTRL - F4) command is used.

Note: If you use CTRL - F4 to issue this command you will need to select an option from the menus displayed in the status line. The three options in the first menu let you specify the type of text to be moved. Since you defined a block of text you will select **B**lock. A second menu appears which lets you tell the program what you want to do with the block. Since you want to move a block, you will select **M**ove.

Select: **E**dit>**M**ove (Cut)
>> Move (CTRL - F4), **B**lock, **M**ove

Your display screen should be similar to Figure 2-7.

FIGURE 2-7

```
The club facilities include 18 lighted tennis courts, 5
racquetball courts, an olympic size swimming pool, Nautilus
equipped weight room, and basketball court. For your comfort
while using the club, the men's and ladies' locker rooms each
have showers, a sauna, and a steam room. A spa for both men and
women is located between the locker rooms. The lounge and cafe
are open to serve you throughout the day and evening.

The regular monthly membership fee is $45.00. Other expenses,
such as league and lesson fees, pro-shop purchases, and charges
at the Courtside Cafe can also be billed to your account. The
charges will be itemized on your monthly statement and added to
your regular monthly fee.

The Sports Club is offering a new program to all its members
which will save you writing a check each month. Upon your
authorization, the bank will send payment of your monthly charges
directly to the club. You will receive a copy of your monthly
statement to confirm the accuracy of your bill. If you are
interested in the automatic fee payment program, please contact
the accounting department to make the necessary arrangements
.
_
Move cursor; press Enter to retrieve.           Doc 1 Pg 1 Ln 6.5" Pos 1"
```

The block of text is temporarily removed from the document. It will remain in temporary memory until ⏎ is pressed.

As long as you do not press ⏎ you can do other simple editing tasks before completing the Move command. For instance, notice that there is a space left before the period at the cursor location. While the cursor is positioned properly, you can delete the space before using the Move command. To delete the space,

Press: BKSP

You can now move the cursor to the location where you want the block to appear. Karen wants it to follow the word "department."

Move to: Ln 6.33" Pos 3.5" (blank space after "department")

You are now ready to retrieve the block. To do this,

Press:

Your display screen should be similar to Figure 2-8.

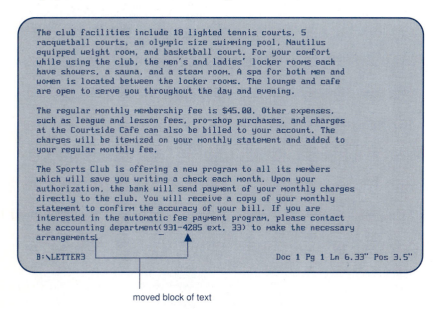

FIGURE 2-8

moved block of text

The telephone number for the accounting department now follows the reference to the department in the sentence.

To insert a space before the opening parenthesis of the telephone number,

Press: Space bar

After looking over the letter for a while, Karen decides she wants to make the following changes:

- enter the current date in the upper right-hand corner
- increase the margin width
- indent the first line of each paragraph
- replace the word "club" with "sports club"
- change the right margin to print ragged

You will follow Karen as she makes these changes to the Welcome letter.

WP62
Creating and Formatting
a Document

Using the Date Command

Karen wants the date to be entered on the first line of the letter. To move to the top of the letter and insert a blank line,

Press: (PGUP)
Press: ⏎
Press: ↑

A blank line has been inserted at the top of the letter where the date will be entered.

The Date command (Tools>Date Code or Date (SHIFT) - (F5), Date Code) inserts the current date into your document. The date inserted into the document is the date you entered when responding to the DOS date prompt.

To use the Date command,

Select: Tools
>> Date (SHIFT) - (F5)

The three date options in the Tools menu (or if you use the function key command, in the menu displayed in the status line) are:

Date Text   inserts the current date as text into your document

Date Code   inserts a WordPerfect code, which automatically updates the date whenever the file is retrieved or printed

Date Format   allows changes to the default date format display

The welcome letter will be mailed to new members as they join the club. Karen wants the current date automatically entered whenever the letter is printed. To do this, the Date Code option is used.

Select: Date Code

Your display screen should be similar to Figure 2-9.

FIGURE 2-9

current date →

```
March 20, 1992_
Dear New Sports Club Member:

Congratulations on your new membership in the Sports Club. All of
us on the staff welcome you and encourage you to participate in
the many tournaments, leagues and club activities offered
throughout the year.

Each month you will receive a newsletter about the upcoming
events at the club. If you have questions about the event or
would like to sign up to participate in an event, just call or
come in to the front desk personnel.

The club facilities include 18 lighted tennis courts, 5
racquetball courts, an olympic size swimming pool, Nautilus
equipped weight room, and basketball court. For your comfort
while using the club, the men's and ladies' locker rooms each
have showers, a sauna, and a steam room. A spa for both men and
women is located between the locker rooms. The lounge and cafe
are open to serve you throughout the day and evening.

The regular monthly membership fee is $45.00. Other expenses,
such as league and lesson fees, pro-shop purchases, and charges
at the Courtside Cafe can also be billed to your account. The
B:\LETTER3                                    Doc 1 Pg 1 Ln 1" Pos 2.4"
```

The current date is entered into the letter at the location of the cursor. It appears as text, not as a WordPerfect code. Whenever this file is retrieved or printed, the current system date will be displayed using this format. You will see shortly how the date is stored as a WordPerfect code.

Note: The date in Figure 2-9 will be different from the date that appears on your display. If you did not enter the current date at the DOS prompt, then the default system date will be used.

Aligning Text Flush with the Right Margin

Next Karen wants the date to end against the right margin or to be **flush right**. The Flush Right command (Layout>Align>Flush Right or Flush Right (ALT) - (F6)) is used to do this. For this command to work correctly the cursor must first be positioned on the first character of the text to be moved and there must be a hard carriage return at the end of the existing line of text. To position the cursor at the beginning of the date,

Press: ⟵

Because the date is a WordPerfect code rather than text you entered character by character, the program considers the date a single character, and the cursor jumps quickly to Ln 1" Pos 1".

To move the date flush with the right margin and reformat the display, using the pull-down menu,

Select: Layout

The Layout menu options affect the design of the document. We will be using many of these options shortly. The Align option controls the placement of text on a line.

Select: Align

Your screen should be similar to Figure 2-10.

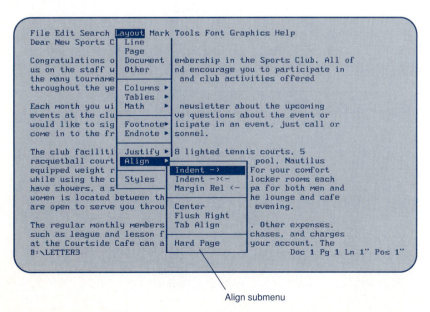

FIGURE 2-10

Align submenu

There are three submenu options which affect the placement of text on a line: Center, Flush Right, and Tab Align. To align the text located to the right of the cursor flush with the right margin,

Select: Flush Right

To reformat the display of the line,

Press: ⬇

Your display screen should be similar to Figure 2-11.

FIGURE 2-11

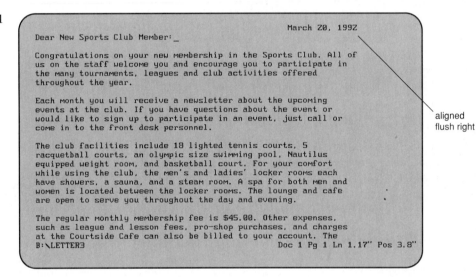

aligned flush right

The date has moved flush with the right margin.

The function key command equivalent is simply Flush Right (ALT) - (F6). In this case, using the function key would be quicker than using the pull-down menus.

The Flush Right command can also be used before typing in new text that you want aligned with the right margin. As you type the text it is entered so that the last character in the line is even with the right margin.

Next Karen wants the date separated from the salutation by four blank lines. To move to the beginning of line 2 and insert four blank lines between the date line and the salutation,

Press: HOME
Press: ⬅
Press: ⏎ (4 times)

The salutation begins on line 1.83".

Setting Margins

Karen would like to change the right and left margin widths from 1 inch (the default setting) to 1-1/2 inches. To change the left and right margin widths of a document, the Line Format (Layout>Line or Format (SHIFT) - (F8)) command is used. The new margin setting must be entered at the beginning of the document so that the entire document below the setting will be formatted to the new margin specifications.

To position the cursor at the top of the document,

Press: (PGUP)

This time, you will use the function key command to set the margins.

Press: Format (SHIFT) - (F8)

Your display screen should be similar to Figure 2-12.

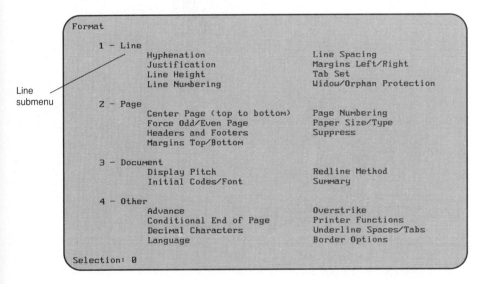

FIGURE 2-12

The document is replaced by a full-screen menu. This menu is divided into four submenus: 1 Line, 2 Page, 3 Document, and 4 Other. Below each submenu the options for that submenu are listed.

The Line, Page, and Other submenu options change the settings from the point they are entered into the document forward. The Document submenu options change the settings for the entire document.

The command to set margins is an option in the Line submenu.

Select: Line

Your display screen should be similar to Figure 2-13.

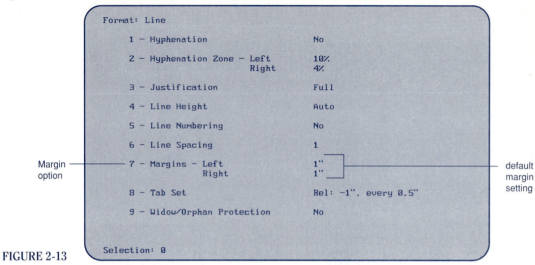

FIGURE 2-13

The Line Format menu is displayed. The left side of the menu lists the 9 options which affect line endings, spacing, numbering, length, and tabs. The right column displays the current settings, in this case the default settings, for each option. The Margins option lets you specify new left and right margins. The default margin settings provide 1 inch of space from the left and right edge of the paper.

Select: Margins

The cursor jumps to the right column under the setting for the left margin. The margin setting can be entered as a decimal or as a fraction. To change the left margin setting to 1-1/2 inches, you could enter either 1.5 or 1 1/2.

Type: 1.5
Press: ⏎

The cursor moves to the right margin setting. To change the right margin,

Type: 1 1/2
Press: ⏎

WordPerfect converts the fraction to a decimal.
   If you wanted you could continue to select other Line Format options. However, Karen first wants to see how the document has changed with the new margin settings. To quickly leave the Line Format menu and return directly to the document, use the Exit command, (F7).

Press: Exit (F7)

The left margin now begins at Pos 1.5"; however, the right margin has not adjusted to the new right margin setting. To reformat the display of text on the screen,

Press: (HOME)
Press: ↓

Your display screen should be similar to Figure 2-14.

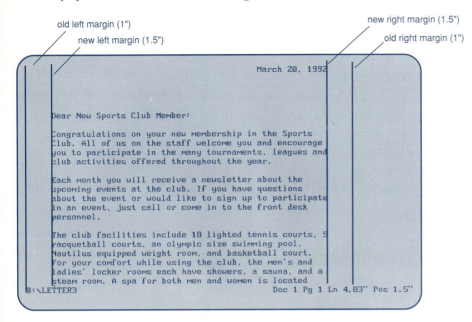

FIGURE 2-14

The letter has been reformatted to fit within the new margin settings.
    To return to the top of the letter,

Press: HOME
Press: ↑

Using and Setting Tabs

Next Karen wants to indent the first line of each paragraph and the closing. The **Tab** key lets you easily indent text on a line. WordPerfect has set the default tab setting at every half inch. As with other default settings, the Tab spacing can also be set to your needs. The Line Format command, (Layout>Line or (SHIFT) - (F8), Line), is used to view and set tabs.

Select: Layout>Line
  >> Format (SHIFT) - (F8) Line

The Line Format menu is displayed. To display the current tab settings,

Select: Tab Set

Your display screen should be similar to Figure 2-15.

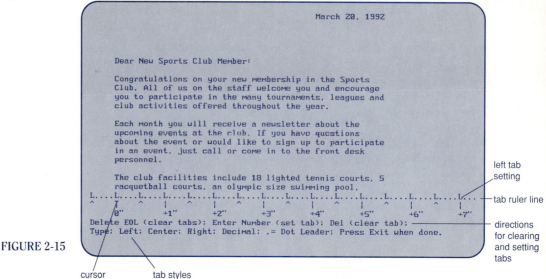

FIGURE 2-15

A Tab Ruler line is displayed at the bottom of the screen. The "L" marks the location of each tab stop from the left margin. The cursor can be moved along the ruler line using → and ←. For Help information about tabs,

Press: Help F3

Your screen should be similar to Figure 2-16.

FIGURE 2-16

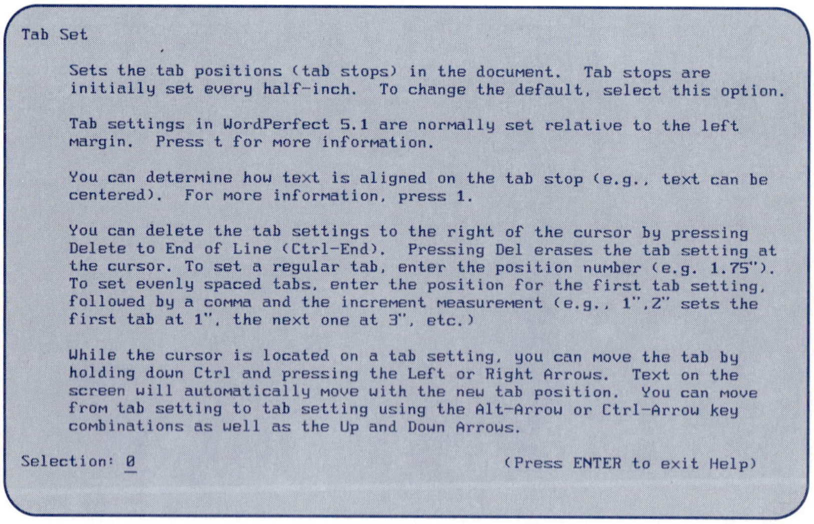

After reading the information on this screen about how to clear and set tabs, following the directions on the screen to obtain more information about tab styles,

Type: 1

This information describes the four styles or types of tabs you can create using the Tab menu.

To return to the document,

Press: ⏎

To review, the basic procedures for clearing and setting tabs are:

- Clear an individual tab setting by placing the cursor on the tab stop and pressing (DEL).
- Clear multiple tab settings by placing the cursor on the first tab stop to be deleted and using (CTRL) - (END) to delete all tab stops from the cursor to the right.
- Enter new left tab settings by moving the cursor to the tab stop and typing L, or by entering the number.

However, Karen is satisfied with the default tab settings and does not want to make any changes. To leave the settings as they are and return to the document,

Press: Cancel (F1) (3 times)

To indent the first line of the first paragraph,

Move to: Ln 2.17" Pos 1.5" (on "C" in "Congratulations")
Press: (TAB)

Your display screen should be similar to Figure 2-17.

```
                                    March 20, 1992



             Dear New Sports Club Member:

indented         Congratulations on your new membership in the Sports
1 tab stop   Club. All of us on the staff welcome you and encourage
(.5")        you to participate in the many tournaments, leagues and
             club activities offered throughout the year.

             Each month you will receive a newsletter about the
             upcoming events at the club. If you have questions
             about the event or would like to sign up to participate
             in an event, just call or come in to the front desk
             personnel.

             The club facilities include 18 lighted tennis courts, 5
             racquetball courts, an olympic size swimming pool,
             Nautilus equipped weight room, and basketball court.
             For your comfort while using the club, the men's and
             ladies' locker rooms each have showers, a sauna, and a
             steam room. A spa for both men and women is located
         B:\LETTER3                          Doc 1 Pg 1 Ln 2.17" Pos 2"
```

FIGURE 2-17

The first line is indented.

In a similar manner, indent the first lines of the next five paragraphs. Notice as you move down through the text that each paragraph is automatically reformatted.

To indent the closing lines,

Move to:	Ln 9.17" Pos 1.5" (on "S" in "Sincerely")
Press:	(TAB) (7 times)
Move to:	Ln 9.83" Pos 1.5" (on "S" of "Sports")
Press:	(TAB) (7 times)
Press:	(↓)

Notice that the last line of the letter is on the last line of the page. Karen feels this does not look good and decides to reset the right and left margins back to the default setting of 1 inch.

Displaying Hidden Codes

Press: (PGUP)

Karen could reset the margins using the Line Format menu. There is another way, however, to return the margins to their original settings.

WordPerfect places hidden **codes** in the document whenever a feature is used that controls the format and display of the document. The codes consist of symbols that tell WordPerfect and the printer what to do. When the program reads the code, it reformats all the text in the document from that point on to the new setting. The codes are hidden so that your document on the display screen looks as close as possible to the text as it will appear when printed. Because the codes are hidden, your display is not cluttered.

The code is entered into the document at the location of the cursor when the command is issued. WordPerfect lets you see the hidden codes in the document so that you can remove the codes you no longer want or need. To see the hidden codes, use the Reveal Codes command (Edit>Reveal Codes or Reveal Codes (ALT)-(F3)).

Select:	**E**dit>**R**eveal Codes
>>	Reveal Codes (ALT)-(F3)

Your display screen should be similar to Figure 2-18.

WP71
Displaying Hidden Codes

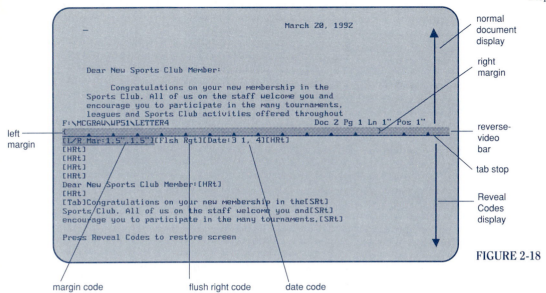

FIGURE 2-18

The screen is divided into two windows by a reverse-video bar, which shows the left ({) and right (}) margins and tab (^) settings. The upper window displays the document as it normally appears. The lower window displays the same text with the hidden codes revealed. This is the Reveal Codes screen. The codes are always displayed in brackets ([]).

The first code displayed in the Reveal Codes screen is [L/R Mar: 1.5",1.5"]. This code controls the left and right margin settings. The first part of the code is an abbreviation of the command used. The selected settings are displayed next. Since the cursor is on this code, it is highlighted.

The next code [Flsh Rgt] is the Flush Right code which aligns the date flush with the right margin. The code [Date:3 1, 4] tells the program to enter the current date into the document. The last code [HRt] stands for a hard carriage return. This code is entered whenever you press ⏎ .

To delete a code, the (BKSP) or (DEL) key is used. The (BKSP) key will delete codes to the left of the cursor, and the (DEL) key will delete codes the cursor is highlighting.

Karen wants to delete the margin code. Since this code is highlighted, to remove it,

Press: (DEL)

Your display screen should be similar to Figure 2-19.

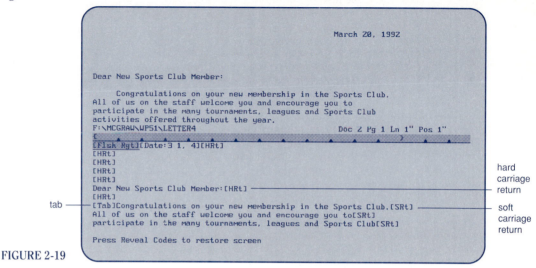

FIGURE 2-19

The code is deleted from the document. When a code is deleted, the document acts as if the code had never been entered. The removal of the margin code causes the margin settings to return to the default settings of one inch. Look in the upper window and you can see that the text is now displayed using the new margin settings.

A code also can be deleted from the document while you are in normal document display mode. That is, you do not have to use the Reveal Codes screen to remove codes. However, if you have forgotten where the code was entered in the text, then it is best to use the Reveal Codes screen while deleting codes. In either display mode, first move the cursor to the location of the code in the document. Then use (BKSP) to delete codes to the left of the cursor and (DEL) to delete codes the cursor is highlighting.

Let's look at the other codes displayed in the Reveal Codes screen. Each of the blank lines between the date and salutation is coded with the [HRt] symbol. The code that tells WordPerfect to indent the paragraph is [Tab]. At the end of each line of the first paragraph a [SRt] code is displayed. This code identifies the location of a **soft carriage return**. As WordPerfect reformats the text on the screen, it enters a [SRt] code at the end of a line. This code shows the location where WordPerfect decided to automatically word wrap to the next line.

When the Reveal Codes screen is in use you can type characters or use any WordPerfect features. The text in the Reveal Codes screen may not wrap the same as the text in the document Editing screen, however. This is because it contains the format codes.

To return to normal document display and hide the codes again, you must reselect the Reveal Codes command. To do this quickly using the function key command,

Press: Reveal Codes (ALT) - (F3)

To see where the letter ends on the page,

Press: (HOME) (HOME) (↓)

As you can see, because the margin widths were decreased, more text can be displayed on a line. Consequently, the last line of the letter is now on Ln 9".

Press: `PGUP`

Searching and Replacing Text

Next Karen wants to find all occurrences of the word "club" in the letter and change it to "Sports Club" where appropriate. The Replace (Search>Replace or Replace `ALT` - `F2`) command will help do this quickly. You will use the pull-down menu to perform this task.

Select: Search

Your screen should be similar to Figure 2-20.

FIGURE 2-20

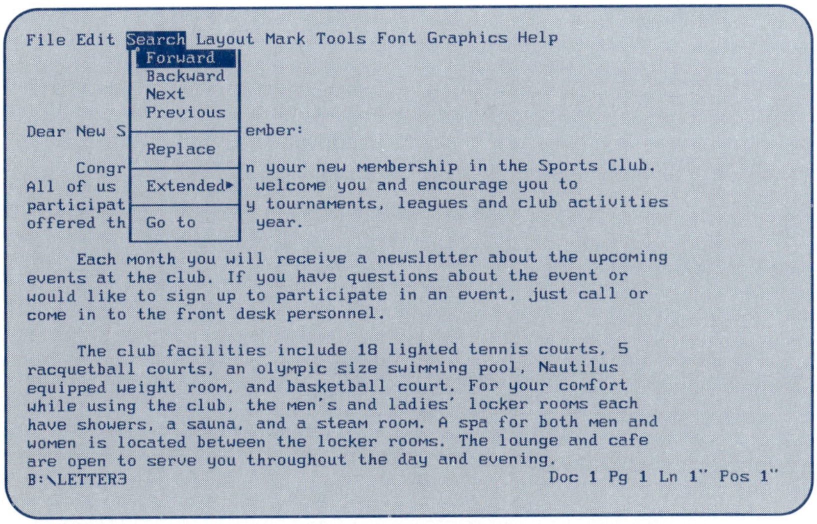

WordPerfect has several commands for **searching** through a file to find a **string**, or specific combination of characters and/or codes. The first two Search menu options, Forward and Backward, move the cursor either forward or backward through the document to locate the first occurrence of the combination of letters, characters or numbers specified. The function key equivalent to the Search>Forward command is Search (`F2`), and for the Search>Backward command it is Search (`SHIFT`) - (`F2`).

The second two options, Next and Previous, tell the program to continue the search by moving to the next occurrence or to the previous occurrence of the matching string.

The next Search menu option, Replace, moves the cursor forward through a document to locate the specified string and replaces it with another. You cannot use Replace to search backward through the text.

Replace is the command Karen wants to use.

Select: Replace

The prompt "W/Confirm? No (Yes)" is displayed in the status line. If you respond **Yes** to the prompt, WordPerfect will display the matching string and ask for confirmation before replacing it. If you respond **No**, WordPerfect will automatically replace every occurrence of the word with the new string.

To selectively replace the word,

Type: Y

The "—> Srch:" prompt is displayed on the status line. The word or phrase you want to find is entered following the prompt. When entering the search string, lowercase letters will match both upper- and lowercase letters in the text. However, if you enter the search string in uppercase letters, only uppercase matches will be found. After entering the search string, do not press ⏎.

Type: club

Next, to search forward in the document,

Press: Search (F2)

The prompt "Replace with" is displayed next. If no replacement string were entered at this prompt, the word "club" would be deleted at every occurrence. You want to replace "club" with "Sports Club." The replacement string must be entered exactly as you want it to appear in your document. Do not press ⏎ after typing the replace string.

Type: Sports Club
Press: Search (F2)

Your display screen should be similar to Figure 2-21.

FIGURE 2-21

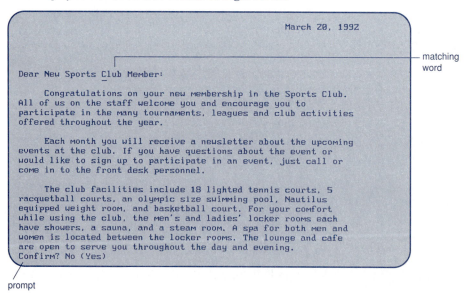

Immediately the cursor moves to the first word matching the search string "club." Notice that the cursor is positioned on "Club." This is because the search string was entered in all lowercase letters, and WordPerfect does not distinguish between upper- and lowercase letters when searching the text for matching strings.

The prompt "Confirm? No (Yes)" is displayed in the Status line. The first occurrence is acceptable as it is (you do not want to replace it),

Type: N (or press ⏎)

The cursor skips to the next occurrence of the word "club" and waits for your response. Again, it is already correct.

Type: N

The cursor moves to the third occurrence of the word "club" and waits for your response. This time Karen wants to replace it with "Sports Club."

Type: Y

The word "club" is replaced with the word "Sports Club." The cursor moves to the next match. Respond to the remaining prompts to replace "club" with "Sports Club" when needed. When no more matches are located the search ends.

Setting Justification

On the screen the welcome letter has even left margins and uneven, or ragged right, margins. But, as you noted at the end of Lab 1, when the letter is printed the text is aligned evenly with both the left and right margin settings. This is called **justification**. To justify text, WordPerfect inserts extra spaces between some of the words on a line to force the line to end even with the right margin setting. Printing a document so that the text aligns against the right and left margins is the default setting in WordPerfect.

Karen wants the welcome letter to be printed with ragged right margins (as it is displayed on the screen). The command to change justification is on the Line Format menu (Layout>Line or Format (SHIFT) - (F8), Line). Using this command inserts a code in the document to control the printing of the text. The code should be entered at the beginning of the document so that the entire letter will be printed with a ragged right margin. If it is not entered at the beginning of the document, the new justification setting will begin at the cursor location and will continue until you insert another code that changes the setting.

To move the cursor to the beginning of the welcome letter and to display the Line Format menu,

Press: (PGUP)
Select: Layout>Line
   >> Format (SHIFT) - (F8), Line

The default justification setting is Full, meaning that both the left and right margins are aligned or justified.

Select: Justification

WP76
Creating and Formatting a Document

The Justify menu at the bottom of the screen displays four justification settings. They have the following effect:

Left	aligns text against left margin, leaving right margin ragged
Center	centers each line of text between the left and right margins
Right	aligns text against right margin, leaving left margin ragged
Full	aligns text against the right and left margins

To change justification to have even left margins and ragged right margins,

Select: Left

The new justification setting "Left" is displayed in the Format Line menu.
To quickly exit the Format Line menu and return to the document,

Press: Exit (F7)

Nothing looks different on the screen. But when the document is printed the right margin will be uneven, as it is displayed.

Note: The pull-down menu option, Layout>Justify, also lets you set the justification of text in your document. It has the same four choices and produces the same effect as using Layout>Line>Justify.

Printing the Document

To print a copy of the welcome letter,

Select: **F**ile>**P**rint
>> Print (SHIFT) - (F7)

The Print menu is displayed.
Let's take a moment to look at the Print options you have not used yet. The second option, Binding Offset, allows you to move the printed document to the right or left side of the paper to allow space for binding. The current setting of 0" is the default. The third option, Number of Copies, allows you to print multiple copies of a document. The default is to print 1 copy. The fourth option, Multiple Copies Generated by, is an option used by some laser printers to print more than one copy of the current print job. The default (1) lets WordPerfect control the number of copies. The last two options, Graphics Quality and Text Quality, allow you to set the quality level at which the graphics or text are printed. The lower quality settings produce a "rough" copy and print faster. The default settings for these options are displayed in the right column.
If necessary, use the Select Printer option to select the printer which is appropriate for your computer system.
To print the letter Karen could select either Full Text or Page from the Print menu, since the welcome letter is only one page long. If the text were longer than a single page, selecting Page would print only the page the cursor is positioned on.

Select: **P**age

Your printed letter should be similar to Figure 2-22.

FIGURE 2-22

WP77
Saving the Document in a New File

```
                                                  March 20, 1992

Dear New Sports Club Member:

     Congratulations on your new membership in the Sports Club.
All of us on the staff welcome you and encourage you to
participate in the many tournaments, leagues and Sports Club
activities offered throughout the year.

     Each month you will receive a newsletter about the upcoming
events at the Sports Club. If you have questions about the event
or would like to sign up to participate in an event, just call or
come in to the front desk personnel.

     The Sports Club facilities include 18 lighted tennis courts,
5 racquetball courts, an olympic size swimming pool, Nautilus
equipped weight room, and basketball court. For your comfort
while using the Sports Club, the men's and ladies' locker rooms
each have showers, a sauna, and a steam room. A spa for both men
and women is located between the locker rooms. The lounge and
cafe are open to serve you throughout the day and evening.

     The regular monthly membership fee is $45.00. Other
expenses, such as league and lesson fees, pro-shop purchases, and
charges at the Courtside Cafe can also be billed to your account.
The charges will be itemized on your monthly statement and added
to your regular monthly fee.

     The Sports Club is offering a new program to all its members
which will save you writing a check each month. Upon your
authorization, the bank will send payment of your monthly charges
directly to the Sports Club. You will receive a copy of your
monthly statement to confirm the accuracy of your bill. If you
are interested in the automatic fee payment program, please
contact the accounting department (931-4285 ext. 33) to make the
necessary arrangements.

     On behalf of the staff of the Sports Club, I hope your
association with the Sports Club is long and enjoyable.

                                                  Sincerely,


                                                  Sports Club Manager
```

Saving the Document in a New File

Karen would like to save the edited version of the welcome letter that is displayed on the screen in a new file named LETTER4. This will allow the original file, LETTER3, to remain unchanged on the diskette in case you would like to repeat the lab for practice. She is also ready to exit the WordPerfect program. To both save the document and exit the program, use the **File>Exit** (Exit (F7)) command.

Select: File>Exit
  >>   Exit (F7)

To respond Yes to the prompt to save the document,

Press: ⏎

To enter the new file name following the "Document to be Saved:" prompt,

Type: LETTER4
Press: ⏎

    The revised letter has been saved on the disk as LETTER4. The printer specifications which were active when the file was saved were also saved with this file. If you were to retrieve this file again, the printer you made active would appear on the Print screen as the selected printer.

    To indicate you are ready to exit the WordPerfect program,

Type: Y

KEY TERMS

word wrap
supplementary dictionary
block
flush right
code

soft carriage return
search
string
justification

MATCHING

1. word wrap —— a. saves file and resumes edit
2. F10 —— b. automatic adjustment of words on a line
3. [HRt] —— c. displays the Line Format menu
4. CTRL-F4 —— d. turns on the Block feature
5. ALT-F6 —— e. moves the cursor a set number of spaces
6. SHIFT-F5 —— f. displays the Date menu
7. margin —— g. hidden code for hard carriage return
8. TAB —— h. displays the Move menu
9. SHIFT-F8 —— i. border of white space around the printed document
10. ALT-F4 —— j. moves text flush with the right margin

PRACTICE EXERCISES

1. This problem will give you practice in creating, combining, and rearranging text.

- Enter the first paragraph from the "Overview to WordProcessing" into a WordPerfect document.
- Save the file as OVER-WP.
- Combine the text in the file DEF-WP (on your data diskette) with your file OVER-WP. The text in the file DEF-WP should be entered at the end of the text in OVER-WP.
- Rearrange the paragraphs in the text so they are in numerical order.
- Rearrange the order of sentence 4. It should read, " The grouping of text data to form words, sentences, paragraphs and pages of text results in the creation of a document."
- Set the justification to have a ragged right margin.
- Enter your name on the last line of the document.
- Print the document.
- Save this new document as OVER-WP.REV.

2. You are the public relations assistant at the local zoo and you are working on a news release about the various fund-raising activities at the zoo.

- Enter the three paragraphs below. Save the file as EVENTS, but do not exit the file. Print the file.

    The zoo Wine Tasting Event is sponsored by the zoo Wine Tasting Society. The second annual event was a 1978 Cabernet Sauvignon tasting party. It raised $3,600 to top off the Roadrunner Exhibit campaign.

    The Aid-to-Zoo National Horse Show is the major fund-raising activity of the Friends of the zoo Auxiliary. This event has raised funds for numerous exhibits throughout the zoo, including the Nocturnal Exhibit, Elephant Exhibit, Galapagos Exhibit, and the Graphic Signage and Deer Exhibit in the Children's zoo. Proceeds from the 1992 Horse Show exceeded $100,000, and were directed toward the Educational Graphics Exhibit.

    The Black-Tie Ball, an annual event held under the stars at the zoo, is sponsored by the men's Wildest Club in Town. Proceeds from the 1992 Black-Tie Ball amounted to $24,000 and are earmarked for architectural drawings for a proposed Bear Exhibit. Past proceeds have gone toward such projects as the Animal Nursery in the Children's zoo.

- Combine the text in the file ZOOFARI (on your data diskette) with the current file. The text in this file should be inserted below the second paragraph. There should be a blank line between paragraphs.
- Change the order of the paragraphs so that the first paragraph is about the Horse Show event, the second paragraph is about the Black-Tie Ball event, the third paragraph is about the Wine Tasting event, and the last

paragraph is about the Zoo-Fari. Again, there should be a blank line between paragraphs.

- Find and replace all occurrences of the word "zoo" with "Zoo".
- Enter your name on line 1 and the current date using the Date command on line 2. Leave one blank line below the date.
- Print the completed document. Save and replace the file as EVENTS. Exit WordPerfect.

3. You are the managing director of the local zoo. Every quarter you need to update the zoo Advisory Board about the current status of the zoo.

- Enter the memo below using margin settings of Left = 1.2", Right = 1.6", Tabs of 1.7" and 2.2" only, and justification left.

```
TO:       Advisory Board
FROM:     [Your Name], Managing Director
DATE:     [Enter current date using Date command]
```

One year after creating a Marketing Department, we are seeing excellent results. We are not budgeting for advertising, and our public relations, promotions, and publications are rapidly improving. With this boost in our profile, we believe that 912,500 attendance figure is within reach and we hope to cross 1,000,000 mark soon.

The major construction project for this quarter continues to be the new Children's Zoo. We expect completion of the project in the next quarter. It has been the largest construction project since our opening twenty-five years ago. Every department at the Zoo has helped in its planning and construction. We are looking forward to its opening scheduled for next quarter.

The other major project this quarter has been the updating of the Zoo Master Plan. The architectural firm and the Society Board have produced a well thought out plan to guide us through the next decade. We hope to begin the renovation of the Arizona exhibit using these guidelines in the next quarter.

The animal inventory has increased this quarter making our collection to this date 292 specimens from 1,280 species. Our collection is well-cared for and its health is excellent. Our breeding success is above normal and our animals enjoy an excellent quality of life, a reflection of our feeding and veterinary programs.

This quarter has been very productive and exciting as we near the completion of the Children's Zoo project.

WP81
Practice Exercises

- Indent each paragraph 1 tab stop.
- Delete the second sentence in the second paragraph using the Move command.
- The animal inventory figures in the fourth paragraph are incorrect. They should be switched to be "1,280 specimens from 292 species." Use the Block/Move command to make these changes.
- Print the memo. Save the file as STATUS.

4. In this problem you will create and format a document.

   - Clear the screen for creation of a new document.
   - Set justification to ragged right.
   - Set margins to left = 2" and right = 1.5".
   - Clear all tab settings. Enter new tab settings of .5" and 3" (save with Exit (F7)).
   - Enter the letter below as follows:

   Begin the letter approximately 2.17" from the top of the page.
   Enter the current date using the Date command.
   Display the date flush with the right margin.
   Enter the letter using the approximate line values as a guide.
   Indent each paragraph 5 spaces.
   Closing begins approximately on position 6.33".
   Use your name in the closing.

(Ln 2.17")   Current Date

(Ln 2.83")   Ms. Peg Mitchell
                  Admissions Department
                  Arizona State University
                  Tempe, AZ 85257

(Ln 3.67")   Dear Ms. Mitchell:

(Ln 4")   Thank you for taking the time to speak with me yesterday about the possibility of employment in your department.

                           I feel my professional background in personnel services and my educational background in higher education would meet many of your requirements.

                           I am enclosing a complete resume and hope that if a position becomes available in the near future you will consider my credentials.

(Ln 6.33")   Sincerely,

(Ln 7.0")   (your name)

WP82
Creating and Formatting
a Document

- Reveal hidden codes.
- Delete the previous margin setting code.
- Enter new margin settings of left = 1.5", right = 1.5".
- Print the letter.
- Save the letter using the file name JOB.

LAB

Merging and Refining Documents

3

CASE STUDY

Karen Barnes, the membership assistant, submitted the final copy of the welcome letter to the membership coordinator. The membership coordinator is very pleased with the content and form of the welcome letter. However he would like it to be more personalized. He wants to include the first name of the new member and an inside address. Karen will create a form letter using WordPerfect's Merge feature to personalize each welcome letter.

As a second project, he would like Karen to write an article for the club newsletter about the new automatic fee payment program. You will follow Karen as she works on these two projects.

The Merge Feature

Boot the system and if necessary, enter the current date at the DOS date prompt. Load the WordPerfect program.
    Retrieve the file WELCOME.
This is the same as the welcome letter you saved as LETTER4 in Lab 2. Notice that the date in the letter is the same as the system date you entered at the DOS prompt. Each time this letter is retrieved or printed, the date will display the system date. This is because of the date code you entered in the document.
    Karen needs to change the welcome letter so that each letter sent to a new member is more personal. The welcome letter will include the new member's first name in the salutation and his or her full name and address as the inside address. To do this Karen will use the Merge feature of WordPerfect.
    The Merge feature will combine a list of names and addresses that are contained in one file with a form letter in another file. The names and addresses are

OBJECTIVES

In this lab you will learn how to:

1. Use the Merge command.
2. Create primary and the secondary merge files.
3. Merge the primary and secondary files.
4. Center, boldface, and underline text.
5. Open two document files.
6. Create a split screen or open a window.
7. Move text between two documents.
8. Define newspaper-style columns.
9. Reformat the screen display.
10. Use the View Document command.
11. Change justification.
12. Use the Hyphenation feature.
13. Save and exit two document files.

WP83

entered (merged) into the form letter in the blank spaces provided. The result is a personalized form letter.

Merge usually requires the use of two files: a **primary file** and a **secondary merge file**. The primary file contains the basic form letter. It directs the merge process through the use of **merge codes**. The merge codes control what information is used from the secondary merge file and where it is entered in the document in the primary file. The welcome letter will be modified to be the primary file.

The secondary merge file, sometimes called an **address file**, contains the information needed to complete the form letter in the primary file. It will contain the new member's name and address data. Each piece of information in the secondary merge file is called a **field**. For example, the member's full name is a field of data, the street address is another field of data, the city a third field of data, and so forth. All the fields of data that are needed to complete the primary document are called a **record**.

The secondary file you will create will contain the following fields of information for each record: Full Name, Street Address, City, State, Zipcode, and First Name. WordPerfect takes the field information from the secondary merge file and combines or merges it into the primary file.

First Karen will modify the welcome letter to accept information from the secondary merge file. Then she will create the secondary merge file, which will hold the new members' names and addresses to be entered into the primary file.

Entering Merge Codes in the Primary File

The welcome letter needs to be modified to allow entry of the name and address information for each new member from the secondary merge file. The inside address will hold the following three lines of information:

>   Full Name
>   Street Address
>   City State Zipcode

The first line of the inside address, which will hold the new member's full name, will be entered as line 5 of the welcome letter.

Move to: Ln 1.67" Pos 1" (blank line above salutation)

How will WordPerfect know to enter the member's full name from the secondary file at this location in the primary file? WordPerfect uses a series of codes, called merge codes, which direct the program to accept information from the secondary merge file at the specified location in the primary file. To display the menu of merge codes use the Tools>Merge Codes or (SHIFT) - (F9) command.

Select: Tools>Merge Codes
  >> **Merge Codes** (SHIFT) - (F9)

Your display screen should be similar to Figure 3-1.

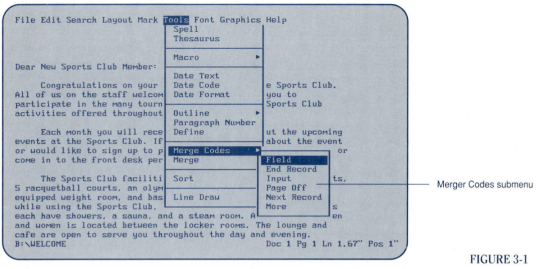

FIGURE 3-1

The Merge Codes submenu (displayed in the status line if you used the function key) consists of five commonly used merge codes. The sixth option, More, allows you to select other merge codes not listed on the menu.

The Merge Codes submenu options have the following meanings:

Field	identifies the field to be inserted from the secondary document into the primary document
End Record	marks the end of a record in the secondary file
Input	stops the merge and waits for keyboard input
Page Off	instructs WordPerfect not to place page breaks after each primary file
Next Record	instructs WordPerfect to move to the next secondary file record during the merge

A Field merge code needs to be entered in the primary file for each field of data you want copied from the secondary file. The location of the Field merge code directs WordPerfect where to enter the data. The cursor is positioned on the line where the new member's full name will appear as the first line of the inside address. The first field you will identify, then, is the Full Name field.

Select: Field

The prompt "Enter field:" is displayed in the status line. Following the prompt you must enter the name you want to assign to the first Field merge code. A field name should be short and descriptive of the contents of the field. You will use the field name "Name."

Type: Name
Press: ⏎

WP86
Merging and
Refining Documents

Your display screen should be similar to Figure 3-2.

FIGURE 3-2

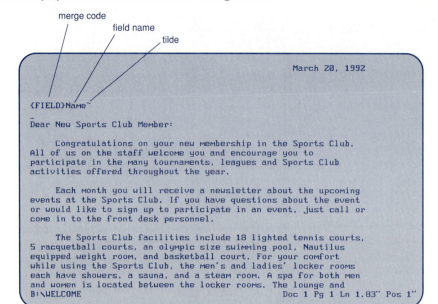

The Field merge code, {FIELD}, followed by the name you assigned the field is displayed at the cursor location. The ~ (tilde) at the end of the field name tells WordPerfect where the field name ends. When the command to merge the documents is used, the information for the new member's full name from the secondary merge file will be entered at this location in the primary file.

The next line of the inside address will contain the street address. To create and move to the next line,

Press: ⏎

To enter the Field merge code for the street address,

Select: Tools>Merge Codes>Field
>> Merge Codes (SHIFT) - (F9), Field

This time, in response to the field name prompt,

Type: Address
Press: ⏎

The second Field merge code is displayed in the welcome letter.

The next line of the inside address will display three fields of data from the secondary file: city, state, and zipcode. They will be identified by the field names City, State, and Zip.

Press: ⏎

To enter the merge code for the next field of data,

Select: Tools>Merge Codes>Field
  >> Merge Codes (SHIFT) - (F9), Field

Type: City
Press: ⏎

To separate the City field from the next field,

Press: Space bar

The State field will be entered on the same line as the City field.

Select: Tools>Merge Codes>Field
  >> Merge Codes (SHIFT) - (F9), Field
Type: State
Press: ⏎

To separate the State field from the next field, Zipcode, and enter the field name,

Press: Space bar (2 times)
Select: Tools>Merge Codes>Field
  >> Merge Codes (SHIFT) - (F9), Field
Type: Zip
Press: ⏎

To enter a blank line between the inside address and the salutation,

Press: ⏎

Your display screen should be similar to Figure 3-3.

```
                                                        March 20, 1992

{FIELD}Name~
{FIELD}Address~
{FIELD}City~, {FIELD}State~ {FIELD}Zip~

Dear New Sports Club Member:

    Congratulations on your new membership in the Sports Club.
All of us on the staff welcome you and encourage you to
participate in the many tournaments, leagues and Sports Club
activities offered throughout the year.

    Each month you will receive a newsletter about the upcoming
events at the Sports Club. If you have questions about the event
or would like to sign up to participate in an event, just call or
come in to the front desk personnel.

    The Sports Club facilities include 18 lighted tennis courts,
5 racquetball courts, an olympic size swimming pool, Nautilus
equipped weight room, and basketball court. For your comfort
while using the Sports Club, the men's and ladies' locker rooms
B:\WELCOME                                 Doc 1 Pg 1 Ln 2.17" Pos 1"
```

FIGURE 3-3

The merge codes to enter the inside address data from the secondary merge file are now complete. If you have made an error, you can edit the merge codes just like any other text entry.

The last field of information (field 6) that needs to be entered in the primary file is the new member's first name in the salutation. First the words "New Sports Club Member" need to be deleted.

Move to: Ln 2.33" Pos 1.5" ("N" of "New")
Press: CTRL - END

To enter the merge code for the first name (field 6) into the salutation,

Select: Tools>Merge Codes>Field
 >> Merge Codes (SHIFT) - (F9), Field
Type: FirstName
Press: ⏎

To end the salutation with a colon,

Type: :

Once all the merge codes that are needed in the primary file are correctly entered, the file must be saved.

A few notes about entering field merge codes in the primary document before saving the file:

n   A field name can be used more than one time in the primary document. For example, the Name field could be used again in the letter without assigning it a new field name.

- The field name should be short and descriptive. It can be a single word or multiple words. If you enter multiple words use a hyphen or underscore to separate the words. Do not use a blank space between words.
- Not all the fields in the secondary file need to be used in the primary file.

To save the primary file as **WELCOME.PF** (the extension .PF identifies the file as a primary file) and clear the screen in preparation for creating the secondary merge file,

Select:	File>Exit
>>	Exit (F7)
Type:	Y
Type:	WELCOME.PF
Press:	⏎
Type:	N

Creating the Secondary File

A blank Wordperfect screen is ready to be used to enter the fields and records for the secondary merge file. The secondary merge file will hold the six fields of data about each new member. The six fields of data for each new member form a record of information.

The primary file calls for the following six fields of data for each record:

Field Number	Field Name
Field 1	Name
Field 2	Address
Field 3	City
Field 4	State
Field 5	Zip
Field 6	FirstName

When entering the data for the secondary merge file, the following rules must be observed:

- At the beginning of the document enter a merge code which identifies the names of each field used in the primary file.
- The order of fields in the primary file determines what order the fields of data should be listed in the secondary merge file. For example, the FirstName field in the primary file is the sixth field of data in a record from the secondary merge file.
- The end of a field of data is marked with an **End Field** merge code.
- The end of a record is marked with an **End Record** merge code.
- Each field of data must be entered in the same sequence for all records and must contain the same type of information.
- The same number of fields must appear in each record.

To enter the merge code that identifies the field names,

Select: Tools>Merge Codes>More
>> Merge Codes (SHIFT) - (F9), More

Your display screen should be similar to Figure 3-4.

FIGURE 3-4

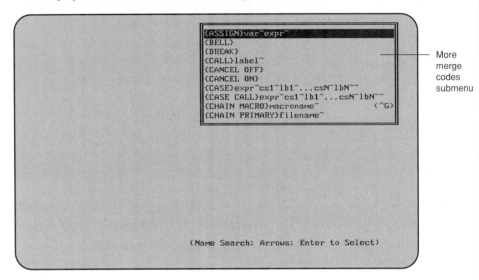

More merge codes submenu

A submenu of other merge codes is displayed. They are listed in alphabetical order. You can use the (↑) and (↓) keys to move the highlight bar through the list of codes, or you can use the mouse. If you use the mouse, position the mouse pointer inside the Merge Codes selection box and drag the mouse to move the highlight. The list will scroll as you drag the mouse. You can also move by "pages" using the (PGDN) or (PGUP) keys.

Using any of these methods, move the highlight to {FIELD NAMES}. To select it,

Press: ⏎ (or press the right mouse button)

The prompt "Enter Field 1:" appears in the status line. In response to the prompt you need to enter the field name of the first field. The field name must be entered exactly as you typed it in the primary file.

Type: Name
Press: ⏎

WordPerfect displays a prompt asking you to enter the name of the second field.

Type: Address
Press: ⏎

Continue to define the remaining four field names. When WordPerfect prompts you to enter the field name for the seventh field,

Press: ⏎

This tells WordPerfect that you are finished. When you are done your screen should be similar to Figure 3-5.

FIGURE 3-5

The {FIELD NAMES} definition code is displayed on the first line of the screen. The name of each field as you typed it and a tilde at the end of each field name are included. The code ends with an extra tilde and an {END RECORD} merge code. WordPerfect treats this merge code as a special record in the secondary file. The page break line separates this record from the other records you will be entering into the document next.

The first record begins immediately below the special record. Your cursor should be on the first line of page 2. Notice that the status line displays "Field: Name." This tells you WordPerfect is ready for you to enter the first field of data, the new member's full name.

Type: Mr. Anthony R. Myers (do not press ⏎)

To tell the program that this is the end of the first field of data, you must enter the End Field merge code. This code can be entered easily using the F9 key, or it can be entered using Tools>Merge Codes> More>{End Field}. Since pressing F9 is much easier, to enter this code,

Press: End Field F9

The End Field code is entered after the first field, and the cursor moves down one line. WordPerfect displays "Field: Address" in the status line to tell you it expects you to enter the data for this field next.

Type: 1452 Southern Ave.
Press: End Field F9

Enter the information for the remaining fields as follows:

Type: Mesa
Press: End Field F9

WP92
Merging and
Refining Documents

Type: AZ
Press: End Field (F9)

Type: 85202
Press: End Field (F9)

Type: Anthony
Press: End Field (F9)

The six fields of information, corresponding to the six field merge codes used in the inside address and saluatation in the primary file, are complete for the first record in the secondary merge file.

To separate this record from the next record and to indicate a page break between documents, the End Record merge code is entered. To enter this code,

Select: Tools>Merge Codes>End Record
>> Merge Codes (SHIFT) - (F9), End Record

Your display screen should be similar to Figure 3-6.

FIGURE 3-6

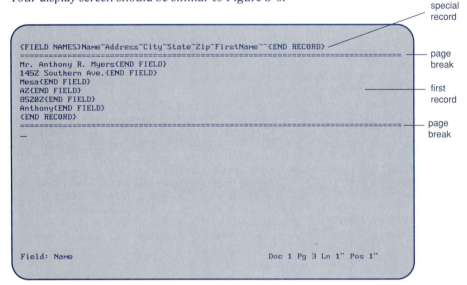

An {END RECORD} code is entered on the line, and the cursor moves to the next line in the file. A double dashed line separates each record. This line indicates a page break. It tells WordPerfect to begin a new page following the page break.

Never separate fields or records with an extra hard carriage return. Also do not insert spaces following the last word in a field and a End Record merge code.

Enter the field information for the second record as follows:

Type: Miss Allycin Miller
Press: End Field (F9)

Type: 128 Forest Ave.
Press: End Field (F9)

WP93
Creating the
Secondary File

Type:	**Tempe**
Press:	End Field (F9)

Type:	**AZ**
Press:	End Field (F9)

Type:	**85285**
Press:	End Field (F9)

Type:	**Allycin**
Press:	End Field (F9)

Select:	**T**ools>Merge Codes>End Record
>>	Merge Codes (SHIFT) - (F9), **E**nd Record

Your display screen should be similar to Figure 3-7.

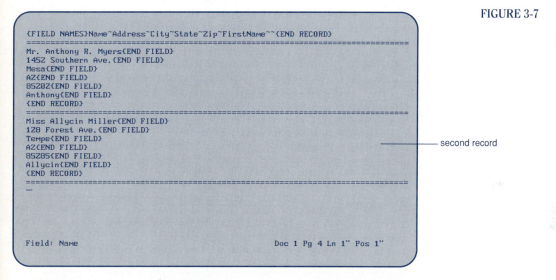

FIGURE 3-7

— second record

Enter your name and address as the third record in the secondary file.

Check your screen and make any corrections as needed. Make sure each field ends with an End Field code and that each record ends with an End Record code.

The number of records you enter into the secondary file is limited only by your diskette space.

To save the secondary file using the file name WELCOME.SF (the file extension .SF identifies this file as the secondary file) and clear the screen in preparation for merging the primary file with the secondary merge file,

Select:	**F**ile>E**x**it
>>	Exit (F7)
Press:	**Y**
Type:	**WELCOME.SF**
Press:	(↵)
Type:	**N**

A blank WordPerfect screen is ready for use.

Merging the Primary and Secondary Merge Files

Now that you have created and saved the primary and secondary merge files, you are ready to combine them to create the new personalized welcome letter.

During this process a third file is created. The original primary and secondary files are not altered or affected in any way. The third file is the result of the merging of the primary and secondary files. It is very important to clear the screen of any document before merging files.

Select: Tools>Merge
>> Merge (CTRL)-(F9), Merge

In response to the prompt to enter the name of the primary file,

Type: WELCOME.PF
Press: ⏎

The primary file is retrieved into the computer's memory.

Next respond to the prompt to enter the name of the secondary file:

Type: WELCOME.SF
Press: ⏎

The status line displays the message "* Merging *." At the completion of the merge, the document containing the three letters is displayed on the screen. To move to the top of the document,

Press: (HOME) (HOME) (↑)

Your display screen should be similar to Figure 3-8.

FIGURE 3-8

```
                                                          March 20, 1992


Mr. Anthony R. Myers
1452 Southern Ave.
Mesa, AZ 85202

Dear Anthony:

        Congratulations on your new membership in the Sports Club.
All of us on the staff welcome you and encourage you to
participate in the many tournaments, leagues and Sports Club
activities offered throughout the year.

        Each month you will receive a newsletter about the upcoming
events at the Sports Club. If you have questions about the event
or would like to sign up to participate in an event, just call or
come in to the front desk personnel.

        The Sports Club facilities include 18 lighted tennis courts,
5 racquetball courts, an olympic size swimming pool, Nautilus
equipped weight room, and basketball court. For your comfort
while using the Sports Club, the men's and ladies' locker rooms
                                            Doc 1 Pg 1 Ln 1" Pos 1"
```

The personalized letter to Anthony Myers is displayed. The fields of data from the secondary merge file have been entered into the primary file at the location of the merge codes.

To see the letter using the data for the second record,

Press: (PGDN)

Finally, to see the letter containing your name and address information,

Press: (PGDN)

Now each time Karen needs to send welcome letters, all she needs to do is to create the new member secondary merge file and issue the Merge command. Because the Date command was used, the date will automatically reflect the date the letter was created.

Save (F10) the current document of three welcome letters as WELCOME.MRG. The letters can be printed like any other document. **Print the letter containing your name and address information only.** Remember to select the appropriate printer for your microcomputer system first.

To leave the document and clear the screen,

Select: File>Exit
   >>   Exit (F7)
Type: N
Type: N

To review, the steps in creating a customized form letter are:

1. Create the primary file. Enter Field merge codes in the document to tell WordPerfect where and what fields of information to use from the secondary merge file. Save the document as the primary file.

2. Create the secondary merge file. It will contain the special record which identifies the field names used in the primary file and the variable data or information needed to complete the primary file for each record. Each field of data must end with an End Field code. Each record must end with an End Record code. As many records as diskette space will allow can be entered in this file.

3. Use the Merge command to combine the primary and secondary files to create a customized document for each record in the secondary merge file.

Centering and Boldfacing Text

The second project Karen needs to work on is the article for the newsletter about the new automatic fee payment program. The membership coordinator already has a file started which contains another article to be entered in the newsletter. He has asked Karen to enter her article at the end of this document.

Retrieve the file ARTICLE.DOC. Your display screen should be similar to Figure 3-9.

FIGURE 3-9

```
           ** NEW MEMBER **
              ORIENTATION
                MEETING

A New Member Orientation meeting will be held on Thursday
evening, November 19 from 7:00 to 8:30 PM in the Adult Lounge.
All new members are encouraged to attend this meeting. Your
picture for the identification card can be taken at this time.
The tennis and racquetball Pro staff will be discussing their
programs, sign-up procedures and costs. The Sports Club
management will also present information on other club events and
programs, procedures and costs. This is your opportunity to meet
the people who can help you make the most of your membership.

This meeting is also open to old members who may have questions
or suggestions to improve the Sports Club. We would like to see
and meet you all!

Refreshments will be served following the meeting.


B:\ARTICLE.DOC                              Doc 1 Pg 1 Ln 1" Pos 1"
```

An article concerning a new member orientation meeting is displayed on the screen.

Karen will begin the article about the automatic fee payment program three lines below the end of the first article. To move to this location,

Press: (HOME) (HOME) (↓)

The cursor should be on Ln 4.67" Pos 1" (three blank lines below the last line of text).

She would like to enter a title for her article similar to the title in the article on the display screen. Notice that each line of this title is centered between the margins. If you have a color monitor, you will also note that it is displayed in color. This is because it has been formatted to be printed in boldface print.

The title for her article is: NEW PROGRAM AUTOMATIC PAYMENT. She will enter it on three lines.

To turn on the capability to enter text in all capital letters,

Press: (CAPS LOCK)

Notice in the status line that "POS" is displayed in uppercase letters. This is how WordPerfect tells you that the (CAPS LOCK) key is on. The (CAPS LOCK) key affects only alphabet keys. Other characters will require that you use the (SHIFT) key.

To **center** text between the margins, the Center (Layout>Align>Center or (SHIFT)-(F6)) command is used. The cursor must be positioned on the left margin before using the command. Otherwise the text will be centered between the cursor location and the right margin.

Select: Layout>Align>Center
>> Center (SHIFT) - (F6)

The cursor jumps to the middle of the screen. As text is typed, it will be centered between the current margin settings.

Karen also wants the title to be printed in **boldface** characters. Boldface text is printed darker than normal text. On the screen it is displayed brighter than surrounding text or in color if you have a color monitor. The command to produce boldfaced text is Bold, (Font>Appearance>Bold or F6). To mark the area in the document to begin bold text and enter the first line of the title,

Select: Font>Appearance>Bold
  \>\> Bold F6
Type: ** NEW PROGRAM **
Press: ⏎

The text is displayed brighter on your screen or in color if you have a color monitor, to show the area that is to be printed in bold text. If yours is not brighter, you may need to adjust the contrast and brightness of your monitor.

Before entering the second line of the heading, the Center command must be used again. Each line you want centered must begin with the Center command. The Bold command continues in effect until turned off by selecting the command again. Since it is quicker to use the function key to initiate the Center command, to center this line,

Press: Center SHIFT - F6
Type: AUTOMATIC
Press: ⏎
Press: Center SHIFT - F6
Type: PAYMENT

To end boldfacing using the function key command and turn off all capital letters,

Press: Bold F6
Press: CAPS LOCK

Karen will begin the text of the article two lines below the heading. To create the blank lines and move to this location,

Press: ⏎ (3 times)

Your cursor should now be on Ln 5.5" Pos 1". Your display screen should be similar to Figure 3-10.

FIGURE 3-10

```
A New Member Orientation meeting will be held on Thursday
evening, November 19 from 7:00 to 8:30 PM in the Adult Lounge.
All new members are encouraged to attend this meeting. Your
picture for the identification card can be taken at this time.
The tennis and racquetball Pro staff will be discussing their
programs, sign-up procedures and costs. The Sports Club
management will also present information on other club events and
programs, procedures and costs. This is your opportunity to meet
the people who can help you make the most of your membership.

This meeting is also open to old members who may have questions
or suggestions to improve the Sports Club. We would like to see
and meet you all!

Refreshments will be served following the meeting.

                    ** NEW PROGRAM **
                       AUTOMATIC
                        PAYMENT




B:\ARTICLE.DOC                             Doc 1 Pg 1 Ln 5.5" Pos 1"
```

Using Two Document Files

Now Karen could begin typing the information about the automatic fee payment program into the document. However, she doesn't want to retype the same information that is in the welcome letter. Instead she will copy the paragraph about the automatic fee payment program from the WELCOME file into the document on the display.

To do this she will use the WordPerfect Switch feature. This feature will let her use two document files at the same time. It does this by creating a new screen for the second document file.

To create a new screen and switch to that screen, the Switch (Edit>Switch Document or (SHIFT) - (F3)) command is used.

Select: Edit>Switch Document
>>   Switch (SHIFT) - (F3)

The screen is blank. The status line indicates, however, that you are in document 2. The ARTICLE.DOC file is still in the computer's memory as document 1, although it is not displayed.

At this point new text could be entered to create a new document, or an existing document can be retrieved. Karen will retrieve the WELCOME file into the new screen.

Retrieve WELCOME.

The welcome letter is displayed on the screen as document 2. Two files are now open and can be used at the same time.

To see and use the file ARTICLE.DOC in the document 1 screen, use Edit>Switch Document or Switch (SHIFT) - (F3) again. It now acts as a toggle to move between the two document screens. Since the function key is quicker,

Press: (SHIFT) - (F3)

The file ARTICLE.DOC is displayed in the document 1 screen.
 The two files can be seen and used by switching from one document screen to another using **SHIFT-F3** or Edit>Switch Document.

Creating a Split Screen

It would be even more convenient for Karen if she could see both documents at the same time on the display screen. This can be done by splitting the display screen into two parts, or **windows**, using the Screen (Edit>Window or **CTRL - F3**) command.

Select: Edit>Window
>>   Screen **CTRL - F3**, **W**indow

The prompt "Number of lines in this window: 24" is displayed in the status line. This is the default window-size setting for a full screen of 24 lines. To divide the full screen into two equal halves,

Type: 12
Press: ⏎

Your display screen should be similar to Figure 3-11.

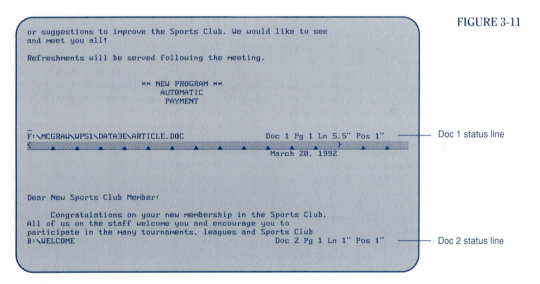

FIGURE 3-11

The screen is divided into two equal parts by a reverse-video bar marked by triangles, which represent the tab stops. Document 1 is displayed in the top window. Document 2 is displayed in the bottom window. The status line at the bottom of each window identifies the file and cursor location.
 The cursor is currently located in document 1. You could now edit the file in this window without affecting the file in document 2. To switch into document 2,

Press: Switch **SHIFT - F3**

The cursor has jumped into document 2.

Note: Mouse users can click on the window to switch from one document to another.

Now you could edit the document in this window without affecting the file in the other window. Notice as you switch from one window to the other that the triangles within the reverse video bar change direction. They point upward when the cursor is in the upper window and downward when the cursor is in the lower window.

The cursor movement keys and command keys operate as they would if only one window or one file was open.

Moving Text Between Documents

Now Karen is ready to move a copy of the paragraph on the automatic fee payment program from the WELCOME file (document 2) into the ARTICLE.DOC file (document 1).

The paragraph to be copied is the fifth paragraph. Using the ↓ key and the status line in document 2 to locate your cursor position,

Move to: Ln 6.17" Pos 1" (left margin of first line of fifth paragraph)

Next, to issue the Move command,

Select: **E**dit>Select>**P**aragraph
>> Move (CTRL) - (F4), **P**aragraph

The whole paragraph is highlighted. The menu displayed in the Status line lets you select whether you want to cut, copy, or delete the marked (highlighted) section of text. To copy the block,

Select: **C**opy

A copy of the paragraph is stored in temporary memory. Karen wants to insert the copy of the paragraph into the ARTICLE.DOC file in document 1. To do this you will switch into document 1 and then retrieve the paragraph from temporary memory.

Press: Switch (SHIFT) - (F3)

The cursor jumps back into document 1. It should be three lines below the heading (Ln 5.5" Pos 1"). If it is not there, before continuing, move it to that location.

To retrieve the paragraph into document 1,

Press: (↵)

The paragraph is copied into the file in document 1. To see the rest of the paragraph,

Press: (HOME) (HOME) (↓)

Your display screen should be similar to Figure 3-12.

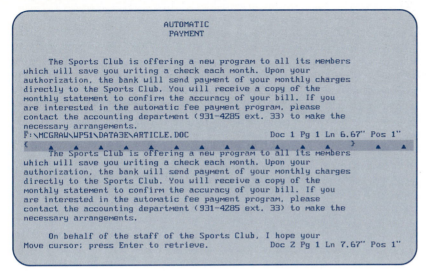

FIGURE 3-12

The copy of the paragraph has been copied from the file in document 2 and inserted into the file in document 1. Using the Split Screen feature to view both documents at the same time made this process very easy.

The documents in each window operate independently of each other. The changes that are made in one document do not affect the other. You can also use the split screen to view two different parts of the same document at the same time.

Closing a Split Screen

Karen no longer needs to see the WELCOME file in document 2. To return to displaying a single document on the screen at one time, the process of creating a window is reversed.

Select: Edit>Window
>> Screen (CTRL)-(F3), Window

To return to a full screen of 24 lines,

Type: 24
Press: ⏎

Your display screen should be similar to Figure 3-13.

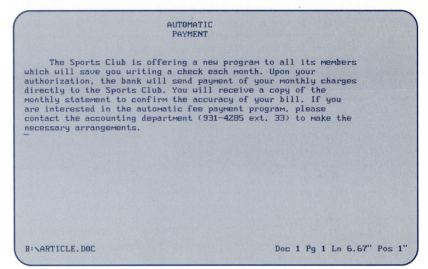

FIGURE 3-13

The screen display returns to a single window of 24 lines, and document 1 occupies the whole screen. Both documents, however, are still open. But document 2 is not visible on the display. When closing a window, the document the cursor is positioned in is the document that will be displayed.

To continue her work on the article, Karen wants to remove the indentation from the first line in the paragraph. To do this she could use the Reveal Codes screen to locate the position of the tab code and then delete it. However, she is sure the tab code is located at the beginning of the line that is indented. So she will remove the code while in normal document display.

Move to: Ln 5.5" Pos 1" (left margin of first line)
Press: DEL

The tab code has been deleted, and the line is no longer indented.

Underlining Text

Finally, Karen wants to **underline** the accounting department telephone number. To underline text which is already entered in a document, the area of text to be underlined must first be defined using the Block feature.

To position the cursor under the "9" in the telephone number, and to turn Block on,

Move to: Ln 6.5" Pos 4.5" ("9" in telephone number)
Select: Edit>Block
   >>   Block ALT-F4

To define the block of text to be underlined (the entire telephone number),

Move to: Ln 6.5" Pos 6.1" (the ")" at end of telephone number)

The telephone number is highlighted on the screen.

To mark this block of text to be underlined, the Underline (Font>Appearance>Underline or (F8)) command is used.

Select: Font>Appearance>Underline
>> Underline (F8)

Your display screen should be similar to Figure 3-14.

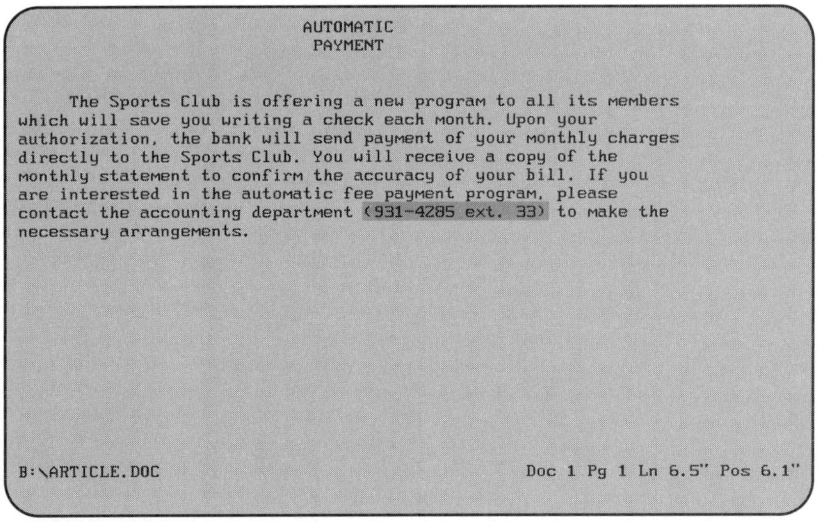

FIGURE 3-14

The marked block of text is underlined, highlighted, or displayed in color, depending upon your monitor. When it is printed, it will be underlined. The hidden code to turn underlining on and off is placed at the beginning and end of the block.

If you want to underline text as you enter it into the document, simply select Underline before typing the text. It then must be turned off by selecting Underline again at the end of the text to be underlined. It is much quicker to use the function key, (F8), to initiate this command than it is to use the pull-down menus.

Defining Columns

The articles will appear in the newsletter as long newspaper-style columns. The WordPerfect Columns (Layout>Columns or (ALT) - (F7)) command lets you easily set the text format of a document into columns.

As with many WordPerfect commands, a hidden code is entered into the document to control the display of the text. The location of the hidden code indicates the point in the document at which the command will take effect. Since both articles need to be displayed in a column format, move the cursor to the top of page 1.

Press: (PGUP)
Select: Layout>Columns
>> Columns/Table (ALT) - (F7), Columns

The Columns submenu (displayed in the status line if you used the function key command) lists three options: On, Off, and Define. They have the following effect:

On	turns columns on at the cursor position
Off	turns columns off at the cursor position
Define	defines the type, spacing, and number of columns

To use the Columns feature, you must first define the column settings.

Select: Define

Your display screen should be similar to Figure 3-15.

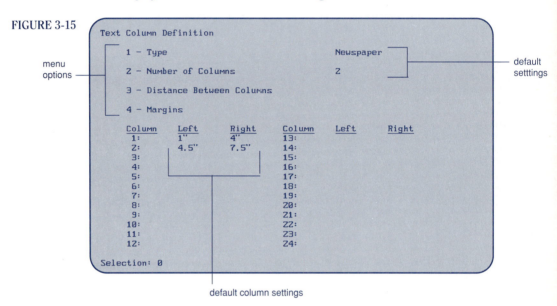

FIGURE 3-15

The Text Column Definition menu replaces the document on the screen. Four menu options are displayed in the upper portion of the screen. The default settings are displayed in the column to the right of each option. The lower portion of the screen shows the right and left margins for the columns based upon the default settings.

The first menu option, Type, lets you specify the type of column you want to create.

Select: Type

The three types of columns which can be created are displayed in the menu in the status line: 1 Newspaper, 2 Parallel, and 3 Parallel with Block Protect. With **newspaper columns**, text runs vertically up and down the page through the columns. With **parallel columns**, text runs horizontally across the page. One of the columns may spill over to the next page while the other does not. The third type of column, Parallel with Block protect, is the same as parallel columns, except that text is protected from being split between two pages.

The default setting is Newspaper. Since the default setting is acceptable, this option does not need to be changed. To leave this menu without changing the default,

Press: ⏎

The second option, 2 Number of Columns, lets you specify how many columns of text you want across the width of the page. The Sports Club newsletter has three columns.

Select: Number of Columns

The cursor is positioned under the default setting. To change the number of columns to three,

Type: 3
Press: ⏎

Your display screen should be similar to Figure 3-16.

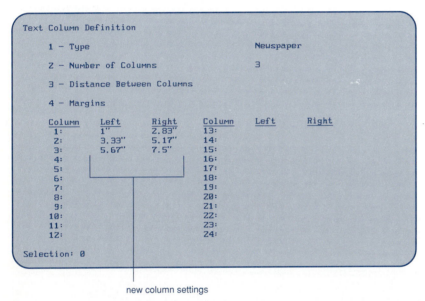

FIGURE 3-16

new column settings

Wordperfect automatically calculates and displays the new left and right margins for the three columns in the lower portion of the screen. The first column will begin at the left default margin of 1" and end at 2.83". The second column will begin at 3.33" and end at 5.16". The third column will begin at 5.67" and end at the right default margin setting of 7.5".

The next option, 3 Distance Between Columns, lets you specify how much space you want between the columns.

Select: Distance Between Columns

The default setting of .5" is displayed. Karen thinks the default setting will be suitable, and decides to leave it as it is.

Press: ⏎

You can also change the default left and right margins by selecting the Margins option. However, for our purposes, the default settings are acceptable. To save the column definitions and exit the menu,

Press: (F7) or ⏎

WP106
Merging and
Refining Documents

The column settings have been defined. A hidden code, [Col Def], containing the column definitions has been entered into the document.

The Columns menu is displayed in the status line again. It allows you to continue making selections. Next you need to direct the program to display the document using the column settings defined. This will enter a [Col on] code in the document. To turn the display of columns on,

Select: On

Reformatting the Screen Display

It appears that nothing has happened. To reformat the display of the text to the new column settings, you could move down through the document using (PGDN) or the cursor movement keys. However, a faster way is to use the Rewrite command, an option in the Screen menu.

Press: Screen (CTRL) - (F3)
Select: Rewrite

The text is reformatted so that it is in newspaper-style columns. Your display screen should be similar to Figure 3-17.

FIGURE 3-17

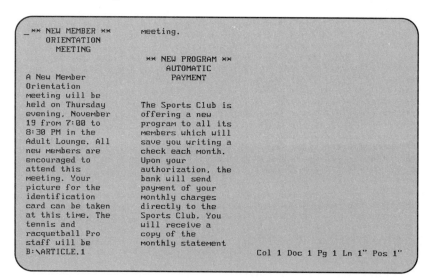

The two articles appear on the screen as two columns of text. Using this option quickly reformats the screen display to the new settings.

To move to the bottom of the page,

Press: (CTRL) - (HOME) (↓)

The cursor is positioned on the last line of the first column. The second column ends before the last line of the page. If there were more text in the second column, it would wrap to the top of the third column.

The following keys can be used move around the document while in column format:

Key	Action
↑, ↓, or PGDN	scroll all columns at the same time
→, ←, or HOME	move cursor inside a column
CTRL - HOME →	move cursor from one column to another
CTRL - HOME ←	
PGUP	move cursor to top of first column

Try moving the cursor around the columns. When you are done, use PGUP to return to the top of the first column.

To edit text while in column format, the delete keys all work within a single column. As in regular document display, the text is automatically reformatted on a line when insertions and deletions are made. You can use most WordPerfect features when in column format, with the exception of Column Definition, Document Comments, Footnotes, and Margins.

In some cases it may be easier to turn off the display of columns, do the editing and changes to the text that are needed, and then turn the column display back on. The display of columns is turned off by selecting the Columns Off/On option in the Columns menu. A [Col off] code is hidden in the document to control the display.

Note: Be careful when turning columns on or off. If the command is not entered in the proper location in the document, any text located between the on and off codes is formatted in columns. The original column definition settings remain in effect in the document unless the code is deleted or another column definition is entered.

Viewing the Document

Before Karen prints the article she wants to view it on the screen as it will appear when printed. The View Document option in the Print menu lets you see how different formats and settings will appear when the document is printed.

To see how the columns will appear when printed,

Select: **F**ile>**P**rint>**V**iew Document
   >>   Print (SHIFT) - (F7), **V**iew Document

After a few moments, the text is generated and displayed in the view document screen. Your display screen should be similar to Figure 3-18 on the next page.

The full page is displayed as close in appearance as possible to the printed page. WordPerfect can display the entire page by changing to a graphics display mode rather than the text display mode.

Note: If your computer does not have graphics capabilities, the View Document feature displays the document in text mode. The instructions in the rest of this

WP108
Merging and Refining Documents

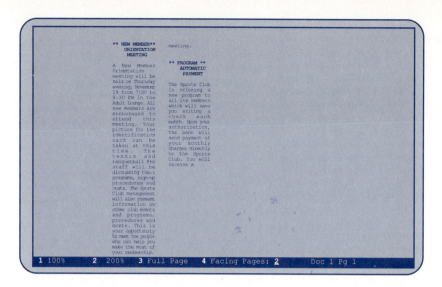

FIGURE 3-18

section do not apply to your computer system. Instead, to see the lower half of the document press (CTRL) (HOME) (↓). To leave the View screen press (F7). Continue the lab by skipping to the next section, "Changing Justification."

The menu at the bottom of the screen lets you enlarge the viewed document. To view the document at its actual size (100%),

Press: 1

Your display screen should be similar to Figure 3-19.

FIGURE 3-19

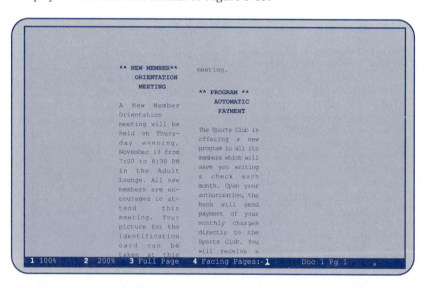

Now the text is large enough to read easily. Because most monitors are not large enough to display an entire page at full size, only the upper postion of the article is visible. To move to the bottom of the page,

Press: (CTRL) - (HOME) (↓)

Karen is not pleased with how the articles will appear when printed. She does not like the large gaps which appear between words. The gaps occur because the justification setting is Full, forcing the program to insert spaces between words to make the right and left margins even. She also does not like how the last line of the first article appears at the top of the second column.

To leave the View screen,

Press: Exit (F7)

Changing Justification

Karen would like to see how the document will appear if the justification setting is changed to Left. To make this change,

Press: (PGUP)
Select: Layout>Line>Justification>Left
>> Format (SHIFT) - (F8), Line> Justification>Left
Press: Exit (F7)

The change in the justification setting does not affect the screen display since the text is displayed with left justification only. When printed, the right margins will be printed as they appear on the screen.

If your computer has graphics capabilities, view the change in the document by selecting **F**ile>**P**rint>**V**iew Document or Print (SHIFT)-(F7), **V**iew Document. You will see that the right margins are no longer even and the large gaps between words have been eliminated. However, now the large gap appears at the right margin, making the right margin too ragged. To leave the View screen, press Exit (F7).

On lines of text where there are several short words, the wrapping of text to the next line is not a problem. On lines where there are long words, the long word is wrapped to the next line, leaving a large gap on the previous line. Hyphenating a long word at the end of a line will help solve this problem.

Using Hyphenation

WordPerfect's Hyphenation feature fits as much of a word as possible on a line before hyphenating the word. The balance of the word wraps to the next line. Hyphenation is set to off by default. To turn it on,

Select: Layout>Line> Hyphenation>Yes
>> Format (SHIFT) - (F8), Line>Hyphenation>Yes

To leave the Line Format menu,

Press: Exit (F7)

To reformat the screen display,

Press: Screen (CTRL) - (F3), **R**ewrite

Your screen should be similar to Figure 3-20.

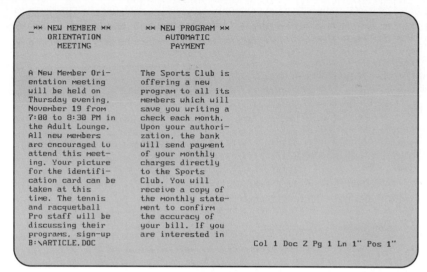

FIGURE 3-20

WordPerfect adds hyphenation to the document. The hyphenation points are determined automatically, based upon the U.S spelling dictionary rules. This dictionary is included in the WordPerfect 5.1 program. If WordPerfect cannot determine how to hyphenate a word, it will prompt you to position the hyphen in any long word that needs hyphenation. The prompt "Position hyphen; Press (ESC)" appears in the status line. Following the prompt the word requiring hyphenation is displayed with the suggested hyphenation. To accept the hyphenation as displayed, press (ESC). To change the hyphenation, move the hyphen with the arrow keys to the correct location and press (ESC). If the word cannot be appropriately hyphenated, press (F7) to cancel hyphenation for that word.

Hyphenating the newsletter has made the right margins much less ragged. Additionally, because more words were able to fit on a line, the last line of the first article now ends at the bottom of the first column, and the second article begins at the top of the second column. Karen is pleased with the appearance of the articles now.

Note: If your computer can display graphics, view the document again using File>Print>View Document or Print (SHIFT) - (F7), View Document. To leave the View screen, press Exit (F7).

Move to the bottom of the second column and enter your name.
If you have printer capability, print a copy of the article. If necessary, select the appropriate printer for your microcomputer system first.

Saving and Exiting Two Document Files

When there are two documents in use, both need to be saved (if needed) and exited from before leaving the WordPerfect program. To save the current document,

Select: File>Exit
   >> Exit (F7)
Type: Y
Type: COLUMNS.DOC
Press: ⏎

The next prompt, "Exit Doc 1?," is new. Whenever there are two open documents at one time, each document needs to be exited.

Type: Y

Document 2, the welcome letter, is displayed on the screen. Since no changes were made to this document, it is not necessary to save the file. To close this document and exit WordPerfect,

Select: File>Exit
   >> Exit (F7)
Type: N
Type: Y

The DOS prompt appears on your display screen.

KEY TERMS

primary file	field	window
secondary merge file	record	underline
merge codes	center	newspaper columns
address file	boldface	

MATCHING

1. End Record~
2. (SHIFT) - (F8) 2
3. Field~
4. (F9)
5. (CTRL) - (F9) 1
6. (SHIFT) - (F9)
7. Layout>Align>Center
8. (F6)
9. (SHIFT) - (F3)
10. (ALT) - (F7)

_____ a. boldfaces text
_____ b. merges files
_____ c. displays merge codes
_____ d. identifies field name
_____ e. switches to other document
_____ f. displays Columns/Table menu
_____ g. displays Page Format menu
_____ h. identifies end of field
_____ i. identifies end of record
_____ j. centers text

WP112
Merging and
Refining Documents

PRACTICE EXERCISES

1. To complete this problem you must first have completed problem 4 in Lab 2. You will change this letter into a form letter and create a secondary file.

- Create a secondary file. Each record will contain seven fields of data. Enter the following records:

    1. Mr. Paul Simone
       Advising Department
       Arizona State University
       Tempe
       AZ
       85257
       Mr. Simone

    2. Mr. Phil Miller
       Southern Telephone Corp.
       56 Highland Way
       Phoenix
       AZ
       85001
       Mr. Miller

    3. Your first and last name
       Your Major Department
       Your School
       City
       State
       Zipcode
       Your last name

- Save the secondary file as JOB.SF.
- Modify the letter in JOB to accept the seven fields of information. Save the primary file as JOB.PF. Print the file.
- Merge the primary and secondary files and print the three letters.

2. The local zoo acknowledges all gifts and donations with a personalized form letter that includes the following fields of data:

Field 1 - full name
Field 2 - street address
Field 3 - city
Field 4 - state
Field 5 - zipcode
Field 6 - donation
Field 7 - designation

- Create a secondary merge file using the data shown below for each of the records.

    1. Mr. and Mrs. Brian Matheson
       1432 Winding Way
       Scottsdale
       AZ
       86942
       $1,000
       Bear Exhibit

    2. Mr. and Mrs. Charles Larson
       732 Decatur St.
       Mesa
       AZ
       85287
       $500
       Otter Exhibit

    3. Your first and last name
       Street
       City
       State
       Zipcode
       Donation
       Designation

- Save the secondary merge file as DONATION.SF.
- The thank you letter for donations is shown on the next page. Create a primary file by entering this letter and the appropriate merge codes reflecting the fields of data in the secondary merge file.

```
[Date Command]


[Field 1]
[Field 2]
[Field 3], [Field 4] [Field 5]

Dear [Field 1]:

The zoo would like to thank you for your generous
donation of [Field 6]. As you specified, your
donation will go toward the [Field 7].

The zoo is continually building new exhibits and
structures, renovating old structures and exhibits,
and upgrading the zoo grounds. It is through the
generosity of donations such as yours that we are
able to continue to improve and grow.

Your gift is greatly appreciated.



Development Director
```

- Save the thank you letter as DONATION.PF. Print the file.
- Merge the primary and secondary files and print the letters.

3. To complete this problem you must first have completed problem 1 in Lab 2. Retrieve the file OVER-WP.REV.

- Enter the title OVERVIEW OF WORD PROCESSING on the first line of the document. It should be in all capital letters and boldfaced. Enter a blank line below the title.
- Underline the title DEFINITION OF WORD PROCESSING.
- Split the screen into two windows of 12 lines each.
- Move into document 2 and retrieve the file TEXT-WP.
- Copy the entire page into document 1. It should be entered at the end of document 1 above your name. Leave two blank lines above the heading "Advantages of Using a Word Processor."
- Clear the window.
- Change this document to be displayed as newspaper-style columns with four columns separated by .3 inches.
- Print the document
- Save the new document as TEXT-WP.REV.

4. To complete this problem, you must first have completed problem 2 in Lab 2. Retrieve the file EVENTS. The text in this file will be used in the zoo member newsletter.

- Enter the heading shown below for the article, centered and in bold, as two lines. (Leave a blank line below your name and date, and two blank lines below the heading.)

  Special Zoo

  Events

- Boldface the name of each event in the first line of each paragraph.
- The article needs an introductory paragraph. This has already been created and saved for you as EVENT1. Create a second window on the screen of 12 lines. Move into the Doc 2 window and retrieve this file. Copy the entire contents of the text in Doc 2 into Doc 1. It should be the first paragraph of the article.
- Clear the window.
- Change the text in Doc 1 to be displayed as two newspaper-style columns. They should be separated by 1 inch.
- Add hyphenation.
- Save the article as EVENT2.
- Print the document.

LAB

Creating a Research Paper

4

OBJECTIVES

In this lab you will learn how to:

1. Create and edit an outline.
2. Draw lines.
3. Generate a table of contents.
4. Enter and edit footnotes.
5. Specify page numbering.
6. Suppress page numbering.
7. Center text top to bottom on a page.
8. Use Block Protection.
9. Prevent widows and orphans.

CASE STUDY

Peg is a senior recreation major at a local university. As part of her degree requirements she must work one semester in an approved internship program. To fulfill this requirement she worked at the Sports Club as an assistant in the swimming program.

As part of the requirements of the internship program, she must write a proposal on how to improve the swimming program. Her proposal is that the club offer an aquatic fitness program. In this lab we will follow Peg as she creates an outline and writes a paper on this topic.

Creating an Outline

Peg has already completed the research she needs and has thought about how the club could begin an aquatics fitness program. She needs to organize her thoughts and topics. To do this she decides to create an outline of the topics she plans to cover in her paper.

Boot the system and load the WordPerfect program.

The WordPerfect Automatic Outlining feature will help her prepare the outline for her proposal. This feature is accessed by selecting the Tools>Outline or Date/Outline (SHIFT) - (F5) command.

Note: If you use the function key command, the Date/Outline menu appears in the status line. The fourth option, Outline, then displays the Outline menu.

Select: Tools>Outline
>>   Date/Outline (SHIFT) - (F5), Outline

WP117
Creating an Outline

To turn on the Automatic Outlining feature,

Select: On

The WordPerfect screen is unchanged except for the message "Outline" displayed in the status line. This tells you that the Outline mode is on. WordPerfect will remain in this mode until you select this option again.

Peg has decided to divide her paper into three sections. In this lab you will learn how to create the outline for the first section of the paper as shown in Figure 4-1.

FIGURE 4-1

I. Introduction

    A. Statement of purpose
        1. Justification for proposal
        2. Organization of proposal
    B. Reasons for aquatic exercise programs
        1. Popularity of swimming
        2. Benefits of aquatic exercise
            a. Adaptable to many people
            b. Less damaging to joints and bones
            c. Improves cardiovascular system
    C. Determining Target Heart Rate (THR)
        1. Define THR
        2. Measure THR
            a. Direct
            b. Indirect
                (1) Karvonen formula
                (2) Percentage of Maximum Heart Rate (MHR)

In Outline mode the ⏎ and TAB keys perform specific functions. You will see how they perform differently as you create the outline. To begin outlining,

Press: ⏎

The Roman numeral "I." appears on the second line of the page. This is called a **paragraph number**. While in Outline mode the ⏎ key, in addition to inserting a blank line in the text, automatically displays a paragraph number. The Roman numeral I indicates that this is the first level of the outline.

To enter the text for the first line of the outline,

Press: Indent F4

The cursor has moved over one tab stop on the line. The Indent key (F4) moves the cursor along the line one tab stop. In normal text entry mode, the Indent key (F4) will align all text with the left tab stop until ⏎ is pressed. You may wonder why you did not use the TAB key to do this. As you will see shortly, the TAB key in Outline mode performs a different function.

To enter the text for this line,

Type: Introduction
Press: ⏎

Your screen should be similar to Figure 4-2.

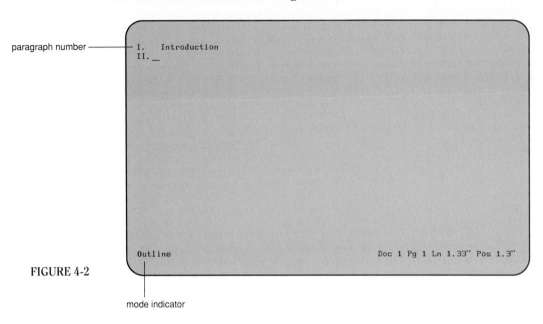

FIGURE 4-2

The Roman numeral "II." is displayed on the next line. Peg wants a blank line below the first outline level. Once a paragraph number is entered on a line, the ⏎ key can be used to insert a blank line.

Press: ⏎

A blank line is created, and Roman numeral II has moved down one line.

Next Peg needs to change the outline level from Roman numeral II to the second level of the outline, A. To do this,

Press: TAB

The cursor moved along the line one tab space, and "II." changed to "A." While outline mode is on, using TAB both changes the outline level number and tabs in one tab stop along the line.

Each time you press TAB the paragraph number advances to the next outline level. Instead of pressing TAB, you could press Space bar five times to advance the cursor to the next tab stop, and the paragraph number would also automatically advance.

Note: If you press TAB too many times and find yourself in the wrong outline level, to back up a tab stop press Margin Release (SHIFT - TAB). The outline number will automatically adjust. If you press BKSP the automatic paragraph number for that line will be deleted. If that happens you will need to press ⏎ at the correct location to insert a new paragraph number.

To indent and enter the text for this level,

Press: F4
Type: Statement of purpose

WordPerfect inserts a hidden code in the outline at each tab location. These codes control the outline levels. To see the hidden paragraph number codes,

Select: Edit>Reveal Codes
   >>   Reveal Codes (ALT) - (F3)

Your screen should be similar to Figure 4-3.

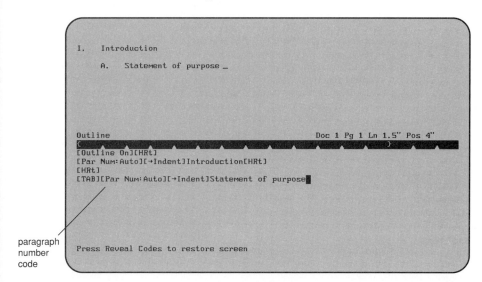

FIGURE 4-3

The first code, [Outline On], was entered when you turned on the Automatic Outlining feature. The hidden code [Par Num:Auto] is automatically entered following a [TAB] or [HRt] code when in Outline mode. The number of tabs along the line determines the paragraph number level that is displayed in the outline. When you delete a [Par Num:Auto] code, the paragraph number disappears. To leave the Reveal Codes screen,

Select: Edit>Reveal Codes
   >>   Reveal Codes (ALT) - (F3)

   To continue the outline,

Press: ⏎

The new paragraph number is "B." When you press ⏎ the new paragraph number is created at the same level as the previous number. In this case, however, the next line of the outline begins at the third level. To change the paragraph number to this level,

Press: (TAB)

The paragraph level number "1." is displayed. To indent and enter the text,

Press: Indent (F4)
Type: **Justification for proposal**
Press: ⏎

The paragraph number "2." appears on the line to allow you to enter the second topic at this outline level. Since this is the correct level for the next line of the outline, you are ready to enter the text for this level.

Press: Indent (F4)
Type: **Organization of proposal**
Press: (↵)

A third-level paragraph number is displayed again. The next outline level to be entered is a second level. To change the level in the opposite direction, or to back up a level, Margin Release ((SHIFT) - (TAB)) is used. This is just the opposite of pressing (TAB) to increase the number's level.

Press: (SHIFT) - (TAB)

The outline number level has decreased one level and is now "B." To enter the text for this level,

Press: (F4)
Type: **Reasons for aquatic exercise programs**
Press: (↵)

Complete the first section of the outline by entering the remaining outline levels as shown in Figure 4-4 using the (↵), (TAB), (SHIFT)-(TAB), and Indent ((F4)) keys. Don't forget to indent before entering the text for each line. If you do forget to indent, you can use the cursor movement keys to move to the first character on the line and then press (F4). The editing and cursor movement keys can be used to correct the text in the outline in the same manner as in regular document entry.

When you are done your screen should be similar to Figure 4-4.

FIGURE 4-4

```
I.   Introduction
     A.   Statement of purpose
          1.   Justification for proposal
          2.   Organization of proposal
     B.   Reasons for aquatic exercise programs
          1.   Popularity of swimming
          2.   Benefits of aquatic exercise
               a.   Adaptable to many people
               b.   Less damaging to joints and bones
               c.   Improves cardiovascular system
     C.   Determining Target Heart Rate (THR)
          1.   Define THR
          2.   Measure THR
               a.   Direct
               b.   Indirect
                    (1)  Karvonen formula
                    (2)  Percentage of Maximum Heart Rate_




Outline                                         Doc 1 Pg 1 Ln 4" Pos 6.7"
```

If you have not done so already, after typing the last line press (↵).
To change the paragraph number to "II,"

Press: (SHIFT) - (TAB) (4 times)

To insert a blank line between section I and II of the outline,

Press: ⏎

The next two sections of the outline have already been completed for you and saved on the file OUTLINE1.W51. **To combine the files, with your cursor positioned immediately after the "II.", retrieve the file OUTLINE1.W51.**
The completed outline consists of three sections. The second topic area discusses the parts of an aquatic fitness routine. The third area discusses how an aquatic fitness program should be modified for people with different physical limitations. **To see the complete outline use ↓ to move to the end of the document.**

Editing the Outline

After looking over her completed outline Peg wants to move a section of the outline to another location. It is easy to edit and move text within an outline while Outline mode is on. To move to the area of the outline that she wants to change,

Press : HOME - ↑ (2 times)

Your screen should look similar to Figure 4-5.

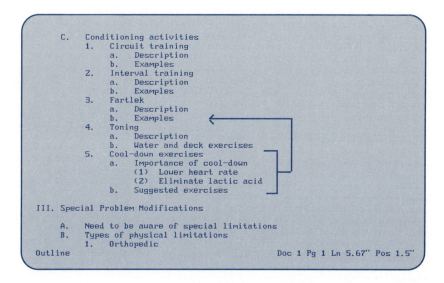

FIGURE 4-5

She wants to move the entire outline section "5. Cool-down exercises" above the section "4. Toning." She also wants to decrease the outline level of section 5 by one level, to level D.
Sections of an outline are grouped into **families**. A family consists of the outline level on the line where the cursor is located, plus any subordinate or lower levels. To move to the first line of the family to be moved,

Move to: Ln 7.83" (outline level "5. Cool-down exercises")
Select: **T**ools>**O**utline
　>> Date/Outline SHIFT - F5, **O**utline

Note: If you used the function key to issue this command, the outline menu will appear in the status line.

Your screen should be similar to Figure 4-6.

FIGURE 4-6

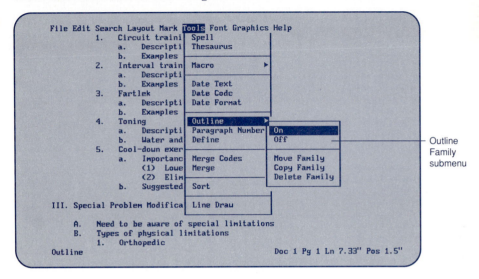

An outline family can be moved, copied, or deleted while in Outline mode using one of the three Family commands displayed in the submenu.

Select: Move Family

Outline level "5. Cool-down exercises" and the two sublevels below it should be highlighted. The highlighted outline family can be moved vertically or horizontally within the outline using the arrow keys.

Peg wants to move the family above the section of the outline beginning with "4. Toning." To move the outline family to this location,

Press:

Your screen should be similar to Figure 4-7.

FIGURE 4-7

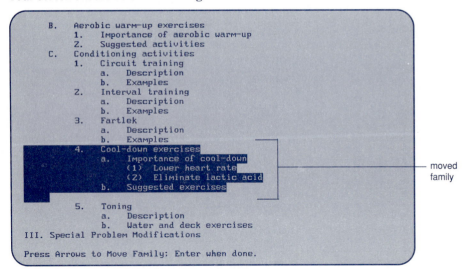

After a few seconds, the family moves up within the hierarchy of the outline and is now "4. Cool-down exercises," and the family below it has changed to "5. Toning."

Peg now wants to change the family from outline level 4 to level D. To do this, the paragraph number level needs to be lowered one level. Moving the highlighted family one level to the left will accomplish this task.

Press: ⬅

The outline family has moved one outline level to the left (horizontally), and all outline level numbers within the family have adjusted appropriately. Notice that the outline levels in the family below it have also adjusted. The new number, "3. Toning," however, is not how Peg wants it to be. She will correct this next.

To fix the highlighted family in place,

Press: ⏎

Next Peg wants to change the outline family beginning at level "3. Toning" to level E.

Move to: Ln 8.33" (outline level "3. Toning")
Select: **T**ools>**O**utline>**M**ove Family
>> Date/Outline (SHIFT) - (F5), **O**utline>**M**ove Family

Press: ⬅
Press: ⏎

The family moved over one tab space on the line, and the paragraph number changed from "3." to "E." All sublevels below it have adjusted appropriately.

Finally, delete the blank line above this outline level by deleting the [HRt] following the word "Exercises" and add a blank line above outline level III. Be careful that you place the cursor correctly before deleting the line or pressing ⏎ to create a blank line. Use Reveal Codes to make sure you are deleting the correct codes.

Your screen should be similar to Figure 4-8.

FIGURE 4-8

```
        C.   Conditioning activities
             1.   Circuit training
                  a.   Description
                  b.   Examples
             2.   Interval training
                  a.   Description
                  b.   Examples
             3.   Fartlek
                  a.   Description
                  b.   Examples
        D.   Cool-down exercises
             1.   Importance of cool-down
                  a.   Lower heart rate
                  b.   Eliminate lactic acid
             2.   Suggested exercises
        E.   Toning
             1.   Description
             2.   Water and deck exercises
   III. Special Problem Modifications
        A.   Need to be aware of special limitations
        B.   Types of physical limitations
             1.   Orthopedic
Outline                              Doc 1 Pg 1 Ln 8.83" Pos 1.5"
```

WP123
Editing the Outline

This same task could be accomplished by deleting or adding [Tab] codes to reduce or increase the paragraph number level, and by using the Block feature to move sections of the outline. When using the Block feature to move a section of the outline, be careful to include all appropriate codes in the block, so that when it is moved the outline levels will adjust appropriately. However, the outline Family feature does the same thing more quickly and accurately. Use Block if the paragraphs you want to manipulate are not a family or if you are not in Outline mode.

Peg feels the outline will help her to organize the topics in her paper. To turn off Outline mode, place the cursor at the end of the outline, and then select Outline Off. To do this,

Press: (HOME) (HOME) (↓)
Select: **T**ools>**O**utline>Off
   >>   Date/Outline (SHIFT) - (F5), **O**utline>Off

The "Outline" indicator in the status line is no longer displayed indicating Outline mode is not on. An [Outline Off] code has been inserted into the document. Now you could continue typing normal text, and the (↵) and (TAB) keys will act as they normally do. However, if you move the cursor into the area of text between the [Outline on] and [Outline Off] codes, the (↵) and (TAB) keys will work as they do in Outline mode.

Peg wants to enter a centered title at the beginning of the outline. To do this,

Press: (PGUP)
Press: **C**enter (SHIFT) - (F6)
Type: **OUTLINE FOR AQUATIC FITNESS PROPOSAL**
Press: (↵)

On the next line center your name and the current date.

To separate the two title lines from the beginning of the outline,

Press: (↵) (2 times)

Your screen should be similar to Figure 4-9.

FIGURE 4-9

```
              OUTLINE FOR AQUATIC FITNESS PROPOSAL
                       Student Name    Date

    I.  Introduction
        A.  Statement of purpose
            1.  Justification for proposal
            2.  Organization of proposal
        B.  Reasons for aquatic exercise programs
            1.  Popularity of swimming
            2.  Benefits of aquatic exercise
                a.  Adaptable to many people
                b.  Less damaging to joints and bones
                c.  Improves cardiovascular system
        C.  Determining Target Heart Rate (THR)
            1.  Define THR
            2.  Measure THR
                a.  Direct
                b.  Indirect
                    (1)  Karvonen formula
                    (2)  Percentage of Maximum Heart Rate
    II. Aquatic Fitness Routine
                                        Doc 1 Pg 1 Ln 1.33" Pos 1"
```

Using Save (F10), save the outline as OUTLINE2.
Print the outline. If necessary select the printer that is appropriate for your computer system.
Clear the screen (Exit (F7)). Do not exit WordPerfect.

Creating Lines

After several days, Peg has written the body of the internship proposal using WordPerfect 5.1 and has saved it on the diskette as PROPOSAL.W51.

To see what she has done so far, retrieve PROPOSAL.W51.

The title page of the report should be displayed on your screen. The first thing Peg would like to do is to draw a line below the title of the report. WordPerfect's Line Draw feature lets you draw lines, boxes, graphs, and other illustrations in your document. The Line Draw feature is an option that is accessed through the Tools menu or (CTRL)-(F3).

Select: **Tools>Line Draw**
>> **Screen (CTRL)-(F3), Line Draw**

Your screen should be similar to Figure 4-10.

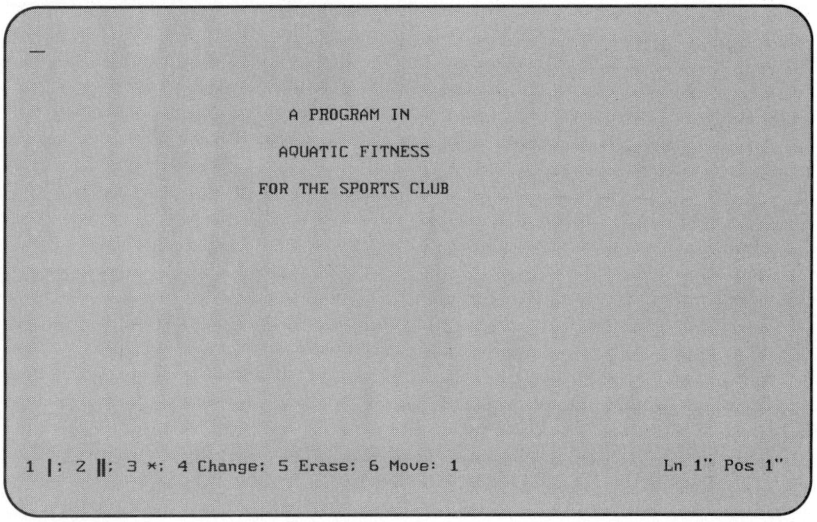

FIGURE 4-10

The Line Draw menu is displayed in the status line. This menu lets you create a single line (1), double line (2), or a line composed of asterisks (3). Change, option 4, lets you change the style of option 3 to something other than an asterisk from a selection of choices. The default is a single line.

Lines are created by using the arrow keys. Once this menu is displayed the arrow keys will automatically begin creating a line if they are pressed. To move the cursor without creating a line, the Move option (6) must be selected. Since Peg wants to create a line below the title, she needs to move the cursor to the line and position where the line is to begin. To do this,

Select: **Move**

The Line Draw menu is still displayed. Following the colon at the end of the menu, the selected option is displayed. Now the cursor can be moved without creating a line. She wants the line to be two lines below the last line of the title. Using the arrow keys,

Move to: Ln 2.83" Pos 2.6"

Peg wants to create a double line. To do this,

Select: 2

The menu remains on the screen, with the selected option, 2, displayed following the colon in the menu.
To create the line, using the → key,

Move to: Ln 2.83" Pos 6.5"

Your screen should be similar to Figure 4-11.

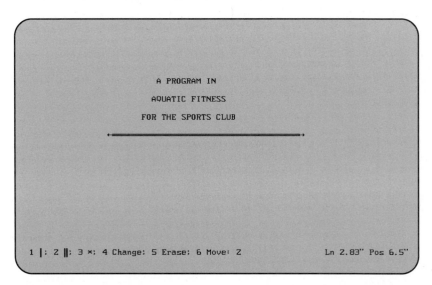

FIGURE 4-11

The line has been created. However, Peg thinks the line is too long. The Erase menu option will let you erase a line or a part of a line.

Select: Erase

To delete part of the line, using ←,

Move to: Ln 2.83" Pos 5.8"

The line is shortened. To turn off the Line Draw feature,

Press: Exit (F7)

You are returned to the document, and the Line Draw menu is no longer displayed.

After looking at the title, Peg thinks that another line above the title would look good.

Move to: Ln 1.5" Pos 2.6" (Use Space bar to move to Pos 2.6")
Select: **T**ools>**L**ine Draw
  >> Screen (CTRL) - (F3), **L**ine Draw

This time she wants to create a single line.

Select: 1
Move to: Ln 1.5" Pos 5.8"

Peg is happy with how the line appears and does not want to make any other changes. To leave the Line Draw feature,

Press: Exit (F7)

When the lines are printed the arrows at the beginning and end of the lines will not be printed.

Complete the title page by entering "By your name" on line 5.67". On line 5.83" enter the title of the course, and on the next line enter the current date as code using the Date command (Tools>Date Code or (SHIFT) - (F5), Date Code). All three lines should be centered on the page.

Creating a Table of Contents

Next Peg needs to create a table of contents for the report. Using ↓,

Move to: Pg 2 Ln 1.5"

The second page of the report contains the heading "TABLE OF CONTENTS" centered on the page. The table of contents can be generated automatically by WordPerfect from text within the document. There are three steps to creating a table of contents:

  Step 1 The text to be used in the table of contents is marked.
  Step 2 The location where the table is to be displayed is specified.
  Step 3 The table is generated or created.

Step 1: Marking Text for the Table of Contents

The Mark menu, or Mark Text (ALT) - (F5), marks the text to be used in the table of contents. Before selecting the command you must first highlight the text to be used as the table of contents heading.

The first heading to be marked is "INTRODUCTION." To move to the top of page 3,

Press: (PGDN)

When a block is defined that will be used in a table of contents, any codes that are included in the block will be included in the table of contents when it is created. Since this heading is in bold and centered, if the [Center] and [BOLD] codes are also included when the block is defined, the heading in the table of contents will appear both boldfaced and centered. Therefore you must be careful when highlighting a block of text to include in a table of contents, that only the codes you want are specified.

To display the codes while blocking the text,

Select: **F**ile>**R**eveal Codes
    >>   Reveal Codes (ALT) - (F3)

The cursor is positioned on the [Center] code, as you can see in the Reveal Codes portion of the window. Peg does not want to include either the [BOLD] code or the [Center] code in the block. To move the cursor to the right of the codes,

Press: (CTRL) - (→)

The cursor should be on the "I" in "INTRODUCTION." Next you need to highlight the word "INTRODUCTION," which will be used in the table of contents. While in Reveal Codes screen you can use the Block feature to highlight text; or you can use the mouse.

To turn on the Block feature,

Select: **E**dit>**B**lock
    >>   Block (ALT) - (F4)

"Block on" flashes in the status line of the upper part of the window, and a [Block] code is displayed in the Reveal Codes area. To highlight "INTRODUCTION,"

Press: (END) (←) or drag the mouse

Your screen should be similar to Figure 4-12.

FIGURE 4-12

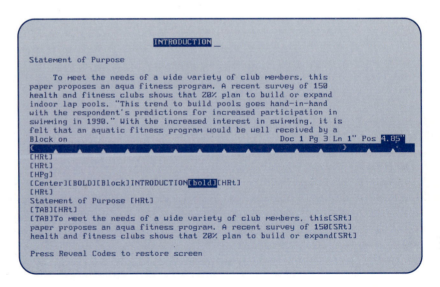

"INTRODUCTION" is highlighted in the upper screen, and the cursor is positioned on the ending [bold] code in the Reveal Codes screen. None of the codes surrounding the text will be included in the block.

To leave the Reveal Codes screen,

Select: Edit>Reveal Codes
>> Reveal Codes ALT - F3

The Block On feature should still be active.

Next, to tell WordPerfect that this block of text is to be used in a table of contents, it must be marked. The Mark menu, or Mark Text (ALT - F5), lets you specify the type of text you want to identify.

Select: Mark
>> Mark Text ALT - F5

Your screen should be similar to Figure 4-13. (If you used the function key command (ALT - F5) the menu is displayed in the status line.)

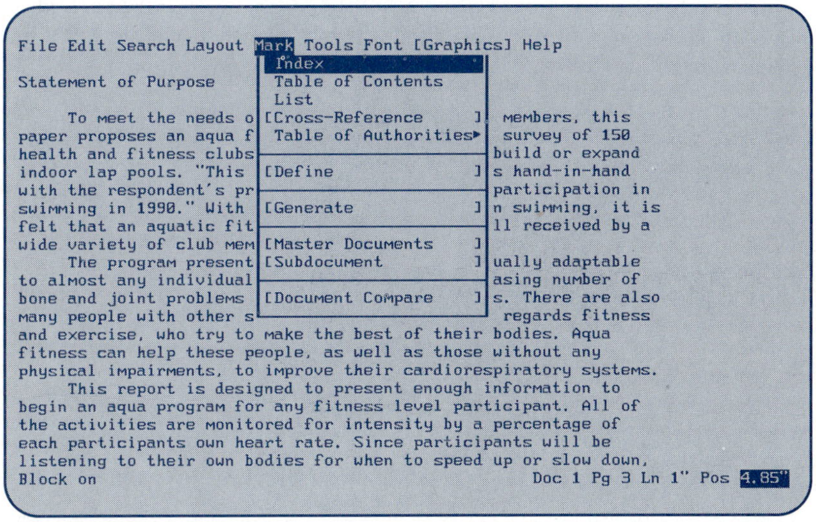

FIGURE 4-13

As you can see from the menu, text can also be marked to create a list, an index, a cross reference, or a table of authorities. The ToC option will mark a block for use in a table of contents by placing a [Mark] code at the beginning of the block and an [End Mark] code at the end of the block of text.

Select: Table of Contents
>> ToC

The prompt "ToC Level:" is displayed.

A table of contents can have up to five levels of heads. The selection of the level of heads determines how the table of contents will look. A **level one head** is the main head. A blank line is placed before all first-level entries. The **level two head** is subordinate to the level one head and is not separated from it by blank lines. Level two heads appear indented under the level one head. For example:

> This is a level one head.
> > This is a level two subhead.
> > This is a level two subhead.
>
> This is a level one head.
> > This is a level two subhead.

Peg wants to create a table of contents that will display the three main topics (I, II, and III in the outline) as level one heads. To identify the blocked text as a level one head,

Type: 1
Press: ⏎

You are returned to the document. The heading "INTRODUCTION" has been marked to be part of the table of contents.

The next heading to be marked is "Statement of Purpose" on line 1.33". Since there are no codes surrounding this block of text, you can simply highlight the block. This heading will be a second-level head in the table of contents.

Move to: Pg 3 Ln 1.33" Pos 1" (on "S" in "Statement")
Select: Edit>Block
>> Block (ALT) - (F4)

Highlight "Statement of Purpose". The cursor should be on Pos 3".
Then, to mark the text as a second-level head in the table of contents,

Select: Mark>Table of Contents
>> Mark Text (ALT) - (F5), ToC
Type: 2
Press: ⏎

To see the hidden codes marking the text for level one and level two table of contents heads,

Select: Edit>Reveal Codes
>> Reveal Codes (ALT) - (F3)

Your screen should be similar to Figure 4-14.

WP131
Creating a
Table of Contents

FIGURE 4-14

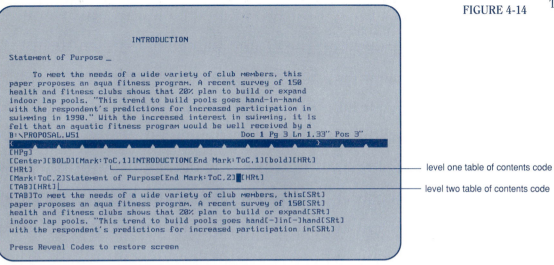

The mark text codes are displayed surrounding the text to be used in the table of contents. The two levels are also differentiated within the codes. If you needed to delete a table of contents heading, you would simply delete the code surrounding the text.

To return to the document,

Select: Edit>Reveal Codes
   >> Reveal Codes (ALT) - (F3)

Mark the next two headings as level two table of contents heads. They are:

Reasons for Aquatic Exercise Program - Pg 3 Ln 6.5"
Determining Target Heart Rate (THR) - Pg 4 Ln 1.83"

Next mark AQUATIC FITNESS ROUTINE (Pg 5 Ln 8") as a level one table of contents head. Be careful not to include the center and bold codes when blocking the heading.

Finally, mark the next two headings as level two table of contents heads:

Warm-up Stretches - Pg 6 Ln 1"
Aerobic Warm-up Exercises - Pg 6 Ln 4.67"

Note: You will complete marking the remaining table of contents heads in a practice exercise at the end of this lab.

Step 2: Define Table of Contents Location

The second step is to define where the table of contents is to be inserted into the document.

Move to: Pg 2 Ln 1.5" Pos 1" (3 lines below the heading "TABLE OF CONTENTS")

The Mark menu (or ALT - F5) option Define lets you specify the location for the table.

Select: **M**ark>**D**efine
>>   Mark Text (ALT) - (F5), **D**efine

Your screen should be similar to Figure 4-15.

FIGURE 4-15

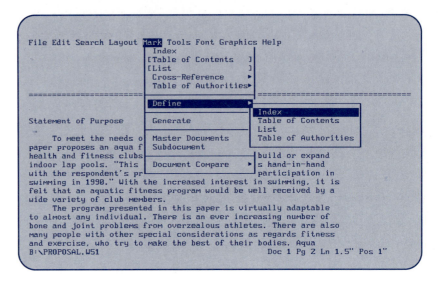

Note: If you used the function key to issue this command, the document is replaced by a full-screen menu of five options. They are the same choices which are available in the Define submenu.

Select: Table of **C**ontents
>>   Define Table of **C**ontents

Your screen should be similar to Figure 4-16.

FIGURE 4-16

```
Table of Contents Definition

    1 - Number of Levels            1

    2 - Display Last Level in       No
        Wrapped Format

    3 - Page Numbering - Level 1  Flush right with leader
                         Level 2
                         Level 3
                         Level 4
                         Level 5




Selection: 0
```

A full-screen menu is displayed. This is the Table of Contents Definition menu. Option 1 Number of Levels displays the default setting of 1 as the number of levels used in the table of contents. Since you defined two levels in the table of contents, change this setting to 2.

Select: Number of Levels
Type: 2

The second option lets you specify whether you want the second-level entries to wrap, or to each be displayed on a separate line. You want each level to be displayed on a separate line. This is the default, and requires no adjustment.

The third option lets you select the page numbering style for each level. The default will display the page numbers flush with the right side of the page with a series of dots, or **leaders**, between the header and the page number. To select this option,

Select: Page Numbering

The five numbering styles are displayed in the status line. To leave the page numbering style as it is for both levels and to exit this menu,

Press: Exit (F7)

To leave the Table of Contents Definition menu,

Press: ⏎

You are returned to the document. To see the codes,

Select: Edit>Reveal Codes
>> Reveal Codes (ALT) - (F3)

The code [Def Mark ToC,2:5,5] has been entered into the document at this location. This code will tell WordPerfect where to place the table of contents when it is generated.

Select: Edit>Reveal Codes
>> Reveal Codes (ALT) - (F3)

Step 3: Generate the Table of Contents

Finally, you are ready for WordPerfect to do a little work. Once all the headings are marked and the table of contents definitions completed, the table of contents can be generated.

Select: Mark>Generate
>> Mark Text (ALT) - (F5), Generate

The Mark Text: Generate menu is displayed. To generate the table of contents,

Select: Generate Tables, Index, Cross-References, etc.

The prompt at the bottom of the screen asks you to confirm that you want any existing tables deleted. Since there are no other tables created in this document, you can accept the default response of Yes.

Type: Y

The message displayed at the bottom of the screen tells you that generation has started. The "Pass:" and "Page:" indicators help you keep track of its progress. When complete the table of contents should be displayed.

Your screen should be similar to Figure 4-17.

FIGURE 4-17

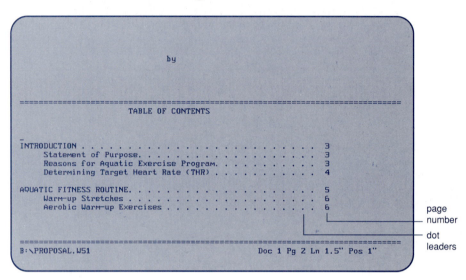

The table of contents for the first few pages of the report is displayed. A blank line separates the first-level heads. The level two heads appear indented under the level one heads. The page numbers are displayed flush with the right side of the page. A series of dots, or leaders, separates the heads from the page numbers, as specified.

Creating Footnotes

Next Peg needs to enter footnotes into her paper. WordPerfect can help her do this by automatically numbering the footnotes and placing them properly at the bottom of the page. The Footnote (Layout>Footnote or Footnote (CTRL) - (F7), 1) command is used to create footnotes.

Before using the Footnote command, the cursor must be positioned in the text where the footnote number is to be inserted. Peg's first footnote will appear following the quote in the first paragraph of the Statement of Purpose on page 3.

Press: (PGDN)
Move to: Ln 2.5" Pos 2.8" (after the quotes (") on the sixth line of the first paragraph of page 3)
Select: Layout
>> Footnote (CTRL) - (F7)

The Layout menu options, Footnote and Endnote (displayed in the status line if you used the function key), let you create and edit footnotes or endnotes. The procedure for both is very similar. The difference is that footnotes are printed at the bottom of the page where the reference is made, and endnotes are compiled as a list at the end of the document.

To create a footnote,

Select: Footnote

Your screen should be similar to Figure 4-18.

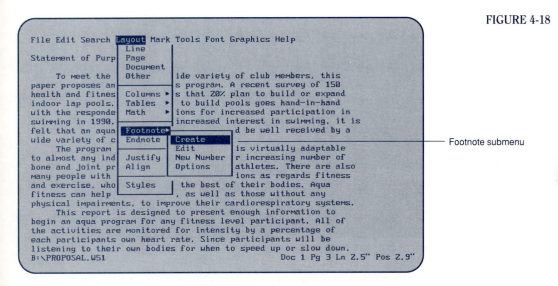

FIGURE 4-18

The four Footnote submenu options (displayed in the status line if you used the function key command) let you create and edit footnotes. To create a footnote,

Select: Create

The text has been replaced by a nearly blank screen. This is a special editing screen used to enter the text for the endnote or footnote. The note can be up to 16,000 lines long. The number 1 displayed on the screen shows that this is the first footnote entered in the text.

To enter a space after the number and before the text of the footnote,

Press: Space bar

When entering a footnote, the same commands and features you use in the normal document editing can be used.

Type: "Participation Up, Swimming Forecast Looks Strong," Athletic Business, July 1988, p. 37. (do not press Enter)

Your screen should be similar to Figure 4-19.

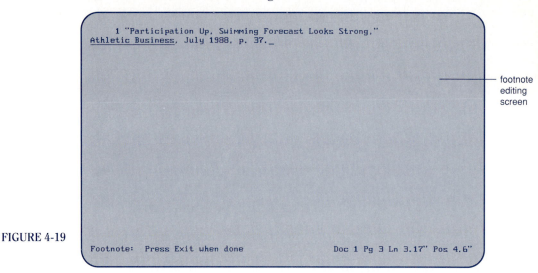

FIGURE 4-19

To save the footnote and return to the document,

Press: Exit (F7)

Your screen should be similar to Figure 4-20.

FIGURE 4-20

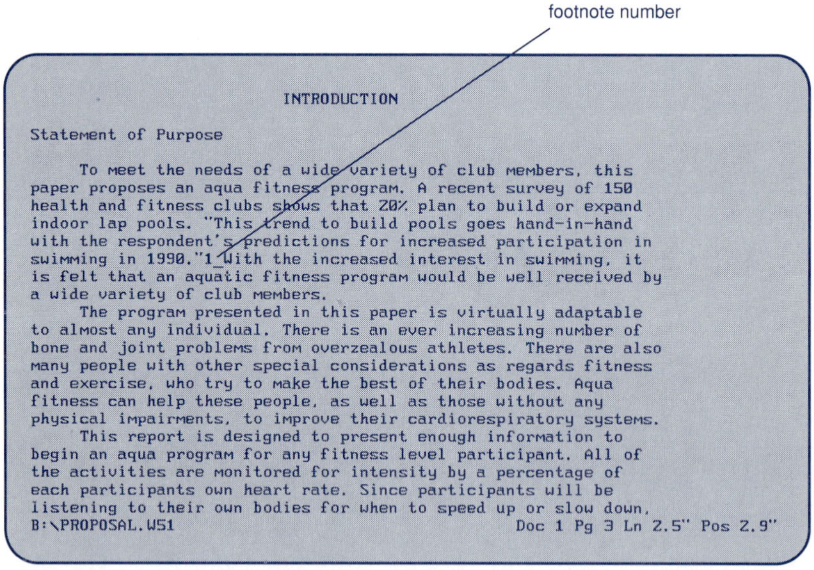

The footnote number, 1, is entered in the text at the location of the cursor. On some screens it may appear highlighted or superscripted. It will appear as a superscript number when printed. The footnotes will not appear on the screen. When the page or entire report is printed, they will be automatically printed on the bottom of the page containing the footnote number.

To enter the second footnote,

Move to: Pg 3 Ln 8.67" Pos 4.8" (space after "water." on third line of sixth paragraph)

WP137
Creating Footnotes

Select: Layout>Footnote>Create
>> Footnote CTRL - F7, Footnote>Create

Notice that the footnote number on the screen is 2.

Press: Space bar
Type: President's Council on Physical Fitness and Sports, Aqua Dynamics: Physical Conditioning Through Water Exercises, p. 1.
Press: Exit F7

The second footnote number is entered in the text.

Peg forgot to enter a footnote earlier in the text.

Move to: Pg 3 Ln 7.33" Pos 6.8" (space after the word "activity." on fourth line of fifth paragraph)
Select: Layout>Footnote>Create
>> Footnote CTRL - F7, Footnote>Create

Notice that this footnote is number 2. WordPerfect automatically adjusted the footnote numbers when the new footnote was inserted.

Press: Space bar
Type: Ibid.
Press: Exit F7

Notice that both footnotes are still displayed as footnote 2. To update the screen display using the Rewrite feature,

Select: Screen CTRL - F3, Rewrite
Move to: Pg 4 Ln 1"

Your screen should be similar to Figure 4-21.

FIGURE 4-21

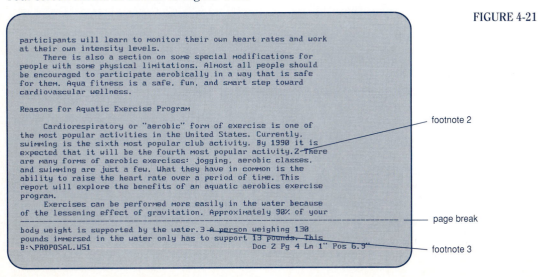

The footnote number for the third footnote changed to 3. Also notice that the sentence containing the third footnote moved to the top of page 4. This is because WordPerfect determined there would not be enough space at the bottom of page 3 to display two footnotes and the associated text.

Editing a Footnote

Peg realizes that she forgot to enter the date in the footnote text for the third footnote. The Edit option in the Footnote submenu lets you change the information in an existing footnote. To edit a footnote you can be anywhere within the document. To edit footnote 3,

Select: Layout>Footnote>Edit
>> Footnote (CTRL) - (F7), Footnote>Edit

The prompt to enter the number of the footnote that you want to edit is displayed. If the correct footnote number is displayed following the prompt you can press (⏎) to accept it. Otherwise you must type in the footnote number following the prompt. Since you want to edit footnote number 3,

Type: 3
Press: (⏎)

The text for footnote 3 is displayed on the screen. To add the date before the page number of the footnote,

Move to: Ln 1.67" Pos 6.7"
Type: 1981,
Press: Space bar
Press: Exit (F7)

Now Peg wants to see how the page containing the footnotes will appear when printed. To see how the footnotes on page 3 will appear when printed move to anywhere within page 3, then

Select: File>Print> View Document
>> Print (SHIFT) - (F7), View Document

After a few moments page 3 is generated and displayed in the View Document screen.

Note: If your computer does not have graphics capabilities, your screen cannot display the entire page as in Figure 4-23. Instead it will display the first 24 lines of the page with the margins and other print options as close as possible to how it will appear when printed. The instructions that follow do not apply to your computer system. Instead, to see the footnotes as they will appear when printed press (CTRL) - (HOME) (↓). The footnotes will appear as they will be printed; however, the footnote numbers will not appear in superscript. To leave the View screen press (F7). Continue the lab by skipping to the next section, "Numbering Pages."

If you are not viewing the bottom of the page and your View screen is not 100%,

Select: 1 100%
Press: (HOME) (↓)

The text is large enough to read easily. Notice that the footnote number is displayed in superscript, and the footnotes appear at the bottom of the page as they will be printed.

To leave the View screen,

Press: Exit (F7)

Numbering Pages

Next Peg wants to instruct WordPerfect to print page numbers for each page in the report. The code to create page numbering is entered on the page where you want page numbering to begin. Generally this is the beginning of the document. To move to the top of page 1,

Press: (HOME) (HOME) (↑)

The Layout>Page, or Format (SHIFT) - (F8), Page, command is used to specify page numbering.

Select: Layout>Page
   >>   Format (SHIFT) - (F8), **P**age

The Page Format menu is displayed. The Page Numbering option lets you specify the placement of numbers on the pages.

Select: Page **N**umbering

The Format: Page Numbering menu is displayed. The four options let you control how and where page numbers are inserted. To turn on page numbering from the cursor position forward, you need to specify where you want the page number placed on the page. The Page Number Position option shows the default is to display no page numbers. To change this setting and specify where you want the number placed,

Select: Page Number **P**osition

Your screen should be similar to Figure 4-22.

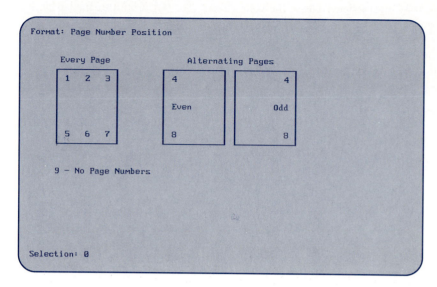

FIGURE 4-22

The Format: Page Number Position menu is displayed. The numbers displayed on the page layout let you specify where the page number will appear. The option number corresponds to its position on the page layout. Peg wants each page number centered on the bottom of every page (option 6),

Select: 6

The new page number position, bottom center, is displayed. To return to the document,

Press: Exit (F7)

The page numbers will not appear on the screen. However, when the document is printed the page numbers will appear on the margin of the location specified. If new pages are inserted or others deleted, WordPerfect will automatically renumber the pages.

Suppressing Page Numbers

Peg realizes that she really does not want the title and table of contents pages to be numbered. She can turn off the page numbering for specified pages using the Page Format menu. To do this, the cursor must be positioned at the beginning of the page to be unnumbered.

The cursor should already be on the first line of page 1. If it is not, move it there.

Select: Layout>Page
   >>

The option "Suppress (this page only)" will turn off page numbering for the page the cursor is on.

Select: Suppress (this page only)

Your screen should be similar to Figure 4-23.

FIGURE 4-23

```
Format: Suppress (this page only)

    1 - Suppress All Page Numbering, Headers and Footers
    2 - Suppress Headers and Footers
    3 - Print Page Number at Bottom Center    No
    4 - Suppress Page Numbering               No
    5 - Suppress Header A                     No
    6 - Suppress Header B                     No
    7 - Suppress Footer A                     No
    8 - Suppress Footer B                     No




Selection: 0
```

A menu of eight options is displayed. The options allow you to suppress or temporarily turn off different page format settings. To turn off page numbering and return to the document,

Select: Suppress **P**age Numbering
Type: Y
Press: Exit (F7)

Use the Reveal Codes screen to look at the codes inserted at this location in your document. It should display [Pg Numbering:Bottom Center][Suppress:PgNum].
Exit the Reveal Codes screen.
Following the procedure above, suppress the page numbering for the Table of Contents page (page 2).

Centering Text Top to Bottom

Next Peg would like the text on the title page to be centered between top and bottom margins of the page. Before this command is used the cursor needs to be positioned at the top left margin of the page to be centered.

Press: (HOME) (HOME) (↑)

The cursor should be on the left margin of the first line of page 1. The Center Page option (1) in the Page Format menu will automatically center the text vertically on a page.

Select:	**L**ayout>**P**age
>>	Format (SHIFT) - (F8), **P**age
Select:	**C**enter Page (top to bottom)
Type:	Y
Press:	Exit (F7)

Again, not until you print or view the page will you see how the text is centered on the page. It will position the text on this page so that an equal number of blank lines lie above and below the first and last line of text.

Center the text on the table of contents page. Use the Reveal Codes screen to view the codes entered at this location.

Using Block Protection

Peg has one last concern. She wants to make sure that text that should remain together on one page, such as a table or a long quote, is not divided over two pages. This situation frequently occurs because WordPerfect automatically calculates the length of each page and inserts a **soft page break** when needed without discrimination as to the text. The position of a soft page break will change as text is added or deleted.

To control where a page ends you could enter a **hard page break** to make WordPerfect begin a new page. A hard page break is entered by pressing (CTRL) - (⏎). However, if you continue to edit the document by adding and deleting text that affects the length of the document, the location of the hard page break may no longer be appropriate. Then you would need to delete the hard page break code and reenter it at the new location. To do this is time consuming.

One solution is to use the Block Protection command (Edit>Protect Block or Block (ALT) - (F4), Format (SHIFT) - (F8)) to keep a specified block of text together on a page. Before using Block Protection, the block of text must be marked. The area of text which Peg does not want to be split between two pages is on page 5.

Move to: Pg 5 Ln 1.5" Pos 1" ("W" in "With")

To specify the first block of text to protect,

Select:	**E**dit>**B**lock
>>	Block (ALT) - (F4)

Highlight the text on lines 1.5" through 2.33". The highlight should cover the lead-in sentence and the following three lines of formulas.

Select: **E**dit>**P**rotect Block

To see the hidden codes entered into the text as a result of using this command,

Select: Edit>Reveal Codes
 >> Reveal Codes (ALT) - (F3)
Press: ↑ (2 times)

Your screen should be similar to Figure 4-24.

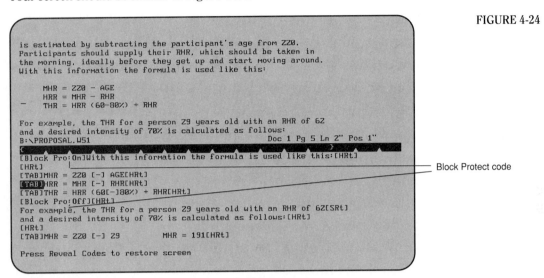

FIGURE 4-24

A [Block Pro:On] code is inserted at the beginning of the block, and a [Block Pro:Off] code is inserted at the end of the block. Now, when WordPerfect formats this page for printing, the text between these codes will never be divided between two pages. If there is not enough space on a page to accommodate the entire block of text a page break is inserted above the [Block Pro:On] code, and the entire block is moved to the next page.

However, in this case it appears that there are enough lines left on this page to keep the entire block of text together, and no page break is inserted. It is always a good idea to turn on Block Protection even though it currently may appear that it is not needed. Later editing of the document may change the location of the block in the text, resulting in a split between two pages.

To remove the Reveal Codes screen,

Select: Edit>Reveal Codes
 >> Reveal Codes (ALT) - (F3)

The next block to be protected begins on Pg 5 Ln 2.5" through Ln 3.33". This block begins with the words "For example" and ends after the third line of formulas.
Block this area of text.
To protect this block, you will use the function key equivalent this time. It is (SHIFT) - (F8).

Select: Format (SHIFT) - (F8)

The prompt "Protect Block?" appears in the status line. To turn on protection,

Type: Y

As Peg looks through the document she notices that a chart which begins on page 5 is divided between two pages. To move to the bottom of page 5,

Press: CTRL - HOME ↓

As you can see, the fitness table which begins on page 5 continues on page 6.

Following the above procedure, protect the table and lead-in sentence (beginning with the word "Once") to prevent the text from appearing on separate pages. (The block should extend through Pg 6 Ln 1.5".)

Your screen should be similar to Figure 4-25.

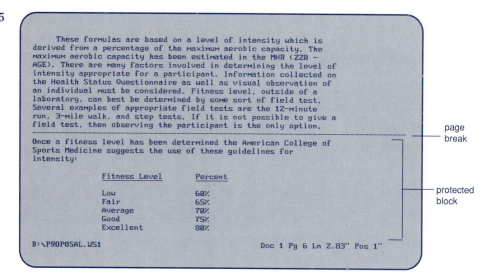

FIGURE 4-25

This time a page break is inserted by the program so that the entire block begins on the following page. Using Block Protection Peg could add more lines of data within the block codes, and the protection would remain in effect.

Preventing Widows and Orphans

The second way to control how text is divided between two pages is to turn on Widow/Orphan Protection. When the first line of a paragraph is the last line on a page it is called a **widow**. When the last line of a paragraph appears at the top of a new page it is called an **orphan**. To prevent this type of problem from occurring, the Widow/Orphan Protection command is used.

The Widow/Orphan Protection command (Layout>Line>Widow/Orphan Protection or SHIFT - F8, Line>Widow/Orphan Protection) should be entered at the beginning of the document so that all the following text will be affected. To move back to the beginning of the document and to use this command,

Press: (HOME) (HOME) (↑)
Select: **L**ayout>**L**ine
>> Format (SHIFT) - (F8), **L**ine

The Line Format menu is displayed. The last option, 9, Widow/Orphan, will turn on this protection.

Select: **W**idow/Orphan Protection

The cursor moved to the default for this option. To turn on Widow/Orphan Protection,

Type: Y
Press: Exit (F7)

To see the hidden codes,

Select: **E**dit>**R**eveal Codes
>> Reveal Codes (ALT) - (F3)

Your screen should be similar to Figure 4-26.

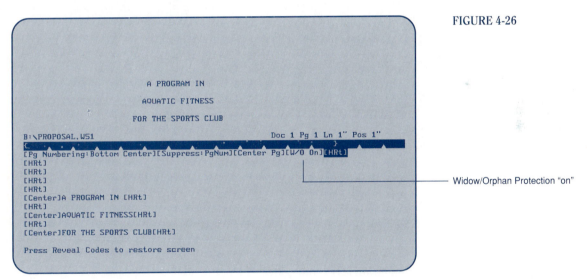

FIGURE 4-26

The four page-format codes you entered at the beginning of the document are displayed. The code [W/O on] will will automatically determine when it is necessary to adjust the text on a page to eliminate widows and orphans. This protection applies only to traditional paragraphs, however.

Select: **E**dit>**R**eveal Codes
>> Reveal Codes (ALT) - (F3)

Printing the Report

Although Peg has a lot more work to do on the report, she wants to print out the first few pages of the text to see how the page settings and footnotes will appear.

Select: File>Print
   >>   Print SHIFT - F7

Next select the printer you want to use to print this document.
The option Multiple Pages will let you specify which pages of the on-screen document to print.

Select: Multiple Pages

The prompt "Page(s):" allows you to print the entire document (All), which is the default, individual pages, or any range of pages.

To print pages 1 through 3, 5, and 6,

Type: 1-3,5,6
Press: ⏎

The prompt "Document may need to be generated. Print?" is displayed. In response to this prompt,

Type: Y

The specified pages should be printing.
Check to see that the page numbers are displayed as specified, that the first two pages are centered, and that the footnotes are correct.
To leave the Print menu,

Press: ⏎

Save the edited report as FITNESS and exit WordPerfect.

Key Terms

paragraph number
family
level one head
level two head
leader
soft page break
hard page break
widow
orphan

Matching

1. (SHIFT)-(F5), 4 _____ a. allows you to specify the placement of page numbers
2. [Par Num:Auto] _____ b. turns on the Outline feature
3. (CTRL)-(F3), 3 _____ c. reformats the display of the screen
4. (ALT)-(F5), 1, 2 _____ d. the View Document command
5. (ALT)-(F5), 6 _____ e. the code for an outline paragraph number
6. (CTRL)-(F7), 1 _____ f. creates a footnote
7. (CTRL)-(F3), 2 _____ g. centers a page top to bottom
8. (SHIFT)-(F7), 6 _____ h. generates a table of contents
9. (SHIFT)-(F8), 2, 1 _____ i. accesses the Line Draw feature
10. (SHIFT)-(F8), 2, 6 _____ j. creates a second level table of contents head

Practice Exercises

1. Retrieve the file FITNESS (created at the end of the lab). You will complete the table of contents for the report.

   ■ Continue marking the level one and two heads as shown below. Do not include bold, center, or underline codes.

   Level one head:

   Special Problem Modifications

   Level two heads:

   Conditioning Activities
   Cool-Down Activities
   Toning
   Orthopedic
   Diabetes
   Asthmatic
   Obesity
   Hypertension
   Seizures
   Elderly

- Return to page 2 of the report and delete the table of contents definition marker code [DefMark ToC,2].
- Enter a new definition marker code at this location. This time specify that the page numbers are displayed flush right but without dot leaders.
- Generate the new table of contents. Make sure that you respond "Yes" to the prompt to confirm that you want any previous tables deleted.
- Print the table of contents page only.
- Save the revised report as FITNESS1.

2. Retrieve the file FITNESS1 created in problem 1. You will enter several more footnotes in the report.

- Enter the fourth footnote at the end of the sentence on Pg 4 Ln 5". The footnote is:

    Judy Seigel, "Children's Target Heart Rate Range," <u>Journal of Physical Education, Recreation & Dance</u>, 59, April 1988.

- Enter the fifth footnote at the end of the sentence on Pg 5 Ln 4.33". The footnote is:

    Joseph McEnvoy, <u>Fitness Swimming: Lifetime Programs</u>, 1985, p. 12.

- Enter another footnote at the end of the first sentence on Pg 4 Ln 8. This footnote is:

    <u>Ibid</u>.

    What number is this footnote? Use the Rewrite feature to update the footnote numbering. What number is the footnote in the middle of page 5?

- Edit footnote number 4. It needs the page reference, "p. 78," added to the end of the footnote.
- Save the report as FITNESS2.
- Print pages 4 and 5.

3. In the next two problems you will create an outline for a paper and write a short paper using WordPerfect. The paper can be any paper you have written in the past.

- Create an outline for your paper. The outline for your paper should have a minimum of three main topic heads (I., II., III.).
- Under the three topic heads you must have a minimum of two subheads (A., B.).
- You must show at least two paragraph level three and level four numbers (1., 2., and a., b.).

Minimally, your outline should look like this:

I.
    A.
        1.
        2.
            a.
            b.
    B.

II.
    A.
    B.

III.
    A.
    B.

4. Write a paper based upon the outline you created in problem 3. The paper can be a paper you have written in the past. It must be a minimum of five pages. You must demonstrate the following:

- Title page

    The title of the paper must be centered and boldfaced.

    The title must have a double line above and below it.

    Your name and the current date (using the Date command) must appear near the bottom of the title page. They must be centered.

    The entire title page should be centered top to bottom.

- Table of contents

    The heading on this page should be centered and boldfaced.

    The table of contents should show the three main headings from the outline as level one heads. The structure of your report will determine the number of level two heads.

    The page numbers should appear right justified. There should not be any dot leaders before the page numbers.

- Body of the report

    There must be a minimum of three pages of text.

    You must enter a minimum of four footnotes.

- The report must have pages numbered on the top right of every page. Suppress page numbering for the title page and the table of contents.
- Turn on Widow/Orphan Protection.
- Turn right justification off.
- Print the report.

SUMMARY
WordPerfect 5.1

Glossary of Key Terms

Active printer: The selected printer used to print the document.

Address file: The secondary merge file used in a merge. It typically contains name and address data to be combined with the primary file document.

Block: A selected area of text, which can vary in size from a single character to the entire document, that is to be copied, moved, or deleted.

Boldface: Printed text that appears darker than surrounding text as a result of printing over the text several times.

Buffer file: A temporary file used to store the last three deletions made to the document.

Center: To position text in a line evenly between the margins.

Code: A hidden symbol entered in the text when a command that affects the format of the text—such as justification, margins, and boldfacing—is used.

Context sensitive: The ability of the Help system to automatically display information about the command in use.

Cursor: A flashing underscore or box that indicates where the next character you type will appear on the screen.

Default: The predefined program settings used initially by the program. Generally, these settings are the most commonly used settings.

Delete: To erase or remove a character, word, or block of text from the document.

Document: A WordPerfect file containing text and codes.

Edit: To correct or change the text or format of a document file.

Endnote: A note of reference in a document displayed at the end of the text.

Family: A section of an outline that consists of the outline level at the cursor location and any subordinates or lower levels.

Field: Each piece of data contained in a record of information in the secondary merge file for use in the merge process.

File extension: The last one to three characters of a filename following a period. Some software packages use this to identify which files were created using that package.

Filename: A unique name for identifying different documents and programs. Each filename consists of from one to eight characters, followed by a period (.) and an optional file extension.

Flush right: Positions a line of text so that the rightmost character is aligned with the right margin.

Footnote: A note of reference in a document displayed at the bottom of the page where the reference occurs.

Hard carriage return: Moves the cursor to the beginning of the next line or inserts a blank line into a text file when ⏎ is pressed.

Hard page break: A page break entered by pressing (CTRL - ⏎). A new page will begin following a hard page break regardless of the amount of text on the page.

Insert mode: Allows new text to be entered in a document at the cursor location by moving all existing text to the right.

Justification: When on, the text is aligned with both the left and right margins, producing even or straight margins on both the right and left sides of the document.

Leader: A series of dots or other characters between the header and the page number in the table of contents.

Level one head: The main head used in the table of contents.

Level two head: The second level head used in the table of contents.

Line: A single row of text. The WordPerfect default setting is 54 lines to a printed page.

Menu bar: The top line of the screen which, when activated by pressing ALT - = , displays the nine menus that can be opened.

Menu cursor: The highlight that covers the name of the selected menu.

Merge codes: WordPerfect codes entered in the primary file that control which fields are used from the secondary merge file and where they are entered in the primary file.

Mnemonic letter: The highlighted letter associated with the menu or submenu name.

Move: To remove a marked block of text from one location in a document and place it in a different location.

Newspaper columns: Columns of text that are read down the page and wrap to the top of the next column on the same page, like a newspaper.

Option: A list of command menu choices from which the user selects.

Orphan: The last line of a paragraph that is printed as the first line of a new page.

Page: The number of lines that can be printed on a single sheet of paper.

Paragraph number: The lettering/numbering system used in the Outline command to identify the topic levels and define the structure of the outline.

Parallel columns: Columns of text that are read across a page of text rather than down.

Position: The location of the cursor on a line.

Primary file: The file containing the form letter or master document that controls the merge process using merge codes.

Prompt: A question or other indication that the computer is waiting for a response from the user.

Pull-down menu: A list of commands displayed in a box below the selected menu that are available for selection.

Record: All the fields of data in the secondary merge file that may be used to complete the primary file during the merge process.

Reformat: Automatic readjustment of the text on a line after the text has been changed so that the justification is reestablished.

Repeater: The ESC key in WordPerfect causes a command or function to be repeated a certain number of times.

Replace: To substitute a new version of a document for the old version when saving.

Repositioning: The message displayed in WordPerfect when the cursor is directed to move to a new location.

Save: To write the current document to a diskette so that when the computer is turned off, the document will remain intact.

Scroll: To move quickly line by line, screen by screen, or page by page through the document.

Search: To move backward or forward through a document to locate a specified character string in the document.

Secondary merge file: A file used in a merge. It typically contains name and address data to be combined with the primary file document.

Soft carriage return: Carriage return entered automatically by the word wrap feature, which determines when a line of text should end.

Soft page break: A page break automatically entered by the program when the entire page is filled. The location of the page break changes automatically as text is added or deleted.

Status line: The bottom line of the screen display, which displays the document number, page, line, and position of the cursor in the document. It may also display a menu or program prompts if a command is issued.

String: A specific combination of characters and/or codes.

Submenu: Another list of commands available for selection when a command that displays a > symbol following the command name is selected.

Supplementary dictionary: A secondary dictionary used by the Speller consisting of words added by the user. Whenever the Speller does not locate the word in the main dictionary, it will check the supplemental dictionary.

Switch: To move from one document into another document file when two documents are in use at one time.

Typeover mode: Activated by pressing the (INS) key. In the typeover mode, new text replaces the existing text by typing over it.

Underline: An underscore appears under every character or space in the selected block of text.

Widow: The first line of a paragraph that is printed as the last line of a page.

Window: Division of the display screen into two parts, which allows you to view two different documents at the same time or two parts of the same document at the same time.

Word wrap: Feature that automatically determines when to begin the next line of text. The user does not press ⏎ at the end of a line unless it is the end of a paragraph or to insert a blank line.

Functional Summary of Selected WordPerfect Commands

To start WordPerfect: WP
To display Menu bar: [ALT] - =

Function	Command	Action
Cursor movement	→	One character right
	←	One character left
	↑	One line up
	↓	One line down
	[CTRL] - →	One word right
	[CTRL] - ←	One word left
	[HOME] - → or [END]	Right end of line
	[HOME] ←	Left edge of screen
	[HOME] ↑ or - (minus sign)	Top of screen
	[HOME] ↓ or + (plus sign)	Bottom of screen
	[CTRL] - [HOME] ↑	Top of current page
	[CTRL] - [HOME] ↓	Bottom of current page
	[CTRL] - [HOME] page n	Top of the page n specified
	[PGUP]	Top of previous page
	[PGDN]	Top of next page
	[HOME] [HOME] ↑	Top of document
	[HOME] [HOME] ↓	Bottom of document
	[CTRL] - [HOME] →	One column right
	[CTRL] - [HOME] ←	One column left
	[ESC] n, command	Repeat command n times
	[ESC] n, arrow	Move cursor n spaces or lines
Insert	[INS] on	Insert text
	[INS] off	Typeover text
	↵	Insert blank line/end line
Delete	[DEL]	Delete at cursor
	[BKSP]	Delete left of cursor
	[CTRL] - [BKSP]	Delete word
	[CTRL] - [END]	Delete to end of line
	[CTRL] - [PGDN]	Delete to end of page
Retrieve	[SHIFT] - [F10] File>Retrieve	Retrieve a file
Save	[F10] File>Save>Y	Save file, resume edit
	[F7] Y File>Exit>Y	Save file, clear screen
Blocks	[ALT] - [F4] Edit>Block	Block on/off
	[CTRL] - [F4] Edit>Select	Move, copy, delete, or append a sentence, paragraph, page

WP154
Summary: WordPerfect

Function	Command	Action
Format	`F6` Font>Appearance>Bold	Bold on/off
	`F8` Font>Appearance>Underline	Underline on/off
	`SHIFT` - `F6` Layout>Align>Center	Center text
	`ALT` - `F6` Layout>Align>Flush Right	Flush right
	`SHIFT` - `F8`, **1 7** Layout>Line>Margins	Set margins
	`SHIFT` - `F8`, **1 8** Layout>Line>Tab Set	Set tabs
	`SHIFT` - `F8`, **1 3** Layout>Line>Justification	Set justification
Print	`SHIFT` - `F7` **1** File>Print>Full Document	Print full document
	`SHIFT` - `F7` **2** File>Print>Page	Print a page
	`SHIFT` - `F7` **6** File>Print> View Document	View Document
	`SHIFT` - `F7` **S** File>Print>Select Printer	Selects printer
Outline	`SHIFT` - `F5` **4 1** Tools>Outline>On	Outline mode on
	`SHIFT` - `F5` **4 2** Tools>Outline>Off	Outline mode off
	`SHIFT` - `F5` **4 3** Tools>Outline>Move Family	Move family
	`SHIFT` - `F5` **4 4** Tools>Outline>Copy Family	Copy family
	`SHIFT` - `F5` **4 5** Tools>Outline>Delete Family	Delete family
Line Draw	`CTRL` - `F3` **2** Tools>Line Draw	Begins Line Draw
	`CTRL` - `F3` **2 1** Tools>Line Draw>1	Creates single line
	`CTRL` - `F3` **2 2** Tools>Line Draw>2	Creates double line
	`CTRL` - `F3` **2 3** Tools>Line Draw>3	Creates line of asterisks
	`CTRL` - `F3` **2 4** Tools>Line Draw>Change	Creates line of your design
	`CTRL` - `F3` **2 5** Tools>Line Draw>Erase	Erases a line
	`CTRL` - `F3` **2 6** Tools>Line Draw>Move	Moves the cursor without creating a line
Table of Contents	`ALT` - `F5` **1** Mark>Table of Contents	Marks selected text to be used in TOC
	`ALT` - `F5` **5** Mark>Define>Table of Contents	Specifies location and design for TOC

WP155
Functional Summary of Selected
WordPerfect Commands

Function	Command	Action
Table of Contents (*continued*)	ALT - F5 **6 5** Mark>Generate>Generate	Generates TOC Tables, Indexes, Cross-References, etc.
Footnotes	CTRL - F7 **1** Layout>Footnote>Create	Allows entry of footnote references and specifies location of footnote in text
	CTRL - F7 **2** Layout>Endnote>Create	Allows entry of endnote references and specifies location of endnote in text
	CTRL - F7 **1 2** Layout>Footnote>Edit	Allows you to edit footnote references
Page Format	SHIFT - F8 **2 6** Layout>Page>Page Numbering	Specifies placement of page numbers
	SHIFT - F8 **2 8** Layout>Page>Suppress	Surpresses page numbering
	SHIFT - F8 **2 1** Layout>Page>Center Page	Centers text vertically on a page
	SHIFT - F8 **1 9** Layout>Line>Widow/Orphan Protection	Turns on Widow/Orphan protection
	SHIFT - F8 Edit>Protect Block	Turns on block protection for a selected block of text
Merge	SHIFT - F9 **1** Tools>Merge Codes>Field	Define field names
	SHIFT - F9 **2** Tools>Merge Codes>End Record	End of record
	SHIFT - F9 **6** Tools>Merge Codes>More	Advanced Merge Codes
	F9 Tools>Merge Codes>More>{End of Field}	End field
	CTRL - F9 **1** Tools>Merge	Merge primary and secondary files
Columns	ALT - F7 **1 3** Layout>Columns>Define	Define column settings
	ALT - F7 **1 1** Layout>Columns>On	Turn on column settings
	ALT - F7 **1 2** Layout>Columns>Off	Turn off column settings
Search	F2 Search>Forward	Search forwards
	SHIFT - F2 Search>Backward	Search backwards
	ALT - F2 Search>Replace	Search and replace
Utilities	SHIFT - F3 Edit>Switch Document	Switch to document 2
	F3 Help>Help	Help

WP156
Summary: WordPerfect

Function	Command	Action
Utilities *(continued)*	`F5` File>List Files	List files
	`ALT`-`F3` Edit>Reveal Codes	Reveal codes
	`F1` Edit>Undelete	Cancel/Undelete
	`CTRL`-`F3` 1 Edit>Window	Windows
	`SHIFT`-`F5` 1 Tools>Date Text	Date text
	`SHIFT`-`F5` 2 Tools>Date Code	Date as code
	`SHIFT`-`F5` 3 Tools>Date Format	Date Format
	`CTRL`-`F2` Tools>Spell	Begins Spell Checking
	`ALT`-`F1` Tools>Thesaurus	Begins Thesaurus
	`CTRL`-`F3` 3	Rewrites display of text on the screen
	`CTRL`-`↵`	Hard page break
Exit	`F7`>**NY**	Abandons file without saving and exits WP
	`F7` **Y Y** File>Exit **Y Y**	Saves file and exits WP

INDEX

Address files:
    creating, WP89-93
    defined, WP84, WP150
    merging with letter files, WP94-95
Aligning flush right, WP63-64
Appending text, defined, WP58

Binding, allowing for in printing, WP76-77
Block protection, WP142-43
Blocks:
    defined, WP4, WP150
    marking, WP59-60
    marking for contents, WP127-31
    marking for underline, WP102-3
    moving, WP59-61
    moving, in Outline mode, WP121
    summary of commands, WP153
    See also Block protection
Boldfacing:
    defined, WP4, WP150
    text, WP95-WP97
Booting up, WP6
Brackets, for codes, WP72

Canceling menu selections, WP12
Caps Lock key, WP96
Carriage returns:
    hard, WP38, WP71, WP150
    soft, WP72, WP150
    and word wrap, WP52
Centering:
    defined, WP4, WP150
    text, WP95-97
    text top to bottom, WP141-42
Character string:
    defined, WP4
    text, WP73-74
Characters:
    deleting, WP29-31
    inserting, WP32-35
    repeating, WP37
Codes:
    for Block Protect, WP143
    for columns, WP103
    defined, WP150
    deleting, WP72

    displaying, WP70-72
    hiding, WP72
    merge, WP84-89, WP151
    in Outline mode, WP119, WP122-24
    removing Reveal Codes, WP119
    for tables of contents, WP127-28
Columns:
    commands for, WP155
    defining, WP103
    editing in column format, WP107
    newspaper style, WP104
    parallel, WP104
    turning settings on/off, WP106
Commands:
    Block, WP59-61, WP124
    Block Protect, WP142-44
    Bold, WP97
    canceling, WP12
    Center, WP96
    for columns, WP155
    Date, WP62-63
    Delete, WP153
    Exit, WP42, WP48
    Flush Right, WP71
    Footnote, WP155
    Format, WP65-67
    formatting, WP66
    and function key template, WP8
    GOTO, WP24, WP25
    for Line Draw, WP125-27
    Line Format, WP67, WP75
    List Files, WP42-43
    Math/Columns, WP103-6
    Merge, WP94
    Merge Codes, WP84
    Move, WP57-59
    Page Format, WP155
    Print, WP45
    Replace, WP73-75
    Retrieve, WP10
    Reveal Codes, WP70-72
    Rewrite, WP106-7, WP109
    Save, WP49, WP55
    Screen, WP99, WP101
    Search Backward, WP73
    Search Forward, WP73
    summary of, WP153

    Switch, WP98-99
    for tables of contents, WP154
    Underline, WP102
    for utilities, WP155
    Widow/Orphan Protect, WP144-45
Contents, table of:
    creating, WP127-34
    defining location of, WP131-34
    generating, WP134-35
    leaders in, WP133
    levels of heads in, WP129
    marking text for, WP127-31
    summary of commands, WP154
Copying text:
    between documents, WP98-99
    within a document, WP58
Cursor:
    defined, WP8, WP150
    jumping to beginning, WP24
    jumping to end, WP24
    moving, WP19-27
    moving between columns, WP107
    position, in Status Line, WP8
    summary of commands, WP153
    using a mouse, WP27-28
Customizing form letters. *See* Merging

Dates:
    code for, WP62
    Date/Outline menu options, WP62
    entering into documents, WP62
    entering when booting, WP6
Default settings:
    defined, WP8
    justification, WP75
    left margin, WP21
    line spacing, WP21
    right margin, WP21
    tabs, WP21
Deleting:
    blank lines, WP38-39
    characters with backspace key, WP29-31
    characters with Del, WP31
    codes, WP70
    in column format, WP107
    defined, WP4, WP58, WP150
    to end of line, WP36

Index

- several lines, WP37-38
- summary of commands, WP153
- tabs, WP69
- words, WP35-36

Directory, listing files in, WP42-43

Displaying:
- formatted footnotes, WP137-38
- Help screens, WP12
- hidden codes, WP70-72
- pages on screen, WP137-38
- tab settings, WP67-70

Documents:
- creating, WP50-52
- defined, WP150
- editing, WP28-41
- exiting, WP42, WP48
- footnotes in, WP134-38
- moving text between, WP100-1
- printing, WP45-47, WP76-77, WP146
- saving, WP44-45
- saving and exiting two, WP111
- saving in a new file, WP77-78
- using two, WP98-99
- viewing on screen, WP107-9, WP138-39
- *See also* Files

Drawing lines, WP125-27

Editing:
- in column format, WP107
- defined, WP150
- deleting characters, WP29-31
- deleting words, WP35-36
- documents, WP28-41
- footnotes, WP138
- inserting text, WP32-35
- summary of keys used, WP27, WP41

Endnotes:
- creating and editing, WP135
- defined, WP150
- summary of commands, WP155

Erasing. *See* Deleting

(ESC) key as repeater, WP37-38, WP151

Exiting a document:
- with Exit command, WP42, WP44-45, WP48, WP77, WP156
- with two documents in use, WP111

Extensions in file names:
- defined, WP43
- .PF for primary files, WP89, WP94
- .SF for secondary files, WP94

Fields:
- in address files, WP85, WP89
- defined, WP150

File names:
- defined, WP150
- entering, WP42
- extensions, WP43, WP89, WP91, WP150
- rules for, WP42

Files:
- combining, WP56, WP98-99
- jumping to beginning/end, WP26
- listing, WP42-44
- merging, WP94-95
- opening, WP11-WP12
- primary merge, WP84-89, WP94-95
- replacing, WP44-45
- retrieving, WP17-19
- saving, WP44-45
- saving and exiting two, WP111
- saving in a new file, WP77-78
- secondary merge, WP89-93
- using two, WP98-99
- *See also* Address files; Documents

Flush right:
- aligning text, WP63-64
- code for, WP71
- defined, WP4, WP150

Footnotes:
- creating, WP134-38
- defined, WP150
- displaying, WP137-38
- editing, WP138
- numbering, WP135
- saving, WP136
- summary of commands, WP155

Form letters. *See* Merging

Formatting:
- in columns, WP103-7
- defined, WP5
- summary of commands, WP154

Function keys:
- combining with other keys, WP27
- (F1) (Cancel), WP12, WP17, WP69
- (F2) (Search Forward), WP73
- (F3) (Help), WP12, WP16
- (F5) (List Files), WP42-WP43
- (F7) (Exit), WP41-42, WP48
- (F8) (Underline), WP102
- (F10) (Save), WP42-43
- template for, WP8-9
- *See also* Commands

GOTO command, WP24, WP25

Hard carriage returns, WP38, WP71, WP150

Hard page breaks, WP142

Heads, in tables of contents, WP129, WP151

Help screen:
- clearing, WP13
- displaying, WP12

Hidden codes:
- for columns, WP103
- displaying, WP70-72
- hiding, WP72

Home key, WP21-23

Hyphenation, WP109-10

Indenting first line of paragraph, WP69

Insert mode:
- defined, WP151
- editing in, WP32-33

Inserting:
- blank lines, WP38-39
- in Insert mode, WP32-33
- summary of commands, WP153
- in Typeover mode, WP34-35

Justifying:
- changing, WP109
- defined, WP5, WP151
- setting margins for, WP75-76

Keys:
- arrow, WP19-24
- (BACKSPACE), to delete, WP29-31, WP71, WP118
- (CAPS LOCK), WP96
- for cursor movement, WP19-27
- (DEL), WP31, WP38, WP71
- for deleting, WP29-31, WP35-36, WP107
- editing, WP36, WP41
- (END), WP21
- (ESC), WP37-38
- for GOTO, WP24, WP25
- (HOME), WP21-26
- Indent, WP117
- (INS), WP41
- Mark Text, WP116, WP129
- (NUM LOCK), WP19
- in Outline mode, WP116-24
- (PGDN), WP24-25, WP27
- (PGUP), WP24-25, WP27
- summary of functions, WP153-56
- (TAB), WP118, WP120
- *See also* Commands; Function keys

Leaders, in tables of contents, WP133

Letters, personalized. *See* Merging

Line Draw feature:
- to draw boxes, WP125-27
- summary of commands, WP154

Lines:
- blank, inserting and deleting, WP38-39
- creating, WP125-27
- and cursor position, WP8
- defined, WP151
- deleting, WP37-38
- double, WP126

Index

Listing file names, WP42-44
Loading WordPerfect, WP6-9

Margins:
   aligning flush right, WP63-64
   code for, WP70
   justifying, WP5, WP75, WP151
   left, default for, WP21
   ragged right, WP75, WP76
   right, default for, WP21
   setting, WP65-67
Memory, temporary, WP152
Menus:
   Date/Outline, WP62
   Footnote, WP135
   Format, WP65
   Line Draw, WP126
   Line Format, WP75
   List Files, WP42
   Mark Text, WP116, WP132
   Math/Columns, WP103-6
   Merge/Sort, WP94
   Move, WP57-59, WP60
   options in, WP43
   Page Numbering, WP139
   Print, WP45, WP76-77
   Screen, WP124
   Pull-Down, WP9-13
   Table of Contents Definition, WP132-33
   Text Column Definition, WP103-5
Merging:
   addresses with form letter, WP83-95
   codes for, WP84-89, WP151
   defined, WP5
   summary of commands, WP155
   See also Primary files; Secondary files
Modes:
   Insert, WP4, WP32-33, WP151
   Outline, WP116-46
   Typeover, WP5, WP34-35, WP152
Mouse, using a, WP13-17
   to move the cursor, WP27-28
Moving the cursor, WP19-28
Moving text:
   between documents, WP100-1
   with Block command, WP59-61
   defined, WP151
   with Move command, WP57-59
   in Outline mode, WP121

Newspaper-style columns, WP104, WP151
Numbering:
   footnotes, WP135-36
   pages, WP139-40
   paragraphs in outlines, WP117
   suppressing, WP140-41
Numeric keypad, and NumLock, WP19

Opening files, WP11-12
Options. *See* Commands; Menus
Orphans:
   defined, WP144, WP151
   preventing, WP144-45
Outlines, creating, WP116-23
Overstriking, defined, WP5

Page breaks:
   hard, WP142
   preventing, WP142-44
Page Format, commands for, WP155
Pages:
   centering top to bottom, WP141-42
   defined, WP151
   displaying on screen, WP138-39
   numbering, WP139-40
   preventing page breaks, WP142-44
   and Status Line, WP8
   suppressing numbering, WP140-41
   See also Formatting
Paragraph numbers, WP117, WP151
Parallel columns, WP104, WP151
Primary files, for merging:
   creating, WP84-89
   defined, WP84, WP151
   merging with secondary files, WP89-93
Printing documents:
   allowing for binding, WP76-77
   merged letters, WP95
   with Print command, WP45-47
   using Print Options menu, WP76-77
   specifying range of pages, WP146
   summary of commands, WP154
Prompts, WP17, WP151
Protecting blocks from page breaks, WP142-44

Ragged-right margins, setting, WP75-76
Records, in address files, WP84, WP151
Reformatting:
   in columns, WP106-7
   defined, WP151
   display of text, WP66
Repeater, (ESC) key as, WP37-38, WP151
Replacing character string, WP73-75
Replacing existing files, WP44-45, WP151
Repositioning message, WP24, WP151
Research paper, creating, WP116-46
Retrieving files, WP17-19, WP153
Revealing codes:
   removing Reveal Codes, WP119
   on screen, WP70-72
Ruler line, tab, WP68

Saving documents:
   commands for, WP153
   defined, WP152
   and exiting, WP55
   and exiting two documents, WP111
   with (F10), WP42-43
   in a new file, WP77-78
   and replacing files, WP44-46
   with two documents in use, WP111
Saving footnotes, WP136
Screens:
   clearing, WP41-42
   closing split screens, WP101-2
   components of, WP8
   creating split screens, WP90-100
   reformatting in columns, WP106-7
   updating footnote numbers on, WP138-39
   View Document, WP138-39
Scrolling between columns, WP107
Search and replace, WP5
Searching:
   backward and forward, WP73
   defined, WP5, WP152
   summary of commands, WP155
Secondary merge files:
   creating, WP89-93
   defined, WP84, WP152
   fields in, WP84, WP89
   merging with primary file, WP89-93
Soft carriage returns, WP72, WP152
Split screens:
   closing, WP101-2
   creating, WP99-100
   to reveal hidden codes, WP70
   and Status Line, WP8
Status Line:
   and cursor location, WP8
   defined, WP152
   information in, WP12
Strings:
   defined, WP73
   upper- and lowercase in, WP74
Suppressing page numbers, WP140-41
Switching between documents, WP98-99, WP152

Tab ruler line, WP68
Table of contents:
   creating, WP127-34
   defining location of, WP131-33
   generating, WP134-35
   leaders in, WP133
   levels of heads in, WP129
   marking text for, WP127-31
   summary of commands, WP154

Index

Tabs:
    default settings for, WP8
    deleting, WP69
    displaying current settings, WP67, WP69
    in Outline mode, WP117-19, WP124-25
    removing, WP69
    setting, WP67-70
Templates:
    defined, WP5
    function key, WP8
Temporary memory, WP152
Text:
    aligning flush right, WP63-64
    appending, WP58
    boldfacing, WP95-97
    centering, WP95-97
    centering top to bottom, WP141-42
    in column format, WP103-7
    copying, WP58
    deleting, WP58
    entering, WP50-52
    indenting, WP69
    justified, WP5, WP75, WP151
    moving, WP57-59
    moving, between documents, WP100-1
    moving, in Outline mode, WP121
    protecting from page breaks, WP142-44
    ragged right, WP75
    reformat display of, WP66
    underlining, WP102-3
    unjustified, WP75
    See also Formatting
Typeover mode:
    defined, WP5, WP152
    editing in, WP34-35

Underlining text, WP102-3, WP152
Unjustified text, defined, WP5
Utilities, summary of, WP155-6

Viewing documents on screen, WP107-9, WP138-39

Widows:
    defined, WP144, WP152
    preventing, WP144-45
Windows. *See* Split screens
Word processing:
    advantages of using, WP3-4
    defined, WP3
    terminology, WP4
Word wrap, WP5, WP50, WP152
WordPerfect:
    exiting, WP39, WP42, WP156
    Help system for, WP8
    loading, WP6-9
Words, deleting, WP35-36

Lotus 1-2-3
Release 2.2

Copyright © 1991 by McGraw-Hill, Inc. All rights reserved. Printed in the United States of America. Except as permitted under the United States Copyright Act of 1976, no part of this publication may be reproduced or distributed in any form or by any means, or stored in a database or retrieval system, without the prior written permission of the publisher.

34567890 KPKP 90987654321

P/N 048808-8

ORDER INFORMATION:
ISBN 0-07-048808-8

Lotus and 1-2-3 are registered trademarks of Lotus Development Corporation.
IBM, IBM PC, and PC DOS are registered trademarks of International Business Machines, Inc.

CONTENTS

Overview Electronic Spreadsheets SS3
Definition of Electronic Spreadsheets SS3
Advantanges of Using an Electronic Spreadsheet SS3
Electronic Spreadsheet Terminology SS4
Case Study for Labs 1–5 SS5

Lab 1 Creating a Worksheet: Part 1 SS6
Loading the Lotus 1-2-3 Program SS6
Examining the Worksheet SS7
Moving Around the Worksheet SS8
Using the Function Keys SS11
Using Scroll Lock SS12
Entering Labels SS13
Editing a Cell Entry SS17
Using the UNDO Feature SS22
Using 1-2-3 Menus SS23
Using the Help System SS25
Retrieving a File SS26
Entering Values SS29
Entering Formulas SS31
Recalculating the Worksheet SS32
Saving a Worksheet SS33
Printing a Worksheet SS35
Key Terms SS37
Matching SS37
Practice Exercises SS38

Lab 2 Creating a Worksheet: Part 2 SS42
Using the Copy Command SS42
Highlighting a Range SS45
Copying Formulas SS48
Entering an @Function SS51
Using the Erase Command SS53
Changing Column Widths SS54
Formatting a Value SS57
Inserting Rows SS61
Using the Repeat Label Prefix Character SS61
Inserting Columns SS63
Saving and Replacing a File SS64
Printing a File SS65
Key Terms SS66
Matching SS66
Practice Exercises SS66

Lab 3 Managing a Large Worksheet SS69
Locating and Correcting a Circular Reference SS69
Freezing Titles SS72
Creating and Scrolling Windows SS75
Displaying a Percent SS77
Using What-If Analysis SS79
Using an Absolute Cell Reference SS82
Extracting Worksheet Data SS85
File Linking SS87
Entering the System Date SS90
Justifying Text SS92
Using Compressed Printing SS94
Key Terms SS96
Matching SS96
Practice Exercises SS97

Lab 4 Creating and Printing Graphs SS101
Using the Access System SS101
Selecting the Type of Graph SS104
Labeling the X Axis SS106
Specifying the Data to Be Graphed SS107
Viewing the Graph SS107
Entering Graph Titles SS108
Naming the Graph Settings SS113
Saving Graphs for Printing SS114
Switching the Graph Type SS114
Resetting Graph Specifications SS115
Defining Multiple Data Ranges SS116
Entering Legends SS117
Creating a Stacked-Bar Graph SS118
Creating a Pie Chart SS120
Shading the Pie Slices SS121
Exploding a Slice of the Pie SS123
Recalling Named Graphs SS125
Saving the Worksheet SS126
Printing a Graph SS127
Key Terms SS130
Matching SS130
Practice Exercises SS130

Lab 5 Creating Templates and Macros SS134
Naming a Range SS134
Using the @IF Function SS139
Creating a Template SS141
Creating an Interactive Macro SS141
Planning the Macro SS142
Entering the Macro SS143
Naming the Macro SS145
Testing the Macro SS146
Editing the Macro SS147
Using a Repetition Factor SS150
Documenting the Macro SS152
Using the Learn Feature SS153
Protecting Cells SS159
Creating an Autoexecute Macro SS160
Key Terms SS162
Matching SS162
Practice Exercises SS163

Summary Lotus 1-2-3 Release 2.2 SS167
Glossary of Key Terms SS167
Functional Summary of Selected Lotus 1-2-3
    Commands SS170
Function Keys SS173

Index SS174

OVERVIEW
Electronic Spreadsheets

In contrast to a word processor, which manipulates text, an electronic spreadsheet manipulates numerical data. The first electronic spreadsheet software program (Visi-Calc) was offered on the market in 1979. Since then more than 5 million electronic spreadsheet programs of differing brands have been sold. In a 10-year period, spreadsheets have revolutionized the business world.

Definition of Electronic Spreadsheets

The electronic spreadsheet, or worksheet, is an automated version of the accountant's ledger. Like the accountant's ledger, it consists of rows and columns of numerical data. Unlike the accountant's ledger, which is created on paper using a pencil and a calculator, the electronic spreadsheet is created using a computer system and an electronic spreadsheet applications software program.

The electronic spreadsheet eliminates the paper, pencil, and eraser. With a few keystrokes the user can quickly change, correct, and update the data. Even more impressive is the spreadsheet's ability to perform calculations—from very simple sums to the most complex financial and mathematical formulas. The calculator is replaced by the electronic spreadsheet. Analysis of data in the spreadsheet has become a routine business procedure. Once requiring hours of labor and/or costly accountants' fees, data analysis is now available almost instantly using electronic spreadsheets.

Nearly any job that uses rows and columns of numbers can be performed using an electronic spreadsheet. Typical uses of electronic spreadsheets are for budgets and financial planning in both business and personal situations.

Advantages of Using an Electronic Spreadsheet

Like a word processor, the speed of entering the data into the worksheet using the keyboard is not the most important advantage gained from using an electronic spreadsheet. This is because the speed of entering data is a function of the typing speed of the user and the user's knowledge of the software program. The advantages are in the ability of the spreadsheet program to quickly edit and format data, perform calculations, create graphs, and print the spreadsheet.

The data entered in an electronic spreadsheet can be edited and revised using the program commands. Numeric or text data is entered into the worksheet in a location called a cell. These entries can then be erased, moved, copied, or edited. Formulas can be entered that perform calculations using data contained in specified cells. The results of the calculations are displayed in another cell.

The design and appearance of the spreadsheet can be enhanced in many ways. There are several commands which control the format or display of a numeric entry in a cell. For instance, numeric entries can be displayed with dollar signs or with a set number of decimal places. Text or label entries in a cell can be displayed centered or left- or right-justified (aligned) to improve the spreadsheet appearance. Columns and rows can be inserted and deleted. The cell width can be changed to accommodate entries of varying lengths.

You have the ability to "play" with the values in the worksheet, to see the effect of changing specific values on the worksheet. This is called "what-if," or sensitivity, analysis. Questions that once were too expensive to ask or took too long to answer can now be answered almost instantly, and with little cost. Planning that was once partially based on instinct has been replaced to a great extent with facts. However, any financial planning resulting from the data in a worksheet is only as accurate as that data and the logic behind the calculations. Incorrect data and faulty logic only produce worthless results.

Most electronic spreadsheets also have the ability to produce a visual display of the data in the form of graphs. As the values in the worksheet change, a graph referencing those values automatically reflects the new values. The graphs produced by most spreadsheet programs are a tool for visualizing the effects of changing values in a worksheet. Thus, they are analytic graphs. An electronic spreadsheet program is not designed to produce graphs exclusively, as many presentation graphics programs are. As a result the graphs may appear crude compared to those produced by a pure graphics software program.

Electronic Spreadsheet Terminology

Absolute cell reference: The cell address in a formula does not change when the formula is copied to another cell. A $ character entered before the row number and/or column letter causes absolute addressing.

Arithmetic operators: Special characters assigned to basic numerical operations (e.g., + for addition, * for multiplication).

Automatic recalculation: The recalculation of all formulas in a worksheet whenever a value in a cell changes.

Cell: The space created by the intersection of a horizontal row and a vertical column. It can contain a label, value, or formula.

Circular reference: A formula in a cell that directly or indirectly references itself.

Column: The vertical line on the spreadsheet identified by letters.

Copy: A spreadsheet command that duplicates the contents of a cell or range of cells to another location in the worksheet.

Format: The feature that controls how values in the spreadsheet are displayed (currency, percent, number of decimal places, etc.).

Formula: A numeric computation containing cell references and arithmetic operators.

Freeze: A spreadsheet feature that stops the scrolling of specified rows and/or columns on the display.

Function: A set of built-in or preprogrammed formulas.

Global: Command that affects all rows and columns in the spreadsheet.

Graph: The visual representation of ranges of data in the worksheet. Some graph types are line, bar, stacked-bar, and pie chart.

Justification: The alignment of a label in a cell to the left, centered, or right in the cell space.

Label: A text entry in a cell used to describe the data contained in the row or column.

Manual recalculation: Recalculation of the formulas in a worksheet is performed only when specified by the user.

Mode: Displays the status or condition the program is currently operating in. The three main categories of operation are READY, EDIT, and MENU.

Move: The command which relocates the contents of a cell(s) to another area in the worksheet.

Range: A cell or rectangular group of adjoining cells.

Relative cell reference: The adjustment of the cell address in a formula to reflect its new location in the spreadsheet when copied.

Row: The horizontal line on the worksheet identified by numbers.

Value: A number displayed in a cell.

What-if analysis: A process of evaluating the effect of changing the contents of one or more cells in the spreadsheet to help in decision making and planning.

Case Study for Labs 1–5

Paula Nichols is the manager of the Courtside Cafe at the Sports Club. She has proposed expanding the menu of the cafe and has been asked by the board of directors to prepare a budget for the first 6 months of operation.

In Lab 1, Paula learns how to use a spreadsheet program to assist her in preparing this budget. She enters descriptive row and column titles and enters the values for the expected sales for food and beverages. She also enters a formula to compute a total value.

Lab 2 continues the building of the cafe budget by entering the values for expenses using copying. Functions are introduced. The worksheet is formatted to display currency.

In Lab 3, Paula expands the cafe budget to cover a 1-year period. The problems of managing a large worksheet are handled in this lab by freezing titles and creating windows. What-if analysis on the worksheet is used to achieve the objectives of a 20 percent profit margin by the end of a year of operation.

Lab 4 deals exclusively with creating graphs. It requires that the computer can display and print graphs. The case used in this lab follows Fred Morris as he prepares several graphs to show trends in membership growth of the Sports Club over 5 years. A line, bar, stacked-bar, and pie chart are created.

In Lab 5, Fred creates a bi-weekly membership enrollment report which uses macros to help speed up the data entry and report generation process. You will learn how to create, test, and edit macro commands.

LAB

Creating a Worksheet: Part 1

1

OBJECTIVES

In this lab you will learn how to:

1. Move around the worksheet.
2. Enter labels.
3. Edit worksheet entries.
4. Use the UNDO feature.
5. Use the Main menu.
6. Use the Help system.
7. Enter values.
8. Enter formulas.
9. Save a worksheet file.
10. Print a file.

CASE STUDY

Paula Nichols is the manager of the Courtside Cafe at the Sports Club. She has proposed that the menu of the Courtside Cafe be expanded. The board of directors, before approving the expansion, want her to prepare a budget for the first 6 months of the proposed cafe expansion.

During the next three labs, you will follow Paula as she creates and uses a worksheet for the cafe budget using Lotus 1-2-3. In this lab, you will follow Paula as she learns to enter descriptive row and column titles for the worksheet. She will enter the expected sales values for food and beverages. A simple formula to calculate the expected sales total value will also be entered.

Loading the Lotus 1-2-3 Program

To load the Lotus 1-2-3 Release 2.2 program, boot the computer with the DOS diskette in drive A. After you respond to the DOS date and time prompts, the A> should be on your display. Remove the DOS diskette. Place the Lotus 1-2-3 System Disk in drive A and your data diskette in drive B.

Note: If you have a hard disk or network system, consult your instructor for instructions.

At the A>,

Type: 123
Press: ⏎

The computer loads the Lotus 1-2-3 Release 2.2 program into memory. After a few moments your display should be similar to Figure 1-1.

SS7
Examining the Worksheet

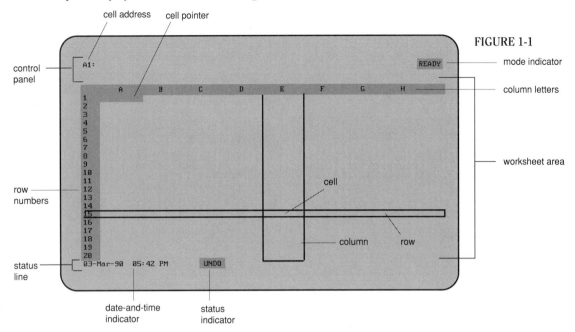

FIGURE 1-1

Examining the Worksheet

Figure 1-1 is a blank Lotus 1-2-3 **worksheet**. It is similar to a financial spreadsheet in that it is a rectangular grid of rows and columns used to enter data.

The worksheet screen is divided into three areas: the worksheet area, the control panel, and the status line.

The **worksheet area** is located in the center of the display screen and occupies the largest amount of space on the screen. The worksheet consists of a rectangular grid of **rows** and **columns**. The border of **row numbers** along the left side of the worksheet area identifies each row in the worksheet. The border of **column letters** across the top of the worksheet area identifies the columns.

The intersection of a row and column creates a **cell**. The cell that is highlighted on your display is A1. The highlight box is called the **cell pointer**. It identifies the **current cell**, which is the cell your next entry or procedure affects.

The **control panel** is located above the column letters. It consists of three lines that display information about the worksheet. On the left side of the first line, the **cell address** of the current cell is displayed. The cell address always consists of the column letter followed by the row number of the current cell. Since the cell pointer is located in cell A1, the cell address displays "A1." The highlighted box on the right side of the first line is the **mode indicator**. It tells you the current **mode**, or state, the 1-2-3 program is in. The current mode is READY. When READY is displayed, you can move the cursor, make a cell entry, use the function keys, or initiate a command. There are 14 different modes of operation. As you are using the program, the mode indicator will display the current mode. The other modes will be discussed as they appear throughout the labs.

The control panel shows other information in the second and third lines as commands are executed and entries are made in the worksheet. You will be referring to this area of the worksheet often throughout this series of labs.

The bottom line of the display screen contains the **status line**. This line is used to display the date-and-time indicator, status indicators, and error messages. Currently the **date-and-time** indicator is displayed on the left side of the status line. This indicator shows the date and time as maintained by DOS. As you are using the program, **error messages** may replace the date-and-time indicator to tell you the program detects an error or cannot perform a task. The highlighted box containing the word "UNDO" is a **status indicator**. (If UNDO is not displayed, this feature has been turned off on your system.) Status indicators tell you that a certain key or program condition is in effect. Currently it tells you that the UNDO feature is in effect. Other status indicators will be displayed as they are activated and will be discussed as they appear throughout the labs.

Moving Around the Worksheet

The arrow keys, (HOME), (END), (PGUP), (PGDN), and (TAB) keys allow you to move the cell pointer around the worksheet. They are called the **pointer-movement keys**. The arrow keys on the numeric keypad move the cell pointer in the direction indicated by the arrow.

To move the cell pointer to cell E3,

Press: → (4 times)
Press: ↓ (2 times)

Your display screen should be similar to Figure 1-2.

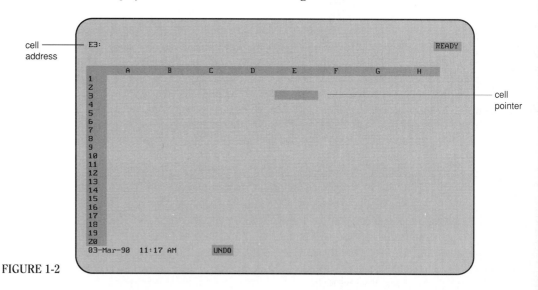

FIGURE 1-2

The cell pointer is in cell E3, making this cell the current cell. The control panel reflects the new location of the cell pointer in the worksheet by displaying the cell address E3 (column E row 3).

Press: ← (5 times)

The computer beeped, because the cell pointer cannot be moved beyond the limits of the row or column borders.

To practice moving around the display screen using the four arrow keys,

Move to: E10
Move to: C6
Move to: G18

To return quickly to the upper left-hand corner, cell A1, of the worksheet,

Press: HOME

Wherever you are in the worksheet, pressing HOME will move the cell pointer to the upper left-hand corner of the worksheet.

The worksheet is much larger than the part you are viewing on your display screen. The worksheet actually extends many columns to the right and many rows down. The worksheet in Lotus 1-2-3 has 256 columns and 8192 rows.

The part of the worksheet you see on your display screen is called a **window**. The current window shows rows 1 through 20 and columns A through H.

To move one full window to the right of the current window,

Press: TAB

Your display screen should be similar to Figure 1-3.

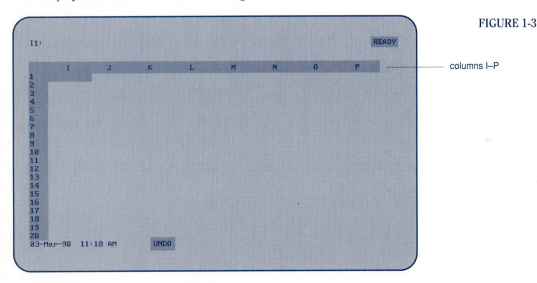

FIGURE 1-3

The window is now positioned over columns I through P and rows 1 through 20 of the worksheet.

To return to the previous window,

Press: SHIFT - TAB

The window is now positioned over columns A through H again.

The same movement of the window can be made using CTRL - → instead of TAB, and CTRL - ← instead of SHIFT - TAB.

To move down one full window on the worksheet,

Press: PGDN

Your display screen should be similar to Figure 1-4.

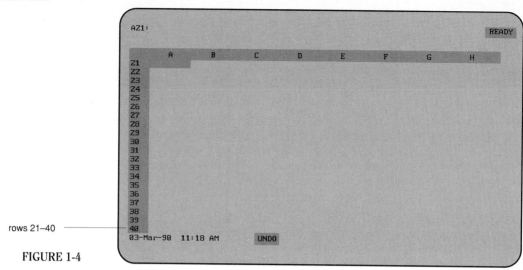

rows 21–40

FIGURE 1-4

The window is positioned over rows 21 through 40 of the worksheet. Columns A through H have remained the same.

To move up a window on the worksheet,

Press: (PGUP)

The window is positioned over rows 1 through 20 of the worksheet again.

If you hold down the arrow keys, the (TAB) or (SHIFT)-(TAB) keys, or the (PGUP) or (PGDN) keys, you can quickly move through the worksheet. This is called **scrolling**. You will try this by holding down (TAB) for several seconds. Watch your display screen carefully as the columns quickly change window by window.

Press: (TAB) (hold down for several seconds)

To quickly return to cell A1,

Press: (HOME)

The (END) key followed by an arrow key will move the cell pointer to the last cell of that row or column. To quickly move the cell pointer to the last row of column A in the worksheet,

Press: (END)

Notice the word "END" displayed in the status line. This is a status indicator. The status line will display different status indicator messages about a particular program or key condition as they are used. In this case it tells you the (END) key is on.

Press: (↓)

The cell pointer moved to the last row, 8192, of column A in the worksheet.

To move to the rightmost column in row 8192,

Press: (END)
Press: (→)

Your display screen should be similar to Figure 1-5.

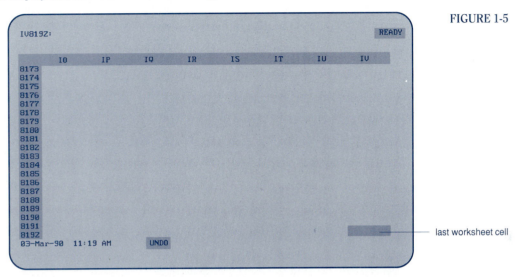

FIGURE 1-5

last worksheet cell

The cell pointer is positioned in cell IV8192. This is the last cell in the Lotus 1-2-3 worksheet. Columns are labeled A to Z, AA to AZ, BA to BZ, and so forth, through IA to IV.

Using the Function Keys

The function keys on your keyboard (located to the left of the typewriter keys or above the typewriter keys, depending upon your computer keyboard) perform special operations. Each function key, except the (F6) key, performs two operations. One operation is executed by pressing the function key alone, another by pressing the (ALT) key and the function key in combination. The function keys are named according to the operation they perform. The function keys and their operations are listed in Table 1-1 below.

TABLE 1-1

HELP	EDIT	NAME	ABS	GOTO	WINDOW	QUERY	TABLE	CALC	GRAPH
(F1)	(F2)	(F3)	(F4)	(F5)	(F6)	(F7)	(F8)	(F9)	(F10)
(ALT)	(ALT)	(ALT)	(ALT)	(ALT)		(ALT)	(ALT)	(ALT)	(ALT)
(F1)	(F2)	(F3)	(F4)	(F5)		(F7)	(F8)	(F9)	(F10)
COMPOSE	STEP	RUN	UNDO	LEARN		APP1	APP2	APP3	APP4

The GOTO function key ((F5)) will move the cell pointer to a specific cell in a worksheet.

Press: (F5) GOTO

Notice the second line in the control panel. It displays the prompt, "Enter address to go to:" followed by the address of the current cell pointer position. A **prompt** is how the program tells you it is waiting for a user response. In this case, the prompt is asking the user to enter the cell address that you want to move the cell pointer to. The cell address you want to move the cell pointer to is entered in either upper- or lowercase letters. To move the cell pointer to cell AL55,

Type: AL55
Press: ⏎

Your display screen should be similar to Figure 1-6.

FIGURE 1-6

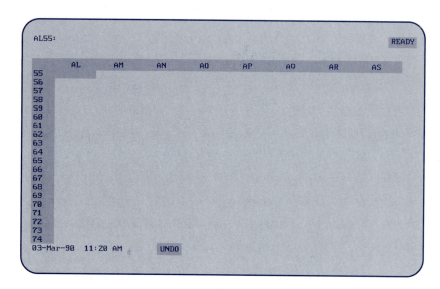

The cell pointer is positioned in cell AL55. The cell you specified at the GOTO prompt is placed in the upper left-hand corner of the window.

Using Scroll Lock

Move to: AP60

Rather than moving the cell pointer around the screen, the cell pointer can remain stationary while the worksheet columns and rows move. This is done by using the SCROLL LOCK key (located at the upper right-hand corner of the keyboard).

Press: SCROLL LOCK

The status indicator "SCROLL" appears in the status line. It tells you that this key is in effect.

Press: ↑ (3 times)

The cell pointer remained in cell AP60 while the rows moved in the direction indicated by the pointer-movement keys.

Press: [→] (4 times)

The cell pointer is still in cell AP60 while the columns moved four columns to the right.

To turn off (SCROLL LOCK),

Press: (SCROLL LOCK)

The SCROLL status indicator is no longer displayed. Pressing (SCROLL LOCK) acts as a toggle to turn on and off the scroll feature. You will find the scroll lock feature helpful if you want to bring into view an area of the worksheet a few rows or columns outside the window without moving the cell pointer from the current cell.

To review, the following keys are used to move around the worksheet:

Key	Action
[↓] [↑] [→] [←]	Move cell pointer one cell in direction of arrow
(TAB) or (CTRL) - [→]	Moves cell pointer right one full window
(SHIFT) - (TAB) or (CTRL) - [←]	Moves cell pointer left one full window
(PGDN)	Moves cell pointer down one full window
(PGUP)	Moves cell pointer up one full window
(HOME)	Moves cell pointer to cell in upper left-hand corner of worksheet
(END) [↓]	Moves cell pointer to last row in worksheet
(END) [→]	Moves cell pointer to last column in worksheet
(F5) (GOTO)	Moves cell pointer to specified cell
(SCROLL LOCK)	Holds cell pointer stationary while worksheet scrolls (on)

Practice moving the cell pointer around the worksheet using each of the keys presented above.

When you are ready to go on,

Move to: A1

Entering Labels

Now that you know how to move around the worksheet, you will begin creating the cafe budget. By the end of this lab, you will have entered part of the cafe budget as shown in Figure 1-7 on the next page.

SS14
Creating a Worksheet: Part 1

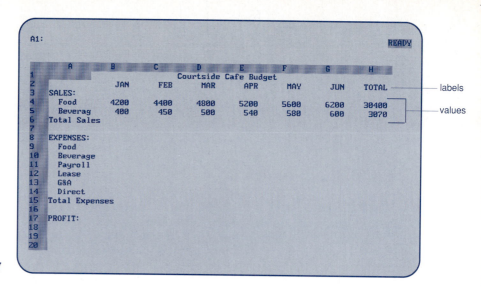

FIGURE 1-7

Entries into a worksheet are defined as either a label or a value. **Labels** create the structure of the worksheet and describe other worksheet entries. The months in row 2 are labels. **Values** are numbers (data) or results of formulas or functions. The entry in cell B4, 4200, is a value.

The column labels in this worksheet consist of the months (January through June) and a Total (sum of entries over 6 months) located in row 2, columns B through H.

The row labels in column A describe the following:

Sales:
    Food   Income from sales of food items
    Beverage   Income from sales of beverages
    Total Sales   Sum of food and beverage sales

Expenses:
    Food   Cost of food supplies
    Beverage   Cost of beverage supplies
    Payroll   Hourly personnel expenses
    Lease   Monthly cost of space used in club
    G & A   General and Administrative
    Direct   Other expenses (insurance, utilities, etc.)
    Total Expenses Sum of Food, Beverage, Payroll, Lease, G&A, and Direct Expenses

Profit: Total Sales minus Total Expenses

To create the structure for this worksheet, you will begin by entering the column labels. The column label for January will be entered in cell B2. Type the label exactly as it appears below.

Move to: B2
Type: january

Your display screen should be similar to Figure 1-8.

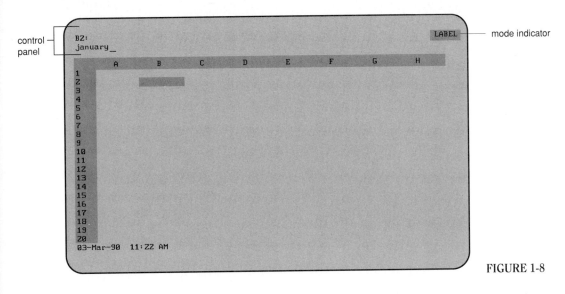

FIGURE 1-8

Several changes have occurred on the display screen. As you type, the second line in the control panel displays each character. It should display "january." The blinking cursor marks your location on the line.

Note: If you made an error while typing the label, use the (Bksp) key (the left-facing arrow key located above the ⏎ key) to erase the characters back to the error. Then retype the entry correctly.

Look at the mode indicator next. It changed from READY to LABEL as the current mode of operation in the worksheet. This tells you that the entry in this cell is defined as a label.

The first character of an entry into a cell determines whether the cell contents are defined as a label or a value. All entries beginning with a space, an alphabetic character (A to Z), ', ", ^, or any other characters not considered a value, define a cell as a label. All entries beginning with a number from 0 to 9, +, -, ., (, @, #, and $ define a cell entry as a value. The entry in cell B2 is defined as a label because it begins with the alphabetic character "j."

Although the label is displayed in the control panel, it has not yet been entered into cell B2 of the worksheet. To actually enter the label into cell B2,

Press: ⏎

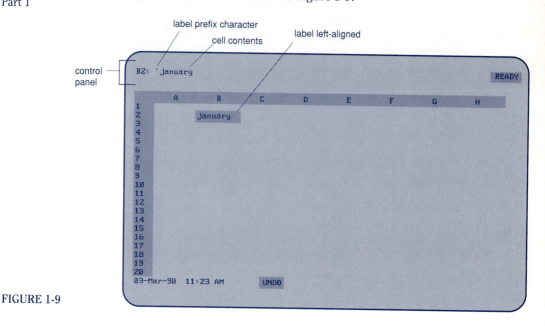

FIGURE 1-9

The label "january" is displayed in cell B2. Notice that the label is placed flush with the left side of the cell space.

Note: If you find that the entry in the cell is not correct or that it is in the wrong cell, you can cancel the entry by immediately pressing (ALT) - (F4). This is called the UNDO feature. The UNDO indicator in the status line must be displayed for this feature to work. This command will be discussed in greater detail later in the lab.

Following the cell address in the control panel, the contents of the cell are displayed. The apostrophe (') preceding the label is a **label prefix character**, which is automatically entered by Lotus 1-2-3. The label prefix character determines how the label will be displayed in the cell space. A label can be displayed flush with the left side of the cell space, centered within the cell space, or flush with the right side of the cell space. The three label prefix characters that control the placement of a label in a cell are:

Character	Alignment
'(apostrophe)	Flush left (this is the default)
" (quotes)	Flush right
^(caret)	Centered

The apostrophe is the **default** label prefix character. Defaults are options or settings automatically provided by 1-2-3. Generally they are the most commonly used settings. The apostrophe is automatically placed before any label entry unless one of the other label prefixes is entered. Notice how the label entry "january" is aligned to the left side of the cell space. The apostrophe positioned the label flush left within the cell space.

Editing a Cell Entry

Paula would like to change the label from "january" to "Jan."

An entry in a cell can be changed or edited in either the READY mode or the EDIT mode. To use the READY mode, simply retype the entry the way you want it to appear. For example, with the cell pointer on cell B2,

Type: Jan
Press: ⏎

Your display screen should be similar to Figure 1-10.

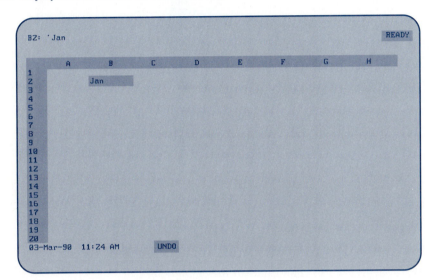

FIGURE 1-10

The new label "Jan" is entered into cell B2, replacing "january."

Next Paula wants to change the placement of the label in the cell. She wants it to be displayed flush with the right side of the cell space. To do this, she needs to change the apostrophe to quotes.

Rather than retyping the entire contents of the cell again, she can use the EDIT mode. The EDIT function key, (F2), is used to edit a cell.

Press: (F2) EDIT

Your display screen should be similar to Figure 1-11.

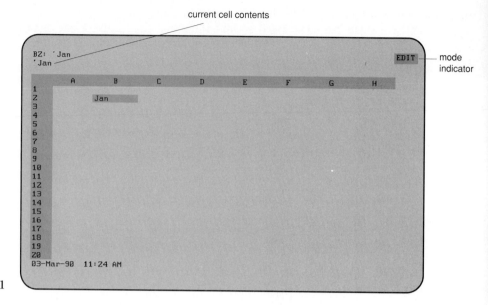

FIGURE 1-11

The control panel displays the current cell contents, and the mode indicator shows the new mode of operation as EDIT. The cursor is positioned at the end of the label in the control panel.

In the EDIT mode, the following keys can be used:

Key	Action
(HOME)	Moves cursor to beginning of entry
(END)	Moves cursor to end of entry
(DELETE)	Erases character at cursor
(Bksp)	Erases character to left of cursor
(INS)	Overwrite mode in effect when on
(TAB)	Moves cursor 5 characters to right
(SHIFT) - (TAB)	Moves cursor 5 characters to left
(→)	Moves cursor 1 character right
(←)	Moves cursor 1 character left

To change the label prefix character at the beginning of the label from an apostrophe (') to quotes ("),

Press: (HOME)

The cursor moves to the beginning of the cell entry.

Press: (DELETE)

The apostrophe is removed.

Type: "
Press:

Your display screen should be similar to Figure 1-12.

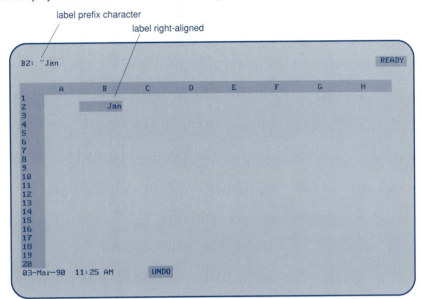

FIGURE 1-12

The label is placed to the right side of the cell. As you can see, editing would be particularly useful with long or complicated entries.

Finally, Paula wants the labels to be in all capital letters.

Press: (CAPS LOCK)

Notice that the CAPS indicator appears in the status line. The (CAPS LOCK) key affects only the letter keys. To produce the characters above the number or punctuation keys, you must use the (SHIFT) key.

Using the EDIT mode, you will change "Jan" to "JAN."

Press: (F2) EDIT
Press: (Bksp) (2 times)

The letters "an" are erased.

Type: AN

The characters "AN" are inserted into the label.

Press: ⏎

To turn off (CAPS LOCK),

Press: (CAPS LOCK)

Your display screen should be similar to Figure 1-13.

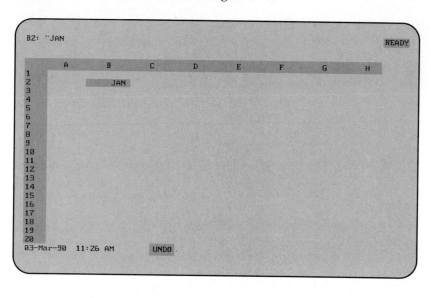

FIGURE 1-13

The next label to be entered is "FEB." You will practice using the READY and EDIT modes while entering this label in cell C2 as follows:

Move to: C2
Type: february
Press: ⏎

To change "february" to "Feb" in the READY mode,

Type: Feb
Press: ⏎

Using the EDIT mode next, change "Feb" to "FEB." First position the label flush right in the cell as follows:

Press: (F2) EDIT
Press: (HOME)

Another way to replace the apostrophe is to type over it with the quotes. This is done by pressing (INS).

Press: (INS)
Type: "

Pressing (INS) changes the entry of characters into a cell to overwrite. Anything you type will write over existing text that is already in the cell. The status indicator OVR is displayed whenever (INS) is pressed. Overwrite is turned off when you leave the EDIT mode or by pressing (INS) again.

To change the label to all capital letters,

Press: →
Press: CAPS LOCK
Type: EB
Press: ↵

Your display screen should be similar to Figure 1-14.

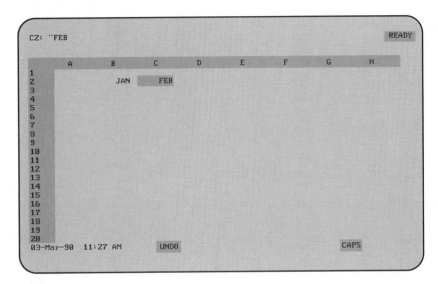

FIGURE 1-14

Notice that the OVR status indicator has disappeared. The CAPS status indicator is still displayed, showing that the CAPS LOCK key is still on.

The label for March needs to be entered in cell D2 next.

Move to: D2
Type: "MAR
Press: →

Using the → key entered the label into the cell. It also moved the cell pointer one cell to the right. You are now ready to enter the label for April into cell E2. Moving the cell pointer to any other cell will both enter the label or value into the cell and move the cell pointer in the direction of the arrow.

The labels "APR," "MAY," "JUN," and "TOTAL" need to be entered into the worksheet in cells E2 through H2. Enter them in all capital letters. They should be displayed flush right in the cell. After typing the label "TOTAL," use ↵ rather than the arrow key to enter the label into the cell, and then turn off CAPS LOCK.

Your display screen should be similar to Figure 1-15.

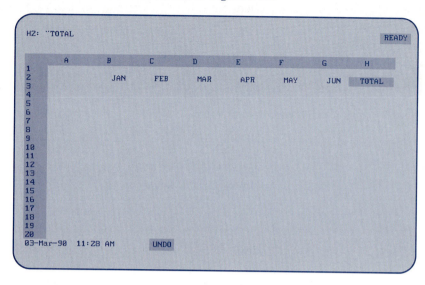

FIGURE 1-15

Using the UNDO Feature

Above the column headings, in row 1, Paula wants to enter a title for the worksheet.

Move to: D1
Type: Courtside Cafe Budget
Press: ⏎

Your display screen should be similar to Figure 1-16.

FIGURE 1-16

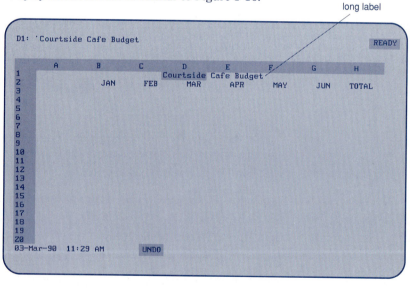

Notice that the worksheet title is longer than the 9 spaces in cell D1. When a label is longer than the cell's column width, it is called a **long label**. 1-2-3 will display as much of the label as it can. If the cells to the right are empty, the whole label will be displayed. If the cells to the right contain an entry, the overlapping part of the label will not be displayed.

Note: If UNDO is not displayed in the status line, this feature has been turned off. Consult your instructor for directions to turn on this feature, or skip to the next section, "Using 1-2-3 Menus."

Paula thinks the worksheet title is not descriptive enough.

<mark>Use the EDIT mode to change the title in cell D1 to "Estimated Budget for the Courtside Cafe."</mark>

After looking at the new title, Paula feels the first title looked better. Rather than reentering the first title, you can cancel the most recent operation that changed worksheet data or settings by using the UNDO function key ((ALT) - (F4)). This feature restores the worksheet to the way it was the last time 1-2-3 was in the READY mode.

Press: (ALT) - (F4) UNDO

The original worksheet title is redisplayed. The worksheet appears exactly as it did before you entered the last label. The UNDO key, like (SCROLL LOCK), acts as a toggle to jump back and forth between the two most recent operations. To see how this works,

Press: (ALT) - (F4) UNDO

The worksheet displays the previous title. You just undid the effect of the UNDO operation.

Press: (ALT) - (F4) UNDO

The worksheet is redisplayed with the title the way Paula wants it to appear. In order to do this, 1-2-3 creates a temporary backup copy of the worksheet each time you press a key that might lead to a worksheet change. In this way, each time you press UNDO, you are switching between the backup copy and the current worksheet.

Using 1-2-3 Menus

The row labels are entered into the worksheet in a similar manner to entering column labels. The only difference is that they are entered down column A rather than across row 2. We have already entered the row labels for you and saved them in a file on your data diskette.

To see the file containing the row labels, you will need to retrieve the file named ROWS.WK1 using the **Main menu**. This menu is accessed by pressing the slash (/) key. (Be careful not to use the backslash (\) key.)

Press: /

SS24
Creating a Worksheet: Part 1

Your display screen should be similar to Figure 1-17.

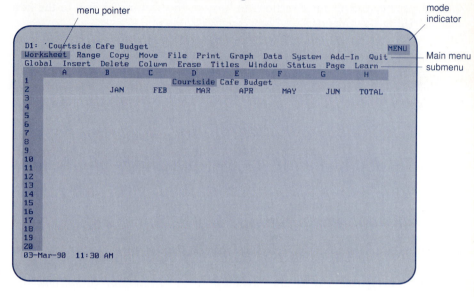

FIGURE 1-17

The second line of the control panel now displays a list or menu of 11 commands, beginning with Worksheet and ending with Quit. The **menu pointer** is the rectangular highlight, which is currently positioned over Worksheet.

The third line of the control panel displays 10 **submenu** commands, beginning with Global and ending with Learn. The submenu commands currently displayed are associated with the highlighted main menu command, Worksheet.

To tell you that you are using the 1-2-3 menus, the mode indicator displays "MENU."

Press:

The menu pointer moves to the right and is positioned over Range. The third line of the control panel now displays the /Range submenu. The commands listed in the submenu are the lower-level commands associated with the main menu command, Range.

Press:

The menu pointer is highlighting Copy. A brief description of the Copy command is displayed in the third line of the control panel. This is because there are no submenu commands associated with the highlighted main menu command.

Look at the submenus or descriptions associated with each main menu command as you

Press: → (slowly 9 times)

The menu pointer has moved through the list of commands in a circular fashion and is positioned back on Worksheet.

The menu pointer can also be quickly moved to the first or last command from any location in the menu using (HOME) and (END).

Press:

The menu pointer is positioned on Quit. To move back to Worksheet, the first command in the menu,

Press: (HOME)

Using the Help System

Lotus 1-2-3 has a very useful Help system to provide information about any part of the program you are using. The Help function key ((F1)) is used to access the Help system.

Press: (F1) Help

Note: If you are using a 5-1/4 inch disk, follow the directions on your screen to replace the System Disk with the Help Disk. You can run the 1-2-3 program without having the System Disk in the drive, because the entire program has been copied into your computer's memory. However, you cannot use Help unless the Help Disk is in the drive.

Your display screen should be similar to Figure 1-18.

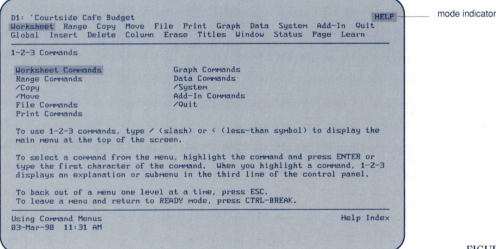

FIGURE 1-18

The worksheet temporarily disappears and a Help screen appears. The mode indicator now displays "HELP." Since you are using the main menu, the Help screen provides information about this feature. This Help screen tells you about the Lotus 1-2-3 commands listed in the control panel and how to select or cancel a command.

More detailed information can be obtained by moving the highlight bar with the arrow keys to any highlighted items and pressing ⏎. Since you want to retrieve a file, to get more help on the File command,

Move to: File Commands
Press: ⏎

Your display screen should be similar to Figure 1-19.

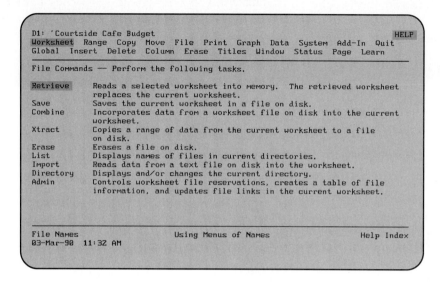

FIGURE 1-19

Information about the /File submenu commands is displayed. Read the information about this command carefully. Since you want to retrieve a file and the highlight is already over "Retrieve," to obtain more information about this command,

Press: ⏎

After reading this screen, to leave the Help screen and return to the worksheet,

Press: ESC

After leaving the Help screen, you are returned to the same place in the worksheet you were before accessing Help. The Main menu is displayed in the control panel. The mode indicator displays MENU again.

Note: If you are using 5-1/4 inch disks, you do not need to remove the Help Disk from the drive. This way, if you want to use Help again, you will not need to swap disks.

Retrieving a File

You are now ready to retrieve the file ROWS.WK1. To select a Main menu command or submenu option, you can use any of the following methods:

- Type the first character of the command name.
- Use → or ← to move the menu pointer to the menu item or submenu option and press ⏎.
- Use any combination of the above methods.

Generally the method that takes the fewest keystrokes is to type the first character of the command name. This is the recommended method.

Note: If you accidentally select the wrong command or submenu option, press the (ESC) key. It will cancel the command selection and take you back one step in the command sequence. Then select the correct Main menu or submenu command. To return directly to the READY mode, press (CTRL) - (BREAK).

Since the Main menu is already displayed, to select File,

Type: F

Your display screen should be similar to Figure 1-20.

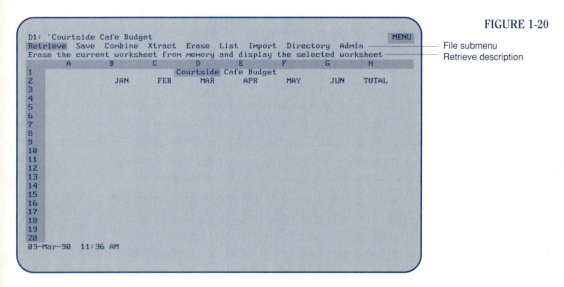

FIGURE 1-20

The /File submenu which was displayed in the third line of the control panel is now displayed on the second line. The third line now presents a brief description of the highlighted command, Retrieve.

Again using (→) and (←), slowly move the menu pointer to each submenu command. Either a description of the highlighted command or more submenu commands (if available) are displayed in the third line of the control panel.

To retrieve a file,

Select: Retrieve

Note: If the message "Disk drive not ready" is displayed, check that your data diskette is properly inserted in the drive and that the disk drive door is completely closed. Press (ESC) to clear the message, and reenter the command.

Your display screen should be similar to Figure 1-21.

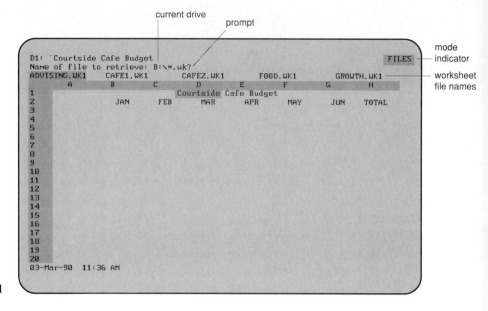

FIGURE 1-21

The second line of the control panel displays the prompt "Name of file to retrieve:." The prompt is followed by the drive that the program will search to locate your data files. If the drive letter displayed following the prompt is not the correct drive for your system, consult your instructor for further directions.

Also notice that the mode indicator has changed from MENU to FILES. This is because 1-2-3 is displaying the names of the available worksheet files in the third line of the control panel. The file names are displayed in alphabetical order. Because there is not enough room on the line to display all the file names, only the first five worksheet file names are listed. If there are more than five files in the directory, more lines of file names can be displayed by using ⬇ and ⬆. To move the menu pointer along a line of file names, use ➡ and ⬅.

You want to read into memory the file ROWS.WK1. In response to the prompt for the name of the file you want to retrieve, you can type the full file name following the prompt, or you can move the menu pointer to the file name and press ⏎ to select the file. Using the menu pointer to select the file,

Move to: ROWS.WK1
Press: ⏎

Note: If the file name ROWS.WK1 is not displayed in the directory of file names, ask your instructor for help.

Your display screen should be similar to Figure 1-22.

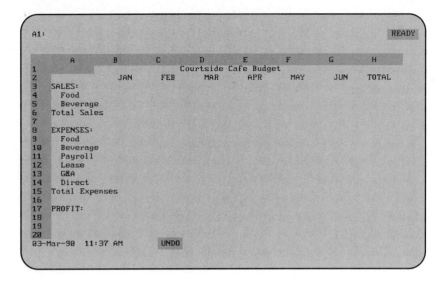

FIGURE 1-22

The current worksheet is erased from the screen and from the computer's memory. The retrieved worksheet file, ROWS.WK1, containing the row and column labels, is displayed.

To review, the command sequence used to retrieve the file ROWS.WK1 was **/F**ile **R**etrieve **ROWS.WK1** ⏎. Throughout the rest of the Lotus 1-2-3 labs, command sequences will be presented as just shown. The character(s) to type will be printed in boldface type.

Entering Values

The next step is to enter the data or values into the cells.

Remember, values can be numbers or the result of a formula or function. All values must begin with a number 0 through 9, or with any one of the **numeric symbols**: + , - , ., @, (, #, or $.

Paula has estimated that the sales of food items during the month of January will be $4,200. To enter the value 4200 into cell B4,

Move to: B4
Type: 4200

The mode indicator displays the new mode of operation as VALUE. Lotus 1-2-3 has interpreted this entry as a value because the first character entered into the cell is the number 4. Do not enter a space before a value. If you do, the cell contents will be interpreted as a label rather than a value.

Press: ⏎

Your display screen should be similar to Figure 1-23.

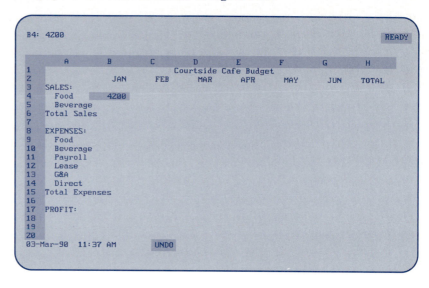

FIGURE 1-23

The value 4200 is displayed in cell B4. The value is displayed almost flush right in its cell space. One space to the right of the value is left blank. It is reserved for special numeric displays such as a ")." Unlike labels, the display of a value in a cell cannot be changed. Values are always displayed to the right side of the cell space.

To complete the data for food sales (row 4), enter the following values into the cells indicated. Use ⟶ to enter the value and move to the next cell.

    cell C4—**4400**
    cell D4—**4800**
    cell E4—**5200**
    cell F4—**5600**
    cell G4—**6200**

Your display screen should be similar to Figure 1-24.

FIGURE 1-24

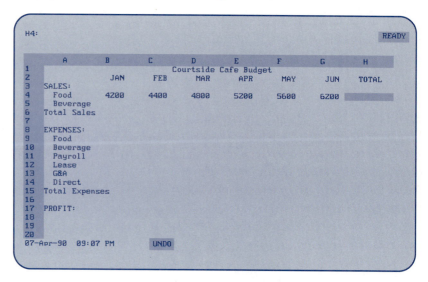

Entering Formulas

A **formula** is an entry that performs a calculation. The result of the calculation is displayed in the worksheet cell. Numeric values or cell addresses can be used in a formula. If cell addresses are used, the calculation is performed using the contents of the cell addresses. As the values in the referenced cell(s) change, the value calculated by the formula is automatically recalculated. A formula is the power behind the worksheet.

Three types of formulas can be entered in a worksheet: numeric, string, and logical. You will use a numeric formula to calculate the sum of the food sales for January through June. To enter a numeric formula, the following **arithmetic operators** are used:

- \+   for addition
- \-   for subtraction
- /   for division
- *   for multiplication
- ^   for exponentiation

A formula must begin with a number or one of the numeric symbols which defines an entry as a value. If a formula begins with a cell address, the cell address must be preceded with a character that defines the cell as a value. Since the formula you will enter will sum the values in cells B4 through G4, you will use a + to begin the entry. Cell addresses can be typed in either upper- or lowercase letters. If you enter a formula incorrectly, Lotus 1-2-3 will beep and change to the EDIT mode to let you correct your entry.

The cells containing the values for food sales for January through June are cells B4 through G4. To sum the values in these cells and display the calculated value in cell H4,

Move to: H4
Type: +B4+C4+D4+E4+F4+G4
Press: ⏎

Your display screen should be similar to Figure 1-25.

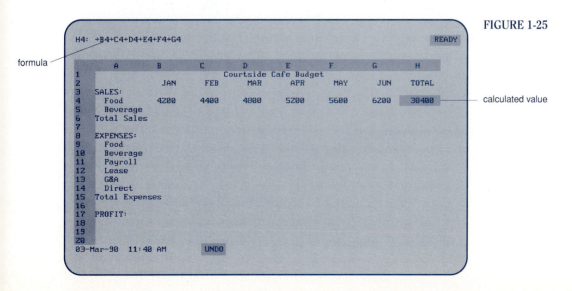

FIGURE 1-25

The formula appears in the control panel. The result of the formula, 30400, is displayed in cell H4.

The values for beverage sales need to be entered into cells B5 through G5 next.

Move to: B5
Type: 400
Press: ⏎

Notice that the label in cell A5 is now displayed as "Beverag." This is because the label exceeds the cell width of 9 spaces. The new entry in cell B5 causes the label to be interrupted after 9 characters.

Move to: A5

The control panel shows the complete row label as entered into the cell. Only the display of the label in cell A5 has been interrupted. You will learn how to change the width of a column in the next lab so that the entire label can be displayed.

Continue entering the values for beverage sales in the cells indicated:

C5—**450**
D5—**500**
E5—**540**
F5—**560**
G5—**600**

Recalculating the Worksheet

Finally, the formula to calculate the total beverage sales needs to be entered in cell H5. It will sum the values in cells B5 through G5. Enter the formula to make this calculation in cell H5. When you are done, your display screen should be similar to Figure 1-26.

FIGURE 1-26

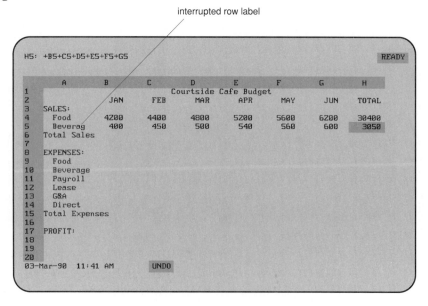

The total for beverage sales, 3050, is displayed in H5.

Paula feels that she has underestimated the beverage sales for the month of May. She wants to change this value to 580.

Move to: F5
Type: 580
Press: ⏎

The formula in cell H5 has automatically recalculated the total. The value displayed is now 3070. The automatic recalculation of a formula when a value in a referenced cell in the formula changes is one of the most powerful features of electronic worksheets. When 1-2-3 recalculates a worksheet, only those formulas directly affected by a change in the data are recalculated. This is called **minimal recalculation**. Without this feature, in large worksheets it could take several minutes to recalculate all formulas each time a value is changed in the worksheet. The minimal recalculation feature decreases the recalculation time by only recalculating affected formulas.

In the next lab you will complete the worksheet by entering the other values and formulas. Before saving the worksheet, enter your first initial and last name in cell A1. Put the date in cell A2. Don't forget to precede it with a label prefix character (for example, "9/08/91).

Saving a Worksheet

To save the current worksheet in a file on the diskette in drive B, you use the File Save command. Always save your current worksheet before retrieving another file or leaving the Lotus 1-2-3 program.

Select: / File Save

The file name of the file you retrieved, ROWS.WK1, is displayed following the prompt "File to be Saved:." The 1-2-3 program has suggested a response to this prompt by displaying the name of the file you retrieved. In response to this prompt you must specify a file name either by accepting the default name, editing the default name, or typing a new name. You will give the file a new name. To save the worksheet as it appears on the display in a new file named CAFE,

Type: CAFE
Press: ⏎

The worksheet data which was on your screen and in the computer's memory is now saved on your data diskette in a new file called CAFE.WK1. A 1-2-3 file name should not be longer than eight characters. It can include any combination of letters, numbers, underscores, and hyphens. However, it cannot contain blank spaces. It is automatically saved with the file extension .WK1. This file extension identifies this file as a worksheet file. Lotus 1-2-3 uses several different file extensions for different types of files that are created using the program.

To see a list of all the worksheet (.WK1) files on the data diskette,

Select: / File List

The first three options, Worksheet, Print, and Graph, list all files of that type in the current directory. These files are differentiated by their file extensions: .WK1, .PRN, and .PIC, respectively. The Other option lists all files regardless of the type of file in the current directory. The Linked option lists all files on the disk that are linked to the current worksheet. You will learn about these other types of files in later labs.

To display all the worksheet files,

Select: Worksheet

Your display screen should be similar to Figure 1-27.

FIGURE 1-27

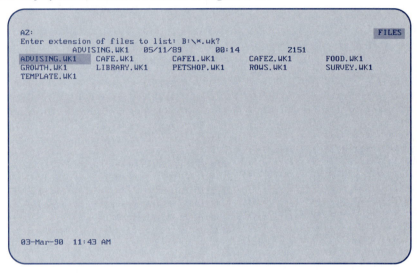

The files ROWS.WK1 and CAFE.WK1 are both listed, along with several other worksheet files you will be using in the next labs.

To return directly to the worksheet,

Press: CTRL - BREAK

The file CAFE.WK1 can be retrieved like any other worksheet file. To erase the current worksheet from the display and from the computer's memory,

Select: /Worksheet Erase

As a safety precaution, Lotus requires that you confirm that you want to erase the worksheet. Since you have already saved the current worksheet on the diskette, to confirm that you want to erase the worksheet from the screen and the computer's memory,

Type: Y

A blank worksheet screen is displayed. To retrieve the file CAFE.WK1,

Select: /File Retrieve CAFE.WK1 ⏎

The worksheet as saved is loaded into memory and displayed. Even the cell pointer is in the cell you left it in when you saved the file.

Be very careful before erasing a worksheet, retrieving a file, or quitting Lotus 1-2-3 that you have saved the current worksheet. Otherwise your hard work will be lost.

Printing a Worksheet

If you have printer capability, you can print a copy of the worksheet. If necessary, turn the printer on and check to see that it is online. Adjust the paper so that the perforation is just above the printer scale (behind the ribbon).

Select: / Print

Two print options are displayed in the control panel, Printer and File. The output can be sent directly to a printer for immediate printing or to a file for printing later. You want to send it to the printer.

Select: Printer

Your display screen should be similar to Figure 1-28.

FIGURE 1-28

```
F5: 580                                                  MENU
Range Line Page Options Clear Align Go Quit
Specify a range to print
                    ─────── Print Settings ───────
  Destination:   Printer

  Range:

  Header:
  Footer:

  Margins:
     Left 4    Right 76   Top 2   Bottom 2

  Borders:
     Columns
     Rows

  Setup string:

  Page length:   66

  Output:        As-Displayed (Formatted)

06-Mar-90  08:27 AM
```

The worksheet is temporarily replaced by the Print Settings sheet. As a part of many commands, 1-2-3 will display a **settings sheet** to help you keep track of the current settings for the options associated with the command you are using. To change the settings displayed in the settings sheet, you must select the appropriate commands from the menu that appears above the settings sheet. The Print Settings sheet currently displays the default print settings. There are many print settings and options available which you will use in future labs. The only print submenu command setting which must be specified is Range.

The Range option specifies the area of cells in the worksheet to be printed. You want the entire worksheet printed from cell A1 through cell H17. A **range** can be a single cell or any rectangular group of adjoining cells in the worksheet. The range is specified by entering the cell addresses of the two most distant cells in the range,

SS36
Creating a Worksheet: Part 1

separated by a period. Typically this will be the upper left corner cell (in this case, A1) and the lower right corner cell (in this case, H17) of the range.

Select: Range

The worksheet is redisplayed to let you see the range of cells you want to specify.

Type: A1.H17
Press: ⏎

The Print Settings sheet is displayed again, and the specified range has been entered following "Range" in the settings sheet.
    Next, to tell the program that the alignment of the paper is at the top of the page and to begin printing,

Select: Align Go

Your printer should be printing out the worksheet. Your printed output should look like Figure 1-29.

FIGURE 1-29

	JAN	FEB	MAR	APR	MAY	JUN	TOTAL
\multicolumn{8}{c}{Courtside Cafe Budget}							
SALES:							
Food	4200	4400	4800	5200	5600	6200	30400
Beverage	400	450	500	540	580	600	3070
Total Sales							
EXPENSES:							
Food							
Beverage							
Payroll							
Lease							
G&A							
Direct							
Total Expenses							
PROFIT:							

When printing is finished,

Select: Page

This command advances the paper to the top of the next page.
    To return to the READY mode,

Select: Quit

If you want to quit or exit the Lotus 1-2-3 program at this time,

Select: / Quit Yes

The DOS prompt appears on the display screen. If it does not, follow the directions on the screen, by replacing the disk in drive A with the disk containing the COMMAND.COM file (usually your DOS disk). Remember, always save your current worksheet before quitting Lotus 1-2-3.

Key Terms

worksheet	mode	default
worksheet area	status line	long label
row	date-and-time indicator	Main menu
column	error message	menu pointer
row number	status indicator	submenu
column letter	pointer-movement keys	numeric symbols
cell	window	formula
cell pointer	scroll	arithmetic operators
current cell	prompt	minimal recalculation
control panel	label	settings sheet
cell address	value	range
mode indicator	label prefix character	

Matching

1. /
2. ^
3. F5
4. INS
5. .WK1
6. F2
7. +C19-A21
8. *
9. D11
10. value

____ a. moves the cell pointer to a specified cell
____ b. accesses EDIT mode
____ c. displays the Main menu
____ d. centers a label
____ e. a cell address
____ f. a number or result of a formula or function
____ g. an arithmetic operator
____ h. switches between overwrite and insert
____ i. a formula subtracting two cells
____ j. a worksheet file extension

SS38
Creating a Worksheet: Part 1

Practice Exercises

1. Identify the parts of the worksheet screen shown below. The first item has been completed for you.

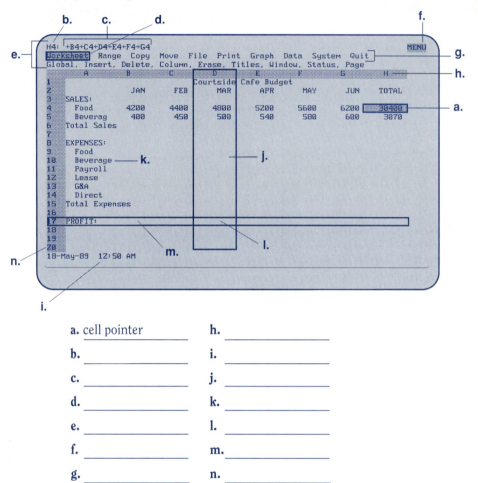

a. cell pointer
b. _____
c. _____
d. _____
e. _____
f. _____
g. _____
h. _____
i. _____
j. _____
k. _____
l. _____
m. _____
n. _____

2. Retrieve the worksheet file SURVEY.WK1. This worksheet contains data from a survey conducted over the years 1978 to 1986. It shows the percentage of college freshmen who expressed interest in careers in computers, education, and business. It contains many errors which you will correct as follows:

- Change the title in cell D2 to all uppercase characters.
- Change the title in cell D4 to Percent of College Freshmen.
- Change the column labels in row 8 to be displayed flush right.
- Change the values in the following cells:
    D10—5
    C14—19
    F12—5.5
    G14—24

- Check the formulas in row 16. Correct as needed.
- Enter your name in cell A1. Enter the date in cell A2.
- Save the file as SURVEY1.
- Print a copy of the file.

3. You have just finished paying off the loan on your old car and you are considering purchasing a new 1991 model car. The new car costs $12,300 and the trade-in value on your old car is $3,700. You can borrow the difference with a four-year loan of 8.9 percent. You decide to create a worksheet to help you analyze whether you should keep the old car or trade it in on a new car.

- Create the worksheet as shown below by entering the labels and values in the cells indicated. Place flush right the Old Car and New Car labels.

```
        A         B           C        D       E        F       G       H
 1   Student Name            Four Year Cost of Ownership
 2   Date                    Old Car   New Car
 3
 4   Expenses:
 5
 6   Loan payment               0      10200
 7   Gas and oil             3428       3000
 8   Insurance               2213       2403
 9   Repairs                 2562       1383
10                          ------------------
11   Total Expenses:
12   Trade-in value:
13                          ==================
14   Net cost of ownership:
15
16   Saved by not trading in:
17
18
19
20
```

- Enter the formulas to calculate the Total Expenses for the old and new cars.
- Save the worksheet as COST.
- Print the worksheet.

You will complete this worksheet as Practice Exercise 3 in Lab 2.

4. You are the manager of Fine Things Jewelry Store. You are having a sales campaign that will reward the salesperson who has the largest average sales over a 4-week period. The winner of the contest will receive a bonus of 5 percent on all

SS40
Creating a Worksheet: Part 1

sales made during the 4 weeks. The regular percent earned is 10 percent. The campaign has been in progress 2 weeks already.

Create the following worksheet to keep track of the sales. The column labels are all flush right. Enter the formula to calculate the total sales for the 2 weeks.

```
         A            B        C        D        E        F        G        H
 1  Student Name           FINE THINGS JEWELRY STORE
 2  Date                      WEEK
 3
 4               Week 1    Week 2   Week 3   Week 4   Total   Average  Percent
 5  Sally         1975      3608
 6  Martin        1500      5298
 7  Phillip       4295      1400
 8  Dorothy       2730      2895
 9  Alyce         4129      2568
10
11  TOTAL        14629     15769
12
13
14
15
16
17
18
19
20
```

You will complete the worksheet as Practice Exercise 1 in Lab 2. Enter your name in cell A1 and the date in cell A2. Save your completed worksheet as JEWELRY. Print a copy of the worksheet.

5. The Assistant Director of the zoo wants to prepare a financial summary for the years 1988, 1989, and 1990.

- Create the worksheet shown below by entering the labels and values in the cells indicated. Right-align the column labels.

```
         A              B         C         D          E          F         G         H
 1  Student Name                        Zoological  Society   Financial Statement
 2  Date                                   1988       1989       1990    TOTAL   AVERAGE
 3  Support & Revenues
 4  Operating                            5613504    6509754    7250692
 5  Fund Raising                          997676     538208     720715
 6  Supporting Org.                       137070     252963     177066
 7  Interest Income                       110154     154771     189723
 8  Total Support & Revenues
 9  Applications/Expenses
10  Operating                            5133565    6247933    6984207
11  Capital Projects                     1150000     744631     871201
12  Fund Raising                          227640     173270     159302
13  Operating Reserve
14  Total Applications/Expenses
15
16
17
18
19
20
```

- Edit the row labels indicated:
    - A3 — All capital letters
    - A4 through A7 — Enter 5 blank spaces before each label
    - A8 — TOTAL S & R
    - A9 — All capital letters
    - A10 through A13 — Enter 5 blank spaces before each label
    - A14 — TOTAL A/E
- Enter formulas to calculate the TOTAL S & R (D8) and TOTAL A/E (D14) for 1988 only.
- Enter the following formula in cell D13: +D8-D10-D11-D12.
- Save the worksheet as ZOOFINAN.

LAB
Creating a Worksheet: Part 2   2

OBJECTIVES

In this lab you will learn how to:

1. Copy cell contents.
2. Highlight and copy a range.
3. Enter @functions.
4. Erase cell contents.
5. Change column widths.
6. Set cell display format.
7. Insert and delete rows.
8. Use the character repeat prefix.
9. Insert and delete columns.
10. Save and replace a file.

CASE STUDY

During Lab 1 Paula Nichols, the manager of the Courtside Cafe at the Sports Club, defined the row and column labels for the cafe budget worksheet. She entered the expected food and beverage sales figures, and she entered formulas to calculate the total sales for food and beverages.

In Lab 2 you will continue to build the worksheet for the cafe. The data for the expenses needs to be entered into the worksheet. The formulas to calculate the total sales, expenses, and profit also need to be entered into the worksheet. The physical appearance of the worksheet will be improved. This will be done by adjusting column widths, inserting and deleting rows and columns, and underlining the column labels.

Using the Copy Command

Load the Lotus 1-2-3 Release 2.2 program. Your data diskette should be in the B drive (or in the appropriate drive for your computer system).

To retrieve the worksheet CAFE1.WK1,

Select: / File Retrieve **CAFE1.WK1** ⏎

Your display screen should be similar to Figure 2-1.

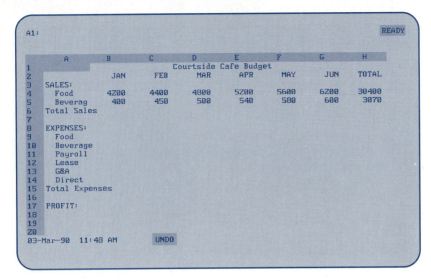

FIGURE 2-1

This worksheet should be the same as the worksheet you created in Lab 1 and saved as CAFE.WK1 on your data diskette.

Paula needs to enter the values for the expenses (rows 9 through 14) into the worksheet. The food and beverage costs are estimated by using a formula to calculate the value as a percent of sales. The remaining expenses are estimated over the 6-month period. They are the same for each month.

In Lab 1 the food and beverage sales values for January through June were entered individually into each cell because the value changed from month to month. But sometimes a value or formula in a cell is the same across several cells. Then it is faster to enter the information by using the Copy command.

Paula will begin by entering the estimated expenses for payroll first. She estimates that payroll expenses, based on the average hourly rate of pay and the number of hours needed per month to operate the cafe, will be $2,250 per month.

Move to: B11
Type: 2250
Press: ⏎

The value in cell B11 is the same value that needs to be entered in cells C11 through G11 for February through June. You could type the same amount into each month, or you could **copy** the value in B11 into the other cells. This is done using the Copy command.

To use the Copy command, with the cell pointer in cell B11,

Select: / Copy

SS44
Creating a Worksheet: Part 2

Your display screen should be similar to Figure 2-2.

FIGURE 2-2

```
B11: 2250
Enter range to copy FROM: B11..B11                                    POINT
        A         B         C         D         E         F         G         H
 1                               Courtside Cafe Budget
 2                JAN       FEB       MAR       APR       MAY       JUN       TOTAL
 3    SALES:
 4       Food    4200      4400      4800      5200      5600      6200      30400
 5       Beverag  400       450       500       540       580       600       3070
 6    Total Sales
 7
 8    EXPENSES:
 9       Food
10       Beverage
11       Payroll  2250
12       Lease
13       G&A
14       Direct
15    Total Expenses
16
17    PROFIT:
18
19
20
03-Mar-90  11:49 AM
```
(prompt points to "Enter range to copy FROM:"; range points to "B11..B11")

The control panel displays the prompt "Enter range to copy FROM:". Remember, a **range** is a cell or rectangular group of adjoining cells in the worksheet. The FROM range is the cell or cells whose contents you want to copy.

Following the prompt, Lotus 1-2-3 automatically enters the current cell pointer location (B11) as the default response to the prompt. Even though this is a single cell, it is displayed as a range (B11..B11). 1-2-3 always displays a range with the upper left-hand and lower right-hand cell addresses of the range separated by two periods.

If the current cell pointer position is not the cell whose contents you want to copy, you can enter the correct range following the prompt. However, since B11 is the cell whose contents you want to copy, to accept the range as displayed,

Press: ⏎

Your display screen should be similar to Figure 2-3.

FIGURE 2-3

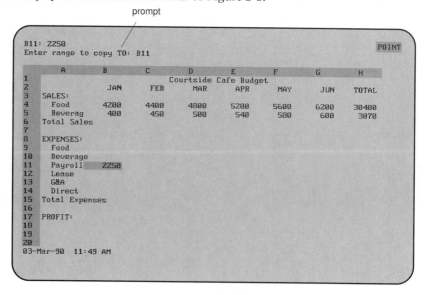

A second prompt appears in the control panel: "Enter range to copy TO:". The range to copy TO is the cell(s) in the worksheet where you want the contents of the FROM range copied. Again 1-2-3 entered the current cell pointer position (B11) following the prompt.

Since you do not want to copy *to* B11, you need to enter the correct range, C11 through G11. To specify this range by typing in the cell addresses,

Type: C11.G11
Press: ⏎

Note: You can enter one or two periods in the range. 1-2-3 will always display a range with two periods. The cell address can be entered in either upper- or lower-case letters.

Your display screen should be similar to Figure 2-4.

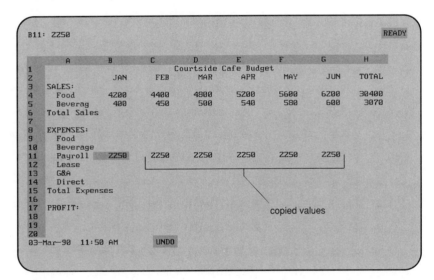

FIGURE 2-4

The value 2250 is quickly entered into cells C11 through G11. As you can see, using the Copy command is very fast. It also eliminates the possibility of typing errors.

Highlighting a Range

Next you will enter the value 500 for the lease expense for January in cell B12 and copy it across row 12 for February through June. To do this,

Move to: B12
Type: 500
Press: ⏎

To copy this value, with the cell pointer positioned in cell B12,

Select: / Copy

To accept the cell range to copy as B12,

Press: ⏎

Another way to specify a data range is by highlighting it using the POINT mode. To do this, the pointer-movement keys are used to expand the cell pointer to highlight the cell or range of cells you want to specify. Whenever 1-2-3 displays "POINT" in the mode indicator, this method can be used. To see how this works, to specify the range to copy TO, C12 through G12,

Press: →

The cell pointer is positioned in cell C12. The cell address, C12, is displayed following the prompt as the first cell in the range to copy TO. Before you can highlight the range, you must **anchor** the cell pointer in the corner cell of the range. To anchor this cell,

Type: . (period)

The period stops the cell pointer from leaving cell C12 and specifies this cell as the beginning or **anchor cell** of the range. You can tell if the cell pointer is anchored by looking at how it is displayed following the prompt. If just a cell address, such as C12, is displayed, it means the cell pointer is not anchored; if, however, a range address, such as C12..C12, is displayed, it means the cell pointer is anchored. If the cell pointer is anchored in the wrong cell, press (ESC) to release it, move to the correct cell, then type a period to anchor it again.

The cell ending the range to copy TO, G12, must be entered next. To specify the range by highlighting,

Press: → (4 times)

Your display screen should be similar to Figure 2-5.

FIGURE 2-5

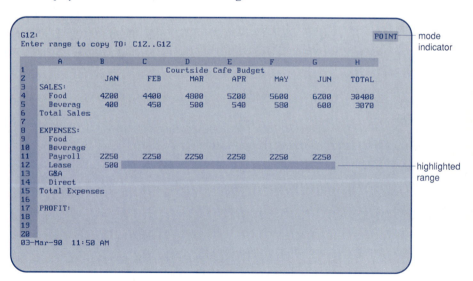

The range to copy TO is highlighted on the display screen. Each time you moved the cell pointer, the highlight bar expanded to cover the entire range of cells from the anchor cell to the cell the pointer is on. The beginning and ending cells of the range (C12..G12) are entered following the prompt in the control panel.

To enter the range as highlighted and complete the command sequence,

Press: ⏎

The value 500 is copied into cells C12 through G12. Using highlighting to specify a range is especially helpful when you have a large worksheet and the entire range is not visible on the screen. Also, highlighting avoids the entry of an incorrect range due to typing errors.

The values for G&A (General & Administrative) and direct expenses need to be entered next. For January enter the values of 175 for G&A expense and 975 for direct expenses as follows:

Move to: B13
Type: 175
Move to: B14
Type: 975
Press: ⏎

To copy the contents of cells B13 and B14 at the same time,

Select: / Copy

Notice that the cell range is anchored already. To highlight the range to include cell B14,

Press: ↑
Press: ⏎

To specify the range to copy TO as the direct and G&A expenses for February through June (cells C14, the lower-left corner cell of the range, through G13, the upper-right corner cell of the range),

Move to: C14
Type: .
Move to: G13
Press: ⏎

Creating a Worksheet: Part 2

Your display screen should be similar to Figure 2-6.

FIGURE 2-6

```
B14: 975                                                    READY

        A         B        C        D        E        F        G        H
 1                         Courtside Cafe Budget
 2                JAN      FEB      MAR      APR      MAY      JUN      TOTAL
 3  SALES:
 4    Food       4200     4400     4800     5200     5600     6200     30400
 5    Beverag     400      450      500      540      580      600      3070
 6  Total Sales
 7
 8  EXPENSES:
 9    Food
10    Beverage
11    Payroll    2250     2250     2250     2250     2250     2250
12    Lease       500      500      500      500      500      500
13    G&A         175      175      175      175      175      175
14    Direct      975      975      975      975      975      975
15  Total Expenses
16
17  PROFIT:
18
19
20
08-Apr-90  07:53 AM              UNDO
```

The values for January G&A and direct expenses (cells B13 and B14) were quickly copied into the February through June G&A and direct expense cells (C13 through G13 and C14 through G14.)

Copying Formulas

The final two expenses that need to be entered into the worksheet are for food and beverage expenses. Paula has estimated that the cost of food and beverage supplies will be 30 percent of sales each month.

The formulas to calculate these values are:

Food expense = monthly food sales * 30%

Beverage expense = monthly beverage sales * 30%

To enter the formula to calculate the food expense for January,

Move to: B9
Type: +B4*30%
Press: ⏎

The calculated value of 1260 is displayed in cell B9, and the formula is displayed in the control panel. 1-2-3 automatically converts the percentage in the formula to its decimal equivilant. You could also have entered .30 instead of 30% and the same result would be calculated.

The formulas to calculate the February through June food expenses (C9 through G9) need to be entered next. **Copy the formula from the January expense cell (B9) to make these calculations, using highlighting to specify the range.**

The calculated values are displayed in the specified cell range. Let's look at the formulas as they were copied into the cells.

Move to: C9

Your display screen should be similar to Figure 2-7.

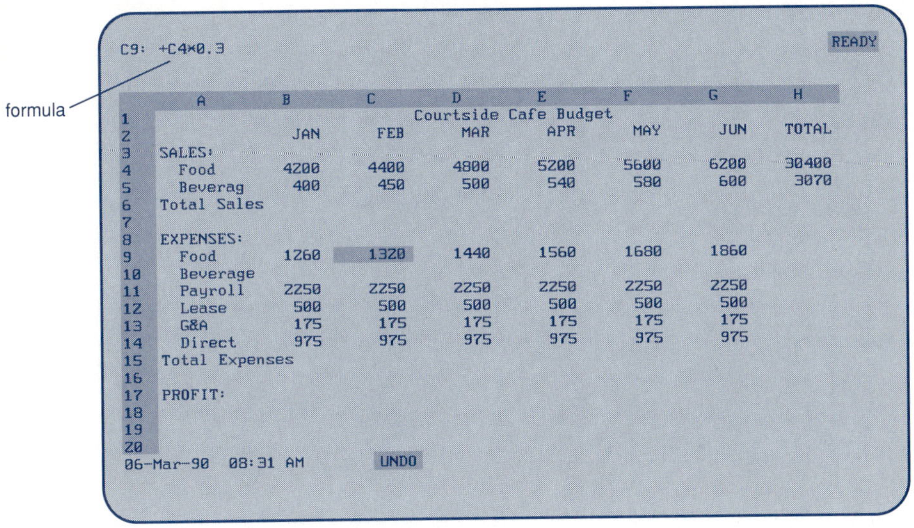

FIGURE 2-7
Copying Formulas

```
C9: +C4*0.3                                          READY

         A        B       C       D       E       F       G       H
    1                         Courtside Cafe Budget
    2              JAN     FEB     MAR     APR     MAY     JUN    TOTAL
    3   SALES:
    4     Food    4200    4400    4800    5200    5600    6200    30400
    5     Beverag  400     450     500     540     580     600     3070
    6   Total Sales
    7
    8   EXPENSES:
    9     Food    1260    1320    1440    1560    1680    1860
   10     Beverage
   11     Payroll 2250    2250    2250    2250    2250    2250
   12     Lease    500     500     500     500     500     500
   13     G&A      175     175     175     175     175     175
   14     Direct   975     975     975     975     975     975
   15   Total Expenses
   16
   17   PROFIT:
   18
   19
   20
   06-Mar-90  08:31 AM       UNDO
```

formula

The value 1320 is displayed in the cell. Look at the formula displayed in the control panel. It is +C4*.3. The formula to calculate the February food expense is not an exact duplicate of the formula used to calculate the January food expense (+B4*.3). Instead, the cell address referenced in the formula has been changed to reflect the new column location. This is because the formula uses a **relative cell reference**. A relative cell reference is a cell or range address in a formula whose location is interpreted by 1-2-3 as relative to the cell that contains the formula. When the formula in B9 was copied, the referenced cell in the formula was automatically adjusted to reflect the new column location so that the relative relationship between the referenced cell and the new column location is maintained.

Look at the formulas as they appear in the control panel as you move to cells D9 through G9. The formula has changed to reflect the new column location in each, and it appropriately calculates the value based on the food sales for each month.

The same formula will be used to calculate beverage expenses. This formula, however, will take the monthly beverage sales values in row 5 and multiply them by 30 percent. You could enter the formula in cell B10 as +B5*30% and then copy it across row 10. Instead you will copy the formula used to calculate the January food expense (B9) to calculate the January through June beverage expenses (B10 through G10) in one step.

Move to: B9

Copy the formula in the January food expense cell to the January thorugh June beverage expense cells, using highlighting to specify the range.
Let's look at how the formulas in these cells have adjusted relative to their new location in the worksheet.

Move to: B10

SS50
Creating a Worksheet: Part 2

Your display screen should be similar to Figure 2-8.

```
B10: +B5*0.3                                                    READY

         A          B         C         D         E        F        G        H
                                   Courtside Cafe Budget
  1
  2                JAN       FEB       MAR       APR      MAY      JUN    TOTAL
  3   SALES:
  4     Food       4200      4400      4800      5200     5600     6200    30400
  5     Beverag     400       450       500       540      580      600     3070
  6   Total Sales
  7
  8   EXPENSES:
  9     Food       1260      1320      1440      1560     1680     1860
 10     Beverag     120       135       150       162      174      180
 11     Payroll    2250      2250      2250      2250     2250     2250
 12     Lease       500       500       500       500      500      500
 13     G&A         175       175       175       175      175      175
 14     Direct      975       975       975       975      975      975
 15   Total Expenses
 16
 17   PROFIT:
 18
 19
 20
06-Mar-90  08:32 AM                  UNDO
```

FIGURE 2-8

The value 120 is displayed in the cell as the cost of beverages. The formula in the control panel has been adjusted relative to the new row. It correctly calculates the value based on the contents of the referenced cell, January beverage sales (B5). **Move across the row and look at how the formulas have been adjusted to reflect both the new row and column location.**

All the expenses have been entered into the worksheet. The total for sales and expenses can be calculated now.

The formula to calculate total sales for January (+B4+B5) needs to be entered in cell B6. Highlighting can also be used to specify the cells in a formula. To do this,

Move to: B6

Type: +

To extend the cell pointer to the cell containing the January food sales, cell B4,

Press: ↑ (2 times)

Cell B4 is entered following the + sign in the control panel. The mode indicator displays "POINT." To continue the formula, the next operator is entered.

Type: +

The cell pointer returns to the cell in which you entered the formula. To move the cell pointer to the cell containing the January beverage sales, cell B5,

Press: ↑

Then to complete the formula,

Press: ⏎

The calculated value of 4600 is displayed in cell B6. The formula +B4+B5 is displayed in the control panel. **Copy the formula in this cell to calculate the total sales values for February through June, using highlighting to specify the range.**

Your display screen should be similar to Figure 2-9.

FIGURE 2-9

```
B6: +B4+B5                                                              READY

        A         B         C         D         E         F         G         H
 1                          Courtside Cafe Budget
 2                JAN       FEB       MAR       APR       MAY       JUN       TOTAL
 3    SALES:
 4      Food      4200      4400      4800      5200      5600      6200      30400
 5      Beverag    400       450       500       540       580       600       3070
 6    Total Sal   4600      4850      5300      5740      6180      6800
 7
 8    EXPENSES:
 9      Food      1260      1320      1440      1560      1680      1860
10      Beverag    120       135       150       162       174       180
11      Payroll   2250      2250      2250      2250      2250      2250
12      Lease      500       500       500       500       500       500
13      G&A        175       175       175       175       175       175
14      Direct     975       975       975       975       975       975
15    Total Expenses
16
17    PROFIT:
18
19
20
03-Mar-90  11:55 AM         UNDO
```

Entering an @Function

Next the formula to calculate the total expenses for January needs to be entered in the worksheet in cell B15 and copied across the row through June.

Move to: B15

You could use a formula similar to the formulas used to calculate the total food and beverage sales (H4 and H5). The formula would be +B9+B10+B11+B12+B13+B14. But there is a shorter way to write this formula.

1-2-3 has a set of built-in formulas called **@functions** ("at functions") that perform certain types of calculations automatically. The @function you will use to calculate a sum of a range of cells is @SUM (list). Let's take a moment to look at the way this function is written.

The structure, or **syntax**, of an @function is:

@function name (argument1, argument2...)

All @functions begin with the @ ("at") character, followed by the function name. After the function name may come one or more **arguments** enclosed in parentheses. An argument is the data the @function uses to perform the calculation. It can be a number, a cell address, or a range of cells.

In the @SUM (list) function, "SUM" is the @function name, and "list" is the argument. The term **list** means an individual cell, a range of cells, or a combination of these, each separated by a comma. A list is one of many different arguments that may be required by the @function.

The @function can be entered in either upper- or lowercase characters. There is no space between the @ sign and the @function name or between the @function name and the arguments. Like a formula, if you incorrectly enter an @function,

Lotus 1-2-3 will beep and change to the EDIT mode to allow you to correct your entry. Alternatively, you could press (ESC) to clear the entry and retype it correctly.

To enter the @function to calculate the total expenses for January in cell B15, using highlighting to specify the range,

Type:	@SUM(
Move to:	B9
Type:	.
Move to:	B14
Type:	)
Press:	⏎

The value 5280, calculated by the @function, is displayed in cell B15.

Copy the @function in the January total expense cell to the February through June total expense cells, using highlighting to specify the range.

The calculated values for the total expenses for January through June are displayed in cells C15 through G15 as specified.

Move to: C15

Your screen should be similar to Figure 2-10.

FIGURE 2-10

@function

```
C15: @SUM(C9..C14)                                                    READY

          A         B         C         D         E         F         G         H
  1                            Courtside Cafe Budget
  2                  JAN       FEB       MAR       APR       MAY       JUN       TOTAL
  3     SALES:
  4       Food      4200      4400      4800      5200      5600      6200      30400
  5       Beverag    400       450       500       540       580       600       3070
  6     Total Sal   4600      4850      5300      5740      6180      6800
  7
  8     EXPENSES:
  9       Food      1260      1320      1440      1560      1680      1860
 10       Beverag    120       135       150       162       174       180
 11       Payroll   2250      2250      2250      2250      2250      2250
 12       Lease      500       500       500       500       500       500
 13       G&A        175       175       175       175       175       175
 14       Direct     975       975       975       975       975       975
 15     Total Exp   5280      5355      5490      5622      5754      5940
 16
 17     PROFIT:
 18
 19
 20
 03-Mar-90  11:56 AM              UNDO
```

The value 5355 is displayed in the cell. Look at the @function as displayed in the control panel. It is @SUM(C9..C14). When an @function is copied, it is adjusted relative to the new cell location just like a formula.

Now that the total sales and expenses are calculated, the formula to calculate profit can be entered in cell B17 and copied across the row through G17. The formula to calculate profit is the difference between monthly total expenses and monthly total sales.

In the January profit cell (B17), enter the formula +B6-B15, using highlighting to specify the cell addresses. Then copy the formula to calculate the February through June profits, using highlighting to specify the range.

Your display screen should be similar to Figure 2-11.

FIGURE 2-11

The profit for January, February, and March shows a loss. Paula is not too concerned about this. In the first few months of operation of the new cafe she does not expect to make a profit.

Using the Erase Command

Finally, the @function to calculate the total sales over the 6 months, @SUM(B6.G6), needs to be entered in cell H6. This @function can then be copied to calculate the total expenses in cells H9 through H17.

Move to: H6

Enter the @function to make this calculation, using highlighting to specify the range. Copy it to calculate the total expenses in cells H9 through H17, using highlighting to specify the range. Your display screen should be similar to Figure 2-12.

FIGURE 2-12

Move to: H16

Look at the contents of cell H16. It displays a zero. The @function was copied into a cell that references empty cells. The command to erase, or remove, the contents of a cell or range of cells is an option under the Range command. To erase the @function from cell H16,

Select: / Range

The eleven /Range commands affect specific cells or ranges of cells. You will be using many of these commands in the next lab.

Select: Erase

The prompt "Enter range to erase:" is displayed in the control panel. As in the Copy command, the range (H16..H16) entered following the prompt is the current location of the cell pointer. To accept the range,

Press: ⏎

The @function is erased from the cell and consequently the value 0 is no longer displayed in the cell. Highlighting can also be used to specify a range of cells whose contents you may want to erase. Do not remove the contents of a cell by entering a blank space. If you do this, although the cell appears empty, it still contains the label prefix character and the cell is considered occupied.

Changing Column Widths

The worksheet is complete. However, Paula wants to improve the appearance of the worksheet. She can do this by adjusting the column widths, inserting and deleting blank rows and columns, using underlining, and displaying dollar signs and commas.

After entering the values for January in column B, many of the long labels in column A were interrupted because they were longer than the 9 spaces available. To allow the long labels to be fully displayed, you can increase the **column width** of column A.

To change the width of an individual column or a range of columns, the Worksheet Column command is used. Begin by positioning the cell pointer anywhere in the column whose width you want to change. You will move to cell A15 which contains the longest label in column A.

Move to: A15
Select: / Worksheet

Ten Worksheet submenu commands are displayed in the second line of the control panel. The Worksheet commands let you control the display and organization of the worksheet. The command you want to use to change the width of specified columns in the worksheet is Column.

Select: Column

Five Column submenu commands are displayed in the control panel. They have the following effects:

Set-Width   specifies the width of the column that contains the cell pointer

Reset-Width   returns the current column width to the default width of 9 spaces

Hide   hides one or more columns to prevent them from being displayed and printed

Display   redisplays hidden columns

Column-Range   changes the width of a range of columns

The quickest way to change the width of a single column is to use the Set-Width command.

Select: Set-Width

The prompt asks you to enter the number of spaces you want to make the new column width. The current width, 9, is displayed following the prompt. The column width can be any value from 1 to 240. If you know the width you want to change the column to, you can simply type in the value following the prompt. However, if you are not sure how much you need to increase the column width, you can press the → or ← key to increase or decrease the column width. To increase the column width,

Press: → (slowly 5 times)

Each time → is pressed, the width of column A expands one space, the value following the prompt increases by one, and the columns to the right of the current column move to the right one space. The label "Total Expenses" is fully displayed in the cell space, and the prompt displays 14 as the column width.

Press: ⏎

Your display screen should be similar to Figure 2-13.

column width setting 14 spaces

```
A15: [W14] 'Total Expenses                                    READY

        A           B       C       D       E       F       G
 1                          Courtside Cafe Budget
 2                  JAN     FEB     MAR     APR     MAY     JUN
 3   SALES:
 4      Food        4200    4400    4800    5200    5600    6200
 5      Beverage    400     450     500     540     580     600
 6   Total Sales    4600    4850    5300    5740    6180    6800
 7
 8   EXPENSES:
 9      Food        1260    1320    1440    1560    1680    1860
10      Beverage    120     135     150     162     174     180
11      Payroll     2250    2250    2250    2250    2250    2250
12      Lease       500     500     500     500     500     500
13      G&A         175     175     175     175     175     175
14      Direct      975     975     975     975     975     975
15   Total Expenses 5280    5355    5490    5622    5754    5940
16
17   PROFIT:        -680    -505    -190    118     426     860
18
19
20
03-Mar-90  12:01 PM         UNDO
```

FIGURE 2-13

Notice that the new column width setting, [W14], is displayed in the control panel following the cell address. Also notice that the Total column, column H, is no longer visible in the window. It was pushed to the right to make space for the increased width of column A.

To bring the Total column back into view in the window, you will decrease the column widths of all other columns in the workhsheet. To do this,

Select: / **W**orksheet **G**lobal

Your screen should be similar to Figure 2-14.

FIGURE 2-14

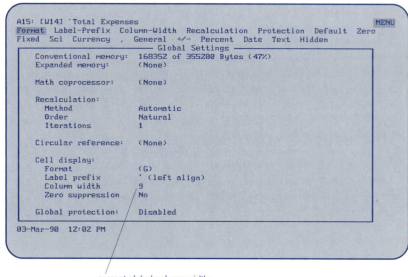

current global column width

The worksheet has been replaced by the Global Settings sheet. Like the Print Settings sheet you saw in Lab 1, the Global Settings sheet is used to help you keep track of the current settings for the options associated with the command you are using. The Global Settings sheet displays the current global settings for the worksheet. **Global** settings are settings that affect the entire worksheet. The setting you want to change is the column width. The Global Settings sheet shows that the current setting for all columns in the worksheet (except those set using the / Worksheet Column command) is 9.

To change the global column width setting, continue the command sequence as follows.

Select: **C**olumn-Width

The worksheet is redisplayed. The prompt "Enter global column width (1..240):" is displayed. To decrease the column width to 8 and see the effect on the worksheet display,

Press: ⟵

The Total column is now visible in the window. Paula wants to see how narrow she can make the columns. To decrease the column widths even more,

Press: ⟵ (3 times)

Your display should be similar to Figure 2-15.

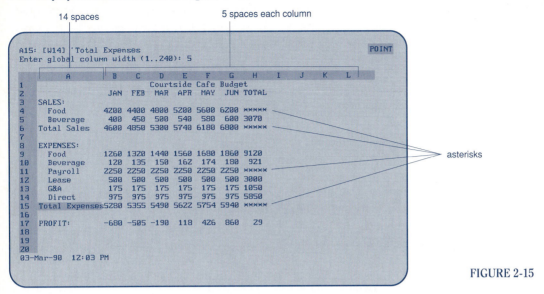

FIGURE 2-15

A series of asterisks (*****) is displayed in cells H4, H6, H11, and H15. Whenever the width of a cell is too small to display the entire value in that cell, a series of asterisks is displayed. To increase the column width back to 7,

Press: → (2 times)

Paula thinks this column width setting looks pretty good. To complete the command,

Press: ↵

All column widths have changed to 7 except for column A, which was set using the Worksheet Column Set-Width command to 14 spaces. The Worksheet command settings always override the Worksheet Global command settings. To see the change in the Global Settings sheet,

Select: / Worksheet Global

The Global Settings sheet shows the new global column width of 7. To cancel this command and return to the READY mode,

Press: CTRL - BREAK

Formatting a Value

Next Paula wants to improve the appearance or **format** of values in the worksheet. The format of values can be changed using the Worksheet Global Format command. Since this is a global command, it will affect all worksheet cells.

Select: / Worksheet Global Format

SS58
Creating a Worksheet: Part 2

The Global Settings sheet shows the default format setting is General (G). The 10 format options are listed in the control panel. For an explanation of these options, use the Help system.

Press: F1

The first Help screen discusses cell formats in general. To see a Help screen on numeric formats,

Move to: Numeric Formats
Press: ⏎

The two Format options Paula wants to try are Comma and Currency. After reading this screen of information, return to the worksheet.

Press: ESC

First Paula wants to see how the comma (,) format will look. To change the worksheet format to this setting,

Select: ,

The prompt in the control panel asks you to specify the number of decimal places you want displayed. To specify no decimal places,

Type: 0
Press: ⏎

Your display screen should be similar to Figure 2-16.

FIGURE 2-16

```
A15: [W14] 'Total Expenses                                              READY

         A           B      C      D      E      F      G      H     I
 1                              Courtside Cafe Budget
 2                      JAN    FEB    MAR    APR    MAY    JUN   TOTAL
 3     SALES:
 4       Food        4,200  4,400  4,800  5,200  5,600  6,200  30,400
 5       Beverage      400    450    500    540    580    600   3,070
 6     Total Sales  4,600  4,850  5,300  5,740  6,180  6,800  33,470
 7
 8     EXPENSES:
 9       Food        1,260  1,320  1,440  1,560  1,680  1,860   9,120
10       Beverage      120    135    150    162    174    180     921
11       Payroll     2,250  2,250  2,250  2,250  2,250  2,250  13,500
12       Lease         500    500    500    500    500    500   3,000
13       G&A           175    175    175    175    175    175   1,050
14       Direct        975    975    975    975    975    975   5,850
15     Total Expenses 5,280  5,355  5,490  5,622  5,754  5,940 33,441
16
17     PROFIT:       (680)  (505)  (190)    118    426    860     29
18
19
20
03-Mar-90  12:04 PM              UNDO
```

The values in the worksheet are displayed with commas where appropriate and no decimal places. Also notice the use of parentheses in cells C19, D19, and E19 to show that they contain negative values.

Next Paula wants to see how the worksheet would look with the format set to Currency. This option will display dollar signs, commas, and decimal places.

Select: / **W**orksheet **G**lobal **F**ormat **C**urrency

The prompt in the control panel asks you to specify the number of decimal places you want displayed. To display 0 decimal places,

Type: 0
Press: ⏎

Your screen should be similar to Figure 2-17.

FIGURE 2-17

```
A15: [W14] 'Total Expenses                                    READY

        A          B      C      D      E      F      G      H      I
                              Courtside Cafe Budget
 1
 2                 JAN    FEB    MAR    APR    MAY    JUN   TOTAL
 3   SALES:
 4      Food      $4,200 $4,400 $4,800 $5,200 $5,600 $6,200 *******
 5      Beverage   $400   $450   $500   $540   $580   $600  $3,070
 6   Total Sales $4,600 $4,850 $5,300 $5,740 $6,180 $6,800 *******
 7
 8   EXPENSES:
 9      Food      $1,260 $1,320 $1,440 $1,560 $1,680 $1,860 $9,120
10      Beverage   $120   $135   $150   $162   $174   $180   $921
11      Payroll  $2,250 $2,250 $2,250 $2,250 $2,250 $2,250 *******
12      Lease     $500   $500   $500   $500   $500   $500  $3,000
13      G&A       $175   $175   $175   $175   $175   $175  $1,050
14      Direct    $975   $975   $975   $975   $975   $975  $5,850
15   Total Expenses$5,280 $5,355 $5,490 $5,622 $5,754 $5,940 *******
16
17   PROFIT:            ($680)($505)($190) $118   $426   $860   $29
18
19
20
08-Apr-90  08:35 AM     UNDO
```

Now the worksheet displays dollar signs and commas in all cells displaying a value. However, a series of asterisks appears in many of the cells. This indicates that the cell width is too small to fully display the value. The additional characters used to display currency (dollar sign and comma) have caused this problem. Before changing the column width, Paula wants to decide which format she prefers. You can switch back and forth between the two formats using the UNDO feature.

Note: Consult your instructor if UNDO is not displayed in the status line.

Press: ALT - F4

The comma format is displayed. To see the currency format again,

Press: ALT - F4

The UNDO feature is useful not only for undoing errors but for switching back and forth between two worksheet settings. You will recall that the UNDO feature works by creating a temporary backup copy of the worksheet each time you begin a command, start an entry, or use certain function keys that affect the worksheet data. The backup copy is stored in memory. When you use UNDO, it displays the worksheet that was stored in memory. Since 1-2-3 does not wait until the command or entry is complete before backing up the worksheet, you must use the UNDO feature immediately after executing the command or making the entry that you want to undo. A backup worksheet is not created if the key you press does not cause a change in worksheet data.

The UNDO feature is an important safeguard against mistakes that may take a lot of time to fix. However, be careful when using this command as you may get some unexpected results.

After looking at the two different formats of the worksheet, Paula decides she likes the currency format best after all. The currency format should be displayed on your screen.

Now she needs to increase the column width to allow display of all the values in their cells. To take a look at how these values are displayed, move the cell pointer to the last-used cell in the row, H15, as follows.

Press: END
Press: →

The formula used to calculate the total expenses for 6 months is displayed in the control panel. In order for the calculated value to be displayed, the width of the cell needs to be increased. Additionally, Paula thinks the columns look crowded because of the extra space required to display the currency format. To increase the width of columns B through H, the Worksheet Column Column-Range command is used.

Select: /Worksheet Column Column-Range Set-Width

In response to the prompt in the control panel you must specify the range of columns whose width you want to change. In response to the prompt, 1-2-3 displays the cell address of the current cell as the default response to range. Notice that the default response is anchored already.

To specify the range of columns, any row can be used. **Since the cell pointer is already on row 15, use highlighting to specify columns B through H as the range.**

The default response was cleared and the new range is displayed following the prompt.

To increase the column width,

Press: →

The width of columns B through H each changed to 8 spaces, and the values in cells H4, H6, H11, and H15 are fully displayed.

Press: ↵

The new column width setting, [W8], is displayed in the control panel because the width of these columns was changed using the Worksheet Column command. The column width for all columns to the right of column H remain at 7 spaces, as they were set using the Global Column-Width command and were not changed when the Worksheet Column Column-Range command was used.

Inserting Rows

The appearance of the worksheet is greatly improved already. However, Paula still feels that it looks crowded. She wants a blank row entered below the worksheet title as row 2.

To insert a blank row into the worksheet, begin by moving the cell pointer to the row where the new blank row will be inserted.

Move to: H2
Select: / Worksheet Insert Row ⏎

Your display screen should be similar to Figure 2-18.

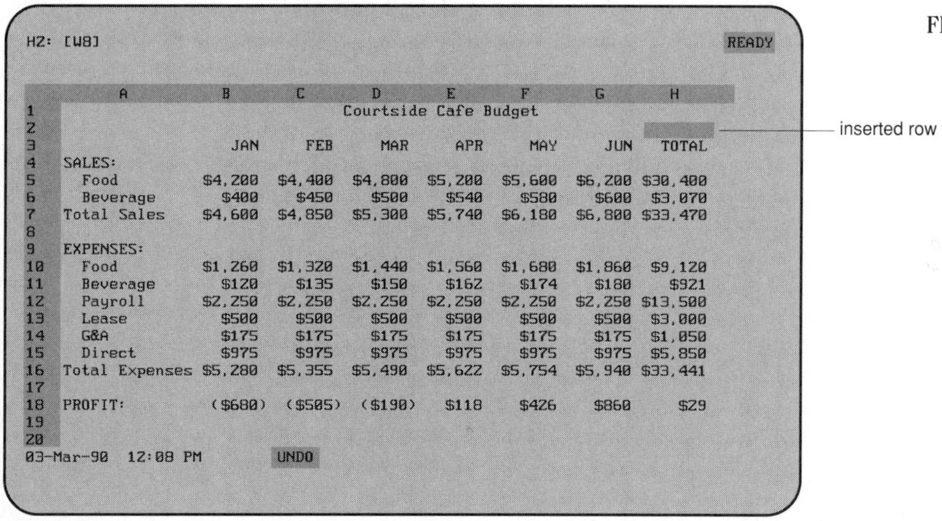

FIGURE 2-18

inserted row

A new blank row has been inserted into the worksheet at the cell pointer location. Everything below row 2 has moved down one row. All formulas and functions have been automatically adjusted to their new row locations.

Next Paula wants to enter a blank row below the column labels. Then she will be able to underline the column labels.

Move to: H4

Insert a blank row in row 4. The rows below row 4 have moved down one row to make space for the blank row. All formulas and functions have again been readjusted.

To delete a row, use the same procedure, except select Delete rather than Insert. Be very careful when using the Delete option because any information in the range specified will be deleted.

Using the Repeat Label Prefix Character

Paula would like the month labels to be offset from the worksheet values by a series of underline characters.

To underline the column heading "TOTAL," with the cell pointer in cell H4, press the minus sign character 8 times as follows:

Type: `--------`

Notice the mode indicator displays "VALUE."

Press: `↵`

The computer beeped and placed the worksheet in the EDIT mode. This is because Lotus 1-2-3 has determined that this is not a valid cell entry and wants you to edit the cell contents.

The first character entered into this cell was a minus sign. This character defined the cell entry as a value. A series of minus signs is not a valid numeric entry. If you want a character that Lotus 1-2-3 interprets as a value to be interpreted as a label, precede it by an apostrophe.

To correct this entry,

Press: `HOME`
Type: `'`
Press: `↵`

A series of underline characters fills the cell.

Another way to fill a cell with a repeated character is by using the fourth label prefix character, a backslash (\).

Move to: `G4`
Type: `\`

To specify the character to be used to fill the cell,

Type: `-`
Press: `↵`

The character following the \ fills the entire cell width. It was not necessary to enter an apostrophe before the minus character because the \ defined the cell contents as a label. The backslash can be used to fill a cell with any repeated characters.

Using the Copy command, underline the January through May column labels.

Your display screen should be similar to Figure 2-19.

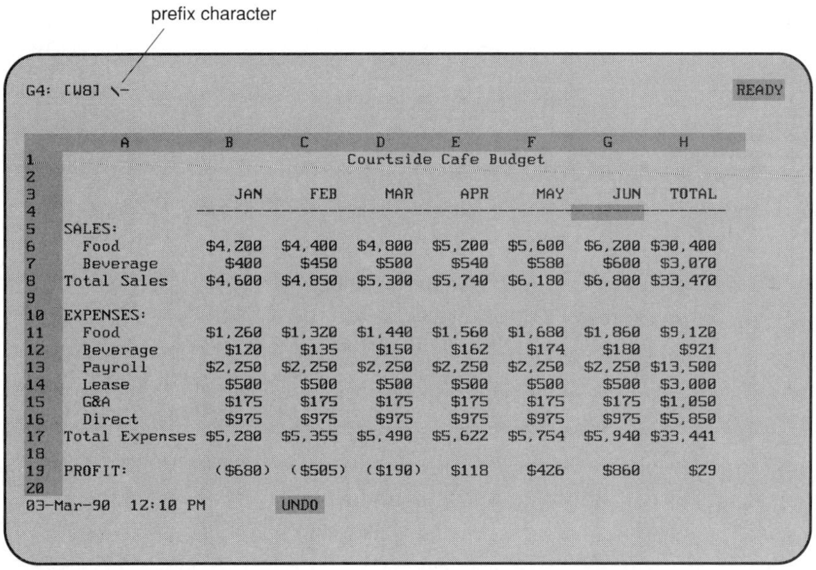

FIGURE 2-19

Inserting Columns

Next Paula wants to separate the row labels from the months by inserting a blank column between column A and column B. The blank column will be column B.

Move to: B4
Select: / **W**orksheet **I**nsert **C**olumn ⏎

Your display screen should be similar to Figure 2-20.

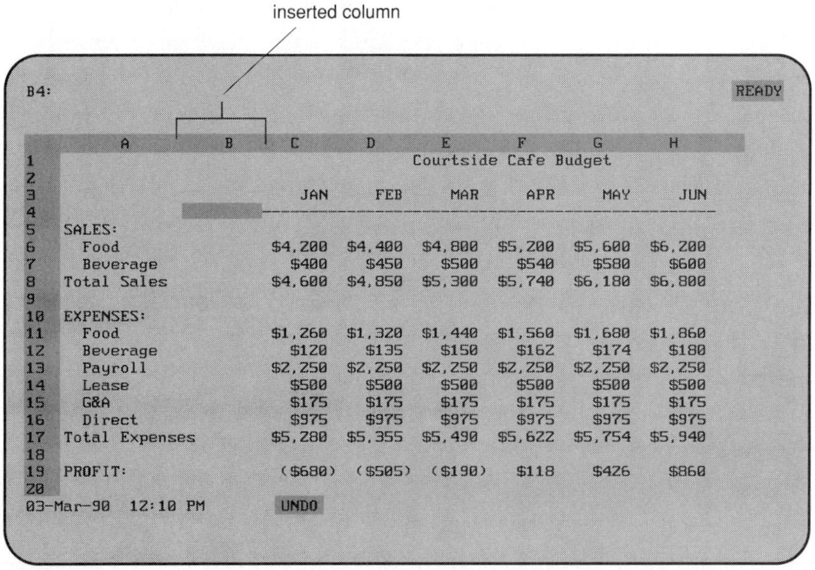

FIGURE 2-20

A blank column has been inserted into the worksheet as column B.
    Notice that the Total column, I, is no longer visible on the display. The inserted column forced it to the right of the window.

SS64
Creating a Worksheet: Part 2

To see the rest of the worksheet, using the (→) key,

Move to: I4

Your display screen should be similar to Figure 2-21.

FIGURE 2-21

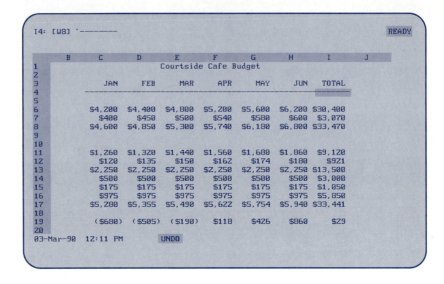

Column I is now visible on the display, but the row labels in column A are not. This makes reading the worksheet difficult, since it is hard to know what the figures mean. You will learn how to handle a worksheet that is larger than a window in the next lab.

A column can also be deleted using the same procedure, except the Delete option is selected rather than Insert. Again, be careful when deleting a column that you do not accidentally delete a column of important information.

Before saving and printing the worksheet, enter your name in cell A1 and the date in cell A2.

Saving and Replacing a File

Whenever you are finished working on a file, be sure to save the current version of the file displayed on the screen to the diskette. If you retrieve another file or leave the Lotus 1-2-3 program without saving the current version of the worksheet, you will lose all your hard work.

When you save a worksheet file you will either give the worksheet a new file name or write over the contents of an existing worksheet file using an old file name.

Before Lotus 1-2-3 saves any worksheet files, it checks to see whether the file name already exists on the diskette. If it does not exist, the worksheet is automatically saved with the new file name. If it does exist, the program asks you to specify whether you want to replace (write over) the contents of the old file with the current worksheet.

You no longer need the file you created at the end of Lab 1, CAFE.WK1. So you will reuse the file name and replace the file contents with the current worksheet.

Select: / File Save

The current worksheet file name, CAFE1.WK1, is displayed after the prompt. To enter a different file name,

Type: CAFE
Press: ⏎

The 1-2-3 program checked the diskette and found that another file already exists with the file name CAFE.WK1. The prompt in the control panel displays three options:

> Cancel — returns 1-2-3 to READY mode without saving the worksheet. You can then reissue the command to save the file using a new file name.
>
> Replace — writes over the worksheet file on disk with a copy of the current worksheet.
>
> Backup — saves the current worksheet using the existing file name and creates a backup copy of the existing file on disk, using the same file name but with the file extension .BAK.

Select: Replace

The file is saved as CAFE.WK1. The Cancel and Replace options are a protection against accidentally writing over a file with the same name.

Printing a File

If you have printer capability, you can print a copy of the worksheet. First turn the printer on and check to see that it is online. Adjust the paper so that the perforation is just above the printer scale.

Press: (HOME)
Select: / Print Printer Range

The entire worksheet range can be specified using highlighting. To anchor the current cell and move the cell pointer to the last used cell in the worksheet,

Type: .
Press: (END)
Press: (HOME)

The range A1..I19 is entered following the prompt.

Press: ⏎

Next, to tell 1-2-3 that the paper is aligned with the top of the page and to begin printing,

Select: Align Go

SS66
Creating a Worksheet: Part 2

After the worksheet is printed, to advance the page and leave the print menu,

Select: Page Quit

Your printout requires two pages to display the entire width of the worksheet. In the next lab you will learn how to print a large worksheet on one page.
If you are ready to leave Lotus 1-2-3, issue the Quit command.

Key Terms

copy	argument
anchor	list
anchor cell	column width
relative cell reference	global
@function	format
syntax	

Matching

1. @ _____ a. globally sets column width
2. \ _____ b. inserts a column
3. POINT _____ c. erases a range of cells
4. / C _____ d. indicates insufficient cell width
5. @AVG(list) _____ e. method of entering cell range
6. / R E _____ f. character used at the beginning of an "at" function
7. / W G C _____ g. moves cursor to last-used cell
8. / W I C _____ h. fills cell with repeated character
9. ********* _____ i. averages a range of cells
10. END - HOME _____ j. copies the contents of a cell or a range of cells

Practice Exercises

1. To complete this problem you must have created the worksheet in Lab 1, Practice Exercise 4. If you have done so already, retrieve the file JEWELRY.WK1. You will continue to build the worksheet for the jewelry store sales campaign.
Enter the following sales figures:

	Week 3	Week 4
Sally	2275	3602
Martin	1898	5900
Phillip	3342	4688
Dorothy	4198	4975
Alyce	3604	2800

■ Copy the weekly total formula in cell C11 to cells D11 through H11.

- Enter @functions to calculate the total sales and average sales for each salesperson.
- The winner of the contest is the salesperson with the largest average sales over the 4 weeks. That person will earn 15 percent on their total sales. All other salespersons will earn 10 percent on their total sales. Enter the formulas to calculate the appropriate percent earned.
- Enter the current date in cell A2. Save the worksheet as JEWELRY.
- Print the worksheet.

2. To complete this problem you must have completed Practice Exercise 1 above. Retrieve the file JEWELRY.WK1. You will improve the appearance of this worksheet by inserting rows, changing column widths, and displaying currency.

- Insert a blank row at row 1. Insert another blank row below the worksheet title. Finally, insert two blank rows below the column headings for the weeks.
- Underline the column heading in row 6.
- Globally format the worksheet to display currency with 2 decimal places.
- Increase the column widths of the range of columns necessary to fully display the values.
- Move your name to cell A1.
- Erase the date from cell A4.
- Enter the current date in cell A2. Save the worksheet as CONTEST.
- Print the worksheet.

3. To complete this problem you must have created the worksheet in Practice Exercise 2 of Lab 1. Retrieve the file COST.WK1. You will continue to build the worksheet for the cost analysis of purchasing a new car versus keeping the old car.

- Enter the trade-in value for the old car as 924 and for the new car as 4637 after 4 years of ownership.
- Enter the formula to calculate the net cost of ownership for the old car. This formula is the difference between the total expenses and the trade-in value. Copy this formula to calculate the net cost of ownership for the new car.
- Enter a formula to calculate the "Saved by not trading in" value. This formula is the difference between the net cost of ownership for the old and new cars. This value should be displayed in the old-car column.
- Format the worksheet to display currency with 2 decimal places. If necessary, increase the column width globally to fully display all values.
- Insert a blank row below the worksheet title and the column headings. Delete row 7.
- Underline the column headings.
- Increase the column width of A to completely display all row labels. Right-align the labels in cells A7 through A10.
- Enter the current date in cell A2, and erase the old date from cell A3.

SS68
Creating a Worksheet: Part 2

- Save the worksheet using the same file name, COST.
- Print the worksheet.

4. To complete this problem you must have created the worksheet in Practice Exercise 5 of Lab 1. Retrieve the file ZOOFINAN.WK1. You will continue to build the worksheet for the 3-year financial statement for the zoo.

- To make the worksheet easier to read, you will insert blank rows and columns. Insert a blank row between the worksheet title and the column headings. The blank row will be row 2.
- Insert a blank row below the column headings. Underline the column headings.
- Enter blank rows as rows 10, 12, and 18 (in that order.)
- Enter underline characters (-) in rows 10 and 18 in columns D through H.
- Delete column B.
- Increase the column width of A to completely display all row labels.
- Change the column width of column B to 4 spaces.
- Copy the formulas used to calculate TOTAL S & R and TOTAL A/E for 1988 to calculate these values for 1989 and 1990. Also copy the formula used to calculate operating reserve for 1989 and 1990.
- Enter @functions to calculate the TOTAL and AVERAGE in cells G6 and H6 respectively. Copy the @functions down the column. Erase the @function from those cells which reference empty cells, and replace the underline where appropriate.
- Erase the old date from cell A3 and enter the current date in cell A2.
- Save the worksheet using the same file name, ZOOFINAN.
- Print the worksheet.

LAB 3
Managing a Large Worksheet

CASE STUDY

Paula Nichols, the manager of the Courtside Cafe at the Sports Club, presented the completed worksheet of the estimated operating budget for the proposed Courtside Cafe expansion to the board of directors. Although the board was pleased with the 6-month analysis, it asked her to extend the budget to cover a full year period. The board also wants her to calculate the profit margin for the proposed cafe expansion over the 12 months. At the end of 12 months the profit margin should be 20 percent. You will follow Paula as she makes the adjustments in the budget.

Locating and Correcting a Circular Reference

After presenting the budget to the board, Paula revised the worksheet, making several of the changes requested.

> When responding to the DOS date prompt, be sure to enter the current date. Load Lotus 1-2-3. The data diskette should be in the B drive (or the appropriate drive for your computer system). To see what Paula has done so far, retrieve the file CAFE2.WK1.

OBJECTIVES

In this lab you will learn how to:

1. Correct a circular reference
2. Freeze row and column titles
3. Create and use windows.
4. Set window synchronization
5. Perform what-if analysis.
6. Use an absolute cell reference
7. Extract worksheet data.
8. Link worksheet data
9. Enter the system date
10. Justify text
11. Use compressed printing

SS70
Managing a Large Worksheet

Your display screen should be similar to Figure 3-1.

FIGURE 3-1

```
A1: [W15]                                                          READY

          A          B        C        D        E        F        G        H
1
2
3                                                 Courtside Cafe Budget
4
5
6                    JAN      FEB      MAR      APR      MAY      JUN      JUL
7        ─────────────────────────────────────────────────────────────────────
8
9   SALES:
10    Food        $4,200   $4,400   $4,800   $5,200   $5,600   $6,200   $7,000
11    Beverage      $400     $450     $500     $540     $580     $600     $700
12  Total Sales   $4,600   $4,850   $5,300   $5,740   $6,180   $6,800   $7,700
13
14  EXPENSES:
15    Food        $1,260   $1,320   $1,440   $1,560   $1,680   $1,860   $2,100
16    Beverage      $120     $135     $150     $162     $174     $180     $210
17    Payroll     $2,250   $2,250   $2,250   $2,250   $2,250   $2,250   $2,250
18    Lease         $500     $500     $500     $500     $500     $500     $500
19    G & A         $175     $175     $175     $175     $175     $175     $175
20    Direct        $975     $975     $975     $975     $975     $975     $975
03-Mar-90 12:16 PM            UNDO                       CIRC
```

The worksheet now contains values for 12 months and a new row label for profit margin. The worksheet extends beyond column H and below row 20.

Note: Although there are quicker ways to move to cells in the worksheet, use the arrow keys when directed. Your display will then show the same rows and columns as the figures in the text.

To see the rest of the row labels, using ⓓ,

Move to: A25

The row label "PROFIT MARGIN:" is now visible on the display. The formula to calculate this value still needs to be entered into the worksheet.

To see the rest of the worksheet to the right of column H, using ⓡ,

Move to: N25

Your display screen should be similar to Figure 3-2.

FIGURE 3-2

```
N25: [W8]                                                                     READY

          F        G        H        I        J        K        L        M          N
6       MAY      JUN      JUL      AUG     SEPT      OCT      NOV      DEC      TOTAL
7     ────────────────────────────────────────────────────────────────────────────────
8
9
10   $5,600   $6,200   $7,000   $5,500   $6,400   $5,500   $6,500   $7,520   $68,820
11     $580     $600     $700     $500     $750     $800     $650     $775    $7,245
12   $6,180   $6,800   $7,700   $6,000   $7,150   $6,300   $7,150   $8,295   $76,065
13
14
15   $1,680   $1,860   $2,100   $1,650   $1,920   $1,650   $1,950   $2,256   $20,646
16     $174     $180     $210     $150     $225     $240     $195     $233    $2,174
17   $2,250   $2,250   $2,250   $2,250   $2,250   $2,250   $2,250   $2,250   $27,000
18     $500     $500     $500     $500     $500     $500     $500     $500    $6,000
19     $175     $175     $175     $175     $175     $175     $175     $175    $2,100
20     $975     $975     $975     $975     $975     $975     $975     $975   $11,700
21   $5,754   $5,940   $6,210   $5,700   $6,045   $5,790   $6,045   $6,389   $69,620
22
23     $426     $860   $1,490     $300   $1,105     $510   $1,105   $8,295   $12,834
24
25
03-Mar-90 12:16 PM              UNDO                       CIRC
```

— circular reference indicator

The TOTAL column and the values for the months of May through December are now visible. Notice the message "CIRC" displayed on the bottom line of the window. This message is a warning that a **circular reference** has been located in the worksheet. This means that a formula in a cell either directly or indirectly references itself. For some special applications, a formula containing a circular reference may be valid. These cases, however, are not very common. Whenever you see this message displayed, stop and locate the cell or cells containing the reference.

Locating the formula containing a circular reference in a worksheet can be very difficult. However, Lotus 1-2-3 has made it easy by providing a status screen. It tells you the specific cell containing the circular reference. The status screen is displayed by using the Worksheet Status command.

Select: /Worksheet Status

The Global Settings sheet is displayed. When using the Worksheet Status command, this settings sheet is displayed to provide information about available memory, recalculation, cell display format, circular references, and global protection. To make changes to the global settings you would need to use the appropriate command. You are interested in the Circular Reference status. It tells you that the cell containing the circular reference is M23.

To clear the settings sheet and return to the worksheet,

Press: any key

Let's look at the formula in cell M23.

Move to: M23

The value in this cell is 8295. Look at the formula in the control panel. It is +M12-M23. The formula in cell M23 incorrectly references itself, M23, as part of the computation.

The formula in this cell should calculate the profit for December using the formula +M12-M21. **Correct the formula in cell M23 to be +M12-M21.**

Your display screen should be similar to Figure 3-3.

FIGURE 3-3

The CIRC message has disappeared, and the affected worksheet formulas were recalculated. The new calculated value, 1907, is displayed in cell M23. This was a simple example of a circular reference error; others may be much more complex. In any case, whenever this message appears, display the status screen to locate the circular reference and determine whether it is valid or not.

Freezing Titles

Looking at the values in the worksheet, you may find it difficult to remember what the values stand for when the row labels in column A are not visible on the display screen. For example,

Move to: M19

The value in this cell is 175. Is this value a lease expense or a beverage expense or a direct expense? Without seeing the row labels, it is difficult for you to know. To see the row labels in column A,

Press: END
Press: ←

Although the row labels are visible again, you cannot see the values in columns I through N. To keep the row labels visible in the window all the time while viewing the values in columns I through N, you will **freeze** column A in the window.

The Worksheet Titles command lets you fix, or freeze, specified rows or columns (or both) on the window while you scroll to other areas of the worksheet. The "titles" can consist of any number of columns or rows along the top or left edge of the window.

To freeze a column of titles, move the cursor one column to the right of the column you want frozen. Since you want to freeze column A on the window,

Move to: B23
Select: /Worksheet Titles

The Titles submenu options in the control panel have the following effects:

Both	freezes both the horizontal and vertical titles
Horizontal	freezes only the horizontal titles
Vertical	freezes only the vertical titles
Clear	unfreezes all titles

The row labels in column A run vertically down the worksheet. To freeze the vertical column of titles (A),

Select: Vertical

Nothing appears different on the display screen until you move the cell pointer.

Press: ←

Lotus 1-2-3 beeped. It will not let you move the cell pointer into column A because it is frozen.

Watch the movement of the columns on the display screen as you use (→) to,

Move to: N23

Your display screen should be similar to Figure 3-4.

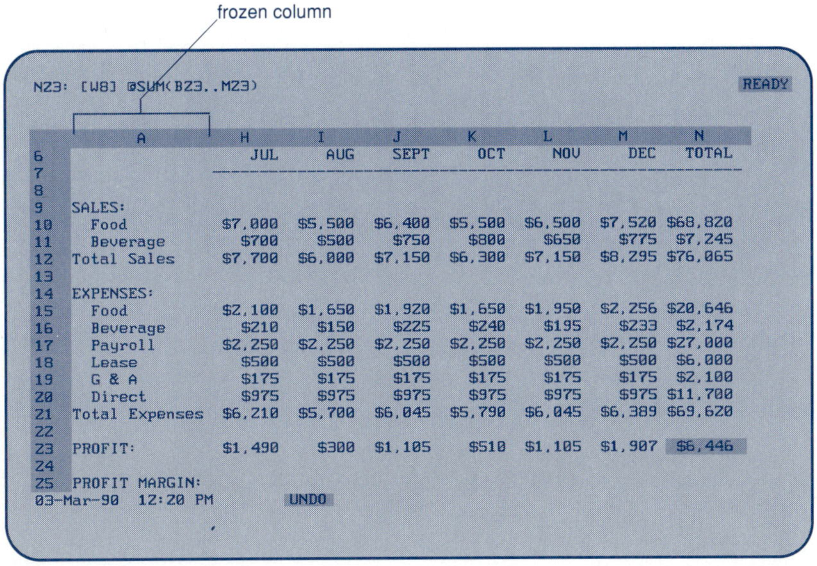

	A	H	I	J	K	L	M	N
6		JUL	AUG	SEPT	OCT	NOV	DEC	TOTAL
7		-----	-----	-----	-----	-----	-----	-----
8								
9	SALES:							
10	Food	$7,000	$5,500	$6,400	$5,500	$6,500	$7,520	$68,820
11	Beverage	$700	$500	$750	$800	$650	$775	$7,245
12	Total Sales	$7,700	$6,000	$7,150	$6,300	$7,150	$8,295	$76,065
13								
14	EXPENSES:							
15	Food	$2,100	$1,650	$1,920	$1,650	$1,950	$2,256	$20,646
16	Beverage	$210	$150	$225	$240	$195	$233	$2,174
17	Payroll	$2,250	$2,250	$2,250	$2,250	$2,250	$2,250	$27,000
18	Lease	$500	$500	$500	$500	$500	$500	$6,000
19	G & A	$175	$175	$175	$175	$175	$175	$2,100
20	Direct	$975	$975	$975	$975	$975	$975	$11,700
21	Total Expenses	$6,210	$5,700	$6,045	$5,790	$6,045	$6,389	$69,620
22								
23	PROFIT:	$1,490	$300	$1,105	$510	$1,105	$1,907	$6,446
24								
25	PROFIT MARGIN:							

FIGURE 3-4

Column A has remained fixed in the window while columns H through N scroll into view. This makes reading the worksheet much easier.

To unfreeze, or clear, the frozen column,

Select: / **W**orksheet **T**itles **C**lear

Column A is no longer visible on the display. To further confirm that column A is unfrozen, to move to cell A23,

Press: (END)
Press: (←)

Since column A is no longer frozen, the cell pointer can be positioned in cell A23.

Titles can also be frozen horizontally, or across a row, as easily as they are frozen vertically down a column. Paula would like to freeze the month labels and the underlining in rows 6 and 7 in the window. The row to freeze is marked by positioning the cell pointer one row below the row to be frozen.

Using (↑),

Move to: A8
Select: / **W**orksheet **T**itles **H**orizontal
Press: (↑)

SS74
Managing a Large Worksheet

Again the cell pointer movement is restricted to unfrozen cells.
Using ⓓ,

Move to: A29

Your display screen should be similar to Figure 3-5.

FIGURE 3-5

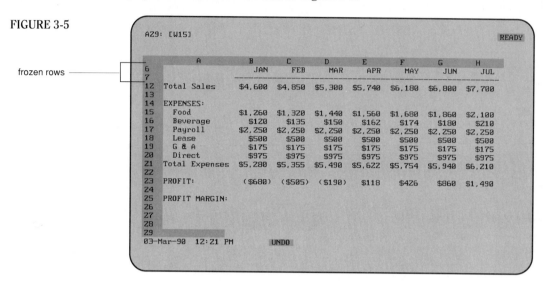

frozen rows

Rows 6 and 7 remained stationary in the window as you scrolled down through the worksheet.
Using ⓡ,

Move to: N29

Although the month labels have remained stationary in the window with the row labels unfrozen, it is again difficult to read the worksheet. Conveniently, both column and row titles can be frozen at the same time.

Press: (HOME)

Notice that the Home position is the upper left-hand corner of the unfrozen worksheet cells rather than cell A1, which is frozen.
Clear the frozen horizontal titles.
To freeze both the horizontal and vertical titles at the same time, position the cell pointer one row below the row to be frozen and one column to the right of the column to be frozen.

Move to: B8
Select: /**W**orksheet **T**itles **B**oth
Press: ⓐ
Press: ⓑ

The rows above and the column to the left of the cell pointer position are frozen. Watch your display carefully as you use your arrow keys to

Move to: N8
Move to: N29

Your display screen should be similar to Figure 3-6.

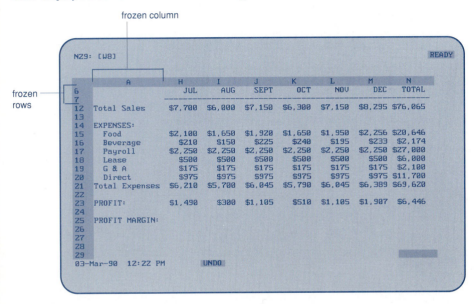

FIGURE 3-6

Both the vertical and horizontal titles remain stationary in the window as you scroll through the worksheet.

Press: (HOME)

The Home position is now the upper left-hand corner of the unfrozen rows and columns, cell B8.

Creating and Scrolling Windows

The frozen titles greatly improve the readability of the worksheet. However, it is still difficult to compare the values in columns that cannot be viewed in the same window. For example, to compare the values in each month to the values in the TOTAL column or to certain other months is difficult. This is because as one column comes into view on the display screen, the other may scroll off due to lack of space in the window.

You could freeze the leftmost column you want to compare and then scroll the worksheet until the column on the right comes into view. But then you would not be able to make any changes or see the other columns to the left of the frozen column. The solution is to create a second window on the display.

Worksheets are viewed through a **window**. The part of the worksheet you can see on your display screen is a window. So far you have had only one window, the full size of the display screen, on the worksheet. The Worksheet Windows command lets you create a second window on the screen through which you can view different areas of the worksheet at the same time.

SS76
Managing a Large Worksheet

To easily compare the values in each month to the values in column N, TOTAL, you will create a second window. This window will divide the display vertically.

Use → to,

Move to: N8

Select: /Worksheet Window Vertical

Your display screen should be similar to Figure 3-7.

FIGURE 3-7

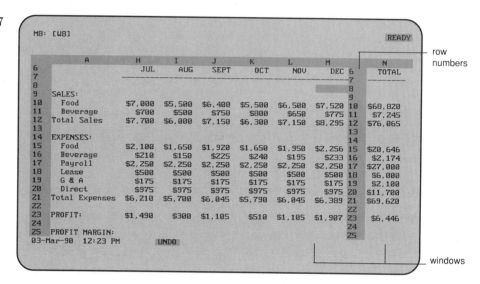

The screen is split vertically into two windows. A new border of row numbers separates the two windows. The cell pointer is positioned in the left window. This is the **active window**.

Watch your display screen carefully as you use ← to,

Move to: B8

Your display screen should be similar to Figure 3-8.

FIGURE 3-8

The columns in the left window move into view as the cell pointer moves across the row. The right window did not change. Now the values in January through June can easily be compared to the total values displayed in the right window.
Using ⊙,

Move to: B29

The rows scrolled together in both windows. When you scroll vertically through a vertical window, the rows in the other window will scroll at the same time, keeping the rows even in both windows. This is called **synchronized** scrolling. If a horizontal window were created on the screen, scrolling horizontally through the window would move the columns together in both windows. This is the default setting for windows in Lotus 1-2-3.

Press: (HOME)

The cell pointer can be moved from one window to the other using the Window function key, (F6)

Press: (F6) Window

The cell pointer is positioned in cell N8 in the right window.
Windows can be changed to scroll independently, or **unsynchronized**. To change to unsynchronized scrolling,

Select: / Worksheet Window Unsync

Using ⊙,

Move to: N29

The rows in the right window moved. The rows in the left window did not move.
Since a window lets you view different parts of the same worksheet, any changes made in one window are made to the entire worksheet and will be seen in either window.
Before continuing, to clear the vertical window,

Select: / Worksheet Window Clear

The display screen returns to one window.

Displaying a Percent

Now that Paula knows how to move around and manage a large worksheet, she needs to enter the formula to calculate the profit margin in cell B25. Using ⊙,

Move to: B25

The formula to calculate profit margin is:

Profit/Total sales*100%

In cell B25, enter the formula +B23/B12 using pointing. Do not multiply it times 100 percent.

Your display screen should be similar to Figure 3-9.

FIGURE 3-9

```
B25: [W8] +B23/B12                                                          READY

        A              B        C        D        E        F        G        H
   6                  JAN      FEB      MAR      APR      MAY      JUN      JUL
   7               -------  -------  -------  -------  -------  -------  -------
   8
   9   SALES:
  10     Food      $4,200   $4,400   $4,800   $5,200   $5,600   $6,200   $7,000
  11     Beverage    $400     $450     $500     $540     $580     $600     $700
  12   Total Sales $4,600   $4,850   $5,300   $5,740   $6,180   $6,800   $7,700
  13
  14   EXPENSES:
  15     Food      $1,260   $1,320   $1,440   $1,560   $1,680   $1,860   $2,100
  16     Beverage    $120     $135     $150     $162     $174     $180     $210
  17     Payroll   $2,250   $2,250   $2,250   $2,250   $2,250   $2,250   $2,250
  18     Lease       $500     $500     $500     $500     $500     $500     $500
  19     G & A       $175     $175     $175     $175     $175     $175     $175
  20     Direct      $975     $975     $975     $975     $975     $975     $975
  21   Total Expenses $5,280 $5,355  $5,490   $5,622   $5,754   $5,940   $6,210
  22
  23   PROFIT:    ($680)   ($505)   ($190)    $118     $426     $860    $1,490
  24
  25   PROFIT MARGIN:       ($0)
  03-Mar-90  12:25 PM       UNDO
```

The value "($0)" is displayed in cell B25. To display the value in this cell as a percent, you need to change the cell format from currency (set globally in Lab 2) to a percent with zero decimal places. Setting the cell format to percent will also multiply the formula in the cell times 100.

In Lab 2 you learned how to change the format of values with the Worksheet Global Format command. The format of a cell or range of cells can also be changed using the Range Format command. This command will affect the display of values in a specified cell or range of cells only. This setting will override the cell format previously set globally.

Select: **/R**ange **F**ormat **P**ercent **0** ⏎ ⏎

Your display screen should be similar to Figure 3-10.

FIGURE 3-10

cell format

```
B25: (P0) [W8] +B23/B12                                                     READY

        A              B        C        D        E        F        G        H
   6                  JAN      FEB      MAR      APR      MAY      JUN      JUL
   7               -------  -------  -------  -------  -------  -------  -------
   8
   9   SALES:
  10     Food      $4,200   $4,400   $4,800   $5,200   $5,600   $6,200   $7,000
  11     Beverage    $400     $450     $500     $540     $580     $600     $700
  12   Total Sales $4,600   $4,850   $5,300   $5,740   $6,180   $6,800   $7,700
  13
  14   EXPENSES:
  15     Food      $1,260   $1,320   $1,440   $1,560   $1,680   $1,860   $2,100
  16     Beverage    $120     $135     $150     $162     $174     $180     $210
  17     Payroll   $2,250   $2,250   $2,250   $2,250   $2,250   $2,250   $2,250
  18     Lease       $500     $500     $500     $500     $500     $500     $500
  19     G & A       $175     $175     $175     $175     $175     $175     $175
  20     Direct      $975     $975     $975     $975     $975     $975     $975
  21   Total Expenses $5,280 $5,355  $5,490   $5,622   $5,754   $5,940   $6,210
  22
  23   PROFIT:    ($680)   ($505)   ($190)    $118     $426     $860    $1,490
  24
  25   PROFIT MARGIN:      -15%
  03-Mar-90  12:26 PM       UNDO
```

The profit margin displayed for January is "-15%."
Setting the cell format to a percent takes the value in the cell and multiplies it by 100. The value is displayed with a percent sign (%). Also notice that when the cell format is specified using the Range Format command, the setting "(P0)" is displayed in the control panel.

Copy the formula in cell B25 across the row through the end of the worksheet, using highlighting to specify the range.

Your screen should be similar to Figure 3-11.

FIGURE 3-11

```
B25: (P0) [W8] +B23/B12                                              READY

        A              B        C        D        E        F        G        H
 6                    JAN      FEB      MAR      APR      MAY      JUN      JUL
 7                   ───────────────────────────────────────────────────────────
 8
 9   SALES:
10     Food        $4,200   $4,400   $4,800   $5,200   $5,600   $6,200   $7,000
11     Beverage      $400     $450     $500     $540     $580     $600     $700
12   Total Sales  $4,600   $4,850   $5,300   $5,740   $6,180   $6,800   $7,700
13
14   EXPENSES:
15     Food        $1,260   $1,320   $1,440   $1,560   $1,680   $1,860   $2,100
16     Beverage      $120     $135     $150     $162     $174     $180     $210
17     Payroll    $2,250   $2,250   $2,250   $2,250   $2,250   $2,250   $2,250
18     Lease         $500     $500     $500     $500     $500     $500     $500
19     G & A         $175     $175     $175     $175     $175     $175     $175
20     Direct        $975     $975     $975     $975     $975     $975     $975
21   Total Expenses $5,280  $5,355   $5,490   $5,622   $5,754   $5,940   $6,210
22
23   PROFIT:       ($680)  ($505)   ($190)    $118     $426     $860   $1,490
24
25   PROFIT MARGIN:  -15%    -10%      -4%      2%       7%      13%     19%
03-Mar-90  12:26 PM          UNDO
```

Notice that not only was the formula copied but also the cell format.
To see what the total profit margin for the year is, move to cell N25.

Press: `END`
Press: `→`

The total profit margin for the year is "8%." The board of directors wants the proposed cafe expansion to show a 20 percent total profit margin during the first year of operation. The total profit margin, using the figures as budgeted for the year, is much below this objective.

Using What-If Analysis

After some consideration, Paula decides that the only way to increase the total profit margin is to reduce expenses. She feels she can reduce payroll by more carefully scheduling the number of hours the employees work. She can decrease the number of employee work hours by scheduling fewer employees to work during slow periods.
The process of evaluating what effect reducing the payroll expenses will have on the total profit margin is called **what-if analysis**. What-if analysis is a technique used to evaluate the effects of changing selected factors in a worksheet. Paula wants to know what would happen if payroll expenses decreased a set amount each month.

SS80
Managing a Large Worksheet

Before you begin, to make the worksheet easier to handle, you will create a vertical window large enough to display two columns of information. To do this,

Move to: M25
Select: /Worksheet Window Vertical

Your display screen should be similar to Figure 3-12.

FIGURE 3-12

```
L25: (P0) [W8] +L23/L12                                                    READY

           A              H       I       J       K       L          M       N
  6                      JUL     AUG    SEPT    OCT     NOV    6    DEC    TOTAL
  7                      ---------------------------------------7
  8                                                             8
  9       SALES:                                                9
 10         Food       $7,000  $5,500  $6,400  $5,500  $6,500 10  $7,520 $68,820
 11         Beverage     $700    $500    $750    $800    $650 11    $775  $7,245
 12       Total Sales  $7,700  $6,000  $7,150  $6,300  $7,150 12  $8,295 $76,065
 13                                                            13
 14       EXPENSES:                                            14
 15         Food       $2,100  $1,650  $1,920  $1,650  $1,950 15  $2,256 $20,646
 16         Beverage     $210    $150    $225    $240    $195 16    $233  $2,174
 17         Payroll    $2,250  $2,250  $2,250  $2,250  $2,250 17  $2,250 $27,000
 18         Lease        $500    $500    $500    $500    $500 18    $500  $6,000
 19         G & A        $175    $175    $175    $175    $175 19    $175  $2,100
 20         Direct       $975    $975    $975    $975    $975 20    $975 $11,700
 21       Total Expenses $6,210 $5,700  $6,045  $5,790  $6,045 21  $6,389 $69,620
 22                                                            22
 23       PROFIT:      $1,490    $300  $1,105    $510  $1,105 23  $1,907  $6,446
 24                                                            24
 25       PROFIT MARGIN:  19%      5%     15%     8%     15%/25    23%      8%
 03-Mar-90  12:27 PM             UNDO
```

First Paula would like to see the effect of reducing the payroll expenses to $2,100 per month.

Move to: B17
Type: 2100
Press: ⏎

The profit margin for January (B25) changed from -15 to -12 percent. **To see the effect of reducing the payroll expenses to $2,100 for each month on the total profit margin, copy the January payroll value to the February through December payroll cells, using highlighting to specify the range.**

The worksheet has been recalculated. The new total profit margin is displayed in cell N25 in the right window. Reducing the payroll expenses to $2,100 per month has increased the total profit margin from 8 to 11 percent. This is still not enough.

Paula realizes that it may take her several tries before she reduces the payroll expenses enough to arrive at a total profit margin of 20 percent. Each time she changes the payroll expense, she has to copy the values across the entire row. A quicker way to enter different payroll expense values into the worksheet is by using a **work cell.** Any blank cell outside of the worksheet area can be used as a work cell.

Paula will use cell O17 in the right window as the work cell.

Press: F6 Window

The cell pointer should be in cell M25 in the right window.

Move to: O17

This time Paula will decrease the payroll expense value to 1900 per month.

Type: 1900
Press: ⏎

The value in the work cell needs to be copied into the payroll expense cells in the worksheet. To do this, a formula referencing the work cell is entered in the payroll expense cells. This formula will tell the program to add the value in cell O17 to the cell contents.

Press: (F6) Window

The cell pointer should be in cell B17. Enter the formula +O17 in cell B17 as follows:

Type: +
Press: (F6) Window

The cell pointer should be in cell O17.

Press: ⏎

Your display screen should be similar to Figure 3-13.

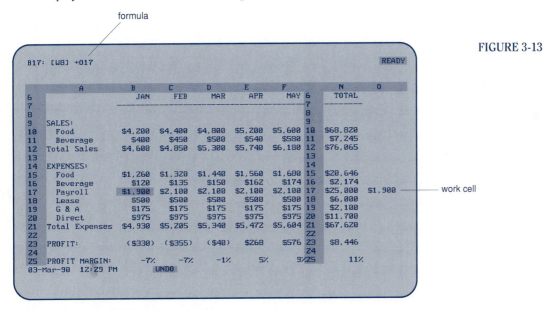

FIGURE 3-13

The value "$1,900" is entered in cell B17. The formula in B17 tells Lotus 1-2-3 to place the value in cell O17 in cell B17.

Copy the formula in the January payroll cell to the February through December payroll cells, using highlighting to specify the range.

Your display screen should be similar to Figure 3-14.

```
B17: [W8] +O17                                                    READY

        A        B      C      D      E      F         N        O
  6              JAN    FEB    MAR    APR    MAY    6  TOTAL
  7                                                  7
  8                                                  8
  9   SALES:                                         9
 10     Food    $4,200 $4,400 $4,800 $5,200 $5,600  10  $68,820
 11     Beverage  $400   $450   $500   $540   $580  11   $7,245
 12   Total Sales $4,600 $4,850 $5,300 $5,740 $6,180 12  $76,065
 13                                                 13
 14   EXPENSES:                                     14
 15     Food    $1,260 $1,320 $1,440 $1,560 $1,680  15  $20,646
 16     Beverage  $120   $135   $150   $162   $174  16   $2,174
 17     Payroll $1,900    $0     $0     $0     $0   17   $1,900    $1,900
 18     Lease    $500   $500   $500   $500   $500   18   $6,000
 19     G & A    $175   $175   $175   $175   $175   19   $2,100
 20     Direct   $975   $975   $975   $975   $975   20  $11,700
 21   Total Expenses $4,930 $3,105 $3,240 $3,372 $3,504 21 $44,520
 22                                                 22
 23   PROFIT:  ($330) $1,745 $2,060 $2,368 $2,676   23  $31,546
 24                                                 24
 25   PROFIT MARGIN:  -7%   36%    39%    41%   43% 25    41%
 03-Mar-90  12:29 PM         UNDO
```

FIGURE 3-14

The worksheet again has been recalculated. However, there is something wrong. The value "$1,900" should appear in cells C17 through M17. Instead the value "$0" appears in those cells.

Move to: C17

The control panel shows the formula in this cell is +P17. This is a blank cell. Since it contains nothing, the value of 0 is entered in C17.

Move to cells D17, E17, and F17. Look at how the formula changes from +P17 to +Q17, +R17, and +S17. The column letter has been adjusted relative to the new column location of the formula in row 17. Each of the formulas in the cells references the cell one column to the right of the previous formula. They were adjusted relative to their location in the worksheet. As you learned in Lab 2, the formula was copied using relative cell references.

Using an Absolute Cell Reference

The formula in B17 needs to be entered so that the column in the referenced cell, O17, will not change when the formula is copied. To do this, you will use an **absolute cell reference**.

Move to: B17
Press: (F2) EDIT

To change the formula in B17 to have an absolute cell reference, enter a $ (dollar sign) character in front of the column letter. You can enter the dollar sign character by typing it in directly or you can use the ABS (Absolute) key, (F4).

When using the ABS key, first position the cursor on or immediately to the right of the cell address you want to change. Since this is the only cell address in this entry, the cursor is already appropriately positioned. To change this cell address to absolute,

Press: (F4) ABS

The cell address now displays a $ character before both the column letter and row number (O17). Because a dollar sign is entered before both the column letter and row number, this cell address is absolute. If this formula were copied to another row and column location in the worksheet, the copied formula would be an exact duplicate of the original formula (O17).

Pressing ABS repeatedly cycles a cell address through all possible combinations of cell reference types.

Press: (F4) ABS

The cell address has changed to display a dollar sign before the row number only (O$17). This is a **mixed cell reference** because only the row number is preceded by an absolute address, not the column letter. A mixed cell reference contains both relative and absolute cell references. If this formula were copied to another column and row, the column in the referenced cell in the formula would be adjusted relative to its new location in the worksheet, but the row number would not change. For example, if the formula in B17 (O$17) were copied from B17 to E13, the formula in E13 would be R$17.

Press: (F4) ABS

Again this is a mixed cell reference. This time the $ character precedes the column letter. Consequently, if this formula were copied to another row and column, the row in the referenced cell in the formula would be adjusted relative to its new location in the worksheet, and the column would not change. For example, the formula in B17 ($O17) would change to $O13 if it were copied to cell B13.

Press: (F4) ABS

The formula returns to relative cell references. You have cycled the cell address through all possible combinations of cell references.

To stop the relative adjustment of the column in the formula when it is copied from one column location to another in the same row, the formula needs to be a mixed cell reference with the column letter absolute. To make this change,

Press: (F4) ABS (3 times)

To accept the formula as displayed in the control panel (+$O17),

Press: (↵)

Copy this formula from the January payroll cell to the February through December payroll cells, using highlighting to specify the range.

The value "$1,900" appears in each cell in row 17.

Move to: C17

SS84
Managing a Large Worksheet

Your display screen should be similar to Figure 3-15.

FIGURE 3-15

```
C17: [W8] +$O17                                                         READY

        A          B        C        D        E        F      N          O
  6                JAN      FEB      MAR      APR      MAY  6  TOTAL
  7                                                        7
  8                                                        8
  9   SALES:                                               9
 10     Food      $4,200   $4,400   $4,800   $5,200   $5,600  10  $68,820
 11     Beverage    $400     $450     $500     $540     $580  11   $7,245
 12   Total Sales $4,600   $4,850   $5,300   $5,740   $6,180  12  $76,065
 13                                                           13
 14   EXPENSES:                                               14
 15     Food      $1,260   $1,320   $1,440   $1,560   $1,680  15  $20,646
 16     Beverage    $120     $135     $150     $162     $174  16   $2,174
 17     Payroll   $1,900   $1,900   $1,900   $1,900   $1,900  17  $22,800   $1,900
 18     Lease       $500     $500     $500     $500     $500  18   $6,000
 19     G & A       $175     $175     $175     $175     $175  19   $2,100
 20     Direct      $975     $975     $975     $975     $975  20  $11,700
 21   Total Expenses $4,930 $5,005  $5,140   $5,272   $5,404  21  $65,420
 22                                                           22
 23   PROFIT:     ($330)   ($155)    $160     $468     $776   23  $10,646
 24                                                           24
 25   PROFIT MARGIN:  -7%     -3%      3%      8%      13% 25      14%
 06-Mar-90  08:39 AM          UNDO
```

The formula displayed in the control panel is an exact duplicate of the formula in B17. It references the cell O17. Using an absolute cell reference easily solved the problem. The absolute cell reference stopped the relative adjustment of the cells in the copied formula by maintaining the particular cell coordinates.

Decreasing the payroll expenses to $1,900 each month has increased the total profit margin to 14 percent (cell N25). This is closer to the 20 percent management objective. But it's still not good enough.

Decrease the payroll expense to $1,700 per month as follows:

Press: [F6] Window

The cell pointer should be in cell O17.

Type: 1700
Press: ⏎

Your display screen should be similar to Figure 3-16.

FIGURE 3-16

```
O17: [W8] 1700                                                          READY

        A          B        C        D        E        F      N          O
  6                JAN      FEB      MAR      APR      MAY  6  TOTAL
  7                                                        7
  8                                                        8
  9   SALES:                                               9
 10     Food      $4,200   $4,400   $4,800   $5,200   $5,600  10  $68,820
 11     Beverage    $400     $450     $500     $540     $580  11   $7,245
 12   Total Sales $4,600   $4,850   $5,300   $5,740   $6,180  12  $76,065
 13                                                           13
 14   EXPENSES:                                               14
 15     Food      $1,260   $1,320   $1,440   $1,560   $1,680  15  $20,646
 16     Beverage    $120     $135     $150     $162     $174  16   $2,174
 17     Payroll   $1,700   $1,700   $1,700   $1,700   $1,700  17  $20,400   $1,700
 18     Lease       $500     $500     $500     $500     $500  18   $6,000
 19     G & A       $175     $175     $175     $175     $175  19   $2,100
 20     Direct      $975     $975     $975     $975     $975  20  $11,700
 21   Total Expenses $4,730 $4,805  $4,940   $5,072   $5,204  21  $63,020
 22                                                           22
 23   PROFIT:     ($130)    $45      $360     $668     $976   23  $13,046
 24                                                           24
 25   PROFIT MARGIN:  -3%     1%       7%      12%     16% 25      17%
 03-Mar-90  12:31 PM          UNDO
```

The value in O17 was quickly entered into the payroll expense cells in row 17 for each month, and the worksheet was recalculated.

By using a work cell and referencing the work cell in a formula in the worksheet using absolute cell referencing, changing the what-if value becomes a simple process.

The total profit margin is now 17 percent. This is still not enough. **Try 1400.** The total profit margin is now 22 percent. That's too high. You know the appropriate payroll expense level is between 1700 and 1400. **Now try 1500.** Your display screen should be similar to Figure 3-17.

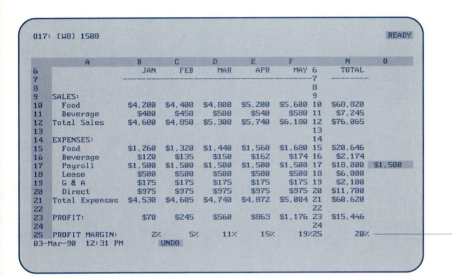

FIGURE 3-17

total profit margin

That's it! The total profit margin is 20 percent if payroll expenses are reduced to $1,500 per month.

Clear the vertical window and then unfreeze the titles.

Press: `HOME`

Extracting Worksheet Data

After looking at the values in the annual budget, Paula is concerned that she may have underestimated some values. She wants the club manager to review the figures before she submits the final budget to the board of directors. She decides to create a summary of the annual budget for him to look at which will contain the worksheet labels and the total values only.

Paula could create this new worksheet by entering the row labels into another worksheet. A quicker way, however, is to save the row labels in column A from the current worksheet to a new worksheet file on disk. The new worksheet file will be named CAFESUM. Figure 3-18 on the next page illustrates this process. (It will not appear this way on your screen, however.)

SS86
Managing a Large Worksheet

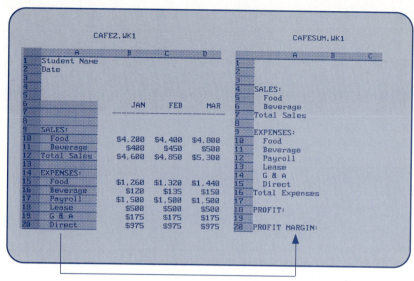

FIGURE 3-18

label extracted from CAFE2.WK1
and copied to CAFESUM.WK1

The command which will save a range of data from the current worksheet to a new worksheet file on disk is / File Xtract.

Select: / File Xtract

Two options, Formulas and Values, are displayed in the control panel. If you select Formulas, 1-2-3 copies all labels, numbers, formulas, and worksheet settings in the specified range. If you select Values, 1-2-3 performs the same function except that the values of formulas are copied, not the formulas themselves. Since the row entries are all labels, either response is acceptable. To accept the default,

Press: ⏎

In response to the next prompt to enter a file name for the extracted file,

Type: CAFESUM
Press: ⏎

Next you must specify the range to be extracted, A6 through A25 (includes three blank rows). Specify this range using highlighting. You will need to press ESC to unanchor the cell address first.

After a few moments the defined range is copied to the new file. The current file is not affected.

Save the current worksheet as CAFE3.

Retrieve the new worksheet file, CAFESUM.

Your screen should be similar to Figure 3-19.

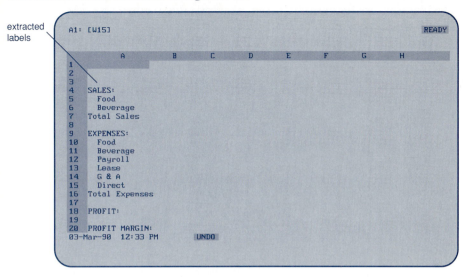

FIGURE 3-19

The column of extracted labels is displayed in the worksheet. 1-2-3 enters the extracted range in the file beginning in cell A1.

File Linking

Next Paula needs to enter the values from the CAFE3 file TOTAL column (N10 through N25) into the CAFESUM worksheet. She decides this may be a good time to see how the **file linking** feature of Lotus 1-2-3 works. This feature allows you to use values from cells in other worksheets in the current worksheet. A linking formula is entered in one file that refers to a cell in another file. When data in a linked cell changes, the worksheet that is affected by this change is automatically updated whenever it is retrieved. The file that receives the value is the **target file,** and the file that supplies the data is the **source file.** The CAFE3 file will be the source file and the CAFESUM file will be the target file. The file-linking process is illustrated in Figure 3-20.

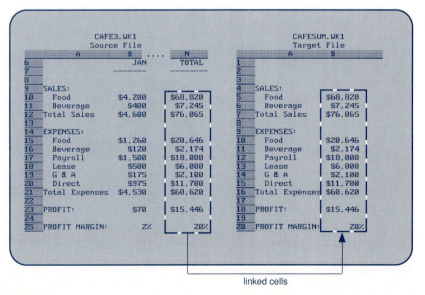

FIGURE 3-20

SS88
Managing a Large Worksheet

To create a link between two files, you enter a **linking formula** in the target file that refers to a cell in the source file. The cell containing the linking formula is called the **target cell**. A linking formula uses the following format:

+<<file reference>>cell reference

The "file reference" is the file name of the source file; it is enclosed in double angle brackets. The "cell reference" is the cell address of the cell in the source file containing the value to be copied into the target file.

Paula needs to enter a linking formula for each row item The first linking formula will be entered in cell B5 of the target file and will link to cell N10 of the source file.

Move to: B5
Type: +<<CAFE3>>N10
Press: ⏎

Your screen should be similar to Figure 3-21.

FIGURE 3-21

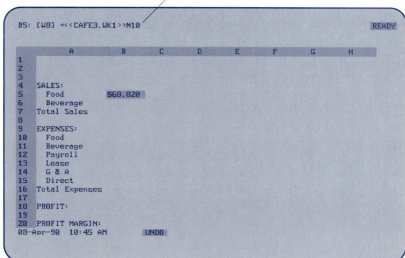

The current value in cell N10, $68,820, was copied from the source file into the target file and displayed in cell B5.

The remaining linking formulas will reference cells N11 through N25 of the source file. Like any other formula, linking formulas can be copied, and the cell addresses will adjust relative to their new location in the worksheet.

Copy the linking formula for food sales down column B through cell B20, using highlighting to specify the range.

Notice that the values are displayed in currency format. When the Xtract command was used, the global worksheet settings were copied along with the column labels.

Erase the formulas in cells B8, B9, B17, and B19.

Correct the cell format of B20 so that the value is displayed as a percent with no decimal places.

Enter the column title "TOTAL" in cell B3. It should be right-aligned.

Enter the worksheet title "Courtside Cafe Budget" in cell A1 and "(Consolidated)" in cell A2. Precede the label in cell A2 with four blank spaces to center it beneath the label in cell A1.

Your screen should be similar to Figure 3-22.

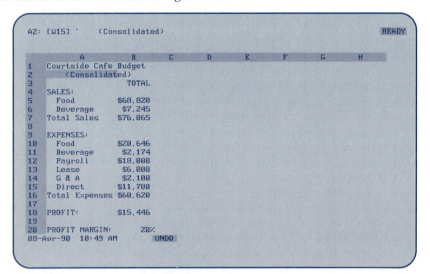

FIGURE 3-22

Save (Replace) the file as CAFESUM.

Paula shows the consolidated worksheet and the annual worksheet to the club manager. He anticipates that the lease expense for the cafe will increase by 10 percent.

To reflect this change in the budget, retrieve the worksheet file CAFE3 and change the lease expense for January through December to $550.

All affected worksheet formulas are recalculated.

Move to: N18

The total lease expense increases to $6,600.

Move to: N25

The total profit margin is still at 20 percent. To see if the consolidated worksheet, CAFESUM, reflects this change in data, the file needs to be retrieved.

First, enter your name in the current worksheet in cell A1 and the date in cell A2, and save the current file as CAFE3.

Retrieve CAFESUM.

Move to: B13

SS90
Managing a Large Worksheet

Your screen should be similar to Figure 3-23.

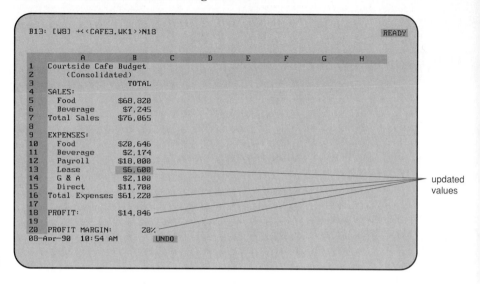

FIGURE 3-23

The target file has been recalculated using the new data. The total lease expense in cell B13, the total expense in cell B16, and the total profit margin have been updated to reflect the change of data in the linked worksheet cells.

Once a linking formula is entered in a worksheet, whenever a value(s) in the cell referenced in the source file changes, the target file is automatically updated when it is retrieved. Another way to update the source file is to use the command **/ F**ile **A**dmin **L**ink-Refresh. This command will immediately update the linked cells.

Paula likes how the file linking feature works. Now, if the board of directors request that she change other worksheet data, it will be quickly reflected in the consolidated budget worksheet.

Entering the System Date

Paula feels that the proposed budget is ready to present to the board of directors again. She would like to include a brief memo of explanation below the consolidated worksheet. Using the arrow keys,

Move to:	A24
Type:	**TO:**
Move to:	B24
Type:	**Board of Directors**
Move to:	A25
Type:	**FROM:**
Move to:	B25
Type:	**Paula Nichols**
Move to:	A26
Type:	**DATE:**
Move to:	B26

The date can be entered automatically into a worksheet using the @NOW function. This @function will display the system date entered at the DOS prompt into the worksheet. The @function calculates the date by assigning an integer to each of the 73,050 days from January 1, 1900 through December 31, 2099. The integers are assigned consecutively beginning with 1 and ending with 73,050. They are called **date numbers**.

Type: @NOW
Press: ⏎

Your display screen should be similar to Figure 3-24.

FIGURE 3-24

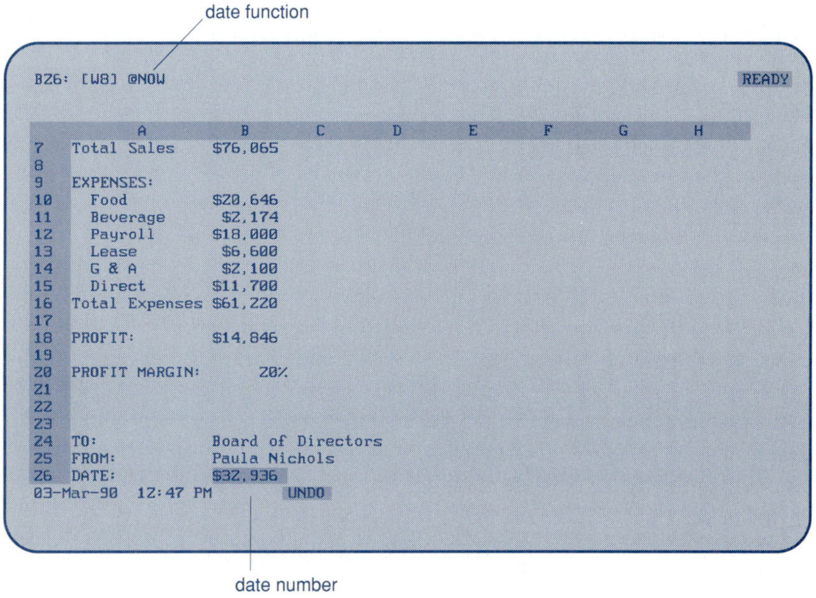

The value displayed in C32 is the date number calculated by the @NOW function displayed in currency format.

Note: The value in this cell will differ depending on the system date you entered at the DOS prompt.

To change the display of this one cell from currency to a date format, you use the Range Format Date command.

Select: /Range Format Date

Options 1 through 5 let you specify how the date will be displayed. The Time option will display the current time as recorded by DOS. You want the date displayed as mm/dd/yy. Use the Help system for information on the different date formats. The option which will display a date as Month/Day/Year is 4 (Long Intn'l).

Select: 4

To accept the range to format as B26,

Press: ⏎

A series of asterisks appears in the cell, indicating the column width is not large enough to display the value. The date format setting is displayed in the control panel as "(D4)."

Use the Worksheet Column Set-Width command to increase the width of column B to 9 spaces to display the date.

Your display screen should be similar to Figure 3-25.

FIGURE 3-25

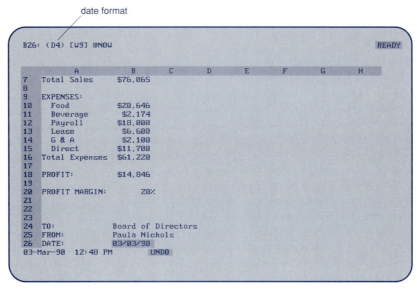

Increasing the column width by one space is all that is needed to display the date.

Note: If you did not enter a date at the DOS date prompt, the DOS default date is entered.

Justifying Text

Continue the memo below. Do not press ⏎ until directed.

Move to: A28

Type: Above is a consolidated budget for the year for the proposed expansion of the Courtside Cafe. The monthly breakdown of this budget is on the following page.

Press: ⏎

The text you have entered is a long label which is displayed as a single line of text. To change this long label into a paragraph of several lines of text no longer than a specified width, the Range Justify command is used. This command rearranges or **justifies** labels to fit within a width you specify. Using highlighting to specify the range,

Select: / Range Justify A28..F28 ⏎

Move to: A32

Your display screen should be similar to Figure 3-26.

SS93
Justifying Text

FIGURE 3-26

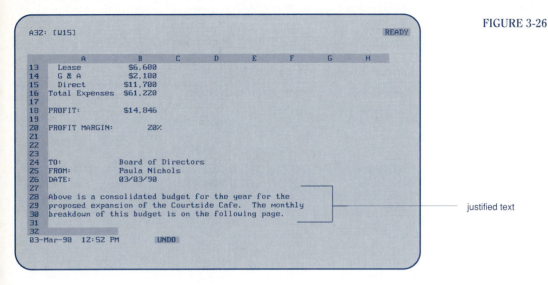

The long label of text in A28 has been divided into three lines of text contained in cells A28 and A30. Neither line extends beyond column F.
To enter the following sentence in cell A32,

Type: To meet the objective of a 20% Total Profit Margin, the payroll expenses were reduced to $1,500 per month.

Press: ⏎

Justify this label using the same range setting as above.
For a better view of the worksheet,

Move to: A35

Your display screen should be similar to Figure 3-27.

FIGURE 3-27

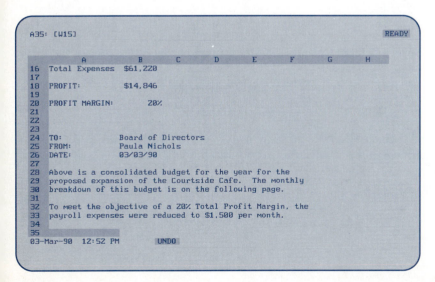

The second paragraph of the memo is now entered into the worksheet.
The worksheet is ready to be printed.

Before saving and printing the worksheet, enter your name in cell A35.

**Save and Replace this worksheet using the file name CAFESUM.
Print the worksheet.**

Next you need to print CAFE3. **Retrieve this file.**

Using Compressed Printing

Because of the width of the worksheet, it will require two pages of paper to print it out. To print the worksheet on one page, the print can be **compressed** by reducing the space between the letters.

Note: The following procedure works on most printers. However, it may not work on yours. Consult your instructor for the correct settings if the following does not produce the proper results.

When defining the print range, make sure the work cell O17 is not included in the range.

Select: / Print Printer Range

Specify the entire worksheet, excluding cell O17, as the print range, using highlighting.

Select: Options

The 8 Print options let you specify how the printed document will appear on the page. The Setup option lets you change the print size.

Select: Setup

The prompt to enter a setup string appears in the control panel. (A string is any sequence of characters.) Compressed print is turned on by entering the string \015.

Type: \015 (use the number zero, not the letter O)
Press: ⏎

The Print Options submenu is still displayed in the control panel to allow you to select other options. The settings sheet displays the setup string you specified.

Select: Margins

When specifying compressed print, move the right margin to the right the maximum number of spaces, 132. This will allow the maximum number of characters to be printed on a line.

Select: Right
Type: 132
Press: ⏎

Your screen should be similar to Figure 3-28.

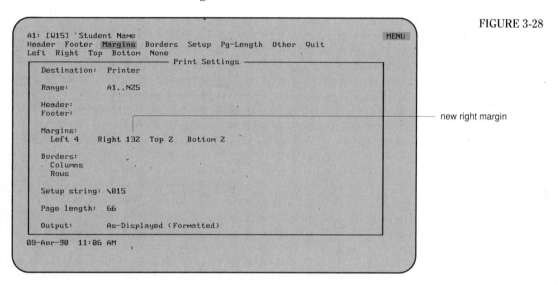

FIGURE 3-28

new right margin

To leave the Print Options submenu,

Select: Quit

To continue the Print command sequence,

Select: Align Go

Your worksheet should be printing. After it has completed printing, to advance the page and return to the READY mode,

Select: Page Quit

Your printed output should be similar to Figure 3-29 on the next page.

Quit Lotus 1-2-3.

Student Name
Date

Courtside Cafe Budget

	JAN	FEB	MAR	APR	MAY	JUN	JUL	AUG	SEPT	OCT	NOV	DEC	TOTAL
SALES:													
Food	$4,200	$4,400	$4,800	$5,200	$5,600	$6,200	$7,000	$5,500	$6,400	$5,500	$6,500	$7,520	$68,820
Beverage	$400	$450	$500	$540	$580	$600	$700	$500	$750	$800	$650	$775	$7,245
Total Sales	$4,600	$4,850	$5,300	$5,740	$6,180	$6,800	$7,700	$6,000	$7,150	$6,300	$7,150	$8,295	$76,065
EXPENSES:													
Food	$1,260	$1,320	$1,440	$1,560	$1,680	$1,860	$2,100	$1,650	$1,920	$1,650	$1,950	$2,256	$20,646
Beverage	$120	$135	$150	$162	$174	$180	$210	$150	$225	$240	$195	$233	$2,174
Payroll	$1,500	$1,500	$1,500	$1,500	$1,500	$1,500	$1,500	$1,500	$1,500	$1,500	$1,500	$1,500	$18,000
Lease	$150	$150	$150	$150	$150	$150	$150	$150	$150	$150	$150	$150	$6,600
G & A	$175	$175	$175	$175	$175	$175	$175	$175	$175	$175	$175	$175	$2,100
Direct	$975	$975	$975	$975	$975	$975	$975	$975	$975	$975	$975	$975	$11,700
Total Expenses	$4,580	$4,655	$4,790	$4,922	$5,054	$5,240	$5,510	$5,000	$5,345	$5,090	$5,345	$5,689	$61,220
PROFIT:	$20	$195	$510	$818	$1,126	$1,560	$2,190	$1,000	$1,805	$1,210	$1,805	$2,607	$14,846
PROFIT MARGIN:	0%	4%	10%	14%	18%	23%	28%	17%	25%	19%	25%	31%	20%

FIGURE 3-29

Key Terms

circular reference	mixed cell reference
freeze	file linking
window	target file
active window	source file
synchronized	linking formula
unsynchronized	target cell
what-if analysis	date numbers
work cell	justify
absolute cell reference	compressed

Matching

1. \015   _____ a. absolute cell reference
2. @NOW   _____ b. justifies a range of text
3. CIRC   _____ c. moves cell pointer to other window
4. / W T B   _____ d. enters system date
5. / W W V   _____ e. causes compressed printing
6. target file   _____ f. displays a range as a percent
7. +C25   _____ g. the file that receives the data in a linking formula
8. / R J   _____ h. freezes both horizontal and vertical titles
9. (F6)   _____ i. creates a vertical window
10. / R F P   _____ j. status indicator for circular reference

Practice Exercises

1. Retrieve the file PETSHOP.WK1. This is a worksheet of an income statement for the Pet Supply Shop. The formulas in the worksheet are:

   Row 11   Gross margin = Sales - Cost of goods sold
   Row 17   Total expense = Marketing + Administrative + Miscellaneous expenses
   Row 19   Net income before taxes = Gross margin - Total expense
   Row 20   Federal taxes = Net income before taxes * .52
   Row 22   Net income after taxes = Net income before taxes - Federal taxes
   Column N Total = Sum over 12 months

   - Locate and correct the formula or @function causing the CIRC reference to be displayed in the worksheet (there may be more than one).

   The owner of the Pet Supply Shop wants to change the worksheet to calculate the cost of goods sold as a percent of sales. He estimates that the cost of goods sold is about 45 percent of sales. You will use a work cell to hold the percent value and change the values in row 9 to be computed using this value as follows:

   - Freeze both titles so that rows 6 through 25 are displayed in the window. Freeze everything above row 7 and to the left of column B.
   - Move to column N. Create a vertical window at column M. Move to column N.
   - Switch to the left window. Move to column B. Scroll rows 22 to 28 into view. Cell B25 is your work cell. A label has already been entered in cell A25 to identify the value you will enter in B25.
   - Enter the value .45 in cell B25. Change the format of this cell to fixed with 2 decimal places.
   - Enter the formula to calculate the cost of goods sold (B8*B25) in cell B9.
   - Copy the formula in B9 to cells C9 through M9. To see how this change has affected the total net income after taxes, look at the value in N22 (right window). What is the value N22?
   - The manager feels he may have been too high in his estimate for the percent cost value. He wants to see the effect on the total of changing the value in cell B25. Change the value in cell B25 to .40. What is the value in cell N22 now?

   Next the manager would like to see the effect of changing the marketing, administrative, and miscellaneous expenses. By calculating these values as a percent of the gross margin, he feels he will be able to plan and budget better for the future.

   - Enter the following values in the cells specified:

	Cell	Value
MKT	B26	.15
ADM	B27	.28
MISC	B28	.08

SS98
Managing a Large Worksheet

- Format cells B26, B27, and B28 to be displayed as fixed with 2 decimal places.
- Change the contents of cells B13 through B15 to be calculated using a formula referencing cells B26 through B28. Copy the formulas from B13..B15 through C13..M15. What is the total net income after taxes (N22) now?
- Leave the percent value for cost at .40. Change the other percent values to arrive at a net total income (N22) value as close to 5500 as possible. What total net income after taxes did you get? What were the percentages used?
- Clear the windows and titles.
- Enter your name in cell A1 and the date in cell A2. Save the worksheet as PETSHOP2.
- Print the worksheet using compressed printing.

2. To complete this problem, you must have created the worksheet in Practice Exercise 4 of Lab 2. Retrieve the file ZOOFINAN. You will extend and expand the worksheet for the 3-year financial statement for the zoo. The assistant director of the zoo would like to project the financial statement for the next three years, 1991, 1992 and 1993.

- Format the worksheet to globally display currency with 0 decimal places. Globally adjust the column width to 13 in order to fully display the values.
- Insert 3 columns between 1990 and TOTAL for the projected years. Enter column headings for the 3 years (columns F, G, and H). Underline the new headings, and extend the underlines in the rest of the worksheet to cover the new columns.
- Insert another blank row above the column headings. Enter the heading "========Projected========" centered above the years 1991 through 1993.
- Freeze the row labels and column headings.
- Enter formulas to calculate the projected income values for the years 1991-1993. The Support & Revenues projections are: operating expenses increase 15 percent over the previous year, supporting organizations 20 percent and Interest income 22 percent. The fund-raising projected income is directly related to the amount of money allocated to fund-raising activities (cell F16). For each dollar allocated they expect to raise $4.25.
- Enter formulas to calculate the projected applications and expenses for the years 1991-1993. Operating expenses are expected to increase 17 percent each year over the previous year, capital projects 17 percent and fund raising 5 percent. The operating reserve is calculated using the same formula as in previous years.
- Copy the formula for TOTAL S & R, and TOTAL A/E for the years 1991 - 1993.

- Change the formulas used to calculate TOTAL and AVERAGE to include the new columns.
- Create a vertical window at column J. Display the years 1991 and 1992 in the left window, and TOTAL in the right window. Print your display screen (SHIFT)-(Prt scr).

In 1994 the zoo plans on adding a new jungle exhibit, which will cost $1.5 million. After looking at the results of the projected statement on the operating reserve, they realize that they will not have enough money for the new project. Currently the amount allocated toward fund raising is based upon a 5 percent increase over the previous year.

- Create a work cell a few rows below TOTAL A/E in cell F22. Format this cell to display fixed format, with 2 decimal places.
- Reference this cell to calculate the percentage increase for money allocated to fund raising in the years 1991 - 1993. Adjust the value in this cell until the total operating reserve is at least $1.5 million by the end of 1993.
- Clear the windows and titles.
- Erase the old date from cell A3, enter the current date in cell A2, and save the worksheet as ZOOFIN3.
- Print the worksheet using compressed printing. Do not include the work cell.

3. As part of an assignment in a nutrition class, you have created a worksheet comparing four foods and the amount of exercise time it takes to burn off the calories from these foods. To see this worksheet, retrieve the file FOOD.WK1.

- In cell C16 enter the following text:

    As part of my research project on calorie burnoff, I have listed four common food items and the number of calories in each.

- Justify this line of text so that it does not extend beyond column G.
- In cell C20 enter:

    I then calculated the number of minutes needed to burn off the calories according to the type of exercise.

- Justify this line of text so that it does not extend beyond column G.
- Enter the system date in cell C24. Format the date to be displayed as Day-Month-Year (12-Jan-88).
- Enter your name in cell A1 and the date in cell A2. Save the worksheet as FOOD2.
- Print the worksheet.

4. To complete this problem, retrieve the file COST created in Practice Problem 3 in Lab 2.

- Enter the following memo below the worksheet in column A.

SS100
Managing a Large Worksheet

The main finding of the data used in this worksheet is that by keeping the old car, the owner would save over $5,000. This is despite the estimate by expert analysts that in four years of steady driving (60,000 miles), repair costs would exceed those of the new car by $1,179 and that the old car would consume more gas.

The offsetting economies are that the old car would have lower insurance premiums and that there would be no financing costs for the old car. These two items are enough to account for nearly 55% of the costs of keeping a new car during the first four years. Therefore, it is better to keep the heap!

- Justify the text so that it is displayed below columns A through D.
- Enter the system date in cell A2. Format the date to be displayed as MM/DD/YY.
- Print the worksheet.
- Save the worksheet as COSTMEMO.

LAB 4
Creating and Printing Graphs

CASE STUDY

The Sports Club annual membership promotion month is in January. As preparation, the board of directors have asked the membership coordinator, Fred Morris, to present a report on the membership growth over the last 5 years.

Fred has maintained the membership data for the past 5 years. He has entered the data into a worksheet using Lotus 1-2-3. Although the data in the worksheet shows the club's growth, he feels the use of several graphs would make it easier for the board of directors to see the trends and growth patterns over the 5 years.

You will follow Fred as he creates several different graphs of the membership data.

Using the Access System

In this lab you will be using 1-2-3 to create graphs, and PrintGraph to print graphs. To make it easier to switch between 1-2-3 and PrintGraph, you will use the 1-2-3 Access system to load the 1-2-3 program. Turn on your computer and load DOS. Your 1-2-3 System disk should be in the A drive and the data diskette should be in the B drive.

To use the Access system to load 1-2-3, at the A>,

Type: LOTUS
Press: ⏎

OBJECTIVES

In this lab you will learn how to:

1. Use the Access System.
2. Create a line graph.
3. Specify the X axis labels.
4. Specify data to be graphed.
5. Enter graph titles.
6. Enter legends.
7. Name and save the graph.
8. Create a bar and a stacked-bar graph.
9. Create a pie chart.
10. Shade and explode the pie chart.
11. Print a graph.

Your screen should be similar to Figure 4-1

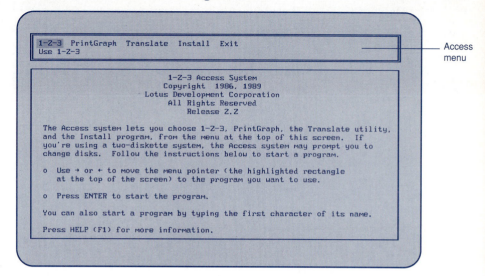

FIGURE 4-1

The Access menu appears at the top of the screen. A description of the highlighted command appears in the next line. Read the information below the menu about how to use the Access system. To load 1-2-3, with the highlight over 1-2-3,

Press: ⏎

The 1-2-3 program is loaded in the usual manner.
To see the worksheet of membership data,

Select: / File Retrieve

Although the files to retrieve are listed in the control panel, only one line of file names can be seen at a time. To display all the files on the screen at once, use the F3 Name key.

Press: F3 Name

A menu of worksheet files is displayed on the screen. The name of the highlighted file and information about its size and date of creation are displayed on the third line of the control panel. To select a file from the menu, use the arrow keys to highlight the file name of your choice and press ⏎ .

Continue the command sequence by selecting GROWTH.WK1.

Your display screen should be similar to Figure 4-2.

FIGURE 4-2

The worksheet lists the four membership categories offered by the Sports Club as row labels in cells B9 through B12. They are defined as follows:

Family	spouse and dependent children
Individual	one-person membership
Youth	individual under 18 years of age
Retired	individual over 55 years of age

The total in row 15 is the sum of the four membership categories. The column labels in row 6 represent the years 1986 through 1990.

Although the worksheet shows the values for each membership category, it is hard to see how the different categories have changed over time. A visual representation of data in the form of a **graph** would convey that information in an easy-to-understand and attractive manner.

Lotus 1-2-3 can produce five types of graphs: line, bar, stacked-bar, XY, and pie. All graph types, except the pie, have some basic similarities. The basic parts of a line or bar graph are illustrated in Figure 4-3.

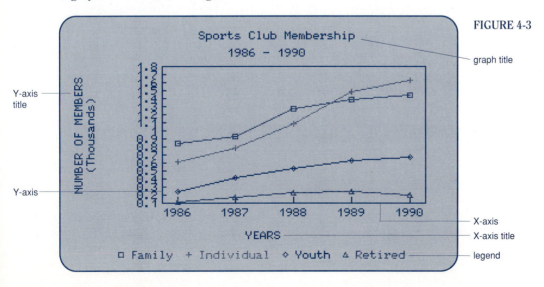

FIGURE 4-3

The bottom boundary of the graph is the **X axis**. It is used to label the data being graphed, such as a value of time or a category.

The left boundary of the graph is the **Y axis**. This axis is a numbered scale whose values are determined by the data used in the graph.

The worksheet data is visually displayed within the X- and Y-axis boundaries. It can be displayed as a line, bar, or stacked bar. Each group of data that is displayed is represented by a symbol. A **legend** at the bottom of the graph describes the symbols used within the graph.

A graph can also contain several different **titles**, which are used to explain the contents of the graph. In Lotus 1-2-3, the two title lines at the top of the graph are called the first and second title lines. Titles can also be used to label the X and Y axes.

In pie charts there are no X or Y axes. Instead, the worksheet data that is graphed is displayed as slices in a circle or pie. Each slice is labeled. A first and second title line can be used; however, legends and X- and Y-axis titles are not used.

Selecting the Type of Graph

The first graph Fred would like to create is a **line graph** to show the total membership growth pattern over 5 years. A line graph represents data as a set of points along a line.

All graphs are drawn from data contained in a worksheet. To graph worksheet data, the Graph menu is used. To open this menu,

Select: / Graph

Your display screen should be similar to Figure 4-4.

FIGURE 4-4

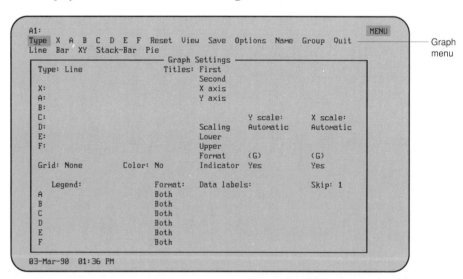

The Graph Settings sheet is displayed on the screen. Like the other settings sheets you have seen, the Graph Settings sheet helps you keep track of the choices you have made. The Graph Settings sheet shows you the current graph settings for the Graph commands displayed in the menu above the settings sheet. Since there are no graph settings specified yet, the settings sheet is empty except for the names of the graph settings and for any default graph settings.

There are 15 Graph menu commands, beginning with Type and ending with Quit. To briefly preview the Graph commands using the Help system,

Press: F1 Help

Read this screen carefully as it describes each of the graph commands you will be using in this lab.
  The first graph command you will use is Type. For further information about this command,

Press: ⏎

The Help screen now tells you about the five types of graphs you can create using 1-2-3. After reading the information on this screen, to return to the Graph menu,

Press: ESC

The first step in creating a graph is to specify the type of graph you want to create. To do this,

Select: Type

Your display screen should be similar to Figure 4-5.

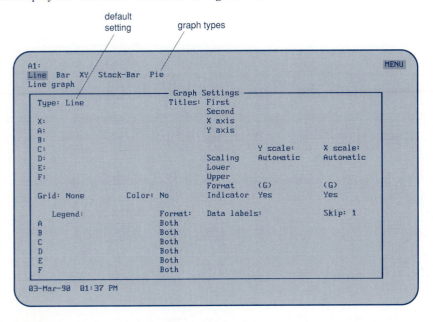

FIGURE 4-5

The five graph types are displayed in the second line of the control panel. The menu pointer is positioned on Line. As you can see from the settings sheet, the default graph type is a line graph. Since this is the type of graph you want to create, to accept the default,

Press: ⏎

Creating and Printing Graphs

If you do not select Type from the Graph menu, a line graph is created by default.

Notice that you are returned to the Graph menu rather than the READY mode so that you can continue defining your graph settings.

Labeling the X Axis

The next step is to specify the labels to be entered along the horizontal or X axis of the graph. In a line graph the X axis usually represents some block of time, such as days, weeks, months, or years. The X axis for Fred's line graph will display the year labels, 1986 through 1990, located in cells C6 through G6.

To define the years as the X-axis labels,

Select: X

The Graph Settings sheet is cleared from the screen and the worksheet is displayed. Now you can see the range of cells in the worksheet containing the data to be specified as the X data range. The prompt "Enter x-axis range:" is displayed in the control panel. The current cell pointer position, A1, is displayed following the prompt. You can specify the range by typing the cell addresses or by highlighting.

Highlight the range of cells containing the year labels 1986 through 1990 as the X-axis labels.

Your screen should be similar to similar to Figure 4-6.

FIGURE 4-6

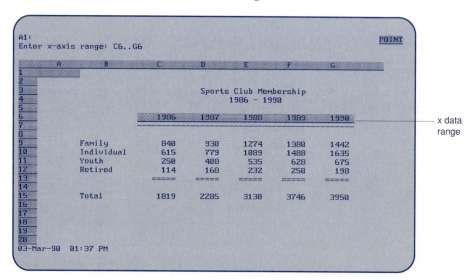

To enter the highlighted range as the X-axis labels,

Press: ⏎

The Graph Settings sheet is displayed again. The range of cells you specified for the X data range is displayed in the settings sheet. If your settings sheet does not display the X data range as C6..G6, respecify the correct X range.

Specifying the Data to Be Graphed

The range of data in the worksheet that contains the numbers to be graphed is specified next. The letters A through F in the Graph menu allow you to specify up to six data ranges to be displayed in the graph.

Fred wants to graph the values that show total membership growth over the 5-year period. This data is in cells C15 through G15. The first range of data you want to graph is entered as the A range. The same procedure you used to specify the X-axis range is used to specify a data range.

Select: A

The prompt "Enter first data range: A1" appears in the control panel. Again, you can type the range or highlight it.

Using highlighting, specify the range of cells containing the total membership growth for the 5 years as the A data range.

Your display screen should be similar to Figure 4-7.

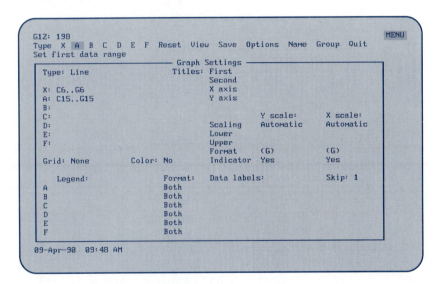

FIGURE 4-7

You are again returned to the Graph Settings sheet, and the A data range setting you specified (C15..G15) is displayed.

Note: All graph data ranges (X and A-F) can be specified in one step using the Graph Group command. However, this command can only be used if the data ranges are in consecutive rows or columns.

Viewing the Graph

Once a data range and the X range have been specified, you can view the graph.

Note: To display graphs you must have a graphics adapter card that is supported by Lotus 1-2-3 and have properly installed the 1-2-3 program. See your instructor if your graph is not displayed.

Select: View

Your display screen should be similar to Figure 4-8.

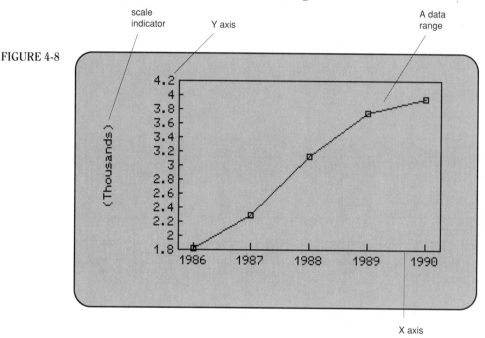

FIGURE 4-8

The years are displayed along the X axis. The data for total membership is displayed within the graph boundaries. Each data point is marked by a square symbol and connected by a line.

The values on the Y axis begin at 1.8 and end at 4.2. The Y axis is automatically set by Lotus 1-2-3 as a scale of values determined by the lowest and highest values in the data range. The notation "(Thousands)" appears along the Y axis to show that the Y-axis values represent numbers in the thousands. This notation is called a **scale indicator**. Scale indicators will appear when appropriate along the X or Y axis to clarify the values displayed along the axis.

The total membership growth pattern over the 5 years is now easy to see. The graph, however, still is not easy to understand. You know what the data stands for because you defined the graph settings. However, someone else would not have any idea what the graph means. The addition of titles to the graph will help explain the graph contents.

To clear the graph from the display and return to the Graph menu,

Press: any key

Entering Graph Titles

Graph titles are not required graph settings. However, without titles, the meaning of the data displayed in the graph is not clear.

Titles can be entered at the top of the graph (two lines) and along the X and Y axes. The command to add titles is a submenu option found in the Graph Options menu. The Graph Options menu is used to refine the appearance of a graph.

Select: Options

Your display screen should be similar to Figure 4-9.

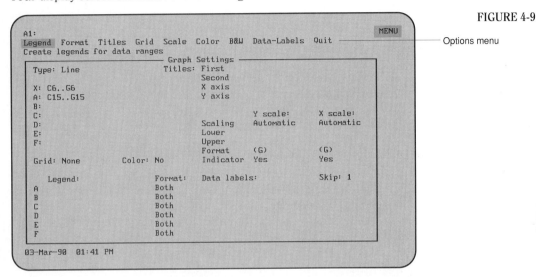

FIGURE 4-9

Options menu

The Options submenu contains eight commands that enhance the appearance of a graph or make it easier to understand. For an explanation of the meaning of these options,

Press: (F1) Help

Your display screen should be similar to Figure 4-10.

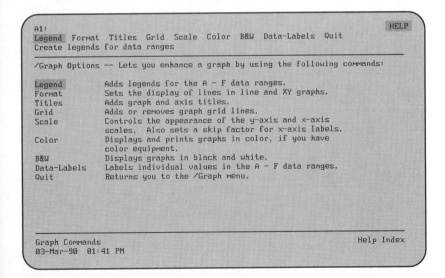

FIGURE 4-10

The Help screen describes the eight graph options. After reading this screen, to return to the Graph Settings sheet,

Press: `ESC`

To add titles to a graph,

Select: `Titles`

The four title alternatives are displayed in the control panel. They have the following effect:

First	puts centered text at the top of the graph
Second	centers a second line of text at the top of the graph
X-Axis	places text along the horizontal axis
Y-Axis	places text along the vertical axis

The same titles used in the worksheet can be copied into the graph, or entirely new titles can be used. The worksheet titles "Sports Club Membership" in cell D3 and "1986-1990" in cell E4 would be appropriate for labeling this graph. Each title can be a maximum of 39 characters long.

To display the worksheet screen so that you can easily refer to cells in the worksheet while specifying the graph title,

Press: `F6` Window

Whenever a settings sheet is displayed on the screen, the `F6` Window key can be used to clear the settings sheet and display the worksheet. The worksheet will continue to be displayed until the `F6` key is pressed again to redisplay the settings sheet.

To enter the first title line of the graph,

Select: `First`

At the prompt "Enter first line of graph title:" you can type any title exactly as you want it to appear in the graph. Alternatively, you can copy a title used in the worksheet. You want to use the same title as the one displayed in the worksheet in cell D3. To copy the contents of a cell into the graph as a title line, you type a backslash (\) character followed by the cell address containing the label. To do this,

Type: `\D3`

Your display screen should be similar to Figure 4-11.

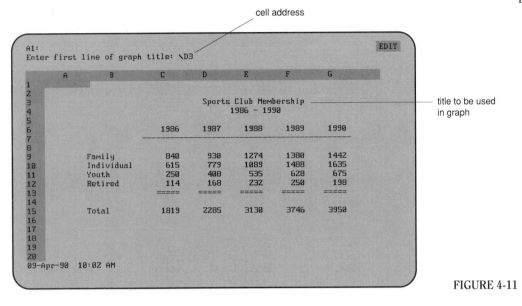

FIGURE 4-11

Press: ⏎

The Graph Options menu is displayed in the control panel again to allow you to continue specifying other options. To redisplay the Graph Settings sheet,

Press: F6 Window

The cell address containing the label you want to use as the first title line of the graph is displayed following "Title: First" in the settings sheet.

The second title line needs to be entered into the graph. It will be the same as the worksheet title in cell E4. To enter a second title,

Select: Titles
Press: F6 Window
Select: Second \E4 ⏎

To leave this menu and view the graph with the title lines as specified,

Select: Quit View

SS112
Creating and Printing Graphs

Your display screen should be similar to Figure 4-12.

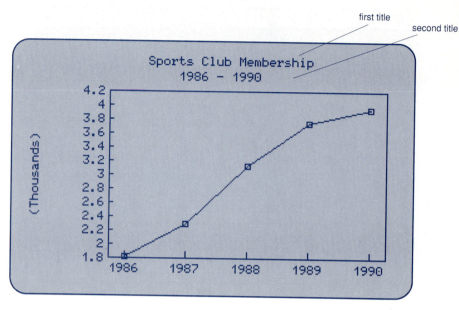

FIGURE 4-12

The two title lines are displayed centered above the graph. Using titles within the graph greatly improves the appearance and meaning of the line graph.
To return to the Graph menu,

Press: any key

The title lines to describe the X and Y axes need to be entered next. The X axis shows the growth in membership over the 5 years. The Y axis shows the number of members. You will label the X axis "YEARS," and the Y axis "NUMBER OF MEMBERS."

The axis titles you want to use in the graph are not labels that are used in the worksheet. Therefore the titles must be typed following the prompt as part of the command sequence. Type the title in all capital letters. A title is displayed in the graph exactly as entered in the command sequence. To redisplay the settings sheet and enter the X- and Y-axis title lines,

Press: (F6) Window
Select: Options Titles X-Axis **YEARS** ⏎
Titles Y-Axis **NUMBER OF MEMBERS** ⏎

The titles as you entered them are displayed in the settings sheet.
To leave the Options submenu and view the graph,

Select: Quit View

Your display screen should be similar to Figure 4-13.

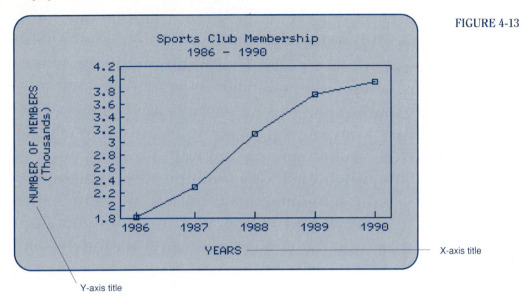

FIGURE 4-13

The title "YEARS" is displayed along the horizontal X axis. The title "NUMBER OF MEMBERS" is displayed along the vertical Y axis.

To return to the Graph menu,

Press: any key

Naming the Graph Settings

The line graph is the first graph created using the data in the worksheet. Many different graphs can be created and stored in a worksheet. To create more than one graph in a worksheet, each graph must be named. Naming the graph settings allows the current graph settings to be stored in the worksheet and recalled for later use. If the current graph settings are not named, the new graph settings as they are defined will write over the current settings.

To assign the current graph settings a name the Graph Name command is used.

Select: Name

The five Name options are:

Use	makes a named graph the current graph
Create	creates or modifies a named graph by storing the current graph settings with the name you specify
Delete	deletes a named graph
Reset	deletes all named graphs in the worksheet
Table	creates a table of named graphs in the worksheet

To store the current line graph settings using the name LINE,

Select: Create

A graph name can be up to 14 characters long and should be descriptive of the contents of the graph. It cannot contain spaces, commas, semicolons, or the characters +, -, /, &, >, <, @, *, #. It can be entered using either uppercase or lowercase characters. 1-2-3 will always display the graph name in uppercase. In response to the prompt to enter the name of the graph,

Type: LINE
Press: ⏎

The line graph settings are stored in the computer's memory for later use. The named graph is not permanently saved on the diskette until the worksheet file is saved using the File Save command.

Saving Graphs for Printing

Although the graph is named, it cannot be printed using the PrintGraph program unless it is also saved on the diskette in a **graph file**. The picture image of the graph is saved on this file. The graph file is distinguished from other files by the file extension .PIC, which is added to the file name by the program.

Before saving this graph for printing, to identify this graph as the graph you created, change the second title line to "By [Your Name]." To do this, use the **/ G**raph **O**ptions **T**itles **S**econd command. Then to clear the exisiting second title, press (ESC). You can then enter a new second title.

To save this graph as a graph file on your data disk,

Select: Save LINE ⏎

After a few seconds the graph is saved on the data diskette. You now have a named graph called LINE and a graph saved for printing called LINE.PIC. Using the same name for both the graph file name and the named graph is perfectly acceptable.

Switching the Graph Type

Once the current graph settings are named, another graph can be created using the worksheet data without erasing the previous graph settings.
    Fred would like to see how the same data displayed in the line graph would look as a bar graph. This can easily be done by changing the type of graph to bar. Since the line graph settings are named, you can change the type of graph to a bar graph without destroying the line graph settings.

Select: Type Bar View

Your display screen should be similar to Figure 4-14.

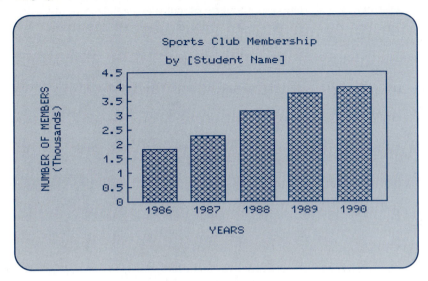

FIGURE 4-14

The data range defined in the line graph for total membership growth over the 5 years is displayed as a **bar graph**. A bar graph displays data as a set of evenly spaced bars. Each bar represents a value in the range. The Y-axis scale is different from the scale used when the data was displayed as a line graph because a bar graph must begin with the scale set at 0.

The only setting that changed was the type of graph. The bar graph is now the **current graph** because it is the one that can be viewed.

To return to the Graph menu,

Press: any key

Resetting Graph Specifications

Fred feels that a better use of the bar graph would be to show growth patterns for the four membership categories rather than the total membership growth.

To display a different range of data in the A range, the A data range needs to be canceled or reset. The Graph Reset command is used to cancel current graph settings.

Select: Reset

The Reset command options are displayed in the control panel. The Reset menu lets you cancel all the current graph settings (Graph), individual data ranges (X and A-F), all data ranges (Ranges), or all graph options (Options).

To cancel the A data range and return to the Graph menu,

Select: A Quit

The Graph Settings sheet shows you that the A data range is no longer defined. To see what has happened to the current bar graph,

Select: View

SS116
Creating and Printing Graphs

The computer beeps and a blank screen is displayed. The A data range has been erased, and consequently a graph cannot be viewed.

Press: any key

Be very careful when using the Reset command that you select the correct submenu command. It can very quickly cancel many graph settings that are very time consuming to respecify.

Defining Multiple Data Ranges

Fred wants the graph to compare the membership growth over the 5 year period for each category of membership (Family, Individual, Youth, and Retired). The A data range will contain the data for family memberships, the B data range will contain the individual membership data, the C data range will contain the youth membership data, and the D data range will contain the retired category of membership data.

Select each data range (A, B, C, and D) to define, and then, using highlighting, specify the appropriate worksheet range.

Note: If you have a color monitor, you can view your graphs in color by issuing the following command sequence: **/ G**raph **O**ptions **C**olor **Q**uit.

To view the graph,

Select: View

Your display screen should be similar to Figure 4-15.

FIGURE 4-15

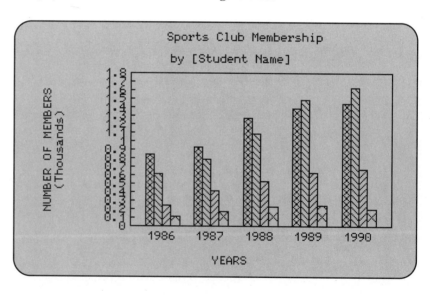

The new bar graph showing the data for each membership category in each year is displayed. Each bar represents one of the four membership categories in each year. But how do you know which bar stands for which category?

Entering Legends

When only one category was graphed, the graph was easy to understand. However, with the addition of the other three membership categories to the graph, it is difficult to distinguish among the four groups.

The use of a different **hatch pattern** (crosshatching design within the bars) or color for each of the four bars helps differentiate the groups. But how do you know which hatch pattern or color goes with which membership category?

To identify or label each hatch pattern, legends are used. A legend is a short descriptive label that helps identify the hatch patterns, or the data symbols in a line graph, that represent the A through F data ranges.

To return to the Graph menu,

Press: any key
Select: Options Legend

Each legend can be entered individually for each data range (A through F) in the same way that titles were entered. Additionally, legends can be entered as a group using the Range command. The Range command allows you to specify a range of cells in the worksheet that contain entries that you want to be the legends for the graph data ranges. 1-2-3 uses the first entry in the range as the A data range legend, the second entry as the B data range legend, and so forth. The labels must be in a continuous range, however. If a blank cell occurs between labels within the range, the blank entry will be used as a legend.

The worksheet labels—Family, Individual, Youth, and Retired— in cells B9 through B12 would be appropriate legends for the graphed data. To use the Range command to define legends for the four data ranges,

Select: Range

Specify the four worksheet labels using highlighting as the range.

The cell addresses are displayed in the settings sheet as if you had entered them individually using the backslash feature. To view the graph and see the legends,

Select: Quit View

Your display screen should be similar to Figure 4-16.

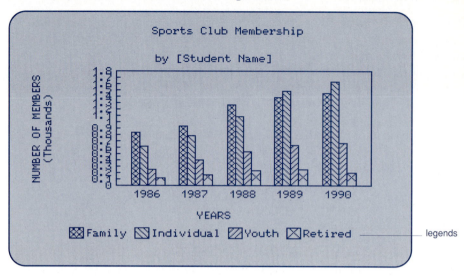

FIGURE 4-16

The four legends are displayed at the bottom of the graph to the right of the corresponding hatch symbol or color. Although 1-2-3 will accept legends up to 19 characters long, it will wrap long legends to a second line if there is insufficient space below the X axis to display the legends on a single line. To avoid this, you may want to abbreviate some of the legend labels.

The addition of legends to the graph makes reading and understanding the graph much easier.

Press: any key

The multiple-bar graph is now the current graph. Before creating another graph or recalling the line graph, the current bar graph settings must be named. Name this graph "BAR" as follows:

Select: Name Create BAR ⏎

Next, you will save this graph for printing as BAR.PIC.

Note: If you are viewing the bar graph in color and you do not have a color printer or plotter, set the color option back to black and white before saving the graph for printing. The command to do this is: **/ G**raph **O**ptions **B&W Q**uit. If you do not turn color off, 1-2-3 will print all ranges in solid blocks of black.

Select: / Graph Save BAR ⏎

There are now two named graphs stored in memory and two graphs saved for printing, LINE and BAR.

Creating a Stacked-Bar Graph

Fred is pleased with the bar graph, but he thinks that a **stacked-bar graph** may display the worksheet data in an even more meaningful manner. The stacked-bar graph will show

the proportion of each type of membership to the total membership in each year.
To change the bar graph to a stacked-bar graph and view it,

Select: Type Stack-Bar View

Note: If you want to view this graph in color, reselect the Color option, then view the graph.

Your display screen should be similar to Figure 4-17.

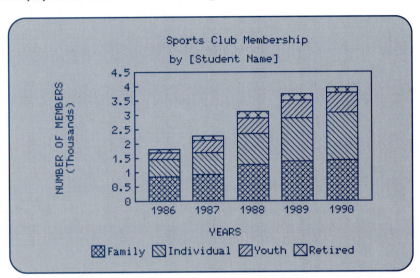

FIGURE 4-17

Rather than the bars being displayed side by side, the bars are stacked upon each other. The Y-axis scale has changed to reflect the new range of data. The new Y-axis range is the sum of the four membership categories, or the same as the total value in the worksheet. It is now easy to compare how much each membership category contributed to the total membership in each year.

Press: any key

The stacked-bar graph is now the current graph. To store the stacked-bar graph settings using the name "STACKED," issue the following command sequence. As you do, notice that the other two named graphs are listed in the control panel.

Select: Name Create STACKED ⏎

Save the graph for printing (set color to B&W first if necessary) as follows:

Select: Save STACKED ⏎

There are now three named graphs stored in memory: LINE, BAR, and STACKED; and three graphs saved for printing using the same names.

SS120
Creating and Printing Graphs

Creating a Pie Chart

The final graph Fred would like to create using the worksheet data is a **pie chart**. A pie chart compares parts to the whole in a similar manner to a stacked-bar graph. However, each value in the range is a slice of the pie or circle displayed as a percentage of the total.

The use of X and A data range settings in a pie chart is different from their use in a bar or line graph. The X range labels the slices of the pie rather than the X axis. The A data range is used to create the slices in the pie. Only one data range (A) is defined in a pie chart.

To cancel all the current graph settings (stacked),

Select: Reset Graph

The settings sheet is now cleared of all graph settings.

Fred wants to compare the four membership categories for the year 1990. The labels for the slices (membership category) will be defined in the X range as B9 through B12. The A data range will be the values for 1990 in cell G9 through G12. Complete the following command sequence:

Select: Type Pie X

Specify the four membership category labels as the X range using highlighting.

Select: A

Specify the values for 1990 as the A data range using highlighting.

Select: View

Note: If you want to view the pie chart in color, you will need to turn the color option back on.

Your display screen should be similar to Figure 4-18.

FIGURE 4-18

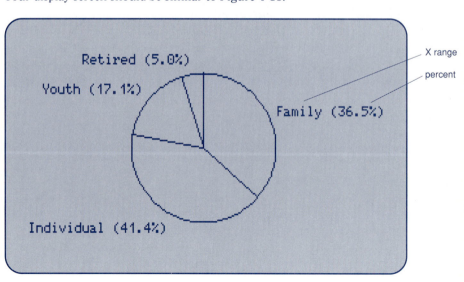

Each membership category, defined in the X range, labels each slice of the pie. Each membership category's percentage of the total membership for 1990 is displayed in parentheses next to the slice label.

To complete this graph, a title needs to be entered. Since the pie chart compares the four membership categories for the year 1990 only, the same title as used in the worksheet would not be appropriate.

Press: any key

Enter the first graph title line as "1990 Membership Comparison" and a second title line as "By [Your Name]."

View the graph.

Shading the Pie Slices

Unlike the bar graphs, the pie chart does not display hatch patterns automatically. To add this feature to a pie chart, you must create a B data range the same size as the A data range and enter a value from 1 to 8 in each cell of the B data range. These values are called **shading values**. Each value assigns a different hatch pattern or color for each slice of the pie. The number 8 leaves a pie slice as a blank. See Figure 4-19.

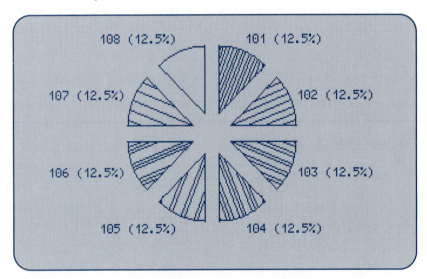

FIGURE 4-19

The shading values can be entered anywhere in the worksheet as long as they are entered as a continuous range of cells. To clear the graph and return to the READY mode,

Press: any key
Select: Quit

You will enter the shading values in column A, next to the worksheet labels.

Move to: A9

Rather than typing the numbers for the shading values into each cell, you can use the Data Fill command to fill the column with a sequence of numbers. To do this,

Select: / Data Fill

First you need to specify the range of cells to fill.

Type: A9..A12
Press: ⏎

Next the prompt asks you to enter the **start value**. This is the value you want to be the first number entered in the range. To begin the range using the number 1,

Type: 1
Press: ⏎

The next prompt is to enter the **step value** or the incrememt between each value in the range. To accept the default of 1,

Press: ⏎

Finally, you need to specify the **stop value**. This is the number 1-2-3 uses as the upper limit for the sequence. Since the range contains only four cells, the end of the range will be encountered before the default stop value (8191) is reached. Therefore, you could enter the number 4 as the stop value or accept the default. To accept the default,

Press: ⏎

Your screen should look similar to Figure 4.20.

FIGURE 4-20

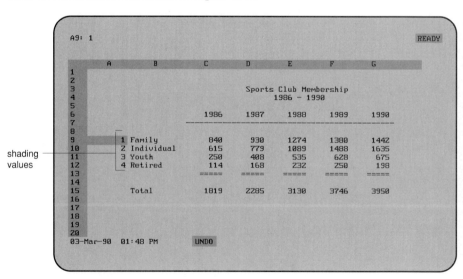

The numbers 1 through 4 are entered in the specified range. As you can see, using the Data Fill command is a real time saver whenever a range of cells needs to be filled with an incremental sequence of numbers.

Now you are ready to define the values you just entered as the B data range values for the pie chart. To do this,

Select: / Graph B

Specify the shading values as the B data range.

The B data range is displayed in the settings sheet. To view the change in the pie chart,

Select: View

Your screen should be similar to Figure 4-21.

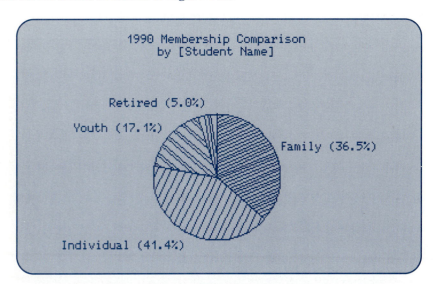

FIGURE 4-21

The shading values in the B data range determine the hatch pattern (or color if you are viewing your graph in color) for each slice of the pie. If you changed the values in the worksheet, the hatch patterns or colors would change accordingly.

Exploding a Slice of the Pie

A slice or several slices of a pie chart can be **exploded** or separated slightly from the other slices in the pie. This lets you emphasize a particular part of the pie chart. To explode a slice, add 100 to the B data range value that corresponds to the slice you want to explode.

To clear the graph and return to the READY mode,

Press: any key
Select: Quit

SS124
Creating and Printing Graphs

To explode the slice of the pie containing the data for the Retired membership category,

Move to: A12
Type: 104
Press: ⏎

The last digit (4) still determines the shading for the exploded slice.
To see the change in the pie chart, you need to view the graph. The current graph can be viewed from the READY mode by using the Graph function key, [F10].

Press: [F10] Graph

Your display screen should be similar to Figure 4-22.

FIGURE 4-22

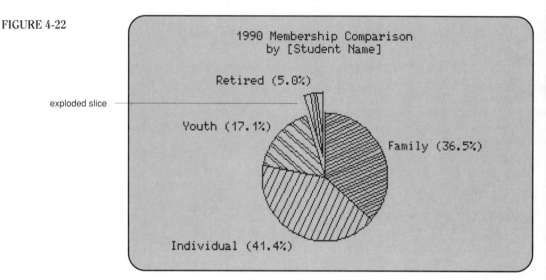

The slice of the pie representing the Retired category is exploded or separated from the other slices of the pie chart.

Fred notices that the Retired membership category represents only 5 percent of the total. He thinks this figure is a little low. To check the data entered in the worksheet for this category, return to the worksheet.

Press: any key

The value in cell G12 is 198. After checking his records, Fred sees that it was entered incorrectly into the worksheet. It should be 298. To change this figure in the worksheet,

Move to: G12
Type: 298
Press: ⏎

The worksheet has been recalculated. But what about the graphs and pie chart using the value in this cell as part of a data range? Do they change to reflect the new value?

To quickly view the current graph again,

Press: `F10` Graph

The pie chart is redrawn to reflect the change in the worksheet value for the Retired membership group. The Retired membership category for 1990 is now 7.4 percent of the total membership. The other percentages have been adjusted accordingly.

Using graphs to visually display the effects of performing what-if analysis in a worksheet is another powerful management tool.

Press: any key

Name the current pie chart settings "PIE."
Save the pie chart for printing (first set the color option to B&W if necessary) as PIE.PIC.

Recalling Named Graphs

There are now four named graphs stored in memory and four graphs saved for printing: LINE, BAR, STACKED, and PIE.

To recall a named graph and view it,

Select: Name Use

The named graphs are displayed in the third line of the control panel. To select a graph to view, move the menu pointer to the graph name and press ⏎ or type in the graph name at the prompt and press ⏎.

To view the line graph,

Select: LINE ⏎

Your display screen should be similar to Figure 4-23.

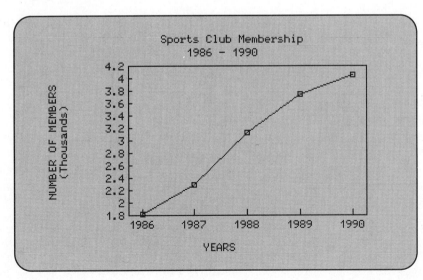

FIGURE 4-23

The line graph whose settings were named and stored in memory is displayed on the screen. Notice that this graph also reflects the change in the data in cell G12. The named graph stores only the settings, not the data in the worksheet. As a result, changes to the worksheet data are automatically reflected in the graph. However, if you change the graph settings, you would need to rename the graph.

To return to the Graph menu,

Press: any key

To view the other two graphs (remember to erase the graph from the display after viewing it by pressing any key),

Select: Name Use BAR ⏎
Name Use STACKED ⏎

Naming graphs is an important feature that allows you to have more than one set of graph settings in a single worksheet. The graph you view on the screen or recalled last is the current graph.

If you have not cleared the graph from the screen,

Press: any key

To leave the Graph menu,

Select: Quit

Saving the Worksheet

To print a graph using Lotus 1-2-3 requires that you leave the 1-2-3 program and then use the PrintGraph program disk. Before leaving 1-2-3 you should save your worksheet containing all the named graph settings. If you do not save the worksheet, the graphs you created and named will be erased from memory when you leave the Lotus program.

To save the named graphs (currently stored only in memory) with the worksheet in a new file called GRAPHS.WK1,

Select: / File Save GRAPHS.WK1 ⏎

It is important to understand the differences between naming a graph, saving a graph for printing, and saving a worksheet. To review:

/ Graph Save   saves a picture of the graph on a file on the diskette with the file extension .PIC for use when the graph is printed.

/ Graph Name   assigns a name to the current graph settings so that these settings can be recalled and used at a later time. The graph settings are stored in temporary memory.

/ File Save   saves the worksheet file with the file extension .WK1 along with any named graphs. The current graph settings are also saved even if they have not been named.

To leave 1-2-3,

Select: / Quit Yes

Printing a Graph

Note: To complete this section, you must have properly installed the PrintGraph program and established the correct hardware setup for your system. Consult your instructor for details.

In a few moments, you are returned to the Access menu rather than to the DOS prompt. The Access menu lets you select the utility program you want to use. To select PrintGraph,

Type: P

If you are using 5-1/4 inch-disks, replace the 1-2-3 disk with the Printgraph disk as directed on the screen and press ⏎.

Note: If you need to load the PrintGraph program directly from the DOS prompt, insert the PrintGraph diskette in drive A. At the A>, type: PGRAPH and press ⏎.

After a few moments your display screen should be similar to Figure 4-24.

```
Copyright 1986, 1989 Lotus Development Corp. All Rights Reserved. V2.2   MENU

Select graphs to print or preview
Image-Select Settings Go Align Page Exit

    GRAPHS    IMAGE SETTINGS                       HARDWARE SETTINGS
    TO PRINT  Size             Range colors       Graphs directory
              Top        .395   X Black              B:\
              Left       .750   A Black           Fonts directory
              Width     6.500   B Black              A:\
              Height    4.691   C Black           Interface
              Rotation   .000   D Black              Parallel 1
                                E Black           Printer
              Font              F Black              Eps FX,RX/lo
              1  BLOCK1                           Paper size
              2  BLOCK1                              Width    8.500
                                                    Length   11.000

                                                 ACTION SETTINGS
                                                    Pause  No   Eject  No
```

FIGURE 4-24

This is the PrintGraph main screen. The PrintGraph menu is displayed in the third line of the control panel, and a description of the highlighted command is displayed in the second line. It is not necessary to press / to display the PrintGraph menu. A PrintGraph menu option is selected in the same way a 1-2-3 menu option is selected.

Note: The hardware settings on your display may differ from those in Figure 4-24.

To print a graph, first you will select the graph to print. Then you will prepare the printer, and finally you will print the graph.

First, to select the graph to print,

Select: Image-Select

Your display screen should be similar to Figure 4-25.

FIGURE 4-25

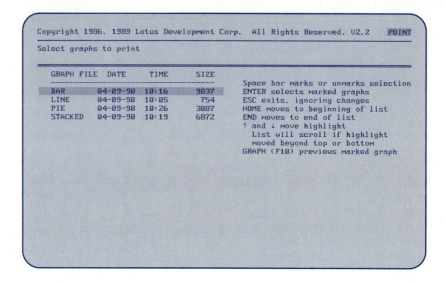

Note: If your screen tells you there are no graph files on the disk, check to see that the directory that PrintGraph is searching is properly defined for your system (Settings Hardware Graphs-Directory) or that the correct disk is in the drive.

The four graph files you saved for printing are listed.

The highlight bar is positioned over the first .PIC file. To select a graph to print, move the highlight bar to the file name and press the space bar.

Select: STACKED.PIC

A # sign appears to the left of the graph name. This indicates it has been selected for printing. If you wanted to cancel a selection, you would press the space bar again, and the # would disappear.

Before printing a graph, it can be previewed on the screen.

Press: F10 Graph

The stacked-bar graph is displayed on the screen. The settings for this graph cannot be altered at this point.

To clear the graph from the display,

Press: any key

Note: If your instructor wants you to print more than one graph, select the additional graph names from the list of names.

When you have selected all the graphs you want to print, to return to the main PrintGraph menu,

Press: ⏎

Your display screen should reflect the graphs you have chosen to print. Turn on the printer. Check to see that it is online and that the perforation in the paper is aligned with the printer scale.

To actually print the selected graph(s),

Select: Align Go

After a few moments, your printed graph should be similar to Figure 4-26.

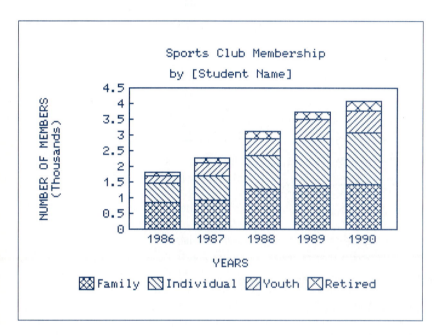

FIGURE 4-26

Note: If your screen tells you there are no graphics printers active, check to see that you have defined and selected the appropriate printer (Settings Hardware Printer).

To advance the paper to the top of the next page and to leave the PrintGraph program,

Select: Page Exit Yes

Again you are returned to the Access menu. To leave the Access system and return to the DOS prompt,

Select: Exit

SS130
Creating and Printing Graphs

Key Terms

graph	current graph
X axis	hatch patterns
Y axis	stacked-bar graph
legend	pie chart
titles	shading values
line graph	start value
scale indicator	step value
graph file	stop value
bar graph	explode

Matching

1. F10 ____ a. specifies the kind of graph
2. PIE ____ b. calls up a named graph for use
3. PIC ____ c. defines the data ranges to graph
4. legend ____ d. displays the current graph on the screen
5. X ____ e. describes the graph
6. A B C D E F ____ f. displays symbols and descriptive labels of the data
7. View ____ g. picture file extension
8. title ____ h. labels the horizontal axis
9. type ____ i. a type of graph
10. / G N U ____ j. displays the current graph from READY mode

Practice Exercises

1. The American dream of owning your own home has become elusive, in part because the prices of homes in most places have risen faster than incomes. The following data shows the average price of a home and the average family income levels from 1976 to 1986.

HOUSING PRICES vs. PERSONAL INCOME
(in thousands of dollars)

	1976	1980	1986
Avg. Home	37	55	89
Personal Income	15	22	30

- Create a worksheet displaying this data. Use the titles and row and column labels shown. Do not leave blank columns between columns of data.
- Create a line graph showing the change in the average cost of a home and family income over the years 1976 to 1986.
- Enter a first title line using the title displayed in the worksheet. Enter a second title line: "By [Your Name]."
- Label the X axis "Years." Label the Y axis "In Thousands of Dollars."

- Enter legends.
- Name the line graph HOUSING.
- Save the line graph for printing as HOUSING.PIC.
- Save the worksheet as HOME.
- Print the line graph, HOUSING.PIC.

2. Financial planners generally recommend that you allocate your capital into five categories: cash, fixed income producers (bonds), real estate, equities, and precious metals. They also recommend changing how much you allocate to each category as you reach different stages of life.

On the average, financial planners recommend that the following percentages of your capital be allocated to the five categories according to three age groups:

PERCENT ASSET ALLOCATION
(by age group)

Asset	In your 20's	In your 40's	In your 60's
Cash	22	9	5
Fixed Income	25	33	45
Real Estate	0	15	25
Equities	53	33	20
Precious Metals	0	0	5

- Create a worksheet using the titles, row and column labels, and data shown above. Do not leave blank columns between columns of data.
- Create a bar graph showing the age group as the X axis label and the percent allocation across the age groups as the data ranges. Specify the legends. Enter a first title line using the worksheet title. Enter a second title line using your name. Enter an X axis title line, "Age Group," and a Y axis title of "Percent Allocation." Name the bar graph BAR3. Save the graph to be printed as BAR3.PIC.
- Change the bar graph to a stacked-bar graph. Name the graph STACKED3. Save it to be printed as STACKED3.PIC.
- Create a pie chart to display the asset allocation for people in their 20's. Enter a first and second (use your name) title line. Add shading to the pie chart and explode the Equities slice. Name the pie chart PIE20S. Save it for printing as PIE20S.PIC.
- Create two more pie charts showing the suggested asset allocation for people in their 40's and 60's. Add shading to the pie charts. Explode the slice(s) with the largest percent allocation. Name them PIE40S and PIE60S. Save them for printing as PIE40S.PIC and PIE60S.PIC.
- Save the worksheet file with the graph settings as ASSETS.
- Print all the graphs you have saved.

3. The U.S. athletic footware market showed continued growth during the years 1983 to 1987. The data presented below shows this growth.

U.S. Athletic Footware Market Retail Sales
(in billions of dollars)

1983	4.03
1984	4.15
1985	5.01
1986	6.87
1987	8.12

- Create a worksheet of this data. Do not leave blank columns between columns of data.
- Create a line graph of this data. It should have two title lines, and an X- and Y-axis title. The second title line should contain your name. Name and save the graph for printing as SHOESL.
- Create a bar graph of this data. It should have two title lines, and an X- and Y-axis title. The second title line should contain your name. Name and save the graph for printing as SHOESB.

In the same worksheet file, create a second worksheet of the following data showing the top five manufacturers of athletic footware and their sales for first half of 1987 compared to the first half of 1988. Do not leave blank columns between columns of data.

1987 First Half Sales vs. 1988 First Half Sales
(in millions of dollars)

	1987	1988
Reebok	488.87	589
Nike	104.16	434
Converse	112.24	140.3
Avia	44.55	99
Adidas	70.52	82

- Create a bar graph of this data comparing the 1987 and 1988 sales figures. Specify the legends. It should have two title lines. The second title line should contain your name. Create X- and Y-axis titles. Name and save the graph for printing as SALES.
- Create two pie charts of this data, one for each year. They should have two title lines. The second title line should contain your name. Add shading to the pie charts. Explode the Avia slice. Name and save the graphs for printing as PIE87 and PIE88.
- Save the worksheet as SHOES.
- Print the graphs.

4. It appears that the exercise boom is losing its strength. Since 1984 the number of Americans participating in athletic activities has plunged. The two activities that have shown an increase are Walking and Bicycling. The following data shows this change.

1984 vs. 1987 Fitness Comparison
(in millions of participants)

Activity:	1984	1987
Running	29.9	27.5
Swimming	74.6	66
Aerobics	23.2	22.8
Tennis	19.9	18.2
Walking	41.1	58.9
Bicycling	50.7	52.2

- Create a worksheet of this data. Do not leave blank columns between columns of data.
- Create a line graph of this data. It should have two title lines, and an X- and Y-axis title. The second title line should contain your name. Specify the legends. Name and save the graph for printing as FITNESSL.
- Create a bar graph of this data. It should have two title lines, and an X- and Y-axis title. The second title line should contain your name. Specify the legends. Name and save the graph for printing as FITNESSB.
- Create two pie charts of this data, one for each year. It should have two title lines. The second title line should contain your name. Add shading to the pie charts. Explode the Swimming slice. Name and save the graphs for printing as FITNES84 and FITNES87.
- Save the worksheet as DECLINE.
- Print the graphs.

LAB 5

Creating Templates and Macros

OBJECTIVES

In this lab you will learn how to:

1. Name a range.
2. Use an @IF function.
3. Create a template.
4. Create an interactive macro.
5. Debug a macro.
6. Use a repetition factor.
7. Document a macro.
8. Use the Learn feature.
9. Protect worksheet cells.
10. Create an autoexecute macro.

CASE STUDY

Fred Morris, the membership coordinator for the Sports Club, would like his assistant to maintain a biweekly membership enrollment report. To help his assistant enter this data, Fred wants to create a worksheet template using Lotus 1-2-3. He also plans to create several macros to simplify and speedup the data entry and report generation process. You will follow Fred as he completes the template and creates the macros.

Naming a Range

Fred has already created much of the worksheet to be used to enter the weekly enrollment data. To see what he has done so far, **load 1-2-3 and retrieve the file TEMPLATE.**

This worksheet displays in column A the names of the three employees who are responsible for membership enrollment: Donna, Pete, and Sue. The five membership categories, Family, Single, Student, Junior and Senior, are displayed across row 5. He also entered some sample data for Donna. It shows that she enrolled three family memberships and two memberships in each of the other categories during this time period.

The worksheet also includes several formulas.

Move to: B11

The formula in this cell calculates the total enrollment for the family membership category. It has been copied across the row through cell H11.

The second formula he entered calculates the total enrollment value earned by each person. To see this formula,

Move to: G7

Your screen should be similar to Figure 5-1.

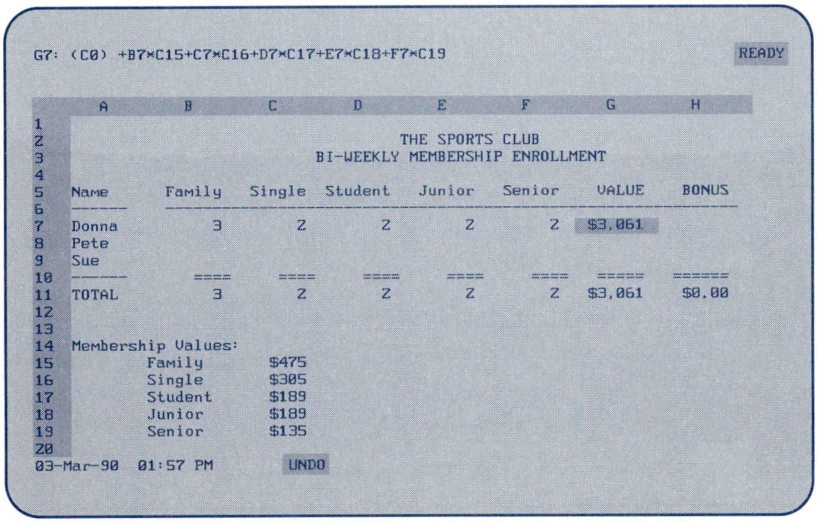

FIGURE 5-1

The VALUE is the sum of the enrollment value of the five membership categories for each person. The enrollment value for each category is calculated by multiplying the number of enrollments times the appropriate membership value.

The membership value for each category is the initiation fee plus one month's dues. This value is calculated and displayed for each category in cells C15 through C19. For example, the family membership value ($475) in cell C15 is the sum of the initiation fee of $400 and one month's dues of $75.

The formula in cell G7 calculates and sums the enrollment value for the five membership categories earned during the two-week period for Donna.

The formula in cell G7, however, is difficult to read because it refers to many different cells in the spreadsheet. To help clarify the meaning of a formula and to simplify entering formulas that repeatedly refer to the same cells or ranges of cells, a name can be assigned to the cell or range of cells. Once a cell or range of cells is named, the name can be used in a formula instead of the cell address. To see how this works you will assign the name Family to cell C15.

Select: / Range Name

Your screen should be similar to Figure 5-2.

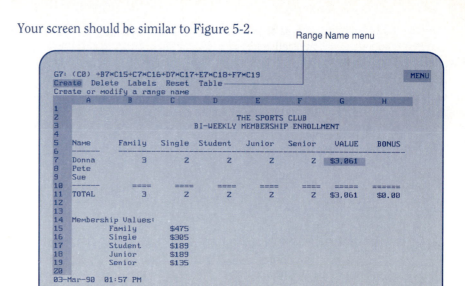

FIGURE 5-2

There are five Range Name menu options. To assign the name FAMILY to cell C15,

Select: Create

The prompt "Enter name:" is displayed. A range name can be up to 15 characters long and should be descriptive of the contents of the cell or range of cells. To enter the name,

Type: family
Press: ⏎

The next prompt asks you to specify the cell or range of cells to be named.

Type: C15
Press: ⏎

Your screen should be similar to Figure 5-3.

FIGURE 5-3

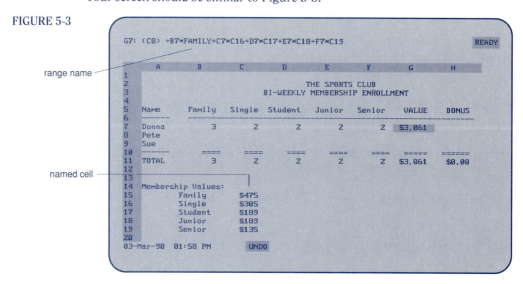

Look at the formula in cell G7 as it is displayed in the control panel. The range name Family has replaced the cell address C15. Using a range name makes the formula easier to understand.

The remaining four membership values in cells C16 through C19 need to be named next. Rather than typing in the range name, an existing spreadsheet label can be used. You will name these cells using the spreadsheet labels displayed in cells B16 through B19. For example, the membership value for the Single category in cell C16 will be named SINGLE.

First the cell pointer must be positioned on one of the corner cells in the range of labels to be used as the range names.

Move to: B16
Select: / Range Name Labels

This option displays four menu choices: Right, Down, Left, and Up. Your selection from this menu depends upon the location of the cell to be named in relation to labels. In this case, the cells to be named are located to the right of the labels.

Select: Right

The prompt to enter the label range is displayed. Enter the range B16..B19 using highlighting.

You are returned to the READY mode. To see the use of the named ranges in the formula,

Move to: G7

Your screen should be similar to Figure 5-4.

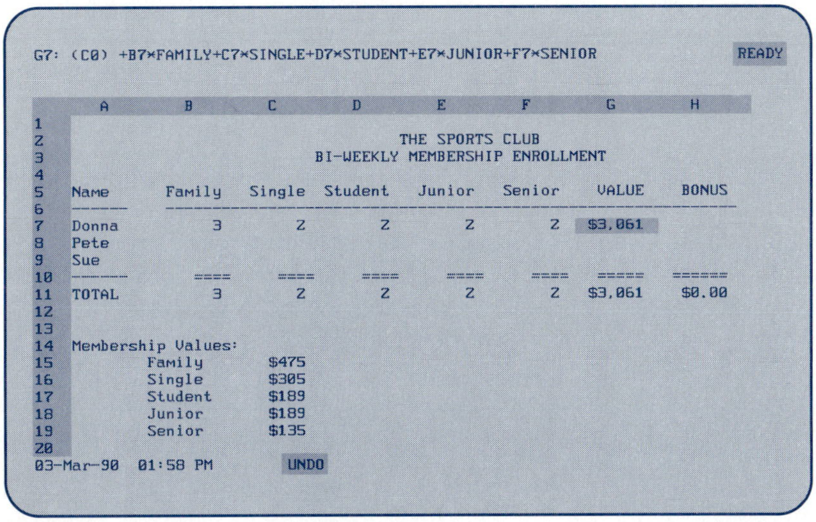

FIGURE 5-4

The labels in cells B16 through B19 have been used to name the cells to their right. The range names are displayed in the formula.

The only time you can use the Labels option to name a cell is if the range to be named is a single-cell range and the labels are located in a cell adjacent to the cells to be named.

A range name can be used in place of cell addresses anytime a range is requested as part of a command or when using the range in a formula or @function.

The three Range Name menu options you have not used are Delete, Reset, and Table. Delete removes an individual range name from the worksheet. Reset deletes all the range names in a worksheet. The Table option creates an alphabetical list of all range names in a worksheet and their corresponding addresses. To see how the Table option works,

Move to: E15
Select: / **R**ange **N**ame **T**able ⏎

Your screen should be similar to Figure 5-5.

FIGURE 5-5

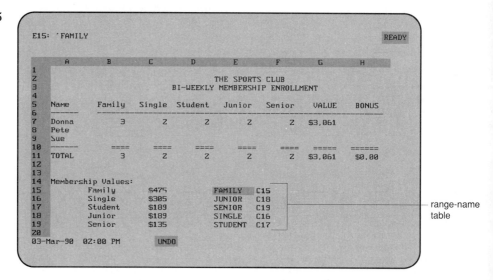

range-name table

The range names and cell addresses are alphabetically displayed. This option is especially useful to someone who is not familiar with the worksheet. They can quickly see all the named ranges and associated addresses used in the worksheet.

When using this option be sure to specify an empty area of the worksheet for display of the table, as it will write over any existing data in the range.

To remove the table, erase the range E15..F19.

Finally, the formula in cell G7 needs to be copied to cells G8 and G9. Since the range names refer to specific cells that you do not want adjusted relative to the new location of the formula when it is copied, the range names must be made absolute.

Move to: G7
Press: (F2) EDIT

The cell addresses, rather than the range names, are displayed in the formula in the second line of control panel.

Since the edit cursor is to the right of C19, to change this cell address to absolute,

Press: (F4) ABS

The cell address C19 now displays the range name preceded by a $ character. A named range can only be relative or absolute, not mixed.

To complete the edit of this formula, change the cell addresses for C15, C16, C17, and C18 to absolute using the ABS key. Remember to position the edit cursor appropriately before pressing (F4).

Copy the formula, which calculates the VALUE for Donna, to calculate the VALUE for Pete and Sue.

Move to: G8

Look at the formula in the control panel. The range names appear exactly as they did in the formula in cell G7. They were copied using absolute cell referencing. The other cell addresses in the formula correctly adjusted relative to the new location in the worksheet.

Using the @IF Function

Next Fred needs to enter a formula in cell H7 to calculate the bonus earned. The club gives a 15 percent bonus on total enrollment values over $3000 and a 10 percent bonus on total enrollment values under $3000 in a two week period.

Lotus 1-2-3 has a special @function, the @IF function, that can check to see if certain conditions are met and then take action based upon the results of the check. The format for this @function is @IF(condition,true,false). This @function contains three arguments: condition, true, and false.

Condition lets you set up an equation to check against. To make this comparison, **logical operators** are used. Logical operators are used in formulas and @functions that compare values in two or more cells. The result of the comparison is either true (the conditions are met) or false (the conditions are not met).

The logical operators are:

Symbol	Meaning
=	equal to
<	less than
>	greater than
<=	less than or equal to
>=	greater than or equal to
<>	not equal to
#NOT#	logical NOT
#AND#	logical AND
#OR#	logical OR

In this case, the condition is whether the total enrollment VALUE (G7) is greater than (>) 3000. The condition argument will be G7>3000.

The true argument contains the instructions that are executed if the condition is true. In this case, if VALUE (G7) is greater than 3000 (true), then G7 is multiplied times 15 percent (G7*15%).

The false argument contains instructions that are executed if the condition is not true, or false. If VALUE (G7) is less than 3000 (false), then G7 is multiplied times 10 percent (G7*10%).

To enter the @IF function,

Move to: H7
Type: @IF(G7>3000,G7*15%,G7*10%)
Press: ⏎

Your screen should be similar to Figure 5-6.

FIGURE 5-6

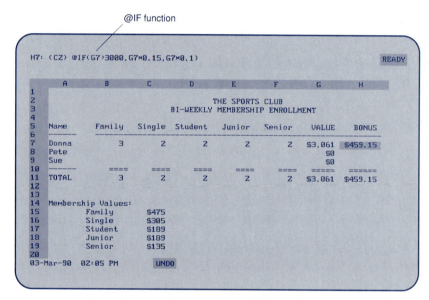

The BONUS earned using the sample data for Donna is $459.15. Since the value in cell G7 was greater than 3000, the bonus was calculated using 15%. To check that the @IF statement is calculating correctly, you will decrease the value in cell G7 to less than 3000 by decreasing the number of Family enrollments to 2.

Move to: B7
Type: 2
Press: ⏎

The value in cell G7 is now $2,586, and the calculated bonus in cell H7 is $258.60, or 10% of the value in cell G7. The @IF function is operating correctly.

Copy the @function used to calculate the BONUS for Donna to calculate the BONUS for Pete and Sue.

Creating a Template

The worksheet is complete. Now Fred is ready to create a blank **template**, or entry form, for his assistant to use for data entry.

Erase the sample membership enrollment data for Donna (B7 through F7).

Press: (HOME)

Your screen should be similar to Figure 5-7.

FIGURE 5-7

```
A1: [W8]                                                         READY

         A        B        C        D        E        F        G        H
1
2                                   THE SPORTS CLUB
3                           BI-WEEKLY MEMBERSHIP ENROLLMENT
4
5   Name       Family   Single  Student   Junior   Senior    VALUE    BONUS
6   -------   -----------------------------------------------------------
7   Donna                                                      $0    $0.00
8   Pete                                                       $0    $0.00
9   Sue                                                        $0    $0.00
10  -------      ====     ====     ====     ====     ====    =====   ======
11  TOTAL           0        0        0        0        0      $0    $0.00
12
13
14  Membership Values:
15          Family      $475
16          Single      $305
17          Student     $189
18          Junior      $189
19          Senior      $135
20
03-Mar-90  02:06 PM        UNDO
```

This is how the blank **template** will appear when Fred's assistant uses it to enter the biweekly enrollment figures. A template is simply a prewritten worksheet that contains blank spaces for entry of data. Templates are useful in any application where input and output is required using the same format. The template saves the user time by not having to redesign the same worksheet form each time the report is needed. The original design can be used repeatedly by saving the worksheet containing the data using a different file name than the file name used to save the template.

Creating an Interactive Macro

To speed the data entry process, Fred will create a macro that will help enter the data into the report. A **macro** is a series of keystrokes and commands that are stored as labels in a worksheet. When the macro is run or executed the series of keystrokes or commands is performed automatically.

Some macros are very simple and are merely a duplication of a series of keystrokes. For example, a macro can be written that moves the cell pointer to the left one cell. A more complex macro may perform a command, such as copying data from one cell to another or changing cell widths. Even more complex macros can be written that let you create and display your own menu and perform conditional tests.

Macros are very useful for replacing a series of commands or keystrokes that are performed repeatedly. Instead of manually entering each keystroke every time you need to perform the same task, you use the macro, which performs the keystrokes automatically for you.

The simplest type of macro represents keys on the keyboard. The macro commands consist of **keystroke instructions** which can be a single-character key or **key names** enclosed in braces ({key name}). The single-character keystroke instructions represent typewriter keys on the keyboard and are identical to the keys they represent. The only exception to this is the ⏎ key. The single-character key which represents ⏎ is the ~ (tilde). Many of the keystroke instructions that consist of a key name enclosed in braces are shown below.

Keyboard Key	Macro Keystroke Instruction
↑	{U} or {UP}
↓	{D} or {DOWN}
→	{R} or {RIGHT}
←	{L} or {LEFT}
HOME	{HOME}
END	{END}
PGUP	{PGUP}
PGDN	{PGDN}
DELETE	{DEL}
ESC	{ESC}
Bksp	{BS}
⏎	~
Waits for keyboard entry (pause)	{?}
F2	{EDIT}
F3	{NAME}
F4	{ABS}
F5	{GOTO}
F6	{WINDOW}
F7	{QUERY}
F8	{TABLE}
F9	{CALC}
F10	{GRAPH}

Creating a macro follows several steps: planning, entering, naming, testing, and editing. You will create a macro to enter data following these steps.

Planning the Macro

The first step in creating a macro is to plan the macro. A good way to plan a macro is to perform the task you want it to do manually, and write down every step on paper as you are doing it. This way you are less likely to forget a step or to perform a step out of sequence.

To demonstrate, you will enter some sample membership enrollment data for Donna manually.

Press:	(F5) GOTO
Type:	B7
Press:	(↵)
Type:	2
Press:	(→)
Type:	4
Press:	(→)
Type:	2
Press:	(→)
Type:	0
Press:	(→)
Type:	1
Press:	(↵)

You will enter a macro in the worksheet to perform each of the keystrokes you just used to enter the data for Donna. The only difference will be that, in place of the numbers that will be entered each time the report is completed, you will enter in the macro a ? character to show that the user should enter data. The recorded keystrokes on paper then would be: (F5), GOTO, B7, (↵), ?, (→), ?, (→), ?, (→), ?, (→), ?, (↵).

Entering the Macro

The second step is to enter the series of keystrokes as a label entry in the worksheet. The text representing the keystrokes is a macro. A macro is usually placed in an area outside of the active area of the worksheet that would not be affected by the later addition or deletion of rows and columns in the worksheet. In a large and complex worksheet, the bottom right-hand corner of the worksheet would be the best place to enter the macro statements. However, to demonstrate the macro creation process more easily, you will use an open area of the worksheet in the same window as the active area of the worksheet.

Several rules should be followed when entering a macro in a worksheet:

- Enter the macro in an empty area of the worksheet.
- Enter the macro as a label. If the macro statement begins with a non-text character, such as a number, a numeric symbol, or a /, use a label prefix character before entering the character so that 1-2-3 will interpret the entry as a label.
- Enter the macro commands using either upper- or lowercase letters. Many people use uppercase letters when entering the key names enclosed in braces and cell addresses. They use lowercase letters for macros that represent the use of the command menu. This makes reading the macro easier.
- Enter the macro in a single cell or in a vertical column of cells.

The first macro command will move the cell pointer to cell B7 using the GOTO (F5) feature. The keystroke instruction that represents the F5 function key is {GOTO}.

Move to: E14
Type: {GOTO}

Because the first character in this macro command begins with a {, the entry is interpreted as a label. Therefore it was not necessary to begin the macro with a label prefix character.

Next the cell location to move the cell pointer to must be specified.

Type: B7

To complete the GOTO command, the ⏎ macro symbol (~) must be entered.

Type: ~

The next macro statement allows you to enter data. The keystroke instruction that will do this is {?}. A macro that uses this keystroke instruction is called an **interactive macro** because it temporarily stops the action of the macro to allow the user to enter data into the worksheet.

Type: {?}

Next you want the macro to both enter the data and move right one cell. To do this,

Type: {RIGHT}

To enter the macro into the cell,

Press: ⏎

Your screen should be similar to Figure 5-8.

FIGURE 5-8

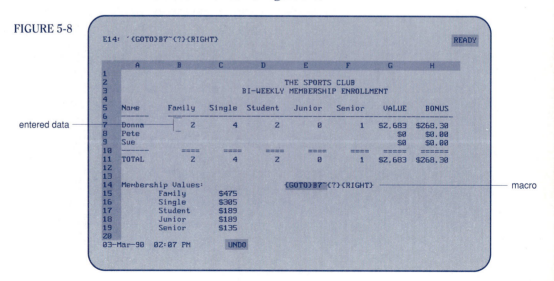

The remaining macro commands could be added to cell E14 as one long label, or they can be placed in a series of continuous cells in a single column. It is often easier to enter the macro commands in segments as a column of cells. This makes it easier to correct or edit the macro later.

Move to: E15

The next series of macro statements allow you to enter data and move the cell pointer. This time you will use the short version of the {RIGHT} macro key name, {R}.

Type: {?}{R}{?}{R}{?}{R}{?}~
Press: ⏎

Your screen should be similar to Figure 5-9.

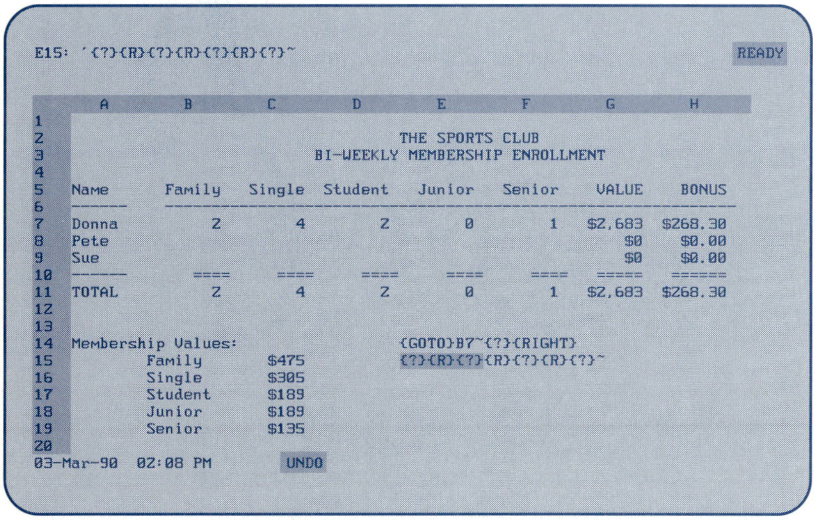

FIGURE 5-9

Be sure you entered the macro commands exactly as they appear in cells E14 and E15 in Figure 5-9. If they are different, correct your entry by editing the cell as you would any other entry.

Naming the Macro

The macro commands to enter data in the first row of the report should now be complete. The next step is to name the macro. Macros are named using the Range Name Create command.

Move to: E14
Select: / Range Name Create

The prompt to enter a name is displayed in the control panel. Notice that all the range names you entered earlier are also displayed in the control panel.

There are two ways to name a macro. The first method consists of a backslash (\) character followed by a single letter (A to Z). The second method follows the same rules for naming a range. That is, the name can consist of any combination of 15 characters.

You will use the first method to name this macro. When assigning a macro a single-letter name, it is a good idea to use a letter which is descriptive of the action of the macro.

Since this macro allows **d**ata entry to the right, you will name it \D.

Type: \D
Press: ⏎

The prompt to enter the range of cells to be named is displayed in the control panel. When naming a macro, only the cell containing the first macro statement needs to be entered. Since the cell pointer is positioned on this cell, to accept the default,

Press: ⏎

Each macro you create in a worksheet needs to be assigned a name. If you use a single-letter name, you cannot use the same letter more than once.

Testing the Macro

The fourth step is to test or run the macro. When a macro is run, it executes the commands in the first cell of the range specified when the macro was named, from left to right. It will continue executing the commands in the next cell in the same column until it reaches a blank cell, a numeric cell, or a Quit command.

To run a macro whose name consists of a \ and a single letter, the (ALT) key is held down while pressing the letter key you named the macro (D).

Press: (ALT) - D

The first command, {GOTO}B7~, has been executed and the cell pointer is positioned in cell B7. Notice the indicator "CMD" displayed at the bottom of the screen. This tells you that a macro is in progress and is pausing for user input. The next command, {?}, temporarily stopped execution of the macro to allow you to enter data into the cell.

Type: 3

To resume execution of the macro commands following a {?}, you must press ⏎.

Press: ⏎

The macro continues execution by performing the next command, {RIGHT}. The cell pointer moved to the right one cell. It continues execution by performing the commands in cell E15 next from left to right. The first command in this cell, {?}, causes the macro to pause and await user input.

Continue using the macro by entering the following data (remember to press ↵ to resume macro execution after entering the data):

Cell	**Value**
C7	**4**
D7	**1**
E7	**2**
F7	**0**

Your screen should be similar to Figure 5-10.

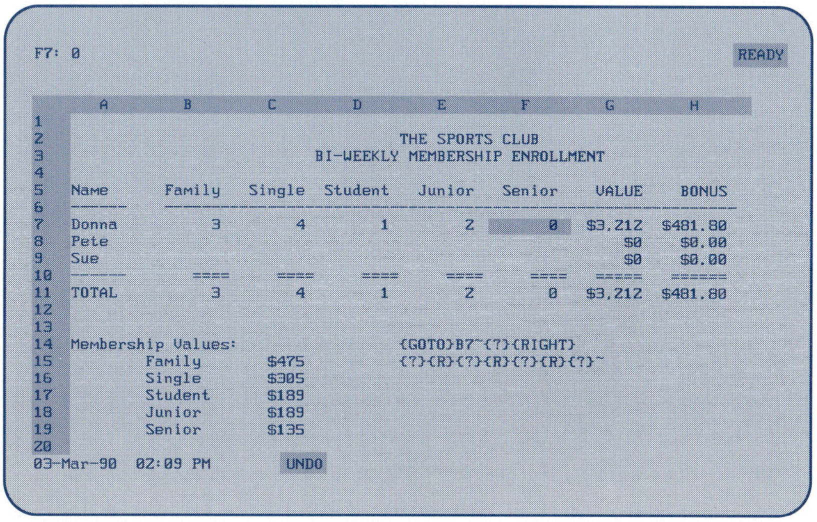

F7: 0 READY

	A	B	C	D	E	F	G	H
1								
2					THE SPORTS CLUB			
3				BI-WEEKLY MEMBERSHIP ENROLLMENT				
4								
5	Name	Family	Single	Student	Junior	Senior	VALUE	BONUS
6	------	------	------	------	------	------	------	------
7	Donna	3	4	1	2	0	$3,212	$481.80
8	Pete						$0	$0.00
9	Sue						$0	$0.00
10	------	====	====	====	====	====	=====	======
11	TOTAL	3	4	1	2	0	$3,212	$481.80
12								
13								
14	Membership Values:				{GOTO}B7~{?}{RIGHT}			
15		Family	$475		{?}{R}{?}{R}{?}{R}{?}~			
16		Single	$305					
17		Student	$189					
18		Junior	$189					
19		Senior	$135					
20								

03-Mar-90 02:09 PM UNDO

FIGURE 5-10

Editing the Macro

If you are very careful when entering a macro, it will execute properly the first time. Then you will not need to make corrections to the macro, or **debug** it, so that it performs correctly. However, not all macros will run correctly the first time. Some common errors are missing commands, and misplaced spaces and tildes.

To demonstrate an error and how to correct it, you will enter three errors in the macro you just created. The first error will demonstrate the effect of a misspelled keystroke instruction.

Move to: E14

Edit this macro so that {RIGHT} is spelled {RIGH}.

Move to: E15

The second error will demonstrate the effect of a missing command, and the third error will show the effect of an extra space.

Edit the macro in cell E15 by deleting the third {?} and entering a space before the last {?}. When edited, this macro should look like: **{?}{R}{?}{R}{R} {?}~**.

To see what happens when a macro contains an error, you will run the macro.

Press: (ALT) - D
Type: 4
Press: ⏎

Your screen should be similar to Figure 5-11.

FIGURE 5-11

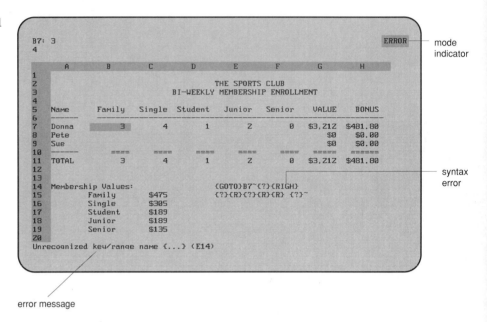

error message

Macro execution has been interrupted and the mode indicator flashes "ERROR," The error message displayed in the status line tells you that the error is due to an unrecognized key or range name and that the location of the error is in cell E14. To clear the message,

Press: (ESC)

You are returned to the READY mode. This type of error is called a **syntax error**. It is an error that is the result of a technical mistake made when entering the command. Another common mistake that causes a syntax error is a missing { or }.

A macro can be edited like any other cell entry. Since you know the cause of this error, simply change {RIGH} to {RIGHT} in cell E14.

To see how the errors in cell E15 affect the macro, invoke the macro again.

Press: (ALT) - D

Enter 4 as the enrollment figure for the first three categories for Donna.

You should now be about to enter the enrollment figure for the Junior category. However, the cursor is positioned on cell F7 waiting for entry of the data for the Senior category. This time an error message is not displayed and the macro continues execution.

The macro performed exactly as it should have by moving the cell pointer two cells to the right. After entering the value for the student category in cell D7, the cell pointer moved two cells right, skipping the junior category (E7). This is because the macro reads {R}{R}. The error in this macro command is a **logic error**. Because the macro is syntactically correct, an error message does not interrupt the macro execution. The macro executed the command exactly as entered in the cell.

Now watch your screen carefully as you enter the value in cell F7.

Type: 4
Press: ⏎

Your screen should be similar to Figure 5-12.

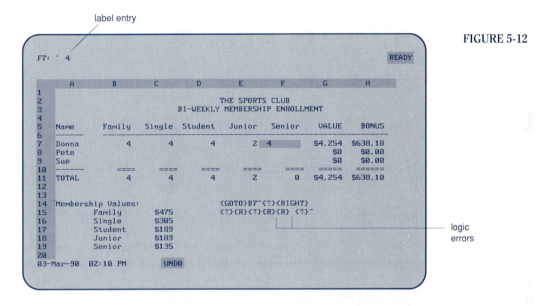

FIGURE 5-12

The entry in cell F7 begins on the left side of the cell space with a blank space, followed by 4. This is because the blank space in the macro had the same effect as beginning a cell entry with a space, that is, the mode changes to LABEL and a blank space is the first character entered in the cell. Therefore, the next character entered, 4, is interpreted as a label.

In both cases, although an error message was not displayed, the macro did not execute as intended due to a logic error. If you need to interrupt the execution of a macro because it is not performing correctly, press (CTRL) - (BREAK). "ERROR" will flash in the mode indicator. To clear the error message and return to the READY mode, press (ESC).

You have demonstrated two types of errors to be aware of: a syntax error that produces an error message, and a logic error. The macro containing a logic error may be syntactically correct, therefore Lotus 1-2-3 does not interrupt the macro execution. However, the intended task is not performed correctly.

Correct the macro in cell E15 to be: {?}{R}{?}{R}{?}{R}{?}~.

The macro should now appear as it was originally entered and it should run correctly.

Using a Repetition Factor

Next Fred wants to add to the macro to allow entry of the data for Pete in row 8. After entering the last value for Donna in cell F7, he needs to move down a row and left four cells to begin entry of the values for Pete in row 8.

Move to: E16

The macro key that moves the cell pointer down is {D}.

Type: {D}

Next, to move the cell pointer left four cells, the macro key {L} could be typed four times. However, whenever you need to repeat a macro key a number of times, a **repetition factor** can be included within the macro key. A repetition factor specifies how many times to repeat the use of the same key. A space must be entered following the macro key name before entering the repetition factor number.

Type: {L 4}

The number 4 within the macro key tells 1-2-3 to repeat the command four times.
  If the macro were executing, the cell pointer would now be in cell B8. Next, to allow entry of data in this cell and to move right one cell space, continue the macro as follows:

Type: {?}{R}
Press: ⬇

To continue the macro to allow the entry of data in row 8, the same sequence of keys as in the macro commands in cell E15 can be used. A macro, like any other worksheet entry, can be copied.
  Copy the macro in cell E15 to cell E17.
  To complete the macro so that the data for Sue can be entered, the macro commands in cells E16 and E17 can be used.
  Copy the contents of E16 and E17 to E18.

Your screen should be similar to Figure 5-13.

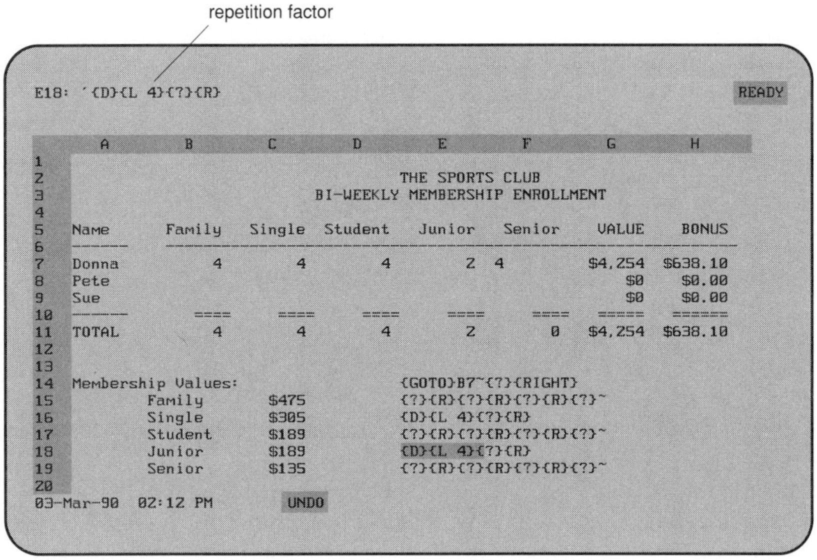

FIGURE 5-13

You have extended the macro so that it now consists of the commands in cells E14 through E19. Although you have added several lines to the original macro named \D, it is not necessary to rename the macro. By entering the additional macro commands into the cells immediately below the original commands, the macro will automatically continue executing the commands.

To test the macro,

Press: ALT-D

Enter 3 as the enrollment figure for all categories for Donna, 2 for all categories for Pete, and 1 for all categories for Sue. If your macro does not run correctly, locate and correct the error and rerun the macro.

Your screen should be similar to Figure 5-14.

FIGURE 5-14

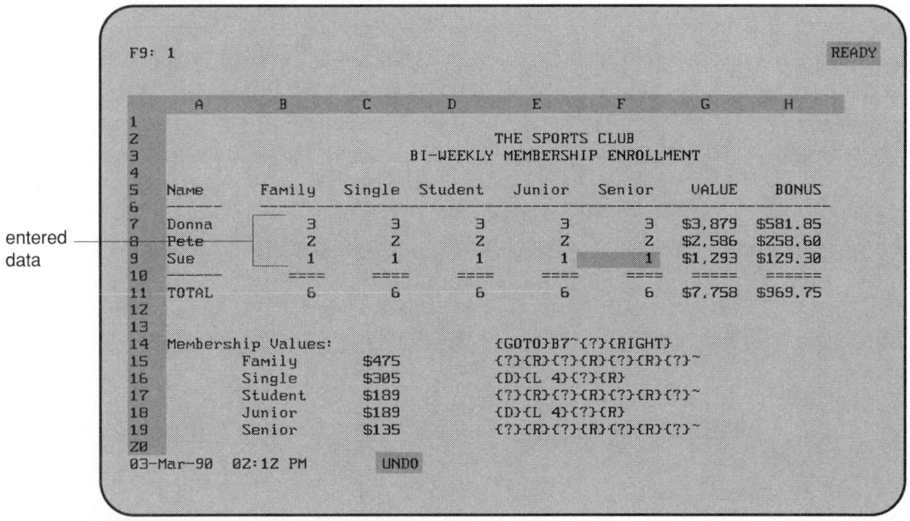

SS152
Creating Templates
and Macros

Fred feels this macro will help his assistant enter the data for the report easily.

Now that the macro is complete, you will move it out of the worksheet window to cell B25 as follows:

Move to: E14
Select: / Move E14..E19 ⏎ B25 ⏎

To see the new location of the macro statements,

Press: PGDN

Lotus 1-2-3 automatically adjusts the macro range to its new location in the worksheet.

Documenting the Macro

A macro tells 1-2-3 to perform certain commands and procedures. A worksheet can contain many macros. To avoid confusion and inform other users of the meaning of the macros in a worksheet, it is important to document the macros. Usually the name assigned to the macro is displayed to the left of the macro, and explanatory text is placed to the right.

Move to: A25
Type: \D
Move to: F25
Type: Enrollment Data Entry
Press: ⏎

Your screen should be similar to Figure 5-15.

FIGURE 5-15

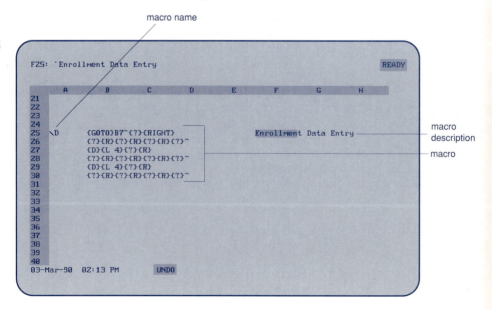

Using the Learn Feature

Next Fred would like to create a macro that will print a copy of the report after the data has been entered and save the worksheet using a new file name.

Move to: B32

First you will enter the macro to print the report. The command sequence to print the report is: **/ P**rint **P**rinter **R**ange **A1..H11** ⏎ **A**lign **G**o **P**age **Q**uit. The macro statement to perform this command is the same as the keystrokes you would use to enter the command manually. In addition to typing macros directly into worksheet cells, you can use the Learn feature to record your keystrokes as a macro at the same time as you perform them.

Before using this feature you must define a range in the worksheet where the macro commands will be recorded. This is called the **learn range**. This range is a single-column range which needs to be large enough to contain all the macro instructions. When specifying the learn range, specify a range that is much larger than you think you will need and in an area of the worksheet which will not interfere with other worksheet data.

To define the range,

Select: **/ W**orksheet **L**earn **R**ange **B32..B40** ⏎

To have 1-2-3 record your keystrokes as a macro, turn on the Learn feature by pressing the Learn key, (ALT) - (F5).

Press: (ALT) - (F5)

Your screen should look similar to Figure 5-16.

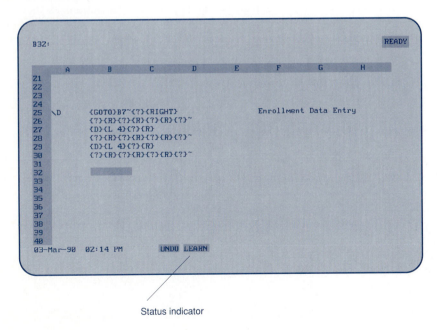

FIGURE 5-16

Status indicator

Notice the status indicator displays "LEARN." Now anything you type or any commands you enter will be recorded as a macro. To create the macro to print the worksheet,

Select: / Print Printer

To define the first cell of the range to print,

Select: Range
Press: (HOME)
Press: . (period)

To define the area of the worksheet to print,

Press: ↓ (10 times)
Press: → (7 times)
Press: ↵

To tell the printer to align to the top of the page, print the report, advance to the top of the next page, and then leave the print menu,

Select: Align Go Page Quit

The report should be printing. The keystrokes to print the report have also been recorded as a macro in the learn range. To turn off the Learn feature,

Press: (ALT) - (F5)

The LEARN indicator is no longer displayed. The macro instructions as they were recorded using the Learn feature have been entered in the learn range. To display all the macro statements,

Move to: B34

Your screen should be similar to Figure 5-17.

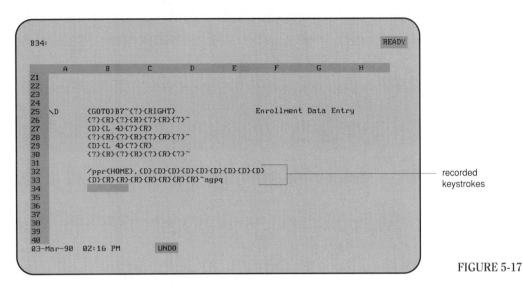

FIGURE 5-17

The macro commands are displayed in the learn range. Notice that it records each {D} and each {R} key name individually. The Learn feature cannot use a repetition factor within key names. Consequently the macro takes up much more worksheet space.

If you enter more characters than your learn range can hold, 1-2-3 will turn off the Learn feature and tell you the learn range is full. The learn range will contain all the macro instructions entered up to that point. You can erase the contents of the range, define a larger range, and begin again; or you can define a larger range and start where you left off.

Now you are ready to name the macro. The second method of naming a macro lets you assign a name up to 15 characters long. Again the name should be descriptive of the function of the macro. You will name the macro PRINT.

Move to: B32
Select: / Range Name Create **PRINT** ⏎ ⏎

Document the macro statement by putting the macro name in cell A32 and a short description of the macro, such as "Prints the Report," in cell G32.

Your screen should be similar to Figure 5-18.

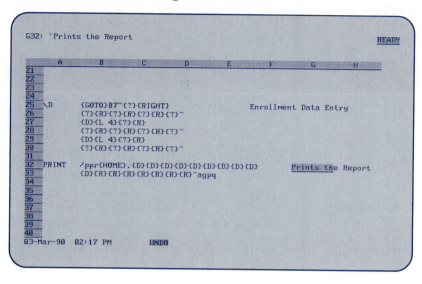

FIGURE 5-18

To run a macro which has been named using the second method, you must use the Run (ALT - F3) key. The Run key can be used to run any macros, including those named with the backslash character.

Press: ALT - F3

The prompt "Select the macro to run:" is displayed in the second line of the control panel, and all the range names used in the worksheet are listed in the third line. This makes it difficult to distinguish between range names and macro names. To help distinguish between the two types of range names, you may want to begin all macro names in a worksheet with the same character, such as a \, to help you distinguish the macro names from the range names.

The macro named PRINT is the third range name listed. To see additional range names,

Press: ↓

An additional line of range names is displayed. The \D macro name is the last range name.

Rather than leave the macro name as PRINT, you will change it to \PRINT. To cancel the Run command,

Press: CTRL - BREAK

To delete the macro name PRINT and create the macro name \PRINT,

Select: / Range Name Delete PRINT ⏎
Select: / Range Name Create \PRINT ⏎ B32 ⏎

To run the \PRINT macro,

Press: ALT - F3
Press: ↓

Your screen should be similar to Figure 5-19.

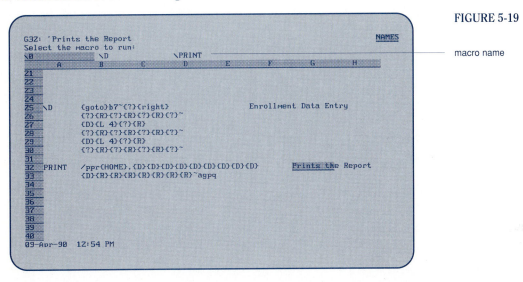

FIGURE 5-19

macro name

Now both the macros appear at the end of the named ranges and begin with a \ character.

Select: \PRINT

The printer should be printing the report. If your macro did not operate correctly, locate and correct the error and retest the macro.

The next macro command will save the worksheet using a new file name. Since each report is for a different two-week period in a month, Fred wants his assistant to name the file using the name of the month that the report covers followed by a 1 or a 2 to indicate the first or second two-week period. For example, JAN1 would be the file name for the report covering the first two weeks in January.

The command sequence to save a file with a new file name is: **/ F**ile **S**ave file name ⏎. You will enter this macro into the worksheet directly by typing the macro commands. Since the file name will change each time the report is saved, the {?} macro keystroke instruction is used in place of the file name.

When entering a macro that begins with a /, you must begin the entry with an apostrophe to indicate that a label is being entered in this cell. If you do not begin the macro statement with a label prefix character, when you press /, the main menu will appear in the control panel rather than a / being entered in the cell. Also be careful not to enter any blank spaces in the command sequence, as a blank in a command sequence can stop the macro execution.

Move to: B34
Type: '/fs{?}~
Press: ⏎

The macro commands to save the worksheet will continue as part of the PRINT macro. Therefore it is not necessary to assign the save macro commands a new macro name.

Enter a description of the macro, such as "Saves the worksheet," in cell G34.

Your screen should be similar to Figure 5-20.

FIGURE 5-20

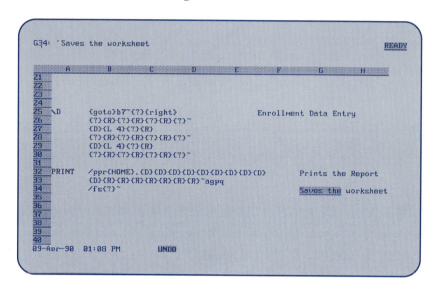

Enter your name in cell A1 and the current date in A2.

To review, the following steps should be followed when developing a macro.

Plan   Careful planning of the steps you want the macro to perform is essential to the macro development process. Writing down the steps while you are actually performing the task will greatly improve the accuracy of the macro you enter.

Enter The macro is entered as a label in any open area of the worksheet. It is recommended that this area be outside the active worksheet space. It must be entered in a continuous range of vertical cells. A macro can also be entered by defining a learn range (/ Worksheet Learn Range) and then using the Learn feature ((ALT) - (F5)) to record your keystrokes as a macro.

Name   A macro is assigned a name using the Range Name Create command. A macro name can consist of a \ (backslash) followed by a single letter or any combination of up to 15 characters.

Test   To see if the macro is operating correctly and to locate any errors, run the macro. If the macro name consists of a \ and a single letter, press the (ALT) key and the letter name of the macro to execute the macro. If the macro name consists of any combination of characters, press (ALT) - (F3) (the Run key) and select the appropriate macro name. Testing the macro is also known as debugging, since the purpose is to locate both syntax and logic errors.

Edit If errors are located or if you need to change a macro, it can be edited like any other worksheet entry.

Before testing this macro, Fred wants to make a few other adjustments to the worksheet.

Protecting Cells

Fred is concerned that the formulas and the macro statements in the worksheet may be accidentally altered or erased. To prevent this from happening, he will protect those cells from changes by enabling the Worksheet Protection feature.

To turn on the Worksheet Cell Protection feature,

Select: / Worksheet Global

The Global Settings sheet tells you that global protection is disabled. This is the default. To turn protection on,

Select: Protection Enable

When this feature is used, all cells in the worksheet are protected. This means that you cannot enter or change an entry in any cell in the worksheet. Notice that "PR" is displayed in the control panel to show you that the current cell is protected.

To allow his assistant to enter data into the worksheet, Fred needs to unprotect the range of cells where the data will be entered. To see this area of the worksheet,

Press: (HOME)
Move to: B7

To show the effect of trying to enter data into a protected cell,

Type: 5
Press: ⏎

The computer beeped and "ERROR" flashed in the mode indicator. The message in the status line tells you that this is a protected cell.

To clear the message,

Press: (ESC)

To unprotect the range of cells to be used to enter data, B7 through F9,

Select: / Range Unprot B7..F9 ⏎

Your screen should be similar to Figure 5-21.

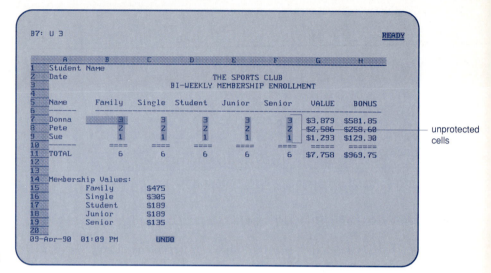

FIGURE 5-21

Notice that the control panel now displays "U" to show that these are unprotected cells. Whenever worksheet protection is enabled, the control panel will display either PR or U. The unprotected cells may also appear highlighted on your screen.

Next Fred needs to erase the sample data in the worksheet.

Select: / Range Erase **B7..F9** ⏎

He now has a blank template that can be used by his assistant to enter the biweekly enrollment data. Each time this worksheet is retrieved it will contain a blank entry template with the macro commands. His assistant will save the worksheet with the data entered in it using a different file name each time. Therefore the template will always be blank.

Creating an Autoexecute Macro

The final change Fred wants to make to the worksheet is to have the \D macro automatically begin execution as soon as the file is retrieved. This is called an **autoexecute macro**. To do this a special macro name is used, \0 (zero). Only one macro in a worksheet can be named \0. To make the \D macro to an autoexecute macro,

Select: / Range Name Create **\0** ⏎ **B25** ⏎

This macro is now named both \D and \0. Before testing the macro execution, with the cell pointer in cell A1, save your revised worksheet using the file name ENROLL.

Fred has the enrollment data for the first two weeks in October. He will use this data to demonstrate to his assistant how to use the template.

Retrieve the file ENROLL.

The data entry macro automatically began execution and the cell pointer is positioned in cell B7.

Enter the following data:

	Family	Single	Student	Junior	Senior
Donna	3	5	2	0	0
Pete	2	1	0	3	1
Sue	4	2	0	0	0

If you made an error when entering the data, either rerun the entire macro using \D or edit the cell containing the error.

To print the report and save the worksheet as OCT1,

Press: ALT - F3
Select: \PRINT
Type: OCT1
Press: ⏎

By using the template named ENROLL and saving the completed report using a new file name, the template will always be retrieved with empty cells in the worksheet space for entry of the new data.

It is also good procedure when creating a template for others to use to include documentation within the worksheet. Many templates use the HOME position in the worksheet for this documentation. It should include:

Template identification   Information such as the name of the template, who designed it, the date it was last revised, and a contact person for assistance if problems occur.

Template purpose   Should briefly describe what information is needed to complete the template and what output is generated from the template.

Template instructions   Should briefly discuss steps for completing the template, such as the names of any macros that need to be used and what they do, how to move to different areas of the worksheet, and how to interrupt a macro.

Template procedures   Should describe how to name and save the report file so that the original template is not destroyed.

Figure 5-22 shows an example of template documentation.

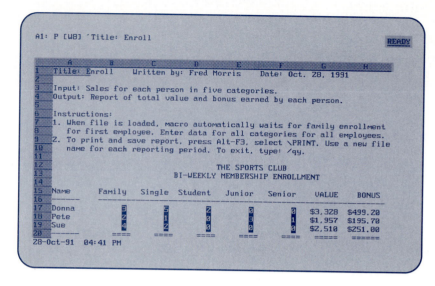

FIGURE 5-22

Always make a backup copy of the original template in case it is accidentally erased, overwritten, or lost.

Quit 1-2-3.

Key Terms

logical operators	debug
template	syntax error
macro	logic error
keystroke instruction	repetition factor
key name	learn range
interactive macro	autoexecute macro

Matching

1. / R N L L
2. / R N T
3. <=
4. {?}
5. ~
6. {Up 5}
7. \0
8. Alt-S
9. / W G P E
10. '/

____ a. less than or equal to
____ b. enters the / character as a label in a cell
____ c. creates a table of range names
____ d. the range name for an autoexecute macro
____ e. invokes the macro named \S
____ f. enables worksheet protection
____ g. allows user input during a macro
____ h. assigns labels to the left of the cell pointer position as range names
____ i. moves cell pointer up 5 cells
____ j. macro command for ⏎

Practice Exercises

1. The DMAB Publishing Company pays its book salespeople a base salary plus a bonus based upon an annual quota of $500,000 of sales. You will create a worksheet to be used as a template to calculate the annual salary of these employees. Set up the worksheet as if there were only 5 book salespeople, using the following information:

The base salary and annual sales for the 5 employees are:

Employee	Base Salary	Sales
A	39958	625211
B	26500	265479
C	23400	525863
D	32650	341982
E	21985	456989

The company uses two methods to calculate the bonus. The first method awards $3,000 to all salespeople who achieve 90 percent of the quota, but do not reach quota, The second method is used for all employees who achieve quota. They earn a bonus of 3 percent on the $500,000 quota minimuim plus 5 percent on the amount of sales over quota. If a salesperson does not fit either category, no bonus is paid.

- Create a worksheet calculating the bonus earned for the five employees. You should have 6 column heads: Employee, Base Salary, Sales, Annual Bonus (1), Annual Bonus (2), Total Salary.
- Enter the percents earned that determine the bonus and the quota amount as cell values. Enter descriptive labels to identify the cell values. For example:

Quota	500000
Achieve	3%
Over	5%

- Name these ranges using the Range Name Labels command. Use the named ranges in the formulas.
- Enter the formula for Annual Bonus (1) to calculate the bonus earned by salespeople that achieve quota. The formula for Annual Bonus (2) will calculate the bonus earned if the employee met 90% of quota (but less than quota).
- Enter the formula to calculate the total salary.
- Format the display of the worksheet.
- Enter a title for the worksheet. Put your name in cell A1 and the current date in cell A2.
- Save the worksheet as QUOTA.
- Print the worksheet.

2. Begin this problem with a blank worksheet. You will create a macro following the steps below.

- In cell C12 enter the macro command to move the cell pointer to cell A1.
- In cell C13 enter the macro command to enter the phrase "This was typed by a macro" into cell A1.

- Name the macro \N.
- Execute the macro. If necessary debug and reexecute the macro until it works correctly.
- In cell C14 enter the macro command to increase the width of column A to 26 spaces.
- Execute the macro. If necessary debug and reexecute the macro until it works correctly.
- In cell C15 enter the macro command to move down one cell (to cell A2) and enter your name in cell A2.
- In cell C16 enter the macro command to move to cell A3, format the cell to display a date as MM/DD/YY, and enter the current date into cell A3 using the date function.
- Execute the macro. If necessary debug and reexecute the macro until it works correctly.
- In cell C17 enter the macro to copy your name in cell A2 to cells A4..A10 using highlighting.
- Execute the macro. If necessary debug and reexecute the macro until it works correctly.
- Edit the macro so that your name is displayed right-aligned in the cell space.
- Edit the macro so that it is more efficient. (Hint: eliminate the unnecessary tildes (~).)
- Execute the macro. If necessary debug and re-execute the macro until it works correctly.
- Save the worksheet as [YOURNAME].
- Print the entire worksheet.

3. Begin this problem with a blank worksheet. You will create a macro using the Learn feature following the steps below.

- Specify a learn range as C12..C25

Turn on the Learn feature and perform the following:

- Move the cell pointer to cell A1 and enter the label "This was typed by a macro."
- Increase the width of column A to 26 spaces.
- Move down one cell (to cell A2) and enter your name (right-aligned) in cell A2.
- Move to cell A3, format the cell to display a date as MM/DD/YY, and enter the current date into cell A3 using the date function.
- Copy your name in cell A2 to cells A4..A10.

Turn off the Learn feature and do the following:

- Erase the contents of cells A1 through A10. Set the width of column A back to 9.
- If you made mistakes while using the Learn feature to record your keystrokes, edit the macro.

- Name the macro and run it again.
- If necessary debug and reexecute the macro until it works correctly.
- Save the worksheet as LEARN.
- Print the entire worksheet.

4. Retrieve the file ADVISING.WK1. This is a blank template used by the college advising office to track the flow of students. The worksheet row headings list the four main categories of advising. The academic advisors maintain a daily checksheet of the number of students they advise and the reason for the appointment. Each month the checksheets are totaled and the values entered into this template.

The advising coordinator wants to improve the worksheet by creating several macros which will automate the process of entering the data.

- Each month the blank template needs to be copied to allow entry of the next month's data. Create a macro to the right of the worksheet that will copy the blank template for January (cells A5 through G15) to rows A19 through G27. Assume the cell pointer is on cell A6 when you begin the Copy command. Use pointing. The month heading for February is already entered in the worksheet. Name and document the macro.
- Use this macro again to copy the template to allow entry for data for March. Enter the March month heading.
- The second macro will assist in the entry of the data to complete each month's report. Write a macro that will move the cell pointer and pause for user entry of data. Assume that the cell pointer is positioned on the first category to be entered before the macro is executed. Name and document the macro.
- Use the macro to enter data of your choice for January and February.
- Enter your name in cell A1 and the current date in cell A2.
- Write a macro to save and replace the worksheet using the same file name. Execute and document the macro.
- Print the entire worksheet.

5. In this problem you will create 12 very common and handy macros. These macros can be copied into other worksheets using the / File Combine command. This saves having to recreate the same macros each time you create a new worksheet. The file containing your frequently used macros is called a macro library.

To begin this problem, retrieve the file named LIBRARY. This file contains data in columns A, B, and C that you will use to test the macros as your create them. A duplicate set of data is available beginning in cell A40. This is provided as a backup in case your macro damages the data in rows 1 through 20 as you are testing the macros.

You will use column D to display the macro name, column E to contain the macro commands, and column F to display a description of each macro. You will enter the first macro in cell E1. Remember to leave a blank cell between each macro.

- Enter a macro to name a macro in cell E1. Assume the cell pointer is on the first cell in the macro to be named. Name it \N. You will test this macro by using it to name the next macro you will create. Use this macro to name all the other macros you will create.

- Enter a macro beginning in cell E3 to move the cell pointer to cell A1 and enter your name in that cell. Name this macro \Y using the \N macro. Execute the macro. Debug and edit if necessary.

- Enter a macro in cell E6 to format a cell to display a date as MM/DD/YY and enter the current date using the date function. Name it \D. Test the macro by moving to cell A2 and executing the macro.

- Write a macro beginning in cell E9 that will change the column width. Use the interactive macro key {?} to allow you to enter the new width setting. Test the macro by changing the column width of column B to 4 and column E to 14.

- Many macro commands can be open-ended. This means the macro begins the command sequence, and the user finishes the command by completing a range or specifying information at the prompt. The Copy command can be used in this manner. Enter a macro in cell E11 that will copy the contents of the cell that the cell pointer is on. Leave it open-ended so that the range to copy TO can vary. Test your macro by copying the value in cell A11 to B11..B12.

- Enter a macro in cell E13 to help you fill a cell with a double-ruled line and copy it to a range. Name it \L. Test this macro by moving to cell A13 and executing the macro. Copy the line through cell C13.

- Enter a macro in cell E15 to help you fill a cell with a single ruled line and copy it across a range. Name it \M. Test this macro by moving to cell A15 and executing the macro. Copy the line through cell C15.

- Enter a macro in cell E17 to erase a range. Use the {?} macro command to allow you to specify the range to erase. Name it \E. Test the macro by erasing the contents of cells A17..A18.

- Enter a macro in cell E19 to format a cell to currency with 0 decimal places. Name it \F. Test the macro by formatting the value in cell A19.

- Enter a macro in cell E21 to format a range to currency with 0 decimal places. Name it \R. Test the macro by formatting the values in cells A21..C21.

- Enter a macro in cell E23 to save and replace a file. Name it \S. Test the macro by saving and replacing this file.

- Enter a macro in cell E25 to print an entire worksheet. Since the Print command retains previous settings, such as the range, it is a good idea to clear all previous print settings as part of this macro. The print option to clear settings is Clear All. Include this option in your macro. You will also want the macro to advance the page before you quit the command. Name it \Print. Test this macro by printing your current worksheet.

To use this list of macros in another worksheet, you will want to erase all the test data in the worksheet. Then move the macro commands and documentation so they begin in cell A1. Then you can use the / File Combine command to copy the macros into the current worksheet. For information about this command use the Help system. Check with your instructor before making these changes to your file if you want to use the same file name. Otherwise assign the file a new name when saving it so that the current file remains unchanged on your diskette.

SUMMARY
Lotus 1-2-3
Release 2.2

Glossary of Key Terms

Absolute cell reference: A $ character entered before the column letter or row number (or both) of a cell address in a formula will make the cell address remain the same (absolute) when copied.

Anchor: To freeze the cell pointer in the corner cell of a range when specifying the range using highlighting.

Anchor cell: The beginning cell of a range.

Argument: The data the @function can work on. It can be a number, a cell address, or a range of cells.

Arithmetic operators: Arithmetic signs (+, –, /, *, and ^) entered in a formula that control the arithmetic function to be performed in the formula.

Autoexecute macro: A macro that begins execution as soon as the file is retrieved. It must be named \0.

Bar graph: The data values displayed as a set of evenly spaced bars. Each bar represents a value in the range.

Cell: The space created by the intersection of a vertical column and a horizontal row.

Cell address: The column letter and row number displayed in the control panel that tells the user the current location of the cell pointer in the worksheet.

Cell pointer: A highlighted bar that shows the current cell being used.

Circular reference: A formula in a cell that directly or indirectly references itself.

Column: A vertical block of cells, one cell wide, in the worksheet.

Column width: The number of characters that the cells in a column can display.

Compressed: Printed text that is reduced in size by making the space between lines and letters smaller.

Control panel: The top three lines of the worksheet screen that display cell addresses, cell contents, program prompts, and command menus.

Copy: To duplicate the contents of a cell to other cells.

Date numbers: The integers assigned to the days from January 1, 1900 through December 31, 2099.

Date-and-time indicator: The current date and time maintained by DOS is displayed in the status line.

Debug: To run a macro to locate and correct errors.

Default: Worksheet settings automatically provided by 1-2-3.

Erase: To remove or delete the contents of a cell.

Error message: A message displayed in the status line to tell you the program detects an error or cannot perform a task.

Exploded: The slice of a pie chart is separated slightly from the other slices in the pie.

Format: The appearance or display of numeric values in the worksheet.

Formula: A mathematical expression that yields a numeric value based on the relationship between two or more cells in the worksheet.

Freeze: To hold specified rows or columns (or both) in place on the screen when scrolling.

@function: A set of built-in formulas that performs a calculation automatically.

Global: Settings that affect the entire worksheet.

Graph: The visual representation of data in a worksheet.

Graph file: A file containing the picture image of the graph used to print the graph. It has a .PIC extension.

Hatch patterns: The crosshatch designs used in bar or pie charts to differentiate the bars or slices when the graph is being viewed with a black and white monitor.

Interactive macro: A macro that temporarily stops to allow the user to enter data.

Justify: To take a long label of text and break it into several lines of text no longer than a specified number of columns.

Key name: Special words or symbols that represent specific keys on the keyboard. They are enclosed in curley braces ({keyname}).

Keystroke instruction: Macro instructions that represent keystrokes.

Label: A cell entry that begins with an alphabetic character or a label prefix character.

Label prefix character: A character that precedes a label and controls the display of the label within the cell space. A label can be displayed flush left, centered, or flush right in the cell.

Learn range: A single-column range where macro commands are recorded when using the Learn feature to enter the macro.

Legend: A brief description of the symbols used in a graph to represent the data ranges.

Line graph: Data represented in a graph as a set of points along a line.

Linking formula: A formula entered in the target file that refers to a cell in the source file, creating a link between two files.

List: An argument used in an @function that could be a cell, a range of cells, a range name, or a combination of these.

Logic error: A macro that is syntactically correct; however, it does not perform the intended task.

Logical operators: Symbols used in formulas that compare values in two or more cells.

Long label: A label entry in a worksheet that extends beyond the width of the cell it is entered in.

Macro: A series of keystrokes and commands that are stored as labels in a worksheet. When the macro is run, the keystrokes and commands are performed automatically.

Main menu: The Lotus 1-2-3 commands displayed in the second line of the control panel when the / key is pressed.

Menu pointer: The highlight bar used to select a command from the command menu.

Minimal recalculation: The recalculation of only the formulas in a worksheet that are affected by a change of data.

Mixed cell reference: A cell address that is part absolute and part relative.

Mode indicator: The condition or state of operation of the program displayed in the upper right-hand corner of the worksheet.

Numeric symbol: Any of the symbols +, -, ., @, (, #, or $ that define an entry as a value.

Pie chart: A graph that compares parts to the whole. Each value in the data range is a wedge of the pie (circle).

Point: To use the cell pointer to define the beginning and ending cells of a range.

Pointer-movement keys: The keyboard keys consisting of (↓), (↑), (→), (←), (HOME), (PGUP), (PGDN), and (TAB), which move the cell pointer around the worksheet.

Prompt: A program message displayed in the control panel which shows that the program is waiting for user input.

Range: A single cell or any rectangular group of adjoining cells in the worksheet.

Relative cell reference: The automatic adjustment of the cell addresses in a formula to its new location in a worksheet when the formula is copied or moved.

Repetition factor: A numerical entry following a macro keystroke instruction that specifies how many times to repeat the keystroke.

Reset: To cancel all graph settings or specified data ranges.

Row: A horizontal block of cells, one cell long, in the worksheet.

Run: To invoke or execute the macro commands.

Scale indicator: The notation that appears next to an axis to clarify the values displayed along the axis.

Scroll: To move more than one screen at a time horizontally or vertically through the worksheet.

Settings sheet: Displays the current settings for the options associated with the command you are using.

Shading values: Values assigned as the B data range in a pie chart that determine the hatch pattern or color for each slice of the pie.

Source cell: The file that supplies the data in a linking formula.

Stacked-bar graph: A graph that displays the data values as bars stacked upon each other.

Start value: The value that begins the range in the Data Fill command.

Status indicator: A message displayed in the bottom line of the screen that tells the user a particular key or program condition is in effect.

Status line: A line located at the bottom of the worksheet screen that displays the date-and-time indicator, status indicators, and error messages.

Step value: The increment between values in the range in the Data Fill command.

Stop value: The upper limit for the sequence of values in the range in the Data Fill command.

Submenu: The commands that are subordinate to the main menu commands.

Synchronized: Simultaneous scrolling of rows or columns in both windows at the same time.

Syntax: The structure or format for entering an @function.

Syntax error: An error that is the result of a technical mistake made when entering a command.

Target file: The file that receives the values from the linking formula.

Template: A prewritten blank worksheet that is used repeatedly to enter data.

Title: A descriptive label used in a graph at the top of the graph and/or along the X axis and Y axis lines.

Unsynchronized: Independent scrolling of rows or columns when there are two windows on the display.

Value: A number (0 to 9) or the result of a formula or an @function.

What-if analysis: A technique used to evaluate the effect of changing certain values in the worksheet to see what effect it has on other values in the worksheet.

Window: The portion of the worksheet that can be seen at any one time on the display screen.

Worksheet: A grid of vertical columns and horizontal rows used to enter and manipulate data.

Worksheet area: The largest area of the worksheet screen, located between the control panel and the status line and used to enter information.

X axis: The horizontal axis of a graph.

Y axis: The vertical axis of a graph.

Functional Summary of Selected Lotus 1-2-3 Commands

Function	Command	Action
Change appearance of the worksheet	/**R**ange **L**abel	Change label alignment
	/**R**ange **F**ormat	Change the appearance of numbers
	/**W**orksheet **G**lobal **L**abel-Prefix	Change alignment of labels for the entire worksheet
	/**W**orksheet **G**lobal **F**ormat	Change the appearance of numbers for the entire worksheet
	/**W**orksheet **G**lobal **C**olumn-Width	Change the column widths for the entire worksheet
	/**W**orksheet **C**olumn **S**et-Width	Change column width for a specified column
	/**W**orksheet **C**olumn **C**olumn-Range **S**et-width	Change the width of a range of columns
	/**C**opy	Copy part of the worksheet to another part
	/**R**ange **F**ormat **T**ext	Display the formulas used in each cell
	/**W**orksheet **C**olumn **Hi**de	Hide a column from view
	/**W**orksheet **I**nsert	Insert blank columns or rows
	/**W**orksheet **T**itles	Freeze rows or columns on the screen
	/**M**ove	Move data from one part of the worksheet to another

SS171
Functional Summary of Selected
Lotus 1-2-3 Commands

Function	Command	Action
Change appearance of the worksheet (*continued*)	/ **R**ange **J**ustify / **W**orksheet **D**elete / **W**orksheet **W**indow	Justify a range of text Delete rows or columns Split the display into two windows
Copying data	/ **C**opy / **F**ile **I**mport / **F**ile **C**ombine	Copy part of the worksheet to another area Incorporate data from a text (ASCII) file Incorporate data from another worksheet file
Erasing data	/ **W**orksheet **D**elete / **F**ile **E**rase / **R**ange **E**rase / **W**orksheet **E**rase	Delete rows or columns Erase a file from diskette Erase a range of the worksheet Erase the entire worksheet
Graphing data	/ **G**raph **O**ptions **L**egend / **G**raph **O**ptions **T**itles / **G**raph **O**ptions **D**ata-Labels / **G**raph **O**ptions **G**rid / **G**raph **O**ptions **S**cale / **G**raph **R**eset / **G**raph **V**iew / **F**ile **L**ist **G**raph / **G**raph **N**ame / **G**raph **X**, **A–F** / **G**raph **G**roup / **G**raph **S**ave / **G**raph **T**ype	Add descriptive legends Add descriptive titles Label individual data points Overlay a horizontal and/or vertical grid on the graph Specify the numeric scale of the X and Y axes Erase all graph settings Display the graph on the screen Display a list of graph (.PIC) files Save the current graph settings for later use Define the data ranges to graph Specifies the X and A-F data ranges in a graph in one step Save the current graph as .PIC file Define the type of graph
Hiding data	/ **W**orksheet **C**olumn **H**ide / **W**orksheet **C**olumn **D**isplay / **R**ange **F**ormat **H**idden	Hide entire column from view Redisplay a hidden column Hide contents of a cell
Loading data	/ **F**ile **I**mport / **F**ile **C**ombine / **F**ile **R**etrieve	Incorporate text (ASCII) file into worksheet Incorporate data from another worksheet Load a worksheet file
Moving data	/ **M**ove / **F**ile **X**tract	Move data to another part of the worksheet Save specified data in a separate worksheet file
Printing your work	/ **P**rint **P**rinter **L**ine / **P**rint **P**rinter **P**age	Advance printer paper one line Advance printer paper to the top of the page

Summary: Lotus 1-2-3

Function	Command	Action
Printing your work (*continued*)	/ **P**rint **P**rinter **G**o	Begin printing
	/ **P**rint **P**rinter **O**ptions	Change printer settings
	/ **P**rint **P**rinter **O**ptions **O**ther **C**ell-Formulas	Print cell formulas instead of cell values
	/ **W**orksheet **C**olumn **H**ide	Hide certain columns
	/ **P**rint **P**rinter **C**lear	Remove current printer settings
	/ **P**rint **F**ile	Send worksheet data to a text (ASCII) file
	/ **P**rint **P**rinter **O**ptions **H**eader/**F**ooter	Set header/footer for printed page
	/ **P**rint **P**rinter **O**ptions **M**argins	Set margins for printed page
	/ **P**rint **P**rinter **A**lign	Set paper to top of page
	/ **P**rint **P**rinter **R**ange	Specify range of the worksheet to print
	PrintGraph Program	Print a graph
Protecting data	/ **F**ile **S**ave P	Assign a password to a worksheet
	/ **W**orksheet **G**lobal **P**rotection **E**nable	Turn on protection facility
	/ **R**ange **P**rotect	Prevent changes to a range of cells
	/ **R**ange **U**nprotect	Remove protection of certain cells
	/ **R**ange **I**nput	Restrict cell pointer to movement among unprotected cells
Saving your work	/ **F**ile **X**tract	Extract and save part of the worksheet
	/ **G**raph **S**ave	Save a graph as a .PIC file for printing
	/ **F**ile **S**ave	Assign a password to the worksheet
	/ **F**ile **S**ave **B**ackup	Save current worksheet and create a backup file with a .BAK extension
	/ **P**rint **F**ile	Save the worksheet as a text (ASCII) file
Working with files	/ **F**ile **L**ist	Display the names of files in the current directory
	/ **W**orksheet **G**lobal **D**efault **U**pdate	Save default settings in 1-2-3 configuration file
	/ **F**ile **D**irectory	Specify directory where 1-2-3 will look for files this session
	/ **W**orksheet **G**lobal **D**efault **D**irectory **U**pdate	Specify directory where 1-2-3 will look for files in future sessions
Miscellaneous	/ **W**orksheet **S**tatus	Display current worksheet settings
	/ **W**orksheet **G**lobal **D**efault **S**tatus	Display configuration settings for printer, current directory, etc.
	/ **Q**uit	Exit 1-2-3

Function	Command	Action
Miscellaneous *(continued)*	/ **W**orksheet **G**lobal **D**efault	Specify configuration settings for printer, current directory, etc.
	/ **W**orksheet **G**lobal **R**ecalculation	Specify how and when to recalculate formulas
	/ **F**ile **A**dmin **L**ink-Refresh	Immediately updates the linked cells in the worksheet files.
	/ **D**ata **F**ill	Fills a range of cells with a sequence of numbers.
	/ **W**orksheet **L**earn **R**ange	Defines range of cells where the macro commands will be recorded when using the Learn feature.

SS173
Functional Summary of Selected
Lotus 1-2-3 Commands

Function Keys

Key	Name	Action
F1	HELP	Displays a 1-2-3 Help screen.
F2	EDIT	Puts 1-2-3 in EDIT mode and displays the contents of the current cell in the control panel.
F3	NAME	Displays a menu of range names.
F4	ABS	Cycles a cell or range address between relative, absolute, and mixed.
F5	GOTO	Moves cell pointer directly to a particular cell.
F6	WINDOW	Moves cell pointer between two windows. Turns off the display of setting sheets (MENU mode only).
F7	QUERY	Repeats most recent /Data Query operation.
F8	TABLE	Repeats most recent /Data Table operation.
F9	CALC	Recalculates all formulas (READY mode only). Converts formula to its value (VALUE and EDIT modes).
F10	GRAPH	Draws a graph using current graph settings.
ALT - F1	COMPOSE	When used with alphanumeric keys, creates characters you cannot enter directly from the keyboard.
ALT - F2	STEP	Turns on STEP mode, which executes macros one step at a time for the purpose of debugging.
ALT - F3	RUN	Displays a menu of named ranges in the worksheet so you can select the name of a macro to run.
ALT - F4	UNDO	Cancels any changes made to the worksheet since 1-2-3 was last in READY mode. Press again to redo changes.
ALT - F5	LEARN	Turns Learn feature on and records keystrokes in the learn range. Press again to turn off the Learn feature.
ALT - F7	APP1	Activates add-in program assigned to key, if any.
ALT - F8	APP2	Activates add-in program assigned to key, if any.
ALT - F9	APP3	Activates add-in program assigned to key, if any.
ALT - F10	APP4	Activates add-in program assigned to key, if any, or displays /Add-In meu if there is no add-in assigned to keys.

INDEX

Absolute cell address:
    defined, SS4
    and range names, SS138
    using, SS82-85
Addition, in worksheets, SS31
Address, cell:
    absolute, SS4, SS82-85
    defined, SS7
    mixed, SS83
    range name used in place of, SS138
    relative, SS5, SS49
    typing, SS31
Analysis, what-if:
    defined, SS5
    using, SS79-82
Apostrophe, for flush left labels, SS16, SS17, SS18
Arguments:
    in @functions, SS51-52
    in @IF functions, SS139-40
Arithmetic operators, SS4, SS31
Arrow keys, SS8
Asterisks, displayed in cells, SS57
@functions:
    arguments in, SS51-52
    copying, SS52-53
    correcting errors in, SS51
    defined, SS51
    entering, SS51-53
    @IF, SS139-40
    @NOW, SS91
    statistical, SS50
    @SUM, SS51
    types of, SS51
Autoexecute macros, SS160-62
Automatic recalculation, SS4
Axes on graphs:
    defined, SS104
    labeling, SS106-7, SS112-13

Backslash (\):
    in macro names, SS145
    to repeat characters, SS62-63
Bar graphs:
    creating, SS115
    crosshatching designs on, SS117-18
    entering legends on, SS117-18
    multiple ranges for, SS116
    stacked-bar graphs, SS118-19
Booting up, SS6-7
Braces for macros key names, SS142

Canceling command selection, SS27
Capital letters for labels, SS19
Caret for centering labels, SS16
Cell addresses:
    absolute, SS4, SS82-85, SS139
    defined, SS7

mixed, SS83
    range names used in place of, SS138
    relative, SS5, SS49
    typing, SS31
Cell pointer, SS7, SS13
Cells:
    asterisks displayed in, SS57
    defined, SS4, SS7
    editing entries in, SS17-22
    protecting, SS159-60
    work, SS80
Character repeat label prefix, SS61-63
Charts, pie, SS120-21
Circular references:
    defined, SS4
    locating and correcting, SS69-72
Color, viewing graphs in, SS116
Columns:
    defined, SS4, SS7
    deleting, SS64
    entering labels for, SS13-16
    freezing, SS72-75
    inserting, SS63-64
    letter labels for, SS11
    widths, changing, SS54-57
Command macros, SS153-59
Commands:
    canceling, SS27
    Copy, SS42-45, SS170, SS171
    for copying data, SS171
    Erase, SS53-54
    for erasing data, SS171
    File, SS26
    File List, SS33
    File Retrieve, SS34
    File Save, SS33, SS126
    Graph, SS104-6
    for graphing data, SS171
    for hiding data, SS171
    Justify, SS92
    for loading data, SS171
    for moving data, SS171-72
    Print, SS35, SS65, SS94
    for printing, SS172
    for protecting data, SS172
    Quit, SS36
    Range, SS54
    Range Erase, SS54, SS160
    Range Format Date, SS91
    Range Format Percent, SS78
    Range Justify, SS92
    Range Name, SS135-39, SS145, SS160
    Range Unprotect, SS159
    for saving, SS172
    summary of, SS170-73
    Worksheet Column, SS54
    Worksheet Erase, SS34
    Worksheet Global Column-Width, SS56-58

Worksheet Global Format, SS57
Worksheet Global Protection Enable, SS159
Worksheet Insert Column, SS63
Worksheet Insert Row, SS61
Worksheet Status, SS71
Worksheet Titles, SS72-74
Worksheet Window, SS75-77, SS80
Compressed printing, SS94-95
Control panel, SS7
Copy command, SS42-45, SS171
Copying:
    @functions, SS52-53
    commands for, SS171
    defined, SS4
    underline, SS62-63
    values, SS43-45
Currency format, SS58

Data, specifying for graphs, SS107
Date, entering, SS90-92
Debugging macros, SS147-49
Deleting. See Erasing
Displaying:
    filenames, SS26
    graphs, SS108, SS116
    negative values, SS58
    percents, SS77-79
Division in worksheets, SS31
Documentation:
    for macros, SS152
    for templates, SS161
Dollar sign in formulas, SS82-83

EDIT mode, SS17, SS19
Editing:
    cell entries, SS17-22
    labels, SS17-22
    macros, SS147-49
Electronic spreadsheets:
    advantages of using, SS3-4
    defined, SS3
    terminology for, SS4-5, SS167-70
Entering:
    @functions, SS51-53
    date, SS90-92
    formulas, SS31-32, SS48-50
    graph titles, SS108-12
    labels, SS13-16
    labels for X axis, SS106
    legends on graphs, SS117-18
    macros, SS143-45
    system date, SS90-92
    titles on graphs, SS108-13
    titles for worksheets, SS22-23
    values, SS29-30
Erase command, SS53-54
Erasing:
    columns, SS64

Index

commands for, SS171
   a range, SS54, SS160
   worksheets, SS34
Errors, correcting:
   in @functions, SS51
   circular references, SS69-72
   in command selection, SS25
   logic, SS148-49
   in macros, SS147-49
   syntax, SS148-49
Executing macros, SS141
Exponentiation in worksheets, SS31

File command, SS26
File List command, SS33
File Retrieve command, SS34
File Save command, SS33, SS126
Filenames:
   displaying, SS26
   .PIC extension, SS114
   writing over, SS65
Files:
   picture, SS114
   printing, SS65
   replacing, SS64-65
   retrieving, SS26-29
   saving, SS64-65, SS114, SS147
Formatting:
   as currency, SS58
   defined, SS4
   as percents, SS77-79
   values, SS57-60
Formulas:
   absolute cell address in, SS82-85
   defined, SS4, SS31
   entering, SS31-32, SS48-50
   for percents, SS77-79
   types of, SS31
Freezing:
   defined, SS5
   titles, SS72-75
Function keys:
   (F1) (Help), SS25
   (F2) (Edit), SS17
   (F5) (GOTO), SS11
Functions, @:
   defined, SS5
   entering, SS51-53
   @IF, SS139-40
   @NOW, SS91
   @SUM, SS51
   types of, SS51

Global commands. *See* Worksheet commands
GOTO key ((F5)), SS11
Graph command, SS104-6
Graphics adapter card, SS108
Graphs:
   adapter card, for displaying, SS108
   for analysis, SS4
   axes on, SS100, SS106-7, SS112-13
   bar, SS115-18
   canceling settings, SS120
   commands for creating, SS171

creating, SS101-27
   crosshatching designs on, SS117-18
   data for, specifying, SS107
   defined, SS5
   displaying, SS108, SS116
   labeling the axes, SS106-7, SS112-13
   legends, entering, SS117-18
   line, SS104-14
   multiple ranges for, SS116
   naming settings, SS113-14
   options for, SS109
   pie charts, SS120-21
   printing, SS127-29
   recalling, SS125-26
   saving, for printing, SS114
   selecting type of, SS104-6
   specifying data for, SS107
   stacked-bar, SS118-19
   titles on, SS104, SS108-13
   types of, SS103
   viewing, in color, SS116

Hardware:
   color monitor, SS116
   graphics adapter card, SS108
HELP mode, SS25
Help system:
   accessing with (F1), SS25
   using, SS25-26
Hiding data, commands for, SS171
Highlighting, SS45-48
Home position, SS8-9, SS24

@IF function, SS139-40
Inserting:
   columns, SS63-6
   rows, SS61
Interactive worksheets, SS141

Justify command, SS92
Justifying:
   defined, SS5
   text, SS92-94

Key names in macros:
   entering, SS143-44
   errors in, SS147
   repetition factor in, SS150-52
Keys:
   arrow, SS8
   backslash (\), SS62-63, SS145
   (CAPS LOCK), SS19
   in EDIT mode, SS17
   (END), SS10, SS24
   (ESC), SS27, SS52
   GOTO, SS11
   (HOME), SS8-9, SS24
   (INS), SS18, SS20
   for moving around worksheets, SS13
   (PGUP) and (PGDN), SS10
   (SCROLL LOCK), SS12
   slash (/), SS22
   See also Function keys; Key names
Keystroke instructions in macros, SS142

Label prefix characters, SS16, SS17
Labels:
   defined, SS5, SS14
   editing, SS17-22
   entering, SS13-16
   position in cells, SS16
   for X axis on graphs, SS106
   See also Titles
Learn feature, using, SS153-59
Legends on graphs:
   defined, SS104
   entering, SS117-18
Line graphs:
   entering titles, SS108-13
   labeling the X axis, SS106-7
   specifying, SS100-1
   specifying data for, SS107
List in @functions, SS51
Loading data, commands for, SS171
Loading Lotus 1-2-3, SS6-7
Logic errors in macros, SS147-49
Logical operators, SS139-40
Lotus 1-2-3:
   loading, SS6-7
   maximum size of worksheet, SS9
   quitting, SS36

Macros:
   autoexecute, SS160-62
   automating with, SS134-66
   command, SS146-47
   creating, SS134, SS146-47
   debugging, SS147
   documenting, SS152
   editing, SS147-49
   entering, SS143-45
   errors in, SS147-49
   executing, SS141
   interactive, SS141, SS144
   key names in, SS142-43
   keystroke instructions in, SS142
   moving, in worksheets, SS152
   naming, SS145-46
   planning, SS142-43
   for printing, SS153-59
   protecting macro cells, SS159-60
   repetition factor in, SS150-52
   testing, SS146-47
Main menu, using, SS23-24
Manual recalculation, SS5
Memos in worksheets, SS92-94
MENU mode, SS22
Menu pointer, SS22
Menu, Main, SS23-25
Mixed cell addresses, SS83
Mode indicator, SS7
Modes:
   defined, SS5
   EDIT, SS17, SS19
   HELP, SS25
   Highlight, SS45
   MENU, SS24
   mode indicator, SS7
   overwrite, SS17, SS19

Index

Modes: (*continued*)
    READY, SS7, SS20
    VALUE, SS29-30
Move command:
    defined, SS5
    to move macros, SS152
Moving data, commands for, SS171-72
Multiplication in worksheets, SS31

Naming:
    graph settings, SS113-14
    macros, SS145-46
    ranges, SS134-39
Negative values, displaying, SS58
@NOW function, SS91
Numeric formats, SS58
Numeric keypad, SS8

Operators:
    arithmetic, SS4, SS31
    logical, SS139-40
Overwriting, to edit, SS17, SS19

Percents, displaying, SS77-79
Picture files, SS114
Pie charts, SS120-25
Pointing ranges
    for copying, SS46-48
    for printing, SS65
Print command, SS35, SS65, SS94
PrintGraph program, SS127-28
Printing:
    commands for, SS172
    compressed, SS94-95
    files, SS65
    graphs, SS127-29
    macros for, SS153-59
    ranges for, SS35, SS65, SS94
    saving graphs for, SS114
    worksheets, SS35-37, SS65
Prompts, defined, SS12
Protecting cells, SS159-60, SS172

Question mark, in macros, SS144
Quitting, SS36

Range command, SS54
Range Erase command, SS54, SS160
Range Format Date command, SS91
Range Format Percent command, SS78
Range Justify command, SS92
Range Name command, SS135-39, SS145, SS160
Range Name table, SS138-39
Range Unprotect command, SS159
Ranges:
    for copying values, SS44-45
    defined, SS5
    erasing, SS54, SS160
    formatting as percents, SS77-79

justifying, SS92-94
moving, SS152
multiple, for graphs, SS116
naming, SS134-39
pointing, SS46-49
for printing, SS35, SS65, SS94
protecting, SS150-60
unprotecting, SS160
READY mode, SS7, SS20
Recalculation:
    automatic, SS4
    manual, SS5
References, circular:
    defined, SS4
    locating and correcting, SS69-72
Relative cell addressing, SS5, SS49
Repeating characters, SS61-63
Repetition factor in macros, SS150-52
Replacing files, SS64-65
Retrieving files, SS26-29
Rows:
    defined, SS5, SS7
    freezing, SS72-75
    inserting, SS61

Saving:
    commands for, SS172
    files, SS64-65, SS114, SS147
    graph settings, SS113-14
    graphs for printing, SS119
    macros for, SS157-58
    worksheets, SS33-35, SS126-27
    worksheets with graph settings, SS126-27
Screens, split, SS76-77, SS80
Scroll Lock, SS12
Scrolling:
    defined, SS10
    with (SCROLL LOCK), SS12
    synchronized, SS77
    unsynchronized, SS77
    windows, SS75-77
Slash key (/), SS22
Spreadsheets. *See* Worksheets
Stacked-bar graphs, SS118-19
Status indicator, SS10
Status window, displaying, SS71
Subtraction in worksheets, SS31
@SUM function, SS51
Synchronized scrolling, SS77
Syntax errors in macros, SS148-49
System date, entering, SS86-89

Templates for data entry:
    creating, SS141, SS160-61
    documenting, SS161
Terminology for worksheets, SS4-5, SS167-70
Testing macros, SS146-47
Text, justifying, SS92-94
Tilde (~) as macro key name, SS142

Titles:
    entering on worksheets, SS21
    freezing, SS72-75
    on graphs, SS104, SS108-13
    longer than cell, SS22
    See also Labels

Underlining headings, SS61-63
Unprotecting cells, SS160
Unsynchronized scrolling, SS77

VALUE mode, SS29-30
Values:
    copying, SS43-45
    defined, SS5, SS14
    entering, SS29-30
    formatting, SS57-60
    negative, displaying, SS58
    percent, displaying, SS77-79
    See also Formulas

What-if analysis:
    defined, SS5
    using, SS79-82
Windows:
    defined, SS9
    moving around in, SS9-10
    scrolling, SS75-77
    split-screen, SS76-77, SS80
    status, displaying, SS71
Work cells, using, SS80
Worksheet Column command, SS54
Worksheet Erase command, SS34
Worksheet Global Column-Width command, SS56-SS58
Worksheet Global Format command, SS57
Worksheet Global Protection Enable command, SS159
Worksheet Insert Column command, SS63
Worksheet Insert Row command, SS61
Worksheet Status command, SS71
Worksheet Titles command, SS72-74
Worksheet Window command, SS75-77, SS80
Worksheets:
    advantages of using, SS3-4
    autoexecuting, SS160-61
    automating, SS134-66
    defined, SS3, SS7
    erasing, SS34
    interactive, SS141, SS144
    macros in, SS134-66
    maximum size of, SS9
    memos in, SS92-94
    moving around, SS8-13
    printing, SS35-37, SS65
    printing compressed, SS94-95
    protecting cells in, SS159-60, SS172
    saving, SS33-35, SS126-27
    saving, with graph settings, SS126-27
    terminology for, SS4-5, SS167-70

dBASE III PLUS

Copyright © 1990 by McGraw-Hill, Inc. All rights reserved. Printed in the United States of America. Except as permitted under the United States Copyright Act of 1976, no part of this publication may be reproduced or distributed in any form or by any means, or stored in a database or retrieval system, without the prior written permission of the publisher.

      6 7 8 9 0   KGP KGP   9 5 4 3 2 1

P/N 047884-8

ORDER INFORMATION:
ISBN 0-07-047884-8

dBASE III PLUS is a registered trademark of Ashton-Tate.
IBM, IBM PC, and PC DOS are registered trademarks of International Business Machines Corp.

CONTENTS

Overview Database DB3
Definition of Database DB3
Advantages of Using a Database DB4
Database Terminology DB4
Case Study for Labs 1–4 DB5

Lab 1 Creating a Database DB6
Loading dBASE III PLUS DB7
Using the Dot Prompt DB8
Using the Assistant DB9
Defining the Database File Structure DB12
Creating Field Names DB16
Inputting Records DB23
Appending Records to the Database DB30
Printing the Database DB31
Quitting dBASE III PLUS DB33
Key Terms DB33
Matching DB33
Practice Exercises DB34

Lab 2 Modifying, Editing, and Viewing a Database DB37
Opening a Database File DB37
Modifying the Database Structure DB39
Browsing the Database Records DB42
Editing Database Records DB49
Marking Records for Deletion DB50
Positioning the Record Pointer DB51
Displaying Database Records DB59
Recalling Records Marked for Deletion DB61
Listing Database Records DB61
Removing Records Marked for Deletion DB62
Printing Selected Records DB62
Key Terms DB64
Matching DB64
Practice Exercises DB64

Lab 3 Sorting, Indexing, and Summarizing Data DB67
Displaying a Disk Directory DB67
Displaying the File Structure DB68
Sorting the Database Records DB70
Creating a Multilevel Sort File DB73
Creating an Index File DB76
Opening Index Files DB80
Using the Seek Command DB82
Using the Dot Prompt DB84
Summarizing Data DB86
Printing a Simple Report DB88
Key Terms DB89
Matching DB90
Practice Exercises DB90

Lab 4 Creating a Professional Report DB92
Examining the Report Screen DB92
Entering the Report Title DB95
Specifying the Report Column DB97
Viewing the Report DB103
Modifying the Report DB104
Creating Subtotals DB112
Printing the Report DB115
Key Terms DB118
Matching DB118
Practice Exercises DB118

Summary dBASE III PLUS DB122
Glossary of Key Terms DB122
Functional Summary of Selected dBASE III PLUS Commands DB124

Index DB125

OVERVIEW
Database

A word processor helps you enter and manipulate text. An electronic spreadsheet helps you enter and analyze numerical data. A computerized database helps you enter and manage information or data in record format.

Databases have been in existence for many years. Paper records organized in a filing cabinet by name or department are a database. The information in a telephone book, organized alphabetically, is a database. The records maintained by a school of teachers, classes, and students is a database.

Before computers, most database records were kept on paper. With computers, the same data is entered and stored on a diskette. The big difference is that an electronic database can manipulate—sort, analyze, and display—the data quickly and efficiently. What took hours of time to pull from the paper files can be extracted in a matter of seconds using a computerized database.

Definition of a Database

A **database** is an organized collection of related data that is stored in a file. The data is entered as a record which consists of several fields of data. Each record contains the same fields. For example, a school has a database of student records. Each record may contain the following fields of data: name, address, social security number, phone number, classes, and grades. All the records for each student in the school are stored in a single file.

Some **database** programs only access and manipulate the data in a single file. Others allow the user to access and relate several files at one time. For example, the school may have a second database file containing data for each student's current class schedule. At the end of the semester the grades are posted in this file for each student. The data in one file can then be merged into the other file by using a common field, such as the student's name, to link the two files.

The database program contains commands that allow the user to design the structure of the database records and enter the data for each record into the file. This is the physical storage of the data. How this data is retrieved, organized, and manipulated is the conceptual use of the data.

Advantages of Using a Database

A computerized database system does not save time by making the data quicker to enter. This, as in most programs, is a function of the typing speed of the user and his or her knowledge of the program.

One of the main advantages to using a computerized database system is the speed of locating the records, updating and adding records to the file, and organizing the records to meet varying needs.

Once data is entered into the database file, the data can be located very quickly by record number or field data. In a manual system, usually a record can be located by knowing one key piece of information. For example, if the records are organized by last name, to find a record you must know the last name. In a computerized database, even if the records were organized by last name, the record could still be located without knowing the last name. Any other field, such as address or social security number, could be used to locate the record. Because specific records can be located quickly, the data in the fields can easily be edited and updated.

A second advantage to a computerized database system is its ability to arrange the records in the file according to different fields of data. The records can be organized by name, department, pay, class, or whatever else is needed at a particular time. This ability to produce multiple file arrangements helps provide information in a more meaningful manner. The same records can provide information to different departments for different purposes.

A third advantage is the ability to perform calculations on different fields of data. Instead of pulling each record from a filing cabinet, recording the piece of data you want to use, and then calculating a total for the field, you can simply have the database program sum all the values in the specified field. It can even selectively use in the calculation only those records meeting certain requirements. Information that was once costly and time-consuming to get is now quickly and readily available.

Finally, a database program can produce either very simple or complex professional-looking reports. A simple report can be created by asking for a listing of specified fields of data and restricting the listing to records meeting specified conditions. A more complex professional report can be created using the same restrictions or conditions as the simple report. But the data can be displayed in columnar format, with titles, headings, subtotals, and totals.

In manual systems, there are often several files containing some of the same data. A computerized database system can allow access by more than one department to the same data. Common updating of the data can be done by any department. The elimination of duplicate information saves space and time.

Database Terminology

Create: The process of defining the database file structure.
Delete: To remove a record from the database file.
Edit: To change or update the data in a field.
Field: A collection of related characters, such as last name.
File: A database of records.
Index: The display of records in a file according to a specified key field.
Record: A collection of related fields, such as class time, class name, or grade.
Report: A listing of specified fields of data for specified records in the file.
Scope: The number of records in a file to be processed by the command.

Search: To locate a specific record in a file.

Sort: To arrange the records in a file in a specified order.

Structure: The attributes (name, type, width) and order of fields in the record.

Type: The content of a field can be Character (alphanumeric), Numeric, Logical, or Date.

Case Study for Labs 1–4

Two separate cases are used in the dBASE III PLUS labs. The first case study demonstrates the basic features of creating, updating, and finding records in a database file. The second case study emphasizes organizing and using records to produce information and reports.

Labs 1 and 2   The Sports Club membership is growing rapidly. Their current method of maintaining membership data consists of a filing system of 3 × 5 index cards. This system was fine when the club was small. But now that the club has grown so much, the system no longer works.

The membership coordinator, Fred Morris, recently purchased dBASE III PLUS. He will use the program to create a database file of member records. We will follow Fred as he creates the database file structure, enters records, and edits, deletes, and locates records in the file. He will also retrieve and print a listing of specified records from the database file.

Labs 3 and 4   In the second case, Donna McIntyre, the assistant manager of the Sports Club, has a dBASE III PLUS file of employee records. We will follow Donna as she organizes the records in the file using sorting and indexing. The records are analyzed using the three numeric functions in dBASE III PLUS—Count, Add, and Average. A simple report is produced in Lab 3. Lab 4 deals exclusively with the Report Generation program of dBASE III PLUS. First a report is created listing all employees alphabetically, the rate of pay, hours worked, and weekly pay. A second report is produced summarizing the same employee data by job category.

LAB
Creating a Database

1

OBJECTIVES

In this lab you will learn how to:

1. Load dBASE III PLUS.
2. Issue commands at the dot prompt.
3. Use The Assistant to issue commands.
4. Use the Help facility.
5. Define the database structure.
6. Input records to a database.
7. Append records to a database.
8. Use the editing keys.
9. Print the database records.
10. Quit dBASE III PLUS.

CASE STUDY

Fred Morris is the membership coordinator for the Sports Club. One of Fred's responsibilities is to keep track of all the club's membership records. Currently, this information is stored on 3 × 5 note cards like the one shown below.

```
Account No:    1001
Membership Date:   May 21, 1983
First Name:   Edward
Last Name:   Becker
Street:   1036 W. 5th Place
City:   Mesa
State:   AZ
Zipcode:   85205
Age:   45
Auto Payment:   Yes
```

This system was fine when the club was small. Now, however, the club is much larger, and Fred is having problems with this manual database system.

To automate the membership records, Fred has purchased dBASE III PLUS. We will follow him as he learns how to use dBASE III PLUS to create a membership database, insert records, and print the database.

Loading dBASE III PLUS

Load DOS and respond to the date and time prompts. The A> should appear on the display screen. Remove the DOS diskette from drive A.
    Place the dBASE III PLUS Sampler Disk 1 in drive A. To start the dBASE III PLUS program, in upper- or lowercase letters,

Type: **DBASE**
Press: ⏎

After a few moments your display screen should look similar to Figure 1-1.

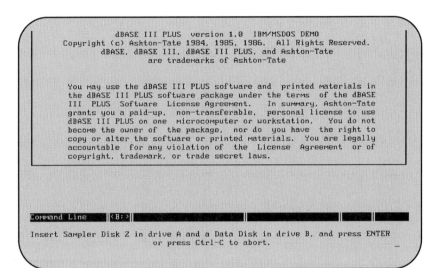

FIGURE 1-1

This screen discusses the license agreement to using the dBASE III PLUS program. Following the instructions at the bottom of the screen, remove the sample Disk 1 from drive A and insert the sampler Disk 2 in drive A. Your data diskette should be in drive B.

Your display screen should look similar to Figure 1-2.

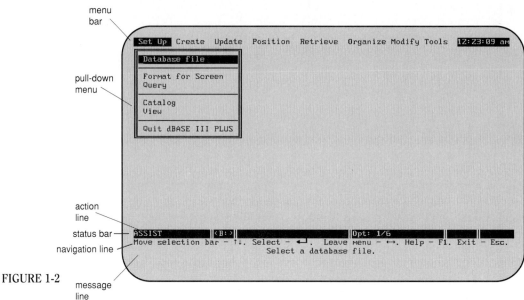

FIGURE 1-2

This is The Assistant. **The Assistant** is a collection of menus that help you perform dBASE III PLUS commands and operations. There are two ways to issue commands in dBASE III PLUS. One way is to use The Assistant to select and build the commands. The other way is to use the dot prompt to directly enter the commands.

Using the Dot Prompt

To leave The Assistant and display the dot prompt,

Press: (ESC)

Your display screen should be similar to Figure 1-3.

FIGURE 1-3

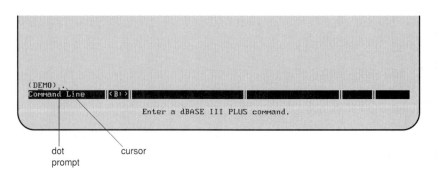

The Assistant has been replaced by a nearly blank display screen. Near the bottom of the screen, immediately following "(DEMO)", is the **dot prompt** (a period) followed by a blinking cursor.

dBASE III PLUS commands are entered following the dot prompt. The cursor shows you where the next character you type will appear as you enter the command. For example, the dBASE III PLUS dot command "Assist" will return you to The Assistant from the dot prompt.

To issue this command, in either upper- or lowercase letters,

Type: ASSIST
Press: ⏎

Note: If an error message appears on your display screen, you probably made an error entering the command. Press (ESC) and type the command again.

You should be returned to The Assistant. Your display screen should be similar once again to Figure 1-2.

Many experienced dBASE III PLUS users prefer using the dot prompt to issue commands. After you have completed these labs, you may also find it quicker to use the dot prompt to issue many commands.

However, the Assistant eliminates many typing and other kinds of potential errors. Beginners (as well as many more experienced users) find that The Assistant is a very effective means of issuing commands. Next we will learn how to use The Assistant to issue dBASE III PLUS commands. Throughout this series of labs we will use The Assistant rather than the dot prompt to issue most commands.

Using the Assistant

The Assistant is a menu-driven tool used to issue dBASE III PLUS commands. As selections are made from The Assistant menu, the dBASE III PLUS dot command is created and displayed.

The top line of the screen, beginning with "Set Up" and ending with "Tools," is called the **menu bar.** It lists the eight **menus** that can be opened.

Directly below the menu bar is a box containing a **pull-down menu** of options that are available for selection.

At the bottom of the screen there are four lines of information: the action line (currently blank), the status bar, the navigation line, and the message line.

We will be discussing in detail the different areas of The Assistant screen as we use them throughout the lab.

The **menu highlight bar,** currently over "Set Up" in the menu bar, allows you to select and open a menu. The current open menu is Set Up.

The pull-down menu lists the six menu **options** associated with the open Set Up Menu that can be selected. Within the pull-down menu, the **selection bar** is currently highlighting "Database file". Notice that the **message line** (the last line on the screen) displays a brief description of the highlighted menu option.

The ⬅ and ➡ keys, located on the numeric keypad, are used to select and open a menu from the menu bar. Watch your display screen as you

Press:

Your display screen should be similar to Figure 1-4.

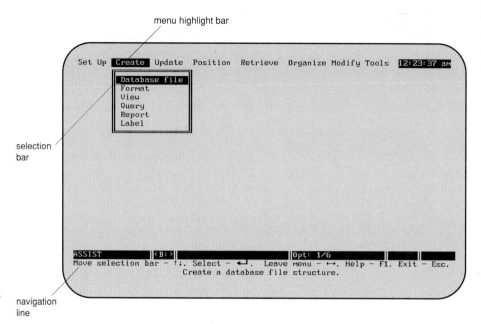

FIGURE 1-4

The menu highlight bar is now positioned over "Create" and a new pull-down menu appears in a box below the open menu. This box displays the six menu options that are associated with the open Create Menu.

Each time → is pressed, the menu highlight bar moves to the right to open the next menu. The pull down menu of options associated with the highlighted (open) menu is displayed. To open the other six menus and see the associated pull-down menu of options, slowly

Press: → (6 times)

The menu highlight bar should be positioned over "Tools". To move quickly back to the beginning of the menu bar, watch your display screen as you

Press: →

The menu highlight bar wraps around to the beginning of the menu bar. It should be positioned over "Set Up" again.

The menu highlight bar can also move to the left through the menu by using ←. Watch your display screen as you

Press: ← (4 times)

The highlight bar moves one menu to the left each time ← is pressed. It should be positioned over "Retrieve".

The (HOME) and (END) keys can be used to move the menu highlight bar to the first menu, Set Up, or to the last menu, Tools, from any location in the menu bar. To demonstrate,

Press: (HOME)

The menu highlight bar moved quickly to Set Up when (HOME) was pressed.

Press: (END)

Although we were at the beginning of the menu when (END) was pressed, using the (END) key will take you to Tools from any location in the menu bar.

To quickly move the menu highlight bar to open a specific menu, the first letter of the menu name can be typed. To quickly move back to Create,

Type: C

The Create Menu is open. The selection bar is positioned over the Database file option in the pull-down menu.

Instructions on how to move the selection bar are given in the **navigation line** (second line from the bottom of the screen). It tells you that the selection bar is moved by using the (↑) and (↓) keys. (The ↑↓ displayed in the navigation line represents the (↑) and (↓) keys.)

To move the selection bar to the Format option,

Press: (↓)

Your display screen should be similar to Figure 1-5.

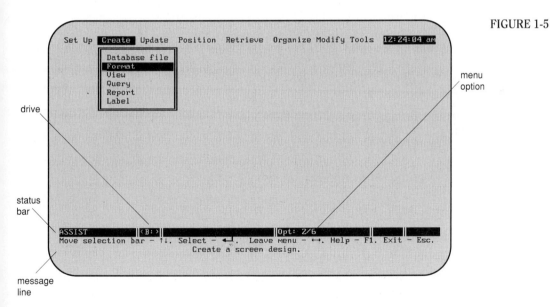

FIGURE 1-5

The selection bar is positioned over the Format option. The message line briefly tells you that this option will let you "Create a screen design".

Notice that the information in the status bar (highlighted bar at the bottom of the screen) has changed. The **status bar** is divided into six areas. It tells you where you are in the menu and the state of various optional settings. As the settings change, the information displayed in the boxes changes.

Right now the first box in the status bar tells you that you are using The Assistant. The second box displays the drive you are using. The third box is blank until a file is in use, at which time it will display the filename. The fourth box displays "Opt: 2/6". The highlighted option, Format, is the second (2) of six (6) options available. Each time the selection bar moves, the option number changes. The last two boxes are blank. They will display the status of the (INS), (CAPS LOCK), and (NUM LOCK) keys when they are on.

Note the changes in the message line and the status bar as you

Press: ⬇ (slowly, 5 times)

The selection bar moved down through the options and back up to "Database file". It wrapped around through the options in a manner similar to the movement of the menu highlight bar.

To move the selection bar quickly to the last option in a pull-down menu,

Press: ⬆

Like the menu highlight bar, the selection bar can move in either direction through the options and wraps around its menu. Unlike the menu highlight bar, however, the selection bar cannot be moved by typing the first letter of the desired option name.

Defining the Database File Structure

Now that you are familiar with how to move the menu highlight bar and the selection bar, we will follow Fred as he defines the structure for the database.

A database file consists of rows (records) and columns (fields) of information. A **field** is a collection of related characters, such as a person's name. The column titles are called **field names.** A **record** is a collection of related fields, such as a person's name, address, and phone number.

Fred's first step is to do a little planning. Fred decides that each member will be represented as a record in his database. Each member's record will consist of the same 10 pieces of information that are currently stored on 3 × 5 index cards. The 10 fields will be:

    Account Number
    Membership Date
    First Name
    Last Name
    Street
    City
    State
    Zipcode
    Age
    Fee Payment Method—Automatic Payment

Once the fields are determined, the database structure can be defined. A database file is created and the fields are defined using the Create Database file command.

The Create Menu should be open, and if the selection bar is not already on the Database file option,

Move to: Database file

Each of the six pull-down menu options in the Create Menu corresponds to a different type of file that can be created in dBASE III PLUS. Although the message line gives you a brief description of each option, more detailed information is provided by pressing the Help ((F1)) key.

With the selection bar on the option you want more information about, in this case Database file,

Press: (F1)

Your display screen should be similar to Figure 1-6.

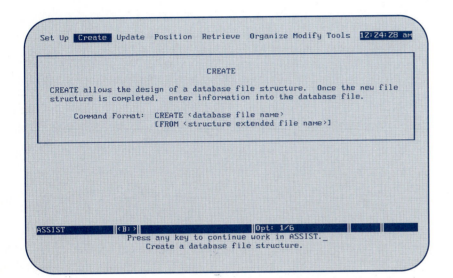

FIGURE 1-6

Information about the Create Database file command and the format for entering this command at the dot prompt are displayed. You can access information about each pull-down menu option from The Assistant screen simply by pressing (F1), Help.

To clear the information and return to The Assistant screen,

Press: any key

For information on how to select a pull-down menu option, refer to the navigation line. First the selection bar is moved to the option you want to use. Following the directions in the navigation line select the option by pressing ⏎. (The ↵ displayed on the navigation line represents the ⏎ key.)

With the menu pointer on Create and the selection bar on Database file,

Press: ⏎

Note: If you accidentally select an incorrect menu option, press (ESC) to cancel the selection and return to the previous selection.

Your display screen should be similar to Figure 1-7.

FIGURE 1-7

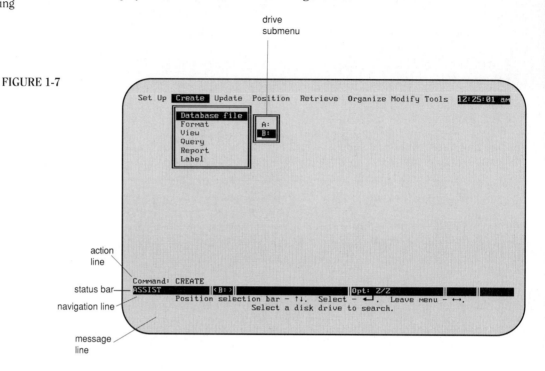

There are several changes on the screen. Now, another box appears displaying a **submenu** of options. The two options, "A:" and "B:", represent the disk drives available. (Your screen may display several more drive selections. The drives presented will reflect your particular system.)

The **action line** (above the status bar) displays the dBASE III PLUS command "CREATE". As pull-down menu and submenu options are selected using The Assistant, the action line will display the dBASE III PLUS dot command as it is being built.

The status bar displays "Opt: 2/2". This means that the selection bar is on the second of two possible submenu options.

The message line provides information concerning the submenu. In this case, we must specify the disk drive where the database file will be saved. The disk drive we want to use to hold the new file is the B drive. (Your system may be different. Consult your instructor if you are not sure of the drive to select.)

To select the B drive, with the selection bar over "B:", following the directions in the navigation line,

Press:

Your display screen should be similar to Figure 1-8.

DB15
Defining the Database File Structure

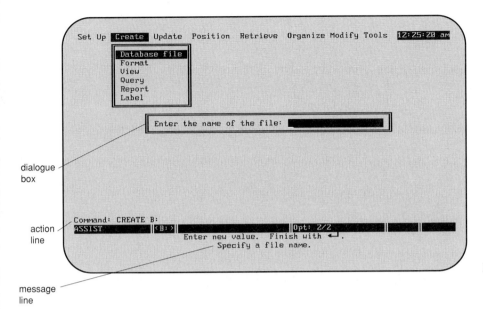

dialogue box

action line

message line

FIGURE 1-8

The action line now shows the dot command "CREATE B:". Another box appears on the display screen. It replaces the drive selection submenu box. This box is called a **dialogue box** because it contains a **prompt**. A prompt is a dBASE III PLUS message that requires a user response. In this case, the dialogue box wants you to "Enter the name of the file:". The message line tells you to specify a filename.

The filename should be descriptive of the contents of the database. It cannot be longer than eight characters. Nor can it include any blank spaces, periods, or special characters. Do not enter a filename extension. dBASE III PLUS automatically assigns a special extension to the filename.

Since Fred's database file will contain information on each club member, he has decided to name the file MEMBERS. In either upper- or lowercase characters,

Type: MEMBERS

If you made an error, use the (Bksp) key to delete the characters back to the error. Then retype the filename correctly. Watch the action line closely to see the complete dBASE III PLUS command as you

Press: ⏎

The complete command in the action line was CREATE B: MEMBERS. If you used the dot prompt to directly enter the command to create a database file, it would be entered exactly as displayed in the action line.

The Assistant, through the use of menu and submenu options, help information, and dialogue boxes, helps the user to build and execute the dBASE III PLUS commands. The actual dot commands are displayed in the action line as the user selects options from the menus.

Your display screen should be similar to Figure 1-9.

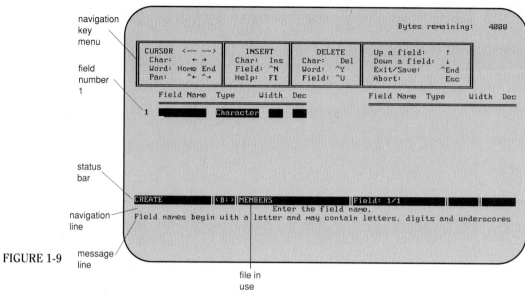

FIGURE 1-9

The Assistant screen has been replaced by the Create screen. This screen is used to define the structure of your database file.

The **navigation key menu** across the top of the screen contains editing and cursor navigation keys to use while in the Create screen.

The central area of the screen contains two identical sets of column headings: Field Name, Type, Width, and Dec (decimal places). These are the four pieces of information that are needed to define each field in the record.

Under the left set of column headings is a highlighted area beginning with the number 1. This is where the first field will be defined.

The first three boxes in the status bar now tell you that the Create Menu is the current menu, the B drive is in use, and the filename is MEMBERS. The fourth box, which used to display the menu option number, now tells you which field the highlight bar is on, "Field: 1/1".

The navigation line tells you that dBASE III PLUS wants you to enter a field name. The message line briefly defines the characteristics of a field name.

Creating Field Names

The first field to be defined is Account Number. The field name needs to be entered first. It should be descriptive of the contents of the field data. It can be up to 10 characters long and may contain letters, digits, and underscores. It cannot contain blank spaces. The blinking underscore or cursor will show where each character will appear as you type.

Fred has decided to use the field name ACCT_NUM. The name can be typed in either upper- or lowercase letters. dBASE III PLUS will display them as all uppercase. An underscore is entered by using the (SHIFT) key and the dash (the key to the right of 0).

Type: ACC_NUM

Fred sees that he has made an error already. He forgot the "T" in "ACCT". Look at the navigation key menu. The "CURSOR" (left) section shows that the ⬅ and ➡ keys will move the cursor character by character. The other three sections of the navigation key menu tell you how to insert and delete characters and fields, how to move between fields, and how to save your work or abort the command.

To correct the entry, we will move the cursor back to the location of the error and retype it correctly as follows:

Press: ⬅ (4 times)
Type: T_NUM

Your display screen should be similar to Figure 1-10.

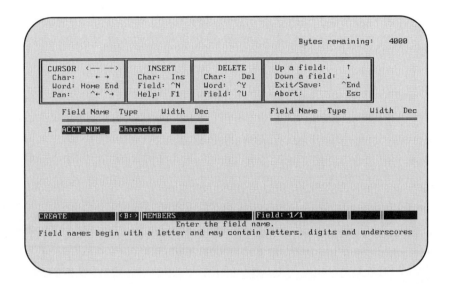

FIGURE 1-10

The new characters typed over the existing letters.

Now that the field name is correct, to indicate you are finished defining the field name,

Press: ⏎

The cursor skips to the Type column and waits for input. The field type, "Character", is already displayed in this space because it is the default setting. There are five **field type** choices:

Character (C) contains any alphanumeric characters (letters, punctuation, numbers that are not used in calculations).

Numeric (N) contains only digits, a decimal point, and a sign. All numbers that will be used in calculations or will be sorted.

Logical (L) contains either a Yes (Y) or No (N) or True (T) or False (F) response.

Date (D) contains a numeric date entry.

Memo (M) contains free-form text.

Although the account number is a numeric entry, no calculations will be made using it. Therefore, Fred decides to define it as a Character field type.

The field type can be selected in two ways. One way is to type the first letter of the field type.

Type: C

(Since "Character" was already displayed, we could also have simply pressed ⏎ to accept the default setting.)

The cursor moves to the next column, Width. **Field width** is the number of spaces needed to hold the largest possible entry into that field.

A Character field can be 1 space to 254 spaces wide as noted in the message line. Logical, Date, and Memo field types are automatically assigned field widths by dBASE III PLUS. A numeric field width must also include the space for the decimal point, the number of decimal places, and the sign.

Fred has determined that the largest account number will occupy four spaces. To specify 4 as the field width,

Type: 4
Press: ⏎

Your display screen should be similar to Figure 1-11.

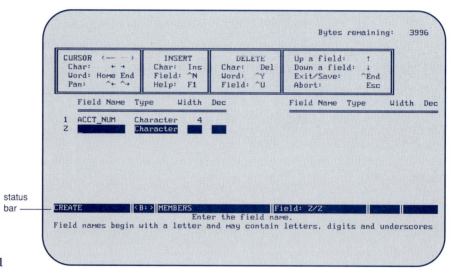

FIGURE 1-11

The cursor skips the Dec (decimal) column because the field type was not defined as numeric. The program waits for you to enter the field name of the second field. Notice that the status bar shows that you are working on the second field of a total of two fields ("Field: 2/2").

The second field is the Membership Date (MEMB_DATE). To enter the second field name,

Type: MEMB_DATE
Press: ⏎

The program is waiting for definition of the field type. This field will display the date the member joined the club in the form of month/day/year. The field type choice which will display the date in this format is Date.

For the last field type specification, we typed the first letter (C for Character) of the field type. An alternative way is to use the space bar to change the default choice. Watch the field type change as you

Press: space bar (5 times)

To set the field type to Date, press the space bar until Date appears, and then,

Press: ⏎

Your display screen should be similar to Figure 1-12.

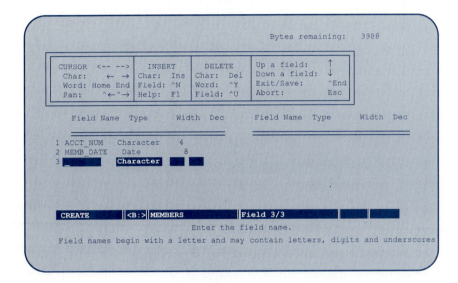

FIGURE 1-12

Notice that the field width for the Date type was automatically entered as eight (mm/dd/yy) spaces by dBASE III PLUS. The program is now waiting for the definition of the third field.

The third field will hold the member's last name. The field name is LAST_NAME. The field type is Character, and the field width is 18 spaces. Complete the third field specifications as follows:

Type: LAST_NAME
Press: ⏎
Press: ⏎
Type: 18
Press: ⏎

The fourth field is FIRST_NAME, Character, 15.

Type: FIRST_NAME

dBASE III PLUS beeped and moved the cursor to the Type column. This occurred because the field name was the maximum length of 10 characters. Whenever a field entry equals the maximum allowable space, the cursor will automatically move to the next column.

Continue defining the field characteristics for FIRST_NAME as follows:

Press: ⏎
Type: 15
Press: ⏎

Your display screen should be similar to Figure 1-13.

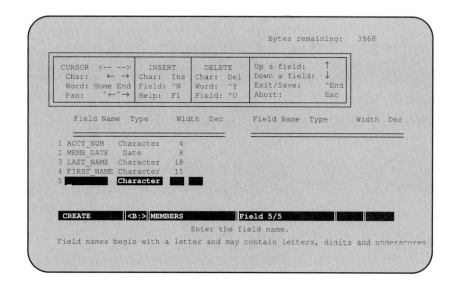

FIGURE 1-13

Enter the information for the next four fields. They are defined as follows:

Field Name	Type	Width	Dec
STREET	C	22	
CITY	C	15	
STATE	C	2	
ZIPCODE	C	5	

You will notice that the field type for ZIPCODE is defined as Character. Again, although this field contains numbers, it will not be used in calculations. Also, by specifying the type as Character, any leading 0s (for example, the zipcode 07739) will be preserved. Leading 0s in a Numeric type field are dropped (which would incorrectly make this zipcode 7739).

When you have completed the four fields, your display screen should be similar to Figure 1-14.

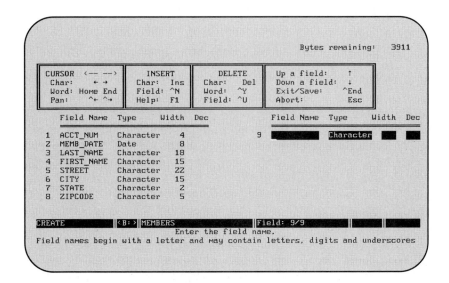

FIGURE 1-14

The cursor has moved over to the right-hand column under Field Name. The program is waiting for you to define the ninth field.

To enter the field information for the ninth field, Age,

Type: AGE
Press: ⏎
Type: N

Numeric is displayed in the Type column. This field is defined as a Numeric type because the data may be used to perform calculations. The cursor skipped to the field width column. The maximum number of spaces needed in this field is two.

Type: 2
Press: ⏎

Since the field type is defined as Numeric, the program is waiting for the Dec column to be defined. The member's age is a whole number. Therefore, we want zero decimal places displayed.

Type: 0
Press: ⏎

Simply pressing ⏎ would also have entered the default decimal place setting of zero.

The last field, 10, will indicate whether the member participates in the automatic fee payment program.

To enter the field name,

Type: AUTO_FEE

Fred decides this is not a good field name for this field. He wants to change it to AUTO_PAYMT. To erase the last three letters, "FEE,"

Press: (Bksp) (3 times)

(Bksp) erases the characters to the left of the cursor.

Type: PAYMT

The AUTO_PAYMT field type is Logical. The data that will be entered in this field is a response to the question "Is the member using the automatic fee payment program?" The answer will be either a true/yes or a false/no entry. Remember, you can either type the first letter of the type (L) or you can use the space bar to display the field types and press ⏎ to select it.

Select: Logical

dBASE III PLUS automatically defines the field width as 1 space for a Logical field type. The data entered in this field is displayed as a single character, T/Y or F/N.

Your display screen should be similar to Figure 1-15.

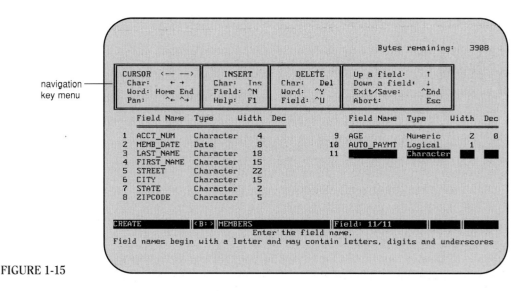

FIGURE 1-15

After looking over the database file structure, Fred decides to increase the STREET field width from 22 to 25 spaces. Again, referring to the navigation key menu, (↑) and (↓) are used to move up or down between fields. To move right one word (END) is used, and to move left one word (HOME) is used.

Press (↑) to move the highlight bar to field 5, STREET.

To move the cursor to the field width column,

Press (END) (2 times)

You can also use ⏎ to move the highlight bar to the next field to the right.

Finally, to change the STREET field width to 25 spaces,

Type: 25
Press: ⏎

Your display screen should be similar to Figure 1-16.

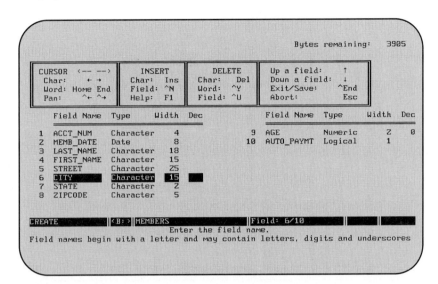

FIGURE 1-16

Carefully check your screen to ensure that all field names, types, and widths match exactly those in Figure 1-16. If your screen does not match, correct it now.

Once you are satisfied that your field entries are correct, the database file structure needs to be saved to the diskette. The navigation key menu shows you that the key sequence to Exit and Save is ^End (the ^ stands for the CTRL key). The CTRL key is held down while pressing the END key.

Press CTRL-END

The navigation line instructs you to press ⏎ to confirm that you want to leave the Create screen. If you wanted to continue in the Create screen, you would press any other key. To leave the Create screen,

Press: ⏎

The drive light goes on briefly, and the structure for your file is saved on the diskette using the filename MEMBERS.

Inputting Records

The next prompt in the action line from dBASE III PLUS is "Input data records now? (Y/N)". You can enter records immediately after specifying the database structure by responding "Yes" (Y) to the prompt. Or you can return to The Assistant by responding "No" (N).

Fred has a meeting to go to in just a few minutes, but he would like to enter a few records before leaving. To enter records, in response to the prompt,

Type: Y

Your display screen should look similar to Figure 1-17.

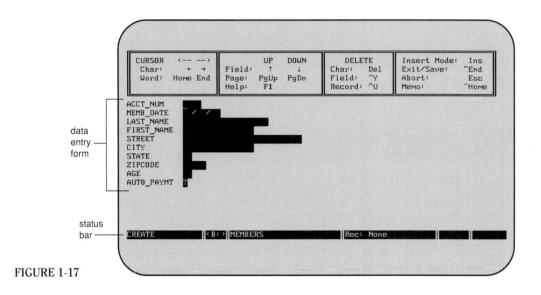

FIGURE 1-17

The main area of the screen displays a blank **data entry** form. It consists of the 10 field names you just defined and a shaded area following each field name. The size of the shaded area corresponds to the width of the field.

The MEMB_DATE field displays slashes (/) to separate the month, day, and year. The AUTO_PAYMT field contains a "?". This means that no response has been entered into this field yet and that the field has been defined as Logical.

The status bar shows "Rec: None". This area of the status bar will display the total number of records in a file and the number of the record that dBASE III PLUS is positioned on.

The data for the first record is:

Field Name	Field Data
ACCT_NUM	1001
MEM_DATE	May 21, 1983
LAST_NAME	Becker
FIRST_NAME	Edward
STREET	1036 West 5th Place
CITY	Mesa
STATE	AZ
ZIPCODE	85205
AGE	45
AUTO_PAYMT	Y

The cursor is positioned to accept entry of the data for the first field, ACCT_NUM.

Type: 1001

dBASE III PLUS beeped and automatically moved the cursor to the next field. The program will do this when the contents of the field fill all the spaces.

Complete the MEMB_DATE field as follows:

Type: 054183

Your display screen should be similar to Figure 1-18.

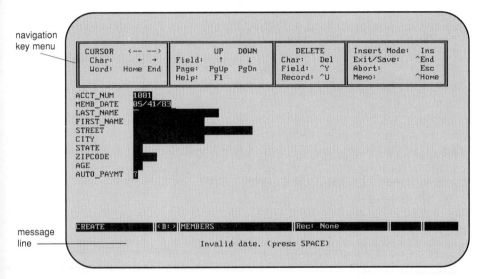

FIGURE 1-18

dBASE III PLUS beeped again. However, this time it did not move the cursor to the next field. Notice the message line. It tells you that this is an invalid date. dBASE III PLUS makes some logic checks on the data entered. In this case, the date entered (05/41/83) could not be correct—no month has 41 days.

To correct the date entry, following the directions in the message line,

Press: space bar

The cursor moves to the beginning of the date field. To correct the date,

Press: ⟶ (2 times)
Type: 2
Press: ⟵

The data you enter in a record must be typed just as you want it to appear. Unlike field names, which are displayed in all uppercase letters (even if you typed the field name in all lowercase characters), the field data you enter for each record is displayed just as you type it. It is very important to be consistent when entering field data. It should be entered the same way for every record. For example, if you decide to use all uppercase characters to enter the LAST_NAME field data, then every record should have the last name entered in all uppercase characters. Also, be careful not to enter a blank space before or after a field entry. This can cause problems when using the database to locate records.

Enter the LAST_NAME data exactly as shown below:

Type: Becker
Press: ⏎

Enter the FIRST_NAME data as follows:

Type: Edward
Press: ⏎

The STREET field is next.

Type: 1026 W 50th Place
Press: ⏎

Fred notices that he entered the address incorrectly. It should be **1036 West 5th Place.**

To correct this entry, we will use several of the cursor-movement and editing keys shown in the navigation key menu.

To move back up to the STREET field,

Press: ↑

First the house number needs to be corrected. To move the cursor under the "2" and change it to a "3",

Press → (2 times)
Type: 3

The "3" replaced the "2" in the house number.

The cursor can move word by word to the right or left by using (HOME) and (END). To position the cursor on the space after the "W",

Press: (END)
Press: →

Next, we want to add the letters "est" to make the word "West". To insert characters into existing text, turn on the Insert mode as follows.

Press: (INS)

The status bar displays the message "Ins" to tell you that this mode is in operation. While Ins is on, characters you type are inserted into existing text. They do not type over the existing text.

Type: est

The characters were inserted into the existing text by moving the existing text to the right to make space.
To turn off the Insert mode,

Press: (INS)

To correct the rest of the street address,

Press: (→) (2 times)
Press: (DEL)

The "0" and the space it occupied are deleted. The (DEL) key deletes the character at the cursor location.
To move to the next field,

Press: (↵)

Enter the data into the CITY field as follows:

Type: Scottsdale
Press: (↵)

Another error. Fred was looking at the wrong record when typing in the city. It should be Mesa. To completely delete the field entry, the (CTRL)-Y key combination is used (hold down (CTRL) while pressing Y).

Press: (↑)
Press: (CTRL)-Y

This editing command deletes all characters from the cursor location to the right. Since the cursor was positioned at the beginning of the entry, the entire entry was deleted. It can be used to delete part of an entry by moving the cursor to the place in the entry where you want everything to the right deleted.

Type: Mesa
Press: (↵)

Enter the data for the remaining fields, typing the information exactly as it appears below. If you make typing errors, practice using the editing keys demonstrated above.

Field Name	Field Data
STATE	AZ
ZIPCODE	85205
AGE	45
AUTO_PAYMT	Y

The data for the first record is now complete. A second blank data entry form is displayed on the screen. The status bar displays the message "EOF/1". This means that the program is currently viewing a blank record at the **E**nd **O**f the **F**ile (EOF) and that there is one record in the file (/1). dBASE III PLUS assigns each record in the file a **record number.** The record number is determined by the order the record is entered into the file. Since this is the first record entered into the file, it is assigned record number 1. The program also keeps track of its location in the file by using a **record pointer.** Only one record can be used or displayed at a time. The record pointer is positioned on the record in use. In this case, the record pointer is positioned on a blank record located at the end of the file.

To review, the cursor-movement and editing keys that we have used are shown below.

Key	Result
⏎	Moves cursor to next field
→	Moves cursor one space forward
←	Moves cursor one space backward
↑	Moves cursor up one field
HOME	Moves cursor one word forward
END	Moves cursor one word backward
DEL	Deletes character at cursor
INS	Turns Insert mode on or off
Bksp	Deletes character left of cursor
CTRL-Y	Deletes all characters from the cursor to the right

Fred has just enough time to enter a second record before going to his meeting. Enter the following data into the second record.

Field Name	Field Data
ACCT_NUM	0683
MEMB_DATE	February 24, 1986
LAST_NAME	Christianson
FIRST_NAME	Phillip
STREET	1766 N. Extension #17-24
CITY	Scottsdale
STATE	AZ
ZIPCODE	85205
AGE	26
AUTO_PAYMT	Y

When you have completed entering the data for the second record, a blank data entry form is displayed on the screen again. The program is ready for input of data for the third record. The status bar displays "EOF/2". This means the record pointer is located at the end of the file on a blank data entry form and there are two records in the file. The second record has been assigned the record number 2.

To view the contents of record number 1,

Press: PGUP (2 times)

Your display screen should be similar to Figure 1-19.

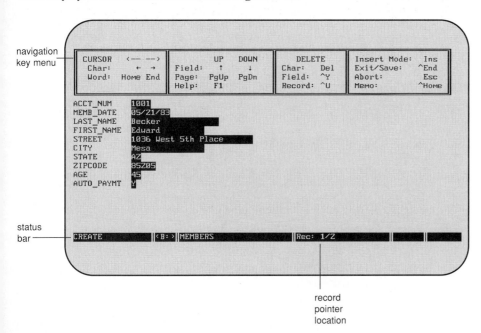

FIGURE 1-19

The membership information for Edward Becker, record number 1, is displayed on the screen. Look at the status bar. It shows that the record pointer is positioned on the first of two records ("Rec: 1/2"). Pressing (PGUP) or (PGDN) will move the record pointer up or down through the records in the file and display the record the pointer is positioned on.

Check your record entries carefully. Edit if necessary.

Fred has to go to his meeting and wants to end the process of adding records to the file. The navigation key menu shows that the command to exit and save is (CTRL)-(END). This is the same key sequence you used to save the file structure to the diskette. Before you use this command, make sure the record pointer is not on a blank data entry form. If it is on a blank data entry form when the records are saved to the diskette using (CTRL)-(END), a blank data entry form will be saved as a record.

Move to any completed record in the database.

To end the process of adding records to the file, to save the last record entered onto the diskette, and to return to The Assistant,

Press: (CTRL)-(END)

Note: You may have noticed that when you moved the record pointer to another record, the drive light went on briefly. By moving to another record, the program automatically saves the last record entered to the diskette.

Another way to end the process of adding records to the file is to simply press (↵) when the record pointer is on the EOF (blank entry form). The blank entry form will not be saved as a record in the file.

If you did not want to save changes made to the current record, press (ESC) to exit.

Appending Records to the Database

Fred left the computer running while he attended his meeting. Now that he has returned from the meeting, he wants to add more records to the MEMBERS database file. To add more records to the end of the database file,

Move to: Update
Select: Append

Your display screen should look similar to Figure 1-20.

FIGURE 1-20

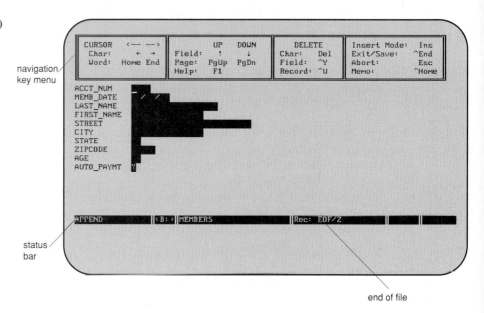

navigation key menu

status bar

end of file

This is the Append screen. It is the same screen we used to enter records immediately after creating and saving the file structure. A blank data entry form is displayed on the screen. The status bar shows that the record pointer is on the end of the file and that there are two records in the file.

The navigation key menu at the top of the screen is the same as the one in the Create screen. It tells you how to move around the screen and edit entries.

Enter the following two records into the database.

Field	Record #3	Record #4
ACCT_NUM	0728	0839
MEMB_DATE	October 10, 1982	March 3, 1984
LAST_NAME	Salvana	Johnson
FIRST_NAME	Lori	William
STREET	2061 Winchester Rd.	1622 E. Donner Dr.
CITY	Apache Junction	Tempe
STATE	AZ	AZ
ZIPCODE	85220	85284
AGE	31	23
AUTO_PAYMT	N	N

After you have inserted records 3 and 4, move to each of the records and check them for accuracy. Edit any entries that are incorrect.

Remember, do not have the record pointer on the end of the file (blank record) when you save and exit the Append screen. If you do, a blank record will be saved to your file.

Press: CTRL-END

You are returned to The Assistant.

Printing the Database

Fred would like to view and print a hard copy of the four records in his file. The Retrieve Menu options let you view and print a database file. The List option will scroll the records in the file on the display screen and will also let you print the records. Using the menu highlight bar and the selection bar,

Select: Retrieve
Select: List

Your display screen should be similar to Figure 1-21.

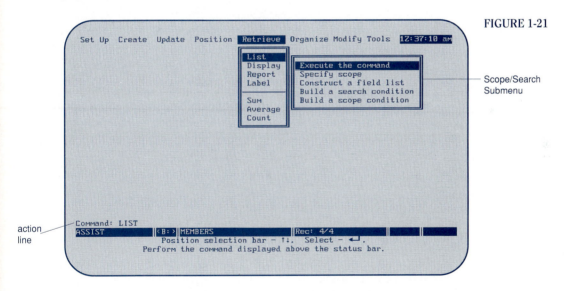

FIGURE 1-21

A new submenu is displayed. It lists options for limiting the **scope** (range or number of records) and specifying conditions for the List command to follow. We will be using and explaining many of the options in the Scope/Search submenu in the next lab.

Notice the dot command in the action line. It is simply "LIST". Watch the action line to see the dot command as you continue the command sequence using The Assistant.

To list all the records and all the fields in each record in the database file (the default setting),

Select: Execute the command

A dialogue box appears containing the prompt "Direct the output to the printer? [Y/N]".

If you have printer capability, make sure the printer is on. To specify that you want the output to be printed,

Type: Y

If you do not have printer capability (or if you simply do not want a printed copy of the records),

Type: N

Regardless of your response to this prompt, you will still see the output on the display screen. Your display screen should be similar to Figure 1-22.

FIGURE 1-22

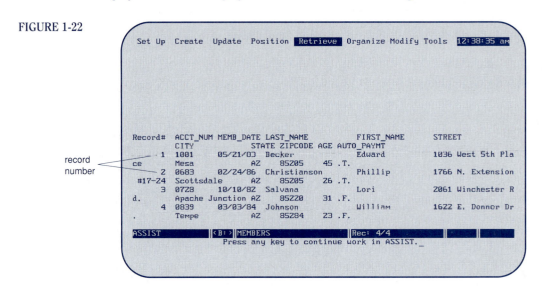

record number

The four records are listed on the display screen and printed if specified. The field names and the contents of each record wrap around to a second line because the record length is too long to fit on one line. This makes reading a listing of records difficult. The next lab will demonstrate other ways of specifying and displaying the contents of a file.

The record number assigned to each record as it was entered into the file is displayed in the first column. Notice that the data entered in the AUTO_PAYMT field is either a T or an F. Even though we entered Y and N, dBASE III PLUS will display the data in a logical field as a T or an F.

To clear the display screen and return to The Assistant,

Press: any key

Notice in the status bar that the record pointer position is now "Rec: EOF/4". After the contents of a file have been listed, the record pointer is placed at the end of the file.

Quitting dBASE III PLUS

We will continue to follow Fred as he builds and uses his database file of membership records in the next lab. The command to end a dBASE III PLUS session is an option in the Set Up Menu.

Select: Set Up

To quit dBASE III PLUS,

Select: Quit dBASE III PLUS

Quit closes all open database files and returns you to the DOS prompt. Always use Quit when ending a dBASE III PLUS session. If you end the session by turning off or rebooting your computer without selecting Quit, you may damage the open database file. This could cause loss of data.

Key Terms

The Assistant	field name
dot prompt	record
menu bar	submenu
menu	action line
pull-down menu	dialogue box
menu highlight bar	prompt
options	navigation key menu
selection bar	field type
message line	field width
navigation line	record number
status bar	record pointer
field	scope

Matching

1. Rec: 4/4
2. Dot prompt
3. Opt: 1/6
4. Create
5. (F1)
6. (CTRL)-(END)
7. Append
8. (CTRL)-Y
9. EOF/12
10. scope

____ a. defines the range or number of records to be used
____ b. record pointer is on the end of the file containing 12 records
____ c. Assistant command to add records
____ d. accesses Help
____ e. deletes characters from cursor to right
____ f. shows location of selection bar
____ g. allows direct entry of command
____ h. exits and saves work to diskette
____ i. record pointer is on record 4 of a total of four records in a file
____ j. Assistant command to enter the file structure

DB34
Creating a Database Using dBASE III PLUS

Practice Exercises

1. Identify the parts of the dBASE III PLUS screen by entering the appropriate letters in the blanks below.

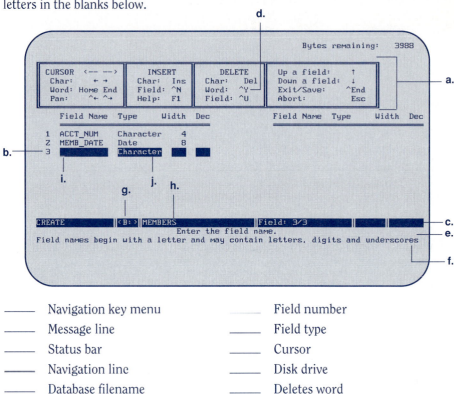

_____ Navigation key menu   _____ Field number
_____ Message line   _____ Field type
_____ Status bar   _____ Cursor
_____ Navigation line   _____ Disk drive
_____ Database filename   _____ Deletes word

2. Susannah owns a small business that sells custom-made ceramic tiles. She currently keeps her client orders and payment records in a small accounting ledger. Her business has grown considerably since she first started it a year ago, and she decided to invest in a computer. She wants to keep track of her client orders and payments using dBASE III PLUS. She has defined the fields as follows:

Field Name	Type	Width	Dec
LAST_NAME	C	12	
FIRST_NAME	C	10	
ADDRESS	C	20	
CITY	C	12	
STATE	C	2	
ZIP	C	5	
PHONE	C	8	
DATE	D		
UNIT_COST	N	5	2
QUANTITY	N	4	
PAID	L		

- Load dBASE III PLUS.
- Create a database file using the field information defined above. Name the file TILES.
- Enter the two records shown below.

Record 1	Record 2
Doyle	Miller
Marilyn	Phillip
298 Winding Way	46 South View
Fairview	Albion
PA	PA
07392	09523
298-1374	468-9238
02-12-89	03-21-89
3.75	4.85
125	75
N	N

- Enter your name and appropriate information as the third record using Append.
- Print a copy of the three records.
- Exit dBASE III PLUS.

3. Joe is a full-time college student. He is in his third full semester of school. He wants to create a database file of all the courses he has taken to date. His fields are:

```
COURSE_NUM   Character  6
TITLE        Character  20
SEMESTER     Character  4
GRADE        Numeric    1
```

The semester is entered as f=fall, sp=spring, followed by the year. The year is entered as "88" for 1988.
The grade is on a 4.00 grading scale with 4=A, 3=B, 2=C, 1=D, 0=F.

- Load dBASE III PLUS.
- Create a database file named SCHOOL using the fields as defined above.
- Enter the data below in numbered order (shown in parenthesis). You will have 10 records. Check your data carefully before saving and exiting.

(1) ENG101
    Freshman English
    F 88
    C

(2) MAT 210
    Calculus
    F 88
    D

(6) ENG102
    Freshman English
    Sp 89
    B

(7) MAT210
    Calculus
    Sp 89
    C

(3) BUS 100
    Intro to Business
    F 88
    B

(4) PSY 100
    Intro to Psychology
    F 88
    B

(5) PED101
    Physical Education
    F88
    A

(8) ACC 120
    Accounting 1
    Sp 89
    B

(9) ART 100
    World Art
    Sp 89
    B

(10) PED102
    Physical Education
    Sp89
    A

For the eleventh record, enter your name in the field TITLE and leave the other fields blank.

- Print a copy of the database records.
- Exit dBASE III PLUS.

4. Lynne is the recording secretary for the Future Entrepreneurs Club. To help keep track of the club members, she decides to create a database to include each member's full name, complete address, home telephone number, and major.

- Load dBASE III PLUS.
- Create a database file named ENTRE.
- Define a record structure appropriate for Lynne's needs using 9 fields.
- Enter your name and appropriate related information in the first record.
- Enter 19 additional records using either real or fictitious data.
- Print a copy of the database records.
- Exit dBASE III PLUS.

LAB 2
Modifying, Editing, and Viewing a Database

CASE STUDY

Fred continued to work on appending records to the database file. After a short period of time, he had 20 records in the file. Before adding more records, he wants to show the club manager a printout of the records in the file. The manager suggests that another field, SEX, may be useful in analysis of the membership records. We will follow Fred as he modifies the database structure to include this new field of data.

Throughout the day Fred receives several notes asking him for information or telling him about changes that need to be made to various member records. Updating records and providing information to other staff members from the membership data is a routine part of his job. We will follow Fred as he locates, edits, adds, and deletes records in the database file.

Finally, he has one last job for the day. The accounting department would like a list of members participating in the automatic fee payment program. Fred will use dBASE III PLUS to produce this list.

OBJECTIVES

In this lab you will learn how to:

1. Open a database file.
2. Modify the database structure.
3. Browse the database records.
4. Edit the database records.
5. Mark records for deletion.
6. Position the record pointer.
7. Display database records.
8. Recall records marked for deletion.
9. List all and selected records.
10. Delete records from the file.
11. Print selected records.

Opening a Database File

Load dBASE III PLUS. Follow the directions in Lab 1 if you are uncertain of the procedure.

Note: Many of the commands in dBASE III PLUS are made of a sequence of selections from The Assistant. The command sequences you are to issue will appear on a single line following the word "Select:". Each command selection will be separated by a slash (/). If the menu item can be selected by typing the first letter of the command, the first letter will appear in boldface. Anything you are to type will also appear in boldface text.

To use or **open** an existing database file,

Select: Set Up / Database file / B:

Your display screen should be similar to Figure 2-1.

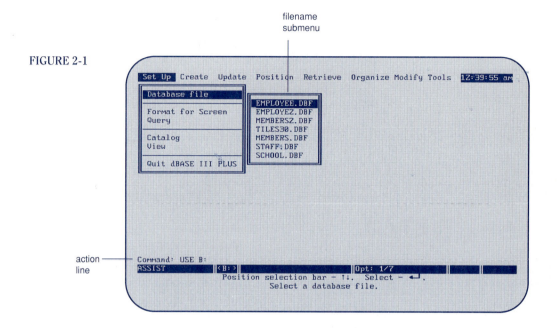

FIGURE 2-1

The names of all the database files on the data diskette are displayed in the submenu. Notice the file extension .DBF following the file names. This extension is automatically added to a database file name by dBASE III PLUS. The extension identifies the file as a database file. The file you created in Lab 1, MEMBERS.DBF, as well as several others we will be using in the next two labs, are listed.

Note: The file names listed on your screen may be different from those in Figure 2-1 depending upon the homework problems you have completed.

The file with 20 member records in it is MEMBERS2.DBF. It is the same as the file MEMBERS.DBF you created in Lab 1, except that it now contains 20 records.

Select: MEMBERS2.DBF

Your display screen should be similar to Figure 2-2.

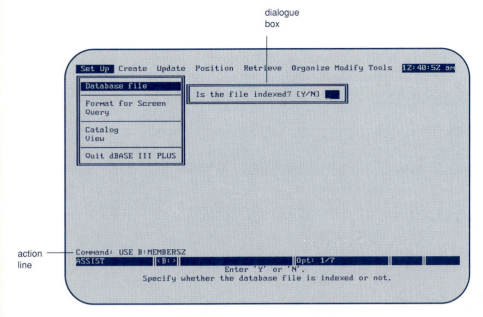

FIGURE 2-2

Notice the command in the action line, "USE B:MEMBERS2". If you used the dot prompt to issue the command to open a database file, the command would be entered exactly as displayed in the action line.

The dialogue box prompt "Is this file Indexed?" is waiting for a response of either Yes (Y) or No (N). We will be explaining file indexing in the next lab. For now the response is No.

You can either type the letter **N** or press ⏎. Pressing ⏎ will respond to the prompt as if **N** had been typed. Whenever a Yes or No response is needed in a dBASE III PLUS command, the default is No.

Type: N (or press ⏎)

After a few seconds the file is read from the diskette and becomes the open database file. The Assistant Menu is available for selections.

The status bar shows that the file MEMBERS2 is open and that the record pointer is on record 1 of 20 (Rec: 1/20). Whenever a file is opened, the record pointer is automatically placed on the first record in the file.

Modifying the Database Structure

First Fred wants to add the new field, SEX, to the database file structure. To change, or **modify,** the structure of a database file, use the Modify Menu.

Move to: Modify

DB40
Modifying, Editing, and Viewing a Database

The six Modify Menu options are displayed. The Modify Menu allows you to edit the structure of a dBASE III PLUS file. The Modify Menu options are the same six options listed under the Create Menu. Any files you create can be modified.

To modify a database file,

Select: Database file

Your display screen should be similar to Figure 2-3.

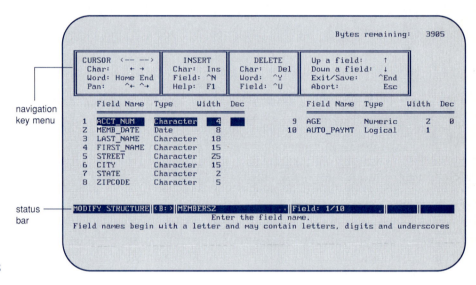

FIGURE 2-3

This screen should be familiar to you. It is the same screen that was displayed when you created the database file structure. The only difference is that it contains the data you entered to define the field structure. However, the status bar shows that the screen form in use is Modify Structure rather than Create.

After looking at the order of the fields, Fred decides that he wants to add the new field, SEX, between the eighth field, ZIPCODE, and the ninth field, AGE. The new field will be field number 9.

To add a new field to the file structure, a blank field line must be inserted into the structure. The navigation key menu displays the command to insert a field. It is ^N ((CTRL)-N).

First move to the location in the structure where you want the field inserted. To quickly move the highlight bar to field 9, AGE,

Press: (CTRL)-(→)

To insert a blank field line,

Press: (CTRL)-N

Your display screen should be similar to Figure 2-4.

DB41
Modifying the Database Structure

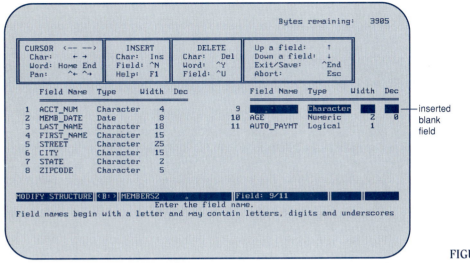

FIGURE 2-4

The AGE field has moved down one line to become field number 10. A blank field line is ready to be defined as field number 9.

Enter the following new field information:

Field name: **SEX**
Type: **C**haracter
Width: **1**

Your display screen should be similar to Figure 2-5.

FIGURE 2-5

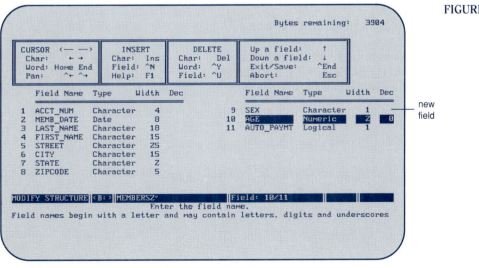

The new field has been added to the database file structure. To exit the Modify Structure screen, to save the structure changes to the diskette, and to return to The Assistant,

Press: `CTRL`-`END`

In response to the prompt, to confirm or save the changes made to the file,

Press: `↵`

The disk drive light goes on briefly as the changes to the file structure are saved on the diskette. Saving the changes to the file structure does two things. dBASE III PLUS creates a new file with the new file structure using the original file name. Then it changes the original file to a backup file using the file extension .BAK. The records that were in the original file are copied into the new file. As the records are copied to the new structure, the progress of the number added is displayed on the bottom of the screen,
    You can modify the structure of your database at any time if you are careful. Sometimes, however, certain changes can cause loss of all data or of data in that field. For example, if you change the field name, do not change its width or type at the same time. If you do, data will be lost. Also, do not delete or insert new fields and change field names at the same time. Data will be lost.

Browsing the Database Records

Next, Fred needs to add the data for the new field, SEX, to the records in the database.

Select: `Update`

The Update Menu has commands that let you display and change information in your database file. Eight submenu options let you add, edit, and delete data and records.
    The Browse command allows full-screen viewing and editing of multiple records in the file. It is especially useful for changing the data in the same field for many records.

Select: `Browse`

Your display screen should be similar to Figure 2-6.

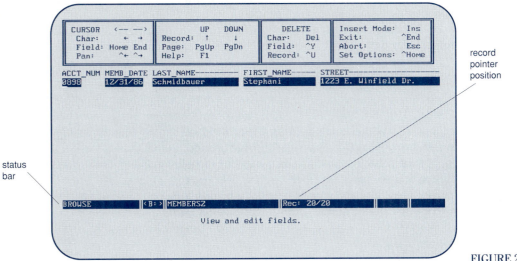

FIGURE 2-6

The status bar shows that we are using the Browse command and that the record pointer is located on record 20, the last record in the file. The data for record 20, Stephani Schmidbauer, is displayed. To display a full screen of records,

Press: (PGUP)

Eleven records are displayed on the screen. Browse displays as many records as possible on a screen. Each record occupies one line. The highlight bar indicates the record pointer location, and the blinking cursor shows your location in that record. The record number is not displayed.

The last field visible on the screen is STREET. To see the fields to the right of STREET, watch your screen closely as you

Press: (CTRL)-(→) (4 times)

Your display screen should be similar to Figure 2-7.

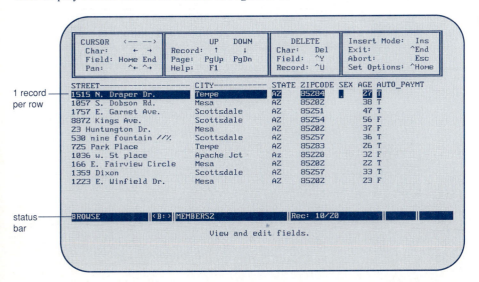

FIGURE 2-7

DB44
Modifying, Editing, and Viewing a Database

The remaining fields are displayed on the screen. However, the fields to the left of STREET are no longer visible. The process of moving right and left to bring a field into view on the screen is called **panning.**

The column of data for the SEX field needs to be entered for each record. The contents for each record can be determined by looking at the member's name.

Press: CTRL ← (2 times)

The LAST_NAME and FIRST_NAME fields are visible on the screen, but the SEX field is not. Whenever the fields in a record extend beyond a single window, reading and knowing what data belongs with which record is difficult.

Fortunately, Browse has its own menu of commands to make it easier to move around and see particular fields. Before displaying this menu, let's make the screen easier to read and allow more records to be displayed on the screen at one time. To do this, turn off the display of the navigation key menu.

Press: F1

Once a menu item has been selected, the F1 key no longer displays a Help screen. It now turns on or off the navigation key menu. To completely fill the screen with records,

Press: PGUP

Seventeen records are displayed on the screen. The highlight bar is positioned on record 1, Becker. The navigation key menu can be turned back on by pressing F1 at any time.

To access the Browse Menu,

Press: F10

Your display screen should be similar to Figure 2-8.

FIGURE 2-8

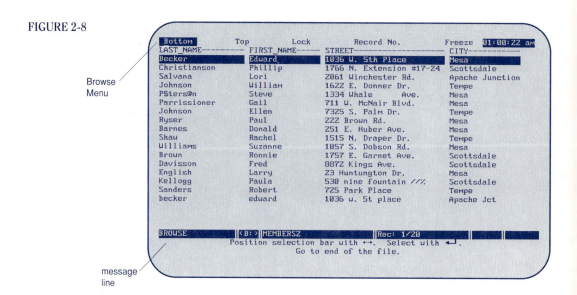

Browse Menu

message line

The Browse menu bar appears at the top of the screen. You can select a menu item by moving the highlight bar to the option and pressing ⏎. Or you can type the first letter of the menu item.

Read the message line as you slowly

Press: → (5 times)

The six menu items have the following effect:

    Bottom   moves cursor to the last record in the file
    Top   moves cursor to the first record in the file
    Lock   stops the scrolling of specified fields
    Record No.   moves cursor to a specified record number
    Freeze   specifies a single field to edit

Fred needs to enter the data for the SEX field to every record. To do this, he needs to be able to see the FIRST_NAME and LAST_NAME fields while entering the data in the SEX field for each member.

To stop the scrolling of, or **lock,** these two fields on the screen when he moves to the SEX field to enter the data,

Select: Lock

A dialogue box appears prompting you to enter the number of columns to lock. Counting from the left side of the screen, LAST_NAME and FIRST_NAME occupy the first two columns. To lock these fields,

Type: 2
Press: ⏎

The Browse menu bar disappears from the screen. Watch your screen carefully as you pan to the right.

Press: CTRL-→ (4 times)

Your display screen should be similar to Figure 2-9.

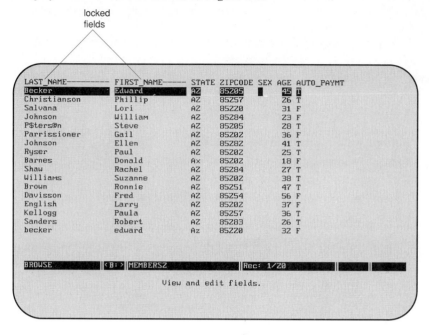

FIGURE 2-9

The two locked fields have remained stationary on the screen while the fields to the right have scrolled into view. The SEX field column can now be viewed at the same time as the name fields.

Fred can now easily look at the FIRST_NAME field data and complete the data for the SEX field.

The Browse Menu option Freeze allows you to restrict, or **freeze,** the movement of the cursor to a single field. To call up the Browse menu bar again and select this option,

Press: F10
Select: Freeze

In response to the prompt in the dialogue box to "Enter the field name to freeze:", in either upper- or lowercase letters,

Type: SEX
Press: ⏎

Your display screen should be similar to Figure 2-10.

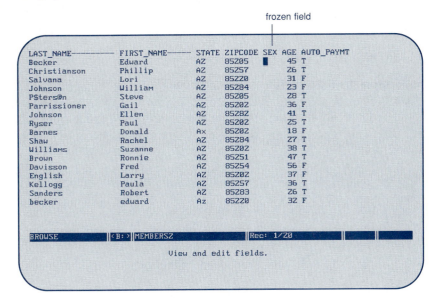

FIGURE 2-10

The cursor jumps to the specified field, SEX. The member in the first record is a male. To enter this data as a capital letter,

Press: CAPS LOCK
Type: M

dBASE III PLUS beeped, the disk drive light went on, and the cursor skipped to the next record.

Continue entering the data for this field, looking at the FIRST_NAME field to determine whether the member is male or female. When you complete the data for the last record displayed on the screen, another record will scroll into view to be edited. This continues until the last record in the database file is displayed.

After entering the sex for the last record, your display screen should be similar to Figure 2-11.

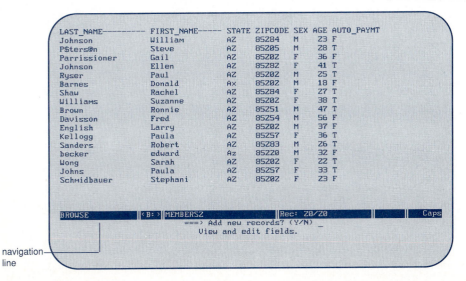

FIGURE 2-11

The prompt in the message line asks "Add new records?". While in Browse, new records can be added to the end of the file. Since we do not need to add any new records at this time,

Type: N (or press ⏎)

Did you notice several errors in the records as you were entering the data in the SEX field? For example, the second record displayed on the screen has several errors in the LAST_NAME. Fred also noticed that he entered the data for Edward Becker twice, as record number 1 and as record number 17. Record 17, however, contains several errors. He figures there are probably several other errors in other fields that are not visible on the screen.

Editing a single field column in Browse is easy. However, editing fields that span more than a single screen display becomes awkward. You have to keep panning the screen. An alternative method of editing data is to use Edit.

Let's leave Browse to use Edit to correct the errors in the other records. First move the record pointer to the top of the file and unfreeze and unlock the fields as follows:

Press: F10
Select: Top

The cursor is positioned on the first record in the file. To unfreeze the SEX field,

Press: F10
Select: Freeze
Press: ⏎

The SEX field is unfrozen. You can now move the cursor to any field.

Unlock the columns in a similar manner.

Press: F10
Select: Lock
Press: ⏎

To verify that the fields are unlocked and unfrozen, pan the screen to the left.

Press: CTRL-← (6 times)

The ACCT_NUM column should be visible on the screen again.

Finally, turn on the display of the navigation key menu and turn off CAPS LOCK as follows:

Press: F1
Press: CAPS LOCK

To save the changes made while using Browse and to return to The Assistant,

Press: CTRL-END

Another method of leaving Browse is to press ESC. However, if the cursor is still on the record you last made changes to, the changes to that record will not be saved.

Editing Database Records

Fred wants to correct the errors and delete the duplicate record in the database file. To do this, he will use the **Edit** command. This is another option in the Update Menu.

Select: Edit

Your display screen should be similar to Figure 2-12.

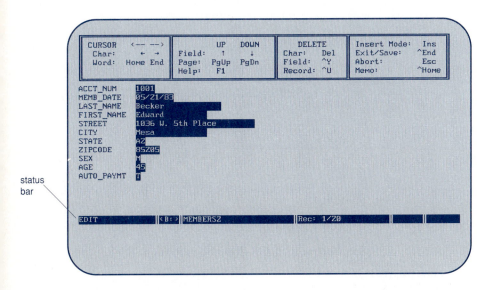

FIGURE 2-12

This screen should look familiar. It is identical to the Append screen. The status bar shows that we are using Edit and that the record pointer is on record number 1. The record displayed by the Edit command will always be the record the record pointer is positioned on at the time the command is issued.

You cannot see more than one record at a time using Edit. But you can see and edit the fields more easily within a record.

To move up and down through the records, the (PGUP) and (PGDN) keys are used.

Move to: Record 5

This is the first record containing several errors. The same editing and cursor-movement keys that are used in Append are used in Edit. They are displayed in the navigation key menu.

Correct the LAST_NAME to **Paterson** and the street to **1334 W. Hale Ave.**

DB50
Modifying, Editing, and Viewing a Database

Your display screen should be similar to Figure 2-13.

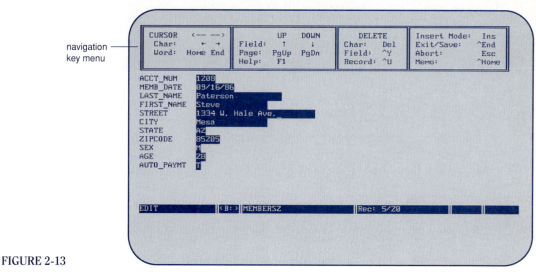

FIGURE 2-13

Examine the other records as you move to records 9 and 15. Make the corrections to the two records shown below:

Record 9   STATE should be **AZ**
Record 15 STREET should be **530 Nine Fountains Dr.**

Marking Records for Deletion

The duplicate record for Becker is record 17. To remove, or **delete,** an entire record from a file is a two-step process. The first step is to mark the record for deletion. The second step is to actually remove the record from the database file.

The navigation key menu shows you that the command to delete a record is ^U ((CTRL)-U). First, the record pointer must be on the record to be deleted.

Move to: Record number 17

When marking a record for deletion, the cursor can be on any field in that record. To mark the record for deletion,

Press: (CTRL)-U

Your display screen should be similar to Figure 2-14.

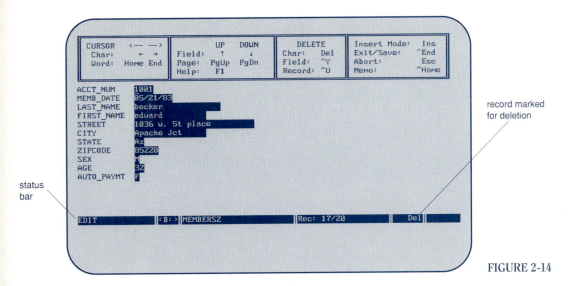

FIGURE 2-14

The status bar displays "Del" to show that this record is marked for deletion. A record can be marked for deletion in the same manner while using Browse and Append.

The "Del" marking can be removed from a record by pressing (CTRL)-U a second time. The record pointer must be on the record marked for deletion.

To save the changes made in Edit and return to The Assistant,

Press: (CTRL)-(END)

Fred has completed the first step in removing a record from a database file by marking it for deletion. The record is still part of the file until the second step, which will actually remove the record from the database file, is completed. The second step is accomplished by using the Pack command in the Update Menu. Before Fred uses the Pack command to actually remove this record from the database file, he has several other changes he wants to make to other database records. They are to:

- Change Ellen Johnson's last name to Foran.
- Delete record 5 for Paul Ryser, who canceled his membership.
- Display record 15 to get address information.

Positioning the Record Pointer

To make the changes to these records, Fred needs to find the specific records in the database file. He could use Edit to move the record pointer to each record. However, that can take a lot of time, especially if the database is large. Instead he will use the dBASE III PLUS Position Menu options to quickly locate a specific record in a database. Once the record is located it can then be updated or displayed.

The first change Fred needs to make is a name change. Ellen Johnson married and her last name changed to Foran. To quickly locate this record,

Select: Position

There are five Position Menu options. Notice that "Seek" and "Continue" are displayed in dimmed letters and that you cannot move the selection bar to those options. In order to use these options, certain other conditions must be met first. "Locate", "Skip", and "Goto Record", however, are available for selection.

The Skip and Goto Record options require that you know the record number. Fred does not know the record number for Ellen Johnson, only her name. However, the Locate option will find a record by searching the database file for specific data in a field that matches the data you specify in the command.

Select: Locate

Your display screen should be similar to Figure 2-15.

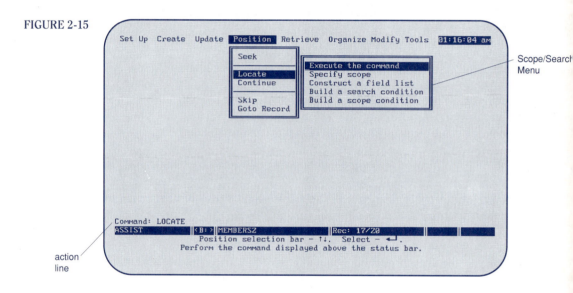

FIGURE 2-15

Five submenu options are displayed which allow you to specify the scope (range) of records in the database to search or the criteria (conditions) to search on. This is the same Scope/Search Menu that was displayed when you used the Retrieve List command in Lab 1.

Fred needs to specify the field content, or **search condition,** for the command to use.

Select: Build a search condition

Your display screen should be similar to Figure 2-16.

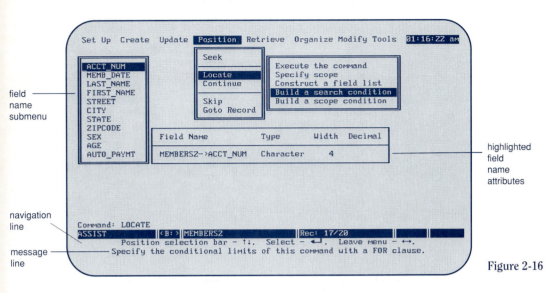

Figure 2-16

The field name submenu on the left lists all the field names in the database. The information box in the center displays the field name and attributes of the highlighted field. The message line asks you to specify the conditional limits of the search condition with a FOR clause.

This may all sound very confusing. However, it is really quite simple. First, the command wants you to select from the field submenu the field name you want to use to locate the record. Then, it wants you to enter the specific data within the selected field that you want the program to find in the database file. Fred wants to locate the record using the field LAST_NAME. To select a field name, following the directions in the navigation line, move the selection bar with ⬆ and ⬇ and press ⏎.

Select: LAST_NAME

Your display screen should be similar to Figure 2-17.

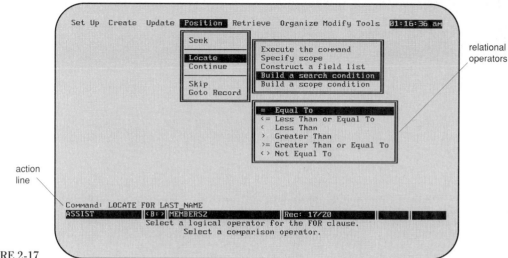

FIGURE 2-17

Another submenu appears displaying six **relational operators.** Relational operators allow the program to compare character or numeric data in a field to the data specified as part of the command. In this case, Fred wants to search FOR LAST_NAME *equal to* the character string "Johnson".

Select: = Equal To

A dialogue box appears prompting you to enter the condition to search on. The search condition must be a character string because the selected field, LAST_NAME, is defined as a Character type. It must be entered exactly as it appears in the record.

Type: Johnson
Press: ⏎

A submenu of **logical operators** is displayed. This submenu will allow you to specify a second search condition which can be compared to the first condition. To indicate that this is the only field to search on,

Select: No more conditions

The action line displays the completed command as "LOCATE FOR LAST_NAME='Johnson' ". If you were entering this command at the dot prompt, it would be entered exactly as displayed in the action line.
   The Scope/Search Menu is again available for selections. We want dBASE III PLUS to search all records in the database file until it locates a record matching the search condition. Since this is the default scope setting, it is not necessary to select Specify scope from the Scope/Search Menu.

We are now ready to tell the Locate command to begin the search. The selection bar can be moved quickly to the first option or last option in a submenu, using (PGUP) or (PGDN). To move to and select "Execute the command",

Press: (PGUP)
Press: ⏎

Your display screen should be similar to Figure 2-18.

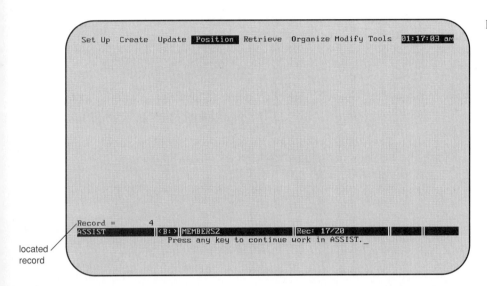

FIGURE 2-18

located record

The first record in the file to exactly match the specified search condition of "LAST_NAME Equal To Johnson" is record number 4. Only the record number is displayed at the bottom of the screen.

Note: If your command did not locate this record, reissue the command and make sure you enter the name Johnson exactly as shown.

To return to The Assistant,

Press: any key

Notice that the record pointer is now positioned on record number 4.
What if there are other records in the database with a last name of Johnson? Notice that the "Continue" option is no longer in dimmed letters, indicating that this option can now be selected. The Continue option can be used to look for the next record that meets the conditions specified in the Locate command.
To continue searching the file to locate the next record that meets the same search conditions,

Select: Continue

The next record meeting the Locate conditions is record number 7. Are there others?

Press: any key
Select: Continue

The screen display shows the message "End of LOCATE scope". This means that all the records in the file have been searched and there are no more records meeting the Locate search condition.

Now Fred knows that record numbers 4 and 7 both have last names of Johnson. How can he find out which is Ellen Johnson? He could go into Edit and look at both records. But that defeats the purpose of using Locate.

What he will do is make his conditions more specific. He will search for both last and first names.

To return to The Assistant,

Press: any key

Select: Locate / Build a search condition / LAST_NAME / = Equal To / **Johnson** ⏎

Reminder: Command sequences that combine several menu selections will appear as written above. The slash (/) separates the menu selections. Letters in boldface are to be typed.

Your display screen should be similar to Figure 2-19.

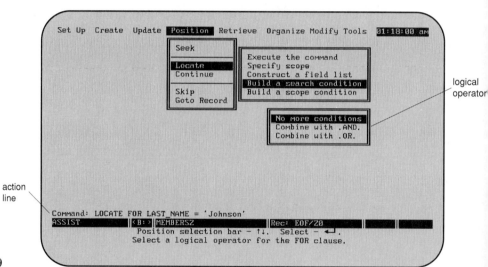

FIGURE 2-19

The submenu of logical operators is displayed. To specify a second search condition, LAST_NAME can be combined with either an AND or an OR to a second condition.

Select: Combine with .AND.

Watch the action line as you continue to build this command.

Select: FIRST_NAME / = Equal To / **Ellen** ⏎ / No more conditions / Execute the command

Record number 7 is displayed on the screen. Since there were only two Johnsons, there is no need to select Continue. The more specific the conditions are in the search, the more accurate and efficient the Locate command can be.

To return to The Assistant,

Press: any key

Notice that the record pointer is on record number 7. To edit this record,

Select: Update / Edit

Ellen Johnson's record is displayed. The Edit option will display the record that the record pointer is currently on.

Change LAST_NAME to **Foran.**

Press: CTRL-END

The second note on Fred's desk asks him to delete record number 5 for Paul Ryser. If the record number is known, then the Goto Record command is the quickest way to position the record pointer.

Select: Position
Select: Goto Record

Your display screen should be similar to Figure 2-20.

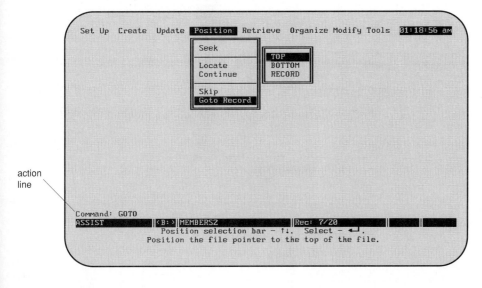

FIGURE 2-20

action line

Your choices are to position the record pointer to the TOP (first record) or BOTTOM (last record) of the file or to a specific RECORD number. We want to move the pointer to record number 5.

Select: RECORD
Type: 5
Press:

The completed command in the action line was "GOTO RECORD 5". This would have been a simple command to enter at the dot prompt.

The status bar indicates that the record pointer is positioned on record 5. Since the record pointer is on the record we want to remove, a quick way to mark that record for deletion is to use the Delete option in the Update Menu.

Select: Update / Delete

The default setting for the Delete command is to mark for deletion the current record, number 5. The Scope/Search Menu is displayed. Since record number 5 is the record we want to delete, we do not need to specify conditions or scope. Using the Delete option is also useful for marking for deletion a number of records with common data in a field. You would do this by specifying scope and search conditions.

Select: Execute the command

The screen shows that one record has been marked for deletion. The command in the action line was simply "DELETE". Many times, using the dot prompt to issue commands is faster.

To return to The Assistant,

Press: any key

The last note on Fred's desk asks for the address of record number 15. Another way to move the record pointer is Skip.

Select: Position / Skip

Your display screen should be similar to Figure 2-21.

FIGURE 2-21

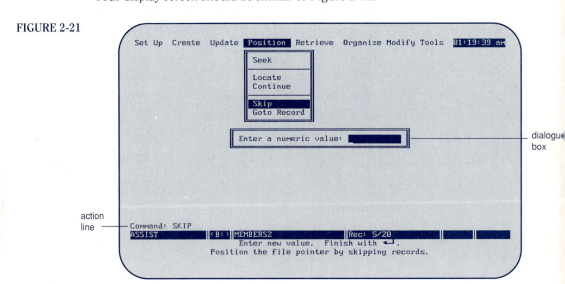

The record pointer is currently on record number 5. Fred wants to move the pointer to record number 15, which is 10 records past the current record pointer location.

In response to the prompt in the dialogue box,

Type: 10
Press: ⏎

The status bar shows that the record pointer is now on record number 15. The command in the action line was "SKIP 10".

Displaying Database Records

Fred does not need to change the data in this record, he just needs to get the address information. He can quickly do this using Display, an option under the Retrieve Menu.

Select: Retrieve / Display

The Scope/Search Menu is displayed again. We do not need to specify a search condition or scope because the default setting for Display is to display the current record.

Select: Execute the command

Your display screen should look similar to Figure 2-22.

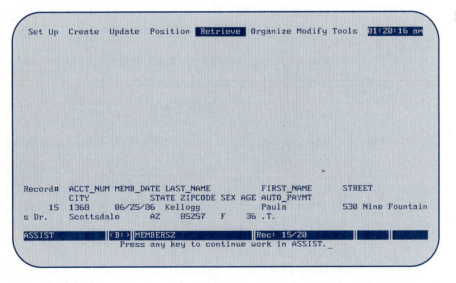

FIGURE 2-22

The data for record 15 is displayed on the screen. Fred can now respond to the request for address information.
To return to The Assistant,

Press: any key

Before Fred uses the Pack command to remove the two records marked for deletion from the file, he would like to see a list of all the records. It is always a good idea to check the records you have marked for deletion before using the Pack command. Once Pack is selected, the records are gone for good.

Select: Display / Specify scope

The options in the Scope submenu allow you to specify how many records in the file will be processed. Move the highlight bar to each of the options. Read the message line for a description of each. The default scope setting for Display is the current record.

To display all the records,

Select: ALL / Execute the command

Your display screen should be similar to Figure 2-23.

FIGURE 2-23

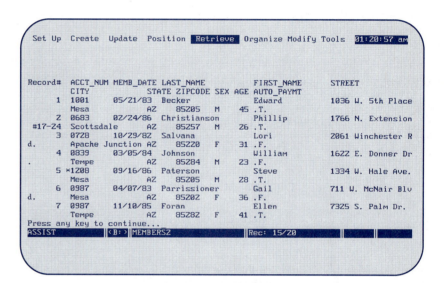

Record numbers 1 through 7 are displayed on the screen. Display automatically pauses the scrolling of the records when the screen is full.

Look at record number 5. The asterisk between record number and the data in the first field shows that this record is marked for deletion. Fred sees, however, that this is the record for Steve Paterson, not Paul Ryser. He must have been given an incorrect record number. There is no need to panic. The delete marking can be easily removed, as we'll demonstrate shortly.

To see the next screenful of records,

Press: any key

The next screenful of records is displayed. The field names appear at the top of each column. Notice that Paul Ryser's record, number 8, is not marked for deletion as it should be.

Press: any key

The last screenful of records is displayed. Note that the duplicate record for Becker, number 17, is correctly marked for deletion.

To return to The Assistant,

Press: any key

After displaying all the records, the record pointer is positioned on the end of the file.

Recalling Records Marked for Deletion

Fortunately Fred had only marked the records for deletion and, as you can see, the records are still in the file.

dBASE III PLUS allows you to easily **recall,** or remove, the delete marking with the Recall option in the Update Menu.

Select: Update / Recall

The Scope/Search Menu is displayed. Since Fred wants to reinstate only one of the two records he has marked for deletion, he needs to specify the record to be recalled.

Select: Specify Scope / Record / 5 ⏎ / Execute the command

The message on the screen tells you that one record has been recalled.

Press: any key

To mark Paul Ryser's record, number 8, for deletion,

Select: Delete / Specify Scope / Record / 8 ⏎ / Execute the command

As you can see, it is always a good idea to check that the correct records are marked for deletion before issuing the Pack command.

Listing Database Records

Since we want to see all the records, we will use the List command to verify that the records for Becker and Ryser are still marked for deletion and that Paterson's record has been recalled,

Press: any key
Select: Retrieve / List / Execute the command / N

The List command quickly scrolls the records in the file without pausing, as the Display command did. If you watched carefully, you could see that the two records marked for deletion were correct and that record 5 was not marked for deletion.

Press: any key

If you missed seeing the marked records, reissue the command and use (CTRL)-**S** to stop the scrolling of the records when the screen is full. Press any key to continue scrolling.

Removing Records Marked for Deletion

Finally, Fred is ready to remove the marked records from the database. The step which actually erases a marked record from the database is Pack.

Select: Update / Pack

The command is executed immediately. The disk drive light goes on while the command is executed, and after a few moments your display screen should be similar to Figure 2-24.

FIGURE 2-24

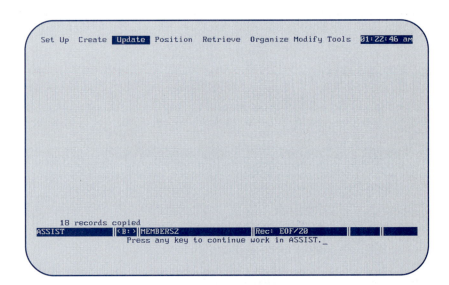

The message displayed, "18 records copied", tells you that the two marked records have been removed from the database. Pack also renumbers the remaining records to fill in the empty spaces left by the deleted records.
    To return to The Assistant,

Press: any key

Printing Selected Records

Fred still has one last thing to do, for the accounting department. He needs to print a list of the records in the database of all members who are using the automatic payment program. To do this,

Select: Retrieve / List / Build a search condition / AUTO_PAYMT

The submenu of relational operators is not displayed. This is because AUTO_PAYMT is a logical field, and dBASE III PLUS assumes you want the true condition.
    To continue the command sequence,

Select: No more conditions / Execute the command

If you have printer capability,

Type: Y

If you do not have printer capability,

Type: N

Your printed output should be similar to Figure 2-25.

FIGURE 2-25

```
RECORD# ACCT_NUM MEMB_DATE LAST_NAME       FIRST NAME   STREET
        CITY              STATE ZIPCODE SEX AGE AUTO_PAYMT
      1 1001     05/21/83  Becker          Edward       1036 W. 5th Place
        Mesa              AZ    85205   M   45  .T.
      2  683     02/24/86  Christianson    Phillip      1766 N. Extension
  #17-24 Scottsdale        AZ    85257   M   26  .T.
      5 1208     09/16/86  Paterson        Steve        1334 W. Hale Ave.
        Mesa              AZ    85205   M   28  .T.
      7  987     11/10/85  Foran           Ellen        7325 S. Palm Dr.
        Tempe             AZ    85282   F   41  .T.
      9  756     08/07/83  Shaw            Rachel       1057 S. Dobson Rd
        Tempe             AZ    85284   F   27  .T.
     10  756     08/07/83  Williams        Suzanne      1057 S. Dobson Rd
        Mesa              AZ    85202   F   38  .T.
     11  755     06/10/84  Brown           Ronnie       1757 E. Garnet Av
  e.    Scottsdale        AZ    85251   M   47  .T.
     14 1368     06/25/86  Kellog          Paula        530 Nine Fountain
  s Dr. Scottsdale        AZ    8527    F   36  .T.
     15  357     02/17/83  Sanders         Robert       725 Parl Place
        Tempe             AZ    85202   F   26  .T.
     16  876     05/28/84  Wong            Sarah        166 E. Fairview
  Circle
        Mesa              AZ    85202   F   22  .T.
     17 1599     07/18/87  Johns           Paula        1359 Dixon
        Scottsdale        AZ    85257   F   33  .T.
```

Only the records whose AUTO_PAYMT field contents are true are listed.

Although the database of member records is far from complete, the sample list will show the accounting department the type of report that dBASE III PLUS is capable of producing.

To return to The Assistant,

Press: any key

To leave dBASE III PLUS,

Select: Set Up / Quit dBASE III PLUS

DB64
Modifying, Editing, and Viewing a Database

Key Terms

open	delete
modify	search condition
panning	relational operators
lock	logical operator
freeze	recall

Matching

1. CTRL-N   ____ a. accesses the Browse Menu
2. F1   ____ b. stops scrolling of records
3. F10   ____ c. unmarks record marked for deletion
4. Freeze   ____ d. identifies record marked for deletion
5. CTRL-→   ____ e. marks record for deletion
6. CTRL-U   ____ f. inserts a blank field line
7. Pack   ____ g. stops display of navigation key menu
8. CTRL-S   ____ h. allows edit of a single field
9. Recall   ____ i. removes records marked for deletion from file
10. *   ____ j. pans screen to right

Practice Exercises

1. This problem requires that you have completed Lab 2 and have modified the file MEMBERS2.DBF as specified in that lab.

   - Edit record 1 by entering your first and last name in the appropriate fields.
   - Print the entire database.
   - Mark records 4, 5 and 15 for deletion, and change Rachael Shaw's age to 28.
   - Print the entire database.
   - Recall record 4.
   - Remove all records that are marked for deletion.
   - Print only those records for male members.
   - Print all records for members whose age is less than 35 and zip code is 85202.

2. Open the database file TILES30.DBF. This file has the same database structure as the file created in Practice Exercise 2 in Lab 1 and saved as TILES.DBF. Susannah continued to enter her clients' information into her database file. It now contains 30 records.

   Edit record 1 by entering your first and last name.
   - Edit the following records:

Record 3   FIRST NAME is Thomas
Record 12 ADDRESS is 8903 W. Longmore
Record 20 CITY is Hightown
Record 25 UNIT_COST is 12.50
Record 28 STATE is PA
Record 29 PAID is True (T)

- While in Edit, mark records 23 and 28 for deletion.
- Use your name and address information as a new record to be added to the database file. Today, you have ordered 56 tiles at a cost of $3.25 each. Your account is not paid.
- Use the Position Menu to Locate the record for Carol King. Display the record. How many tiles were ordered and what was the unit cost?
- Skip eight records. Display this record. What is the quantity ordered for this record?
- Recall record 10.
- Goto Record 24. What is the client's last name?
- List all the records. How many are marked for deletion? What is the total number of records?
- Recall the record marked for deletion with a last name of Reed.
- Remove the marked records from the file. How many records are in the file now?
- Print all records having a city of Albion.

3. This problem requires that you have completed Practice Exercise 3 in Lab 1, by creating the database file named SCHOOL.DBF. Open the database file SCHOOL.DBF.

- Confirm that your name has been entered as record 11. If it has not, enter your name in the field TITLE and leave the other fields blank.
- Joe has decided that he needs to add another field of data to his file structure. This field will contain the number of credit hours earned for each class taken. Insert this new field as field number 4. The field name is HOURS. It is a Numeric field with a field width of 1 and 0 decimal places.
- Use the Freeze command in the Browse submenu to enter the data for the HOURS field for each record in the file. All the classes are 3 credit hours except MAT210 which is 5 credit hours and Ped101 and Ped102 which are each 1 credit hour. Do not enter data for record 11.
- Enter the courses you took and the grades you earned last semester as new records in this file. Begin with record 12.
- Remove the record for MAT210 taken in Fall 1988 from the database file.
- Print a list of all the classes in which a grade of B was earned.

DB66
Modifying, Editing, and Viewing a Database

4. Bob is a manager for a small manufacturing company. One of his responsibilities is to keep weekly records for each of the company's 20 employees. Bob has created a database using dBASE III PLUS to help him.

- Open the database file STAFF.DBF.
- Edit record 1 by entering your first and last name.
- Modify the structure to include a new field SEX to be inserted between the existing fields PAY and HRS.
- Based on the FIRST_NAME for each employee, enter either F or M for SEX. If you cannot determine whether the first name is for a male or female, enter a question mark (?).
- Edit the following records:

    Record 5   FIRST_NAME is Robert
    Record 17 Hours is 35

- Delete records 3, 7, and 10.
- Print the entire database.
- Print only those employees who work in Accounting and earn less than $4.75.

LAB 3
Sorting, Indexing, and Summarizing Data

CASE STUDY

Donna McIntyre is the assistant manager of the Sports Club. As part of her responsibilities she maintains all employee records and produces weekly and monthly employee status reports.

The database structure and all the hourly employee data have been entered into a file using dBASE III PLUS by her assistant. We will follow Donna as she organizes the records in the file, analyzes the information in the database, and produces a simple report.

Displaying a Disk Directory

Donna's assistant created the database file of hourly employee records. He left the diskette and a note containing a description of the file structure in Donna's in-basket before leaving on vacation.

Upon seeing the diskette and note, Donna decides to take a look at the file. However, she realizes her assistant neglected to tell her the name of the file. Donna hopes that by looking at a list of all the files on the diskette, she will be able to pick out the file.

Load dBASE III PLUS.
To see a listing of all the files on the diskette,

Select: Tools

The Tools Menu performs mostly operating system functions such as setting the disk drive, listing the disk files (directory), copying, erasing, and renaming files. To see a directory of files on the diskette in the B drive,

Select: Directory / B:

OBJECTIVES

In this lab you will learn how to:

1. Display the disk directory.
2. Create a sorted database file.
3. Create a multilevel sorted file.
4. Create an index file.
5. Open index files.
6. Use the Seek command.
7. Use the dot prompt.
8. Perform basic numeric calculations.
9. Create and print a simple report.

DB68
Sorting, Indexing, and
Summarizing Data

Note: If you are using a drive other than B to hold your data files, select the appropriate drive from the drive submenu.

Your display screen should be similar to Figure 3-1.

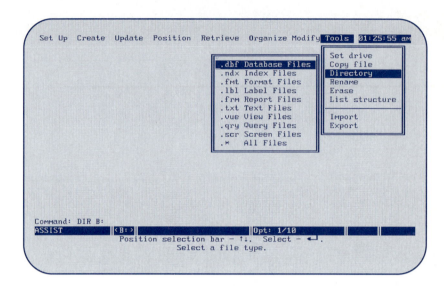

FIGURE 3-1

The nine types of files that can be created using dBASE III PLUS and the file extensions associated with each type are displayed in the submenu. We created and used database files (.DBF) in Labs 1 and 2. In this lab we will create index files, which have an .NDX file extension. This submenu allows you to view only the files with a specific file extension or to view all the files on the diskette.

To see a complete list of files on the diskette (use (PGDN)),

Select: .* All Files

All files on the diskette are listed. This includes files that are accessed by other types of software, such as files created by a word processor, as well as the files created by dBASE III PLUS.

This screen also shows the total number of bytes used by the files, total number of files on the diskette, and the total number of bytes remaining on the diskette.

Donna looks through the list of file names and sees a database file named EMPLOYEE.DBF. This file name is descriptive of the contents of the file she is looking for.

To return to The Assistant,

Press: any key

Displaying the File Structure

Donna wants to open the EMPLOYEE.DBF file and then view its structure to confirm that this is the file she wants to use.

Select: Set Up / Database file / B: / EMPLOYEE.DBF / **N**

The EMPLOYEE.DBF file is open. The List structure option in the Tools Menu lets you display and print the structure of the open database file. To display, but not print, the structure of this file,

Select: **T**ools / List structure / **N**

Your display screen should be similar to Figure 3-2.

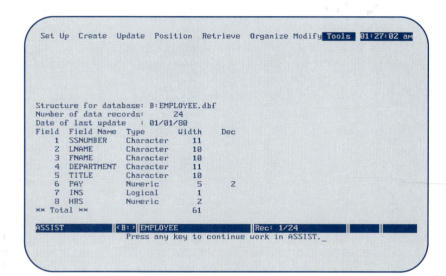

FIGURE 3-2

The first three lines display the name and drive location of the database file (B:EMPLOYEE.dbf), the number of database records (24) in the file, and the date of last update.

The eight field names and their attributes are displayed next. Below the list of field names the total number of bytes (spaces), plus 1, used by the eight fields is displayed. dBASE III PLUS adds one extra space for marking records for deletion.

The EMPLOYEE.DBF file contains eight fields of data. The written description left by Donna's assistant of each field (shown below) confirms that this is the correct file.

SSNUMBER   The employee's social security number. This field is defined as a Character field since no numeric calculations would be made using it. The width was set at 11 to allow for two dashes within the nine-digit number.

LNAME   The employee's last name.

FNAME   The employee's first name.

DEPARTMENT   The division of the club the employee works in.

TITLE   The employee's job title.

PAY   The employee's hourly rate of pay. This is a Numeric field, displaying two decimal places.

INS   This field indicates whether the employees chose to participate in the insurance program offered by theclub. It is a Logical field.

HRS   The number of hours per week the employee works. This is a Numeric field with no decimal places.

To return to The Assistant,

Press: any key

To view the records in the database file,

Select: **R**etrieve / List / Execute the command / **N**

Your display screen should be similar to Figure 3-3.

FIGURE 3-3

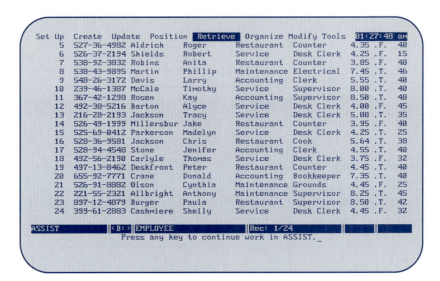

Each record occupies only a single line because the record length is short enough to be completely displayed in a window. The Sports Club has 24 hourly employees. Notice that the records are not ordered in any sequence other than the original record number order they were assigned as the data was entered into the file.

To return to The Assistant,

Press: any key

Sorting the Database Records

Donna would like to organize the records in the database file in a more meaningful way. She wants the records **organized,** or arranged, in alphabetical order by last name. To do this, the Organize Menu is used. The Organize Menu helps you arrange the order of records in your file.

Select: **O**rganize

There are three menu options: Index, Sort, and Copy. The Index and Sort commands allow you to change the order of records in a file. The Copy command makes a copy of all or selected portions of the file.

To sort the records in the file by last name,

Select: Sort

Your display screen should be similar to Figure 3-4.

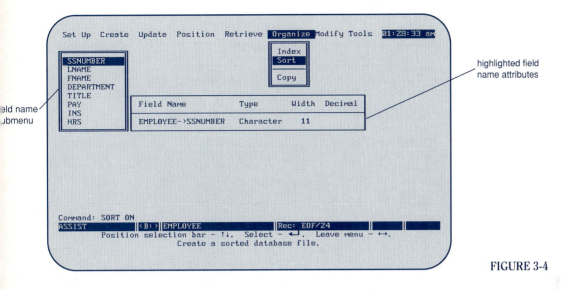

FIGURE 3-4

A field name submenu is displayed. Donna wants the records arranged in alphabetical order by LNAME. The field on which a database is sorted is called the **key field.** To select a key field, following the instructions in the navigation line, move the highlight bar to the field name and press ⏎.

Select: LNAME

To leave the field name submenu,

Press: ⟶

The Sort command creates a new database file. It contains a duplicate of all the records in the original database file arranged in the order specified. To specify the drive to create the new sorted file on,

Select: B:

The new file needs a file name. Enter the file name for the new sorted database file as follows:

Type: LASTNAME
Press: ⏎

The completed command shown in the action line was "SORT ON LNAME TO B:LASTNAME".

The B disk drive light goes on, and the file is sorted and saved on the diskette. After a few moments your display will tell you the percentage and number of records sorted.

The new database file is a duplicate of the original EMPLOYEE.DBF file. It has been saved as LASTNAME.DBF on the diskette in the B drive. The only difference between the two files is that the records in the new file are arranged alphabetically by last name.

To return to The Assistant,

Press: any key

To open the new database file of sorted records,

Select: Set Up / Database file / B: / LASTNAME.DBF / N

The status bar shows that the database file in use is LASTNAME. To view the records in this file,

Select: Retrieve / Display / Specify scope / All / Execute the command

Your display screen should be similar to Figure 3-5.

FIGURE 3-5

The sorted database file, LASTNAME.DBF, contains the same data as the original file, EMPLOYEE.DBF. But the records in the sorted database are listed in ascending alphabetical order by last name. Notice that the records have been renumbered.

Look at record numbers 12 and 13. Both the employees have the same last name, Jackson. Donna would like the records to be sorted so that the first names are alphabetized within same last names. This would change the order so that Chris Jackson's record would come before Tracy Jackson's.

DB73
Creating a Multilevel Sort File

To see the next screenful of records,

Press: any key

To return to The Assistant,

Press: any key

Creating a Multilevel Sort File

A file can also be sorted on more than one key field. This is called a **multilevel sort.** To alphabetize the employees' first names within identical last names, two key fields, LNAME and FNAME, are specified.

Select: Organize / Sort /

To select more than one key field, simply move the selection bar to each field you want to select from the field name submenu and press ⏎. When sorting on multiple key fields, the most important key field is selected first.

Move to: LNAME
Press: ⏎
Move to: FNAME
Press: ⏎
Press: →
Select: B: / Namesort ⏎

The action line displays the command as "SORT ON LNAME, FNAME TO B:NAMESORT". Multiple key fields are separated by commas in the dot command.
    To return to The Assistant and open the file NAMESORT.DBF,

Press: any key
Select: Set Up / Database file / B: / NAMESORT.DBF/ N

    The open database file is now NAMESORT.DBF. To view the records in their new sorted order,

Select: Retrieve / List

    Rather than displaying all the fields in each record, you can restrict the listing to display only the fields we are interested in seeing, i.e., LNAME and FNAME. To specify which fields to display,

Select: Construct a field list

Your display screen should be similar to Figure 3-6.

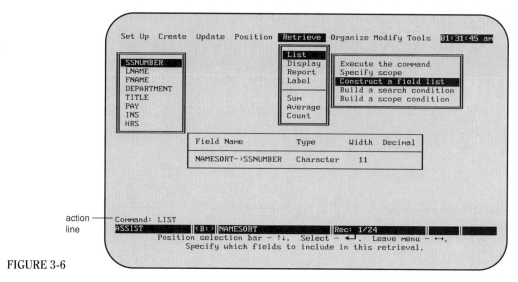

FIGURE 3-6

The field name submenu is displayed. The order in which the fields are selected from the field name submenu will determine the order they are displayed on the screen.

Select: FNAME
Select: LNAME
Press: ⟶
Select: Execute the command / **N**

The command in the action line was "LIST FNAME, LNAME".
Your display screen should be similar to Figure 3-7.

FIGURE 3-7

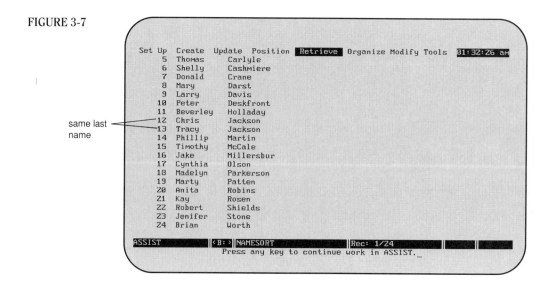

The employee names are displayed with the first name before the last name. Chris Jackson's record is now number 12. It comes before Tracy Jackson's record, which is number 13. Donna is pleased with the results of the multilevel sort.

To return to The Assistant,

Press: any key

Donna needs to update the open database file, NAMESORT.DBF, by adding a new employee record.

Select: Update / Append

A blank entry form is displayed on the Append screen. The record pointer should be positioned on EOF/ 24.

Enter the following data:

Field Name	Field Data
SSNUMBER	187-49-0213
LNAME	Fischer
FNAME	Sarah
DEPARTMENT	Service
TITLE	Desk Clerk
PAY	3.55
INS	N
HRS	40

Another blank entry form is displayed. To verify that the data for Sarah Fischer was entered correctly,

Press: PGUP

Record number 25 is displayed on the screen. Edit if necessary.

To save the new record and exit the Append screen,

Press: CTRL-END

Do not press CTRL-END when a blank record form is displayed on the screen. If you do, a blank record will be added to the file.

To view the records in the file,

Select: Retrieve / List / Execute the command / **N**

The record for Sarah Fischer is the last record in the file. Each time a record is added to a file using Append, it is added to the end of the file. The file would need to be resorted in order to have the records arranged in alphabetical order.

In addition, the original file, EMPLOYEE.DBF, and the other sorted database file, LASTNAME.DBF, do not contain the record for Sarah Fischer. Her record would need to be added to each of these files to make them up to date.

Press: any key

As you can see, the Sort command has some serious drawbacks:

- Each time a file is sorted using the Sort command, a new duplicate file is created. With a large database, this duplication of data uses a lot of your diskette space.
- The renumbering of the records in the sorted file makes locating a record by record number unlikely. Each time the file is sorted, the record number may change.
- Sorting a large database takes a lot of time, sometimes several hours.
- Each time a change, addition, or deletion to the original file is made, the sorted file becomes out of date. The original file would need to be resorted, or the sorted file would need to be updated.

For these reasons, using the Sort command is usually limited to files that do not change frequently. Donna feels that the file of employee records will change frequently as people are added and deleted and changes are made to individual records. Many of these problems can be resolved by creating index files.

Creating an Index File

Donna wants to create an index file using the file EMPLOYEE.DBF.

To close the sorted file, NAMESORT.DBF, and open the original unsorted file, EMPLOYEE.DBF,

Select: Set Up / Database file / B: / EMPLOYEE.DBF / **N**
Select: **O**rganize

To use Help for information on the Index option,

Press: F1

Your display screen should be similar to Figure 3-8.

FIGURE 3-8

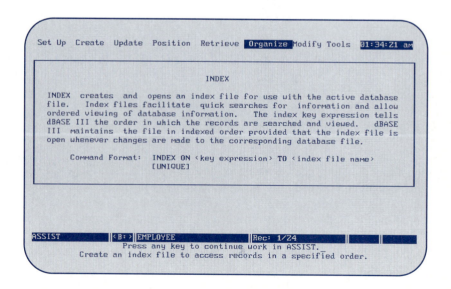

DB77
Creating an Index File

Read this screen carefully. The Index command is used to create index files which control the order of display of records in the open database file.
    To return to The Assistant,

Press: any key

To use the Index option to arrange the records ordered alphabetically by last name and first name.

Select: Index

Your display screen should be similar to Figure 3-9.

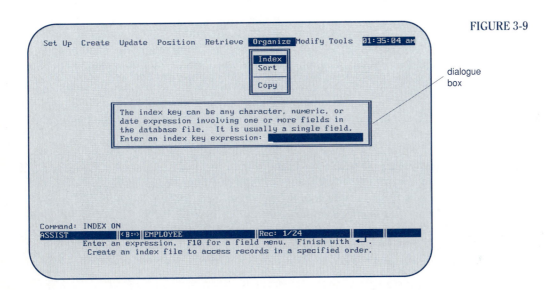

FIGURE 3-9

dialogue box

The message in the dialogue box prompts you to enter a **key expression.** In the Sort command, the key field to sort on was specified. Here, the index key expression must be specified. This is simply the field or fields that will determine the order of the records.
    There are two ways to enter the index key expression. You can type the field name exactly as it appears in the database file following the prompt in the dialogue box. Or you can select the field name from a field name submenu. To display the field name submenu,

Press: F10

As in previous screens where the field name submenu is displayed, move the selection bar to the desired field name and press ⏎ to select it.

Select: LNAME

Your display screen should be similar to Figure 3-10.

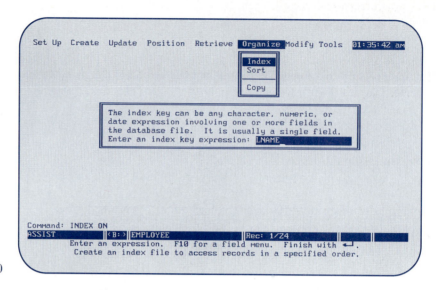

FIGURE 3-10

LNAME is entered as the key expression in the dialogue box. The field name submenu is no longer displayed.

To complete the entry Donna could simply press ⏎, and the file would be indexed on the LNAME field only. However, to have first names alphabetized within same last names, a second index key expression must be specified.

In a manner similar to the multilevel sort, we will index the file on both last name and first name. This is called **multilevel indexing.**

The cursor is positioned after LNAME in the dialogue box. To add a second index key expression,

Type: +
Press: F10
Select: FNAME

Your display screen should be similar to Figure 3-11.

FIGURE 3-11

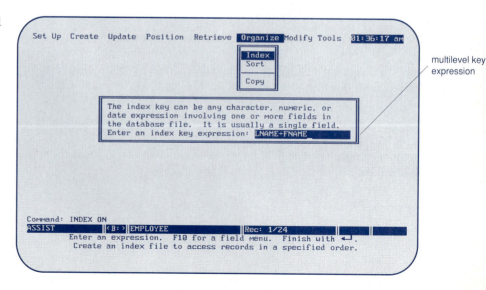

multilevel key expression

DB79
Creating an Index File

Both fields are displayed as key expressions in the dialogue box. To end the specification of the key expressions,

Press:

The Index command creates a new file with a file extension .NDX. To complete the command sequence, enter the drive where the indexed file will be saved and the file name for the indexed file as follows:

Select: B: / EMPNAME ⏎

The completed command in the action line was "INDEX ON LNAME+FNAME TO B:EMPNAME".
  The action line shows that 100 percent of the records have been indexed. To return to The Assistant,

Press: any key

As soon as an index file is created, the records in the EMPLOYEE.DBF database file are reordered according to the key expressions. The index file does not need to be opened, as the sortfile did. It is put into use immediately. To view the records in the EMPLOYEE.DBF file,

Select: Retrieve / Display / Specify scope / All / Execute the command

Your display screen should be similar to Figure 3-12.

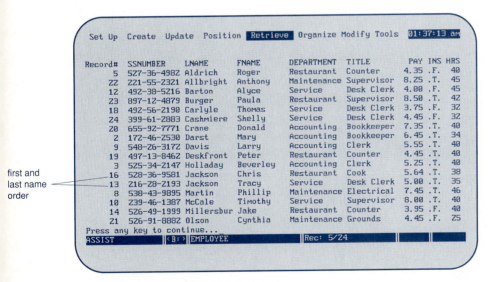

FIGURE 3-12

first and last name order

DB80
Sorting, Indexing, and Summarizing Data

The index file has taken control over the order of display of the records of the open database file, EMPLOYEE.DBF. The records are arranged in the same order as in the multilevel sort file NAMESORT.DBF. The records for the two Jacksons are in alphabetical order by last and first names.

Each record still has the original record number it was assigned when it was entered into the database file. The records have not been physically reordered in the file as they were when the Sort command was used. Indexing uses an index **pointer** which controls the order of display of the records in the EMPLOYEE.DBF file.

The Sort command creates a duplicate database file. The records are physically reordered and renumbered. The Index command creates an index file containing pointers (the index key expression values and corresponding record numbers) to records in the open database file. Since the entire record is not copied into the index file, this file takes up much less diskette space.

To continue to view the rest of the file and return to The Assistant,

Press: any key (2 times)

The club manager has asked Donna for a list of all employees by department. To do this, Donna needs to create a second index file. This one will arrange the employee records alphabetically within departments. The most important key expression is selected first.

Select: Organize / Index / **DEPARTMENT+LNAME+FNAME** / B: / **EMPDEPT** ⏎

To return to The Assistant and view the records in the new index order,

Press: any key
Select: Retrieve / List / Execute the command / N

The new index file, EMPDEPT.NDX, now controls the order of display of the records in the database file EMPLOYEE.DBF. The records are organized first by department, next by last name, and finally by first name.

The first index file, EMPNAME.NDX, is closed.

Before preparing the report for the club manager, Donna needs to add the data for Sarah Fischer to the EMPLOYEE.DBF file. (Remember that her record was added only to the sorted database file, NAMESORT.DBF.)

Opening Index Files

The new record can be added to the original database file, EMPLOYEE.DBF and both index files at the same time. To do this, both index files must be open.

To open both index files,

Select: Set Up / Database file / B: / EMPLOYEE.DBF

This time in response to the prompt "Is the file indexed?",

Type: Y

Your display screen should be similar to Figure 3-13.

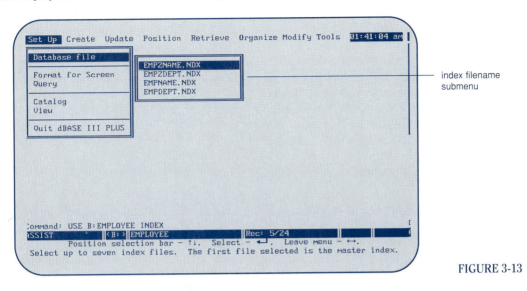

FIGURE 3-13

An index file name submenu appears. It displays all the index files on this diskette (including index files you will use in the next lab). To open an index file, move the selection bar to the index file name and press ⏎.

Select: EMPNAME.NDX

Your display screen should be similar to Figure 3-14.

FIGURE 3-14

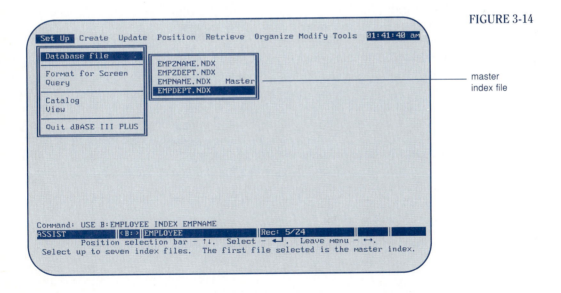

The word "Master" appears next to the file name. The first index file that is opened is called the **master index.** This index file will control the order of display of the records in the EMPLOYEE.DBF file.

To open the second index file,

Select: EMPDEPT.NDX

As additional index files are selected they are numbered 2, 3, and so on. They are open, but they are not in control of the order of display of records on the screen. They are called **secondary indexes.**

The command in the action line is "USE B:EMPLOYEE INDEX EMPNAME, EMPDEPT".

To leave the index submenu,

Press: ⟶

Whenever a file is updated, it is important that all related index files are open so that they will be automatically updated at the same time. dBASE III PLUS will update open index files *only*. You can open as many as seven index files at once. Of course, the more index files that are open, the longer the update process takes because each index file has to be updated at the same time.

If you wanted to use the EMPLOYEE.DBF file without using an index file, you would respond "No" to the prompt "Is your file indexed?".

Add the data for Sarah Fischer to the database file as follows:

Select: Update / Append

Enter the data below exactly as it appears:

Field Name	Field Data
SSNUMBER	187-49-0213
LNAME	Fischer
FNAME	Sarah
DEPARTMENT	Service
TITLE	Desk Clerk
PAY	3.55
INS	N
HRS	40

Check the record for accuracy and edit if necessary.

To save the record and leave the Append screen (remember, do not have a blank record form on the screen),

Press: CTRL-END

Using the Seek Command

To verify that Sarah Fischer's record was added to the master index file, the Seek option in the Position menu can be used. This command can be used only on files that are indexed. If an index file is not open, this option will not be available for selection through The Assistant.

To quickly locate the record,

Select: Position / Seek

Your display screen should be similar to Figure 3-15.

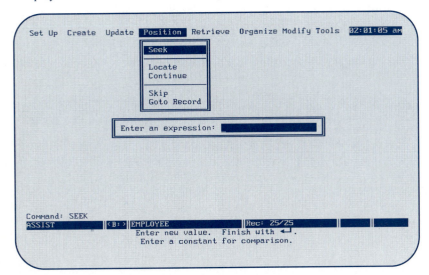

FIGURE 3-15

A dialogue box appears prompting you to "Enter an expression:". Any key expression field value entry that matches the first index key expression in the master index file can be entered. The first index key for the master file is LNAME. The expression to enter in this Seek command can be any last name in the EMPLOYEE.DBF file. You will enter the last name, Fischer, of the record we want to locate, as the seek expression.

The expression must be entered exactly as it appears in the file. dBASE III PLUS is case-sensitive, which means it searches for strings exactly as they are entered in the dialogue box—uppercase, lowercase, or a combination of the two. For this reason, when entering your data into the file, you need to be consistent with your use of upper- and lowercase letters.

If the expression is a character field, it must be enclosed in quotes (') or brackets([ ]).

Type: 'Fisher'
Press: ⏎

The message displayed at the bottom of the screen tells you that there are no records in the file that match the expression. Donna notices that she spelled the last name incorrectly. To try it again,

Press: any key
Select: Seek / **'Fischer'**
Press: ⏎

No error message is displayed this time. Although nothing appears to have happened, the record was found. The pointer is now located on that record. The Seek command quickly locates the first record in an indexed file that matches the specified expression.

To return to The Assistant,

Press: any key

To display the record located by the Seek command,

Select: Retrieve / Display / Execute the command

Your display screen should be similar to Figure 3-16.

FIGURE 3-16

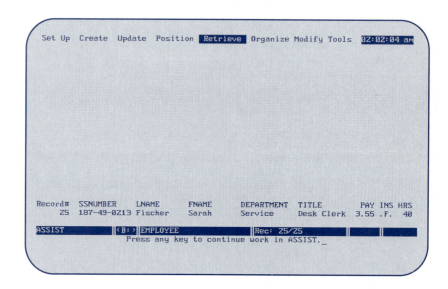

The record for Sarah Fischer is displayed. Although not apparent with this small database, using Seek to find a record in a large indexed file is faster and more efficient than using Locate.

To return to The Assistant,

Press: any key

Next, we want to verify that Sarah Fischer's record was added to the other index file. To do so, we need to change the master index file to EMPDEPT.NDX. We could use The Assistant to select Set Up / Database file / B: / EMPLOYEE.DBF / Y / EMPDEPT.NDX EMPNAME.NDX. However, changing the master index file can be done easily and more quickly at the dot prompt.

Using the Dot Prompt

To get to the dot prompt screen,

Press: ESC

A dBASE III PLUS dot command can be typed in either upper- or lowercase letters.

To enter the command to change the order of the index files so that the secondary index file, number 2, becomes the master index file,

Type: SET ORDER TO 2
Press: ⏎

The message displayed on the screen tells you that the master index file is EMPDEPT.NDX.

Note: If you entered the command incorrectly and have an error message on the screen, press ESC and retype the command.

This is easy, assuming you remember the index filenames and the order the index files were opened. In case you do not remember the index file names, you can have a directory of index files displayed as follows.

Type: DIR *.NDX
Press: ⏎

Your display screen should be similar to Figure 3-17.

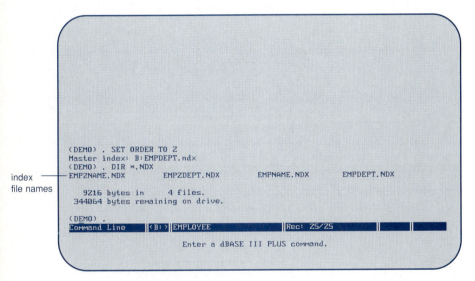

FIGURE 3-17

All the index files on the diskette are displayed. If you do not remember the order you used to open the index files,

Type: DISPLAY STATUS
Press: ⏎

We are interested only in the first four lines following the command. It tells you the current database file in use, the master index file, and other open index files. The keys used in the indexed files are also displayed.

There is a lot of other information about the current dBASE III PLUS session provided using this command. To see the next screen of information and return to the dot prompt,

Press: any key

To return to The Assistant, you can type ASSIST or use the F2 key.

Press: F2

The master index file is EMPDEPT.NDX. The records will be displayed in order by department, last name, and first name.
To verify that Sarah Fischer's record was added to this index file,

Select: Retrieve / List / Execute the command / N

Your display screen should be similar to Figure 3-18.

FIGURE 3-18

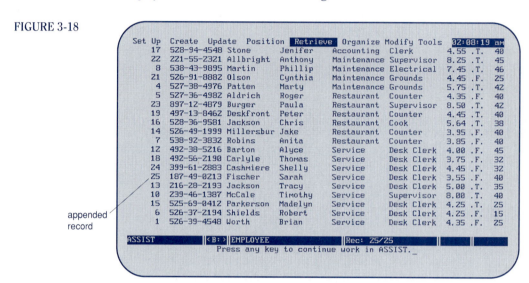

appended record

Sarah Fischer, record number 25, is displayed alphabetically within the service department. Since both index files were open at the time the record was added to the EMPLOYEE.DBF file, both index files were updated with the new record.
To return to The Assistant,

Press: any key

Using indexed files has many advantages over Sort.

- Accessing records is faster with Seek.
- The indexed file takes up much less diskette space because only the pointers to records in the database are stored in the file.
- All open index files are automatically updated if changes are made in the database file.

Summarizing Data

The club manager wants to know the number of employees, average pay rate, and total hours worked for all employees in the service department.

Now that the database is up to date, Donna can proceed to analyze the data. To do this, Donna will use the dBASE III PLUS **numeric functions.** These functions can average, sum, or count the specified records in a database.

To find out how many employees there are in the service department, use the Count command. This is an option under the Retrieve Menu.

Select: Retrieve / Count / Build a search condition / DEPARTMENT / = Equal To / **Service** / No more conditions / Execute the command

Your display screen should be similar to Figure 3-19.

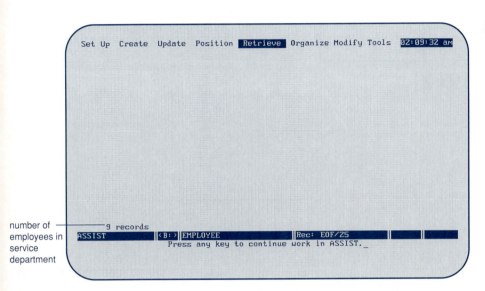

FIGURE 3-19

number of employees in service department

The number of records (9) meeting the specifications is displayed.
To return to The Assistant,

Press: any key

To find the average hourly rate of pay for all employees in the service department,

Select: Average / Construct a field list

Notice that only the Numeric fields are available for selection from the field name submenu.

Select: Pay / Build a search condition / DEPARTMENT / = Equal To / **Service** / No more conditions / Execute the command

Your display screen should appear similar to Figure 3-20.

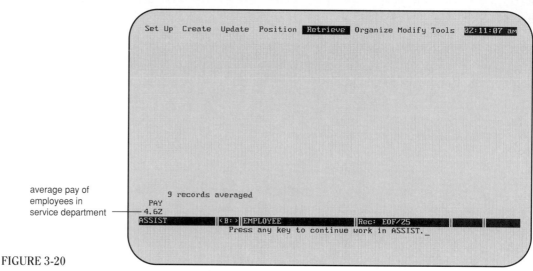

average pay of employees in service department

FIGURE 3-20

The number of records averaged and the computed average pay rate of 4.62 are displayed.

To return to The Assistant,

Press: any key

To calculate the total number of hours worked last week by employees in the service department,

Select: Sum / Construct a field list / HRS / Build a search condition / DEPARTMENT / = Equal To / **Service** / No more conditions / Execute the command

The number of records summed and the total number of hours worked by all employees in the service department, 289, are displayed.

To return to The Assistant,

Press: any key

Printing a Simple Report

Donna is ready to create the report listing all employees by department for the club manager. The only fields of data he wants to see in the list are department, last and first names, job title, and rate of pay.

The master index file is EMPDEPT.NDX. Therefore, the display of records will be in the desired order.

To produce a printed report of this information,

Select: **R**etrieve / List / Construct a field list / DEPARTMENT, LNAME, FNAME, TITLE, PAY / Execute the command

If you have printer capability,

Type: Y

If you do not have printer capability,

Type: N

Your printed output should be similar to Figure 3-21.

FIGURE 3-21

```
Record#  DEPARTMENT   LNAME       FNAME     TITLE        PAY
     20  Accounting   Crane       Donald    Bookkeeper   7.35
      2  Accounting   Darst       Mary      Bookkeeper   6.45
      9  Accounting   Davis       Larry     Clerk        5.55
      3  Accounting   Holladay    Beverly   Clerk        5.25
     11  Accounting   Rosen       Kay       Supervisor   8.50
     17  Accounting   Stone       Jenifer   Clerk        5.25
     22  Maintenance  Albright    Anthony   Supervisor   4.55
      8  Maintenance  Martin      Phillip   Electrical   7.45
     21  Maintenance  Olson       Cynthia   Grounds      4.45
      4  Maintenance  Patten      Marty     Grounds      5.75
      5  Restaurant   Aldrich     Roger     Counter      4.35
     23  Restaurant   Burger      Paula     Supervisor   8.50
     19  Restaurant   Deskfront   Peter     Counter      4.45
     16  Restaurant   Jackson     Chris     Cook         5.64
     14  Restaurant   Millersbur  Jake      Counter      3.95
      7  Restaurant   Robins      Anita     Counter      3.85
     12  Service      Barton      Alyce     Desk Clerk   4.00
     18  Service      Carlyle     Thomas    Desk Clerk   3.75
     24  Service      Cashmiere   Shelly    Desk Clerk   4.45
     25  Service      Fischer     Sarah     Desk Clerk   3.55
     13  Service      Jackson     Tracy     Desk Clerk   5.00
     10  Service      McCale      Timothy   Supervisor   8.00
     15  Service      Parkerson   Madelyn   Desk Clerk   4.25
      6  Service      Sheilds     Robert    Desk Clerk   4.25
      1  Service      Worth       Brian     Desk Clerk   4.35
```

Donna is pleased with the report she has created. However, she would like the report to look more professional. We will demonstrate how to prepare a professional report in the next lab.

To return to The Assistant,

Press: any key

To quit dBASE III PLUS,

Select: Set Up / Quit dBASE III PLUS

Key Terms

index   pointer
key field   organize
multilevel sort master index
key expression secondary index
multilevel indexing numeric functions

Matching

1. .NDX
2. DIR *.DBF
3. SET ORDER TO 4
4. DISPLAY STATUS
5. F2
6. master
7. Sort
8. Index
9. Count
10. pointer

_____ a. a numeric function that counts the number of records in a file

_____ b. index key values and record numbers contained in the index file

_____ c. displays The Assistant

_____ d. dot command to display a directory of database files

_____ e. dot command to change the open index file 4 to the master

_____ f. file extension for indexed files

_____ g. dot command that provides information about the current dBASE III PLUS session

_____ h. the index file opened first

_____ i. organizes a file on a key expression

_____ j. creates an index file

Practice Exercises

1. This problem requires that you have completed Lab 3 and have created the indexed files as specified in that lab. Open EMPLOYEE.DBF with the index file EMPNAME.NDX.

   - Edit record 1 by entering your first and last name in the appropriate fields.
   - Sort the records by TITLE and LAST_NAME. Name the sorted file STITLE.
   - Print the database file STITLE.
   - Index the file EMPLOYEE on TITLE. Name the index file EMPTITLE.
   - Change EMPLOYEE's master file to EMPTITLE.
   - Print the database file EMPLOYEE.DBF.
   - Print a report displaying FIRST_NAME, LAST_NAME, DEPARTMENT, and TITLE, organized by TITLE.

2. To complete this problem you must first have completed Practice Exercise 2 in Lab 2. Open the database file TILES30.DBF.

   - Use the LOCATE command to confirm that your name has been entered into the database. If it has not, enter your first and last name as a record.
   - Index the file on UNIT_COST. Name the index file COST. What is the unit cost of the tile that is ordered most often?
   - Index the file on DATE. Name the index file DATE. How many orders were placed in September?
   - Sort the records by LAST_NAME and FIRST_NAME. Name the sorted file TILESORT. Open the sorted file. How many records have a last name of King?
   - Open the file TILES30.DBF. Open the index file COST.NDX first and DATE.NDX second.

- Using the dot command, change the order of the index files so that DATE.NDX is the master index file.
- Print a list of all paid accounts displaying the LAST_NAME, QUANTITY, and UNIT_COST fields only, organized by date.

3. To complete this problem, you must first have completed Practice Exercise 3 in Lab 2. Open the database file SCHOOL.DBF.
    - Use the LOCATE command to confirm that your name has been entered into the database. If it has not, enter your name in the field TITLE of record 11.
    - Index the file on COURSE_NUM. Name the index file COURSE.
    - Index the file on GRADE. Name the index file GRADE.
    - Use the Sum function to calculate the total number of hours earned. What is Joe's total hours earned?
    - Use the Count function to calculate how many B's Joe has earned. How many B's has Joe earned?
    - Print a simple report showing the course TITLE and GRADE, categorized by GRADE.
    - Print another report displaying COURSE_NUM and HOURS organized by COURSE_NUM.

4. To complete this problem you must first have completed Practice Exercise 4 in Lab 3. Open the database file STAFF.DBF.
    - Use the LOCATE command to confirm that your name has been entered into the database. If it has not, enter your first and last name as a record.
    - Sort the file on DEPARTMENT. Name the sorted file DEPTSTAF.
    - Print the file STAFF.DBF.
    - Print the file DEPTSTAF.DBF.
    - Index the file STAFF on DEPARTMENT and TITLE. Name the index file DEPT.
    - Print the file STAFF.DBF.
    - Use the number functions to determine:
        a. The number of people in the Accounting department.
        b. The average pay in the Maintenance department.
        c. The total number of hours worked (for all departments).
    - Print a simple report displaying LAST_NAME and DEPARTMENT, by DEPARTMENT.
    - Print a report displaying FIRST_NAME, LAST_NAME, DEPARTMENT, and TITLE organized by DEPARTMENT.

LAB 4
Creating a Professional Report

OBJECTIVES

In this lab you will learn how to:

1. Use the report generator feature.
2. Specify a title for a report.
3. Specify report columns.
4. View the report.
5. Modify a report.
6. Define subtotals.
7. Print a report.

CASE STUDY

The club manager is pleased with the data analysis and report Donna produced. Next, he would like a weekly report listing the employee's name, hourly pay rate, hours worked, and weekly pay. He would also like a second report on a monthly basis. This report will list the employees by department, hourly pay, hours worked, and monthly pay. To create the reports, Donna will use the dBASE III PLUS report generator.

Examining the Report Screen

At the end of Lab 3, Donna McIntyre, the assistant manager of the Sports Club, had updated the EMPLOYEE.DBF file, sorted and indexed the file, and performed some basic analysis of the data. We will use the database file EMPLOYE2.DBF in this lab. This file should be the same as the file EMPLOYEE.DBF after you completed Lab 3.

Load dBASE III PLUS.
Open the file EMPLOYE2.DBF as follows:

Select: Set Up / Database file / B: / EMPLOYE2.DBF

Donna will open the index file EMP2NAME.NDX. This index file arranges the records by last name and first name. This is the order in which she wants the names to be arranged in the report.

To complete the command sequence,

Select: Y / EMP2NAME.NDX ⟶

DB92

The basic format of a report consists of:

Margin settings   top, bottom, left, and right

Page title   up to four lines of text, displayed at the top of each report page

Column titles   up to four lines of text, displayed over each column of information

Column contents   the fields of data to display in the column

Column totals   the sum of the column contents displayed beneath each column of data

The first report Donna needs to create is the weekly report listing each employee's name, pay rate, hours worked, and weekly pay. It will look like the report shown in Figure 4-1.

FIGURE 4-1

```
              Employee Payroll Report         ── page title
              Week of May 16, 1994

Last Name     First Name    Pay      Hours      Weekly      ── column title
                                     Worked     Pay

Aldrich       Roger         4.35     40         174.00
Allbright     Anthony       8.25     45         371.25
Barton        Alyce         4.00     45         180.00
Burger        Paula         8.50     42         357.00
Carlyle       Thomas        3.75     32         120.00
Cashmiere     Shelly        4.45     32         142.40
Crane         Donald        7.35     40         294.00
Darst         Mary          6.45     34         219.00
Davis         Larry         5.55     40         222.00
Eberley       Peter         4.45     40         178.00
Fisher        Sarah         3.55     40         142.00
Holladay      Beverley      5.25     40         210.00
Jackson       Chris         5.64     38         214.32      ── column content
Jackson       Tracy         5.00     35         175.00
Martin        Phillip       7.45     46         342.70
McCale        Timothy       8.00     40         320.00
Millersbur    Jake          3.95     40         158.00
Olson         Cynthia       4.45     25         111.25
Parkerson     Madelyn       4.25     25         106.25
Patten        Marty         5.75     42         241.50
Robins        Anita         3.85     40         154.00
Rosen         Kay           8.50     40         340.00
Shields       Robert        4.25     15          63.75
Stone         Jennifer      4.55     40         182.00
Worth         Brian         4.35     25         108.75
*** TOTAL ***
                                     921        5127.47     ── column total
```

The Create Report command is used to specify and save the various settings for the report in a **report format file.** The file extension used by dBASE III PLUS to identify a report format file is .FRM. To use this command and to specify the filename for the report format file as EMPWEEK,

Select: Create / Report / B: / **EMPWEEK** ⏎

Your display screen should be similar to Figure 4-2.

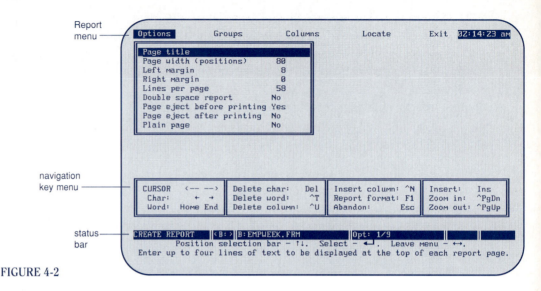

FIGURE 4-2

This is the Create Report screen. The status bar shows that you are using the Create Report command and that the file being created is called EMPWEEK.FRM. The filename extension, .FRM, identifies the file as a report format file.

Across the top of the screen is a menu bar. It contains five menu choices: Options, Groups, Columns, Locate, and Exit. Each of the five menu items assists in building the report form as follows:

Options allows you to specify the title for the report, page width and length, margins, and spacing

Groups specifies what data fields and headings will be used for subtotals

Columns specifies each column of data that will appear in the report and the column heading for each

Locate allows you to move to and edit a specific column while designing the report

Exit saves the report form and returns you to The Assistant

The Report menu bar works just like The Assistant menu bar. As a menu item is opened, a pull-down menu of options appears in a box for selection. A series of submenus and entry areas (similar to dialogue boxes) appear frequently to assist in creating the report.

At the bottom of the screen a navigation key menu is displayed.

Press: F1

Your display screen should be similar to Figure 4-3.

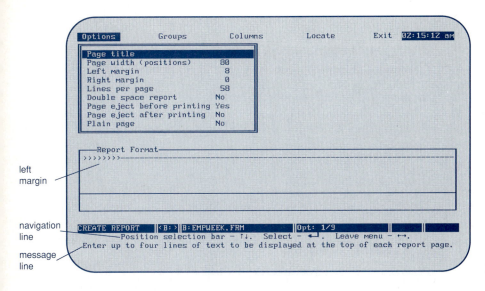

FIGURE 4-3

The navigation key menu is cleared from the screen. The Report Format box is displayed. This box will display a coded diagram of the layout of the report as it is being created. The only **code** currently displayed in the Report Format box is a series of >>>'s on the left side of the box. This code shows the location and size of the left margin. Pressing (F1) changes this area of the Create Report screen to display either the navigation key menu or the Report Format box.

The navigation line and message line work the same as they do in The Assistant.

Entering the Report Title

The title of this report will be "Employee Payroll Report for the Week of May 16, 1994." A menu option is selected by moving the selection bar to the item and pressing (⏎). Use the navigation line for help in making selections and moving around the screen.

Select: Options / Page title

An empty box, called an **entry area,** appears on the screen. These blank entry areas will appear frequently while creating the report. They are used to enter the information needed by the selected menu option. The blinking cursor within the entry area shows you where the next character you type will appear. If you make an error while typing the entry, use the (Bksp) key to erase the characters back to the error. Then retype the entry correctly.

Type: Employee Payroll Report
Press: ⏎

The cursor moved to the second line. To enter the rest of the title as a second title line,

Type: for the Week of May 16, 1994

Your display screen should be similar to Figure 4-4.
The title occupies two lines in the entry area. You can have up to four lines of title

FIGURE 4-4

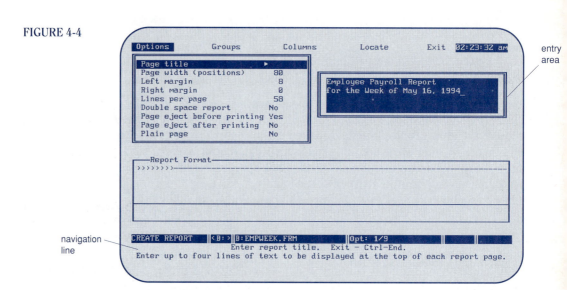

displayed in a report. Although the text is left-justified in the entry area, dBASE III PLUS will center each title line on the page when the report is displayed or printed.
Notice that the navigation line shows that the command to exit this menu is the (CTRL)-(END) key combination.

Press: (CTRL)-(END)

You are returned to the Options Menu. The first eight letters of the title are displayed following the Page title option in the pull-down menu.

The other selections under Options allow you to set the page width, margins, spacing, and page eject options. The default values displayed next to each option are acceptable for now. They are appropriate for most purposes.

Specifying the Report Column

Next the contents, heading, and size of each column of data to appear in the report are specified.

Select: Columns

Your display screen should be similar to Figure 4-5.

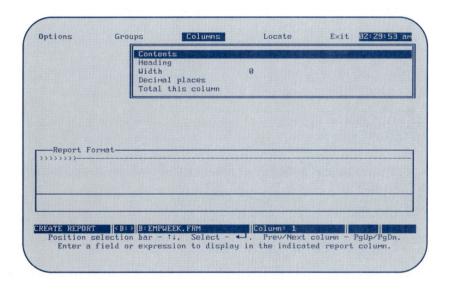

FIGURE 4-5

The first three menu options, Contents, Heading, and Width, are displayed in high intensity. They can be selected and defined immediately. The last two, Decimal places and Total this column, are displayed in regular intensity. They are not available for selection yet.

Each column of data that will appear in the report must be defined. The status bar shows that the current column being used is "Column: 1". First the field of data from the database file that will appear as the **column contents** is specified by selecting the Contents option. The first column will display the information in the LNAME field.

Select: Contents

DB98
Creating a Professional Report

The entry area for the column contents is the space to the right of the option name. A triangle followed by a blinking cursor appears in the entry area to show that the option is waiting to be defined. There are two ways that you can enter the column contents. The first is to type the field name exactly as it appears in the database file. The second is to select the field name from a field name submenu. Using the field name submenu eliminates the possibility of typing errors and incorrect field names.

To display the field name submenu,

Press: F10

Your display screen should be similar to Figure 4-6.

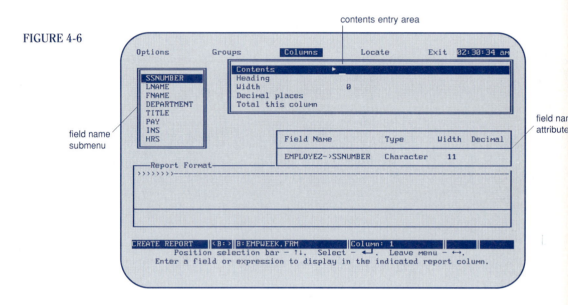

FIGURE 4-6

A field name submenu and a box showing the highlighted field name attributes are displayed.

Move to: LNAME

Notice that the attribute box shows the field width for the LNAME field is 10 spaces.

Press: ⏎

LNAME is entered at the cursor location on the contents entry area. To accept this field as the contents to be displayed in column 1,

Press: ⏎

Your display screen should be similar to Figure 4-7.

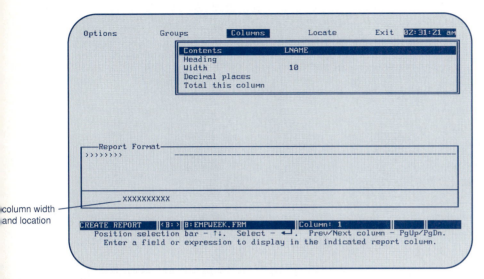

column width and location

FIGURE 4-7

Notice that the **column width** has been defined as 10. dBASE III PLUS automatically enters the field width from the database file structure as the column width.

The Report Format box displays a series of X's. This code marks the location of the first column of data. The number of X's corresponds to the width of the field.

The next Column setting to be specified is Heading. The **column heading** is the column title which will describe the data in the column.

Select: Heading

Another blank entry area appears on the screen. The column heading will be entered in this space. It can be up to four lines of text.

Type: Last Name
Press: CTRL-END

The column heading is displayed in the heading line. The Report Format box also displays the heading over the column.

The third option, Width, is acceptable as displayed. The column width will be 10 spaces. This is the same as the field width for the LNAME field in the database file.

The last two options, "Decimal places" and "Total this column", are not available for specification. They can be specified only when the contents of the column is a numeric field type of data.

Press: PGDN

DB100
Creating a Professional Report

A blank Column menu box appears for entry of information for the second column. The status bar shows that you are working on "Column: 2". The contents of column 2 will be FNAME, with a column heading of "First Name" and a column width of 10 spaces.

Define the second column as follows:

Select: Contents
Press: F10
Select: FNAME
Press: ⏎
Select: Heading
Type: First Name
Press: CTRL-END

When you have completed defining the second report column, your display screen should be similar to Figure 4-8.

FIGURE 4-8

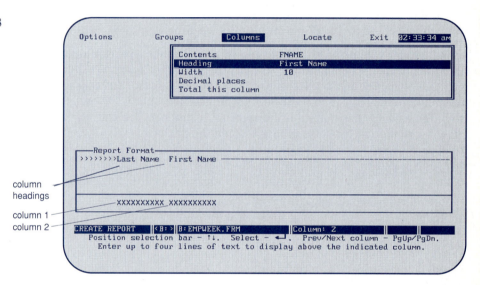

column headings
column 1
column 2

The first two columns of data have been defined. The Report Format box shows how they will appear in the report. dBASE III PLUS automatically inserts one blank space between the columns. The next column of data will hold the hourly rate of pay.

Press: PGDN

Following the above procedure, define column 3 as follows:

Contents: **PAY**
Heading: **Pay**

Your display screen should be similar to Figure 4-9.

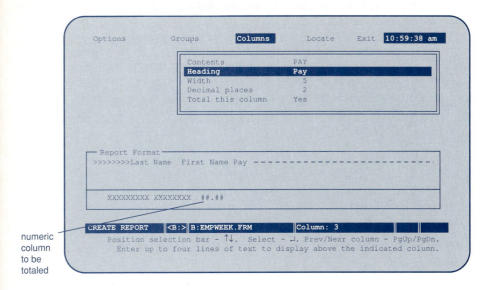

numeric column to be totaled

FIGURE 4-9

The settings for Width, Decimal places, and Total this column were automatically defined by dBASE III PLUS. Width is set for five spaces, allowing for two decimal places and a period. The setting for Decimal places is 2. These are the same as the settings used for the PAY field in the database file structure. Both these settings are acceptable.

The setting in Total this column is "Yes". Also notice the display of # # . # # in the Report Format box. This means that the values in this column will be totaled in the report. dBASE III PLUS automatically totals numeric columns unless you tell it not to. However, we do not want the column of hourly pay rates totaled. To change the setting in "Total this column" to "No".

Select: Total this column

Simply selecting this menu option automatically changed the setting to "No." The code of # # . # # in the Report Format box has changed to 99.99. This code means this is a numeric column that is not to be totaled.

Press: (PGDN)

Define column 4 using the following information. (Refer to the navigation line if you need assistance while making selections.)

Contents: HRS
Heading: **Hours Worked**
Width: 12
Decimal places: 0
Total this column: Yes

Notice that the width of the column was determined this time by the number of characters in the column heading and not the field width. The larger of the two will determine the column width setting.

The final column of data, which will display the weekly pay, is a calculated field. To calculate the values that will be displayed in the column requires that the hours worked be multiplied by the hourly rate of pay (HRS*PAY).

Press: (PGDN)
Select: Contents
Press: (F10)
Select: PAY

The field PAY is entered in the Contents entry area. To multiply (*) the PAY by HRS,

Type: *
Press: (F10)
Select: HRS
Press: (↵)

Enter the column heading as Weekly Pay.

Your display screen should be similar to Figure 4-10.

FIGURE 4-10

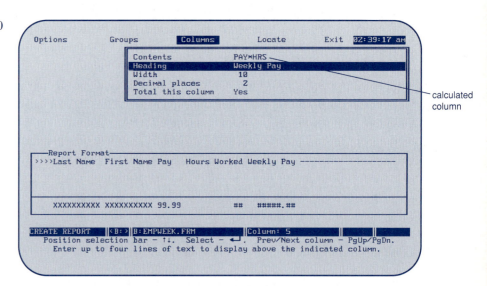

The settings for Width, Decimal places, and Total this column are acceptable.

We have defined the five columns of data. Now we are ready to see how the report looks.

Select: Exit

To save the report format on the diskette,

Select: Save

After a few seconds, the file is saved and you are returned to The Assistant.

Viewing the Report

Donna would like to view the report before printing out a copy of it in case there is anything she wants to change.

Select: Retrieve / Report / B: / EMPWEEK.FRM / Execute the command / N

The report scrolls onto the screen. When "Page No." appears at the top of the screen, to stop the scrolling of the screen,

Press: CTRL-S

Your display screen should be similar to Figure 4-11.

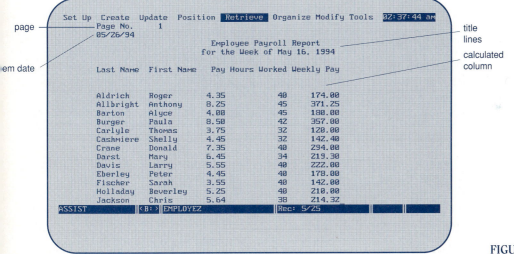

FIGURE 4-11

The page number and system date are displayed in the upper left-hand corner of the report. Donna would like to eliminate these two lines.

The title lines are centered in the middle of the page. However, because the columns of data are not evenly spaced on the page, the title looks off-center.

The report title would look better if it just read "Employee Payroll Report" on the first line and "Week of May 16, 1994" on the second line.

The employee names are listed in alphabetical order. The order of records in the database file is controlled by the master index file, EMPNAME.NDX. The report will display the column data in the same order as the master index file.

The Weekly Pay column values were calculated according to the formula entered as the Weekly Pay column contents.

The column headings for Hours Worked and Weekly Pay would look better if entered on two lines.

To see the rest of the report,

Press: any key

Your display screen should be similar to Figure 4-12.

FIGURE 4-12

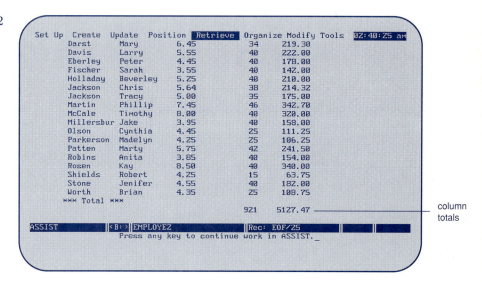

column totals

The bottom line of the report displays the total for the Weekly Pay and Hours Worked columns as specified. The Pay column is not totaled.

Modifying the Report

Donna would like to make several changes to the layout of the report format file.

To return to The Assistant,

Press: any key

To modify the report format file,

Select: Modify / Report / B: / EMPWEEK.FRM

Your display screen should be similar to Figure 4-13.

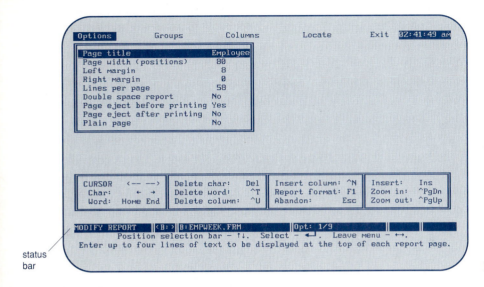

FIGURE 4-13

status bar

The Modify Report screen is displayed. It is the same as the Create Report screen except that it contains the specifications for the report file EMPWEEK.FRM. The navigation key menu is displayed at the bottom of the screen.

Donna wants to change the report title first.

Select: Page title

Your display screen should be similar to Figure 4-14.

FIGURE 4-14

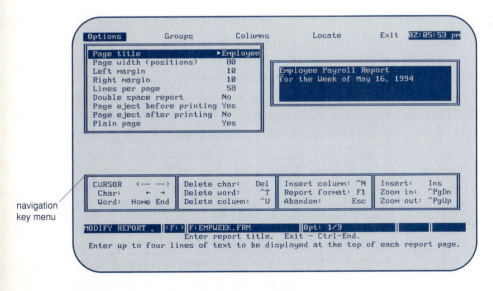

navigation key menu

DB106
Creating a Professional Report

The current title is displayed in the entry area. To change the second line of the title to "Week of May 16, 1994,"

Press: ⏎

The cursor is positioned at the beginning of the second title line.
Donna wants to delete the words "for the" from this line. Notice in the navigation key menu that the key sequence to delete a word is CTRL-T.

Press: CTRL-T (2 times)

The two words are deleted from the second line of the title. To return to the Options Menu,

Press: CTRL-END

The option which allows Donna to turn off the display of the page number and system date from the report is Plain page. To change the setting from "No" to "Yes",

Press: PGDN
Select: Plain page

Simply selecting this option changed the setting to "Yes". The report will not display page numbers and the system date. Changing this setting to "Yes" will also stop the printing of a report title on each page of the report. It will be printed on the first page only.
Next, Donna would like to change the column headings for the Hours Worked and Weekly Pay columns. To quickly locate a specific column,

Select: Locate

Your display screen should be similar to Figure 4-15.

FIGURE 4-15

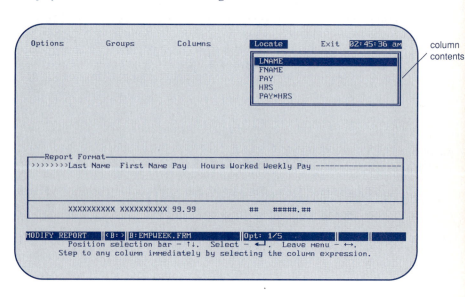

column contents

DB107
Modifying the Report

The five field names specified as the column contents for the five columns are displayed in the menu box.

Select: HRS

The menu highlight bar jumped to the Columns Menu. The Hours Worked column information is now displayed in the box. The Report Format box replaces the navigation key menu on the screen.

Using Locate is especially helpful with a report that has many columns. This is because it eliminates paging down through all the column screens to locate the column you want to use.

Select: Heading

Donna wants to change the title so that "Hours" is on the first line and "Worked" is on the second line.

To move the cursor to the beginning of the word "Worked",

Press: END

To delete the word "Worked" from the first line,

Press: CTRL-T

To move to the second line and enter the word "Worked" on this line,

Press: ⏎
Type: Worked
Press: CTRL-END

Your display screen should be similar to Figure 4-16.

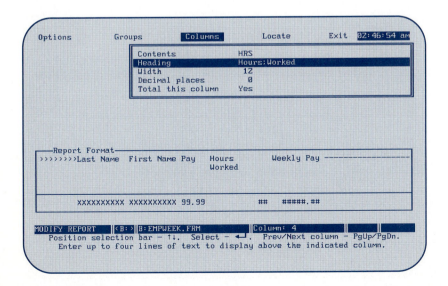

FIGURE 4-16

Notice that a semicolon is displayed between the two words in the Heading entry area. The semicolon indicates a carriage return and the end of the first line.

The column width is still 12. It did not change to reflect the smaller length of the title line.

The Report Format box displays the new column heading on two lines. Notice, however, that because the column width is still set at 12, the code, ##, marking the location of the column contents, is not displayed below the column heading.

To correct this, change the column width to six spaces (the number of characters in the word "Worked") as follows:

Select: Width
Type: 6
Press: ⏎

The contents of the Hours Worked column are now displayed under the column heading.

Press: PGDN

In the same manner, change the column heading for the Weekly Pay column so that it is displayed on two lines. Set the column width to seven spaces. When you are done, your display screen should be similar to Figure 4-17.

FIGURE 4-17

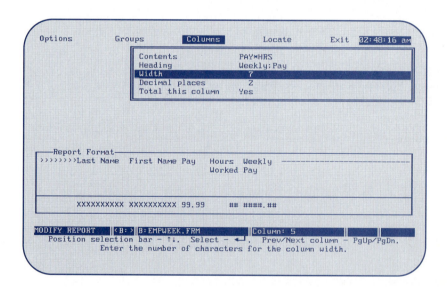

Look at the Report Format box. Donna is still not happy with the layout of the columns. They are not evenly spaced across the width of the page.

DB109
Modifying the Report

To evenly space the columns on the page, we will enter six blank spaces in front of the column headings for the Pay, Hours Worked, and Weekly Pay columns.

Press: `PGUP` (2 times)

The Pay column information is displayed.

Select: Heading
Press: `INS`
Press: space bar (6 times)
Press: `CTRL`-`END`

Your display screen should be similar to Figure 4-18.

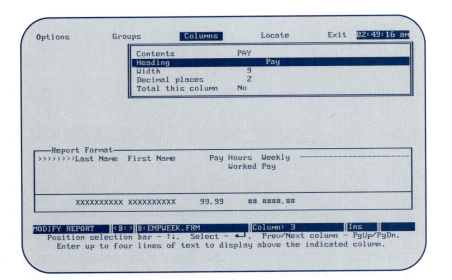

FIGURE 4-18

The column width has increased to nine spaces. As you can see in the Report Format box, the entire column has moved to the right six spaces on the page.

Press: `PGDN`

DB110
Creating a Professional Report

Enter six blank spaces before the Hours Worked and Weekly Pay column headings as follows:

Select: Heading
Press: space bar (6 times)
Press: ⏎
Press: space bar (6 times)
Press: CTRL-END

Press: PGDN
Select: Heading
Press: space bar (6 times)
Press: ⏎
Press: space bar (6 times)
Press: CTRL-END

To turn off the Insert mode,

Press: INS

When you have finished, your display screen should be similar to Figure 4-19.

FIGURE 4-19

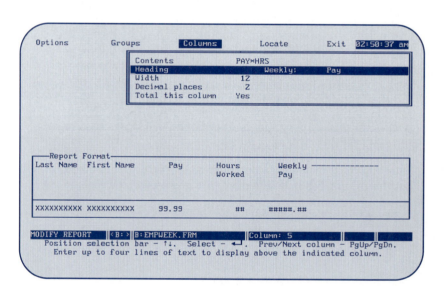

Notice that the column widths automatically adjusted to reflect the increased size of the column headings.

The columns appear more evenly spaced across the width of the page, as you can see in the Report Format box.

Next, to center the columns on the page, the right- and left-margin settings will be increased to 10 spaces. The command to change margins is under Options.

Select: Options / Left margin / **10** ⏎
Select: Right margin / **10** ⏎

Your display screen should be similar to Figure 4-20.

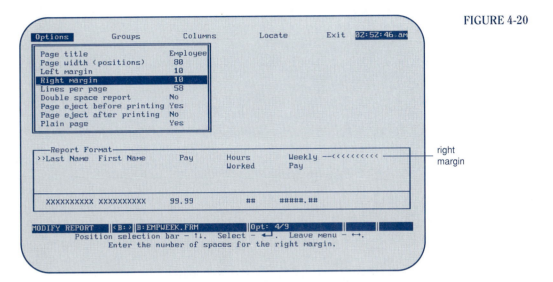

FIGURE 4-20

The Report Format box displays the new layout of the report. The entire width of the page cannot be displayed at one time in the Report Format box. Therefore, the left-margin setting shows only two >'s, while the right-margin setting displays all 10 <'s.

Finally, to turn off Page eject before printing the report,

Select: Page eject before printing

Donna thinks this will be a lot better. To save these changes,

Select: Exit / Save

The Assistant is displayed on the screen again.
To view the report,

Select: **R**etrieve / Report / B: / EMPWEEK.FRM / Execute the command / **N**

Press (CTRL)-**S** to stop the scrolling of the report as soon as the report title scrolls to the top of the screen.

Your display screen should be similar to Figure 4-21.

```
 Set Up   Create  Update  Position  Retrieve  Organize Modify Tools    02:53:42 am
                        Employee Payroll Report
                          Week of May 16, 1994

         Last Name   First Name      Pay        Hours        Weekly
                                                Worked         Pay

         Aldrich     Roger          4.35          40         174.00
         Allbright   Anthony        8.25          45         371.25
         Barton      Alyce          4.00          45         180.00
         Burger      Paula          8.50          42         357.00
         Carlyle     Thomas         3.75          32         120.00
         Cashmiere   Shelly         4.45          32         142.40
         Crane       Donald         7.35          40         294.00
         Darst       Mary           6.45          34         219.30
         Davis       Larry          5.55          40         222.00
         Eberley     Peter          4.45          40         178.00
         Fischer     Sarah          3.55          40         142.00
         Holladay    Beverley       5.25          40         210.00
         Jackson     Chris          5.64          38         214.32
         Jackson     Tracy          5.00          35         175.00
ASSIST            <B:> EMPLOYE2             Rec: EOF/25
```

FIGURE 4-21

Well, that's an improvement over the first time!

After viewing the entire report, press any key to return to The Assistant.

Creating Subtotals

The second report Donna needs to produce is a monthly report of all employees by department. It will show each department's monthly totals for hours worked and monthly pay.

Many of the same columns of data will be used in this report as are used in the weekly report. Rather than redefine many of the same columns and headings, Donna can modify the current report format to meet the new report specifications. To do this, she needs to make a copy of the EMPWEEK.FRM file. She can then change the copy of the report format file to create the new monthly report format file. The command to copy a file is an option in the Tools Menu. She will name the new file EMPMONTH.FRM.

Complete the command sequence below.

Select: Tools / Copy file / B: / EMPWEEK.FRM / B: / **EMPMONTH.FRM** ⏎

To modify the report file,

Select: Modify / Report / B: / EMPMONTH.FRM

Change the Page title to:

Employee Payroll Report
for May, 1994

DB113
Creating Subtotals

The data in this report will be **grouped,** or organized, by department. Each numeric column of data within the group will display a subtotal if the Total this column option is "Yes".

Select: Groups
Select: Group on expression

The field name to group the data by is entered on this line. To call up a field name submenu,

Press: F10
Select: DEPARTMENT
Press: ⏎

The printed heading that will appear at the start of each group in the report is entered next.

Select: Group heading
Type: Department
Press: ⏎

    The last change Donna needs to make to the report format is in the Weekly Pay column. The formula to compute the monthly pay rate and the column heading need to be changed.

Select: Locate / PAY*HRS / Contents

    We will change the formula in this column to be Pay*Hrs*4 (number of weeks in a month). Since the cursor is located at the end of the formula, to edit the formula,

Type: *4
Press: ⏎

    To change the column heading to Monthly Pay,

Select: Heading
Press: END
Press: CTRL-T
Type: Monthly
Press: CTRL-END

    Save the changes and view the new report as follows:

Select: Exit / Save / Retrieve / Report / B: / EMPMONTH.FRM / Execute the command / N

DB114
Creating a Professional Report

Watch the screen as the department titles scroll past. Stop the scrolling several times using CTRL-S for a better look at the report. The last screen of the report should be similar to Figure 4-22.

```
Set Up  Create  Update  Position  Retrieve  Organize  Modify  Tools  03:02:21 am
        ** Department Accounting
           Rosen    Kay          8.50         40         1360.00
        ** Subtotal **
                                              40         1360.00

        ** Department Service
           Shields  Robert       4.25         15          255.00
        ** Subtotal **
                                              15          255.00

        ** Department Accounting
           Stone    Jenifer      4.55         40          728.00
        ** Subtotal **
                                              40          728.00

        ** Department Service
           Worth    Brian        4.35         25          435.00
        ** Subtotal **
                                              25          435.00
        *** Total ***
                                             921        20509.88

ASSIST          <B:> EMPLOYEZ          Rec: 5/25
                Press any key to continue work in ASSIST.
```

FIGURE 4-22

The employees are grouped, or categorized, by departments. However, many of the departments are displayed more than once. Consequently, the subtotals are all incorrect. This is because the wrong master index file was in control at the time the report was run. Whenever groups are specified in a report format file, the database file in use must be indexed or sorted by the same field that is selected for the group expression.

To return to The Assistant,

Press: any key

To access the dot prompt and change the master index file to EMP2DEPT.NDX, which is indexed by department,

Press: ESC
Type: Set index to EMP2DEPT.NDX
Press: ⏎
Press: F2

To view the report again,

Select: **R**etrieve / **R**eport / B: / EMPMONTH.FRM / **E**xecute the command / **N**

Stop the scrolling of the screen as soon as the title reaches the top line of the screen. Your display screen should be similar to Figure 4-23.

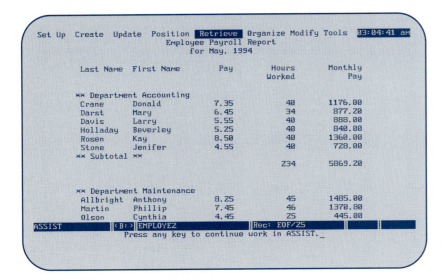

FIGURE 4-23

Notice that now each department is listed only once. The subtotals under each department are accurate. This report will provide the management of the club much valuable information.

Continue to scroll the report on the screen. Press any key to return to The Assistant.

Printing the Reports

If you have printer capability, print a copy of the monthly employee report as follows:

Select: **Retrieve / Report / B: / EMPMONTH.FRM / Execute the command / Y**

DB116
Creating a Professional Report

Your printed output should be similar to Figure 4-24.

```
                      Employee Payroll Report
                        Week of May, 1994

         Last Name      First Name      Pay         Hours        Monthly
                                                    Worked       Pay

         ** Department Accounting
         Crane          Donald          7.35        40           1176.00
         Darst          Mary            6.45        34           877.20
         Davis          Larry           5.55        40           888.00
         Holladay       Beverley        5.25        40           840.00
         Rosen          Kay             8.50        40           1360.00
         Stone          Jennifer        4.55        40           728.00
         *** Subtotal ***
                                                    234          5869.20


         ** Department Maintenance
         Allbright      Anthony         8.25        45           1485.00
         Martin         Phillip         7.45        46           1370.80
         Olson          Cynthia         4.45        25           445.00
         Patten         Marty           5.75        42           241.50
         *** Subtotal ***


         ** Department Restaurant
         Aldrich        Roger           4.35        40           696.00
         Burger         Paula           8.50        42           1428.00
         Eberley        Peter           4.45        40           712.00
         Jackson        Chris           5.64        38           857.28
         Millersbur     Jake            3.95        40           632.00
         Robins         Anita           3.85        40           616.00
         *** Subtotal ***


         ** Department Service
         Barton         Alyce           4.00        45           720.00
         Carlyle        Thomas          3.75        32           480.00
         Cashmiere      Shelly          4.45        32           569.60
         Fisher         Sarah           3.55        40           568.00
         Jackson        Tracy           5.00        35           700.00
         McCale         Timothy         8.00        40           1280.00
         Parkerson      Madelyn         4.25        25           425.00
         Shields        Robert          4.25        15           255.00
         Worth          Brian           4.35        25           435.00
         *** Subtotal ***
                                                    289          5432.60

         *** Total ***
                                                    921          20509.88
```

FIGURE 4-24

Next, change the master index file to EMPNAME.NDX and print the weekly employee report as follows:

Select: **R**etrieve / **R**eport / **B:** / **EMPWEEK.FRM** / **E**xecute the command / **Y**

Your printed output should be similar to Figure 4-25.

```
                  Employee Payroll Report
                    Week of May 16, 1994

Last Name      First Name     Pay       Hours        Weekly
                                        Worked       Pay

Aldrich        Roger          4.35      40           174.00
Allbright      Anthony        8.25      45           371.25
Barton         Alyce          4.00      45           180.00
Burger         Paula          8.50      42           357.00
Carlyle        Thomas         3.75      32           120.00
Cashmiere      Shelly         4.45      32           142.40
Crane          Donald         7.35      40           294.00
Darst          Mary           6.45      34           219.00
Davis          Larry          5.55      40           222.00
Eberley        Peter          4.45      40           178.00
Fisher         Sarah          3.55      40           142.00
Holladay       Beverley       5.25      40           210.00
Jackson        Chris          5.64      38           214.32
Jackson        Tracy          5.00      35           175.00
Martin         Phillip        7.45      46           342.70
McCale         Timothy        8.00      40           320.00
Millersbur     Jake           3.95      40           158.00
Olson          Cynthia        4.45      25           111.25
Parkerson      Madelyn        4.25      25           106.25
Patten         Marty          5.75      42           241.50
Robins         Anita          3.85      40           154.00
Rosen          Kay            8.50      40           340.00
Shields        Robert         4.25      15            63.75
Stone          Jennifer       4.55      40           182.00
Worth          Brian          4.35      25           108.75
*** TOTAL ***
                                        921          5127.47
```

FIGURE 4-25

To review, the following steps are used when creating a report:

- Open the Create Report screen and specify a filename.
- Define the options—report title, line spacing, margins, and so on.
- Define Groups if you want the data categorized and subtotals displayed.
- Define the Column Contents, Headings, and Width.
- Save the report format file.
- View the report.
- Modify the report format file if necessary.
- Print the report.

To leave dBASE III PLUS,

Select: Set Up / Quit dBASE III PLUS

Or from the dot prompt,

Type: Quit

DB118
Creating a Professional Report

Key Terms

report format file   column heading
code   column width
entry area   group
column contents

Matching

1. .FRM
2. >>>>>
3. 99.99
4. XXXX
5. F1
6. column: 4
7. F10
8. ##.##
9. CTRL-T
10. *

____ a. multiplication
____ b. code for a numeric column to be totaled
____ c. deletes word
____ d. right margin code
____ e. report format file extension
____ f. displays field name submenu
____ g. code for column width
____ h. displays Report Format box or navigation key menu
____ i. code for a numeric column not to be totaled
____ j. current column position

Practice Exercises

1. This problem requires that you make a copy of the file EMPLOYE2.DBF. Name this new file PROB1.DBF.

- Open the file PROB1.DBF.
- Index this file by TITLE and name the indexed file JOBTITLE.
- With the index set to JOBTITLE.NDX, create a report format file named JOBANAL.
- Enter the first line of the page
  Title: Job Class Analysis.
  Enter the second linr: (Enter your name).
- Setthe column contents to be TITLE, PAY, DEPARTMENT, FNAME, and LNAME to have the headings Job, Wage, Department, First Name, and Last Name respectively. Wage is to be displayed with two decimal places.
- View this report. Modify it(*do not,* however, turn off the page number and system date) to improve the appearance of the reportby adjusting headings and column widths. Set the left and right margins to 8. Change the Option "Page eject before printing" to "NO". Save and print the report.
- Index PROB1 by DEPARTMENT and name the indexed file JOBDEPT.
- With the index set to JOBDEPT.NDX, create another report file named DEPTANAL by copying JOBANAL.FRM into DEPTANAL.FRM.

- Modify DEPTANAL.FRM by: Changing the first title line to "Job Class Analysis by Department", group the data by department, and specify the group heading to be "Department".
- View this report: Modify it (do turn off the page number and system date) to improve the appearance of the report: Save and print the report.

2. To complete this problem you must first have completed Practice Exercise 2 in Lab 3. Open the database file TILES30.DBF. Using the data in this file and the index files DATE.NDX and COST.NDX, you will create and print two report files.

- The first report Susannah wants to create will display last names, phone numbers, amount owed (unit cost * quantity), and whether the account is paid or not. The data in this report will be organized by date.
- Name this report file AMTDUE.
- Enter the title for the report on two lines. The title is AMOUNT DUE REPORT; BY DATE ORDERED.
- There will be five columns. Accept the default column width. Do not total column 4. Enter the following column information:

Column Number	Column Contents	Column Heading
1	DATE	DATE;ORDERED
2	LAST_NAME	LAST NAME
3	PHONE	PHONE;NUMBER
4	UNIT_COST*QUANTITY	AMOUNT;OWED (Do not total column.)
5	PAID	PAID

- Save the report format.
- View the report.
- Modify it if necessary to be displayed so that it looks balanced on the page. Change column 4 to be totaled. Change "Page eject before printing" to "NO".
- Print the report.
- The second report Susannah wants to create will show her the unit cost, quantity ordered, and total due (unit_cost * quantity). The data in this report will be categorized by the unit cost.
- Name this report file ORDERS.
- Title the report COST AND QUANTITY DATA; your name.
- Group the data by UNIT_COST.
- Title the group heading UNIT COST.

DB120
Creating a Professional Report

- There will be three columns of data. Accept the default column widths. Do not total column 1. Enter the following column information:

Column Number	Column Contents	Column Heading
1	UNIT_COST	UNIT COST (Do not total this column.)
2	QUANTITY	AMOUNT;ORDERED
3	UNIT_COST*QUANTITY	TOTAL

- Save the report.
- View the report.
- Modify the report by adjusting the column placement and margins.
- Do not have a page number displayed. Turn off page eject before printing.
- Save, view, and print the report.

3. To complete this problem, you will need to have completed Practice Exercise 3 in Lab 3. Using the data and index files in SCHOOL.DBF, create and print a report showing the course title, hours, and grade earned as follows:

- Name the report file GRADES.
- Title the report COURSES AND GRADES EARNED: Your Name.
- The columns should contain the course title, hours, and grade. Enter appropriate column headings. Total where needed. Adjust headings, column width and margins as needed. (Turn off "Page eject before printing."
- Save, view, and print the report.
- Modify GRADES.FRM to group on Semester. Title the group heading appropriately.
- Index the file on SEMESTER. Name the index file SEMESTER.
- View the report. Modify it if necessary.
- Print the report.

4. Tom has a modest but growing library of 20 books. He wants to create a database file to record the title, author, publisher, category (i.e. fiction, biography, reference and textbook) copyright, date, and page length for each book.

- Create a database file LIB.DBF.
- Appropriately define the structure.
- Use either your personal library or your school's library to enter data for records 1 through 20.
- Create a report format file named LIBLIST.
- Page Title: Personal Library; (enter your name)
- Specify the column headings to be TITLE, AUTHOR, PUBLISHER, COPYRIGHT.
- Order the records alphabetically by the author's name.

- View this report, modify (*do* turn off the page number and system date) to improve the appearance of the report. Turn off page eject before printing. Print the report.
- Create another report file named CATEGORY.
- Copy LIBLIST.FRM into CATEGORY.FRM.
- Modify CATEGORY by changing the first page title line to "Personal Library by Category." Group the data by category, and specify the group heading to be Category.
- View the repor: Modify it (*do* turn off the page number and system date) to improve the appearance of the report. Print the report.

SUMMARY
dBASE III PLUS

Glossary of Key Terms

Action line: Displays the dBASE III PLUS command as it is built while you are selecting menu options from The Assistant.

The Assistant: A menu driven method of entering dBASE III PLUS commands.

Column contents: The field of data that will determine the contents of a column in a report format file.

Column heading: Specifies the label that will appear above each column of data defined in a report format file.

Column width: The number of spaces each column in a report format file can display.

Codes: The characters displayed in the report format box which symbolize the location and format of the columns in a report format file.

Delete: To mark a record to be removed from the database file when the Pack command is used.

Dialogue box: An entry area that appears on the screen to allow entry of information in response to a command selection or prompt.

Dot prompt: The dBASE III PLUS prompt, represented by a dot, that allows direct entry of commands.

Edit: Allows updating of a single record at a time.

Entry area: A blank area that allows entry of report format specifications.

Field: A collection of related characters, such as a person's name, that makes up a single item in a record.

Field name: The name assigned to a field of information in a record. It can be up to 10 characters long, consisting of letters, numbers, and underscores. It cannot contain any blank spaces and must begin with a letter.

Field type: Determines the type of data that can be entered in a field. The five types are Character, Date, Numeric, Logical, and Memo.

Field width: The number of spaces assigned to a field.

Freeze: A Browse Menu item that restricts cursor movement to a specified field column only.

Groups: Specifies the fields to be grouped together and subtotaled in a report format file.

Index file: Organizes the records in a file according to the specified index key expression. Affects only the display of the records in the database file.

Key expression: The field or fields used to determine the order of records in an index file.

Key field: A field used in sorting the database. It determines the order of records in the sorted file.

Lock: To hold in place specified fields at the left edge of the screen when panning the screen in Browse.

Logical operator: Used to relate logical expressions by selecting either .AND., .OR., or .NOT..

Master index file: The first index file opened. It controls the display of the records in the database file.

Mathematical operators: Used to generate numeric results. They are + for addition, – for subtraction, * for multiplication, and / for division.

Menu: The list of commands displayed in the menu bar.

Menu bar: A selection of menu items, displayed at the top of The Assistant screen, from which you select the operation or command you want to use.

Menu highlight bar: The highlight bar that is used to select the menu you want to use.

Message line: Displays information on the highlighted menu option.

Modify: To make changes to the structure of existing dBASE III PLUS files using the Modify Menu.

Multilevel index: An index file that controls the arrangement of the records in a database file using more than one key expression.

Multilevel sort: A sorted file whose records are organized by the first key field specified and within that by the second key field.

Navigation key menu: Displays the edit and cursor-movement keys available for use.

Navigation line: The line of information at the bottom of the screen that tells you how to move around the menu display.

Numeric functions: A set of built-in formulas that allow calculations on numeric fields of data. They are Sum, Average, and Count.

Open: To use a dBASE III PLUS file.

Options: Command choices available when a menu is opened.

Organize: Arranges the records in a file according to the order specified.

Pan: To scroll into view in the window fields that are off-screen to the right or left while in Browse.

Pointer: The index key values and record numbers of the records in a database file that make up the index file.

Prompt: A message displayed in a dialogue box that requires a user response.

Pull-down menu: A list of options that is displayed when a menu is opened.

Recall: To remove the delete marking from a record.

Record: A collection of related fields of information.

Record number: A unique number automatically assigned by dBASE III PLUS to each record as it is entered into a file.

Record pointer: The number of the current database record.

Relational operators: Used to generate logical results. They are > for greater than, < for less than, = for equals, <> for not equal, <= for less than or equal to, >= for greater than or equal to, $ for substring comparison.

Report format box: Displays a coded layout of the report as columns are defined and options selected.

Report format file: The file created to hold the report specifications. It has an .FRM extension.

Scope: Limits the records to be searched in a file to the range specified.

Search condition: A way to locate records in a file whose field contents meet the specification.

Secondary index: An index file that is opened after the master index file has been selected. It will be updated, but it does not determine the display of records.

Selection bar: The highlighted bar that is used to select pull-down menu options and submenu options when using The Assistant.

Status bar: A highlighted bar at the bottom of the screen that is divided into six areas. It keeps you posted on where you are in The Assistant screen and tells you the state of various optional settings.

Submenu: A list of options that appears when a selection is made from the pull-down menu.

Functional Summary of Selected dBASE III PLUS Commands

dBASE: Starts dBASE III PLUS.

Execute the command: Performs the command as displayed in the action line.

Specify scope: Specifies the range of records in the file to be processed when the command is executed.

Construct a field list: Specifies the fields to include in the retrieval when the command is executed.

Build a search condition: Specifies the conditional limits of the command with a FOR clause.

Build a scope condition: Specifies the conditional limits of the scope condition with a WHILE clause.

Function	Command	Action
Set Up	Database file	Opens an existing database file for use.
	Quit dBASE III PLUS	Quits the dBASE III PLUS program, closes all open files, and returns you to DOS.
Create	Database file	Creates a new database file (.DBF).
	Report	Creates a report format file (.FRM).
Update	Append	Adds new records to the open database file.
	Edit	Allows you to change the contents of a record. One record at a time is displayed on the screen.
	Browse	Allows you to change the contents using full-screen editing. Up to 17 records can be displayed at one time, one record per row.
	Delete	Marks record(s) for deletion.
	Recall	Reinstates all or selected records marked for deletion.
	Pack	Permanently removes all records marked for deletion.
Position	Seek	Locates the first record in an indexed file that matches the key expression.
	Locate; Continue	Moves the record pointer to the first record that matches the specified expression. Continue is then used to find subsequent records.
	Skip	Moves the record pointer forward or backward a specified number of records.
	Goto Record	Moves the record pointer to a specified record number.

DB125
Functional Summary of Selected dBASE III PLUS Commands

Function	Command	Action
Retrieve	List	Lets you view and print all or selected fields and records. Does not pause when screen is full.
	Display	Lets you view all or selected fields and records. Pauses when screen is full.
	Report	Lets you display or print a report using the report format file.
	Sum	Computes the sum of numeric fields.
	Average	Computes the average of numeric fields.
	Count	Counts the number of records meeting a specified condition.
Organize	Sort	Creates a database file (.DBF) that physically rear ranges the records in a database based on specified key fields.
Modify	Database file	Allows changes to the field structure of an existing database file.
	Report	Allows changes to the settings stored in a report file.
Tools	Set drive	Changes the default drive for the program to locate the data files.
	Copy file	Duplicates the contents of any type of file to another file.
	Directory	Displays a listing of files on a specified disk drive.
	List structure	Displays and prints the file structure of the open database file.

INDEX

Action line, DB8, DB9
Analysis of database data, DB86-DB88
Appending records, DB30-DB31, DB75, DB82
Assistant, The:
    and dot commands, DB9
    screen for, DB8
    using, DB9-DB12
Averaging data, DB87

Browsing records, DB42-DB48

Character field type:
    advantages for using, DB20
    defined, DB17-DB18
Code, in Report Format box, DB95
Columns, in reports:
    contents of, DB97-DB98
    headings for, DB99
    modifying layout of, DB108-DB111
    numeric, DB101
    specifying, DB97-DB103
    subtotals for, DB112-DB115
    width of, DB99

Commands:
    Append, DB30-DB31, DB75, DB82
    Assist, DB9
    Browse, DB42-DB48
    Continue, DB52, DB55
    Copy, DB70
    Copy file, DB112
    Count, DB87
    Create Report, DB94
    Database file (Create), DB10, DB12, DB23
    Database file (Modify), DB39-DB42
    Database file (Set UP), DB38-DB39, DB80
    Delete, DB50-DB51, DB58
    Directory, DB67-DB68, DB85
    Display, DB59, DB60, DB79, DB84
    Edit, DB49-DB50, DB57
    entering, DB9, DB37-38
    Goto Record, DB52, DB57
    Index, DB76-DB80
    List, DB31, DB61, DB62-DB63, DB70, DB73, DB75, DB80, DB86, DB88
    List structure, DB69
    Locate, DB52, DB55-DB56

Index

Pack, DB59-DB60, DB62
Quit, DB33, DB117
Recall, DB61
Report (Create), DB93
Report (Modify), DB104-DB112
Report (Retrieve), DB103, DB111, DB113, DB114, DB115-DB116
Retrieve, DB59
Seek, DB52, DB82-DB84
Set drive, DB125
Skip, DB52, DB58
Sort, DB70-DB76
summary of, DB124
Conditional searching, DB52-DB56
Copying files, DB70, DB112
Counting records, DB87
Create Menu:
    Database file, DB10, DB12, DB23
    Report, DB93
Create Report screen:
    Columns, DB97-DB103
    Exit, DB111, DB113
    Groups, DB113
    Locate, DB106, DB113
    Options, DB95, DB111
Creating file structure:
    defined, DB4
    entering field names, DB16-DB23
Cursor:
    freezing movement of, DB46
    unfreezing, DB48

Data:
    analyzing, DB86-DB88
    grouped, in reports, DB113
Data entry (*see* Inputting records)
Database files (*see* Files)
Databases:
    advantages of using, DB4
    defined, DB3
    See also Structure, file
Date field type:
    defined. DB17, DB19
    entering invalid dates, DB25
dBASE III PLUS:
    loading, DB7-DB8
    quitting, DB33, DB63, DB69, DB117
    report generator, DB92-DB117
    See also Assistant, The
Deleting characters, DB15
Deleting records:
    defined, DB4
    marking for deletion, DB50-DB51, DB58
    packing to remove, DB59-DB60, DB62
    undeleting, DB51, DB61
Dialogue boxes, DB15
Directories, disk, displaying, DB67-DB68, DB85
Disk directories, displaying, DB67-DB68
Disk drives, specifying, DB14, DB125
Displaying:
    disk directories, DB67-DB68
    file structures, DB68-DB70
    indexed records, DB79, DB80
    records with List, DB31
    reports, DB103-DB104, DB114-DB115
    specific records, DB59-DB60, DB79, DB84

Dot prompt, DB8-DB9

Editing:
    defined, DB4
    during data entry, DB26-DB27
    previously entered records, DB49-DB50, DB57
Entry areas, on Report screen, DB95
EOF/1 (End Of the File) message, DB27
Errors, correcting, DB15, DB17
    during data entry, DB26-DB27
    in report generator, DB96
Fields:
    character, DB17, DB18, DB20
    date, DB17, DB19, DB25
    defined, DB4, DB12
    defining, DB12-DB23
    key, DB71, DB73
    locking, DB45
    logical, DB17, DB22
    memo, DB17
    names for, DB16
    numeric, DB17, DB21, DB87, DB101
    panning, DB44
    and searching for records, DB53
    submenu, DB53-54
    types of, DB5, DB17
    width of, DB22
File names:
    for database files, DB15, DB38
    for index files, DB68
    for report format files, DB93
File structure:
    defining, DB12-DB23
    displaying, DB68-DB70
    saving, DB23, DB42
Files:
    appending to, DB30-DB31, DB75, DB82
    copying, DB70, DB112
    creating, DB10, DB12, DB23
    defined, DB4
    index, DB79, DB80-DB82, DB85, DB88
    indexing, DB4, DB68, DB76-DB82, DB86
    modifying, DB39-DB42
    opening, DB37-DB39, DB68, DB72, DB73, DB80, DB92
    printing, DB31-DB32
    quitting, DB33, DB63, DB89, DB117
    report format, DB93, DB104
    sorting, DB70-DB76
    See also File names, File structure
Formatting reports, DB93
Freezing cursor movement, DB46
    unfreezing, DB48
Function keys:
    F1, DB13, DB44
    F10, DB48, DB98

Goto Record command, DB52, DB57
Grouped data, in reports, DB113

Help function (F1), DB13, DB44

Index files:
    displaying directory of, DB85
    filename extension for, DB79

Index

master, DB82
opening, DB80-DB82
printing reports with, DB88-DB89
secondary, DB82
Indexing:
    advantages over sorting, DB86
    defined, DB4
    filename extension used, DB68
    on multiple key fields, DB76-DB80
Inputting records, DB23-DB29
    appending records, DB30-DB31
    consistency in, DB25
    correcting errors, DB26-DB27
    editing when entering, DB26-DB27
    saving and existing, DB29
Insert mode, DB26, DB110

Key expressions, DB77
Key fields:
    multiple, DB73
    for sorting, DB71
Keys:
    Backspace, DB15, DB28
    Ctrl-Y, DB27, DB28
    cursor, DB9-DB12, DB17, DB28
    Del, DB27, DB28
    for editing, DB26-DB27, DB28
    End, DB10, DB11, DB26, DB28
    Esc, DB13, DB29
    Home, DB10, DB28
    Ins, DB26-DB27, DB28
    for modifying structure, DB40
    Pgdn, DB31, DB68
    Pgup, DB28, DB31, DB43
    See also Function keys

Listing:
    file structures, DB69
    records, DB31, DB61, DB62-DB63, DB70, DB73, DB75, DB80, DB86, DB88
Loading dBASE III PLUS, DB7-DB8
Locating records, DB55-DB56
Locking fields, DB45
Logical field type:
    defined, DB17
    creating, DB22
Logical operators, DB54

Master index, DB82
Mathematical operators, DB123
Memo field type, defined, DB17
Menu bar:
    for The Assistant, DB9
    for Browse, DB45
    for Report screen, DB94
Menu highlight bar, DB9, DB10
Menus:
    action line, DB8, DB9
    Browse, DB45
    canceling selection, DB13
    menu bar, DB8, DB9
    message line, DB8, DB9
    navigation line, DB8, DB9, DB10, DB16
    pull-down, DB8, DB9
    selecting and opening, DB9-DB10
    selection bar, DB9, DB10

status bar, DB8, DB9
submenus, DB14
summary of functions, DB124-DB125
    See also individual menus: The Assistant, Create, Modify, Organize, Position, Retrieve, Set Up, Tools, Update
Message line, DB8, DB9
Modes (*See* Insert mode)
Modify Menu:
    Database file, DB39-DB42
    Report, DB104-DB112
Modifying database structure, DB39-DB42
Modifying reports, DB104-DB112
Multilevel:
    indexes, DB76-DB80
    sorts, DB73-DB76

Navigation key menu, DB27, DB22, DB40, DB49, DB94
Navigation line, DB8, DB9, DB10, DB16
Numeric field types:
    creating, DB21
    defined, DB17
    and numeric functions, DB87
    in reports, DB101
Numeric functions, DB87

Opening files:
    database, DB37-DB39, DB68, DB72, DB73, DB80, DB92
    index, DB80-DB82
Operators:
    logical, DB54
    mathematical, DB123
    relational, DB54
Options, scope, DB31
Organize Menu:
    Copy, DB70
    Index, DB76-DB82
    Sort, DB70-DB76

Packing records, DB59-DB60, DB62
Panning fields, DB44
Pointer:
    index, DB80
    record, DB28, DB32, DB51-DB61
Position Menu:
    Continue, DB52, DB55
    Goto Record, DB52, DB57
    Locate, DB52, DB55-DB56
    options, DB52-DB52
    Seek, DB52, DB82-DB84
    Skip, DB52, DB58
Printing:
    database files, DB31-DB32
    reports, DB88-DB89, DB115-DB117
    selected records, DB62-DB63
Prompts:
    in dialogue boxes, DB15
    dot, DB8-DB9
Pull-down menus, DB8, DB9
Quitting dBASE III PLUS, DB33, DB63, DB69, DB117

Recalling deleted records, DB61

Index

Records:
  analyzing data in, DB86-DB88
  appending, DB30-DB31
  blank forms, DB75
  browsing, DB42-DB48
  counting, DB87
  defined, DB4, DB12
  deleting, DB4, DB50-DB51, DB58, DB62
  displaying with List, DB31
  editing, DB49-DB50, DB57
  finding, DB51-DB61
  indexing, DB4, DB68, DB76-DB80, DB86
  inputting, DB23-DB29, DB30-DB31
  listing, DB31, DB61, DB62-DB63, DB70, DB73, DB75, DB80, DB86, DB88
  locating, DB55-DB56
  marking for deletion, DB50-DB51, DB58
  numbers for, DB28
  packing to remove, DB59-DB60, DB62
  printing, DB31-DB32, DB62-DB63
  recalling deleted records, DB61
  record pointer, DB28, DB32, DB51-DB61
  removing delete marks, DB51, DB61
  saving, DB29
  scope options, DB31, DB60-DB61
  searching for, DB51-DB59, DB82-DB84
  sorting, DB5, DB70-DB76, DB86
  summing, DB87-DB88
Relational operators, DB54
Report format box, DB95
Report format file
  file name extension for, DB93
  modifying, DB104-DB112
Report generator, DB92-DB117
Reports:
  columns in, DB97-DB103
  creating, DB92-DB117
  defined, DB4
  displaying, DB103-DB104, DB114-DB115
  entering the title, DB95-DB97
  formatting, DB93
  modifying, DB104-DB112
  numeric functions in, DB101
  printing with index file, DB88-DB89, DB115-DB117
  retrieving, DB103, DB111, DB113-DB116
  subtotals in, DB112-DB115
Retrieve Menu:
  Count, DB87
  Display, DB59, DB60, DB79, DB84
  List, DB31, DB61, DB62-DB63, DB70, DB73, DB75, DB80, DB86, DB88
  Report, DB103, DB111, DB113, DB114, DB115-DB116

Saving:
  changes to file structure, DB42
  file structure, DB23, DB42
  files, DB29

records entered, DB29
Scope/Search submenu:
  options, DB31, DB60
  for recalling deleted records, DB61
  scope defined, DB4
Screens:
  Append, DB30
  The Assistant, DB8
  Columns, DB97
  Create, DB16, DB23
  Create Report, DB94
  Modify, DB40
  Modify Report, DB105
  panning records on, DB44
  Report, DB92-DB95
Scrolling:
  with List option, DB31
  locking fields, DB45
  in reports, DB103, DB114
  See also Browsing records
Search condition, DB52-DB56
Searching:
  conditional, DB52-DB56
  defined, DB5
Secondary indexes, DB82
Selection bar, DB9
Set Up Menu:
  Database file, DB38-DB39, DB80
  Quit, DB33, DB117
Slash, in commands, DB38, DB56
Sorting records:
  compared to indexing, DB86
  defined, DB5
  disadvantages of, DB76
  multilevel, DB73-DB76
  on one field, DB70-DB73
Status bar, DB8, DB9
Structure, file:
  defined, DB5
  defining, DB12-DB23
  listing, DB69
  modifying, DB39-DB42
Summing records, DB87-DB88

Tools Menu:
  Copy file, DB112
  Directory, DB67-DB68, DB85
  List structure, DB69
  Set drive, DB125
Type, field (*see* Field type)

Update menu:
  Append, DB30-DB31, DB75, DB82
  Browse, DB42-DB48
  Delete, DB50-DB51, DB58
  Edit, DB49-DB50, DB57
  Pack, DB59-DB60, DB62
  Recall, DB61

Local Area Network

Copyright © 1990 by McGraw-Hill, Inc. All rights reserved. Printed in the United States of America. Except as permitted under the United States Copyright Act of 1976, no part of this publication may be reproduced or distributed in any form or by any means, or stored in a database or retrieval system, without the prior written permission of the publisher.

4 5 6 7 8 9 0 KGP KGP 9 5 4 3 2 1

P/N 047890-2

ORDER INFORMATION:
ISBN 0-07-047890-2

IBM, IBM PC, and PC DOS are registered trademarks of International Business Machines, Inc.

CONTENTS

Overview Local Area Network   NET3
Definition of Local Area Network   NET3
Advantages of Using a Local Area Network   NET4
Local Area Network Terminology   NET4

Lab 1 Using a Local Area Network   NET5
The Club Manager   NET6
   Starting the LAN   NET6
   Logging on to the LAN   NET7
   Examining the Manager's Menu   NET9
   Sending Express Mail   NET10
The Activities Director   NET13
   Logging on to the LAN   NET13
   Examining the Activities Director's Menu   NET14
   Receiving Express Mail   NET14
   Retrieving and Printing the Daily Activity Schedule   NET16
   Using a Specific Applications Software Program   NET19
   Sending Regular Mail   NET22
The Front Desk   NET24
   Logging on to the LAN   NET24
   Using LAN Special Screens   NET25
The Club Manager   NET26
   Receiving Regular Mail   NET27
   Using a Common Data File   NET27
   Signing off the LAN   NET29
Key Terms   NET30
Matching   NET31

Summary Local Area Network   NET31
Glossary of Key Terms   NET31

Index   NET32

OVERVIEW
Local Area Network

Now that you know how to use several different applications programs, wouldn't it be nice if you could access files on a diskette in another area of the building? Or if you could use that new software program the accounting department just purchased? Walking to the other office and finding the diskette the program is on takes time. Of course, you can copy the file onto another diskette, but what happens if later on someone updates the version on his or her diskette? Then your copy is no longer up to date. You then have two copies of the same file being used that contain different data. How will someone else who wants to use the data in this file know which is more up to date?

A communications network can be the answer to this problem. By linking computers together, the same file can be accessed by several people. They can update it as necessary and use it knowing that the file is the most recent version with the most up-to-date data. No longer do you need to run around the building to get the one diskette containing the file, or create and maintain duplicate files containing perhaps different data. The savings in time and duplication of effort are dramatic.

Definition of Local Area Network

A **network** is any system that allows two or more computers to communicate. The task of communication between computers is accomplished by connecting the computers with a communications channel. The channel can be a plain telephone line or a cable dedicated solely to the transmission of data between computers.

In a **local area network (LAN)** system, communication between computers is over a limited geographic area. It can be within a large department of a business, within a single building, or between several adjacent buildings (such as on a college campus). The communications channel in a LAN is usually by cable.

To take advantage of a network system, a communications software program is needed that will allow the computers to talk to one another. It controls the transfer of files to the microcomputers, the transfer of data to the printer, and electronic mail. Usually one central computer, called the **control unit** or **file server,** is responsible for the smooth operation of the network system.

Advantages of Using a Local Area Network

Perhaps one of the most obvious advantages to a network is the common access to files, or **information resources sharing.** This eliminates duplication of files and data and lets several users update and use the data in the same file.

Perhaps a not-so-obvious advantage is that the applications software programs, as well as the data files, can be shared. Rather than each user needing a diskette containing the software program, he or she simply accesses the program through the LAN. It is then loaded into the memory of that user's microcomputer.

Another important advantage to a network system is **hardware resources sharing.** The most common hardware resource that can be shared is a printer. Instead of purchasing several expensive laser printers which can each be accessed by a single microcomputer, one laser printer can be networked for use by all the microcomputers on the LAN.

Most LANs have an **electronic mail** system that allows the users to send and receive messages. The message can be read only by the user to whom it is sent. This is accomplished by entering the recipient's account number or password code. One of the big advantages to electronic mail is that it helps to eliminate telephone tag. If the recipient is not in the office, the message is there just waiting for him or her to return.

Local Area Network Terminology

Communications channel: A cable or telephone line that provides the means for transmission of data between computers.

Electronic mail: The transmission of messages electronically.

File server: A central computer that controls the transfer of data between microcomputers, to the printers, and electronic mail. Also called the control unit.

Local area network (LAN): A communications network consisting of computers connected by cable within a building or group of adjacent buildings in a limited geographic area.

Login: The sign-on procedure used to access the communications network.

Network: The linking of two or more computers to allow communication between computers.

Password: A secret code assigned to each authorized user to control access to the computer network.

Shared hardware resources: The common access to hardware such as printers by all microcomputers linked to the network.

Shared information resources: The common access to data files and applications software programs by all microcomputers on the network.

LAB 1
Using a Local Area Network

CASE STUDY

The Sports Club recently installed a local area network (LAN) system that links the five microcomputers located in different areas within the club. The microcomputer users will be able to access common data files and software programs and to send and receive messages by an electronic mail system. A floor plan of the club (see below) shows the location of the microcomputers and how they are linked to the file server and to one another.

As you can see from the floor plan, there is a microcomputer in the membership office, the manager's office, the accounting office, the activities office, and at the front desk. Each microcomputer is linked to the file server,

OBJECTIVES

In this lab you will learn how:

1. A local area network operates.
2. To create and send a message by electronic mail.
3. To retrieve and use files from the file server.

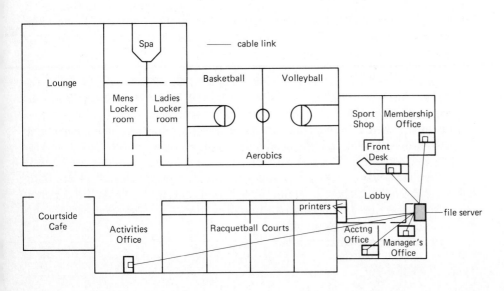

NET5

which is in the manager's office. There are two printers, a dot-matrix printer and a laser printer. Both can be accessed by any of the microcomputers.

During this lab we will observe three employees of the Sports Club as they use the LAN while performing their jobs. The three employees are Ernie Powell, the club manager; Ann Davis, the activities director; and Tom Carlyle, a front desk clerk. They have jobs with different levels of responsibility. Consequently, their use of and access to files within the LAN vary.

The day begins when Ernie Powell, the club manager, opens the club at 6:00 A.M., starts up the LAN for the club, and accesses the LAN on his microcomputer. We will take a look at his menu and follow him as he creates and sends a message to the activities director by electronic mail.

A little while later, Ann Davis, the activities director, turns on her microcomputer and accesses the LAN. She receives and acknowledges the message sent by Ernie. Ann proceeds to use the LAN to retrieve two data files, use the printer, and send a message back to Ernie.

Next we will follow Tom Carlyle, the front desk clerk, as he uses the LAN to check in club members as they enter the club and record the types of activities they plan to use that day.

Finally, toward the end of the day, we will return to watch Ernie as he receives electronic mail and reads his messages. He retrieves and uses a data file that was created by Ann. He ends his day by signing off the LAN.

To begin this lab, you need to turn on your computer and load DOS, responding to the date and time prompts in the usual manner. Place your data diskette in the A drive. The program you will use to run this lab, NETWORK.COM, is on your data diskette. This program will show how the LAN operates at the Sports Club. We will load this program shortly. The A> should be on your display screen.

The Club Manager

Ernie Powell, the club manager, is responsible for the day-to-day operation of the club as well as for long-range planning. Since he is the manager, all club employees either directly or indirectly report to him. The Sports Club opens daily at 6:00 A.M. Frequently Ernie will be the first employee there in the morning. On this particular day (Monday, December 4, 1991), Ernie has just opened the club. We will follow him as he starts up the LAN, logs on to the LAN, and uses the LAN to send a message using the electronic mail system.

Starting the LAN   Since all the microcomputers at the club are linked by the LAN, Ernie's first job of the day is to start up the LAN by turning on the **file server**. The file server is very similar to the system unit on your computer. The file server is a large-capacity hard disk that contains the network operating system for starting up the LAN, for controlling the microcomputers and printers connected to it, and for sending electronic mail. It also holds the common software programs used by the club. They are a word processing program, WordPerfect; a spreadsheet program, Lotus 1-2-3; and a database program, dBASE III PLUS. It also holds the common data files that are used by personnel throughout the club. Next, Ernie goes to his desk and turns on his microcomputer.

To load the program for this lab,

Type: **NETWORK**
Press: ⏎

Your display screen should be similar to Figure 1-1.

FIGURE 1-1

The H> is the LAN system prompt. You are more familiar with the A>. In a LAN, your microcomputer typically has access to much greater storage space than is available on the local diskette drives or the hard disk. This storage space is located in the file server and in this case is identified as the H drive.

Logging on to the LAN The LAN is prompting Ernie to enter his **Login** information. The login information is required of any user who wants to access the LAN; it acts as a means of security. All authorized users of the LAN are assigned a **login identification** and **password.** If the login information you enter at this prompt does not match the information in the file server, you will be denied access to the system.

The login identification and password also control which data files and programs the employee can access. Not all users of the LAN need to have access to all the data files on the file server to perform their jobs. For example, Ernie, as club manager, does need to be able to access all data files and application software programs on the file server. In contrast, Ann, the activities director, has access only to data files that are related to activity scheduling.

Note: All commands you type in this lab must be entered in all capital letters. Use the (CAPS LOCK) key to create all capital letters. If your computer beeps, you are either entering an incorrect character or you are not entering the correct character as a capital letter. If at any time you wish to exit the lab, press: (CTRL)-(BREAK) or (CTRL)-(SCROLL LOCK).

Ernie's login identification is simply his first name. To login,

Type: **ERNIE**
Press: ⏎

Your display screen should be similar to Figure 1-2.

FIGURE 1-2

His login identification has been accepted and now he must enter his **password.** As further security, each employee who uses the LAN has a password. Ernie's password is 7237. You will notice that as you enter the password, it is not displayed on the screen. Instead, as each character of the password is typed, an asterisk is displayed. In this way, anyone watching your screen while you enter your password will not be able to see the password.

NET8
Using a Local Area Network

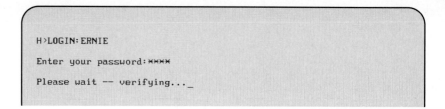

Your display screen should be similar to Figure 1-3.

FIGURE 1-3

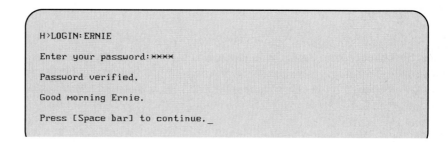

The LAN is verifying that Ernie's login and password are acceptable by checking them against a list of stored login identifications and passwords in the file server. Once they have been verified, your display screen should be similar to Figure 1-4.

FIGURE 1-4

Ernie's password has been verified. The LAN greets him.
To continue, following the directions on the display,

Press: Space bar

Your display screen should be similar to Figure 1-5.

FIGURE 1-5

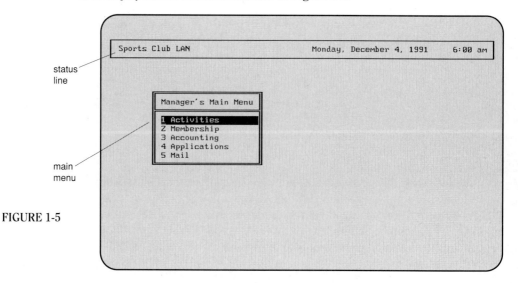

Examining the Manager's Menu This is the LAN customized menu designed for the club manager. The status line at the top of the screen displays the name of the LAN system, the current date, and the time. The central area of the screen displays a menu of five menu options.

This menu lets Ernie access all data files and applications software programs stored on the file server. Because he is the club manager, he has unrestricted access to all files on the file server.

The first menu item, Activities, allows him to access the routine files used by the activities director. The second and third, Membership and Accounting, contain data files used specifically by employees in those areas. The fourth menu item, Applications, allows Ernie to use a specific applications software program to create or edit a file. The fifth menu item, Mail, lets him use the LAN electronic mail system.

The number to the left of the menu item is used to select the item. For example, to access files used by the activities director,

Type: 1
Press: ⏎

Your display screen should be similar to Figure 1-6.

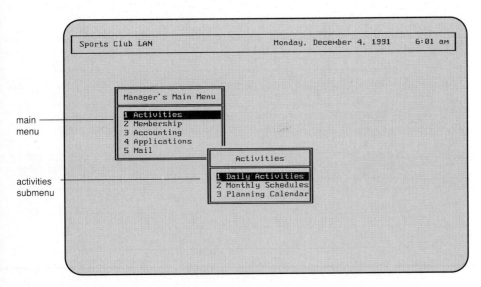

FIGURE 1-6

Upon selecting Activities, a submenu of three options is displayed. Suppose Ernie selected the first submenu option, Daily Activities. The word processing program WordPerfect would be loaded and a text file of the current day's schedule of activities would be automatically retrieved and displayed by the LAN. We will see how this works when we watch Ann, the activities director, check and print the daily schedule.

The other two submenu options, Monthly Schedule and Planning Calendar, access the appropriate applications software program and data files showing activities for the month and year.

To leave the Activities submenu and return to Ernie's main menu,

Press: ESC

Ernie's main menu is displayed again. He can access the other main menu items in the same manner to use files in the accounting and membership areas.

Sending Express Mail Before Ernie makes his daily facility inspection, he wants to send a message to Ann, the activities director. Ann has been working on an analysis of the club activity usage for January through June. Ernie needs to have the completed analysis today so that he can present the data at the board of directors' meeting the next day.

To find out the status of the analysis and to let Ann know that he needs the completed report by the afternoon, he could use the telephone. But it is unlikely that she is in her office yet. He could leave a message with her assistant telling her to call him back about the status of the activity analysis. But he may not be in his office to receive the message and then he would need to return her call. To eliminate the possibility of telephone tag, he will send a message through the LAN electronic mail system.

There are three steps to using the LAN electronic mail system. First the message must be created, then saved, and finally sent. To access the LAN electronic mail system, select the Mail menu item as follows:

Type: 5
Press:

Your display screen should be similar to Figure 1-7.

FIGURE 1-7

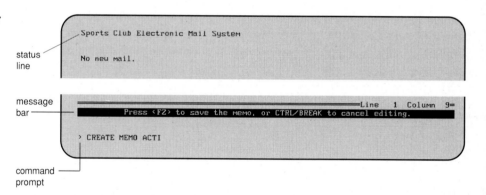

The status line at the top of the screen shows that Ernie has entered the Sports Club electronic mail system. He can use this system to send and receive messages to and from any microcomputer user on the LAN.

The message on Ernie's screen tells him he has not received any new mail. The highlighted bar at the bottom of the screen displays "LAN messages". Right now the message bar tells you to enter a command. The > at the bottom of the screen is the LAN command prompt, followed by the cursor. The LAN is waiting for Ernie to enter a LAN command. The LAN command to create a message is CREATE MEMO followed by the message name. Since this is a memo to Ann about the activity analysis, he will name the message ACTI.

Type: CREATE MEMO ACTI
Press:

Your display screen should be similar to Figure 1-8.

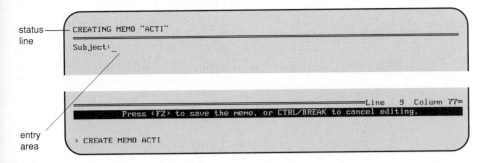

FIGURE 1-8

Notice that the status line now shows that you are CREATING MEMO "ACTI", and the word "Subject:" appears in the entry area followed by the cursor. The content of the memo is entered at the cursor location. The current line number and column location of the cursor are displayed on the bottom right-hand side of the entry area.

Ernie types his message to Ann. To see the message he has typed,

Press: space bar

Your display screen should be similar to Figure 1-9.

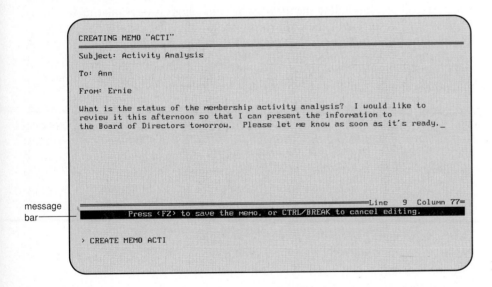

FIGURE 1-9

Next, the memo needs to be saved on the file server, and then it can be sent to Ann. Notice the message in the message bar. It tells you to use the function key (F2) to save the memo.

Press: (F2)

Your display screen should be similar to Figure 1-10.

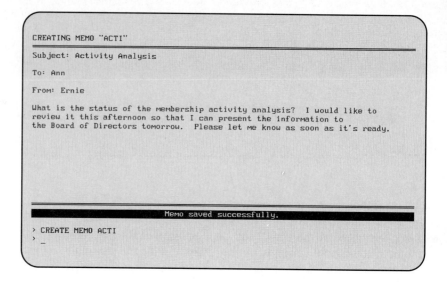

FIGURE 1-10

The message bar indicates that the memo has been successfully saved.

The next step is to send the message. The LAN command is SEND MEMO, followed by the message name and the recipient's login identification. However, Ernie has a choice of sending the message by either **express** or **regular mail** delivery. Express mail is similar to the mail carrier delivering mail directly to your home, knocking on your door, and requiring your signature. Electronic express mail will send the mail to the recipient, display a message on the screen telling the recipient that mail is waiting, and lock the keyboard until the recipient acknowledges the message on the screen.

Regular mail will send the mail to the recipient and store it in his or her electronic "mailbox." This is similar to the way the mail carrier usually delivers mail to your home, by putting it in your mailbox. To find out if you have mail, you must check the mailbox. This is the same with regular electronic mail—you must check your electronic mailbox to find out if you have received any mail.

Ernie wants to send the message using express mail to ensure that Ann sees the message right away. To send the memo by express mail,

Type: SEND EXPRESS MEMO ACTI TO ANN
Press: ⏎

Your display screen should be similar to Figure 1-11.

FIGURE 1-11

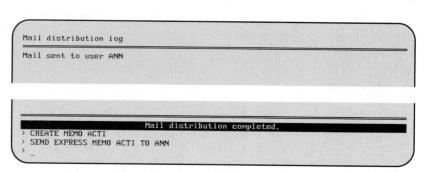

The screen tells Ernie that his mail has been successfully sent (distributed) to Ann. If she is already on the LAN, she will be interrupted by the express mail notification message. If she is not on the LAN, as soon as she logs on the mail notification will be displayed.

After writing and sending a few other messages to other employees in the club, Ernie returns to his main menu by issuing the command to quit.

Type: QUIT
Press: ⏎

Ernie's main menu is displayed again. He has nothing else he needs to do using the LAN right now. So he leaves his office to make his daily inspection of the club.

The Activities Director

The second person we will observe using the LAN is Ann, the activities director. We will follow Ann as she receives the express mail notification and reads the memo from Ernie. She will use her menu to retrieve and print the WordPerfect file containing the daily activity schedule. She will also complete the activity analysis for Ernie using Lotus 1-2-3. Finally, she will send Ernie a message to tell him the analysis is ready for his review.

Logging on to the LAN At about the same time Ernie was creating his memo to Ann, she was logging on to the LAN. Her login procedure is very similar to Ernie's, except her user login identification and password are different.

Ann has turned on her computer. To see her display screen,

Press: space bar

The H> is displayed on the screen.
To enter Ann's login identification,

Type: ANN
Press: ⏎

The prompt to enter the password is displayed on the screen. Ann's password is 1964. To enter the password,

Type: 1964
Press: ⏎

The password and identification are being verified. Once the password is verified, to see Ann's main menu,

Press: space bar

Your display screen should be similar to Figure 1-12.

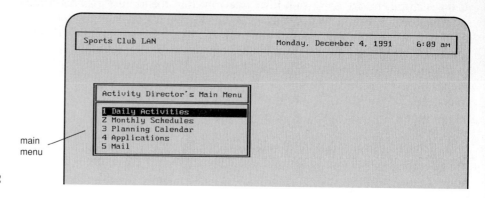

main menu

FIGURE 1-12

Examining the Activities Director's Menu You will notice that Ann's main menu is not the same as Ernie's. However, it should look familiar (see Figure 1-5). The first three menu items in Ann's main menu are the same three submenu options that were displayed when Ernie selected Activities from his main menu.

Since Ann has different job responsibilities, she does not need access to the same files as Ernie. For example, Ann's main menu does not allow her to access the accounting files because her job responsibilities do not require the information in those files. However, Ann's main menu does include Applications and Mail, the same as Ernie's.

Receiving Express Mail Each morning Ann updates and checks the daily activity schedule. Once it is correct, she prints a copy of the schedule using the laser printer and posts it at the front desk.

Just as she is about to select the Daily Activities menu item, she is interrupted by an express mail message notification.

Press: space bar

Your display screen should be similar to Figure 1-13.

FIGURE 1-13

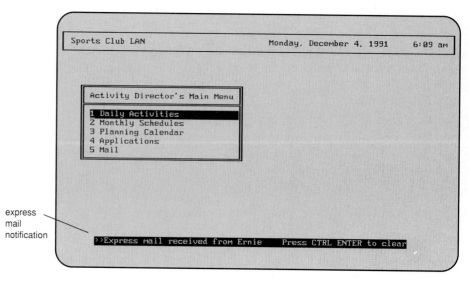

express mail notification

The computer beeped and the keyboard is temporarily frozen. A message appears telling Ann that express mail from Ernie has been received. Until she acknowledges receiving the notification, she cannot continue to use the LAN.

Following the directions on the display, to clear the message and acknowledge receipt of the notification,

Press: CTRL ⏎

The keyboard is freed up for use again and the mail notification message is cleared from the display. Knowing that express mail is only used for important messages, she decides to read the message right away. To read the mail from Ernie, select the Mail menu.

Type: 5
Press: ⏎

Your display screen should be similar to Figure 1-14.

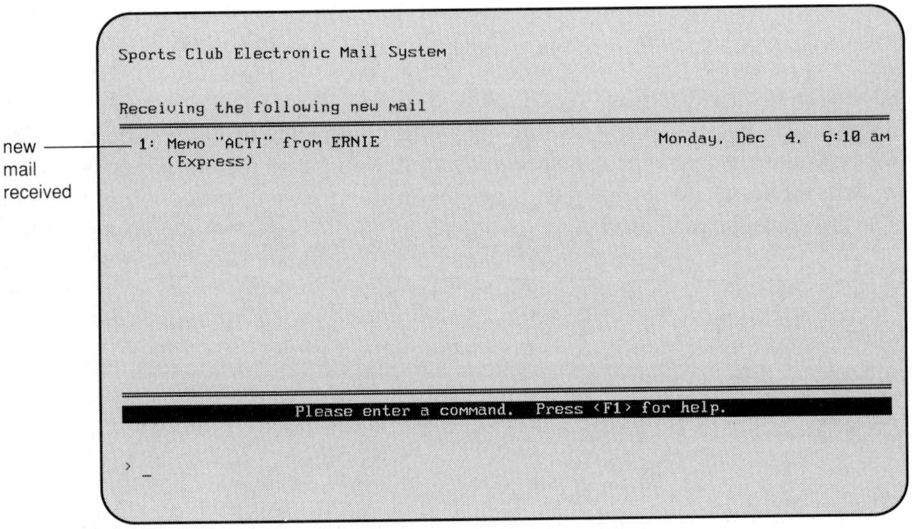

FIGURE 1-14

```
Sports Club Electronic Mail System

Receiving the following new mail

 1: Memo "ACTI" from ERNIE          Monday, Dec  4,  6:10 am
    (Express)




                    Please enter a command.  Press <F1> for help.

> _
```

new mail received

The status line shows that Ann is using the Sports Club Electronic Mail system. The mail screen shows that one piece of new mail has been received. Each piece of mail is numbered to the left of the name, followed by the name of the person who sent the mail.

To read the mail, the LAN command Read is entered at the command prompt followed by the number of the mail item to be opened. To read Ernie's memo,

Type: READ 1
Press: ⏎

Your display screen should be similar to Figure 1-15.

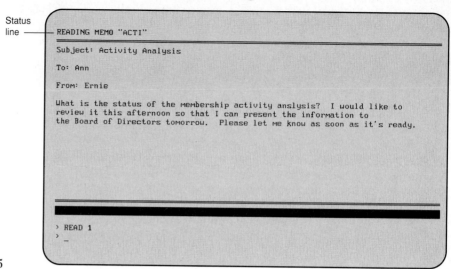

FIGURE 1-15

Ernie's message to Ann is loaded from the file server, read into her computer's memory, and displayed on the screen. The status line shows the current system activity as READING MEMO "ACTI". Ann is almost done with the activity analysis. However, before she completes the analysis and responds to Ernie's message, she needs to quickly check the daily activity schedule and print a copy of it to be posted at the front desk.

To leave the mail menu,

Type: QUIT
Press: ⏎

Retrieving and Printing the Daily Activity Schedule Ann's main menu is displayed again. To select Daily Activities,

Type: 1
Press: ⏎

Your display screen should be similar to Figure 1-16.

FIGURE 1-16

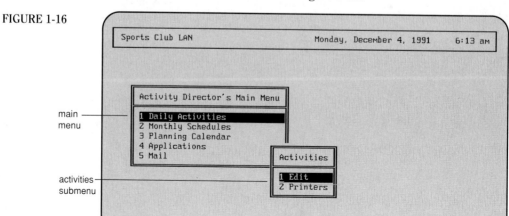

A new submenu is displayed which offers two options, Edit or Printers. The Edit option will load the daily activity document file and software program it runs on to allow Ann to view and edit the file if necessary. The Printers option allows her to select the type of printer, dot-matrix or laser, for the document to be printed on. The printers are a **shared hardware resource** that can be used by any computer linked to the LAN. This saves the club the expense of having a printer attached to each microcomputer.

First, Ann will select the printer.

Type: 2
Press: ⏎

Your display screen should be similar to Figure 1-17.

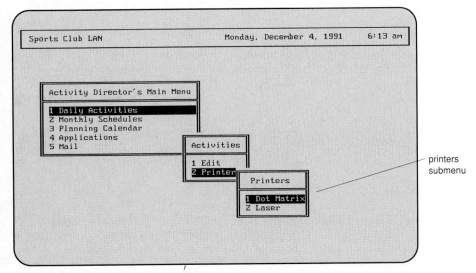

FIGURE 1-17

A third submenu displays the two choices of printers, dot-matrix or laser. Since the daily activity schedule is posted at the front desk, she wants it printed on the laser printer.

Type: 2
Press: ⏎

Your display screen should be similar to Figure 1-18.

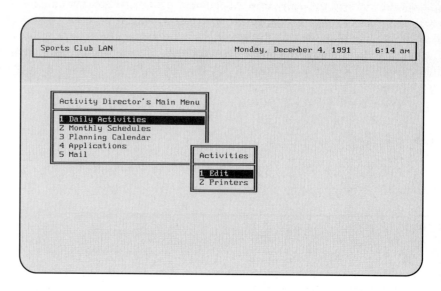

FIGURE 1-18

She is returned to the second submenu.

Next, Ann needs to check the daily activity schedule before printing it. To retrieve the daily activity schedule document and edit it if necessary,

Type: 1
Press: ⏎

Your display screen should be similar to Figure 1-19.

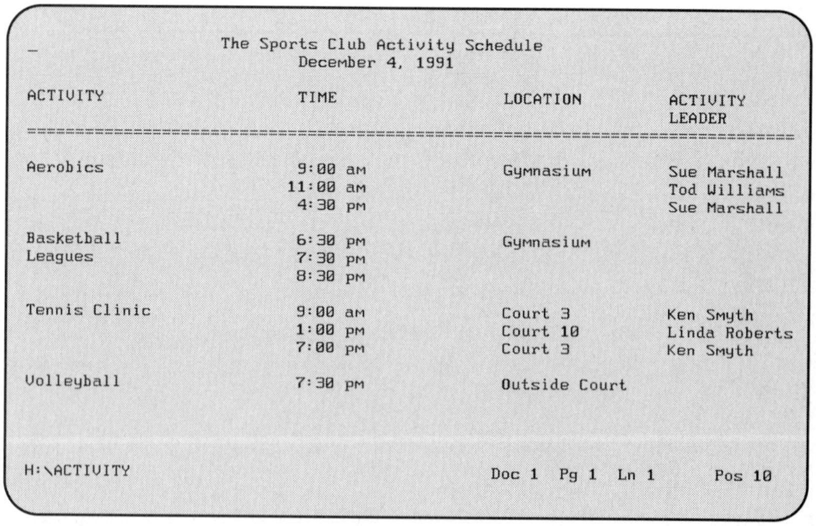

FIGURE 1-19

This screen may look familiar to you. It is a WordPerfect document screen. When Ann selected the Daily Activities menu item and the Edit submenu option, the word processing program and the document file named ACTIVITY were automatically loaded from the file server into the memory of her microcomputer. The LAN program quickly loads the appropriate software program and file when a specific menu item is selected.

Ann checks the schedule and finds no errors. The schedule is ready to be printed. Using the WordPerfect command to print,

Press: `SHIFT`-`F7`

The WordPerfect Print menu is displayed at the bottom of the screen. To print the full text,

Type: `1`

The text to be printed is sent to the file server and routed to the laser printer for printing.

Ann is ready to leave the WordPerfect program. Using the WordPerfect command to exit,

Press: `F7`

In response to the prompt on the screen to save the document, since it was not altered,

Type: `N`

In response to the prompt to exit WP,

Type: `Y`

Using a Specific Applications Software Program Ann is returned to her main menu. Now she can complete the membership activity analysis for Ernie. She has created a special worksheet file named ANALYSIS using the applications software program Lotus 1-2-3. The Applications menu item lets her select the type of applications program.

Type: `4`
Press: `↵`

Your display screen should be similar to Figure 1-20.

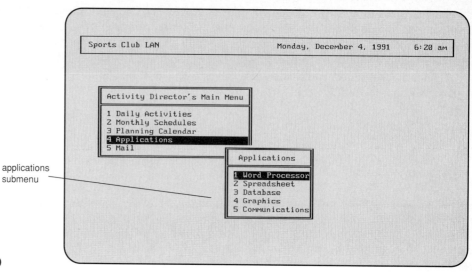

FIGURE 1-20

A submenu of five applications programs is displayed. Each submenu option lets Ann load a specific applications software program. The Word Processor option will load the WordPerfect program. The Spreadsheet option will load Lotus 1-2-3, and the Database option loads dBASE III PLUS. The other two options, Graphics and Communications, load a specialized graphics program called PC Paint and a communications program called Crosstalk.

To load the spreadsheet program from the file server into the memory of her microcomputer,

Type: 2
Press: ⏎

Your display screen should be similar to Figure 1-21.

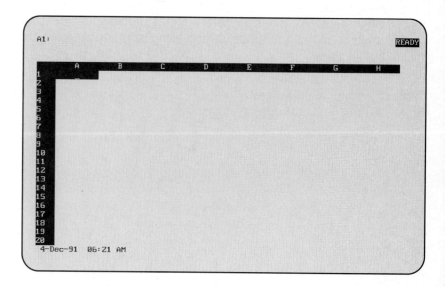

FIGURE 1-21

A blank Lotus 1-2-3 worksheet is displayed. To retrieve the file ANALYSIS, using the Lotus 1-2-3 command to retrieve a file,

Press: /

To select File,

Type: F

To retrieve the file,

Type: R

Since the file ANALYSIS.WK1 is the only file in the listing of filenames, and the highlight bar is over the correct filename, to select it,

Press: ⏎

After a few seconds, your display screen should be similar to Figure 1-22.

FIGURE 1-22

```
A20: [W12]                                                    READY

           A          B       C       D       E       F       G       H
 1
 2                         Activity Analysis
 3                         January - June 1991
 4
 5                        Jan     Feb     Mar     Apr     May     Jun    TOTAL
 6                        ------------------------------------------------------
 7
 8     Aerobics           425     455     380     360     325     350    2295
 9
10     Basketball         180     223     248     208     156     112    1127
11
12     Racquetball        224     256     212     177     154      96    1119
13
14     Tennis             498     508     425     530     600     688    3249
15
16     Volleyball          60      52      44      90     129     150     525
17
18     Weightroom         275     306     289     267     248     212    1597
19
20                       1662    1800    1598    1632    1612    1608    9912
     4-Dec-91  06:22 AM
```

All Ann needs to do to complete the worksheet is to enter the row label TOTAL in cell A20. Since the cursor is already in this cell,

Type: TOTAL
Press: ⏎

The row label TOTAL has been entered in the worksheet in cell A20. Ann makes a final check of the figures in the worksheet. Then she saves the revised version of the file, using the Lotus command to save a file as follows.

Press: /

To select File,

Type: F

To select Save,

Type: S

To save the file using the same filename,

Press: ⏎

To select Replace,

Type: R

The completed version of the file is saved on the file server.
   Next, Ann needs to send a message to Ernie telling him that the analysis is ready for his review.
   To leave Lotus and return to her main menu,

Press: /

To select Quit,

Type: Q

In response to the prompt, to confirm that you want to quit,

Type: Y

The activities director's main menu is displayed again.

Sending Regular Mail   To send a message to Ernie,

Type: 5
Press: ⏎

Your display screen should be similar to Figure 1-23.

FIGURE 1-23

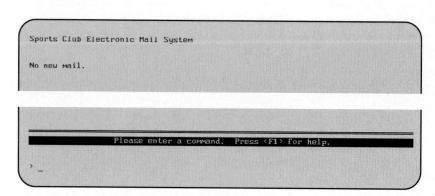

```
Sports Club Electronic Mail System

No new mail.




                    Please enter a command.  Press <F1> for help.

> _
```

The message on the display screen shows that Ann has received no new mail. After reading Ernie's message, it was automatically removed from the new mail list. If she had received any new mail in the meantime, it would be listed on the display.

To send a message to Ernie to notify him that the analysis is complete, at the command prompt,

Type: **CREATE MEMO COMP**
Press: ⏎

The screen changes to allow her to enter her message to Ernie. To see the memo she typed,

Press: space bar

Your display screen should be similar to Figure 1-24.

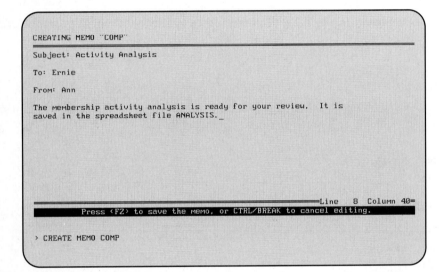

FIGURE 1-24

To save the memo,

Press: F2

The memo has been saved on the file server and can now be sent to Ernie. She knows that Ernie is expecting a message from her and feels she does not need to send the message express. She will send it by regular mail, which will put the message in his electronic mailbox rather than displaying a message notification on the screen.

To send the message regular mail,

Type: **SEND MEMO COMP TO ERNIE**
Press: ⏎

The screen tells you the message has been distributed. To leave the mail menu,

Type: **QUIT**
Press: ⏎

Ann's main menu is displayed again.

That's all Ann needs to do on the LAN right now. She leaves her office to pick up the printout of the daily activity schedule from the laser printer and post it at the front desk.

The Front Desk

The next club employee we will follow as he uses the LAN is Tom. Tom works at the front desk and greets members as they enter the club. He checks them into the club by entering their membership number from their ID card. He also records the type of activity they plan to use that day and gives them the time and location of the activity. Since Tom's job responsibilities are very limited, he does not have a menu to select from. Instead, his access to the LAN is limited to only two screens, which allow him to enter the member number and record the activity. When Ann arrives at the front desk to post the daily activity schedule, Tom is just starting his work shift.

Logging on to the LAN   To log in his user identification, Tom reboots the computer.

Press: space bar

The LAN system prompt is displayed on the screen. Tom's login procedure is similar to Ernie's and Ann's. To enter his login identification,

Type: TOM
Press: ⏎

To enter his password,

Type: FD06
Press: ⏎

Once the login information has been verified, following the directions on the display,

Press: space bar

Your display screen should be similar to Figure 1-25.

```
          The Sports Club Activity Schedule
                 December 4, 1991

 ACTIVITY              TIME            LOCATION         ACTIVITY
                                                        LEADER
 ==========================================================================

 Aerobics              9:00 am         Gymnasium        Sue Marshall
                      11:00 am                          Tod Williams
                       4:30 pm                          Sue Marshall

 Basketball            6:30 pm         Gymnasium
 Leagues               7:30 pm
                       8:30 pm

 Tennis Clinic         9:00 am         Court 3          Ken Smyth
                       1:00 pm         Court 10         Linda Roberts
                       7:00 pm         Court 3          Ken Smyth

 Volleyball            7:30 pm         Outside Court


 Enter Member Account Number: _
```

prompt ⟵

FIGURE 1-25

Using LAN Special Screens You will notice right away that a main menu is not displayed. Instead, the top portion of the screen displays the daily activity schedule prepared by Ann using WordPerfect. When Tom logs on to the LAN, the file server automatically loads and displays a special screen that shows the daily activity schedule. At the bottom of the screen is the LAN prompt "Enter Member Account Number:" followed by the cursor. The prompt on the screen is waiting for Tom to enter the account number of a member.

A member enters the club and shows Tom his ID card. Using the number from the card,

Type: 1001
Press: ⏎

Your display screen should be similar to Figure 1-26.

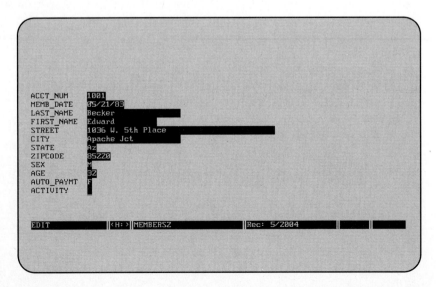

FIGURE 1-26

This screen may look familiar to you. It is a dBASE III PLUS screen displaying the membership data for member number 1001, Ed Becker. When the member account number was entered at the prompt, the LAN automatically loaded the dBASE III PLUS program and the MEMBER data file from the file server. The LAN also automatically displays the field data for the record whose account number was specified.

The cursor is in the Activity field waiting for input of data for this field. In order to restrict the front desk employees to entering data in a single field, the Activity field has been frozen, although the entire member record is visible for viewing

Next, addressing the member by name, Tom asks Ed what facility he plans to use that day. Ed says he plans to play tennis. The type of activity is recorded by entering a numeric code which stands for the activity. The code for tennis is 3.

Type: 3

The activity code is entered into the field. To save the change made to the record on the file, using the dBASE III PLUS command,

Press: CTRL-END

The display automatically returns to the main screen, displaying the daily activity schedule in preparation for checking in the next member.

Employees with varying levels of responsibility and job duties can have access to the LAN without access to all files and programs. The membership director, for example, can access the same MEMBER data file and update and edit all fields and records using dBASE III PLUS. In contrast, the front desk personnel can access the MEMBER file but can change data only in the activity field. The front desk personnel have restricted use of the MEMBER file. They may not even realize or need to know they are using dBASE III PLUS.

The LAN provides the means to share data files and software programs by maintaining the files on the file server for use by authorized personnel. This saves the club the problems of having different versions of data files in effect at the same time. It allows different employees to access the same data files and update and change only the areas for which they are responsible. In this way the data in the file can be altered only by the appropriate employees. The security of the data is maintained.

Throughout his shift, Tom continues to check in each member and enter the activity data.

The Club Manager

Finally, back to Ernie, the club manager. Ernie will check his mail to see if he has received an answer from Ann about the activity analysis report. He will then retrieve the spreadsheet file created by Ann from the file server and review the data for presentation to the board of directors. At the end of the day, Ernie will log off the LAN and leave the club for the day.

Ernie has been having a busy day. After checking the facilities and cafe operations and talking with several people in accounting about the end-of-the-month report, he returns to his office.

NET27
The Club Manager

Receiving Regular Mail Ernie's display is just as he left it. To see his main menu,

Press: space bar

Ernie does not see an express mail notification on the screen. So he decides to check his regular mail to see whether Ann has responded to his memo. To access the Mail menu,

Type: 5
Press: ⏎

Your display screen should be similar to Figure 1-27.

FIGURE 1-27

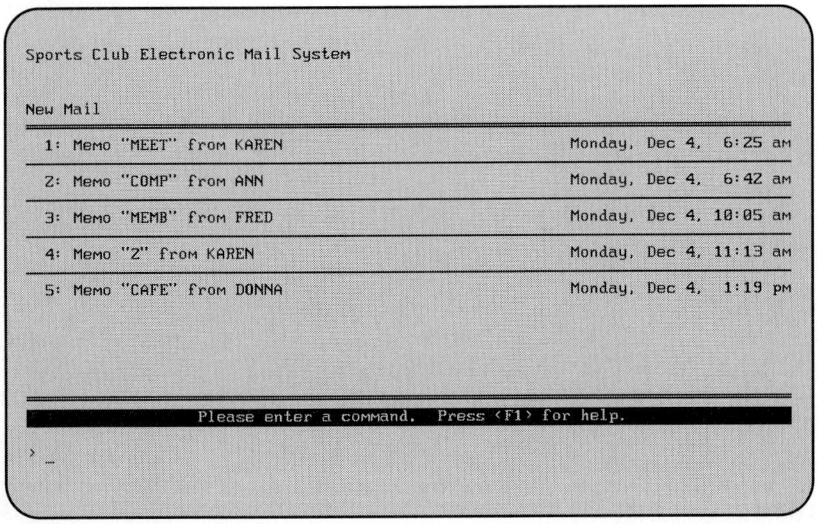

```
Sports Club Electronic Mail System

New Mail

 1: Memo "MEET" from KAREN          Monday, Dec 4,  6:25 am
 2: Memo "COMP" from ANN            Monday, Dec 4,  6:42 am
 3: Memo "MEMB" from FRED           Monday, Dec 4, 10:05 am
 4: Memo "Z"    from KAREN          Monday, Dec 4, 11:13 am
 5: Memo "CAFE" from DONNA          Monday, Dec 4,  1:19 pm




           Please enter a command.  Press <F1> for help.
> _
```

The mail screen shows that he has received five messages. He is most interested in the message from Ann. Ann's message is mail number 2. To read this message,

Type: READ 2
Press: ⏎

Ernie reads Ann's message telling him the activity analysis is ready for his review. Eager to see the analysis, he decides to retrieve the ANALYSIS file before reading his other new mail.

To leave the Mail menu,

Type: QUIT
Press: ⏎

Using a Common Data File Ernie is returned to his main menu. To select the Applications menu,

Type: 4
Press: ⏎

The same five applications software choices that Ann could select from are displayed for Ernie. The file he wants to see is a spreadsheet file. To select this option,

Type: 2
Press: ⏎

The Lotus 1-2-3 software program is loaded from the file server into the memory of Ernie's microcomputer. A blank 1-2-3 worksheet is displayed. To retrieve the file ANALYSIS using 1-2-3 commands,

Press: /

To select File,

Type: F

To retrieve the file,

Type: R

Since the file ANALYSIS.WK1 is the only file in the listing of filenames, and the highlight bar is over the correct filename, to select it,

Press: ⏎

The worksheet file created by Ann using Lotus 1-2-3 and saved on the file server is loaded into the memory of Ernie's microcomputer and displayed on the screen.
    Ernie looks over the worksheet. He decides to graph the data and calculate the average over the 6 months. After making these changes to the file, he saves it. To leave the spreadsheet program,

Press: /

To select Quit,

Type: Q

In response to the prompt, to confirm that you want to quit,

Type: Y

Ernie's main menu is displayed again.
    Now he wants to read his other messages. To select Mail,

Type: 5
Press: ⏎

Your display screen should be similar to Figure 1-28.

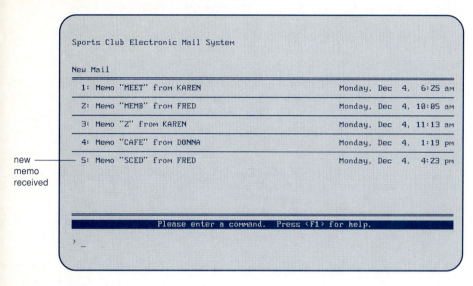

FIGURE 1-28

new memo received

Notice that the message from Ann is no longer listed with the new mail because Ernie has read that message. The other four pieces of mail that were listed when he first checked his mailbox are still displayed because they were not read. In addition, a new piece of mail arrived (number 5, sent regular mail) while Ernie was working on the activity analysis worksheet.

Ernie reads all his messages. To leave the Mail menu,

Type: QUIT
Press: ⏎

Signing Off the LAN He is returned to his main menu. Ernie is ready to leave the club for the day and needs to sign off the LAN.

Press: ESC

Your display screen should be similar to Figure 1-29.

FIGURE 1-29

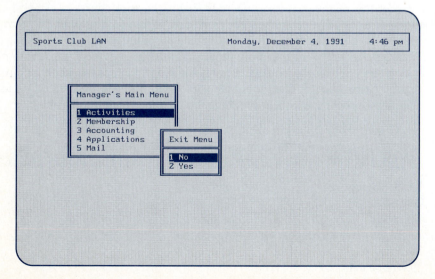

The submenu displayed lets him either exit the system or return to the main menu. To leave the system,

Type: 2
Press: ⏎

The LAN system prompt is displayed. At the prompt,

Type: LOGOFF
Press: ⏎

Your display screen should be similar to Figure 1-30.

FIGURE 1-30

```
H>LOGOFF
Logged off
Goodnight Ernie.
Don't forget to turn the computer and the file server off._
```

Ernie turns off his computer. He does not turn off the file server because the club is open several more hours and other club employees still need to access the file server. The person responsible for closing the club at night will turn off the file server.

As you can see, the club's LAN is a very valuable time-saving tool. It allows multiple users to access the same data files, avoiding the problems of duplicate files with different data. It restricts the data files to only authorized users as determined by the login information. It allows the users to share the same applications programs. It provides the electronic transfer of messages between users, avoiding possible telephone tag problems.

But for all the advantages to the LAN, there are also problems. What happens if the system goes "down"? If the file server fails or needs to be serviced, the LAN is temporarily out of commission. Since all data files and software programs are accessed through the LAN, this can abruptly stop any work that uses the microcomputers. For this reason, it is very important that backup procedures be established. For example, if the LAN were down, the front desk personnel would need to record the member account number and activity data on paper until the LAN is running again. Then they can enter the data from paper into the file. It is also important to make a backup copy of the shared data files on the file server to a diskette or tape on a regular basis. Then, if the file server goes down, the backup file can be used to continue business using the microcomputer on a standalone basis.

Key Terms

local area network
control unit
file server
information resources sharing
hardware resources sharing
electronic mail

login
login identification
password
express mail
regular mail

Matching

1. READ
2. CREATE
3. login
4. Send Express
5. Send
6. H>
7. ****
8. password
9. verifying
10. >

a. identification required to gain access to the LAN
b. transmit mail regularly
c. LAN check of login and password entered
d. LAN command to read mail
e. LAN command prompt
f. causes mail notification to be received
g. hidden code required for access to the LAN
h. allows user to write message
i. LAN system prompt
j. displayed in place of password on screen

SUMMARY
Local Area Network

Glossary of Key Terms

Electronic mail: The transmission of messages electronically.

Express mail: Electronic mail sent to recipient's electronic mailbox that displays a mail notification message on the screen and temporarily freezes the recipient's keyboard until the notification is acknowledged.

File server: A central computer that controls the transfer of data between microcomputers, to the printers, and electronic mail. Also called the control unit.

Local area network (LAN): A communications network consisting of computers connected by cable within a building or group of adjacent buildings in a limited geographic area.

Login: The sign-on procedure used to access the communication network.

Login identification: The first part of the login information entered by each authorized user of the LAN. Used in transmission of electronic mail also.

Password: A secret code assigned to each authorized user to control access to the computer network.

Regular mail: An electronic message that is distributed to the recipient's electronic mailbox.

Shared hardware resources: The common access to hardware such as printers by all microcomputers linked to the network.

Shared information resources: The common access to data files and applications software programs by all microcomputers on the network.

INDEX

Access to files:
    controlled by login, NET7
    for different levels of employees, NET26
Applications software:
    Crosstalk, NET20
    dBASE III PLUS, NET20, NET26
    loading, NET20
    Lotus 1-2-3, NET20-NET22, NET28
    PCPaint, NET20
    WordPerfect, NET20

Backup procedures, NET30

Commands:
    CREATE MEMO, NET10, NET23
    SEND MEMO, NET12, NET23
Communications channels, NET3, NET4
Control unit, defined, NET3
Crosstalk, NET20

Data:
    security, NET7, NET26
    sharing, NET4, NET30
dBASE III PLUS:
    editing, NET26
    entering data, NET26
    loading, NET20

Editing files, NET17, NET26
Electronic mail:
    defined, NET4
    express or regular, NET12
    receiving express mail, NET14-NET16
    receiving regular mail, NET27
    saving express mail, NET11-NET12
    saving regular mail, NET23
    sending express mail, NET10-NET13
    sending regular mail, NET22-NET23
Express mail:
    defined, NET12
    receiving, NET14-NET16
    saving, NET11-NET12
    sending, NET10-NET13

File server:
    defined, NET3, NET4, NET6
    access to, NET30
Files:
    access to, NET7, NET26
    backing up, NET30
    editing, NET17, NET26
    retrieving, NET21, NET28
    sharing, NET4

Hardware resources sharing, NET4, NET17

Information resources sharing, NET4, NET30

Local area networks (LANs):
    advantages of, NET4
    backup procedures for, NET30
    defined, NET3, NET4
    problems with, NET30
    signing off, NET29
    software for, NET3
    starting, NET6
    system prompt, NET7
Logging on, NET7-NET8, NET13, NET24
Login:
    defined, NET4, NET7
    identification, NET7
Lotus 1-2-3
    loading, NET20
    quitting, NET28
    retrieving files, NET21, NET28
    saving files, NET22

Mail (see Electronic mail)
Menus, NET9, NET14

Networks, defined, NET3, NET4

Passwords:
    defined, NET4
    as security, NET7
    verifying, NET8
PCPaint, NET20
Printing, NET17, NET19
Prompt, system, NET7

Regular mail:
    defined, NET 12
    receiving, NET27
    saving, NET23
    sending, NET22-NET23

Security on a LAN:
    and access to files, NET7, NET26
    and passwords, NET4, NET7, NET8
Shared hardware resources, NET4, NET17
Shared information resources, NET4, NET30
Signing off the LAN, NET29
Software for LANs, NET3

WordPerfect, NET20